red dot
design yearbook
2010/2011

living

reddot design award
product design

reddot design award
product design

red dot
Awards for high design quality
Auszeichnungen für hohe Designqualität

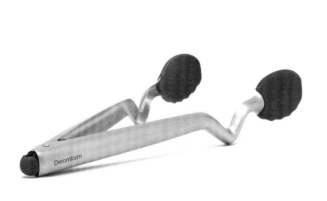

Prof. Dr. Peter Zec

Preface of the editor
Vorwort des Herausgebers

Dear Readers,

Our living environments are continually changing, and every day, new products from all corners of the globe are pushing their way into the market. Under such circumstances, grasping the overall picture isn't always easy. The red dot design award has made it its task to filter out those products that have the best design and that are the most innovative – in short, products with the potential to stay in the market as well as to shape the market. This book presents the results of the jury sessions, during which more than 4,000 products were viewed, tested and evaluated, for the sector "living".

This publication begins (page 14 and on) with presentations of the products awarded with "red dot: best of the best", i.e., products that will set standards in their respective categories and that were distinguished with this highest award of the competition for their groundbreaking design. These presentations also include brief portraits of the creative people behind those outstanding products.

Thanks to the great number of products again submitted for awards this year, our jurors were able to detect trends in the different product groups early on. For example, the chapter "Living rooms and bedrooms" presents furniture that combines well thought-out functions with 1960s design in addition to products in which an Asian sensibility for materials converges with a Western canon of forms. The designers from the "Households and kitchens" category, for their part, concentrate on the careful and clear design of details and on the efficient use of space and energy. In the "Bathrooms, spa and air-conditioning" sector, intelligent technologies are increasingly incorporated into the architecture, resulting in integrative, holistically oriented spaces that are veritable wellness oases. Every product chapter of this book is introduced with a short trend report that summarises the developments of the respective sector.

Liebe Leserin, lieber Leser,

unsere Lebenswelten verändern sich ständig, täglich drängen neue Produkte aus aller Herren Länder auf den Markt – es ist nicht ganz leicht, angesichts dessen den Überblick zu bewahren. Der red dot design award hat es sich zur Aufgabe gemacht, jedes Jahr aufs Neue diejenigen Produkte herauszufiltern, die am besten gestaltet und am innovativsten sind, Produkte, die das Potenzial haben, auch in Zukunft am Markt zu bestehen und diesen zu prägen. Das Ergebnis der Jurysitzungen, in denen mehr als 4.000 Produkte zu sichten, auszuprobieren und zu bewerten waren, präsentieren wir Ihnen für den Bereich „living" in dem vorliegenden Buch.

Gleich zu Beginn dieser Publikation (ab Seite 14) stellen wir Ihnen mit den Preisträgern des „red dot: best of the best" die Produkte vor, die in ihren Kategorien Maßstäbe setzen werden und für ihre wegweisende Gestaltung mit der höchsten Auszeichnung des Wettbewerbs bedacht wurden. Die kreativsten Köpfe, die Menschen, die hinter diesen herausragenden Produkten stehen, haben wir ebenfalls kurz porträtiert.

Die große Anzahl an Produkten, mit denen sich designorientierte Unternehmen auch in diesem Jahr wieder um eine Auszeichnung im red dot design award beworben haben, ermöglicht es unseren Juroren, schon früh neue Trends in den verschiedenen Produktgruppen auszumachen. So finden sich etwa im Kapitel „Wohnen und Schlafen" Möbel, bei denen sich sehr durchdachte Funktionen mit Formen der 1960er Jahre verbinden, ebenso wie Produkte, die Anleihen an die asiatische Materialwelt mit dem westlichen Formenkanon verknüpfen. Die Designer in der Kategorie „Haushalt und Küche" wiederum konzentrieren sich auf die sorgsame und sehr klare Gestaltung von Details sowie auf eine möglichst effiziente Nutzung von Platz und Energie. Im Bereich „Bad, Wellness und Klimatechnik" verschmelzen intelligente Technologien immer mehr mit der Architektur und es entstehen integrative, ganzheitlich orientierte Räume, kleine Wellness-Oasen. Jedem Produktkapitel dieses Buchs haben wir einen eigenen kurzen Trendbericht vorangestellt, der Ihnen gleich zu Beginn einen kompakten Überblick über die Entwicklungen der jeweiligen Branche vermittelt.

However, good design, such as presented in this publication, is not only an expression of a deep understanding of design by designers and companies. Design quality also pays off, as it creates added value for companies and consumers or, as stated succinctly by former IBM President Thomas J. Watson Jr., "Good design is good business." Indeed, in our many years of observing the design sector, the best design companies, regardless of size, were found to demonstrate above-market performance. However, design quality can only be determined through comparison, such as is done by the jury in the red dot design award. Based on the competition evaluations, it is also possible to assess a company's design strength and continuity, to put that in relation to the company results, and to therewith determine the design value of a company. The company Hilti, for example, this year's design team of the year, boasts a successful record of distinctions from the red dot design award that speaks for itself: Over the past 5 years alone, Hilti received 29 awards, among them twice the "red dot: best of the best". The producer of building technological products spearheads the red dot design ranking within its sector by far. For the year 2008, the red dot institute for advanced design studies estimated the company's design value at 2.3 billion euros – the highest of all estimated values.

As you can see, design is a truly multi-faceted and complex theme, as is reflected in every one of the here presented products. I wish you an interesting read!

Sincerely,
Prof. Dr. Peter Zec

Gutes Design, wie wir es Ihnen in der vorliegenden Publikation präsentieren, ist jedoch nicht nur Ausdruck eines tiefen Designverständnisses von Gestaltern und Unternehmern. Designqualität zahlt sich auch aus, weil sie einen Mehrwert für Unternehmen und Konsumenten schafft, oder, wie es der ehemalige IBM-Präsident Thomas J. Watson jr. prägnant formulierte: „Good design is good business." In der Tat zeigen auch unsere langjährigen Beobachtungen der Designbranche, dass sich die besten Designunternehmen unabhängig von ihrer Größe deutlich besser entwickeln als der Markt. Diese Qualität findet man jedoch nur durch Vergleich, so wie es mithilfe der Jury im red dot design award geschieht. Auf Basis der Auswertung des Wettbewerbs ist es auch möglich, die Designstärke und -kontinuität von Unternehmen zu ermitteln, sie in Relation zum Unternehmensergebnis zu setzen und so den Designwert eines Unternehmens zu bestimmen. Hilti, unser diesjähriges Designteam des Jahres etwa, kann im red dot design award eine Erfolgsbilanz vorweisen, die für sich spricht: Allein in den letzten 5 Jahren erhielt Hilti 29 Auszeichnungen, darunter zweimal das Prädikat „red dot: best of the best". Der Hersteller von bautechnologischen Produkten führt das red dot design ranking innerhalb seiner Branche überlegen an und verfügte im Jahr 2008 mit 2,3 Mrd. EUR über den höchsten vom red dot institute for advanced design studies errechneten Designwert innerhalb der Branche.

Wie Sie sehen, ist das Thema Design ausgesprochen vielschichtig und ungemein komplex – ebenso wie jedes einzelne der hier vorgestellten Produkte. Ich wünsche Ihnen eine anregende Lektüre!

Ihr
Prof. Dr. Peter Zec

red dot: design team of the year 2010
Stephan Niehaus
and the Hilti Design Team

red dot: design team of the year 2010
Stephan Niehaus
und das Hilti Design Team

Hilti.

Design as non-verbal brand communication
Design als nonverbale Markenkommunikation

If you mention the word "design", few people are likely to think of rotary hammers, drills and chisels or even jigsaws and reciprocating saws. Yet the interplay of technical functions and innovative design not only promises success for producers of consumer goods but also for the manufacturers of capital goods.

Since its foundation in 1941, Hilti has an impressive track record. Starting as a small family company, it is now a global player with some 20,000 employees. At the headquarters alone, which are based in Schaan, Liechtenstein, approximately 2,000 employees from 60 nations work together. Hilti supplies the global construction industry with technologically cutting-edge products, systems and services and offers innovative solutions that provide building professionals with added value. The products live up to their promise of quality and performance continuing to delight their customers year in, year out.

Die wenigsten Menschen denken beim Stichwort „Design" an Schlagbohrschrauber, Bohr- und Meißelhämmer oder Stich- und Säbelsägen. Dabei ist das Zusammenspiel von technischer Funktion und innovativem Design nicht nur für Hersteller von Konsumgütern Erfolg versprechend, sondern auch für Unternehmen im Investitionsgüterbereich.

Die Firma Hilti schreibt seit ihrer Gründung im Jahr 1941 eine beeindruckende Erfolgsgeschichte. Aus dem kleinen Familienunternehmen ist ein Weltkonzern mit rund 20.000 Mitarbeitenden geworden. Allein am Firmensitz des Unternehmens im liechtensteinischen Schaan arbeiten rund 2.000 Menschen aus über 60 Nationen. Hilti beliefert die Bauindustrie weltweit mit technologisch führenden Produkten, Systemen und Dienstleistungen und bietet für die Bauprofis innovative Lösungen mit Mehrwert. Die Produkte halten, was sie versprechen, und begeistern die Kunden nachhaltig durch ihre Qualität und Leistung.

oben/above
Stephan Niehaus and the Hilti Design Team
Stephan Niehaus und das Hilti Design Team

right page/rechts
2009
Hilti SF 22-A, SFH 22-A cordless drill
Hilti Akku-Bohrschrauber SF 22-A, SFH 22-A

When Stephan Niehaus joined the company as its Chief Designer in 2003, product design at Hilti was still very much dominated by the underlying technology. Designs were conceived individually without any overarching design framework. But if one thing is clear for Stephan Niehaus it is that a systematic design concept is needed if the strengths of consistent product design are to be exploited. Together with his team he has drawn up a master design guideline which applies to all future products of the company and defines the processes needed to realise this guideline in practice. Initially trained as a technical draftsman for engineering applications, he moved on to study product design. With this dual background he brings together product design, corporate design and corporate identity into one consistent brand using a uniform language so as to reflect the values of the Hilti brand, also in its products.

"A master craftsman sizes up a power tool in just seven seconds," says Stephan Niehaus. "We do everything we can to make a lasting impression in these first seven seconds." The design of the product plays a central role in this regard. The design of the tool and the way it lies in your hand provide the user with a clear statement of its qualities in a very short space of time. "We want our customers to sense, literally grasp, the quality, performance and reliability of our products. They should perceive the passion that goes into our products with all of their senses," continues Niehaus. At this Hilti has been successful. Even building professionals, who are not normally accustomed to using the term "design", react unconsciously to the emotional appeal that has run consistently through all product lines since 2003.

Last but not least, the key to success lies in closely observing customers. Watching, listening, and most of all, correctly interpreting customers is the key to creating products that are perfectly tailored solutions to customer needs. Not only the market researchers and project managers closely observe customers at work, the ergonomists and designers do too. Stephan Niehaus: "With everything that we observe and gather, we ask ourselves, is there a simpler or faster way for the customer to operate this device? Will working with it become safer and more productive?" Each grip is registered and analysed before the results are put into a design language that not only expresses the core values of the brand but is also able to communicate the characteristics of the individual products. The effort pays off. For the users, the design strength of Hilti products has in the meantime come to be identified with outstanding quality.

At Hilti, design is far more than just the promise of quality. It is the prime means of non-verbal communication. The design of the products not only expresses their added-value. It also communicates their modern appeal and innovative character. "Hilti customers know instinctively that our products offer more than other products. We don't even have to express this in words any more," claims Stephan Niehaus. The success story of Stephan Niehaus and the Hilti Design Team speaks for itself. In the past five years alone, Hilti has been honoured 29 times in the red dot design award, having been twice honoured with the "red dot: best of the best" award. When a company can exhibit a record like this, it is due to its enormous strength in design and innovation. The manufacturer of products for the construction trade has a superior lead in its category of the red dot design ranking and, at 2.3 billion euros, the highest design value ranking in its category as calculated by the red dot institute in 2008.

The full article on the Hilti Design Team can be found in the "doing" volume of the yearbook.

Als Chefdesigner Stephan Niehaus 2003 ins Unternehmen einsteigt, ist Hilti in der Produktgestaltung noch sehr stark von der Technologie getrieben. Die Designausarbeitung erfolgt individuell, ohne produktübergreifenden Rahmen. Für Stephan Niehaus ist klar: Um die Stärken eines konsistenten Produktdesigns nutzen zu können, braucht es ein systematisches Designkonzept. Gemeinsam mit seinem Team definiert er eine ganzheitlich orientierte Designlinie, die künftig für alle Produkte des Unternehmens gilt, und legt die Prozesse fest, die die konsequente Umsetzung dieser Linie ermöglichen. Der gelernte technische Zeichner im Maschinenbau und studierte Produktdesigner verbindet Produktdesign, Corporate Design und Corporate Identity zu einem konsistenten Markenbild und einer einheitlichen Markensprache, um die Werte der Marke Hilti auch im Produktdesign widerzuspiegeln.

„Ein Bauprofi fällt sein Urteil über ein Gerät in sieben Sekunden", sagt Stephan Niehaus. „Wir tun alles dafür, dass wir ihn in diesen ersten sieben Sekunden nachhaltig begeistern können." Das Design des Produktes spielt dabei eine zentrale Rolle. Die Gestaltung des Gerätes und die Art, wie es in der Hand liegt, geben dem Benutzer in kürzester Zeit ganz klare Informationen über dessen Eigenschaften. „Wir wollen, dass der Kunde die Qualität, Leistung und Zuverlässigkeit unserer Geräte buchstäblich mit Händen greifen kann. Er soll die Leidenschaft, die in unseren Produkten steckt, mit allen Sinnen wahrnehmen", so Niehaus. Das Vorhaben gelingt. Selbst Bauprofis, die mit dem Begriff „Design" wenig anfangen können, reagieren unbewusst auf die emotionale Ansprache, die sich ab 2003 konsequent durch alle Produktlinien zu ziehen beginnt.

Der Schlüssel zum Erfolg liegt nicht zuletzt in der exakten Beobachtung des Kunden. Hinschauen, zuhören und vor allem richtig interpretieren lautet die Devise, wenn es darum geht, die Bedürfnisse des Kunden in maßgeschneiderte Produktlösungen zu übertragen. Nicht nur die Marktforscher und Projektleiter schauen dem Kunden über die Schulter, auch die Ergonomen und Designer. Stephan Niehaus: „Bei allem, was wir beobachten und aufnehmen, fragen wir uns: Kann der Kunde diesen Handgriff nicht einfacher oder schneller durchführen? Wie wird die Arbeit sicherer und produktiver?" Jeder Handgriff wird registriert und analysiert, bevor die Erkenntnisse in eine Sprache umgesetzt werden, die sowohl die Kernwerte der Marke als auch die Eigenschaften der einzelnen Produkte zum Ausdruck bringt. Der Aufwand lohnt sich: Das starke Design der Hilti-Produkte ist mittlerweile zum Äquivalent für hervorragende Qualität im Sinne des Anwenders geworden.

Für Hilti ist Design aber weitaus mehr als ein Qualitätsversprechen. Es ist das non-verbale Kommunikationsmittel erster Wahl. Über das Design der Produkte wird nicht nur deren Mehrwert ausgedrückt, sondern auch der Modernitätsanspruch und der Innovationscharakter der Marke. „Hilti-Kunden spüren instinktiv, dass unsere Produkte mehr bieten als andere. Das muss gar nicht mehr extra ausgesprochen werden", sagt Stephan Niehaus. Die Erfolgsbilanz spricht für sich: Allein in den letzten 5 Jahren erhielt Hilti 29 Auszeichnungen im red dot design award, darunter zweimal das Prädikat „red dot: best of the best". Wenn ein Unternehmen eine derartige Bilanz vorweisen kann, zeugt dies von einer enormen Design- und Innovationsstärke. Der Hersteller von bautechnologischen Produkten führt das red dot design ranking innerhalb seiner Branche überlegen an und verfügte im Jahr 2008 mit 2,3 Mrd. EUR über den höchsten vom red dot institute errechneten Designwert innerhalb der Branche.

Der ausführliche Artikel über das Hilti Design Team ist im Jahrbuchband „doing" nachzulesen.

Stylistic elements of the product design serve as non-verbal communication

The Hilti "face" is a dominant design element containing the product name and logo on the red casing of the product. The silhouette of the product is dynamically concentrated on the focal point of the appliance. The Hilti rib is a frozen stylistic element. The width of the single ribs, their distance to each other, and the breadth of the field are precisely defined. The Hilti rib is used in the product design as well and scaled accordingly.

Stilelemente des Produktdesigns dienen der nonverbalen Kommunikation

Das Hilti-Face ist ein prägnantes Feld auf dem roten Grundkörper des Gehäuses, auf dem der Produktname und das Logo fixiert sind. Die Silhouette ist dynamisch auf den Wirkpunkt des Gerätes ausgerichtet. Die Hilti-Rippe ist ein eingefrorenes Stilelement. Die Breite der einzelnen Rippen, die Abstände zueinander und die Flächenüberspannung sind genau definiert. Die Hilti-Rippe wird auch auf das Design der Produkte übertragen und entsprechend skaliert.

red dot: best of the best
The best products of their category

red dot: best of the best
Die besten Produkte ihrer Kategorie

These products are unique and new. They will essentially influence our living environment in the future. They are leading in their respective categories, and they will set standards: The jury of the red dot design award decides on the best products of our time from 17 different groups and awards them the "red dot: best of the best". This year the red dot jury has selected altogether 45 products to receive the coveted award. Of these, 16 products will be presented on the following pages. They are the expression of a new global lifestyle – products that embellish and enrich our lives in many respects.

Diese Produkte sind einzigartig und neu, und sie werden künftig unsere Lebenswelt entscheidend prägen. Sie setzen Maßstäbe und sind führend in ihrer Kategorie: Aus 17 verschiedenen Bereichen ermittelt die Jury des red dot design award die besten Produkte unserer Zeit, indem sie ihnen die Auszeichnung „red dot: best of the best" verleiht. In diesem Jahr wurde die begehrte Auszeichnung von der red dot-Jury insgesamt 45-mal verliehen. Auf den folgenden Seiten werden 16 dieser Produkte vorgestellt. Sie sind der Ausdruck eines neuen globalen Lifestyles – Produkte, die unser Leben in vielerlei Hinsicht verschönern und bereichern.

Batou CS
Decoration Fabric / Dekorationsstoff

Nya Nordiska Textiles GmbH,
Dannenberg, Germany / Deutschland
In-house design / Werksdesign:
Diete Hansl-Röntgen,
Sybilla Hansl, Alice Pieper
www.nya.com

Dimensions of the hidden

Fabrics have the power to inspire their users, firing up their imagination. As a kind of boundary to the outer world they can create mysterious spaces. A world that is hidden, as is denoted in the French word for venetian blind: "jalousie", a word which also connotes "jealousy", because originally it referred to the protective screens used in Oriental harems. The Batou CS decoration fabric skilfully reflects and picks up on fascination for the hidden, revealing only part of what it covers and hides: when the sun shines through this light transparent weave with its clear graphic pattern, it creates the effect as if one was looking through a venetian blind. This effect is based on a sophisticated and well thought-out design. The pattern of this decoration fabric is created by a soft bulk thread in the weft and, held in place by the slightly "raised" warp threads on one side, drawn together elegantly like a slightly embossed loose network over the hidden yet delicately transparent base. Draped within a room this decoration fabric has a strong three-dimensional effect and, depending on the light source, with changing depths of light and shadow. These features and the fact that it can be railroaded allow the Batou CS decoration fabric to be used in many different interior and arrangement settings. With its elementary aesthetics and architectural quality it reflects the need of our time for clearness and transparency – while its delicate design creates a new dimension of the hidden.

Dimensionen des Verborgenen

Stoffe inspirieren die Phantasie des Betrachters und beflügeln seine Sinne. Als Grenze zur Außenwelt schaffen sie Räume des Geheimnisvollen. Eine verborgene Welt, wie sie auch in dem Wort „Jalousie" anklingt, das aus dem Französischen stammend eigentlich „Eifersucht" bedeutet und in seinem Ursprung einmal den Sichtschutz in den Harems des Orients bezeichnete. Der Dekorationsstoff Batou CS spielt gekonnt mit dieser Faszination des Verborgenen, denn er offenbart stets nur Teilaspekte des Ganzen: Scheint die Sonne durch das zarte Transparentgewebe mit seinem klaren grafischen Muster, wirkt es, als blicke man durch eine Jalousie. Dieser Effekt basiert auf einer inspirierten und durchdachten Gestaltung. Das Dessin des Dekorationsstoffes entsteht durch ein weiches Bauschgarn im Schuss, das wie ein lockeres Geflecht leicht erhaben über einen hauchzarten Fond gezogen wird. Einseitig „herausgehobene" Kettfäden fixieren dieses effektvolle Geflecht und der nahezu unsichtbare Fond gewährt Ein- und Durchblicke. Im Raum schafft dieser Dekorationsstoff eine starke räumliche Tiefe und, je nach Einsatzort, variieren seine Licht- und Schatteneffekte. Diese Eigenschaften wie auch die Option, ihn gestürzt verarbeiten zu können, eröffnen für den Dekorationsstoff Batou CS eine Vielzahl von Einsatzmöglichkeiten im Interieur- und Objektbereich. Mit seiner elementaren Ästhetik und architektonischen Qualität reflektiert er den Wunsch unserer Zeit nach Eindeutigkeit und Transparenz – durch seine feinsinnige Gestaltung kreiert er neue Dimensionen des Verborgenen.

CH04 Houdini
Side Chair and Chair with Armrest / Stuhl und Stuhl mit Armlehne

e15 Design und Distributions GmbH,
Oberursel, Germany / Deutschland
Design: Stefan Diez Design
(Stefan Diez), Munich, Germany /
München, Deutschland
www.e15.com

Bent into shape – inspiration and material
"If you want to build a ship, don't drum up people together to collect wood and don't assign them tasks and work, but rather teach them to long for the endless immensity of the sea." This is one of the messages of the writer and pilot Antoine de Saint-Exupéry, the creator of the renowned novella "The Little Prince". A message that aims at conveying that, above all, inspiration is needed in order to create something new. The history of design gives proof that the versatility of wood, when boldly interpreted and put to creative use, has often been the birth of a new form, such as the Thonet coffee house chair from the 1930s whose design became possible through a new production technique of bending wood. The chair CH04 Houdini by e15 is yet another expression of the design possibilities that emerge when wood as a material is reinterpreted and its shape is defined in the manufacturing process. This chair's proportions and inviting appearance too are intricately linked to the production method itself. Made from thin oak-veneered plywood, it is inspired by a technique hitherto used only in aeroplane model making. The basic shape of this chair is created by first bending two-dimensional plywood by hand around a complexly milled solid wood ring to form the back. In order to make the curved two-dimensional elements stay in position, the scale-like arrangement of the slabs is then glued to the base to produce the self-contained seat shell. With its distinctive form language, this chair is appealing both placed in row at a dinner table and as a single object positioned within a space. Its daring design language captivates the of form captivates the beholder – as if the shape itself has revealed its own inspiration.

Formgebend – Inspiration und Material
„Wenn Du ein Schiff bauen willst, so trommle nicht Männer zusammen, um Holz zu beschaffen, Werkzeuge vorzubereiten, die Arbeit einzuteilen und Aufgaben zu vergeben, sondern lehre die Männer die Sehnsucht nach dem endlosen weiten Meer!" lautet ein Zitat des Schriftstellers und Piloten Antoine de Saint-Exupéry, des Schöpfers der Erzählung „Der Kleine Prinz". Es geht ihm dabei um die Inspiration, die nötig ist, wenn etwas Neues geschaffen werden soll. Der kreative Umgang mit dem vielseitigen Material Holz war in der Designgeschichte schon oft der Ausgangspunkt für neue Formen, so wurde die Gestaltung des Caféhaus-Stuhls von Thonet aus den 1930er Jahren ermöglicht durch den Einsatz eines neuen Biegeverfahrens für Holz. Der Stuhl CH04 Houdini von e15 ist ein weiterer Ausdruck der gestalterischen Möglichkeiten, die sich dann bieten, wenn das Material Holz neu interpretiert wird und ein Fertigungsverfahren die Form definiert. Die Proportionen dieses Stuhls stehen dabei in engem Zusammenhang mit seiner Herstellung. Gefertigt wird er aus mit Eiche furniertem Schichtholz nach einer Methode, die bis dahin vor allem im Flugzeugbau zum Einsatz kam. Die eigentliche Form dieses Stuhls entsteht, indem zunächst zweidimensionale Schichtholzplatten per Hand um einen gefrästen Massivholzring gebogen werden. Damit die gebogenen zweidimensionalen Elemente ihre Form halten können, werden die schuppenartig angeordneten Platten mit der Basis verleimt und bilden die geschlossene Sitzschale dieses Stuhls. In seiner Gestaltung prägnant, wirkt dieser Stuhl in Reihe an einem Esstisch ebenso wie einzeln gestellt im Objektbereich. Seine gewagte Formensprache zieht den Betrachter in ihren Bann – als erschließe sich mit der Form auch der Weg der Inspiration.

Metaphys lucano
Stepstool / Tritthocker

Hasegawa Kogyo Co., Ltd., Osaka, Japan
Design: Hers Experimental Design
Laboratory Inc. (Chiaki Murata),
Osaka, Japan
www.hasegawa-kogyo.co.jp
www.hers.co.jp
www.metaphys.jp

The metaphysics of the new
In famous libraries such as the British Library in London, stepstools are an important element of the inventory; if it was not for them visitors would not be able to reach up to the books on the uppermost shelves. In private households it too plays an important role, because many cupboards and shelves extend up high to the ceiling. Unlike in libraries, however, in private areas stepstools lead a rather shadowy existence: when not in use, they are usually stowed away somewhere in the cellar or a hidden corner in the living area. In order to put an end to this furniture hide-and-seek game, the design of Metaphys lucano reinterprets the classic stepstool as an integrated part of the living area. Aimed at presenting itself self-confidently to the beholder, it is intended to fit harmoniously into the interior. Following this goal, the stepstool surprises the user through a language of form that is overall clear and reduced to the essential. Slim and graceful, it blends neatly into the interior, exuding an appearance of elegance achieved through using only formally matched triangular elements for the legs and steps. To avoid an unnecessarily complex manufacturing process and keep production cost reasonable, the design of Metaphys lucano maintains the basic shape of conventional stepstools. Without adopting any specialised construction method, it nevertheless places particular emphasis on details: each element and component is elaborately designed so that the fastening screws remain invisible. Thus designed, this stepstool enriches the interior – and, in so doing, embodies an interesting metaphysics of the new.

Die Metaphysik des Neuen
In berühmten Bibliotheken wie etwa der British Library in London ist die Trittleiter ein wichtiger Teil des Inventars, ohne sie gelänge der Besucher niemals an die Bücher in den oberen Reihen. Auch im Privathaushalt spielt sie eine wichtige Rolle, da viele Schränke und Regale weit in die Höhe reichen. Anders als in den Bibliotheken fristet die Trittleiter im Privatbereich jedoch ein eher verborgenes Schattendasein: Bei Bedarf wird sie aus dem Keller oder einer nicht einsehbaren Ecke des Hauses hervorgeholt. Um dieses Versteckspiel zu beenden, interpretiert die Gestaltung von Metaphys lucano die klassische Trittleiter als einen integrativen Bestandteil des Innenbereichs. Sie soll sich selbstbewusst dem Betrachter präsentieren und zugleich das Interieur bereichern. Mit dieser Gestaltungsmaxime entstand ein Tritthocker, der mit seiner klaren und auf das Wesentliche reduzierten Formensprache überrascht. Grazil steht er im Raum und wirkt schlank und feingliedrig. Seine elegante Anmutung liegt vor allem darin begründet, dass für die Holme und Sprossen nur formal aufeinander abgestimmte Dreieckselemente verwendet werden. Um den Tritthocker nicht unnötig kompliziert zu machen und um die Herstellungskosten niedrig zu halten, folgt die Gestaltung der Grundbauweise einer klassischen Trittleiter. Metaphys lucano kommt ohne Spezialbauweise aus, der Schwerpunkt liegt vielmehr auf der Ausarbeitung der Details: Die Elemente und Bauteile sind so sorgfältig ausgeführt, dass keinerlei Befestigungsschrauben zu sehen sind. Derart gestaltet bereichert dieser Tritthocker das Interieur – und verkörpert dabei eine interessante Metaphysik des Neuen.

ORIZURU
Chair / Stuhl

Tendo Co., Ltd., Yamagata, Japan
Design: Ken Okuyama, Tokyo, Japan
www.tendo-mokko.co.jp
www.kenokuyamadesign.com

Floating – design and tradition

Origami, the art of folding paper into sculpture figures and geometric objects has a long tradition, particularly in Japan, its country of origin. It required concentration, a lot of time and a high degree of creative imagination. Origami can produce highly complex structures and is made without the use of scissors or adhesive glue from a single square sheet of paper. The design concept of the Orizuru chair adopts the structural folding technique of origami; its shape is inspired by a paper crane. Similar to an origami design, which is folded from only one piece of paper, Orizuru too is made from a single piece of plywood. And just like a paper crane, this chair when seen from the side seems to float in mid-air like a magical object. Despite this visual lightness the chair offers high stability and spring comfort for everyday use yet bearing up to 400 kg of static weight. Its high load-bearing capacity is also derived from the origami technique of structural folding, in combination with the choice of material: the ten layers of plywood include two extra sheets of rice paper to absorb the applied glue in order to strengthen the structure. Even the technology used to actually form this chair is astounding: its complex structure is created via a special single moulding press technique of Tendo Mokko, which already facilitated the shape of the famous "Butterfly" stool in the middle of the 20th century. Due to its design and its embodying a linking of tradition with innovation, the Orizuru chair is an object of high symbolic meaning, an object of complexity that at the same time reflects the meditative simplicity of origami.

In der Schwebe – Design und Tradition

Das Origami, das kunstvolle Falten von Figuren und geometrischen Objekten aus Papier, hat besonders in seinem Ursprungsland Japan eine lange Tradition und erfordert Konzentration, viel Zeit und ein hohes Maß an schöpferischer Vorstellungskraft. Ein Origami ist überaus komplex, es wird aus einem einzigen quadratischen Blatt ohne Schere und Klebstoff gefaltet. Das gestalterische Konzept des Stuhls Orizuru lehnt sich an die Grundprinzipien des Origami an, seine Form ist der Faltfigur eines Kranichs nachempfunden. Wie auch das Origami aus nur einem Blatt Papier gefaltet wird, besteht Orizuru aus einem einzigen Brett Sperrholz. Und wie die Figur eines Kranichs aus Papier scheint dieser Stuhl, von der Seite betrachtet, im Raum zu schweben und wirkt dort wie ein mystisches Objekt. Trotz dieser visuellen Leichtigkeit ist er jedoch alltagstauglich und stabil, mit seiner Federung bietet er Bequemlichkeit für jeden Tag und kann dabei eine Last bis zu einem Gewicht von 400 kg tragen. Seine Belastbarkeit beruht auf den Prinzipien der Origami-Falttechnik wie auch auf der Wahl der Materialien: Das verwendete 10-Schichten-Sperrholz enthält zusätzlich zwei Blätter Reispapier, das den Leim absorbiert und die Struktur des Stuhls dadurch verstärkt. Verblüffend ist auch eine weitere Technik, die bei diesem Stuhl zum Einsatz kommt: Seine komplexe Gestalt entsteht durch eine spezielle Verformungstechnik des Unternehmens Tendo Mokko, die Mitte des 20. Jahrhunderts bereits die bekannte Form des „Butterfly-Hockers" ermöglichte. Durch seine Gestaltung und die darin verwirklichte Verknüpfung von Tradition und Innovation ist der Stuhl Orizuru ein Objekt mit hoher Symbolkraft. In seiner Komplexität zeigt sich zugleich die meditative Einfachheit eines Origami.

Dyson Air Multiplier
Fan/Ventilator

Dyson GmbH, Cologne,
Germany/Köln, Deutschland
In-house design/Werksdesign:
James Dyson
www.dyson.de

In the air – design and imagination
Almost anywhere around the world refreshing air is used, be it via fans or air conditioning – and some indoor areas would be unbearable if it was not for fans running 24 hours around the clock. The working principle of fans is well known: rotating blades create an airflow which in turn creates a cooling effect. Radically questioning the form and principle of fans, the Dyson Air Multiplier is a device with an entirely new appearance. With its filigree loop sitting on top of a cylindrical base, it looks rather like a slender sculpture within a room than a generic fan. Though hard to imagine at first, it works without blades, yet is very powerful and can expel up to 450 litres of cool, uninterrupted air every second. Powered by a brushless and energy-efficient motor, it not only cools efficiently, but is also silent in operation and thus acoustically unobtrusive. The mechanism by which it makes air move is also the result of a high degree of design creativity: air is accelerated through an annular aperture set within the loop amplifier and channelled into a steady and smooth flow of air. The result is a pleasing effect, because – much like in an airplane – the surrounding air is drawn in and cooled without blowing a strong single jet of air towards the user. The sense of user comfort and ease is further enhanced by the possibility of tilting the fan with only a light touch and precisely adjusting and directing the cooling stream of air to where it is needed – a fan that looks like an airy object of the imagination and which, at the same time, embodies a new archetype of its product genre.

In the Air – Design und Imagination
Weltweit wird die Luft im Dienste des Menschen bewegt – es läuft die Air-Condition. Viele Räume sind nur durch die rund um die Uhr arbeitenden Ventilatoren erträglich. Das Prinzip eines Ventilators ist dabei stets dasselbe: Rotierende Flügel beschleunigen die Luft und bewirken so einen spürbaren Kühlungseffekt. Die Form und Arbeitsweise eines Ventilators grundlegend hinterfragend, entstand mit dem Dyson Air Multiplier nun ein Gerät mit einer völlig neuen Anmutung. Ein filigraner Ring sitzt auf einem zylindrischen Unterbau und wirkt im Raum eher wie eine schlanke Skulptur als wie ein Ventilator. Obwohl man es kaum vermutet, ist dieser ohne Flügel gestaltete Ventilator sehr leistungsfähig und kann pro Sekunde 450 Liter kühlende Luft erzeugen. Angetrieben von einem bürstenlosen und energieeffizienten Motor verrichtet er seine Kühltätigkeit zudem sehr leise und ist akustisch nicht wahrnehmbar. Ausdruck eines hohen Maßes gestalterischer Vorstellungskraft ist auch die Art und Weise, wie bei diesem Gerät die kühlende Luft in den Raum gelangt: Über eine ringförmige Öffnung wird die Luft beschleunigt und tritt stetig und gleichmäßig aus. Was sehr angenehm ist, denn wie im Flugzeug wird der Raum ringsum abgekühlt, ohne dass man vom Luftstrom direkt angeblasen würde. Das Gefühl von Ruhe und Komfort hat der Nutzer überdies, wenn er diesen Ventilator ausrichtet, denn mit einer sachten Bewegung wird er nur leicht gekippt, um seine Kühle in die gewünschte Richtung zu verströmen – wobei er wirkt wie ein luftiges Objekt der Imagination, das zugleich einen neuen Archetypus seiner Gattung kreiert.

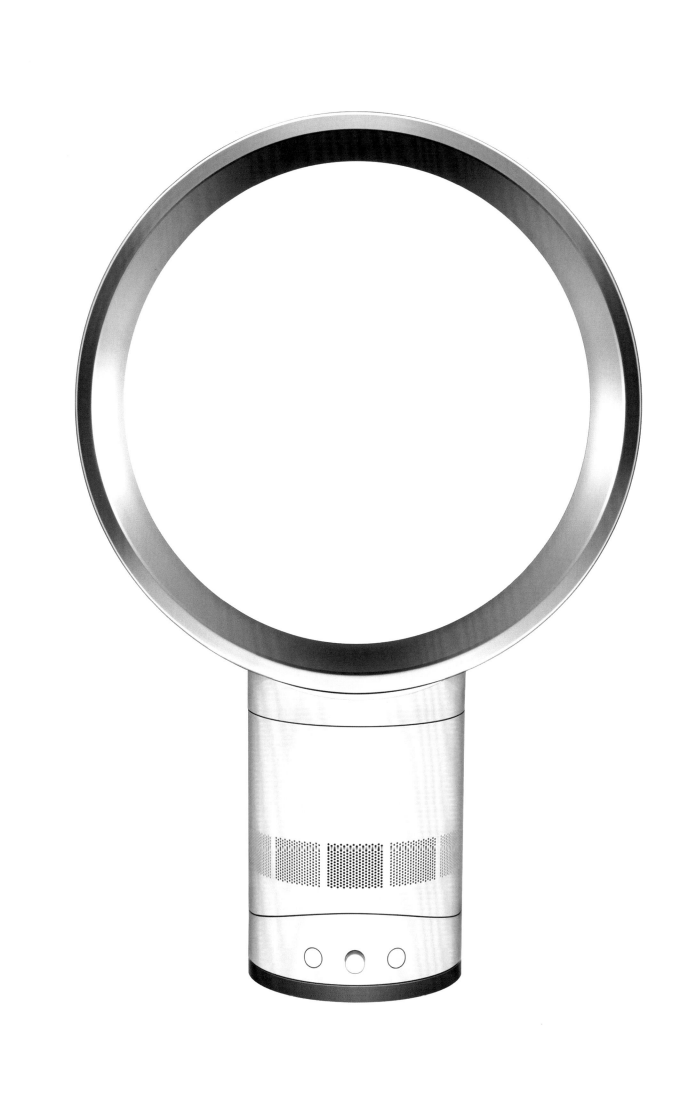

CBNes 6256
BioFresh Freshness Centre /
BioFresh-Frischecenter

Liebherr-Hausgeräte GmbH,
Ochsenhausen, Germany / Deutschland
In-house design / Werksdesign
Design: PRODESIGN Brüssing,
Neu-Ulm, Germany / Deutschland
www.liebherr.com
www.prodesign-ulm.de

Fresh form

They have on their shelves almost any
delicacy that can be found in the region.
Daily and weekly markets worldwide
follow almost the same basic structure and
distributors in Spain, China and Africa are
well informed about the foodstuffs that are
on offer. Be it vegetables, herbs, meat or fish,
high quality and freshness are a top priority.
The dictum of fresh and carefully selected
foodstuffs is reflected by the design of this
refrigerator in the form of a well-balanced
overall appearance. Defining itself as a
BioFresh freshness centre, this refrigerator
combines proven approaches in the storage
and preservation of high-quality foodstuffs
with modern and sophisticated user comfort.
The division of the refrigerator into three
different climate zones ensures storage at
precisely selected temperatures, with the
effect that the foodstuffs are kept fresh for
longer and do not loose flavour over time.
The interior of this freshness centre is clearly
arranged for easy user access, and the high-
quality impression is enhanced by the use of
innovative LED lighting technology. Meant
for daily use, this well thought-out design
is taken up in the freezer drawers, which
are mounted on telescopic rails and thus
open and close very easily. The user panel
featuring the MagicEye control system is
also convenient: all the functions can be
simply operated with a slight touch of a
finger on the self-explanatory electronic
panel. With its design, this well-conceived
refrigerator communicates a high degree
of understatement and at the same time
celebrates the freshness of foodstuffs – an
expression of a refined quality of life.

Frische Form

Sie offerieren alles, was die Region an
Köstlichkeiten zu bieten hat. Die Märkte
und Wochenmärkte sind weltweit in ihrer
Grundstruktur ähnlich, die Händler in
Spanien, China oder Afrika verstehen stets
viel von den jeweils angebotenen Lebens-
mitteln. Von Gemüse über Kräuter bis
hin zu Fleisch oder Fisch sind eine hohe
Qualität und vor allem Frische das oberste
Gebot. Die Maxime frischer und sorgfältig
ausgewählter Lebensmittel bildet die
Gestaltung dieses Kühlgeräts auf eine
stimmige Art und Weise ab. Als BioFresh-
Frischecenter verbindet es das Wissen um
die bestmögliche Lagerung hochwertiger
Lebensmittel mit einem durchdachten und
zeitgemäßen Komfort. Drei gut gegliederte
Klimazonen erlauben eine unterschiedlich
temperierte Lagerung mit dem Ergebnis,
dass die Lebensmittel sich länger halten
und ihr Geschmack durch die Lagerung
nicht leidet. Der Innenraum des Frische-
centers bietet einen guten Überblick, eine
innovative LED-Lichttechnologie vermittelt den Eindruck einer appetitlichen
Warenwelt. Diese tagtäglich erlebbar
durchdachte Gestaltung wird auch bei
den Gefrierfächern fortgeführt, sie laufen
auf Teleskopschienen und lassen sich deshalb sehr gut öffnen und schließen. Komfortabel ist zudem die Bedienoberfläche,
in deren Mittelpunkt die MagicEye-
Steuerung steht: Durch Berühren dieser
selbsterklärenden Elektronik-Oberfläche
werden die Funktionen gesteuert. Mit
seiner Gestaltung kommuniziert dieses
klar gestaltete Kühlgerät ein hohes Maß
an Understatement und zelebriert zugleich
die Frische der Lebensmittel – es wird zum
Ausdruck gehobener Lebensqualität.

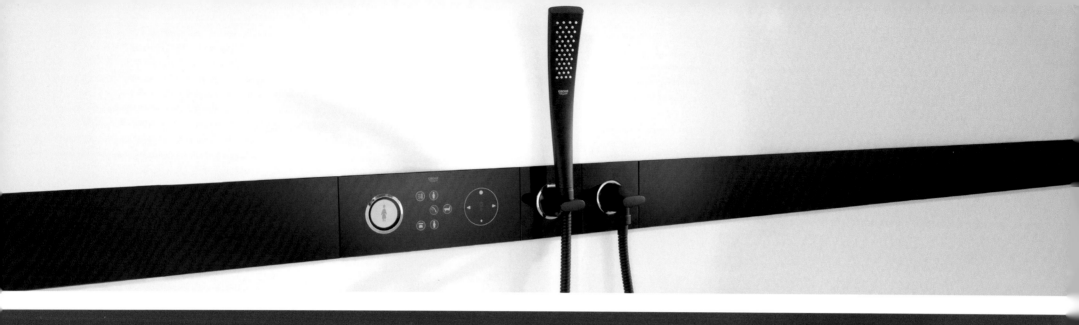

Grohe Ondus Digitecture
Digital Bath / Digitales Bad

Grohe AG,
Düsseldorf, Germany / Deutschland
In-house design / Werksdesign
www.grohe.com

Digital bath – design and architecture
Digitalisation currently contributes to
creating new and highly fascinating worlds
of wellness and comfort. Perfectly adjustable
to the needs and desires of users, modern
technologies facilitate a range of new
experiences, and architecture too focuses
strongly on realising customised user ideas.
Grohe Ondus Digitecture aims at a very
high level of comfort facilitated through
digitalisation and combines it with a new
impressive approach: as a system of modular
elements for the bathroom, it integrates the
architectural planning process right from
the start. The elegant design vocabulary of
this architectural concept is striking: it is
built strictly on the simple 5 x 5 cm grid
system common in architecture and thus
tries to make comfort an integrated part of
architecture, affording architects and users
a high degree of creative freedom. Grohe
Ondus Digitecture allows the preferred
combination of water temperature and
pressure to be programmed and, via an
intuitive interface, be memorised at the
press of a button for the next time of use.
When the pause button is pressed, the
system temporarily stops the water flow for
shampooing and then re-activates the water
at the exact same temperature – taking a
shower thus turns into a interactive and
resource-saving experience. Following a
consistent design approach, Grohe Ondus
Digitecture delivers both new solutions in
architecture and novel user possibilities.
The understanding of luxury too is
surprising and fascinating, as the premium
lifestyle collection comes complete with
a Champagne bucket, integrated storage
and vases, which aid the transition of the
bathroom from a functional space for
cleaning and grooming into a personal
sanctuary for well-being.

Digitales Bad – Design und Architektur
Durch Digitalisierung entstehen aktuell
neue und überaus faszinierende Welten
der Wellness und des Komforts. Die
modernen Technologien bieten exakt
auf die individuellen Bedürfnisse abgestimmte Erlebnismöglichkeiten, und auch
die Architektur richtet sich nach diesen
individuellen Vorstellungen. Grohe Ondus
Digitecture ermöglicht hier eine überaus
komfortorientierte Form der Digitalisierung und verbindet dies mit einem beein-
druckenden neuen Ansatz: Als ein System
aufeinander abgestimmter Module für das
Badezimmer integriert es von Beginn an
die Planungsmöglichkeiten der Architektur.
Auffällig ist die elegante Formensprache
dieses architektonischen Konzepts, das
sich strikt nach dem in der Architektur
gängigen Raster von 5 x 5 cm richtet. Der
Komfort soll damit zu einem integrativen
Teil der Architektur werden und dem Architekten wie auch dem Nutzer ein hohes
Maß an gestalterischem Raum bieten. So
kann bei Grohe Ondus Digitecture die
Wassertemperatur und -menge gespeichert
und auf einem intuitiv zu bedienenden
Menü abgerufen werden. Tippt man die
Pausetaste, wird der Wasserfluss zum
Shampoonieren der Haare unterbrochen
und danach mit der gleichen Wassertemperatur wieder gestartet – das Duschen
wird zu einem die Ressourcen schonenden
interaktiven Erlebnis. Mit einem stringent
verfolgten Konzept bietet Grohe Ondus
Digitecture neue Lösungsmöglichkeiten
für die Architektur und den Nutzer. Über-
raschend und zugleich spannend ist auch
das dadurch verwirklichte Verständnis
von Luxus, denn die Premium-Lifestyle-
Kollektion umfasst außerdem einen
Champagner-Kübel, integrierte Sturäume
sowie Vasen und wandelt so das Bad von
einem funktionalen Ort der Reinigung und
Pflege in eine persönliche Wohlfühl-Oase.

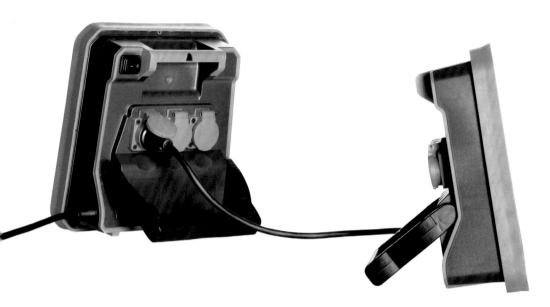

**Gladiator II
Mobile Workplace Luminaire/
Mobile Arbeitsleuchte**

Sonlux GmbH,
Sondershausen, Germany/Deutschland
In-house design/Werksdesign
www.sonlux.de

A ready helper

They turn the night into day. Thanks to good illumination, people working night shifts stay awake longer and work more effectively. British researchers have found out that bright light counteracts fatigue by blocking the production of melatonin in the body, a messenger compound that regulates the sleep-wake cycle. People working on dark building sites or factories are, for various reasons, dependent on sophisticated light sources. Gladiator II is such a well thought-out workplace luminaire, as its functionality harmoniously reflects the reality and illumination demands of today's workplaces. Fascinating design aspects include its robust and ergonomically shaped body, paired with the choice of materials: it consists of a hard, non-breakable and impact-resistant component and a soft one made of durable TPE plastic. Well matched in colour choice, this soft material is pleasing to the touch and, at the same time, lends it an unusual, yet friendly appearance that is very unusual for workplace luminaires. To offer a high degree of mobility that is needed in everyday work, the luminaire features an easy-to-grab handle and a bracket that offers four different angle adjustments; thus this workplace luminaire blends well into many different environments, providing very good illumination even for difficult workspaces. The harmonious concept is also taken up in the choice of the actual light source: the luminaire is equipped with two compact, EVG-powered and energy-saving 36-watt TC-F fluorescent lamps, which provide calm, non-flicker anti-glare illumination – thus designed, this luminaire is a ready helper in today's workplace.

Gewappneter Helfer

Sie machen die Nacht zum Tag. Durch eine gute Beleuchtung bleiben Nachtarbeiter besser wach und arbeiten effektiver. Englische Forscher haben entdeckt, dass helles Licht die aufkommende Müdigkeit vertreibt, da es die müde machende Produktion des Botenstoffes Melatonin im Körper blockiert. Die Menschen, die auf Baustellen oder in Fabriken im Dunkeln arbeiten, sind aus vielerlei Gründen auf eine durchdachte Lichtquelle angewiesen. Gladiator II ist eine sehr intelligent gestaltete Arbeitsleuchte, deren Funktionalität den Arbeitsalltag stimmig abbildet und die das Arbeitsfeld gut ausleuchtet. Faszinierend sind das robuste, ergonomisch gestaltete Gehäuse dieser Leuchte und die Wahl der Materialien: Die Leuchte besteht aus einer schlag- und bruchfesten harten Komponente sowie einem weichen Anteil aus dem langlebigen Kunststoff TPE. Das weiche, farblich abgesetzte Material gibt dieser Leuchte eine angenehme Haptik und verleiht ihr zudem eine für Arbeitsleuchten sehr ungewöhnliche, weil freundliche Anmutung. Für die im Arbeitsalltag nötige Mobilität wurden ein gut greifbarer Tragegriff sowie ein Ausleger integriert, mit dem der Standwinkel in vier Positionen verstellt werden kann. Auf diese Weise kann sich die Arbeitsleuchte unterschiedlichen Situationen anpassen und auch schwierige Arbeitsfelder sehr gut ausleuchten. Das stimmige Konzept wird in der Wahl der Leuchtmittel weitergeführt: Ausgestattet ist diese Arbeitsleuchte mit zwei energiesparenden EVG-betriebenen TC-F-Kompaktleuchtstofflampen mit je 36 Watt, die ein beruhigendes Licht ausstrahlen, welches weder flackert noch blendet – durch ihre Gestaltung ist sie damit ein gut gewappneter Helfer für die Arbeitswelt.

**Velux sun tunnel by Lovegrove/
Velux Tageslicht-Spot by Lovegrove**

Velux A/S, Hoersholm,
Denmark / Dänemark
Design: Ross Lovegrove, London, GB
www.velux.com
www.rosslovegrove.com

Funnelling natural light

The sun plays a key role in many creation
myths, in which the sun is often personified
and represented as a God-like figure. In
Chinese legends, for instance, we find the
story of the sun god Shen Yi. When the
earth was scorched by the heat of ten
suns, he shot down nine with a bow and
arrow to save the world. In Greek-Roman
mythology we have Apollo who is the god
of light and possesses the gift of prophesy.
A fascinating interpretation of what the sun
can also signify is presented by the design
of the Sun Tunnel. Designed according to
the head note "If this is a lamp, the sun
is the bulb", this lamp takes sunlight and
using an innovative approach turns it into a
light source for indoor spaces. The working
principle is simple and highly effective: a
long tube-like tunnel brings natural daylight
from the roof of a building to the ceiling
of otherwise electrically lit rooms. The
formal mediator for the light being directed
from the outside comes in the shape of a
fascinatingly organic-looking lamp body.
This body functions as an additional diffuser
that both enhances the natural light and
spreads it in dynamic light reflections across
the room. Just like almost any electric lamp,
the natural light of this lamp can be directed
and adjusted according to user's needs.
The Sun Tunnel embodies an impressive
lighting concept that not only makes use
of a natural resource, but also offers a new
approach to the experience of sunlight; for
its designer, Ross Lovegrove, it constitutes
"...a contemporary interface between the
tunnel of light and the interior design of
living spaces." With a design marked by
lightness and imaginativeness, this interface
also builds a bridge into the future – in a
figurative sense, it funnels our thinking.

Licht aus dem Tunnel

Die Sonne spielt in Schöpfungsmythen
eine große Rolle und oft wird sie perso-
nifiziert und gottähnlich dargestellt. In
chinesischen Mythen etwa wird erzählt,
dass der Sonnengott Shen Yi, als die Erde
von zehn Sonnen verbrannt zu werden
drohte, neun mit seinen Pfeilen abschoss,
um dadurch die Welt zu retten. Und in
der griechisch-römischen Mythologie ist
Apollon der mit seherischen Fähigkeiten
ausgestattete Gott des Lichts. Eine faszinierende Interpretation der Bedeutung
der Sonne birgt die Gestaltung von
Sun Tunnel. Entworfen mit dem Leitsatz
„Wenn dies eine Lampe ist, dann ist die
Sonne die Glühbirne dafür" wird hier das
Sonnenlicht auf innovative Art und Weise
als Lichtquelle für die Architektur genutzt.
Das Prinzip ist so einfach wie effektiv:
Über einen langen schlauchähnlichen
Tunnel wird das natürliche Licht von
außen in innenliegende Räume geleitet,
wo es das elektrische Licht ersetzt. Der
formale Mittler für das von außen ein-
tretende Licht ist ein faszinierend organisch gestalteter Tageslicht-Spot. Er hat
die Funktion eines Zusatzdiffusors, denn
er verstärkt das Licht und ermöglicht
zugleich spannungsreiche Lichtreflexionen
im Raum. Wie bei einer elektrischen Lampe
kann man diesen Tageslicht-Spot ausrichten und individuell nach seinen Wünschen regulieren. Mit dem Sun Tunnel
entstand ein eindrucksvolles Lichtkonzept,
welches die natürlichen Ressourcen nutzt
und das Sonnenlicht auf neue Weise
wahrnehmbar macht. Für seinen Designer
Ross Lovegrove ist es „.... eine zeitgenössische Schnittstelle zwischen dem Tunnel
des Lichts und der Innenarchitektur der
Wohnräume." Mit einer von Leichtigkeit und Phantasie geprägten Gestaltung
schlägt diese Schnittstelle auch Brücken
in die Zukunft – im übertragenen Sinne
wird sie zu einem Tunnel neuen Denkens.

Juwel Novaplus Evolution
Rotary Clothes Dryer / Wäschespinne

Juwel H. Wüster GmbH,
Garmisch-Partenkirchen,
Germany / Deutschland
Design: Busse Design + Engineering
(Michael Tinius), Elchingen,
Germany / Deutschland
www.juwel.com
www.busse-design.com

Mary Poppins in the garden

Rotary clothes dryers are highly effective helpers in everyday household work since the 1950s. Unlike conventional clothes lines, a rotary clothes dryer can be folded together and stored in a protection cover. The design of the Novaplus Evolution extends this time-proven principle of drying clothes by an exciting aspect of functionality: this rotary clothes dryer can open and deploy the lines "as if all by itself". The opening and deploying mechanism is activated by a short pull of the handle which makes the dryer unfold in a gentle manner. This automatic movement might have the same effect on the user as the exclamation "Supercalifragilisticexpialidocious!" by musical and film character Mary Poppins. Just like this loving nanny who with her umbrella floats, so to speak, through everyday life, the opening and deploying movement of this rotary clothes dryer performs its own magic – with an emotionalising appeal for the user. Moreover, an integrated cover which protects the whole dryer opens with just one turn of the hand, this puts an end to the cumbersome folding process and subsequent search for the right protection cover. Other useful design details are non-stretching lines that do not wear out, as well as the fact that the dryer is easy to install in the garden without concrete – where, due to a helical shaped grounding tube, it withstands all kinds of weather conditions. As if bestowing its users with magic abilities, the design of this product thus embodies a new and almost exhilarating lightness.

Mary Poppins im Garten

Die Wäschespinne ist seit den 1950er Jahren eine sehr effektive und dienstbare Helferin im Alltag. Anders als eine Wäscheleine kann sie zugeklappt unter einer schützenden Hülle verborgen werden und wird erst bei Bedarf aktiv. Diese erprobte Art des Wäschetrocknens bereichert die Gestaltung von Novaplus Evolution um spannende Aspekte der Funktionalität: Diese Wäschespinne kann sich „wie von selbst" öffnen und spannen. Mit einer sanft anmutenden Bewegung wird sie entfaltet, der Öffnen- und Spannmechanismus erfolgt leichtgängig über einen Griff. Es entsteht eine Bewegung, die auf den Nutzer ähnlich wirkt wie die Formel „Supercalifragilisticexpialigetisch!" der Musical- und Filmfigur Mary Poppins. Wie dieses mit magischen Fähigkeiten ausgestattete Kindermädchen, das mit seinem Regenschirm durch den Alltag schwebt, mutet auch die Bewegung dieser Wäschespinne an – das Öffnen und Spannen erfolgt fließend und emotionalisiert den Nutzer. Zudem entfallen das oft mühsame Schließen und das Suchen nach der passenden Hülle, da eine eingebaute Schutzhülle mit nur einem Handgriff über die Spinne gezogen wird. Nützliche Details dieser Wäschespinne sind darüber hinaus Leinen, die sich nicht mehr dehnen und ausleiern können, sowie die Tatsache, dass sie auch ohne Einbetonieren fest im Garten steht – dort trotzt sie, nur über eine Eindreh-Bodenhülse befestigt, den Unbilden des Wetters. Als verleihe sie magische Fähigkeiten, gelingt der Gestaltung dieses Produkts eine neue und geradezu beschwingende Leichtigkeit.

Honda EU 30i Generator

Honda R&D Europe
(Deutschland) GmbH, Offenbach/Main,
Germany / Deutschland
In-house design / Werksdesign:
Honda R&D Co.,
Ltd. Power Products R&D Center,
Asaka-shi, Saitama-ken, Japan
www.world.honda.com

Compact supply

Amber, which in Greek was "electron", had already revealed its secret to the scholars of antiquity: when rubbed briskly, amber builds up an electrostatic charge that can be put to use. The search for new power sources and possibilities for generating electricity from then on inspired crowds of scientists to investigate in this direction. Today electricity flows almost everywhere around the globe, and without it civilisation would have been unthinkable – yet there are many places that are cut off from reliable power networks, such as secluded areas and outdoor terrain, where mobile generators are used to bridge this gap in supply. The Honda EU 30i is such a device, with an innovative and highly compact design of well thought-out and user-friendly functionality. Due to its fully sealed plastic body this generator is conveniently quiet. The material is robust and assures a low weight of just 35 kg. Featuring big wheels and an ergonomic carry handle that folds into its side, this generator is very easy to manoeuvre and allows comfortable loading and transportation. Providing intuitive operability, the device is easy to maintain and handle: all operation elements and outlets are jointly located in the illuminated front panel so that the unit can be easily controlled, even in the dark. As additional technical feature an eco throttle control assures low consumption as well as little noise. Furthermore, the voltage output and frequency are stable at all times, which is important when connecting sensitive electronic equipment such as laptops and TVs. With its design, the Honda EU 30i generator redefines the art of such devices – towards a versatile power supply that aestheticises the way in which energy is sourced.

Kompakte Quelle

Der Bernstein, im Griechischen „Elektron" genannt, offenbarte bereits den Gelehrten der Antike sein Geheimnis: reibt man ihn kräftig, lädt er sich statisch auf und es fließt Strom. Die Suche nach Elektrizitätsquellen und den Möglichkeiten, Strom zu erzeugen, animierte später zahlreiche Wissenschaftler zu entsprechenden Forschungen. Heute ist Elektrizität allgegenwärtig, und ohne sie wäre Zivilisation nicht vorstellbar – dennoch sind viele Orte von einer zuverlässigen Stromzufuhr abgeschnitten. In abseits gelegenem Gelände oder in der freien Natur werden deshalb transportable Stromgeneratoren eingesetzt, um diese Lücke zu überbrücken. Der Honda EU 30i ist ein Gerät für solche Zwecke mit einer innovativen und sehr kompakten Gehäuseform sowie einer durchdachten und nutzerfreundlichen Funktionalität. Durch ein rundherum geschlossenes Kunststoffgehäuse ist dieses Gerät angenehm leise, das verwendete Material ist robust und ermöglicht ein nur geringes Gewicht von 35 kg. Der Generator ist zudem ergonomisch gestaltet und gut transportabel, große Räder und ein seitlich ausklappbarer Griff erleichtern den Transport zu den Einsatzorten. Die Art seiner Bedienung erschließt sich dem Nutzer intuitiv und im Gebrauch: Alle Bedienelemente und Steckdosen sind übersichtlich im Frontpanel angeordnet und gut beleuchtet, sodass man das Gerät auch im Dunkeln bedienen kann. Eine weitere technische Besonderheit ist eine Ökoschaltung, die einen niedrigen Verbrauch bei geringer Lautstärke erlaubt. Außerdem bleiben Spannung und Frequenz stets konstant, weshalb auch empfindliche Geräte wie Laptop oder TV betrieben werden können. Durch seine Gestaltung definiert der Generator Honda EU 30i seine Gerätegattung neu – hin zu einer vielseitigen Stromquelle, die diese Art der Stromerzeugung ästhetisiert.

Fiskars X Range
Axes/Äxte

Fiskars, Billnäs, Finland/Finnland
In-house design/Werksdesign:
Fiskars R&D, Billnäs
www.fiskars.com

Well handled – design and the interpretation of a tool

The axe is one of oldest tools known to mankind. In 1999, near Lake Zug in Switzerland, an axe of the Chassey-Lagozza-Cortaillod culture was found, showing how ergonomic these tools had already become 3,000 years ago. The skills needed to forge a good axe over the open fire and hammer it into shape, was an ability that blacksmiths in later years too acquired only after long years of training, and there were real masters of the art whose expertise was highly sought after. The X Range axes are designed with enhanced blade geometry, which has improved the functionality of the tool. The outcome of a long process, the weight of the head and shaft of these axes was balanced until it reached the best possible distribution to ensure that it rests comfortably in the hand for the most efficient use. Efficiency and safety are matters of great concern when working with an axe to chop firewood, for example, and so the design of the blade too has been retouched. The axes of this series feature a convex-shaped and double-hardened blade; the blade is safe from fracture and its rounded edges ensure easy removal from the log when splitting wood. An additional aspect that makes these axes easy to handle is their ergonomically shaped handle: with their innovative surface structure, these anti-shock handles absorb grip friction when chopping wood and thus ensure a firm and comfortable feel. The safety aspect is further augmented by the hook-shaped end of the handle, which prevent the hands from slipping and thus protects against accidents. In addition, the axes come with a sheath which simultaneously serves as a carrying grip and facilitates easy handling and protection of the blade – a tool that has always been important to mankind thus turns into a true experience of functionality and ergonomics.

Im Griff – Design und die Interpretation eines Werkzeugs

Die Axt ist eines der ältesten Werkzeuge des Menschen. Eine im Jahre 1999 am Zuger See in der Schweiz gefundene Axt der Chassey-Lagozza-Cortaillod-Kultur zeigt, wie ergonomisch diese Werkzeuge bereits vor 3.000 Jahren gestaltet waren. Die Fertigkeit, am offenen Feuer eine gute Axt zu schmieden und sie auszuhämmern, erwarb auch in späteren Zeiten ein Werkzeugschmied erst nach langen Jahren und es gab Meister ihres Fachs, deren Kunst sehr gefragt war. Die Gestaltung der X Range-Äxte verbessert die Klingen-Geometrie und die Funktionalität dieses Werkzeugs. In einem langen Prozess wurde die Gewichtsverteilung zwischen Kopf und Stiel der Axt so lange austariert, bis sie im bestmöglichen Verhältnis stand und die Axt dadurch gut und komfortabel in der Hand liegt. Da es bei der Arbeit mit einer Axt, wie etwa beim Spalten von Brennholz, auch um Effizienz und Sicherheit geht, wurde außerdem die Gestaltung der Klinge neu überdacht. Die Äxte dieser Serie haben eine konvex geformte und doppelt gehärtete Klinge. Diese ist bruchsicher und ihre abgerundeten Kanten erleichtern beim Holzspalten, die Klinge ohne große Schwierigkeit wieder herauszuziehen. Ein weiterer arbeitserleichternder Aspekt ist der ergonomisch gestaltete Griff dieser Äxte: Durch eine innovative Oberflächenstruktur absorbiert er Vibrationen beim Holzhacken, bietet sicheren Halt und fühlt sich haptisch angenehm und griffig an. Die Sicherheit erhöht zusätzlich ein hakenförmig ausgebildetes Griffende, welches verhindert, dass die Hände abrutschen können. Etwaige Unfälle werden deshalb vermieden, ein Klingenschutz, der auch als Tragegriff für diese Äxte dient, ermöglicht zudem eine sichere Aufbewahrung und schützt zugleich den Axtkopf – ein wichtiges Werkzeug des Menschen wird so zu einem Erlebnis von Funktionalität und Ergonomie.

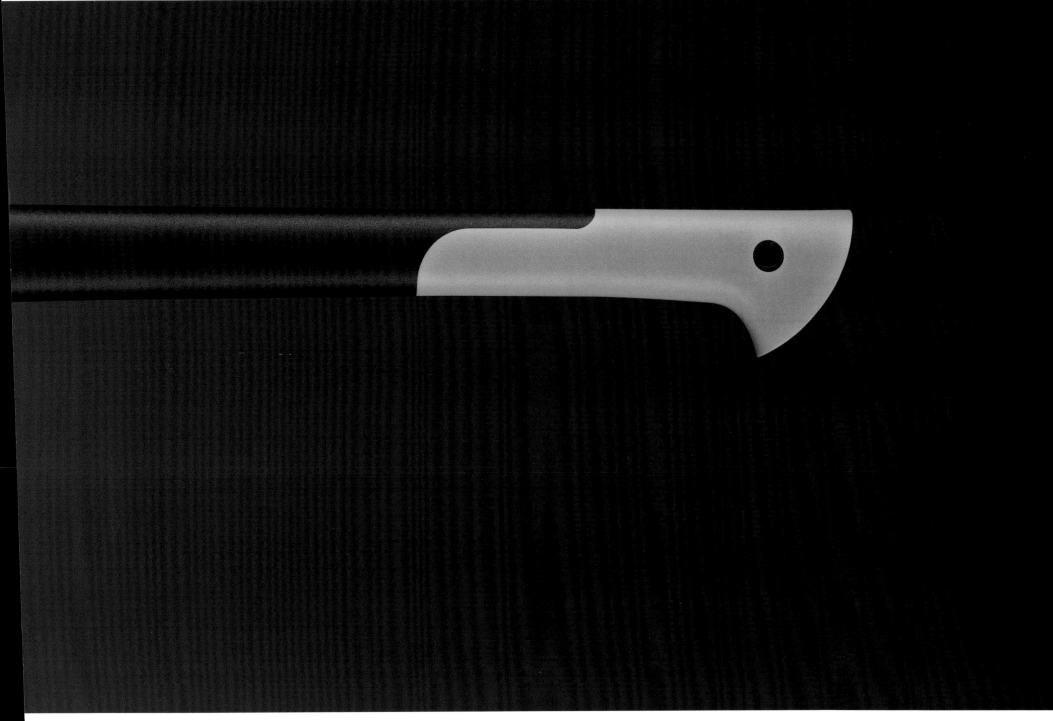

Van Gogh Museum Shop

Design: Day Creative Business Partners B.V. (Gesina Roters, Louk de Sévaux, Mette Hoekstra), Amsterdam, NL
www.day.nu

Among masters

Museums such as the Van Gogh Museum in Amsterdam are true crowd pullers. This museum has a large collection of artworks by Van Gogh and other 19th century artists on display. Closely linked to its significance and popularity is the architecture by Gerrit Rietveld, who was also highly successful as a designer of the De Stijl group. The task to extend the museum shop and at the same time enrich the architecture both in function and aesthetics was therefore a big challenge. The new museum shop was to be larger than before, serve substantially more visitors, and live up to the international reputation of the museum. The architectural conclusion follows an environmental design, which subtly integrates the shop into the existing monumental museum architecture, while at the same time retaining the shop's sense of architectural uniqueness. The entire entrance area was taken into account in order to integrate the shop in the flow of the building. The detailed grid of the building developed by Gerrit Rietveld served as a visual guideline for the shop's interior design: it was used as a point of orientation in proportioning all components of the store into a well-balanced unity. The result is a shop that aims to impress museum visitors though its bold design. With clear lines and balanced contrasts in black and white it embodies an invitingly staged world for visitors and consumers. Dark natural stone, which varies according to sections, and dark shelves meet white installations of sculptural appearance, which also serve as product displays and room partitions. Also visually enticing is the combination of natural and artificial light sources: the products and books as they are presented in the displays look like warmly illuminated objects that amaze and astonish visitors. This shop thus embodies both an architectural as well as consumption-oriented attraction within the museum – users experience it as a unified whole that leaves a lasting impression.

Unter Meistern

Museen wie das Van Gogh Museum in Amsterdam sind wahre Publikumsmagneten. Dieses Museum präsentiert eine große Sammlung der Werke Van Goghs und anderer Künstler des 19. Jahrhunderts. Eng verknüpft mit seiner Bedeutung und Popularität ist die Architektur von Gerrit Rietveld, der auch als Designer der De-Stijl-Gruppe sehr erfolgreich war. Die Aufgabe, den Shop dieses Museums zu erweitern und dabei die Architektur funktional wie auch ästhetisch zu bereichern, war deshalb eine große Herausforderung. Der neue Museumsshop sollte größer werden, die steigenden Besucherzahlen bedienen und auch dem internationalen Ruf des Museums entsprechen. Dem Konzept eines Environmental Designs folgend entstand dabei eine Architektur, die auf eine sehr feinsinnige Art und Weise einen auch architektonisch eigenständig wahrnehmbaren Shop in den vorhandenen Monumentalbau einpasst. Dessen gesamter Eingangsbereich wurde mit einbezogen, um den Shop in die Linienführung des Gebäudes zu integrieren. Als visuelles Leitelement für das Interior Design diente das bereits von Gerrit Rietveld entworfene Gitter-Design des Gebäudes: Es wurde zur Orientierung genutzt, um alle Bestandteile in ein ausgewogenes Verhältnis zu setzen. Das Ergebnis ist ein Shop, der mit seiner mutigen Gestaltung die Museumsbesucher beeindruckt. Mit klaren Linien und ausgewogenen Kontrasten der Farben Schwarz und Weiß stellt er eine einladend inszenierte Warenwelt dar. Ein dunkler und je nach Bereich variierender Naturstein sowie dunkle Regale werden kombiniert mit weißen, sehr skulpturalen, raumgestaltenden Installationen, die als Produktdisplays und Raumgliederungselemente dienen. Überaus spannungsreich ist zudem die Verknüpfung von natürlichem und inszeniertem Licht: Die Produkte und Bücher wirken, teils in Vitrinen präsentiert, wie reizvoll illuminierte Objekte, die zum Staunen und zum Betrachten anregen. Dieser Shop ist damit sowohl eine architektonische wie auch konsumorientierte Attraktion innerhalb des Museums – dem Besucher bietet sich ein als Ganzes wahrnehmbares, unvergessliches Erlebnis.

**Moving Moments –
BMW 7 Series Dealer Drive Event /
Moving Moments –
BMW 7er Händlerveranstaltung**

BMW Group, Munich, Germany /
München, Deutschland
Design: Blue Scope GmbH
(Sylvia Demes, Uwe Prell,
Christoph Schmuck, Mischa Schulze,
Andreas Stephan, Gregor Siber),
Berlin, Germany / Deutschland
Trade fair construction / Messebau:
Nüssli AG, Hüttwilen,
Switzerland / Schweiz
www.bmw.de
www.bluescope.de

A royal stage
They represent luxury and splendid variety.
Baroque castles like the castle grounds of
Schleißheim near Munich were created in a
time, when architecture dealt with manifold
ornamenting elements, and abundance
was a maxim. Between 1701 and 1726
the Schleißheim New Palace was built by
order of Elector Max Emanuel following the
plans of Enrico Zuccalli. With the largest
ceiling painting of its time and an imposing
flight of stairs it expresses Max Emanuel's
exalted attitude towards life as well as his
claim to power. A similar aesthetic, and

with it the implied lifestyle, is taken up in
the temporary architecture for a six-week
product presentation event for the BMW 7
Series, which too embodies an impressive
scenario. Set against the monumental castle
facade, which serves as both the setting for
the presentation of the vehicle fleet and the
gala dinners, the design aims at creating
an atmosphere of luxurious and glamorous
opulence. Even though this might at first
surprise beholders as being a dramaturgically
staged contrast, the concept still manages to
harmoniously combine the castle facade with
the other architectural elements: the pavilion

for the presentation of the vehicles features
a clear layout with flowing lines that make
the outside and the inside spaces blend into
one another, lending the architecture an
exciting feel of transparency. The interior
itself showcases a rather reduced design,
yet with colossal luminaries that create a
visual link to the large-size castle facade.
"Innovation from Tradition" is thus realised
in a highly subtle manner. The staging of
a baroque life thus is brought in line with
the aesthetics and the environment of the
displayed products – the presentation, in the
here and now, of a virtually royal stage.

Königlich inszeniert

Sie verkörpern Luxus und prunkvolle Vielfalt. Barocke Schlösser wie das in der Barockanlage in Schleißheim bei München entstanden in einer Zeit, in der die Architektur mit vielfältigen verzierenden Elementen arbeitete und der Überfluss die Maxime war. Das Neue Schloss Schleißheim wurde zwischen 1701 und 1726 im Auftrag des Kurfürsten Max Emanuel nach Plänen von Enrico Zuccalli erbaut. Mit dem größten Deckengemälde seiner Zeit und einer imposanten Treppenanlage ist es ein Ausdruck des gehobenen Lebensgefühls, aber auch des Machtanspruchs Max Emanuels. An diese Ästhetik und den damit verbundenen Lebensstil knüpft die temporäre Architektur für eine sechswöchige Händlervorstellung des BMW 7ers an und schafft dabei ein eindrucksvolles Szenario. Über die imposante Schlossfassade, die zugleich das Szenenbild für die Enthüllung der Fahrzeugflotte sowie für ein Galadinner liefert, verwirklicht sich die von der Gestaltung angestrebte Atmosphäre des Luxuriösen und Glamourösen. Auch wenn dies den Betrachter als dramaturgisch inszenierter Kontrast zunächst überrascht, gelingt es dennoch, diese Schlossfassade stimmig mit den übrigen architektonischen Elementen zu verbinden: Klar gestaltet ist der Pavillon für die eigentliche Präsentation der Fahrzeuge, fließende Linien lassen im Raum die Wahrnehmung von Innen und Außen verschwimmen und schaffen eine spannungsreiche architektonische Transparenz. Auch das Interieur ist zurückhaltend ausgestattet, wobei überdimensionale Kronleuchter eine visuelle Brücke zur großformatigen Schlossfassade bilden. „Innovation aus Tradition" wird auf diese Weise sehr feinsinnig umgesetzt. Die Vorstellung einer barocken Lebenswelt steht im Einklang mit der Ästhetik und der Lebenswelt des präsentierten Produktes – es wirkt, im Hier und Jetzt, geradezu königlich inszeniert.

Container Scope
Oceanscope

Design: AnL Studio
(Keehyun Ahn, Minsoo Lee),
Seoul, Korea
Art Direction/Planning:
Gilhwang Chang, Busan, Korea
Incheon Metropolitan City
www.incheon.go.kr

A place in the sun

Ports all around the globe have something magical about them; they are passages to the world. While only one hundred years ago it was sailing ships that offloaded precious goods such as silk, pepper and cacao, today harbours are pivots of international trade, with goods being shipped in uniform-sized containers. The design of the Container Scope uses these containers and their symbolism for an architectonically interesting approach that relates them to human beings and the environment. The concept behind this is inspirational and visionary, as it expresses a clear assimilation of the reality in the port city of Incheon in South Korea. In order to lend the many unused containers in its port an architectural significance that the public too benefits from, these containers underwent "recycling", so to speak: they establish observatory platforms by being stacked on top of one another to form geometrical constructions. Since these containers are located next to the historic "sunset place" of Incheon city, the concept centred above all on the view and the possibility to watch the sunset in the port. The arrangement of the containers followed the limitations of the building site, since the ground level was too low to allow a direct view of the sunset, the containers' structures were set at various angles. Visitors are lead via the various staircases and rails upwards to higher positions, each with diverse viewpoints to watch the sun set in their city – in a symbiosis of limitations and imaginativeness thus emerged an architectural object of marked distinction, offering citizens a place in the sun.

Ein Platz an der Sonne

Den Häfen dieser Erde wohnt etwas Magisches inne, sie sind ein Tor zur Welt. Wo noch vor hunderten von Jahren die Segelschiffe kostbare Dinge wie Seide, Pfeffer oder Kakao anlieferten, sind die Häfen heute Dreh- und Angelpunkt des internationalen Handels. Ein Unterschied ist, dass die Güter dabei in fest definierten Einzelräumen, den Containern, verschifft werden. Die Gestaltung von Container Scope nutzt die Container und deren Symbolik architektonisch auf spannende Art und Weise und stellt sie in eine Beziehung zu den Menschen und ihrer Umgebung. Inspiriert und visionär ist der dahinter stehende Ansatz und er hat in der Hafenstadt Incheon an der Nordwestküste Südkoreas einen klaren Bezug zur Realität: Um den zahlreichen ungenutzten Containern im Hafen eine sinnvolle architektonische Bedeutung zu verleihen, die auch der Öffentlichkeit etwas bietet, wurden die Container quasi architektonisch „recycelt": Es entstanden attraktive Aussichtsplattformen, indem mehrere Container übereinander zu geometrischen Bauwerken verschachtelt wurden. Da diese Container in Incheon neben einem historischen „Sonnenplatz" aufgestellt sind, stand vor allem die Aussicht und der Blick auf die Sonne im Hafen im Mittelpunkt des Konzepts. Die Anordnung der Container folgt den Gegebenheiten dieses Aufstellplatzes und da dort eine ebenerdige Aufstellung keinen Blick auf den Sonnenuntergang erlaubt hätte, wurden die Container in verschiedenen Winkeln geneigt. Der Besucher lässt sich nun von Treppen und Geländern auf die nächste Ebene dirigieren und hat stets den Blick auf die Sonne im Hafen seiner Stadt – in einer Symbiose von Imagination und Notwendigkeit entstand ein architektonisches Objekt von zeichenhafter Prägnanz, für die Bewohner ist es ihr Platz an der Sonne.

Ornilux Mikado
Bird–Protection Glass / Vogelschutzglas

Glaswerke Arnold GmbH & Co. KG,
Remshalden, Germany / Deutschland
In-house design / Werksdesign:
Christian Irmscher
www.arnold-glas.de
www.ornilux.de

Discreet lifesaver

They seem to "know" about the special senses of birds. Orb-web spiders, of which there are more than 2,800 species including the garden spider, for instance, protect their laboriously woven nets with a special UV-light reflecting silk from birds flying though them and destroying them. Birds can perceive these reflections of UV light and thus recognise the thin nets as obstacles. By now, ornithologists and engineers also take advantage of this effect with regard to glass architecture: since birds often hurt themselves when crashing unwillingly into transparent or reflecting surfaces, the idea was to use the bird's special ability to perceive UV light and put it to use in protecting them. The design of the Ornilux Mikado bird-protection glass translates this profound discovery into an impressive product: it provides architecture with the possibility of making window panes and glass fronts safer from now on for all birds without the need to resort to special stickers. This innovative bird protection glass was developed in close collaboration with the Max Planck Institute for Ornithology at the Radolfzell ornithological station and its effectiveness was tested in a flight passage with real birds. The result of this collaboration is an innovative coating which is applied to the glass. The highly effective coating which, when looked at against a backlight, seems like a randomly unfolding layer of the game Mikado pick-up sticks, is barely visible to humans and integrates seamlessly into architecture – much like the missing link in the evolution of the species, this bird protection glass is a missing link in terms of form. In its harmonic interplay with the architecture it contributes to the better protection of birds in their environment. At the same time it incorporates a design that creates something new in harmony with nature.

Unscheinbarer Lebensretter

Die besonderen Sinne der Vögel scheinen ihnen „bekannt" zu sein. Radnetzspinnen, zu deren über 2.800 Arten auch die Kreuzspinne zählt, schützen ihr mühevoll gewebtes Netz durch eine spezielle Spinnseide, die das UV-Licht reflektiert. Mit dem Ziel, dass die Vögel, die diese Reflektionen wahrnehmen, nicht durch ihre feinen Netze hindurchfliegen, da sie diese als Hindernis erkennen können. Diese Wirkung nutzen Ornithologen und Ingenieure jetzt auch für die Glasarchitektur: Da Vögel sich sehr oft an durchsichtigen und spiegelnden Glasflächen verletzen, ist es naheliegend, die besondere Wahrnehmungsgabe von UV-Licht gezielt für ihren Schutz zu nutzen. Das Konzept des Vogelschutzglases Ornilux Mikado überführt dieses profunde Wissen nun in ein beeindruckendes Produkt: Es gibt der Architektur die Möglichkeit an die Hand, Fenster und Glasfronten fortan für die Vogelwelt sicherer zu gestalten, ohne dass spezielle Aufkleber nötig sind. Das innovative Vogelschutzglas wurde in Zusammenarbeit mit dem Max-Planck-Institut für Ornithologie an der Vogelschutzwarte in Radolfzell entwickelt und seine Wirksamkeit ist vielfach in einem Vogelflug-Kanal getestet worden. Eine innovative, auf das Glas aufgebrachte Beschichtung ist das Ergebnis dieser Kooperation. Diese sehr effektive Beschichtung, die im Gegenlicht anmutet wie die durcheinander gewürfelten Stäbe eines Mikado-Spieles, ist im architektonischen Gesamtbild kaum sichtbar und integriert sich dort nahtlos – wie das berühmte fehlende Bindeglied der Arten in der Evolution ist dieses Vogelschutzglas damit ein formales Missing Link. Im harmonischen Zusammenspiel mit der Architektur trägt es dazu bei, die Vögel in ihrer Umwelt besser zu schützen. Es ist zugleich Ausdruck einer Gestaltung, die Neues im Einklang mit der Natur entstehen lässt.

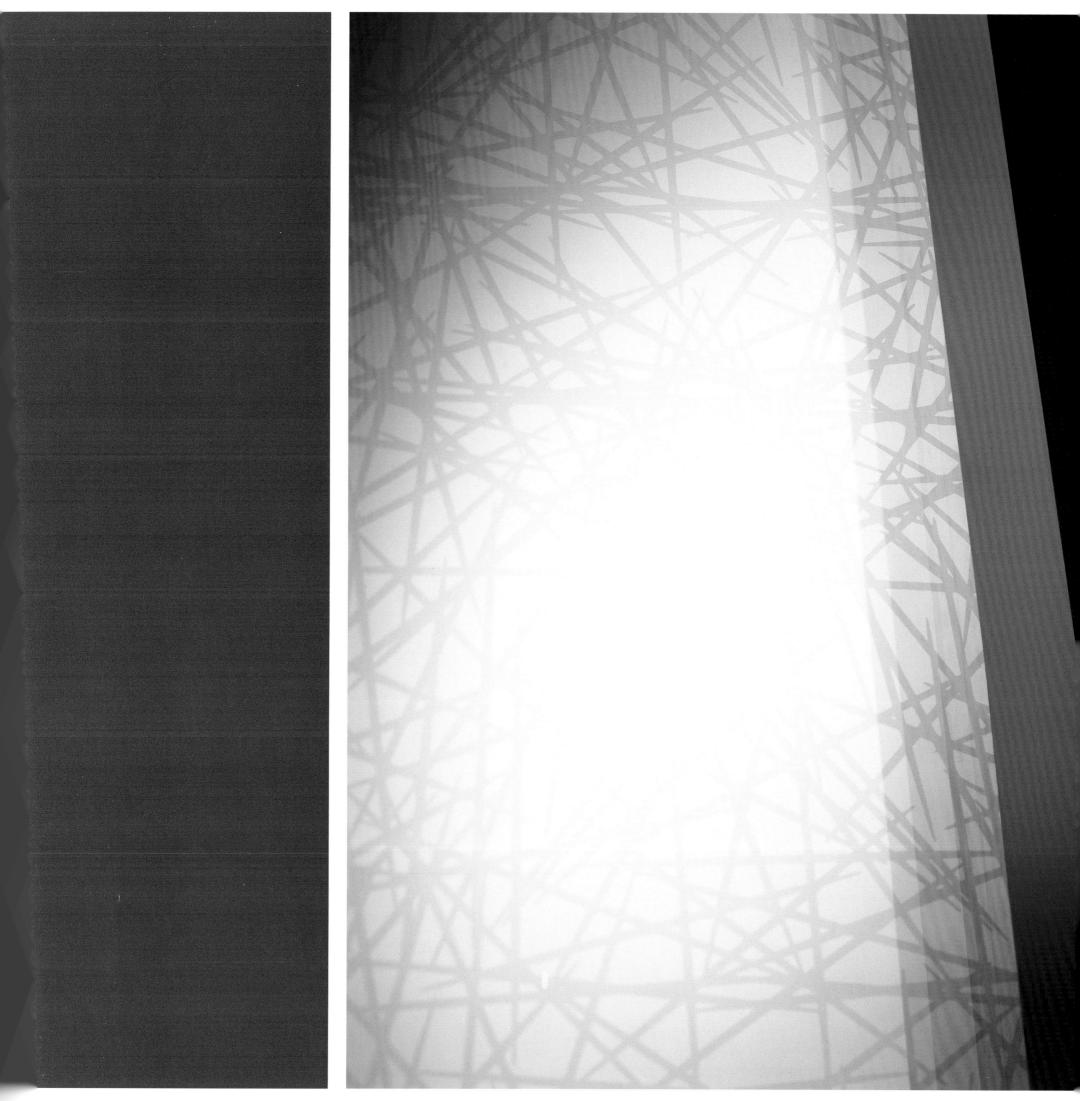

The designers of the "red dot: best of the best"
The best designers of their category

Die Designer der red dot: best of the best
Die besten Designer ihrer Kategorie

In the "red dot award: product design" the jury reserves the distinction of highest design quality for only a very few products. It can nominate three products from each product group for this award. The final selection is then made by democratic vote. Only design with excellent characteristics and maximum innovation receives the coveted "red dot: best of the best" award. The people behind these products, the designers and design teams complete with interviews, statements and photos are presented in the following pages.

Im red dot award: product design verleiht die Jury stets nur sehr wenigen Produkten die Auszeichnung für höchste Designqualität. In jeder Produktgruppe kann sie drei Produkte für diese Auszeichnung nominieren. Die Auswahl erfolgt dann nach einer demokratischen Abstimmung unter den Juroren. Nur Design mit exzellenten Qualitäten und einem Höchstmaß an Innovation erhält den begehrten red dot: best of the best. Auf den folgenden Seiten werden die Menschen hinter diesen Produkten, die Designer und Designteams mit Interviews, Statements und Fotos dargestellt.

CH04 Houdini
Side Chair and Chair with Armrest /
Stuhl und Stuhl mit Armlehne

Page/Seite 18/19

Stefan Diez

Stefan Diez, born in 1971 in Freising, Germany, studied industrial design at the State Academy of Fine Arts and Design in Stuttgart. In 2003 he opened his own studio in Munich, and in 2007 was appointed to a professorship at Karlsruhe University of Applied Sciences as part of a special project; in 2010, this turned into a regular professorship. Together with two partners, he took over the art direction of Authentics from 2008 to 2009. Stefan Diez specialises in product and exhibition design, working for Bree, e15, Established and Sons, Merten, Moroso, Rosenthal, Thonet, Wilkhahn and others; his designs have garnered many awards and are on display in many exhibitions. He is considered one of the most innovative and promising designers.

Stefan Diez, 1971 in Freising geboren, studierte Industriedesign an der Staatlichen Akademie der Bildenden Künste Stuttgart. 2003 eröffnete er sein eigenes Studio in München und wurde 2007 im Rahmen einer Projektprofessur an die Staatliche Hochschule für Gestaltung Karlsruhe berufen; im Jahr 2010 wurde daraus eine reguläre Professur. Zusammen mit zwei Partnern übernahm er von 2008 bis 2009 die Art Direction der Firma Authentics. Stefan Diez ist im Produkt- und Ausstellungsdesign u. a. für Bree, e15, Established and Sons, Merten, Moroso, Rosenthal, Thonet und Wilkhahn tätig; seine Arbeiten wurden vielfach ausgezeichnet und in zahlreichen Ausstellungen präsentiert. Er gilt als einer der innovativsten und vielversprechendsten Designer.

Stefan Diez, what particular challenges did you have to overcome in the conceptualisation, design and realisation of the "CH04 Houdini" chair?
Though we had some design challenges, largely concerning details, the greater difficulties we faced had to do with the technical implementation. The weighing of stability against elasticity with regard to the glue joints took quite a bit of time and required a series of trials.

What has been your biggest challenge to date when working on a project?
I tend to quickly forget everything unpleasant and difficult as soon as a project is finished. So, I'm usually left only with good memories. For that reason I can only think of the obstacles facing me right now, but which I'm of course not supposed to talk about. Therefore, although I do grow and evolve with projects, in retrospect everything appears much easier than how I experienced it. To sum up, the present is always when it's most exciting.

Which current trends is your branch of design currently concerned with?
I think we'll be seeing a significant change in the corporate design of many businesses in the coming years. Most products still speak an industrial design language developed in the 1980s, or else they follow pseudo-emotional design approaches that rob them of any individuality whatsoever. Some firms will succeed in overcoming this and develop an entirely new semantics for their product range.

Which design philosophy influences your work?
I don't have a simple philosophy as such, at least not one that I could summarise in a few words. After all, things aren't always so easy. However, I do believe that, in general, too much is being produced and too little is being tried out and explored. And that is the stance from which I approach my work. It would be fantastic to be able to pack more intelligence into a project. Longer cycles, less waste.

Stefan Diez, vor welche besondere Aufgabe stellte Sie die Gestaltung und Realisierung des Stuhls „CH04 Houdini"?
Neben gestalterischen Schwierigkeiten, die hauptsächlich in den Details lagen, haben wir bei der technischen Umsetzung die größeren Schwierigkeiten gehabt. Das Abwägen zwischen Stabilität und Elastizität der Leimverbindungen hat einiger Zeit bedurft und eine Reihe von Versuchen nötig gemacht.

Welches war Ihre bisher größte Herausforderung bei der Umsetzung eines Projekts?
Ich neige dazu, alles Unangenehme und Schwierige schnell zu vergessen, sobald das Projekt fertig ist. Zurück bleiben die positiven Erinnerungen. Daher fallen mir an dieser Stelle nur aktuelle Hürden ein, über die man natürlich nicht sprechen darf. Außerdem wächst man an den vergangenen Projekten, und es kommt einem im Rückblick alles so viel einfacher vor, als man es damals erlebt hat. Kurz, gerade ist es immer am spannendsten.

Welche Trends sehen Sie derzeit in Ihrer Branche?
Ich glaube, dass wir in den nächsten Jahren eine deutliche Veränderung im Corporate Design vieler Firmen beobachten werden. Die meisten Produkte sprechen nach wie vor die Sprache des Industriedesigns der 1980er Jahre oder haben sich durch ein pseudo-emotionalisiertes Design jeglicher eigenständiger Ausprägung beraubt. Einigen Firmen wird es gelingen, diesen Status zu überwinden und eine komplett neue Produktsemantik für ihr Sortiment zu entwickeln.

Welche Designphilosophie beeinflusst Ihre Arbeit?
Eine Philosophie als solche habe ich nicht, zumindest keine, die man in zwei Worte fassen könnte. Die Dinge liegen ja oft nicht so einfach. Aber ich glaube, dass generell zu viel produziert und zu wenig versucht wird. Das ist die Haltung, mit der ich an meine Arbeit gehe. Es wäre ein Segen, wenn es gelänge, mehr Intelligenz in ein Projekt zu packen. Längere Zyklen, weniger Abfall.

Metaphys lucano
Stepstool / Tritthocker

Page / Seite 20 / 21

Hers Experimental Design Laboratory Inc.

After graduating from Osaka City University in 1982, Chiaki Murata joined Sanyo Electric Co., Ltd. Design Center. In 1986 he established Hers Experimental Design Laboratory, Inc. and created many controversial products in a wide range of designs for products, graphics, and interface design, for which he received many international awards. He proposed the virtual industry system, which links each process of product development to an industry that is specialised in that field, and implemented an IT-type product development system that involves distribution. He has also been involved in inter-corporate coordination, production and consultation works by internally supporting the development of products that utilise each company's core competencies at corporate seminars.

Nach seinem Abschluss 1982 an der Osaka-City-Universität arbeitete Chiaki Murata beim Sanyo Electric Co. Ltd. Design Center. 1986 gründete er Hers Experimental Design Laboratory Inc. und schuf viele kontroverse Produkte mit vielseitigen Gestaltungen in den Bereichen Produkt-, Grafik- und Interfacedesign, für die er mit zahlreichen internationalen Preisen ausgezeichnet wurde. Er führte das virtuelle Industriesystem ein, das jeden Prozess der Produktentwicklung mit einem eigens in diesem Bereich spezialisierten Industriezweig verknüpft, und implementierte das IT-bezogene Produktentwicklungssystem unter Einbindung des Vertriebs. Zudem war er in Projekten für die unternehmensübergreifende Koordination, Produktion und Beratungsarbeit tätig und förderte firmenintern in Unternehmensseminaren die sich auf die Kernkompetenz eines Unternehmens stützende Produktentwicklung.

For Chiaki Murata good design consists of simple shapes with essential lines that point beyond the purely aesthetic. This design understanding is exemplified in his "Metaphys lucano" stepstool, the realisation of which the designer talks about in an interview with red dot:

What particular challenges did you face in the planning, designing and the realisation of your awarded product?
Normally, the sole focus of a stepstool is function, and design does not have an opportunity to play a role. However, the goal of producing the Lucano was to fulfil three criteria: high functionality, good design, and reasonable pricing. This led to the concept of creating a simple form with an original structure, but creating a new image as well as keeping the original structure was a more challenging task than we predicted. In order to achieve the simple form, a lot of effort was put into hiding the screw parts that is originally exposed to the outside. Also, the legs are designed in a triangular shape, however if these legs are in square shape like the general stepstool, there are more lines that come into your eye, which makes it look more complicated. Organizing these visual elements is a difficult task.

What issue are you currently concerned with?
The behaviour of humans over time and a design that is just perfect – this is called behaviour design, and I find it important to design from the stage where the final result is not tied to the shape of the original plan. By studying the psychology of human behaviour, an idea that goes beyond generalisations can be discovered, and a new design can be created.

Which design philosophy influences your work?
Traditional Japanese spiritual culture.

Unter gutem Design versteht Chiaki Murata eine einfache Gestaltung mit wesenhafter und nicht rein ästhetischer Formgebung. Beispielhaft zum Ausdruck kommt diese Auffassung in seinem Tritthocker „Metaphys lucano", über dessen Gestaltung der Designer im Interview mit red dot berichtet:

Welchen speziellen Herausforderungen sind Sie bei der Konzeption und Gestaltung ihres ausgezeichneten Produkts begegnet?
Bei einer Trittleiter spielt die Funktionalität normalerweise die wichtigste und die Gestaltung kaum eine Rolle. Bei der Produktion der „Lucano" sollten jedoch drei Kriterien erfüllt werden: eine hohe Funktionalität, gutes Design und Erschwinglichkeit. So entstand unser Konzept, eine einfache Form zu entwickeln, die ursprüngliche Struktur beibehält und dennoch zugleich ein neues Bild entwirft – und das war herausfordernder, als wir gedacht hatten. Um zu einer einfachen Form zu gelangen, steckten wir viel Mühe in das Verbergen der Schraubelemente, die ursprünglich außen sichtbar waren. Auch die Beine sind dreieckig. Denn wären diese wie bei einer gewöhnlichen Trittleiter rechtwinklig, wären mehr Linien sichtbar, die das Aussehen komplizierter machen würden. Diese visuellen Elemente zu organisieren, war eine schwierige Aufgabe.

Mit welchem Thema beschäftigen Sie sich derzeit?
Das menschliche Verhalten im Laufe der Zeit und ein Design, das einfach perfekt ist – dies nennt man Verhaltensdesign. Für mich ist es wichtig, bei der Gestaltung von der Phase aus zu beginnen, in der das Endresultat nicht mehr an die Form des ursprünglichen Entwurfs gebunden ist. Beim Studium der Psychologie menschlichen Verhaltens kann man Ideen entdecken, die über Generalisierungen hinausgehen und eine neue Art der Gestaltung erzielen.

Welche Designphilosophie beeinflusst Ihre Arbeit?
Die traditionelle japanische geistige Kultur.

ORIZURU
Chair / Stuhl

Page / Seite 22 / 23

Ken Okuyama

Ken Kiyoyuki Okuyama, born in 1959 in Japan, studied automobile design at Art Center College of Design in Pasadena, California. He subsequently worked at General Motors, Porsche, and Pininfarina, eventually as a Chief Designer. He then returned to Art Center College of Design, to teach as a department chairman of Transportation Design. In 2004, he began working as Design Director at Pininfarina where he among many others created the Enzo Ferrari, the Maserati Quattroporte, the Ferrari 612 Scaglietti, and the new generation Porsche 911. In 2007, he left Italy to set up his own design studio, KEN OKUYAMA DESIGN, where his projects span from transportation and furniture to robots and theme parks. Simultaneously, Okuyama launched his own eyewear collection as well as furniture line, and in 2008 he presented his first concept car, k.o7 Spider.

Ken Kiyoyuki Okuyama, geboren 1959 in Japan, studierte Automobildesign am Art Center College of Design in Pasadena, Kalifornien. Anschließend war er bei General Motors, Porsche und Pininfarina tätig, zuletzt als Chefdesigner. Danach kehrte er an das Art Center College of Design in Kalifornien zurück, um als Vorsitzender im Fachbereich Transportation Design zu unterrichten. 2004 begann er als Design Director bei Pininfarina und entwarf u. a. den Enzo Ferrari, den Maserati Quattroporte, den Ferrari 612 Scaglietti und die neue Generation des Porsche 911. 2007 verließ er Italien, um sein eigenes Designstudio KEN OKUYAMA DESIGN zu gründen, dessen Projekte von Transportmitteln über Möbel bis zu Robotern und Themenparks reichen. Zeitgleich brachte Okuyama seine eigene Brillen- und Möbelkollektion heraus und präsentierte 2008 sein erstes Concept Car, den k.o7 Spider.

For Ken Okuyama good design has to be "modern, simple and timeless". The designer, who created the simple yet extraordinary "Orizuru" chair, speaks to us in the interview with red dot about the particular challenges that he faced in the design and realisation of the chair:
To reinforce the chair's strength, a sheet of special paper was rolled into 10 layers to form a 2-metre long sheet of plywood, which was then bent into its final shape using a plywood folding technique inspired by Japanese origami. The plywood is only 10 mm thick, but strong and flexible enough to hold 400 kg of static weight – the result of the effort and skills of Yamagata-based craftsmen. The chair might look decorative at first glance, but its form came from structural reinforcement and a search for essentials. Although the original design theme was introduced last year, developing the stable form of plywood to be used in production took us some time. Now the excellence of the craftsmanship can be finally appreciated all over the world.

What issues is your branch currently concerned with and which development potentials do you see?
Whereas the "Arts and Crafts" started on the rebound of the industrial revolution, and the "Mingei" movement in the 1950s reflected the shortcomings of mass production after World War II, today at the beginning of the new century there are similar movements that are rediscovering local production cultures. Many a manufacturer's egotistic understanding of globalisation will now be overpowered by the customers' willingness to use more "cultural products" in their daily life and thus enrich the lives of us all with more meaning.

Für Ken Kiyoyuki Okuyama muss gutes Design „modern, einfach und zeitlos sein". Der Designer, der den einfachen und zugleich ungewöhnlichen Stuhl „Orizuru" entworfen hat, erzählt im Interview mit red dot von den besonderen Herausforderungen, denen er bei dessen Gestaltung und Umsetzung begegnet ist:
Um die Stärke des Stuhls zu erhöhen, wurde ein Blatt Spezialpapier in zehn Lagen zu einer zwei Meter langen Schalungsplatte zusammengerollt, die dann unter Einsatz einer vom japanischen Origami inspirierten Plattenfalttechnik in ihre finale Form gebogen wurde. Die Schalungsplatte ist nur 10 mm dick, aber stark und flexibel genug, um ein statisches Gewicht von 400 kg zu tragen – das Ergebnis von Fleiß und Geschick der Handwerksfachleute in Yamagata. Der Stuhl mag auf den ersten Blick dekorativ aussehen, doch seine Form resultiert aus der Verstärkung seiner Struktur sowie aus der Suche nach dem Wesentlichen. Obwohl das ursprüngliche Gestaltungsmotiv letztes Jahr vorgestellt wurde, war die Entwicklung einer stabilen Form für die Schalungsplatte zur Herstellung des Stuhls eine zeitintensive Herausforderung. Nun kann die hervorragende Qualität dieser Handwerkskunst endlich überall auf der Welt wahrgenommen werden.

Welche Themen beschäftigen derzeit Ihre Branche und welche Entwicklungspotenziale sehen Sie?
Während „Kunst und Handwerk" im Nachzug der industriellen Revolution seinen Anfang sah und die „Mingei"-Bewegung in den 1950ern die Schwachstellen der Massenproduktion nach dem Zweiten Weltkrieg aufzeigten, gibt es heute zu Beginn des neuen Jahrhunderts ähnliche Bewegungen, die lokalen Produktionskulturen wiederzuentdecken. Das egoistische Verständnis von Globalisierung so manch eines Herstellers wird jetzt von der Bereitschaft der Konsumenten überschattet, mehr „kulturelle Produkte" in ihrem täglichen Leben zu nutzen und so unser aller Leben mit mehr Bedeutung zu bereichern.

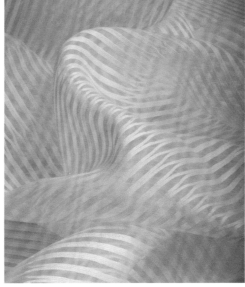

Batou CS
Decoration Fabric / Dekorationsstoff

Page / Seite 16 / 17

Diete Hansl-Röntgen
Sybilla Hansl
Alice Pieper

The design team at Nya Nordiska comprises managing director Diete Hansl-Röntgen, management board member Sybilla Hansl, and head of product development Alice Pieper. Diete Hansl-Röntgen joined Nya Nordiska in 1974 as a draper. Together with her husband and founder of Nya Nordiska, Heinz Röntgen, she expanded the company into an international textile publisher with distinctive textile collections. Sybilla Hansl, their daughter, after holding posts at several international fashion studios, studied textile design and since 1992 has been responsible for, among other things, the technical realisation and quality control of all Nya Nordiska designs. The textile designer Alice Pieper worked with several German companies, and since 2004 has headed the product development and the creative design of the textile collections.

Das Designteam von Nya Nordiska besteht aus Diete Hansl-Röntgen, Geschäftsführung, Sybilla Hansl, Mitglied der Geschäftsleitung, und Alice Pieper, Leiterin Produktentwicklung. Diete Hansl-Röntgen kam 1974 als Textilkauffrau zum Unternehmen und baute es mit ihrem späteren Ehemann, dem Gründer von Nya Nordiska, Heinz Röntgen, zu einem internationalen Textilverlag mit unverwechselbaren Kollektionen aus. Sybilla Hansl, ihre Tochter, studierte nach Stationen in internationalen Modeateliers Textiltechnik und verantwortet seit 1992 u. a. die technische Umsetzung der Entwürfe sowie die Qualitätskontrolle. Die Textildesignerin Alice Pieper arbeitete in verschiedenen deutschen Unternehmen und leitet seit 2004 die Produktentwicklung und kreative Gestaltung der Kollektionslinien bei Nya Nordiska.

Sybilla Hansl on the requirements and the know-how that defined the concept and realisation of the "Batou CS" decorative fabric:
Straightforward design concepts that seem to come easily and effortlessly often require an immense know-how in materials science and textile technology, from development up to production. In the realisation phases we therefore often work hand in hand with our suppliers. For Batou CS, for example, it was particularly difficult.

Alice Pieper on her creative work in textile design and how she handles the requirements of the market:
In fact, the creative process in textile design is one big, never-ending challenge. New materials and new innovations in textile technology continually provide new design possibilities. Colours and threads disappear from the market, while others come to take their place. As a designer, I'm continually in motion, in exchange with others, in the process of learning. The road from idea to woven structure is a genuine creative process with all its highs and lows.

Diete Hansl-Röntgen on the topics and themes that the textile design sector is currently concerned with:
Well, first of all, as for all sectors, the furnishing sector is affected by the current economic conditions. We are experiencing a back-to-the-basics trend. Preference is given to timeless, minimalist designs, to natural materials, and to low-maintenance all-rounders. Authenticity and quality processing are the new high-end attractions. We're also seeing an increased demand for innovative textile solutions, for example, for fabrics with light, heat or odour absorbing qualities or for flame-resistant decorative fabrics for contract use. The development potential of Nya Nordiska was and still is sustained by its immense power of innovation.

Sybilla Hansl über die Anforderungen und das Know-how, die die Konzeption und Realisierung des Dekorationsstoffs „Batou CS" voraussetzten:
Gerade Designentwürfe, die einfach und scheinbar simpel daherkommen, verlangen in der Entwicklung bis zur Produktionsreife oft ein ungeheueres Know-how in Materialkunde und Textiltechnik. Bei der Realisation arbeiten wir daher phasenweise Schulter an Schulter mit unseren Lieferanten. Bei Batou CS, zum Beispiel, war es besonders schwierig.

Alice Pieper über ihre kreative Arbeit im Textildesign und den Umgang mit den Bedingungen des Marktes:
Die kreative Arbeit im Textildesign ist eigentlich eine einzige große, nie endende Herausforderung. Neue Materialien und textiltechnische Innovationen schaffen immer wieder neue Gestaltungsmöglichkeiten. Farben und Garne verschwinden vom Markt, andere kommen hinzu. Als Designerin bin ich ständig in Bewegung, tausche mich aus, lerne dazu. Der Weg von der kreativen Idee zur gewebten Struktur ist ein echter Schaffensprozess mit all seinen Höhen und Tiefen.

Diete Hansl-Röntgen über die Themen und Trends, die die Textilbranche derzeit bewegen:
Der Einrichtungssektor wird wie alle anderen Branchen von den aktuellen Wirtschaftsnachrichten bewegt. Wir erleben einen Trend „back to basic". Den Vorzug erhalten zeitlose, reduzierte Dessins und Naturmaterialien oder pflegeleichte Allrounder. Authentizität und hochwertige Verarbeitung sind der neue Luxus. Gleichzeitig werden aber auch verstärkt innovative textile Lösungen nachgefragt, Stoffe mit Licht, Wärme oder Geruch absorbierenden Eigenschaften und schwer entflammbare Dekorationsstoffe für den Objektbereich. Das Entwicklungspotenzial von Nya Nordiska lag immer und liegt auch jetzt in seiner außerordentlich großen Innovationskraft.

Dyson Air Multiplier
Fan / Ventilator

Page / Seite 24 / 25

James Dyson

James Dyson was born in Norfolk, England, in 1947. While studying at the Royal College of Art during the 1960s, he developed an interest in design and engineering. He began work on his Dual Cyclone vacuum cleaner in 1978. Five years and 5,127 prototypes later, he perfected his no-loss-of-suction vacuum cleaner. Unsuccessful at first in finding a company prepared to manufacture his design, he took the vacuum cleaner to Japan where it was sold under the name G-Force from 1986. The DCO1 was launched in 1993; it was the first vacuum cleaner under his own name. Dyson vacuum cleaners are now sold in forty-seven countries and James Dyson now works alongside 500 engineers in Malmesbury, Wiltshire, developing new and better technology.

James Dyson wurde 1947 in Norfolk, England, geboren. Sein Interesse für Gestaltung und Maschinenbau entwickelte sich in den 1960er Jahren, als er am Royal College of Art studierte. Die Arbeit am Staubsauger „Dual Cyclone" begann 1978. Nach fünf Jahren und 5.127 Prototypen perfektionierte er den Staubsauger ohne Saugkraftverlust. Seine Suche nach einem Unternehmen zur Produktion seiner Erfindung blieb zunächst erfolglos, bis er den Staubsauger in Japan vorstellte, wo er ab 1986 unter dem Namen „G-Force" verkauft wurde. Der DCO1 kam 1993 auf den Markt; dies war der erste Staubsauger unter seinem eigenen Namen. James Dyson arbeitet heute neben 500 Ingenieuren in Malmesbury, Wiltshire, an der Entwicklung neuer und besserer Technologie.

James Dyson, the designer of the "Dyson Air Multiplier" on the background and development process of this startling fan, and the consequences that followed the day he decided to start trusting his instincts instead of listening to what others told him:

I've always been disappointed by fans. Their spinning blades chop up the airflow, causing annoying buffeting and they're hard to clean. So we developed a new type of fan that doesn't use blades. Whilst Dyson engineers were developing the technology behind the Dyson Airblade hand dryer, they observed how fast-flowing air – from a nozzle or aperture – induced surrounding air into its stream. We realised that this inducement, or amplification, effect could be further enhanced by passing airflow over a ramp. And of course this was the point where the idea of a new kind of bladeless fan became a real possibility. One of the most important aspects of the design process was finding the optimum angle from which the air could escape the aperture that runs around the loop amplifier (without it creating too much noise or pressure). The profile of the ramp had to be finely tuned. A 16-degree airfoil-shaped ramp gave the optimum airflow velocity and volume.

A Dyson vacuum cleaner could have looked very different from what it does today, had I listened to the market researchers and retailers who all told me that my idea for a transparent bin was stupid. They thought, "Why would people want to see dirt and grime?" But my instinct told me that people would be fascinated to see how our machines worked and where the dirt was going. It's confirmation of a job well done, so now that is what you see on all our vacuum cleaners.

James Dyson, der Designer des „Dyson Air Multiplier", über den Hintergrund und Entwicklungsprozess des aufsehenerregenden Ventilators und über die Folgen dessen, dass er einst nicht auf andere, sondern auf seinen Instinkt gehört hat:

Ventilatoren haben mich schon immer enttäuscht. Ihre Flügel zerschneiden den Luftfluss, was ein störendes Flattern verursacht, und sie sind schwer zu reinigen. Daher entwickelten wir eine neue Art von Ventilator, der ohne Rotorblätter funktioniert. Während unsere Dyson-Ingenieure die Technologie für den Händetrockner „Dyson Airblade" entwickelten, beobachteten sie, dass Luft, die beschleunigt und durch eine schmale Öffnung geleitet wird, die Umgebungsluft mit in den Luftstrom hineinzieht. Wir stellten fest, dass dieser Sog- oder Verstärkungseffekt noch größer wird, wenn die Luft über eine Schräge geführt wird. Das war der Punkt, an dem die Idee für eine neue Art flügellosen Ventilators möglich wurde. Einer der wichtigsten Aspekte des Gestaltungsprozesses bestand darin, den perfekten Winkel für die Schräge zu finden, über den der Luftstrom beim Verlassen der Öffnung am Luftring geleitet wird (ohne dabei zu viel Lärm oder Luftdruck zu erzeugen). Das Profil der Schräge musste genauestens abgestimmt werden. Die Form einer Tragfläche mit einem Winkel von 16 Grad erzeugte die optimale Luftgeschwindigkeit und Luftmenge.

Ein Dyson-Staubsauger sähe heute wahrscheinlich komplett anders aus, wenn ich damals auf die Marktanalysten und Händler gehört hätte, die mir alle sagten, dass die Idee eines durchsichtigen Auffangbehälters blödsinnig sei. Sie dachten, „warum sollten die Leute den Schmutz und Dreck sehen wollen?" Aber mein Instinkt sagte mir, dass die Leute fasziniert beobachten würden, wie unsere Maschinen arbeiten und wo der Schmutz bleibt. Das ist die Bestätigung für gute Arbeit, und daher sieht man das heute an all unseren Staubsaugern.

CBNes 6256
BioFresh Freshness Centre/
BioFresh-Frischecenter

Page/Seite 26/27

Bernd Brüssing

Bernd Brüssing, born in 1950 in Wuppertal, Germany, studied interior decoration and furniture design at Darmstadt University of Applied Sciences between 1968 and 1973. Until 1983, he worked with Walter Zeischegg, professor and co-founder of Ulm School of Design, before he founded the studio PRODESIGN Bernd Brüssing in 1984. PRODESIGN has managed to remain a creative, team-oriented design company, whose expert employees create entire product developments from first ideas to start of production. The company portfolio encompasses industrial design, engineering, modelling and prototyping, design management, as well as graphic, interface and exhibition design. In the 25 years since its foundation, PRODESIGN has garnered more than 100 national and international design awards.

Bernd Brüssing, geboren 1950 in Wuppertal, studierte von 1968 bis 1973 an der Fachhochschule in Darmstadt Raum- und Möbeldesign. Bis 1983 war er Mitarbeiter von Walter Zeischegg, Dozent und Mitbegründer der Hochschule für Gestaltung Ulm, bevor er 1984 das Büro PRODESIGN Bernd Brüssing gründete. Bis heute ist PRODESIGN ein kreatives, teamorientiertes Designunternehmen, das mit erfahrenen Mitarbeitern komplette Produktentwicklungen von der ersten Idee bis zur Serienreife leistet. Die Tätigkeitsfelder umfassen Industriedesign, Engineering, Modell- und Prototypenbau, Designmanagement, Grafikdesign, Interfacedesign und Ausstellungsdesign. In seinem 25-jährigen Bestehen erhielt PRODESIGN mehr als 100 nationale und internationale Designauszeichnungen.

Bernd Brüssing who as the manager of PRODESIGN Brüssing took the responsibility on the design of the BioFresh Freshness Centre, on the challenges he had to face in its realisation:
The challenges in the design of the BioFresh Freshness Centre were to achieve a consistent continuation of the product line as well as clear, user-oriented design, and to meet challenges relating to economic as well as technical manufacturing conditions.

What topic is currently making waves in your sector and which design philosophy influences your work?
I observe trends, but critically, and I don't use them as a guideline. My aim is rather to achieve timeless and sustainable design. Given the growing scarcity and cost of raw materials, we must all assume responsibility. I share the view of Friedrich Achleitner, who said "Increasingly I see a profound yearning for soft and subtle things, for objects that have no other purpose than to be what they were created for. For things that aren't constantly in your face, that try to educate you, or that insult you with their ignorance."
The roots of my design philosophy are shaped by my many years of collaboration with Walter Zeischegg. Design values such as morals, ethics, aesthetics, and efficiency are still a part of my creative work today. For me, good design therefore must have continuity, and it must be timeless and speak for itself.

Bernd Brüssing, der als Leiter von PRODESIGN Brüssing die Gestaltung des BioFresh-Frischecenters verantwortete, über die Herausforderungen bei dessen Entwicklung:
Die Herausforderungen an der Gestaltung des BioFresh-Frischecenters lagen in der konsequenten Fortführung der Produktlinie, der klaren benutzerorientierten Gestaltung sowie in den konstruktiven Herausforderungen hinsichtlich der ökonomischen und produktionstechnischen Bedingungen.

Welche Trends bewegen derzeit Ihre Branche und welche Designphilosophie beeinflusst Ihre Arbeit?
Trends beobachte ich kritisch und orientiere mich wenig daran. Es geht eher darum, Produkte zeitlos und nachhaltig zu gestalten. In Zeiten immer knapper und teurer werdender Rohstoffe kann man sich nicht aus der Verantwortung stehlen. Ich halte es mit dem Satz von Friedrich Achleitner: „Ich glaube, dass die Sehnsucht nach den leisen Dingen sehr groß geworden ist, nach Gegenständen, die nichts anderes vorhaben als das zu tun, wofür sie geschaffen wurden. Nach Dingen, die einen nicht dauernd anschwatzen, belehren oder durch Dummheit beleidigen."
Die Wurzeln meiner Designphilosophie sind geprägt durch die jahrelange Zusammenarbeit mit Walter Zeischegg. Designwerte wie Moral, Ethik, Ästhetik und Ökonomie beeinflussen meine kreative Arbeit nach wie vor. Für mich muss gutes Design deshalb Kontinuität, Kreativität und Konsequenz beinhalten und es sollte zeitlos sein und sich von selbst erklären.

Grohe Ondus Digitecture
Digital Bath / Digitales Bad

Page / Seite 28 / 29

Grohe In-house Design Team

The in-house design team contributes a wealth of experience, expertise and knowledge to Grohe. Giving the brand a consistent design approach and ensuring Grohe products are both recognisable and enjoyed for the way they look and function. Since 2006, the design team has doubled in size to 15 full-time members, headed by the senior vice president of design, Paul Flowers, who is included on the prestigious "40 under 40" list, established by the European Centre of Architecture, Art, Design and Urban Studies, a list that recognises the top 40 European creative talents under the age of 40. The team reports directly to the chief executive officer of Grohe, David J. Haines, affording them the creative freedom to redefine the industry.

Das In-house Design Team von Grohe verfügt über ein umfangreiches Reservoir an Erfahrung, Know-how und Kompetenz. Es verfolgt mit seiner Gestaltung die konsequente Designlinie der Marke sowie die Wiedererkennbarkeit der Produkte. Seit 2006 wurde die Zahl der Mitarbeiter im Team auf 15 Vollzeitkräfte verdoppelt. Geleitet wird es vom Senior Vice President Design Paul Flowers, der auf der renommierten „40 unter 40"-Liste des European Centre of Architecture, Art, Design and Urban Studies mit den 40 wichtigsten kreativen Köpfen Europas unter 40 Jahren steht. Das Team berichtet direkt an den Chief Executive Officer David J. Haines und erlangt damit die erforderliche Freiheit, um neue und kreative Wege zu gehen.

The Grohe in-house design team on the design and the realisation of the "Grohe Ondus Digitecture", their design philosophy and the design issues that they are currently concerned with:
Our challenge was to create a digital collection which was easy to use, easy to install and easy to specify/plan for in the interior design of the bathroom space. Easy to use: The technology is based on our Ondus digital platform which we have further refined to accommodate the new layout and reduced dimensions. To enable this to function perfectly as an "integrated concept" we had to completely reengineer the sensitivity of the user interface. Easy to install: We have invested a huge amount of time and energy to ensure our patented frame, which is fixed in the wall cavity, is fast and very accurate to install. Easy to specify/plan: We had to create a very simple grid system which would allow architects and interior designers total freedom to create their interior concept but with structure to aid their planning process.

What design issues are you currently concerned with and what are the goals that you focus your efforts on?
We are currently focusing on "Eco Joy", a subject which we are pleased to see has migrated from a "trend" to a consumer expectation. The search for the perfect balance between enjoyment and consumption is where we are currently focusing our efforts. Our goal is to reduce the resources needed to make, transport and use our products without reducing the experience.

Which design philosophy influences your work?
We have developed three simple values for Grohe which guide our design philosophy: Easy, Human, Performance.

Das Grohe In-house Design Team über die Gestaltung und Realisierung des „Grohe Ondus Digitecture", seine Designphilosophie und die Themen, die es derzeit beschäftigt:
Unsere Herausforderung war es, eine digitale Kollektion zu schaffen, die bei der Raumgestaltung eines Badezimmers leicht zu verwenden, zu installieren und zu spezifizieren/planen ist. Leicht zu verwenden: Die Technik basiert auf unserer digitalen Ondus-Plattform, die wir zugunsten des neuen Layouts und reduzierter Dimensionen verbessert haben. Um ihre perfekte Funktionalität als „integriertes Konzept" zu gewährleisten, mussten wir die Berührungsempfindlichkeit der Benutzeroberfläche völlig überarbeiten. Leicht zu installieren: Wir haben enorm viel Zeit und Energie investiert, um sicherzustellen, dass unser patentierter Rahmen, der im Hohlraum in der Wand fixiert wird, schnell und sehr präzise installierbar ist. Leicht zu spezifizieren/planen: Wir mussten ein sehr einfaches Rastersystem entwickeln, das Architekten und Innenarchitekten die vollkommene Freiheit bei der Gestaltung ihres Raumkonzeptes geben würde, aber gleichzeitig auch als Hilfe im Planungsprozess Struktur bietet.

Mit welchem Thema beschäftigen Sie sich derzeit und welche Ziele verfolgen Sie dabei?
Wir beschäftigen uns derzeit mit „Eco Joy", einem Thema, das sich erfreulicherweise von einem Trend zur Erwartungshaltung der Verbraucher weiterentwickelt hat. Die Suche nach der perfekten Balance von Badespaß und Verbrauch steht im Mittelpunkt unserer Bemühungen. Unser Ziel ist die Reduktion des Ressourcenverbrauchs, die bei Produktion, Transport und Gebrauch unserer Produkte entstehen, ohne dabei jedoch das Erlebnis zu schmälern.

Welche Designphilosophie beeinflusst Ihre Arbeit?
Wir haben drei schlichte Werte für Grohe entwickelt, die unsere Designphilosophie bestimmen: Easy, Human, Performance.

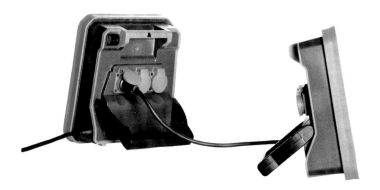

Gladiator II
Mobile Workplace Luminaire /
Mobile Arbeitsleuchte

Page / Seite 30 / 31

Rolf-Dieter Preußat

Rolf-Dieter Preußat, born in 1952, studied engineering at the Technical University of Ilmenau, Germany, and graduated in 1977. Subsequently he worked for many years at VEB Elektroinstallation Sondershausen in the research and development department and since 2000 he has been a constructing engineer with SONLUX, a subsidiary company of RZB-Leuchten. As a manufacturer of spotlights, ceiling and wall lamps, as well as working place light fixtures and safety lamps, RZB-Leuchten is one of the leading companies in this branch of the industry in Germany, delivering products and solutions that meet the photometric, electrotechnical as well as design requirements for a wide spectrum of building projects as well as public spaces both in Germany and abroad.

Rolf-Dieter Preußat, geboren 1952, studierte an der Technischen Universität Ilmenau, die er 1977 als Diplomingenieur abschloss. Anschließend arbeitete er viele Jahre bei dem VEB Elektroinstallation Sondershausen in der Abteilung „Forschung und Entwicklung", und seit dem Jahr 2000 ist er als Konstrukteur bei SONLUX, einem Tochterunternehmen von RZB-Leuchten, tätig. Als Hersteller von Strahlern, Decken- und Wandleuchten, aber auch Arbeits- oder Sicherheitsleuchten zählt RZB-Leuchten zu den führenden Unternehmen seiner Branche in Deutschland und fertigt lichttechnisch, elektrotechnisch und gestalterisch anspruchsvolle Produkte und Lösungen für unterschiedlichste Bauprojekte sowie den öffentlichen Raum im In- und Ausland.

For Rolf-Dieter Preußat good design has to convey quality and safety and should be durable and aesthetically pleasing. Together with the design team at RZB-Leuchten he designed the portable "Gladiator II" working place light fixture and in an interview with red dot told us, among other things, about the special challenge that the design team had to face in its design and realisation:
The challenge of this product consisted of the request to minimise the material usage while at the same time improving the functionality, technical qualities, and the handling.

What was the biggest challenge you had to deal with in a project so far?
The guarantee of a high safety standard for a portable luminaire without adding new components.

What issues is your studio currently concerned with, and what potential developments do you see?
LED and OLED lights are currently the most important trend in our sector, and this also offers great development potential for portable luminaires.

What design project would you like to realise someday?
My dream project is to build courtyard lamps and other lighting fixtures with LED technology in order to provide energy-efficient lighting for public streets and spaces.

Which design philosophy influences your work?
Design is synonymous with innovation.

Für Rolf-Dieter Preußat muss gutes Design Qualität und Sicherheit vermitteln und es soll langlebig und ästhetisch sein. Zusammen mit dem Designteam von RZB-Leuchten hat er die mobile Arbeitsleuchte „Gladiator II" entworfen und erzählt im Interview mit red dot unter anderem von der besonderen Aufgabe, vor die das Designteam bei dessen Gestaltung und Realisierung gestellt wurde:
Bei der Gestaltung dieser Arbeitsleuchte unterlagen wir der Forderung, den Materialeinsatz zu minimieren und dabei gleichzeitig die Funktionalität, die technischen Eigenschaften und das Handling zu verbessern.

Welches war die größte Herausforderung, mit der Sie es bisher bei einem Projekt zu tun hatten?
Die Gewährleistung eines hohen Schutzgrades bei einer ortsveränderlichen Leuchte ohne zusätzliche Komponenten.

Welche Themen und aktuellen Trends bewegen derzeit Ihre Branche und welche Entwicklungspotenziale sehen Sie?
Das Thema LED und OLED ist in unserer Branche zurzeit der wichtigste Trend, der auch bei ortsveränderlichen Leuchten ein hohes Entwicklungspotenzial aufzeigt.

Welches Projekt würden Sie gerne einmal realisieren?
Die Konstruktion von Stand- und Mastleuchten mit LED-Technik zur energieeffizienten Beleuchtung von öffentlichen Wegen und Plätzen ist mein Wunschprojekt.

Welche Designphilosophie beeinflusst Ihre Arbeit?
Design ist gleichbedeutend mit Innovation.

Velux sun tunnel by Lovegrove /
Velux Tageslicht-Spot by Lovegrove

Page / Seite 32 / 33

Ross Lovegrove

Ross Lovegrove, born 1958 in Cardiff, Wales, graduated from Manchester Polytechnic with BA Hons Industrial Design and a Master of Design of Royal College of Art, London. In the early 1980s he worked for Frog Design in Germany on the Walkman for Sony or Computers for Apple; he then moved to Paris as a consultant to Knoll International, and joined the Atelier de Nimes along with Jean Nouvel and Philippe Starck. In 1986 he returned to London, opened his own studio in 1990 and since then has worked for clients such as Cappellini, Moroso, Luceplan, Peugeot, Vitra, LVMH, and Toyo Ito Architects. Ross Lovegrove won numerous international awards, his work has been exhibited in e.g. the Museum of Modern Art, New York, and the Centre Pompidou, Paris.

Ross Lovegrove, geboren 1958 in Cardiff, Wales, machte seinen BA-Abschluss mit Auszeichnung in Industriedesign am Manchester Polytechnic und seinen MA-Abschluss in Design am Royal College of Art in London. In den frühen 1980ern arbeitete er bei Frog Design in Deutschland am Walkman für Sony oder an Computern für Apple. Als Berater für Knoll International ging er dann nach Paris und trat zusammen mit Jean Nouvel und Philippe Starck dem Atelier de Nimes bei. Im Jahr 1986 kehrte er nach London zurück, eröffnete 1990 sein eigenes Studio und arbeitet seither u. a. für Cappellini, Moroso, Luceplan, Peugeot, Vitra, LVMH und Toyo Ito Architects. Ross Lovegrove erhielt zahlreiche internationale Preise und seine Arbeiten wurden u. a. im Museum of Modern Art in New York und dem Centre Pompidou in Paris ausgestellt.

Ross Lovegrove, the designer of the "sun tunnel", on the challenges he faced in designing and realising this luminaire, as well as on his studio's work and the design philosophy that influences him:
The challenge was to take a product that performed a wonderful role in delivering free light into the home and give it a clear and purposeful identity. But the project went very smoothly because we all shared the same intentions … of distributing light in an elegant and peaceful way … to find a solution that worked in harmony with space and that had universal appeal.

What issues is your studio currently concerned with, and what trends or potential developments do you see?
My studio has an open mind and spirit that is looking to contribute to an emerging world and the potential of the times in which we live…

What design project would you like to realise someday?
Maybe a car.

Which design philosophy influences your work?
My philosophy of Organic Essentialism.

Ross Lovegrove, der Designer des „sun tunnel", über die Herausforderungen bei dessen Gestaltung und Umsetzung sowie über die Arbeit seines Studios und die Gestaltungsphilosophie, die ihn leitet:
Die Herausforderung bestand darin, einem Produkt, das in seiner Rolle, freies Licht im Hausinneren zu verteilen, wunderbar funktioniert, eine klare und zielgerichtete Identität zu verleihen. Doch das Projekt verlief sehr glatt, weil wir alle die gleiche Vorstellung hatten, … wie man Licht zugleich elegant und besinnlich gestalten kann, … und darüber, wie eine im Raum harmonisch wirkende und universal anmutende Lösung aussieht.

Welche Themen beschäftigen Ihr Studio derzeit und welche Trends oder Entwicklungspotenziale sehen Sie?
Mein Studio blickt ständig auf eine im Entstehen begriffene Welt und versucht, an dem Potenzial der Zeit, in der wir leben, anzusetzen …

Welches Projekt würden Sie gerne einmal realisieren?
Vielleicht ein Auto.

Welche Designphilosophie beeinflusst Ihre Arbeit?
Meine Philosophie des Organischen Essenzialismus.

Juwel Novaplus Evolution
Rotary Clothes Dryer / Wäschespinne

Page / Seite 34 / 35

Michael Tinius

The Busse Design studio was founded in 1959 and today is one of the largest and most acknowledged design and product development companies in Europe. The studio defines design as encompassing the entire process from the first idea and first concept, to its further development, and to the final design ready for production. The realisations are based on the three core competencies of product aesthetics, engineering and prototyping. Michael Tinius has been the chief designer at Busse Design since 1990. His work focuses on the technical design of consumer and producer goods, for which he has been awarded several international prizes. Alongside lecturing at universities and academies, he also acts as juror in award competitions.

Das 1959 gegründete Büro Busse Design ist eines der größten und renommiertesten Unternehmen für Design und Produktentwicklung in Europa. Unter Design versteht das Büro den gesamten Prozess von der Idee und dem ersten kreativen Design-Entwurf bis hin zum weiterentwickelten, funktionsfähigen und serienreifen Produkt. Die Realisierung erfolgt durch die drei Leistungsbereiche Produktästhetik, Engineering und Prototypenbau. Michael Tinius ist seit 1990 Chefdesigner bei Busse Design. Den Schwerpunkt seiner Tätigkeit bildet die technisch orientierte Gestaltung von Konsum- und Investitionsgütern, für die er zahlreiche internationale Auszeichnungen erhielt. Neben Lehrtätigkeiten an Hochschulen und Akademien ist er als Juror bei Wettbewerben tätig.

In the interview with red dot, Michael Tinius, the designer of the "Juwel Novaplus Evolution" talks about both the challenges that he had to overcome in the design of this rotary clothes dryer, and current trends in his design sector. The designer, who – as he claims – cannot live without music and literature, also reveals to us by what design guideline his work is inspired:
The challenge was to find a convincing visual expression for the innovative functionality of the product – in consideration of materials efficiency and the specific usage environment. As with any project that we are responsible for, the biggest challenge here too was to recognise the actual meaning of the product and to not lose focus during the design process.

What is the issue that your branch of design is currently concerned with and which trends or development potentials do you see?
Many products are getting more complex all the time and therewith less understandable for the user. The challenge of the future will thus increasingly consist of designing the intelligence of these interfaces in ways that are understandable and user-friendly, in order to increase the acceptance of the products.

What design project would you like to realise someday?
To be 100 per cent satisfied with the last one.

Which design philosophy influences your work?
To find the optimal synthesis of rationality and sensuality in form and function.

Im Interview mit red dot spricht Michael Tinius, der Gestalter der Wäschespinne „Juwel Novaplus Evolution", über die Herausforderungen bei deren Gestaltung sowie über die aktuellen Trends der Branche. Der Designer, der – wie er sagt – ohne Musik und Literatur nicht leben kann, erzählt darin auch von der Leitidee, die seine Arbeit inspiriert:
Die Herausforderung war, die innovative Funktionalität des Produktes gestalterisch erkennbar umzusetzen – und zwar unter Berücksichtigung der Ökonomie des Materialeinsatzes und des spezifischen Gebrauchsumfeldes. Wie bei allen Projekten, die wir verantworten, ging es auch hier darum, die tatsächliche Sinnhaftigkeit eines Produkts zu erkennen und sie im Gestaltungsprozess nicht aus den Augen zu verlieren.

Welches Thema bewegt derzeit Ihre Branche und welche Trends oder Entwicklungspotenziale sehen Sie?
Viele Produkte werden immer komplexer und damit unverständlicher für den Nutzer. Es wird in Zukunft also verstärkt darum gehen, die Intelligenz dieser Schnittstellen so zu gestalten, dass sie verständlicher und bedienungsfreundlicher werden, um damit die Akzeptanz der Produkte zu erhöhen.

Welches Wunschprojekt würden Sie gerne einmal realisieren?
Mit dem letzten zu 100 Prozent zufrieden zu sein.

Welche Designphilosophie beeinflusst Ihre Arbeit?
Mir geht es bei meiner Arbeit darum, die jeweils optimale Synthese von Sinn und Sinnlichkeit in Form und Funktion zu finden.

Honda EU 30i Generator

Page / Seite 36 / 37

Honda Design Team

The Honda R&D Co., Ltd. Power Product R&D Center / Design Group is part of the Honda Motor Co., Ltd. in Asaka City, Saitama Prefecture, Japan. The group is independent of the Automobile Design Centre and the Motorcycle Design Centre, and its job is to design general-purpose engines, generators, lawnmowers, snow blowers, tillers, outboard engines and electric wheelchairs, among other things. The range of design work for which designers are responsible is wide and includes the styling of shape, colour and graphics. In the awarded project, the Honda EU 30i generator, the following persons were involved: Kazuo Miyamoto (Design Data), Yuko Fujiki (Graphic Designer), Shuhei Imai (Design Project leader), Joji Maeda (Designer), and Yuya Kato (Designer).

Die Designgruppe „Honda R&D Co. Ltd./Power Product R&D Center" ist Teil von Honda Motor Co. Ltd. in Asaka City in der Präfektur Saitama, Japan. Der Bereich ist unabhängig vom Automobil-Designzentrum und dem Motorrad-Designzentrum, und seine Aufgabe besteht in der Gestaltung von Universalmotoren, Generatoren, Rasenmähern, Schneefräsen, Pflügen, Außenbordmotoren und elektrischen Rollstühlen. Das weite Spektrum an Designarbeiten, für das die Gestalter verantwortlich sind, schließt die Aufmachung von Formen, Farben und Grafik mit ein. An dem preisgekrönten Projekt, dem Generator „Honda EU 30i", waren folgende Personen beteiligt: Kazuo Miyamoto (Designdaten), Yuko Fujiki (Grafikdesigner), Shuhei Imai (Leiter des Designprojekts), Joji Maeda (Designer) und Yuya Kato (Designer).

Shuhei Imai, the leader of the Honda Design Team, on the challenges in designing the Honda EU 30i power generator, the values that Honda cultivates and his personal design values:
We believe that our generator line-up has set a design standard for products in this field. As the competition in this segment gets ever fiercer, our main objective in the development of this new product was to express a new user benefit. So we aimed in the appearance of the design to show the new theme of ease of portability that other products do not yet provide. As generators are a simple power source, we wanted to create a product that people would be proud to purchase and own.

What approach to design do you follow in your work?
I think that for many product designs the functionality is more important than the emotional element, and this is especially true for our power products. But I would like to keep the charm of the design in mind and make an effort to create an attractive product while supplying new benefits to the user. Without that thinking the design of a new product might become too dry.

What are the basic corporate values of Honda?
We are confident that the development of the highest quality power products will offer even better support in accordance with our policy of helping people get things done. The basic sense of value we share in the power products section is based on Mr. Soichiro Honda's conviction that Honda's engine technology could contribute to save Japanese from poverty. The first general-purpose H-type engine was developed at Honda in October 1953.

Shuhei Imai, der Leiter des Honda Design Teams, über die Herausforderungen bei der Gestaltung des Generators „Honda EU 30i", über das Werteverständnis bei Honda und sein persönliches von Design:
Wir glauben, dass unsere Generatoren-Reihe für diese Produktgattung einen neuen Gestaltungsstandard definiert hat. Da der Wettbewerb im Bereich tragbarer Generatoren immer härter wird, bestand unser Hauptanliegen bei der Entwicklung dieses Modells in dem Entwurf eines neuartigen Benutzer-Mehrwerts. Unser Ziel bei der Gestaltung des Gehäuses war, das neue Thema seiner leichten Transportierbarkeit umzusetzen – ein Merkmal, das andere Produkte noch nicht aufweisen. Da Generatoren eine simple Stromquelle sind, wollten wir ein Produkt kreieren, das zu kaufen und zu besitzen die Benutzer mit Stolz erfüllt.

Welcher Gestaltungsansatz beeinflusst Ihre Arbeit?
Ich denke, dass bei vielen Produktgestaltungen die Funktionalität wichtiger ist als das emotionale Element, und das trifft in besonderem Maße auf unsere Power-Produkte zu. Aber ich behalte auch die Anmutung einer Gestaltung im Auge und bemühe mich, ein attraktives Produkt zu entwerfen, das zugleich einen Mehrwert für den Nutzer aufweist. Ohne diesen Denkansatz würde die Gestaltung eines neuen Produktes wahrscheinlich zu unattraktiv werden.

Welche Unternehmenswerte prägen Sie bei Honda?
Wir bei Honda sind zuversichtlich, dass die Entwicklung von Power-Produkten höchster Qualität noch mehr bieten kann – entsprechend unserem Grundsatz, den Menschen zu helfen, ihre Ziele zu erreichen. Unser grundlegendes Werteverständnis, das von allen in der Power-Produktabteilung geteilt wird, basiert auf der Überzeugung des Unternehmensgründers Soichiro Honda, dass die Honda-Motorentechnologie einen Beitrag zum Schutz der Japaner vor Armut leisten könnte. So entwickelte Honda den ersten H-Typ-Universalmotor im Oktober 1953.

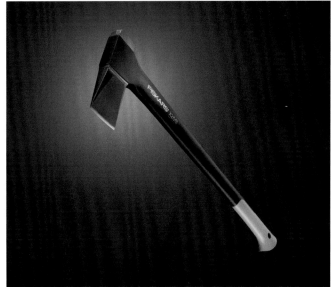

Fiskars X Range
Axes / Äxte

Page / Seite 38 / 39

Fiskars Design Team

The pursuit of perfection is reflected in the way the Fiskars Design Team designs and manufactures its tools. The intention is to reinvent the overall gardening experience, making it simple and pleasurable, by using advanced materials and engineering to produce tools that act like an extension of the body, boost power output, and reduce strain. While very much grounded in its long tradition and design heritage, the Fiskars Design Team is strongly committed to the new in terms of product development and optimised manufacturing processes. Throughout the brand's history, a selected team of dedicated people brings to life Fiskars design credo of creating tools that are durable, lightweight, intuitive and ergonomically sound.

In der Art, wie das Fiskars Design Team seine Werkzeuge gestaltet und herstellt, spiegelt sich das Streben nach Perfektion wider. Sein Ziel ist es, Gartenarbeit insgesamt mit mehr Einfachheit und Freude neu zu definieren, und zwar mit Werkzeugen, die sich – durch den Einsatz hochentwickelter Materialien und Ingenieurskunst – als Verlängerung des menschlichen Körpers verstehen, die die Leistungskraft erhöhen und die Kraftanstrengung vermindern. Das in einer langen Tradition und seinem Gestaltungserbe verankerte Fiskars Design Team sieht sich dem Neuen in Form von Produktentwicklungen und optimierten Herstellungsprozessen verpflichtet. In seiner gesamten Markengeschichte erfüllt ein ausgewähltes engagiertes Team die Gestaltungsmaxime Fiskars mit Leben – Werkzeuge zu schaffen, die langlebig, leichtgewichtig, intuitiv nutzbar und ergonomisch sind.

Fiskars Design Team on the development and design of the X Range:

Building upon 20 years of experience and fine-tuning of details, Fiskars X Range axes truly are an evolution of craftsmanship. The axe head is integrated into the blade design to ensure it remains in place, while the light, durable and glass-fibre reinforced handle minimises fatigue and makes the axe virtually unbreakable. The perfect balance between head and shaft guarantees a safe and efficient swing.

When developing this next generation axes, the biggest challenge facing the R&D team was to improve upon a product that was already great. Although introduced 20 years ago, Fiskars existing axe with its FiberComp™ shaft and integrated blade design is still very innovative today, but manufacturing needed to be optimised according to recent developments in technology. In this process, we were looking to optimise performance and increase the pleasure of work, being careful to ensure that value was truly added and that all new features had purposeful functionality. The subtle, yet ingenious improvement of the blade geometry contributes to a refined user experience, as the rounder edges ensure easier removal from logs when splitting wood. The precision ground convex blade and the double-hardened blade edge makes the axe head less prone to fracture. The optimised, anti-shock, surface structure offers a comfortable, firm grip with just the right feel. The hooked end of the handle prevents the axe slipping from the hand. Particularly challenging was adding a soft touch grip to such a large product, and the special technology for that was developed and patented by Fiskars.

Das Fiskars Design Team über die Entwicklung und Gestaltung der X Range:

Aufbauend auf 20 Jahren Erfahrung und Feinabstimmung von Details, stellen Fiskars' X-Range-Äxte eine echte Evolution dar. Die Integration des Axtkopfes in das Klingendesign stellt sicher, dass sich dieser nicht löst, während der leichte, robuste und glasfaserverstärkte Stiel Ermüdungserscheinungen vermindert und die Axt beinahe unverwüstlich macht. Die perfekte Balance von Kopf und Stiel garantiert einen sicheren und effizienten Schwung.

Die größte Herausforderung bei der Entwicklung dieser Äxte bestand darin, ein bereits großartiges Produkt noch weiter zu verbessern. Obwohl vor 20 Jahren eingeführt, ist der Vorgänger der Fiskars-Axt mit seinem FiberComp™-Schaft und integrierten Klingendesign noch heute sehr innovativ, in der Herstellung musste er jedoch entsprechend den neuesten technologischen Entwicklungen optimiert werden. Bei diesem Prozess versuchten wir, sowohl die Leistung als auch die Arbeitsfreude zu erhöhen, und achteten sorgfältig darauf, dass ein tatsächlicher Mehrwert entsteht und alle neuen Merkmale zweckmäßig und funktional sind. Die subtile, aber neuartige Überarbeitung der Klingengeometrie trägt zu einer verbesserten Benutzererfahrung bei, da die runderen Kanten ein leichteres Herausziehen beim Spalten von Holz gewährleisten. Durch den Präzisionsschliff der Klinge und die doppelt gehärteten Klingenränder ist die Axt zudem noch weniger bruchanfällig. Die stoßfeste Oberflächenstruktur bietet einen komfortablen und sicheren Griff, der sich schlicht gut anfühlt. Das hakenförmige Ende des Stiels verhindert ein Abrutschen der Axt aus der Hand. Eine besondere Herausforderung war die Ausstattung eines derart großen Produkts mit einem weichen Griffprofil, wofür wir bei Fiskars eine Spezialtechnik entwickeln und patentieren ließen.

Moving Moments –
BMW 7 Series Dealer Drive Event /
Händlerveranstaltung 7er BMW

Page / Seite 42 / 43

Blue Scope Communications
Andreas Stephan
Gregor Siber

Blue Scope Communications was founded in Berlin in 2001 and works for clients such as BMW, MINI, Rolls-Royce, and Sony Ericsson, delivering designs, content and dramaturgical creations in the fields of spatial communication as well as live communication. Andreas Stephan trained as a designer and studied pedagogics as well as psychodiagnostics. After working for a while in design management and advertising, from 1990 on he took part in building up Karlsruhe University of Arts and Design. He coordinated several projects in three-dimensional communication such as at EXPO 2000. Gregor Siber graduated in architecture and specialises in, among other things, temporary architecture for exhibitions, trade fairs and presentations, and has repeatedly pushed the limits and qualities of temporary construction for many of the agency's projects.

Blue Scope Communications wurde 2001 in Berlin gegründet und ist u. a. für BMW, MINI, Rolls-Royce und Sony Ericsson in den Bereichen Kommunikation im Raum sowie Live-Kommunikation gestalterisch, inhaltlich und dramaturgisch tätig. Andreas Stephan studierte neben seiner Ausbildung zum Designer Pädagogik und Psychodiagnostik und wirkte nach einer Zeit im Designmanagement und der Werbung ab 1990 am Aufbau der Hochschule für Gestaltung in Karlsruhe mit. Er betreute verschiedene Projekte in der dreidimensionalen Kommunikation, z. B. auf der EXPO 2000. Gregor Siber, Diplom-Architekt, beschäftigt sich u. a. mit temporärer Architektur für Ausstellungen, Messen und Präsentationen und lotete die Grenzen und Qualitäten des temporären Bauens bereits bei vielen Projekten der Agentur neu aus.

In the interview with red dot, Andreas Stephan and Gregor Siber talk about the special challenges that they had to face when designing their award-winning creation "Moving Moments", as well as about their favourite, highly unusual project that they would like to realise sometime:
Temporary architecture offers huge freedoms; however, there are also limitations, such as in regard to modular components and the reuse of already existing materials.

What was the biggest challenge that you ever had to overcome in a project so far?
Each new project has to be understood as the biggest challenge of all. Otherwise it won't work.

What topic is making waves in your branch and what development potentials do you see?
We wish a good sense of quality for all our clients, even when they are faced with shrinking budgets.

What project do you dream of realising at some point in the future?
The Pope's next visit.

Im Interview mit red dot erzählen Andreas Stephan und Gregor Siber von den besonderen Aufgaben, vor die sie die Gestaltung ihrer ausgezeichneten Arbeit „Moving Moments" stellte, und von einem sehr ungewöhnlichen Wunschprojekt, das sie gerne einmal realisieren würden:
Temporäre Architektur schafft große Freiheiten, sie schränkt aber auch ein, etwa durch Systembauteile und den erneuten Einsatz bestehenden Materials.

Welches war die bisher größte Herausforderung, die Sie bei einem Projekt bewältigen mussten?
Jedes neue Projekt muss als die größte Herausforderung verstanden werden. Sonst wird es nichts.

Welches Thema bewegt derzeit Ihre Branche und welche Entwicklungspotenziale sehen Sie?
Auch bei sinkenden Budgets wünschen wir allen Auftraggebern das Gespür für Qualität.

Welches Wunschprojekt würden Sie gerne einmal realisieren?
Den nächsten Papstbesuch.

Ornilux Mikado
Bird-Strike Resistant Glass/
Vogelschutzglas

Page/Seite 46/47

Christian Irmscher

Christian Irmscher, born in 1951, underwent training in natural sciences in Bielefeld, Germany, and Bochum, Germany, and subsequently developed his first works with function and design for the furniture industry. He then moved to the Arnold Glas company, one of the leading European companies in glass refinement, and realised holograms in collaboration with internationally renowned designers, such as the "Eye Fire" hologram together with Michael Bleyenberg for the DFG German Research Foundation as well as the largest open-air hologram together with Martin Hingst in Cologne. In the field of glass art he realised the visions of Olafur Eliasson in the facade of the Munich Opera House (Marstallplatz) as well as in the luminaire for the Copenhagen Opera, and for Michael Lapper the "Der Steg" project at the Institute for Evolutionary Anthropology in Leipzig as well as the façade for the campus project by Novartis in Basle.

Christian Irmscher, 1951 geboren, erhielt eine naturwissenschaftliche Ausbildung in Bielefeld und Bochum und entwickelte anschließend erste Arbeiten mit Funktion und Design für die Möbelindustrie. Er wechselte zu der Firma Arnold Glas, einem der führenden Glasveredeler Europas, und realisierte Hologramme in Zusammenarbeit mit international renommierten Designern, zum Beispiel das Hologramm „Eye Fire" für die Deutsche Forschungsgesellschaft Bonn mit Michael Bleyenberg und das große Freiluft-Hologramm mit Martin Hingst in Köln. Im Bereich der Glaskunst setzte er die Visionen von Olafur Eliasson an der Fassade der Münchner Oper (Marstallplatz) sowie am Leuchter für die Oper Kopenhagen um und mit Michael Lapper realisierte er „Der Steg" am Institut für Anthropologie in Leipzig sowie die Fassade für das Campusprojekt von Novartis in Basel.

Christian Irmscher, the designer of the "Ornilux Mikado", on the challenges in its concept, its design and realisation:
When developing bird-strike resistant glass, the question whether the glass will withstand such an impact comes up from early on in the planning stage – because how can a window be designed to be different from conventional panes so that birds can recognise it? Elaborate functional run-up tests and the design requirement for a coating that is barely visible to humans – these were the big challenges in the design and realisation.

What was the biggest challenge that you ever had to overcome in a project so far?
An aesthetically high-quality glass that consists of a laminate with holographic optical elements puts high demands on the developers and the designers both technically and in the implementation. The holograms must not loose their effect over time, and even when the room is lit, the window pane must be transparent from the inside out. The laminated panes with dichroitic glass (colour effect glass) were equally complicated and challenging, similar to realising the "I see you" project for Louis Vuitton with Olafur Eliasson.

Which topic is currently making waves in your branch and which development potentials do you see?
The big topic is sustainability in glass construction in the field of green buildings. There are enormous development potentials in this, and architects around the globe are aware of it.

Which favourite project would you like to realise one day?
"More light in an enclosed space." To direct light augmented in its intensity via glass surfaces into the inside of a room – using fully transparent glass – would be an exciting project.

Christian Irmscher, der Gestalter des „Ornilux Mikado", über die Besonderheiten bei dessen Konzeption, Gestaltung und Realisierung:
Wenn man ein Glas gegen Vogelschlag entwickelt, kommt schon während der Konzeption die Frage auf, ob es seine Bestimmung dann in der Realität erfüllen wird. Denn wie lässt sich eine Fensterscheibe gestalten, die sich von normalem Glas so unterscheidet, dass ein Vogel sie erkennen kann? Aufwendige Funktionsprüfungen im Vorfeld und ein Designanspruch, der gerade darin liegt, eine Glasscheibe so zu beschichten, dass der Effekt für Menschen kaum wahrnehmbar ist – darin lagen die großen Herausforderungen in der Gestaltung und Realisierung.

Welches war die bisher größte Herausforderung, die Sie bei einem Projekt bewältigen mussten?
Ein ästhetisch hochwertiges Glas, das aus einem Laminat mit holografisch-optischen Elementen besteht, stellt sowohl technisch als auch in der Umsetzung hohe Anforderungen an Entwickler und Designer. Schließlich dürfen die Hologramme ihre Wirkung nicht verlieren, und bei Rückbelichtung muss die Durchsicht der Scheibe gewährleistet bleiben. Ähnlich kompliziert und anspruchsvoll sind die Laminate mit dichroitischen Gläsern (Farbeffektgläser), wie ich sie zusammen mit Olafur Eliasson bei dem Projekt „I see you" für Louis Vuitton umgesetzt habe.

Welches Thema bewegt derzeit Ihre Branche und welche Entwicklungspotenziale sehen Sie?
Das große Thema ist nachhaltiges Bauen mit Glas im Bereich des Green Building. Hier liegen enorme Entwicklungspotenziale, die von Architekten rund um den Globus erkannt werden.

Welches Wunschprojekt würden Sie gerne einmal realisieren?
„Mehr Licht im geschlossenen Raum." Licht über Glasflächen unter Verstärkung ins Rauminnere zu lenken – bei voller Transparenz des Glases –, wäre ein spannendes Projekt.

Container Scope
Oceanscope

Page / Seite 44 / 45

Keehyun Ahn
Minsoo Lee
Gilhwang Chang

Minsoo Lee, born in Korea, is an interdisciplinary working interior architect and interactive designer combining computational media and physical computing into architectural environments. He is co-founder of AnL Studio and Tangible Dots research lab that develop architectural designs and interactive technologies. The architect Keehyun Ahn is co-founder of the AnL Studio and its design director, focused on exploring new realms of technology within the architectural spectrum. He is currently working in the USA, Seoul and Europe. Gilhwang Chang, Art Director at ZZangPD, has been producing and planning many container art projects in Korea, and currently he besides is a committee member of the Pusan International Film Festival.

Minsoo Lee, geboren in Korea, ist ein interdis-ziplinär arbeitender Innenarchitekt und Inter-active Designer, der computerbasierte Medien und Physical Computing in architektonischen Umgebungen miteinander verknüpft. Er ist Mitbegründer von AnL Studio und des For-schungslabors Tangible Dots, die sich mit der Entwicklung von Architekturgestaltungen und interaktiven Technologien beschäftigen. Der Architekt Keehyun Ahn ist Mitbegründer und Design Director von AnL Studio. Er erforscht neue Technologiebereiche innerhalb der archi-tektonischen Bandbreite und arbeitet derzeit in den USA, in Seoul und in Europa. Gilhwang Chang, Art Director bei ZZangPD, hat bereits viele Container-Kunstprojekte in Korea geplant und produziert und ist derzeit u. a. Komiteemit-glied des Pusan International Film Festivals.

Minsoo Lee, Keehyun Ahn and Gilhwang Chang, the designers of the "Container Scope", on the particular challenges and the difficulties that they faced in the design and realisation of their concept, as well as the issues that they are currently concerned with:
Breaking away from the typical stacking system of shipping containers is the one of the essential task in the aspect of this design. In order to both overcome the limitation of a building site where the ground level is too low to view a beautiful sunset and provide people with a dramatic scene with architectural purpose, we suggested that the containers' structure had to be leaned at various angles towards the sky. In the process of the realisation, making the diagonal angles of container units and anchoring them into the concrete base was the one of the big challenges.
The biggest challenge we had to deal with in this project so far was long distance communication between our design firm and the local construction team. Although we (Keehyun Ahn and Minsoo Lee) are originally Korean, our office is currently located in New York City. However, the site is located in In-cheon city in Korea. In the process of the project, this long distance relationship and working environment occasionally caused troubles such as slow decision making and time delays in many ways. But handling this, we learned to trust each other and understand the different circumstances which affected us.

What are the issues that you are currently concerned with?
Both the careful consideration of cultural needs and an analysis of tradition, trends, and social dimensions with a global perspective are the key part of the methodologies of AnL Studio. Basically, our primary goal is to break the tendency towards the simplification of architecture and move beyond a categorical approach towards a more integrated and complex future.

Minsoo Lee, Keehyun Ahn und Gilhwang Chang, die Designer des „Container Scope", über die speziellen Herausforderungen und Schwierigkeiten bei der Gestaltung und Umsetzung dieser besonderen Entwürfe und über die Themen, die sie derzeit beschäftigen:
Eine der, wenn nicht die wesentliche Aufgabe hinsichtlich dieser Gestaltung ist, sich von der üblichen Methode des Über-einanderstapelns von Transportcontainern zu lösen. Um die Begrenzungen des Baugeländes, das für einen freien Blick auf schöne Sonnenuntergänge zu niedrig liegt, zu überwinden und den Menschen eine ergreifende wie architektonisch sinnvolle Szenerie zu bieten, schlugen wir vor, die Containerstrukturen in verschiedenen Winkeln in den Himmel zu neigen. Im Prozess der Realisierung barg dann die Umsetzung der diagonalen Winkel dieser Einheiten und deren Verankerung im Betonfundament eine der größten Schwierigkeiten.
Die größte Herausforderung bestand aber in der Kommunikation zwischen unserem Designbüro und dem Konstruktionsteam vor Ort über die großen Entfernungen hinweg. Obwohl wir (Keehyun Ahn und Minsoo Lee) ursprünglich Koreaner sind, ist unser Büro derzeit in New York City. Und das Baugelände selbst ist in In-cheon in Korea. Im Verlauf des Projektes verursachten diese Fernbeziehung und Arbeitsweise zuweilen Probleme in Form schleppender Entscheidungsprozesse und mehrerer Verzöge-rungen. Doch im Umgang damit lernten wir, uns gegenseitig zu vertrauen und die jeweiligen Umstände zu verstehen.

Welche aktuellen Themen beschäftigen Sie derzeit?
Die sorgfältige Erörterung der kulturellen Erfordernisse sowie die Analyse von Tradition, Trends und der sozialen Dimension aus globaler Sicht gehören zum methodischen Kern von AnL Studio. Unser Hauptziel besteht darin, die Tendenz zur vereinfachten Architektur zu durchbrechen und uns weg von einem katego-rischen Ansatz hin zu einer ganzheitlicheren und komplexeren Zukunft zu bewegen.

Van Gogh Museum Shop

Page / Seite 40 / 41

DAY Creative Business Partners
Louk de Sévaux
Gesina Roters
Mette Hoekstra

Louk de Sévaux, interior designer, is Managing Partner of DAY. He has over ten years experience in general management of design and project management agencies as well as extensive experience with brand retail, interior architecture and events e.g. for Nike, Lego, Porsche, MTV, O'Neill and Orange. Gesina Roters, graphic designer, is Creative Partner of DAY. She develops brand identities, graphic design, packaging, retail and interior design, and works on projects for e.g. Orange, Deutsche Bank, Bugaboo, MTV, Van Gogh Museum and Ziggo. Mette Hoekstra is an interior designer and project leader.

Louk de Sévaux, Interior Designer, ist Managing Partner bei DAY. Er hat mehr als zehn Jahre Erfahrung in der Leitung von Agenturen im Bereich Design- und Projektmanagement sowie umfassende Erfahrungen in Markenvertrieb, Innenarchitektur und Eventmanagement u. a. für Nike, Lego, Porsche, MTV, O'Neill und Orange. Gesina Roters, Grafikdesignerin, ist Creative Partner bei DAY. Sie entwickelt Markenidentitäten, Grafikdesign, Verpackungen, Verkaufs- sowie Interior Design und arbeitet an Projekten u. a. für Orange, Deutsche Bank, Bugaboo, MTV, Van Gogh Museum und Ziggo. Mette Hoekstra ist Interior-Designerin und Projektleiterin.

For Louk de Sévaux, good design has to merge beauty with purpose – without compromising on either one. In an interview with red dot he speaks about, among other things, the philosophy that inspires his designs and the challenge that the design team of the "Van Gogh Museum Shop" faced in its planning and realisation:
The particular challenges that we encounter in almost any project are mostly related to planning constraints, tight budgets, managing expectations, and staff issues. Any big challenge has a bit of all of these. The challenge we encountered with the "Van Gogh Museum Shop" was related above all to its planning: The project was executed from briefing to completion within 5 months, within the given time frame and within the overall budget.

What are the issues that your branch is currently concerned with, which trends or development potentials do you see?
Our branch has started from mono-disciplinary designers and grown into a sector of multi-disciplinary agencies; we now need to integrate into the "real world", learning to appreciate and work with other levels of consultancy to develop integrated services.

What design project would you like to realise someday?
I would love to be involved in the process of building a whole new company, from product to strategy and brand. To create this, together with a team of top-level specialists in every aspect, as a team.

Which design philosophy influences your work?
The current development of Design Thinking and Service Design.

Für Louk de Sévaux muss gutes Design Schönheit mit Zweck vereinen – aber nicht auf Kosten des jeweils anderen. Im Interview mit red dot spricht er unter anderem über die Philosophie, die ihn zu seinen Entwürfen inspiriert, und die Herausforderung, der das Designteam des „Van Gogh Museum Shop" bei der Planung und Realisierung begegnete:
Die besonderen Herausforderungen, mit denen wir es bei Projekten zu tun haben, sind meistens Planungsbeschränkungen, ein knappes Budget, Erwartungshaltungen und Unstimmigkeiten unter Mitarbeitern. Jede große Herausforderung hat von jedem dieser Punkte etwas. Die Herausforderung beim „Van Gogh Museum Shop" lag vor allem in der Planung: Das Projekt wurde vom Start bis zur Vollendung innerhalb von nur fünf Monaten ausgeführt – innerhalb des vorgegebenen Zeitrahmens sowie des Gesamtbudgets.

Welche Themen beschäftigen Ihre Branche derzeit und welche Entwicklungspotenziale sehen Sie darin?
Unsere Branche hat sich von Gestaltern einer Disziplin zu einem Sektor multidisziplinärer Agenturen entwickelt; jetzt müssen wir andere Ebenen der Beratung kennen und schätzen lernen und im Dienste integrativer Serviceleistungen mit ihnen arbeiten.

Welches Projekt würden Sie gerne einmal realisieren?
Ich würde gerne am Aufbauprozess eines kompletten Unternehmens teilhaben, vom Produkt über die Strategie bis zum Branding. Dies zusammen mit einem Team von in jeder Hinsicht hochqualifizierten Spezialisten zu erreichen, würde mich reizen.

Welche Designphilosophie beeinflusst Ihre Arbeit?
Die derzeitigen Entwicklungen im Designdenken und im Service-Design.

Tony K. M. Chang

Dr. Mark Breitenberg

Robert Stadler

Living rooms and bedrooms
Reminiscing old times with a new vision

Wohnen und Schlafen
Reminiszenz an frühere Zeiten in moderner Form

Rigid geometric and supportive structures are interspersed with more relaxed, soft components.

The need for safety and belonging in times of economic instability and ecological challenges is reflected in the "Living rooms and bedrooms" category. Familiar elements of past design styles are taken up and newly interpreted, resulting in a surprisingly large number of features from 1960s design. Rigid, geometric, and supportive structures are interspersed with more relaxed, soft components to generate a feel-good ambience. Asian materials are combined with Western aesthetic forms to create a modern context in the era of globalisation. On the whole, the trend is to forgo maximum flexibility in favour of more specificity. Design concepts are again more solitary and appear to focus on specific lifestyles rather than claiming universality.

Strenge geometrische und haltgebende Strukturen prallen auf auflockernde, weiche Komponenten.

Der Wunsch nach Geborgenheit und Sicherheit in Zeiten wirtschaftlicher Instabilität und ökologischer Herausforderungen findet in der Kategorie „Wohnen und Schlafen" auf verschiedene Arten Ausdruck. Bekannte Elemente vergangener Zeiten werden aufgegriffen und neu interpretiert, sodass sich auffallend viele Anleihen an die Formensprache aus den 1960er Jahren feststellen lassen. Darüber hinaus prallen strenge geometrische und haltgebende Strukturen auf auflockernde, weiche Komponenten, die ein Ambiente des Wohlfühlens vermitteln. Der Prozess der Globalisierung wird ebenfalls gestalterisch aufgegriffen, indem die asiatische Materialwelt mit einem westlichen Formenkanon in einem modernen Kontext verknüpft wird. Insgesamt lässt sich eine Tendenz zur Abkehr von größtmöglicher Flexibilität und Hinwendung zur Spezifität erkennen. Die Entwürfe wirken wieder mehr als Solitär und scheinen sehr bewusst auf bestimmte Lebensstile ausgerichtet zu sein, statt eine Allgemeingültigkeit für sich zu beanspruchen.

Loop – Sofa

Arper Spa, Treviso, Italy / Italien
Design: Lievore Altherr Molina,
Barcelona, Spain / Spanien
www.arper.it
www.lievorealtherrmolina.com

Versatility, soft and clear-cut lines as well
as high-quality finishes are the distinctive
features of this sofa collection. Loop is
available in many shapes and sizes; it adapts
well to all room settings and requirements.
Due to its modular design the sofa can be
used in various combinations or as two- and
three-seater. With its harmonious design
language and a high degree of elegance
this sofa meets the various needs of modern
living. Loop has an upholstered wooden
frame and a cover of fabric. It is mounted on
a framework with brushed steel or aluminium
glides. The sofa and the seat cushions
are available with removable upholstery
featuring hook-and-loop fasteners.

Vielseitigkeit, eine weiche und klare Linienführung sowie hochwertige Oberflächen
sind die Erkennungsmerkmale dieser Sofakollektion. Loop ist in zahlreichen Größen
und Formaten erhältlich und lässt sich
gut an alle Räumlichkeiten und Anforderungen anpassen. Da es modular gestaltet
ist, ist das Sofa kombinierbar im Verbund
sowie als Zwei- oder Dreisitzer nutzbar.
Mit seiner harmonischen Formensprache
und einem hohen Maß an Eleganz wird
dieses Sofa den verschiedenen Anforderungen des modernen Wohnens gerecht.
Loop verfügt über einen Rahmen aus Holz
mit Polsterung und einen Bezug aus Stoff,
es ist auf einem Gestell mit Gleitern aus
satiniertem Stahl oder Aluminium montiert. Das Sofa und die Sitzkissen sind
zudem in einer Ausführung mit einem
Stoffbezug erhältlich, der über Klettver-
schlüsse verfügt und abziehbar ist.

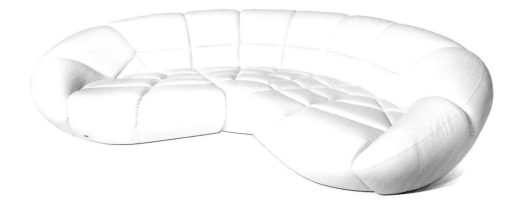

Kautsch Sofa

Bretz, Gensingen,
Germany / Deutschland
In-house design / Werksdesign:
Carolin Fieber
www.bretz.com

This sofa collection represents an innovative combination of stringent, geometric lines and an organic shape. The lines emanating from the centre form padded rhombuses of different sizes that nestle snugly to the body. Specially tempered springs and meticulously balanced, permanently elastic cold foams for each of these rhombuses have been especially selected to provide homogeneous seating comfort. With its traditionally proven substructure Kautsch realises classical values of comfort in an ingenious and optically hidden way, as for example in the kidney support. By this design the sofa offers manifold, individual possibilities of interpretation. In combination with its pleasant design language, revitalising colours and leather variations of the sofa cover are intended to create a home of fairy-like regeneration.

Als innovative Kombination aus strenger geometrischer Linienführung und organischer Formgebung versteht sich diese Sofakollektion. Die aus dem Zentrum entspringenden Linien formen unterschiedlich große Polsterkassetten, die sich an den Körper schmiegen. Speziell gehärtete Federkerne sowie fein austarierte, dauerelastische Kaltschäume für jede dieser Kassetten wurden eigens ausgewählt, sodass ein homogener Sitzkomfort gewährleistet ist. Kautsch setzt mit dem traditionell bewährten Unterbau klassische Komfortwerte wie die Nierenstütze originell und optisch kaschiert um. Derart gestaltet bietet dieses Sofa dem Nutzer vielfältige und individuelle Interpretationsmöglichkeiten. Revitalisierende Farben und Ledervariationen des Sofabezuges sollen in Verbindung mit der anheimelnden Formensprache des Sofas ein feenhaft heiles Zuhause schaffen.

Jalis
Upholstered Furniture/Polstermöbel

COR Sitzmöbel, Rheda-Wiedenbrück,
Germany/Deutschland
Design: Jehs + Laub
(Markus Jehs, Jürgen Laub),
Stuttgart, Germany/Deutschland
www.cor.de
www.jehs-laub.com

The design of Jalis is inspired by the traditional way of life of the Orient and its manner of serenity, hospitality and relaxed communication. By an architecturally pure design language this upholstered furniture wants to deliver such an experience for any home use. Cushion by cushion lines up, and story by story. This is how oases of well-being are created. Special upholsteries provide support and comfort. The cushions with broad surfaces and arranged in rows turn into a seating furniture. Part of this "fabulous" concept is the Patio cover fabric with ornaments woven into it. It becomes visible only when the incidence of light changes and makes the woven patterns look like fine embroidery. Jalis follows a

multifunctional design concept: it can float, rest on pedestals, change levels, and integrate niches and floor recesses. In all these positions its enclosing backrests and deep seats offer a high degree of comfort and security.

Die Gestaltung von Jalis lehnt sich an die traditionelle Lebensweise des Orients und deren Form der Gelassenheit, Gastfreundschaft und entspannten Kommunikation an. Mit einer architektonisch reinen Formensprache will dieses Polstermöbel ein solches Erleben für jeden Wohnbereich ermöglichen. Kissen reiht sich an Kissen, Geschichte an Geschichte. Auf diese Weise entstehen Oasen zum Wohlfühlen, wobei

spezielle Polsterungen Halt und Bequemlichkeit bieten und Kissen in ausladenden Flächen und Reihungen zum Sitzmöbel werden. Teil dieses „märchenhaften" Konzepts ist der Bezugsstoff Patio mit eingewebten Ornamenten. Erst in wechselndem Lichteinfall werden die eingewebten Muster wie eine feine Stickerei sichtbar. Jalis folgt einem multifunktionalen Gestaltungskonzept: Es kann schweben, auf Podesten lagern, Ebenen wechseln sowie Nischen und Bodenvertiefungen mit einbeziehen. In jeder dieser Positionen bieten seine geschlossenen Rückenlehnen und tiefen Sitzflächen ein hohes Maß an Komfort und Geborgenheit.

Cinque
Swivel Armchair / Drehsessel

Machalke Polsterwerkstätten GmbH,
Hochstadt, Germany / Deutschland
Design: Steven Schilte, Naarden, NL
www.machalke.com
www.stevenschilte.nl

The spirited design of Cinque refers to its varied functionality. Elaborate, curved ornamental seams at the seating and leaning area pick up the contours of the armchair and generate an interesting dynamic appeal. The seating is made up of two halves that are linked together by an axis in the centre so that they are rotatable. This structure permits a mobility of 360 degrees. By means of special stainless steel elements several pieces of furniture can be connected and arranged in molecule-like structures of any desired length.

Die schwungvoll anmutende Gestaltung von Cinque weist auf seine vielseitige Funktionalität hin. Aufwendige, geschwungene Ziernähte im Sitz- und Lehnenbereich greifen die Kontur des Sessels auf und verleihen ihm eine interessante Dynamik. Die Sitzfläche besteht aus zwei Hälften, die durch eine Achse in der Mitte drehbar verbunden sind. Dieser Aufbau erlaubt eine volle Bewegungsfreiheit um 360 Grad. Mit speziellen Edelstahlelementen lassen sich mehrere Möbel untereinander verbinden und zu molekülkettenartigen Strukturen in beliebiger Länge anordnen.

Ruché Sofa

Roset S.A., Briord, France / Frankreich
Design: Inga Sempé, Paris,
France / Frankreich
www.ligne-roset.com
www.ingasempe.fr

Garden swing seats have been the inspiration for this extraordinary and comfortable sofa. Like these Ruché joins severity and softness – some air and some material. The frame is made of solid beech. A thick cover with special quilting, quilted upholstery with square patterns and interrupted seams rests on the feet. The fabric partly bulges because it is alternatingly kept together or released by the stitches, which gives it its special look as well as its name (Ruché = ruche). These heights and depths of the cover create varied light reflexes. The fine straight-lined feet and the undulations of the cover form a harmonious interplay of stringent straight lines and soft curves.

Als Inspiration für dieses ungewöhnliche und komfortable Sofa dienten Hollywoodschaukeln. Wie diese will Ruché Strenge mit Weichheit verbinden – etwas Luft und etwas Material. Das Gestell besteht aus massiver Buche. Auf den Füßen ruht eine dicke Decke mit spezieller Absteppung, einer gesteppten Polsterung mit quadratischem Raster und unterbrochenen Nähten. Abwechselnd durch die Stiche gehalten oder wieder freigelassen bauscht sich der Stoff stellenweise auf, was ihm seine besondere Optik sowie seinen Namen (Ruché = Rüsche) verleiht. Aus diesen Höhen und Tiefen des Bezuges entstehen abwechslungsreiche Lichtreflexe. Die feinen geradlinigen Füße und die Wellenbewegungen der Decke bilden ein harmonisches Zusammenspiel von strengen Geraden und weichen Kurven.

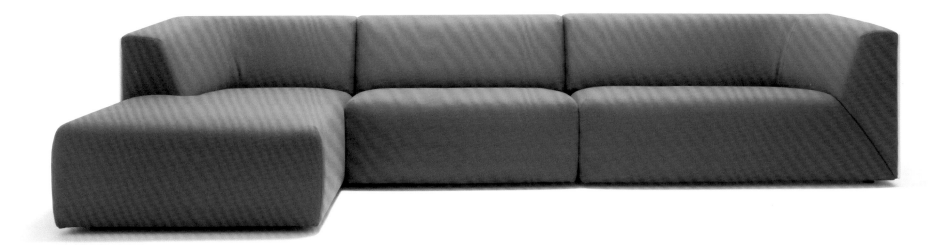

Rolf Benz AMO Sofa

Rolf Benz AG & Co. KG, Nagold,
Germany / Deutschland
Design: Norbert Beck, Markdorf,
Germany / Deutschland
www.rolf-benz.com
www.norbertbeckdesign.de

By its sensuously luxurious aura this representative sofa collection is quite seducing. Voluminous, soft cushions permit comfortable seating pleasure. Rolf Benz AMO can be configured according to the wishes of user: the modular structure allows the most varied combinations from a two-part sofa to a generous seating corner. The thoroughly crafted back shell is optionally available with a different cover fabric, thus creating an individual representation of domestic living culture. An additional feature of this programme's seating culture is thick leather, which nicely accentuates elaborately treated seam details. Rolf Benz AMO is available in two seating heights and is optimally completed by an armchair and an upholstered bench.

Dieses repräsentative Sofaprogramm will mit seiner sinnlich-luxuriösen Aura verführen. Die voluminösen, weichen Polster erlauben einen komfortablen Sitzgenuss. Rolf Benz AMO lässt sich nach Wunsch gestalten: Der modulare Aufbau ermöglicht unterschiedlichste Kombinationen vom zweiteiligen Sofa bis hin zur großzügigen Ecke. Die handwerklich sehr sorgfältig ausgeführte Rückenschale kann auf Wunsch in einem anderen Bezugsmaterial verarbeitet werden – wodurch ein individuelles Stück Wohnkultur entsteht. Ein zusätzlicher Aspekt der Sitzkultur dieses Programms ist Dickleder, welches die aufwendig verarbeiteten Nahtdetails hervorragend zur Geltung bringt. Rolf Benz AMO ist in zwei Sitzhöhen erhältlich und wird durch einen Sessel und eine Polsterbank optimal ergänzt.

Beat
Cushion Cover / Kissenhülle

Bervision GmbH, Münchberg,
Germany / Deutschland
In-house design / Werksdesign
www.bervision.be

Innovative materials and binding methods
enhance the design of the Beat cushion
range. They are the expression of a new
trend. This cushion cover is of a jacquard-
woven quality: it is the result of a method by
which several viscose and polyester yarns are
woven on a fine polyester warp. This binding
method together with an adjusted finish
procedure gives the fabric its special depth
effect. The cushion cover is available in ten
fresh and appealing colours.

Innovative Materialien und Bindeverfahren unterstreichen die Gestaltung der
Kissenserie Beat. Sie sind auch Ausdruck
einer neuen Entwicklungslinie. Diese Kissenhülle besteht aus einem Jacquardge-
webe und ist das Ergebnis einer Methode,
mit der verschiedene Garne aus Viskose
und Polyester auf einem Untergrund aus
Polyesterfäden miteinander verbunden
werden. Dieses Bindeverfahren verleiht
zusammen mit einer darauf abgestimmten
Oberflächenbehandlung dem Stoff seine
besondere Tiefenwirkung. Die Kissenhülle
gibt es in zehn frischen, ansprechenden
Farben.

Aurea Sofa

Intertime AG, Endingen,
Switzerland / Schweiz
Design: Christophe Marchand Design
(Christophe Marchand), Zürich,
Switzerland / Schweiz
www.intertime.ch
www.christophemarchand.ch

The cubic form of the Aurea sofa is plain; its
mature functionality accompanies its owner
through any conceivable situation of life. A
functional cushion serves an upright position
if required, for example when the sofa is
used spontaneously for writing, reading or
multimedia use. A swivel-out shelf provides
an ideal place to deposit the writing material
or notebook. A swivel function allows the
couch to be turned by 90 degrees creating a
comfortable relaxing area.

Die kubische Form des Sofas Aurea ist
schlicht, seine durchdachte Funktionalität
begleitet den Besitzer in allen denkbaren
Lebenssituationen. Ein Funktionskissen
lässt bei Bedarf aufrecht sitzen, zum
Beispiel wenn das Sofa spontan zum
Schreiben, Lesen oder zur Multimedianut-
zung dienen soll. Ein ausdrehbares Tablar
schafft dabei die ideale Ablagefläche für
das Schreibmaterial oder Notebook. Mit
einer Ausdrehfunktion kann die Liege um
90 Grad gedreht werden, wodurch eine
regelrechte Liegelandschaft entsteht.

Liner Sofa

Air Division Pte. Ltd., Singapore
In-house design / Werksdesign:
Jerry Low
www.airdivision.com

This sofa is designed with a clean, simple
and powerful line in mind. Its form language
resonates from the railings of the majestic
1930s ocean liners, when seafaring was the
epitome of travel. An attention to details
and the flow of each structure and joinery
provide an additional strong presence to
the sofa's visual appeal. Time-honoured
traditional craftsmanship along with state-
of-the-art manufacturing technology is
amalgamated into the entire production
process. American black walnut is used for
the structure while white pristine Brazilian
leather completes the aesthetics.

Klare, schlichte und kraftvolle Linien
bestimmen die Form dieses Sofas. Seine
Formensprache spiegelt die Reling der
majestätischen Ozeandampfer aus den
1930er Jahren wider, als eine Seefahrt der
Inbegriff des Reisens war. Die Betonung
von Details sowie fließende Strukturen
und Verbindungen verleihen dem visuellen Charme zusätzliche Aussagekraft.
Altehrwürdiges, traditionelles Handwerk
und modernste Herstellungstechniken
verschmelzen im gesamten Produktionsprozess. Für den Korpus wird amerika-
nisches Schwarznussholz verwendet,
während hochwertiges weißes Leder
aus Brasilien den ästhetischen Eindruck
abrundet.

Kurt
Sofa Bed / Sofabett

Seefelder Möbelwerkstätten GmbH,
Seefeld, Germany / Deutschland
Design: Jan Armgardt Design, Schondorf
am Ammersee, Germany / Deutschland
www.seefelder.com

The versatility and well-conceived comfort of the Kurt sofa offers many options for use. Thereby the classic sofa bed is interpreted in a new way. Presented in a forthright way, the low-seated high-backed sofa with architectural lines serves as a seminal couch. Its sloped seat affords a restful, reclined position. The high backrest is very comfortable and relaxing. If the sofa is closed by folding the backrest forward a consistent corpus in the form of a cuboid is created.

Mit Vielseitigkeit und einem durchdachten Komfort bietet Kurt dem Nutzer viele Einsatzmöglichkeiten. Es interpretiert das klassische Schlafsofa neu. Offen fungiert der tiefliegende Hochlehner mit architektonischer Linienführung als stilbildende Couch. Seine angeschrägte Sitzfläche erlaubt eine bequeme, zurückgelehnte Position. Die hohe Rückenlehne ist sehr komfortabel und entspannend. Schließt man das Sofa, indem man die Rückenlehne mit einem Griff nach vorne klappt, entsteht ein gleichmäßiger Korpus in Form eines Quaders.

Single Sofa

Design: Joine Office for Design
(Maarten Baptist), Eindhoven, NL
www.joine.nl

The Single Sofa is designed for sleeping, lounging and relaxing. It defines a sofa being more than just sitting on. The special aspect of its functionality is that by means of simply lowering one corner of the seat the function of a chaise longue, literally a long chair, has been incorporated into the couch. This integrated reclining chair is formed by the angle of the dip at one end of the seat and the ergonomic slant of the armrest; so the raised and sloping armrest serves as a backrest while the remainder of the seat forms a relaxing support for the legs.

Das Single Sofa eignet sich zum Schlafen, Wohlfühlen und Entspannen. Es zeigt, dass ein Sofa mehr sein kann als nur ein Sitzmöbel. Der besondere Aspekt seiner Funktionalität besteht darin, dass in die Couch ein Longchair integriert wurde. Indem eine Seite heruntergedrückt wird, verwandelt es sich in eine Chaiselongue. Dieser integrierte Liegesessel entsteht durch den Neigungswinkel an einem Ende der Sitzfläche und die ergonomische Schrägstellung der Armlehne. So stützt die aufgerichtete, schräge Armlehne den Rücken, während die Füße angenehm auf dem übrigen Teil der Sitzfläche ruhen.

Dormette
Sofa Bed / Sofabett

Franz Fertig GmbH,
Buchen, Germany / Deutschland
In-house design / Werksdesign
www.die-collection.de

Designed as a multifunctional system this sofa bed allows sitting, relaxing and sleeping in all kinds of variations. Fitted with different mattress qualities and a slatted frame with headrest and footrest adjustment it can be used as sofa, relax lounger and comfortable bed as well. The standard large storage box as well as removable covers complete the comfort of this model. Thanks to a generous workmanship of the bedspread (two-, three- or four-sided depending on the type) the bedding may remain under the spread. In addition, all customary mattresses will fit into it.

Konzipiert als Baukastensystem ermöglicht dieses Sofabett Sitzen, Relaxen und Schlafen in vielfältigen Variationen. Ausgestattet mit unterschiedlichen Matratzenqualitäten und einem Lattenrost mit Kopf- und Fußteilverstellung dient es sowohl als Sofa, Relaxliege wie auch als bequemes Bett. Der standardmäßige große Bettkasten sowie die abnehmbaren Bezüge runden den Komfort dieses Modells ab. Durch die großzügige Verarbeitung der Tagesdecke (je nach Ausführung zwei-, drei- oder vierseitig) kann das Bettzeug auch unter der Decke verbleiben. Es können zudem alle handelsüblichen Matratzen eingelegt werden.

Loft Lounge Chair / Lounge-Sessel

Bernhardt Design Europe,
Hillerød, Denmark / Dänemark
Bernhardt Design, Lenoir, USA
Design: Shelly Shelly,
Los Angeles, USA
www.bernhardtdesigneurope.com
www.bernhardtdesign.com

Loft is a hand-sculpted lounge chair of solid walnut, and in this sense a tangible example of the disappearing art of craftsmanship in furniture making. The Loft lounge chair was designed in a studio course at Art Center College of Design where modern design technologies are combined with age-old construction techniques. 23 pieces of timber and 11 different components of various milling techniques are merged using traditional mortise and tenon wood joinery by placing complex applications of simple geometries. The connections expose the structural element of the chair while highlighting the elegant interplay of the hardwood grains.

Der aus massivem Walnussholz handgefertigte Lounge-Sessel Loft ist ein greifbares Beispiel für die verschwindende Kunst des Handwerks in der Möbelherstellung. Der Lounge-Sessel Loft wurde während eines Lehrgangs am Art Center College of Design entworfen, bei dem moderne Designtechniken mit altbewährten Herstellungsverfahren kombiniert wurden. 23 Holzteile und 11 mit unterschiedlichen Frästechniken hergestellte Elemente wurden mithilfe einer traditionellen Zapfenverbindung zusammengefügt – komplexe Verfahren im Dienste einfacher Gestaltung. Die Verbindungen betonen das konstruktive Element des Sessels und heben das elegante Zusammenspiel der Hartholzfasern hervor.

Hyde Lounge Chair/Lounge-Sessel

Bernhardt Design Europe,
Hillerød, Denmark/Dänemark
Bernhardt Design, Lenoir, USA
Design: FredriksonStallard,
Patrik Fredrikson & Ian Stallard,
London, GB
www.bernhardtdesigneurope.com
www.bernhardtdesign.com
www.fredriksonstallard.com

Trying to combine both, this chair is fashioned as a sculpture that is as much art as it is furniture. The solid walnut frame of Hyde incorporates elegant simplicity with an extreme attention to detail. Hand crafting and carving as well as sophisticated joinery are used for a visually seamless connection of the individual elements. The seat may be upholstered in either fabric or leather, with a back pillow that allows the use of a contrasting fabric or colour. The frame is available in several finishes including natural oil.

Dieser Sessel in Form einer Skulptur ist ebenso sehr Kunst wie Gebrauchsmöbel und versucht, beides zu vereinen. Der stabile Walnuss-Rahmen von Hyde repräsentiert elegante Schlichtheit, wobei das Hauptaugenmerk auf dem Detail liegt. Von Hand geschnitzt zeigt er sich als aufwendige Schreinerarbeit, die die einzelnen Elemente nahtlos miteinander verbindet. Die Sitzfläche gibt es gepolstert in Stoff oder Leder mit einer gleichfalls gepolsterten Rückenlehne, deren Bezug und Farbe durchaus kontrastieren können. Der Rahmen ist in verschiedenen Ausführungen erhältlich, unter anderem geölt.

Jun Zi Chair / Stuhl

Dragonfly Gallery Co. Ltd.,
Taipei, Taiwan
In-house design / Werksdesign:
Jeff Dah-Yue Shi,
Wayne Hung-Wei Liao
www.dragonfly.com.tw

As the material bamboo has been a recognised symbol of a nobleman in Chinese literature, the Jun Zi chair wants to symbolise it through its design. Elegantly, decent, upright, with integrity and vigor of style, the chair achieves the comfort that it should provide in its simple geometric form. The whole structure is composed of bamboo slats. The gaps between provide the ventilation and the delicate arch contributes to its neat and elegant contour. Sitting on it, a sense of slight bounce reflects the natural flexibility of bamboo material. Each slat is carefully processed in special procedure to make sure its solid stability and durability. In order to make sure its durability in various climatic conditions, the bamboo used to make the Jun Zi chair is processed through specific traditional procedures. Therefore, the chair is also a statement about rejoining the craftsmanship into contemporary life and rethinking human's relation to nature.

In der chinesischen Literatur galt Bambus als Symbol des Adels. Das Design des Stuhls Jun Zi nimmt diese Symbolik auf. Elegant, dezent, aufrecht, geradlinig und kraftvoll bietet der Stuhl die Annehmlichkeit, die aufgrund seiner schlichten geometrischen Form von ihm erwartet wird. Seine gesamte Struktur ist aus Bambusleisten gefertigt. Die Zwischenräume sorgen für Belüftung und die feine Bogenform unterstreicht seine glatte, elegante Kontur. Beim Sitzen spürt man eine leichte Schwingung, die die natürliche Biegsamkeit des Bambus vermittelt. Jede Leiste wird in einem speziellen Herstellungsverfahren sorgfältig verarbeitet und sorgt so für große Stabilität und Langlebigkeit. Damit dies auch in unterschiedlichen klimatischen Bedingungen gewährleistet ist, wird der für den Stuhl Jun Zi verwendete Bambus in einem besonderen, traditionellen Verfahren erzeugt. Auf diese Weise dient der Stuhl der Stärkung der Handwerkskunst in der heutigen Zeit und einem Neudenken der Beziehung des Menschen zur Natur.

Qin-Jian Chair/Stuhl

Dragonfly Gallery Co. Ltd.,
Taipei, Taiwan
In-house design/Werksdesign:
Jeff Dah-Yue Shi, Roger Ming-Je Jiang
www.dragonfly.com.tw

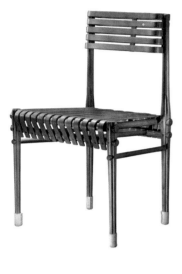

The Qin-Jian chair combines the making and
forming of a traditional material with an
interesting organic design. It is fully made of
the natural material bamboo and is crafted
with traditional techniques developed from
Chinese predecessors' wisdom. This chair
is supposed to be the solution to help the
bamboo factories in JhuShan Township
as well as to bring back the green land of
Taiwan in long-term prospects. The leg of
the chair is ready-made solid bamboo sword
(Zhu-Jian), which is compressed by recycled
waste bamboo strips. The back support and
the seat are composed of straight bamboo
slats, which would show the delicate
flexibility like strings. Starting from the
social and ecological responsibility of design,
this chair also represents the power and the
possibilities of the craft, which is behind it.

Der Stuhl Qin-Jian verbindet die Bearbeitung und Formgebung eines traditionellen Materials mit einer interessanten
organischen Gestaltung. Er besteht ausschließlich aus natürlichem Bambus und
wird in einer überlieferten Verfahrens-
weise, die in der chinesischen Tradition
wurzelt, von Hand gefertigt. Dieser Stuhl
soll eine Lösung zur Erhaltung der Bam-
busverarbeitung in der Gemeinde JhuShan
darstellen und langfristig die grüne Landschaft Taiwans wieder erstehen lassen.
Das Stuhlbein ist ein vorgefertigtes sta-
biles Bambusschwert (Zhu-Jian), das aus
wiederverwerteten, zusammengepressten
Bambusstreifen besteht. Die Lehne und
der Sitz wurden aus geraden Bambus-
latten gefertigt, die biegsam wie Bänder
sind. Ausgehend von der sozialen und
ökologischen Verantwortung des Designs
zeigt dieser Stuhl aber auch die Kraft und
die Möglichkeiten des zugrunde liegenden
Handwerks.

Skeie | Wave
Auditorium Chair System /
Hörsaal–Stuhlsystem

Skeie AS, Sandnes, Norway / Norwegen
Design: Arkitektfirmaet C. F. Møller A/S
(Jon Brøcker, Asger Hartvigsen Jakobsen),
Århus, Denmark / Dänemark
www.skeie.no
www.cfmoller.com

The components of this set of auditorium chairs are anchored in an innovative triangular beam. All seating elements are fastened to this profile allowing for the hidden arrangement of the fittings. A 3D-shaped back, which is characteristic of the look of the whole set, the armrests, and the seat fitting unfold from the beam. The various components form a harmonious unit; they are simple and elegant. The system allows for various seat widths, four back heights adjustable to the step height of the auditoriums, two different desktops and armrests, and two ways of fixing (to the floor and the step risers).

Die Komponenten dieses Systems von Hörsaalstühlen sind verankert in einem innovativen dreieckigen Trägerprofil. An diesem Profil sind alle Sitzelemente befestigt, was eine versteckte Anordnung der Beschläge erlaubt. Ein für die Anmutung dieses Systems charakteristischer 3D-Rücken, die Armlehnen sowie der Sitzbeschlag gehen vom Trägerprofil aus. Die verschiedenen Komponenten bilden ein harmonisches Ganzes, sie sind schlicht und elegant. Das System ermöglicht verschiedene Sitzbreiten, vier Rückenhöhen, angepasst zu den Stufenhöhen in Auditorien, zwei verschiedene Schreibplatten und Armlehnen sowie zwei Befestigungsarten (für den Boden und die Stoßstufen).

Joco
Dining Table / Esstisch

Walter Knoll AG & Co. KG,
Herrenberg, Germany / Deutschland
Design: EOOS Design GmbH
(Martin Bergmann,
Gernot Bohmann, Harald Gründl),
Vienna, Austria / Wien, Österreich
www.walterknoll.de
www.eoos.com

The minimalist design of the Joco dining table offers room for an individual lifestyle. It plays with area and space. The light base – floating and stable at the same time – carries the slimline tabletop. Thus, a modern minimalism and delicate stability find themselves united in its shape. Manufactured in black paint with a soft finish or elegant wood veneers, the long table provides space to seat up to eight people.

Der Esstisch Joco bietet mit seiner minimalistischen Gestaltung Raum für individuellen Lifestyle. Er spielt mit Raum und Fläche, wobei das leichte Gestell – schwebend und sicher zugleich – die dünne Tischplatte trägt. Auf diese Weise vereint sich in seiner Form ein moderner Minimalismus mit filigraner Stabilität. Gefertigt in schwarzem Softlack oder in edlen Hölzern furniert, bietet dieser Esstisch eine lange Tafel mit Platz für bis zu acht Personen.

Cuoio
Chair / Stuhl

Walter Knoll AG & Co. KG,
Herrenberg, Germany / Deutschland
Design: EOOS Design GmbH
(Martin Bergmann,
Gernot Bohmann, Harald Gründl),
Vienna, Austria / Wien, Österreich
www.walterknoll.de
www.eoos.com

The logic of minimalism determines the shape of the Cuoio chair. The recyclable materials leather and steel are the components of the surface and framework of this minimalist and timeless chair. The slits in the seat and back lend the chair its typical shape. The flexible back provides the user with high seating comfort, which is even enhanced by the tailored cut. Cuoio comes both with and without armrests, entirely in black or in natural shades of brown.

Die Logik des Minimalen definiert die Gestaltung des Stuhls Cuoio. Die recyclebaren Materialien Leder und Stahl bilden die Haut und das Gestell dieses reduziert und zeitlos anmutenden Stuhls. Die Ausschnitte in Sitz und Rücken verleihen ihm eine typische Form, wobei der flexible Rücken dem Nutzer ein hohes Maß an bequemem Sitzkomfort bietet, der durch seine Taillierung noch erhöht wird. Cuoio ist erhältlich mit und ohne Armlehnen, komplett in Schwarz oder in natürlichen Brauntönen.

Egon
Table System / Tischsystem

H+H Furniture GmbH,
Arnsberg, Germany / Deutschland
Design: 45 Kilo GbR (Daniel Klapsing,
Phillip Camille Schöpfer), Weimar,
Germany / Deutschland
www.hanshansen.de
www.45kilo.com

This table system consists of a classic steel tube frame with a choice of different tabletops made from HPL. The goal was to improve the famous model of designer Egon Eiermann with regard to material use, disassembly, easy mounting, and especially leg space. The set-up of the legs allow the table to be used equally well from all sides, thereby making the system suitable as a work table as well as a dining table. This all-round frame can be equipped with different tabletops.

Dieses Tischsystem besteht aus einem klassischen Stahlrohrgestell mit unterschiedlichen Auflagen aus HPL. Das Ziel war es, das bekannte Modell des Designers Egon Eiermann in den Punkten Materialeinsatz, Zerlegbarkeit, einfache Montage und vor allem Beinfreiheit zu verbessern. Durch die Anordnung der Beine ist der Tisch von allen Seiten gleichermaßen gut zu nutzen, wodurch das Einsatzgebiet vom Arbeitstisch hin zum Esstisch erweitert wird. Dieses Allroundgestell kann mit verschiedenen Platten ausgerüstet werden.

Origami
Bar Stool / Barhocker

H+H Furniture GmbH,
Arnsberg, Germany / Deutschland
In-house design / Werksdesign:
Hans Hansen
www.hanshansen.de

The Origami bar stool brings meticulously formed sheet metal to high precision. Innovative CNC technology allowed for this unusual product that has a wide range of qualities, including its suitability for contract use. Thanks to its flat surfaces, it lends itself as a flexible advertising medium, in particular in the contract business. Origami is available in stainless steel for outdoor use as well as in powder-coated sheet metal. A variety of project-oriented packages with textile seat solutions can be ordered on demand.

Bei dem Barhocker Origami zeugt akribisch geformter Flachstahl von hoher Präzision. Auf der Basis innovativer CNC-Technologie entstand ein ungewöhnliches Produkt mit vielseitigen und objekttauglichen Qualitäten. Die flächige Interpretation gestattet den flexiblen Einsatz als Werbeträger, vor allem im Objektbereich. Origami ist erhältlich in outdoortauglichem Edelstahl sowie in pulverbeschichtetem Flachstahl. Projektbezogen sind verschiedene Ausstattungspakete mit textilen Sitzergänzungen möglich.

Nano
Coffee Table / Couchtisch

Emoh, Oderzo (Treviso), Italy / Italien
Design: Meneghello Paolelli Associati
(Sandro Meneghello, Marco Paolelli),
Milan, Italy / Mailand, Italien
www.emoh.it
www.meneghellopaolelli.com

Nano is a coffee table system consisting of two units that differ in height. These feature round, methacrylate lacquer tabletops with integrated LED strips that diffuse light from the edges. This gives the table a very discreet, soft feel that accentuates the table form without being too invasive. The table base consists of a single cone that widens downward, ensuring the balanced proportions of this table.

Nano ist ein System, das aus zwei Couchtischen unterschiedlicher Höhe besteht. Es zeichnet sich durch eine runde Tischplatte aus Methacrylat mit einem integrierten LED-Lichtband aus. Da deren Oberfläche lackiert ist, kann das Licht nur von der Tischkante ausstrahlen. Dieser Tisch bietet so ein sehr dezentes, warmes Licht, das die Tischform hervorhebt, ohne aufdringlich zu wirken. Das sich nach unten verbreiternde, kegelförmige Gestell sorgt für ausgewogene Proportionen.

Remix #2 – Desk
Davenport / Sekretär

H+H Furniture GmbH,
Arnsberg, Germany / Deutschland
Design: Gesa Hansen,
Paris, France / Frankreich
www.hanshansen.de
www.gesahansen.com

Following the concept of music, Desk of the Remix collection of the label "The Hansen Family" is considered to be a formal and functional "remix" of the classic davenport. Its form has been reduced to its functions. It can be free standing in the room and it is independent of a partition. It is therefore also used at home and not only as office furniture. With its modern style language this davenport adapts to contemporary as well as very traditional interiors. As a generation-spanning piece of furniture it appeals to people of all ages. It features an extractable work plate and an upper deposit space that can be folded out, and four compartments.

In Anlehnung an das gleichnamige musikalische Konzept versteht sich Desk aus der Remix-Kollektion des Labels „The Hansen Family" als formaler und funktionaler „Remix" des klassischen Sekretärs. Seine Form ist auf seine Funktionen reduziert. Er kann frei im Raum stehen und ist nicht an eine Stellwand gebunden, weshalb er als Wohnmöbel dient und nicht auf das Büro beschränkt ist. Mit seiner zeitgemäßen Formensprache passt sich dieser Sekretär sowohl modernen als auch sehr traditionellen Interieurs an, er eignet sich für jede Altersklasse und ist somit generationsübergreifend. Er besteht aus einer ausziehbaren Arbeitsplatte, einer oberen Ablage, die sich aufklappen lässt, sowie vier Fächern.

Remix #5 – Sideboard

H+H Furniture GmbH,
Arnsberg, Germany / Deutschland
Design: Gesa Hansen,
Paris, France / Frankreich
www.hanshansen.de
www.gesahansen.com

Sideboard of the Remix collection of the label "The Hansen Family" combines Scandinavian forms with the American colours of the 1950s. The drawer fronts are jutting out so that they can easily be pulled out. The design of the furniture was inspired by the boat building of the Danish Folkboat, the outside of which is clinkered in this way. The cross in the centre is designed in one of the four colours of the collection. All Remix products are handcrafted in the studio.

Sideboard aus der Remix-Kollektion des Labels „The Hansen Family" ist ein Mix aus skandinavischen Formen und den amerikanischen Farben der 1950er Jahre. Die Schubladen-Fronten sind nach vorne geschoben, damit sie sich leicht ausziehen lassen. Inspiration war dabei der Bootsbau des dänischen Folkeboots, das außen in dieser Art verklinkert ist. Das Kreuz in der Mitte ist jeweils in einer der vier Farben der Kollektion ausgeführt. Alle Remix-Produkte werden im Atelier in Handarbeit hergestellt.

Bell-Table
Side Table / Beistelltisch

ABR., Barcelona, Spain / Spanien
Design: Sebastian Herkner,
Offenbach / Main,
Germany / Deutschland
www.abrproduccion.com
www.sebastianherkner.com

The Bell-Table serves as a small side or coffee table. Due to a collage of brass and mouth-blown tinted glass it has an interesting appearance and distinctive identity. The play with mass and transparency as well as the lightweight and fragile glass base contrasting the solid brass top element represents an alternative to conventional table designs. Both table elements are put together flush thus forming a single unit. The special combination of materials is merged together as the materials mutually reflect each other.

Der Bell-Table dient als kleiner Beistell- oder Kaffeetisch. Durch eine Collage aus Messing und mundgeblasenem, getöntem Glas schafft er eine interessante Einheit und besitzt eine unverwechselbare Identität. Sowohl das Spiel mit Masse und Transparenz als auch der leichte und zerbrechliche Glassockel im Gegensatz zum festen Messingoberteil stellen eine Alternative zu konventionellen Tischansätzen dar. Beide Elemente des Tisches werden bündig zusammengesteckt und bilden so eine Einheit und Materialverbindung, die zudem durch die gegenseitige Spiegelung der Materialien miteinander verschmilzt.

Wishbone
Side Table / Beistelltisch

Frost A/S, Hadsten,
Denmark / Dänemark
Design: Busk + Hertzog (Flemming
Busk, Stephan Hertzog), London, GB
www.frostdesign.dk
www.busk-hertzog.com

This versatile side table is designed with distinct lines and a significant wishbone, which is positioned asymmetrically on a lacquer-finished aluminium base. The tabletop is the identically shaped matching part of the base and rests on branching of the table leg. The asymmetrical position of the wishbone adds a dynamic momentum to the form of the table and includes an additional functional feature: the tabletop can be placed over the seating area and, for example, be used as a support for laptops. The tabletop is made of lacquer-finished aluminium and comes in several colours.

Dieser vielseitige Beistelltisch ist mit klaren Linien gestaltet, wobei das charakteristisch gegabelte Tischbein asymmetrisch auf dem lackierten Gestell angebracht ist. Die Tischfläche ruht auf der Gabelung des Tischbeins und ist das formgleiche Gegenstück zum Untergestell. Die asymmetrische Position des Gabelbeins bringt Dynamik in die Tischform und birgt eine zusätzliche Funktion: Die Tischplatte kann über dem Sitzbereich platziert und zum Beispiel als Auflage für einen Laptop genutzt werden. Die Tischplatte ist aus lackiertem Aluminium gefertigt und in mehreren Farben erhältlich.

Lulu
Coat Hook / Kleiderhaken

Frost A/S, Hadsten,
Denmark / Dänemark
Design: Busk + Hertzog (Flemming
Busk, Stephan Hertzog), London, GB
www.frostdesign.dk
www.busk-hertzog.com

An open flower, coming to full blossom on the wall, was the inspiration for the design of Lulu. Attractive and easy to use, this functionally designed coat hook can hold hangers, jackets, umbrellas, bags, scarves and much more. An interesting aspect of the Lulu concept is that it is available in five different sizes/depths, and that it can be used as a single hook or a "bouquet of flowers" on the wall. The possibility to combine different elements and to experiment with their arrangement gives users the opportunity to unfold their creativity. Lulu hooks are finished with a soft-touch lacquer that lends them a soft and matt feel and that evokes the velvety feeling of a flower. Lulu is suitable for the wardrobe, the hallway or even the living room.

Eine offene Blume, die an der Wand zu voller Blüte kommt, war die Inspiration für die Gestaltung von Lulu. An diesem funktional gestalteten Kleiderhaken können Kleiderbügel, Jacken, Schirme, Taschen, Schals und vieles mehr dekorativ und einfach aufgehängt werden. Ein interessanter Aspekt des Konzepts von Lulu ist, dass der Haken in fünf verschiedenen Größen/Tiefen erhältlich ist und einzeln wie auch als „Blumenstrauß" an der Wand verwendet werden kann. Die Kombination der Elemente wie auch die Anordnung lassen dem Nutzer einen großen individuellen Spielraum, um seine Kreativität zu entfalten. Lulu hat eine Oberfläche aus einem Soft-Touch-Lack, der diesen Kleiderhaken eine weiche und matte Anmutung verleiht, die dem Samtgefühl einer Blume entspricht. Lulu ist geeignet für die Garderobe, den Flur oder auch das Wohnzimmer.

Kotori
Shoehorn / Schuhlöffel

H Concept Co., Ltd., Tokyo, Japan
Design: Kaichi Design
(Kaichiro Yamada), Kanagawa, Japan
www.h-concept.jp
www.kaichidesign.com

This shoehorn is made from layers of wood twisted to form a unique shape that will easily find its place in the entrance to your home. When placed, its simple shape resembles a bird perched on a branch. Kotori wants to embellish the entrance of a home with its design and please everybody arriving there.

Dieser Schuhlöffel besteht aus mehreren Holzschichten, die zu einer außergewöhnlichen Form gedreht wurden. So findet er im Eingangsbereich der Wohnung einen passenden Platz. Seine schlichte Form gleicht der eines Vogels, der auf einem Ast sitzt. Derart gestaltet, will Kotori den Eingang zur Wohnung bereichern und dort jeden Eintreffenden erfreuen.

Quará Hanger / Bügel

Poly Play, Santa Barbara d'Oeste,
Brazil / Brasilien
Design: Nó Design, São Paulo,
Brazil / Brasilien
www.polyplayplasticos.com.br
www.nodesign.com.br

This hanger addresses the problem of space when hanging up laundry. Thanks to an integrated clothes peg, the Quará hanger can be used to hang clothes on clothes lines, which takes up less space than using conventional clothes pegs. The integrated pegs are designed to stay in place, thus preventing the hangers from sliding up and down the line. Quará is suitable for drying clothes on a line or for hanging them in a wardrobe.

Dieser Bügel löst ein großes Problem in Waschräumen, wo es bei der Verwendung herkömmlicher Wäscheklammern meist zu wenig Platz gibt. Diesem Problem trägt der Bügel Quará Rechnung, indem er die Kleidungsstücke dank der integrierten Wäscheklammer an ihrem Platz hält. Auf diese Weise kann der Bügel mit dem Kleidungsstück auch nicht die Wäscheleine entlangrutschen. Quará eignet sich sowohl zum Trocknen von Kleidungsstücken als auch für die Verwendung im Kleiderschrank.

Tutzi
Coat Stand / Kleiderständer

Taiwan Order Furniture Corp.,
Taipei, Taiwan
Design: Euga Design Studio
(Eugenio Gargioni), Milan,
Italy / Mailand, Italien
www.order.com.tw
www.eugadesign.it

Tutzi is an exciting modular wooden freestanding coat stand made of six triangular section elements joined to create the hexagonal section of the stick. Each one of these elements has three parts: the vertical stick and two slanting elements that are the hook and the base. Since the coat stand has a modular structure it is possible to realise each element with different kind of wood, different colour or finishing or to choose only one material. In this way this product is suitable for very different purposes.

Tutzi ist ein interessanter, freistehender Kleiderständer aus Holz, der auf dem Baukastenprinzip beruht und sich aus sechs dreieckigen Teilelementen zusammensetzt, die den sechsteiligen Aufbau des Ständers bilden. Jedes dieser Elemente hat drei Teile: einen vertikalen Stab und zwei schräge Elemente, welche den Haken und den Fuß bilden. Da sich der Kleiderständer aus Einzelelementen zusammensetzt, ist es möglich, jedes Teil aus einer anderen Holzart mit unterschiedlicher Farbe und Oberfläche oder nur ein Material zu wählen. So eignet sich das Produkt für ganz unterschiedliche Zwecke.

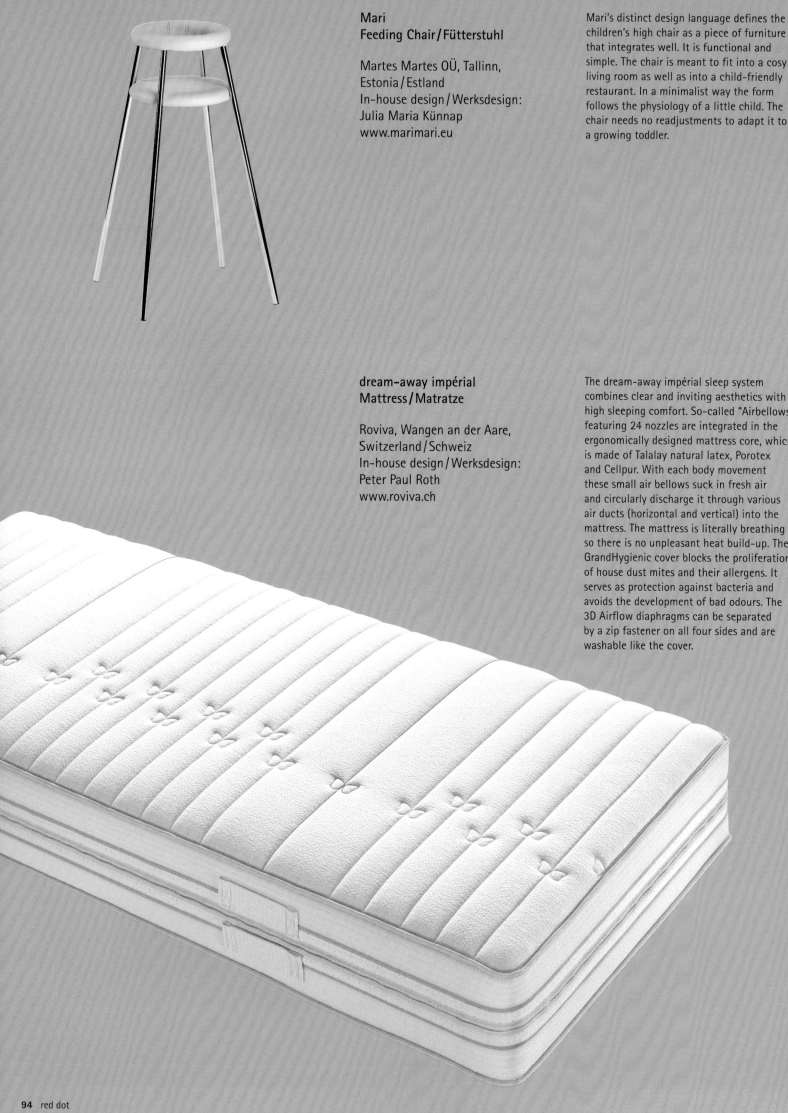

Mari
Feeding Chair / Fütterstuhl

Martes Martes OÜ, Tallinn,
Estonia / Estland
In-house design / Werksdesign:
Julia Maria Künnap
www.marimari.eu

Mari's distinct design language defines the children's high chair as a piece of furniture that integrates well. It is functional and simple. The chair is meant to fit into a cosy living room as well as into a child-friendly restaurant. In a minimalist way the form follows the physiology of a little child. The chair needs no readjustments to adapt it to a growing toddler.

Maris klar strukturierte Formensprache definiert den Kinder-Hochstuhl als ein Möbelstück, das sich gut integriert. Er ist sowohl funktional als auch schlicht gestaltet. Der Stuhl soll in den gemütlichen Wohnraum ebenso passen wie in ein kinderfreundliches Restaurant. Auf minimalistische Weise orientiert sich die Form an der Physiologie eines kleinen Kindes. Der Stuhl muss für das wachsende Kleinkind zudem nicht neu eingestellt werden.

dream-away impérial
Mattress / Matratze

Roviva, Wangen an der Aare,
Switzerland / Schweiz
In-house design / Werksdesign:
Peter Paul Roth
www.roviva.ch

The dream-away impérial sleep system combines clear and inviting aesthetics with a high sleeping comfort. So-called "Airbellows" featuring 24 nozzles are integrated in the ergonomically designed mattress core, which is made of Talalay natural latex, Porotex and Cellpur. With each body movement these small air bellows suck in fresh air and circularly discharge it through various air ducts (horizontal and vertical) into the mattress. The mattress is literally breathing so there is no unpleasant heat build-up. The GrandHygienic cover blocks the proliferation of house dust mites and their allergens. It serves as protection against bacteria and avoids the development of bad odours. The 3D Airflow diaphragms can be separated by a zip fastener on all four sides and are washable like the cover.

Das Schlafsystem dream-away impérial verbindet eine klare und einladende Ästhetik mit hohem Schlafkomfort. In den ergonomisch gestalteten Matratzenkern aus den Materialien Talalay Naturlatex, Porotex und Cellpur sind sogenannte „Airbellows" mit je 24 Düsen eingebettet. Diese wirken wie kleine Luftbälge, denn sie saugen mit jeder Körperbewegung frische Luft an und stoßen diese kreisförmig über die diversen Luftkanäle (horizontal und vertikal) in die Matratze aus. Die Matratze atmet auf diese Weise und jeder unangenehme Wärmestau wird vermieden. Der Bezug GrandHygienic blockiert die Vermehrung von Hausstaubmilben und deren Allergenen, er dient als Bakterienschutz und verhindert die Entstehung lästiger Gerüche. Die 3D-Airflow-Membranen lassen sich über einen 4-Seiten-Reißverschluss trennen und sind, ebenso wie der Bezug, waschbar.

BabyBjörn Bassinet Harmony / BabyBjörn Babykörbchen Harmony

BabyBjörn AB, Solna,
Sweden / Schweden
In-house design / Werksdesign:
Andreas Zandrén, Lisen Elmberg
Design: Ergonomidesign AB
(Håkan Bergqvist), Bromma,
Sweden / Schweden
www.babybjorn.com
www.ergonomidesign.com

The BabyBjörn Bassinet Harmony is a sleeping place where a baby can rest safely and snugly. With a light movement of the hand it can be lulled to sleep. Thanks to its springy base it gently swings through the baby's own movements. Since the bassinet is easy to transport it is no problem to place it in different rooms. It is suitable for both the daytime nap and the night-time sleep. Thanks to its well-conceived design featuring a translucent mesh fabric it is easy to keep an eye on the baby. A canopy is included screening off disturbing light. It can be pulled all around the bassinet to form a mosquito net. The base features sturdy anti-glide strips that also protect the floor. The bassinet's fabric is easy to take off and wash at 40 degrees centigrade.

Das BabyBjörn Babykörbchen Harmony ist ein Schlafplatz, an dem ein Baby sicher und geborgen ruhen kann. Mit einer leichten Handbewegung kann es in den Schlaf gewiegt werden. Dank eines federnden Rahmens wird das Körbchen durch die Bewegung des Kindes sanft geschaukelt. Da es sich gut transportieren lässt, kann das Babykörbchen zudem leicht in verschiedene Räume gestellt werden und eignet sich so für den Mittagsschlaf wie auch für die Nachtruhe. Aufgrund der sehr durchdachten Gestaltung mit einem transparenten, einsehbaren Netzgewebe kann das Baby gut im Auge behalten werden. Zur Ausstattung gehört ein den Lichteinfall abschirmender Himmel, der als Mückennetz um das gesamte Körbchen gezogen werden kann. Die Füße haben robuste, rutschfeste Beläge, die auch den Fußboden schützen. Der Stoff des Babykörbchens lässt sich leicht abnehmen und waschen bei 40 Grad.

Gypsy
Bedlinen Set / Bettwäsche-Set

Lanui GbR, Hamburg,
Germany / Deutschland
In-house design / Werksdesign:
Henrike Reinecke
www.lanui.de

The fresh impression of this bedlinen set originates in the smocked, three-dimensional embroidery that can only be stitched this way by Japanese sewing machines. The bedlinen is made of 100 per cent combed and mercerised cotton and combines the colour white with turquoise, apple green and beige embroidery. The pillow has a little embroidered ruffled edge and the underside of the duvet is smooth. The bedlinen set features an absolutely non-iron finishing since the smocked embroideries produce a marvellous drape – a result that is obtained without any chemical finish.

Die frische Anmutung dieses Bettwäsche-Sets entsteht durch gesmokte, dreidimensionale Stickereien, die nur von japanischen Nähmaschinen auf diese Weise gestickt werden können. Die Bettwäsche besteht zu 100 Prozent aus einer gekämmten und merzerisierten Baumwolle in der Farbigkeit Weiß mit türkiser, apfelgrüner und beiger Stickerei. Das Kopfkissen verfügt über einen kleinen bestickten Rüschenrand, die Bettdeckenunterseite ist glatt. Das Bettwäsche-Set ist völlig bügelfrei, da die gesmokten Stickereien einen sehr schönen Faltenwurf entstehen lassen. Ein Ergebnis, das ohne jegliche chemische Veredelung erreicht wird.

Morsø 7600
Wood-Burning Stove / Kaminofen

Morsø Jernstøberi A/S,
Nykøbing Mors, Denmark / Dänemark
Design: Monica Ritterband,
Frederiksberg, Denmark / Dänemark
www.morsoe.com
www.ritterband.dk

This wood-burning stove made of cast iron is based on the convection principle. It features a clean and effective combustion system with tertiary air supply providing optimal control of the combustion process. It therefore complies with the most stringent environmental standards. Air supply – and therefore combustion and heat – are controlled with one turn of the hand so the handling of this stove is easy and user-friendly. The organically round forms of the stove convey a soft and feminine impression. At the same time, the user has an expansive view of the fire itself.

Dieser Kaminofen aus Gusseisen basiert auf dem Konvektionsprinzip. Er verfügt über eine saubere und effektive Verbrennung mit tertiärer Luftzufuhr, was zu einer optimierten Steuerung des Verbrennungsprozesses führt und deshalb die Einhaltung strengster Umweltnormen ermöglicht. Da die Luftzufuhr, und damit die Verbrennung und Wärme, nur über einen einzigen Handgriff gesteuert werden, ist dieser Ofen leicht und nutzerfreundlich zu handhaben. Die Gestaltung mit organisch abgerundeten Formen verleiht dem Kaminofen eine weiche und feminine Anmutung, gleichzeitig bietet sich dem Nutzer ein großzügiger Einblick auf das Feuer.

H35T Stove / Ofen

NIBE Stoves, Markaryd,
Sweden / Schweden
In-house design / Werksdesign:
Anders Ralsgard
Design: Vitreindustridesign
(Marie Rubin, Susanne Ek),
Barsebäck, Sweden / Schweden
www.nibefire.se

With its oblong shape and soft lines this stove harmonises well with the pure Scandinavian living style. As a discrete piece of interior of high living standard it suitably blends into the room. The design reflects the high importance to performance optimisation, user-friendly functionality, and high energy efficiency. Thanks to an elevated combustion chamber with large glass panels the fire is widely visible. Its height makes it easy to put another log on the fire and discharge the ashes. This model has an efficiency factor of 80 per cent and allows for quick heating by radiation heat as well as stored heat.

Mit seiner länglich-rechteckigen Form und weichen Linien passt sich dieser Ofen gut dem klaren skandinavischen Wohnstil an. Er fügt sich in den Raum ein und ist ein diskret anmutendes Einrichtungsstück mit hohem Wohnwert. Die Gestaltung legte großes Gewicht auf die Leistungs-optimierung, eine nutzerfreundliche Funktionalität und eine hohe Energie-ausbeute. Die erhöhte Brennkammer mit hohen Seitenscheiben macht das Feuer weithin sichtbar. Die Höhe erleichtert das Nachlegen von Holz und das Entleeren der Asche. Das Modell hat einen Wirkungs-grad von 80 Prozent und ermöglicht eine schnelle Erwärmung, sowohl durch Strah-lungs- wie auch durch Speicherwärme.

Jøtul F 470 Concept
Wood-Burning Stoves / Kaminöfen

Jøtul AS, Fredrikstad,
Norway / Norwegen
Design: Hareide Designmill
(Anna Oren, Einar J. Hareide), Moss,
Norway / Norwegen
www.jotul.com
www.hareide-designmill.no

This range of cast-iron wood-burning stoves is designed with an appealing teardrop shape and has a large curved glass door with guillotine solution. The stove with flue outlet at the top and turn plate can be rotated a full 360 degrees and thus aimed at every corner of the room. Slim lines give it a lighter and more elegant look in comparison to the traditional cast-iron stoves. Integrated sides create well-balanced proportions. A conspicuous aesthetic element of this wood-burning stove consists in beautiful blue-grey soapstone sides serving heat storage. The large, curved glass panel extending to the sides of the stove offers a pleasant view to the flames from any viewpoint.

Diese Serie von gusseisernen Kaminöfen ist in einer attraktiven Tropfenform gestaltet und verfügt über eine große gebogene Glastür mit Hebefunktion. Der Ofen kann mit Obenabgang und Drehpodest um volle 360 Grad gedreht werden und ist so in jede Ecke des Raumes ausrichtbar. Eine schlanke Linienführung verleiht ihm ein leichteres und eleganteres Aussehen im Vergleich zu traditionellen Gussöfen, integrierte Seiten schaffen ausgewogene Proportionen. Ein auffälliges ästhetisches Element dieses Kaminofens sind schöne, blaugraue Specksteinseiten, die der Wärmespeicherung dienen. Die große, bis in die Seiten des Ofens gebogene Glasscheibe bietet aus jeder Perspektive einen guten Blick auf das Feuer.

rugs kristiina lassus
Carpet Collection / Teppichkollektion

Kristiina Lassus Studio,
Stresa (Verbania), Italy / Italien
Design: Kristiina Lassus
www.kristiinalassus.com

The subtle design of this carpet collection unites different patterns in an expressive style. Matching human needs, these interesting floor textiles are at the same time rooted in tradition and conscious of modern interior concepts. They have been devised to furnish contemporary spaces, whether modern or classic, urban or rural. They are made by hand in 80 or 100 knot qualities; some flat weaves are also produced in durrie quality. As they are knotted by hand, these rugs are hard-wearing and long-lasting. Their low pile displays an appearance of reserved elegance. Colour variations, haptics and abrasive quality of these rugs have been carefully designed and adjusted.

Mit einer feinsinnigen Gestaltung vereint diese Teppichkollektion unterschiedliche Dessins in einer ausdrucksstarken Formensprache. Auf menschliche Bedürfnisse ausgerichtet, stellen diese Bodentextilien eine interessante Verbindung dar aus Tradition und dem Verständnis für zeitgemäße Interieurs. Sie wurden entworfen, um heutige Räume, ob modern oder klassisch, in der Stadt oder auf dem Land, einzurichten. Gefertigt werden sie von Hand in einer Qualität von 80 oder 100 Knoten, einige Flachwebarten entstehen auch in einer Durrie-Qualität. Da sie handgeknüpft werden, sind diese Teppiche widerstandsfähig und langlebig, ihr niedriger Flor verleiht ihnen die Anmutung zurückhaltender Eleganz. Sorgfältig gestaltet und abgestimmt wurden auch das Farbspektrum, die Haptik sowie die Abriebqualität der Teppiche.

Starck by Fletco
Carpet Tiles / Teppichfliesen

Fletco Carpet Tiles A/S, Bording,
Denmark / Dänemark
Design: Philippe Starck Network
(Philippe Starck),
Paris, France / Frankreich
www.fletco.com
www.starck.com

The exclusive Starck by Fletco collection includes a plethora of tiles in different designs, where the individual figures, icons and patterns and the background can be combined freely in 12 different colours, making the collection the first choice for creative architects, interior architects and designers who want to add an extra dimension to the sensuous expression of their work. Philippe Starck has managed to develop a deeply rich and very versatile implement at the disposal of architects: "And what's more, it's easy. Magical squares for my friends, particularly my architect friends. Good luck! Enjoy … To you, and to us."

Zur exklusiven Kollektion Starck by Fletco gehören eine Fülle von verschieden gestalteten Fliesen, bei denen Figuren, Symbole und Muster sowie der Hintergrund in zwölf verschiedenen Farben frei kombiniert werden können. Dies macht die Kollektion zur ersten Wahl für kreative Architekten, Innenarchitekten und Designer, die dem sinnlichen Ausdruck ihrer Arbeit eine zusätzliche Dimension verleihen wollen. Philippe Starck ist es gelungen, ein ästhetisch ausdrucksvolles und sehr flexibel einsetzbares Werkzeug für Architekten zu entwickeln: „Außerdem ist es ganz einfach: Zauberquadrate für meine Freunde, besonders meine Architektenfreunde. Viel Glück! Einfach nur genießen! … Auf euch und auf uns."

Black Art Vulcano
Carpet / Teppichboden

Object Carpet GmbH, Denkendorf,
Germany / Deutschland
In-house design / Werksdesign
www.object-carpet.com

The design of the Black Art carpet collection drew its inspiration from the fundamental idea of capturing powerful elements of nature: volcanoes and their colossal eruptions, lava flows as they determine their paths, or pebbles on a beach, shaped by the elementary power of the sea. Magical images, black art – the perfect motifs for carpets. The collection was created with a three-dimensional weaving technique. It is very hard-wearing and suitable for contract use.

Der inspirierende Grundgedanke für die Gestaltung der Teppichboden-Kollektion Black Art waren kraftvolle Elemente der Natur: Vulkane und ihre gewaltigen Eruptionen, Lavaströme, die ihren Weg suchen. Kieselsteine am Strand, von der Urkraft des Meeres geformt. Magische Bilder, schwarze Kunst, wie geschaffen, um sie auf Teppichböden abzubilden. Diese Strukturen entstehen durch eine dreidimensionale Webtechnik, die sehr strapazierfähig und damit gut für den Objektbereich geeignet ist.

Encore3
Carpet / Teppich

Hanna Korvela Design Oy,
Kuopio, Finland / Finnland
Design: Hanna Korvela
www.hannakorvela.fi

By combining paper yarn and cotton an
elegant carpet of appealing, minimalist
character is created. A deep carbon black
dominates the smooth paper yarn surface
of Encore3. Cotton runs through the black
filling and gives the carpet an air of softness
and a three-dimensional look. At the same
time, this colour scheme creates a new
element, which may develop a subdued
and calm effect or communicate dynamic
and extravagant qualities depending on the
individual choice of colour. The carpets of the
collection unfold their effects individually
as well as in combination with the carpets
of other collections. They interact with each
other and with the surrounding area. The
carpets are dust-free, durable and recyclable.

Durch die Kombination aus Papiergarn
und Baumwolle entsteht ein elegant
anmutender Teppich mit ansprechendem,
minimalistischem Charakter. Ein tiefes
Rußschwarz dominiert bei Encore3 die
glatte Oberfläche des Papiergarns. Baumwolle, die den schwarzen Schuss durch-
bricht, gibt dem Teppich etwas Sanftes
und verleiht ihm eine dreidimensionale
Optik. Gleichzeitig entsteht durch dieses
Farbschema ein neues Element. Dieses
kann, je nach individueller Farbwahl,
eine gedämpfte und ruhige Wirkung entfalten oder Dynamik und Extravaganz
kommunizieren. Die Teppiche der Kollektion entfalten sowohl einzeln als auch in
Kombination mit den Teppichen anderer
Kollektionen ihre Wirkung, sie interagie-
ren miteinander und mit dem umgebenden
Raum. Die Teppiche sind zudem staubfrei,
langlebig und recycelbar.

Connect
Carpet / Teppich

Carpet Sign, Asten, NL
In-house design / Werksdesign:
Carpet Sign Studio
www.carpetsign.nl

A great number of yarn types have been combined in this custom-made carpet. The result is an exciting carpet that is full of brilliance and pleasing to touch. Connect is a combination of both a cut- and a loop pile structure in one carpet, connected by a bright silk stripe. The loop pile retains a subtle vintage character; it seems to be flowing and looks as if it is knitted. The cut pile however is soft and has an appealing streak. The planes can be scaled individually by positioning the silk stripe and choosing the size of each structure on either side.

Eine Vielzahl von Garnen wurde für diesen individuell gefertigten Teppich miteinander vereint. Das Ergebnis ist ein spannender Teppich voller Glanz, der sich angenehm anfühlt. Connect ist eine Kombination aus Schnitt- und Schlingenpol in einem Teppich, deren verbindendes Element eine glanzreiche Seidenlinie ist. Der Schlingenflor hat einen leichten Vintage-Charakter, wirkt fließend und fast gestrickt. Der Schnittflor ist dagegen weich und hat einen ansprechenden Strich. Die Flächenverteilung kann durch die Positionierung der seidenen Verbindungslinie und die Größe der Struktur auf beiden Seiten individuell gewählt werden.

Delta_And
Carpet / Teppichboden

Anker-Teppichboden, Düren,
Germany / Deutschland
In-house design / Werksdesign:
Ines Binder
www.anker.eu

An unusual structural aesthetics and polarity as design principle are characteristic of the appearance of this carpet. A high-tech thermo-engraving creates filigree design patterns – a delicate structure of the dichotomies high-low, soft-hard and matt-shining. Thanks to the innovative TG+ technology the original product Delta Deco is transformed into individual carpeting. Along with the Jacquard and printing technology this technology opens up a new scope for design for unique languages of style.

Eine ungewöhnliche Strukturästhetik sowie Polarität als Gestaltungsprinzip prägen die Anmutung dieses Teppichbodens. Eine Hightech-Thermogravur bringt filigrane Designfiguren hervor und führt gleichzeitig zu einer Metamorphose des Materials. Dabei entsteht eine interessante Struktur von Gegensätzlichkeiten – hoch-tief, weich-hart und matt-glänzend. Durch die innovative TG+-Technologie erfährt das Ursprungsprodukt Delta Deco so die Wandlung zum individuellen Bodenbelag. Neben der Jacquard- und Drucktechnik eröffnet diese Technologie ein neuartiges Gestaltungsfeld für besondere Formensprachen.

Arrakis
Decoration Fabric / Dekorationsstoff

Nya Nordiska Textiles GmbH,
Dannenberg, Germany / Deutschland
In-house design / Werksdesign:
Diete Hansl-Röntgen, Sybilla Hansl,
Alice Pieper
www.nya.com

The Arrakis decoration fabric is a transparent weave of extensive design. Manufactured in Scherli technique this fabric shows large circles on a surface with rhombus-like gaps. They alternate with rhombus-like areas, which are crossed by a stripe pattern. This alternating arrangement and the changing alignment of rhombuses creates a very dynamic graphic pattern to which the viewer's attention is attracted again and again. The circle elements are outlined by effective glazed yarns and Lurex. Four different colours give the design an individual look-and-feel in each case.

Der Dekorationsstoff Arrakis ist ein Transparentgewebe mit einem raumgreifenden Dessin. Gefertigt in der Scherli-Technik zeigt dieser Stoff große Kreise auf einem rautenförmig ausgesparten Fond. Diese stehen im Wechsel mit rautenähnlichen Flächen, die von einem Streifenmuster durchzogen werden. Durch diese alternierende Anordnung und wechselnde Ausrichtung der Rauten entsteht ein äußerst dynamisches, grafisches Muster, das die Aufmerksamkeit der Augen immer wieder neu gewinnen kann. Die Kreis-Elemente sind mit effektstarken Glanz- bzw. Lurexgarnen herausgearbeitet. Vier verschiedene Farbstellungen verleihen dem Design eine jeweils andere Anmutung.

Panel Track / Flächenvorhang
Decoration Fabric / Dekorationsstoff

Nya Nordiska Textiles GmbH,
Dannenberg, Germany / Deutschland
In-house design / Werksdesign:
Diete Hansl-Röntgen, Sybilla Hansl,
Alice Pieper
www.nya.com

This decoration fabric was designed for use in panel tracks. The interesting linen character offers a high degree of homely comfort. The stiffened Trevira CS weave is flame-resistant and therefore suitable for properties. It is available in three different designs. The long sides of the panels do not have to be seamed due to a thermo cut. In combination with the Nya Artline System Quattro, which is available in any RAL colour, twelve monochrome colours, a laser cut version as well as a hole pattern version offer multiple possibilities of combination.

Dieser Dekorationsstoff wurde konzipiert für den Einsatz als Flächenvorhang. Der interessante Leinencharakter verleiht ihm ein hohes Maß an Wohnlichkeit. Das versteifte, schwer entflammbare und damit gut objekttaugliche Trevira CS-Gewebe ist in drei Dessinvarianten wählbar. Da dieser Stoff in einem Thermoschnitt gefertigt wird, entfällt das Säumen der Stoffbahnen an den Längsseiten. In Verbindung mit dem in jeder RAL-Farbe erhältlichen Nya Artline System Quattro erlauben zwölf Unifarben sowie eine Laser-Cut- und eine Lochmuster-Variante dem Nutzer vielfältige Kombinationsmöglichkeiten.

Mumble Sofa

Felicerossi, Casorate Sempione,
Italy / Italien
Design: UAU (Francesco Mansueto),
Turin / Los Angeles
www.felicerossi.it
www.uaueb.it

Mumble is a highly mouldable sofa system that is well accepted in any atmosphere. Due to its modular design, it can be arranged in a central position lined up as a corner system or as an island according to the necessity of the client. Its sinuous and wrapping form allows comfort and relaxation.

Mumble ist ein hochgradig formbares Sofasystem, das sich in die unterschiedlichsten Umgebungen einfügt. Dank seiner baukastenartigen Gestaltung kann es zentral als Ecksystem oder als Insel aufgestellt werden, je nach Bedarf des Nutzers. Seine kurvige und umhüllende Form vermittelt Bequemlichkeit und Wohlbehagen.

Stuben-Hocker
Stool / Hocker

Stuben-Hocker, Brühl,
Germany / Deutschland
Design: Ralf Hennig, Brühl,
Germany / Deutschland
www.stuben-hocker.com

The Stuben-Hocker is conceived as additional seating. It is suited for putting the feet up, as deposit space or as eye-catcher. Featuring a brand logo it can be used for presentations, trade fairs and events. The covers are merely slipped over the seat. They are made of 100 per cent new wool and available in 36 different colours. They permit a quick change of decoration with impressive colour variations.

Der Stuben-Hocker ist als zusätzliche Sitzgelegenheit gedacht. Er dient dem Beinehochlegen, als Ablagemöglichkeit oder als Eye-Catcher. Mit einem Firmenlogo versehen, findet er Einsatz auf Präsentationen, Messen und Veranstaltungen. Die nur übergestülpten Hussen aus 100 Prozent Schurwolle sind in 36 verschiedenen Farben erhältlich. Sie erlauben einen schnellen und farblich eindrucksvollen Dekowechsel.

Nuna Leaf™
Infant Seat / Kindersitz

Nuna International, Amsterdam, NL
In-house design / Werksdesign
Design: Iron Mountains
www.nuna.eu

The innovative motion of this infant seat enables the baby to calm down and relax. A gentle push is enough to make the seat swing automatically. Without electricity or batteries a swinging motion is generated that is more natural than rocking. The main focus was placed on safety aspects, thus the infant seat is easily locked and disassembled for transportation. This infant seat fits well in home interiors since its design turns it into a stylish piece of furniture.

Aufgrund der neuartigen Bewegung dieses Kindersitzes kann sich das Baby beruhigen und entspannen. Ein leichter Stoß reicht aus, um den Sitz selbsttätig schwingen zu lassen. Ohne Strom und Batterien entsteht eine Schwingbewegung, die natürlicher als ein Schaukeln ist. Sicherheitsaspekte betonend kann der Kindersitz leicht arretiert und für den Transport demontiert werden. Da seine Gestaltung ihn als ein attraktives Möbelstück interpretiert, harmoniert dieser Kindersitz gut mit der Inneneinrichtung.

Flex
Chair / Stuhl

Guangzhou Songdream Furniture Co., Ltd.,
Guangzhou, China
In-house design / Werksdesign: Yi Han
www.songdream.com.cn

This chair was inspired by the random placement of a curve ruler. An elegant curvature runs through the design of the chair. The twin-colour design places additional emphasis on the perfect combination of line and surface. The seat pad of the Flex chair is formed without any support force, its internal structure without any metal parts. The framework is completely made of wood. The internal structure of Flex allows remodelling it into another chair by minor changes.

Dieser Stuhl ist inspiriert von der zufällig gezogenen Linie eines Kurvenlineals. Ein eleganter Bogen zieht sich durch den ganzen Stuhl. Das zweifarbige Design betont die perfekte Verbindung von Linie und Oberfläche. Die Sitzfläche des Stuhls Flex kommt ohne Stützelemente aus, seine innere Struktur ohne Metall, denn der Rahmen ist komplett aus Holz gefertigt. Dank der inneren Rahmenkonstruktion lässt sich Flex mit wenigen Änderungen in einen anderen Stuhl verwandeln.

Abile
Folding Table / Klapptisch

Grüne Erde GmbH, Scharnstein,
Austria / Österreich
In-house design / Werksdesign:
Stefan Radner
www.grueneerde.com

The rounded edges of this delicate and long-lasting wooden table elegantly unite with the trestle made of beech scantlings. In the "high" position it serves as dining table, writing desk or conference table. When it is folded down to a height of 33 cm it can be used as a low coffee or "Japanese" table

Die abgerundeten Kanten dieses zartgliedrigen und langlebigen Holztisches verbinden sich elegant mit dem Fußgestell aus Buchenkanthölzern. In „Hoch"-Stellung dient er als Ess-, Schreib- und Besprechungstisch. Auf 33 cm Höhe geklappt als niedriger Sofa- oder „Japan"-Tisch.

Rado Swing
Dining Chair / Essstuhl

Accente Einrichtungsgesellschaft mbH,
Viersen, Germany / Deutschland
Design: Design Ballendat
(Martin Ballendat), Simbach am Inn,
Germany / Deutschland
www.accente.com
www.ballendat.de

This dining chair focuses on the essentials: minimalist elegance pleases the eye while continuous contours convey lightness. A high-quality chromed metal frame encloses an ergonomically curved seat and backrest.

Dieser Essstuhl besinnt sich auf das Wesentliche: Formal reduzierte Anmut verwöhnt das Auge und eine durchgehende Linienführung vermittelt Leichtigkeit. Die Seiten werden von einem hochwertigen verchromten Metallrahmen beschlossen, dazwischen wölbt sich die ergonomische Sitz- und Rückenschale.

WK 565 ponte Sofa

WK Wohnen GmbH & Co.
Möbel Marketing KG,
Dreieich, Germany / Deutschland
Design: Michael Plewka,
Berlin, Germany / Deutschland
Production / Produktion:
Molinari srl, Tione di Trento, Italy / Italien
www.wkwohnen.de

The design of this sofa unites contour and comfort. It consists of a slim cushion carcass that is floatingly supported by a filigree square frame. This emphasises the contrast to heavy, close-to-the-ground upholstery. The free suspension impressively separates the upholstery volume and the framework allowing fascinating perspectives. The large span of the framework and its sophisticated construction surprises: a design language that follows contemporary architecture and technology.

Kontur mit Komfort verbindet die Gestaltung dieses Sofas. Es besteht aus einem schlanken Polsterkörper, der schwebend von einem filigranen Vierkant-Gestell getragen wird. Dies stellt einen Kontrast zu den bodennahen, schweren Polstermöbeln dar. Die freie Aufhängung führt eindrucksvoll zur Trennung von Polstervolumen und Gestell und lässt spannende Perspektiven zu. Die große Spannweite des Gestells verblüfft und ist konstruktiv durchdacht ausgeführt. Eine Formensprache, die sich an der zeitgenössischen Architektur und Technik orientiert.

Aura
Bed / Bett

Accente Einrichtungsgesellschaft mbH,
Viersen, Germany / Deutschland
Design: Design Ballendat
(Martin Ballendat), Simbach am Inn,
Germany / Deutschland
www.accente.com
www.ballendat.de

The harmony of contrasts determines the shape of this bed. Gently and invitingly the lying surface flows over a compact flat base that serves as deposit space at the sides. Setting a charming accent the side inlays reiterate the colour of the base and emphasise the evenly curved linear design.

Die Harmonie der Gegensätze bestimmt die Form dieses Bettes. Leicht fließt die einladende Liegefläche über einen kompakt und flach gestalteten Korpus, der an den Seiten als Abstellfläche dient. Als schöner Akzent wiederholen die Seitenblenden die Farbwahl des Korpus und betonen die gleichmäßig geschwungene Linienführung.

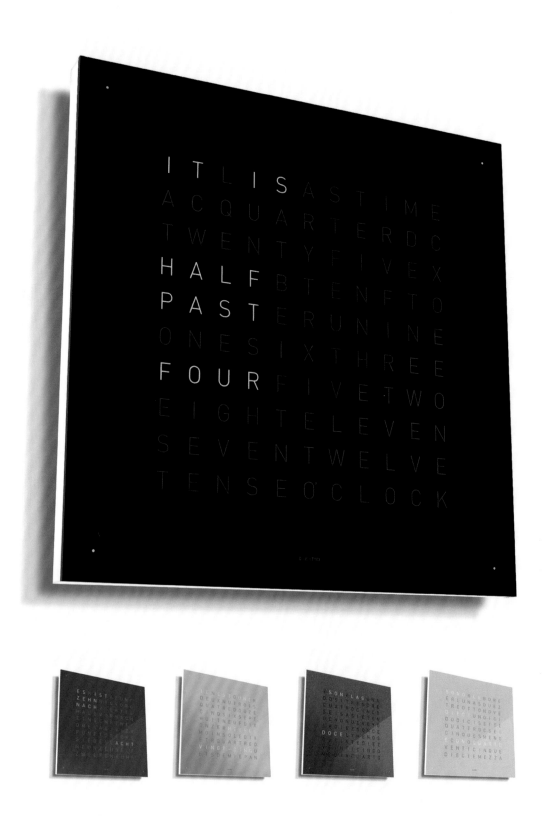

Qlocktwo
Wall and Table Clock/
Wand- und Tischuhr

Biegert & Funk, Schwäbisch Gmünd,
Germany/Deutschland
In-house design/Werksdesign:
Marco Biegert, Andreas Funk
www.biegertfunk.com

This clock forms a perfect square and seems
to hover freely at the wall. A matrix with
symmetrically arranged characters constitutes
another square. Some of these characters shine
in pure white to form words that describe time.
The front surface is made of polished acrylic
glass; the lacquered wooden body supports it by
means of eight magnets. When it is activated,
the timer sets itself exact to the second and
adjusts the brightness of the characters to
ambient light.

Ein perfektes Quadrat scheint frei an der Wand
zu schweben. Eine Matrix mit symmetrisch
angeordneten Schriftzeichen bildet im Inneren
ein weiteres Quadrat. Einige dieser Zeichen
leuchten in reinem Weiß und formen so
Worte, welche die Zeit beschreiben. Die
Frontfläche besteht aus poliertem synthe-
tischem Glas und wird mit acht Magneten
von einem Korpus aus lackiertem Holz
getragen. Nach dem Einschalten stellt sich
der Zeitmesser sekundengenau ein und
passt die Helligkeit der Schriftzeichen dem
Umgebungslicht an.

wodtke daily.nrg
Pellet Stove / Pellet-Primärofen

Wodtke GmbH, Tübingen,
Germany / Deutschland
In-house design / Werksdesign
www.wodtke.com

Carbon dioxide-neutral heating with wood pellets
as fuel and pioneering microprocessor-controlled
technology provide for high effectiveness and
energy efficiency. An automatic feed screw
ensures that there are always enough pellets in
the burner pot. A clear-cut design combining
steel with black decorative glass and the omission
of a visible handle underscore the style of this
typical wodtke line. With a modulating range of
2–6 kW for thermal output and an innovative
room-air-independent air supply system this
stove is especially designed for use in homes
with controlled room ventilation.

Kohlendioxidneutrales Heizen mit dem Brennstoff Holzpellets und zukunftsweisende, über
einen Mikroprozessor gesteuerte Technologie
ermöglichen einen hohen Wirkungsgrad und
Energieeffizienz. Eine Förderschnecke sorgt
automatisch dafür, dass immer ausreichend
Pellets im Brennertopf sind. Eine klare Formgebung, Stahl mit schwarzen Dekorgläsern,
und der Verzicht auf eine sichtbare Griff-
Variante unterstreichen die typische wodtke-
Linie. Die Wärmeleistung, modulierend
zwischen 2–6 kW, und die innovative raum-
luftunabhängige Luftzuführung sind speziell
auch für den Einsatz in Gebäuden mit
kontrollierter Wohnraumlüftung abgestimmt.

Park
Wallpaper / Tapete

Rasch Tapetenfabrik,
Bramsche, Germany / Deutschland
Design: Iris Maschek Wallpapers
(Iris Maschek),
Cologne, Germany / Köln, Deutschland
www.rasch.de
www.irismaschek.com

This wallpaper brings up new formal and
aesthetic ways of expression made possible by
digital printing techniques. The design wants
to overcome the traditional serial character of
wallpapers aiming at a modern reinterpretation
of the ornament and the development of
complex murals.

Diese Tapete zeigt neue formale und ästhetische Ausdrucksmöglichkeiten, die durch
digitale Druckverfahren entstehen. Im Fokus
der Gestaltung liegt die Überwindung des
traditionell seriellen Charakters der Tapete
hin zu einer modernen Re-Interpretation des
Ornaments und der Entwicklung komplexer
Wandbilder.

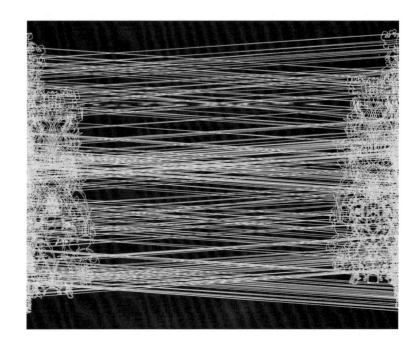

Prof. Renke He

Sebastian Conran

Satyendra Pakhalé

Households and kitchens
Solid design with clever details

Haushalt und Küche
Durchdachtes Design mit raffinierten Details

Carefully selected and precision-finished materials reflect the products' high quality.

The "Households and kitchens" sector has always been strongly determined by cultural aspects and needs. In design, this calls for a high degree of sensibility for the differences and nuances of those phenomena. As the products in this sector have already matured, there is little room for groundbreaking innovations or experimental approaches. Yet, innovation is realised through well-thought-out features, such as integrated LED lighting systems or simplified, user-friendly operation. Carefully selected and precision-finished materials reflect the products' high quality. Overall, product design in the "Households and kitchens" sector emphasises maximum efficiency in the use of space and energy as well as high standards with regard to hygiene and comfort.

Sorgsam ausgesuchte und präzise verarbeitete Materialien hinterlassen einen hohen Qualitätseindruck.

Gerade im Bereich „Haushalt und Küche" spielen kulturelle Aspekte und Bedürfnisse seit jeher eine wichtige Rolle, sodass für das Design eine hohe Sensibilität für die jeweiligen Unterschiede von großer Bedeutung ist. Da die Produkte hier schon sehr ausgereift sind, lassen sich keine revolutionären Innovationen oder auffallend experimentellen Ansätze feststellen. Vielmehr sind durchdachte Details ausschlaggebend, so zum Beispiel integrierte LED-Lichtsysteme oder eine vereinfachte, nutzerfreundliche Bedienungsführung. Sorgsam ausgesuchte und präzise verarbeitete Materialien hinterlassen einen hohen Qualitätseindruck. Insgesamt wird bei der Gestaltung der Produkte im Bereich „Haushalt und Küche" auf eine möglichst effiziente Nutzung von Platz und Energie Wert gelegt, die gleichzeitig höchsten Standards in Bezug auf Hygiene und Komfort entspricht.

KGF39S50, KGF39S20, KGF39S71
Fridge-Freezer /
Kühl-Gefrier-Kombination

Robert Bosch Hausgeräte GmbH,
Munich, Germany / München,
Deutschland
In-house design / Werksdesign:
Robert Sachon, Ralph Staud,
Thomas Tischer
www.bosch-home.com

The use of glass front panels for cooling appliances is taken to the second generation with the new ColorGlass Edition. The design concept, which boasts a completely frameless glass front in white, black and metal behind glass, is to convey the look of a piece of furniture rather than a mere appliance. The elegant look of this model is created using an innovative sandwich construction, in which a stainless steel layer is laminated behind clear glass in a special procedure. The altered depth perception that results gives the front its special appeal, which goes beyond the more functional appearance of previous models. In keeping with the minimalist style, the handles are laterally integrated into metal profiles. The interior of this floor-mounted appliance offers state-of-the-art technology, glare-free LED lighting and mirror-finished applications.

Der Einsatz des Materials Glas bei Kühlgerätfronten wird mit der neuen ColorGlass Edition in die zweite Generation geführt. Das Gestaltungskonzept verfolgt dabei die Zielsetzung, Kühl- und Gefrierschränke visuell zu wohnlichen Küchenmöbeln aufzuwerten und nutzt vor allem die Wirkung einer komplett rahmenlosen Glasfront in Weiß, Schwarz und Metall hinter Glas. Die hochwertige Anmutung dieses Modells wird durch eine innovative Sandwichkonstruktion erzielt, mittels derer eine Edelstahlschicht in einem speziellen Verfahren hinter das transparente Glas laminiert wird. Die dadurch changierende Tiefenwirkung gibt der Gerätefont ihr attraktives Erscheinungsbild, welches über das funktionale Gesamtbild früherer Geräte hinausgeht. In allen drei Ausführungen runden seitlich in Echtmetallprofile integrierte Griffe die puristische Formgebung stringent ab. Im Inneren bietet das Standgerät eine zeitgemäße Technologie, eine blendfreie LED-Beleuchtung sowie hochglanzgebürstete Applikationen.

KSR38S70, GSN32S70
TwinCenter
Fridge/Freezer/
Kühlgerät/Gefriergerät

Robert Bosch Hausgeräte GmbH,
Munich, Germany / München,
Deutschland
In-house design / Werksdesign:
Robert Sachon, Ralph Staud,
Thomas Tischer
www.bosch-home.com

The spacious TwinCenter has a sleek,
compact look thanks to its frameless
glass front backed by a sheet of stainless
steel. The unconventional layering of
these two different shiny materials has
a strong aesthetic impact. A model of
the ColorGlass range, the TwinCenter is
equipped with distinctive metal handles that
rest comfortably in the hand. The austere,
straight form is reflective of the high value
of the product. With French doors, the extra-
wide appliance provides enough space for
frozen foods on one side and refrigerated
foods on the other. Thanks to its up-to-date
technology, the fridge/freezer is exceptionally
energy-efficient.

Seine visuelle Prägnanz verdankt das
großzügige TwinCenter einer rahmenlosen Glasfront, die mit einem dahinter
liegenden Layer aus Edelstahl visuell in
Szene gesetzt wird. Die unkonventionelle
Schichtung der beiden unterschiedlich
glänzenden Materialien entfaltet dabei
eine besonders ästhetische Tiefenwirkung.
Das TwinCenter der ColorGlass-Reihe
wurde zudem mit markanten Metall-
Griffleisten, die gut in der Hand liegen,
ausgestattet. Darüber hinaus visualisiert
eine stringent geradlinige Formensprache
die Wertigkeit des Produkts. Als French-
Door-Konzept bietet die Extrabreite des
Geräts genügend Volumen, um auf einer
Seite das Kühlgut und auf der anderen das
Gefriergut zu lagern. Dank seiner aktuellen Technologie zeichnet sich das Gerät
durch sehr niedrige Verbrauchswerte aus.

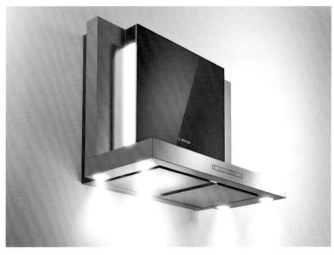

DWB099660, DWB099620,
DWB099650
Wall—Mounted Chimney Hood Range/
Wandessen—Reihe

Robert Bosch Hausgeräte GmbH,
Munich, Germany/München,
Deutschland
In-house design/Werksdesign:
Robert Sachon, Christoph Ortmann,
Alexander Marsch
www.bosch-home.com

The characteristic L-shape of the wall-mounted chimney hood range is divided into remarkable design units and represents a break with the shape of conventional extractor hoods. Supplemented by a striking illumination concept the generous individual surfaces of the appliance body attract attention. Apart from two-dimensionally designed chimney elements, the covered filter surfaces at the lower side contribute to its independent appearance. A flush-integrated MetalTouch operating panel allows comfortable control of the powerful chimney hood. In addition to the function light of four halogen lamps, aligned with the cooking zone, there is a flexibly switchable ambient light source at the sides of the chimney, which laterally shines into the room. Different, attachable décor panels matching the appliance are available to integrate the chimney individually into a timely homelike kitchen environment. They make it possible to pick up the material ambience of the surrounding furniture fronts and consistently continue its impression.

Die charakteristische L-Form dieser Wandessen-Reihe bricht mit den konventionellen Dunstabzugsbauformen und gliedert sich in markante Gestaltungseinheiten. Ergänzt durch ein auffälliges Beleuchtungskonzept, fallen die großzügigen Einzelflächen des Gerätekorpus auf. Zum eigenständigen Erscheinungsbild tragen neben den flächig konstruierten Kaminelementen auch die verdeckten Filterflächen auf der Unterseite bei. Eine flächenbündig integrierte MetalTouch-Bedienleiste erlaubt die komfortable Steuerung der leistungsstarken Wandesse. Zusätzlich zum Funktionslicht der vier auf die Kochzone gerichteten Halogenlampen befindet sich an den Seiten des Kamins ein flexibel zuschaltbares Ambient-Light, das seitlich in den Raum leuchtet. Um den Kamin individuell in ein zeitgemäß wohnliches Küchenumfeld zu integrieren, sind passend zum Gerät unterschiedliche, aufsetzbare Dekorscheiben erhältlich. Diese ermöglichen es, das Materialambiente der umgebenden Möbelfronten aufzugreifen und konsequent fortzuführen.

HBA78B9B0, HBC36D7B3,
HBC86K7B3, HSC140B1
Built-In Appliance Series/
Einbaugeräte-Serie

Robert Bosch Hausgeräte GmbH,
Munich, Germany/München,
Deutschland
In-house design/Werksdesign:
Robert Sachon, Christoph Ortmann,
Ulrich Goss
Design: Busalt-Industriedesign
(Gerhard Busalt),
Traunreut, Germany/Deutschland
www.bosch-home.com

The design of this series of built-in
appliances features a partially matted
surface specially developed by Schott, giving
the glass a novel look, depth and feel. The
devices feel silky soft, are easy to clean
and virtually impervious to fingerprints. In
cooperation with Alno, an integrated kitchen
concept was developed where the appliance
front panels are harmoniously matched to
the frameless glass fronts of the kitchen
furniture, thus allowing for the trend of
merging kitchen and living environments.

Die Einbaugerätereihe weist als beson-
deres Designmerkmal eine partiell mattierte Oberfläche auf, die speziell von der
Fa. Schott entwickelt wurde und die dem
Glas eine neuartige Anmutung, Tiefenwirkung und haptische Qualität verleiht. Die
Geräte fühlen sich samtig weich an, sind
leicht zu reinigen, und Fingerabdrücke
verschwinden darauf fast wie von selbst.
In Zusammenarbeit mit der Fa. Alno entstand ein ganzheitliches Möbelkonzept,
bei dem die Gerätefronten auf die rahmenlosen Glasfronten der Küchenmöbel
abgestimmt sind und somit dem Trend der
Verschmelzung von Küchen- und Wohnumfeld Rechnung tragen.

SKS50E18EU
Free-Standing Compact Dishwasher /
Stand-Kompaktspüler

Robert Bosch Hausgeräte GmbH,
Munich, Germany / München,
Deutschland
In-house design / Werksdesign:
Robert Sachon, Thomas Ott
www.bosch-home.com

As a free-standing compact appliance this
dishwasher displays an independent style and
was designed as a solution that meets the
requirements of single households, offices
and small-scale kitchens. The curved shape
of the wide handle element is contrasting
the straight-lined structure of the appliance.
Due to modern technology it is not necessary
to renounce usability or capacity. Up to
six programmes are intuitively operated
via a rotary selector with integrated start
button. Special functions, which optimise the
programme performance, can be addressed
if required. A clearly laid out LED display
informs on the respective programme routine
and fill level. In addition to a silver version,
the appliance is available in many more
colours.

Als Stand-Kompaktgerät weist dieser
Geschirrspüler eine eigenständige Formensprache auf. Konzipiert wurde er
als bedarfsgerechte Produktlösung für
Singlehaushalte, Büros oder Kleinkü-
chen. Das breite Griffelement steht in
seiner geschwungenen Gestaltung im
Kontrast zur geradlinigen Gerätestruktur. Eine zeitgemäße Technologie stellt
sicher, dass weder auf Bedienkomfort
noch auf Fassungsvermögen verzichtet werden muss. Die Bedienung der bis
zu sechs Programme erfolgt über einen
Drehwähler mit integrierter Starttaste und
erschließt sich intuitiv. Bei Bedarf können
Sonderfunktionen abgefragt werden, die
die Programmleistungen optimieren. Ein
übersichtliches LED-Display informiert
über den jeweiligen Programmverlauf und
Füllstand. Neben der silbernen Ausführung ist das Gerät noch in vielen weiteren
Farben erhältlich.

SBV69T20EU
Fully Integrated Dishwasher/ Vollintegrierter Geschirrspüler

Robert Bosch Hausgeräte GmbH, Munich, Germany / München, Deutschland
In-house design / Werksdesign: Thomas Ott
www.bosch-home.com

The innovative, zeolite-based technology that accelerates the drying process by means of an absorbent mineral makes this dishwasher very energy-efficient. The clear arrangement of its piezo touch controls from left to right allows for easy, intuitive operation. Energy consumption and cleaning performance are enhanced with novel features such as a heat exchanger, aqua sensor and automatic detergent aware. A specially designed catch tray in the upper basket ensures the targeted dissolution of the detergent tabs. A flexible basket system with three load levels offers a high storage capacity in the extra-large interior. Solid wire baskets with stainless steel handle elements enhance the value of the appliance.

Die innovative Zeolith-Technologie, bei der ein absorbierender Mineralstoff den Trocknungsprozess unterstützt, lässt diese Geschirrspülmaschine zu einer sehr energieeffizienten Produktlösung werden. Die klare Anordnung der Piezo-Touch-Bedienelemente in Leserichtung gewährt eine intuitiv leichte Bedienung. Um den Verbrauch und das Reinigungsergebnis entscheidend zu verbessern, verfügt das Gerät über zeitgemäße Ausstattungsdetails wie Wärmetauscher, Aquasensor und Reinigerautomatik. Eine speziell gestaltete Auffangschale im Oberkorb unterstützt die gezielte Auflösung von Reinigertabs, zudem bietet ein flexibles Korbsystem mit drei Beladungsebenen viel Stauraum im XL-Innenraum. Stabile Drahtkörbe mit Edelstahl-Griffelementen unterstreichen die Wertigkeit des Gerätes.

SBI69T25EU
Integrated Dishwasher/ Integrierter Geschirrspüler

Robert Bosch Hausgeräte GmbH, Munich, Germany / München, Deutschland
In-house design / Werksdesign: Thomas Ott, Robert Sachon
www.bosch-home.com

The design of this built-in dishwasher focuses on the essential. Consequently, the clear text display merges with the grip opening to form a unit thus characterising the distinctive front of the appliance. It is ergonomically operated from above by means of touch sensors that are intuitively arranged from left to right. The energy consumption of 0.86 kWh is supposed to set new standards. An intelligent sensor technology optimises water consumption and the cleaning performance. The interior impresses with various adjustment possibilities of the basket system and the use of high-quality materials.

Die Gestaltung dieses einbaubaren Geschirrspülers konzentriert sich auf das Wesentliche. Die Klartextanzeige verbindet sich deshalb mit der Grifföffnung zu einer Einheit und prägt damit die markante Gerätefront. Die Bedienung erfolgt ergonomisch günstig von oben mittels intuitiv in Leserichtung angeordneten Touch-Sensoren. Mit einem Energieverbrauch von 0,86 kWh sollen neue Maßstäbe gesetzt werden, wobei eine intelligente Sensortechnik den Wasserverbrauch und das Reinigungsergebnis optimiert. Der Innenraum glänzt durch zahlreiche Verstellmöglichkeiten des Korbsystems und die Verwendung hochwertiger Materialien.

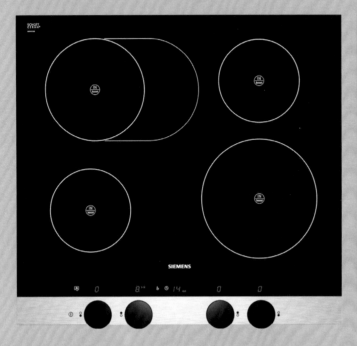
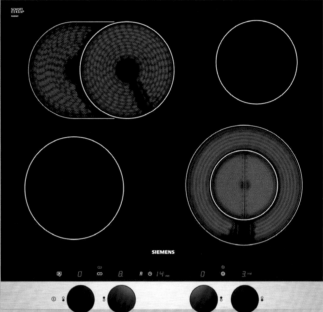

**Siemens ET 685 DN 11D,
ET 885 DC 11D, EH 685 DB 11E,
EH 885 DB 11E, EH 885 DL 11E
Hob Product Line/Kochstellen-
Produktlinie**

Siemens-Electrogeräte GmbH, Munich,
Germany/München, Deutschland
In-house design/Werksdesign:
Andreas Hackbarth, Gerd E. Wilsdorf
Design: Digitalform, Munich,
Germany/München, Deutschland
www.siemens-hausgeraete.de

This flush-integrated built-in ceramic hob
meets high aesthetic standards. The interplay
of minimalist design elements is visually
enhanced by the contrasting materials. The
manufacturer-specific front edge closes
off with a robust metal panel that holds
four cylindrical disks. Each disc controls a
cooking zone and can be turned from the
front as well as from the top. Thereby precise
magnetic detents that match the setting
on the display generate positive tactile
feedback. This innovative discControl hob
offers both the user-friendliness of rotary
knobs and the advantage of easy-to-clean
touch controls. The discs can be completely
removed from the control unit to facilitate
thorough cleaning of the hob. The appliance
is available in five different models, each of
which features a different arrangement of
the cooking zones.

Diese flächenbündig einbaubare Glaskera-
mik-Kochstelle zeigt eine ästhetisch hochwertige Formensprache, wobei das Zusammenspiel puristischer Gestaltungselemente
durch den Kontrast der Materialien visuell
unterstützt wird. Die herstellertypische
Frontfacette schließt an der Vorderkante mit
einem massiven Metallprofil ab, in welches
vier zylindrische Scheiben eingelassen
sind. Jede dieser Disc-Scheiben steuert eine
Kochzone direkt an, wobei sie von vorn
wie auch von oben auf der Zylinderfläche
bedienbar sind. Eine präzise, magnetische
Rastung, die synchron zur Anzeige im Display erfolgt, gibt dabei ein positives taktiles
Feedback. Mit dieser Steuerungseinheit bietet die innovative discControl-Kochstelle die
Bedienfreundlichkeit eines Drehknopfes und
die Reinigungsfreundlichkeit einer Touch-
Kochstelle. Eine gründliche Reinigung wird
dadurch erleichtert, dass die Disc-Scheiben
komplett aus dem Bedienfeld herausgenom-
men werden können. Das Gerät ist in fünf
unterschiedlichen Ausführungen erhältlich,
die eine Auswahl der individuell passenden
Kochfeldanordnung erlauben.

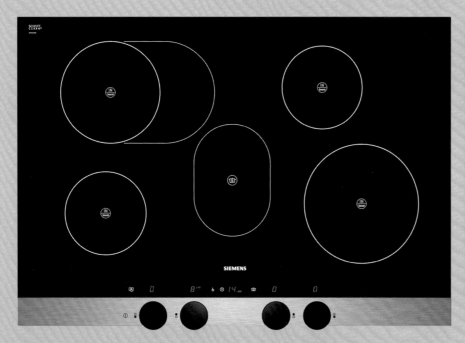

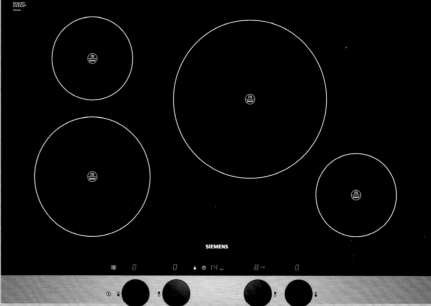

**Siemens HG 19551 OME
Range Cooker**

Siemens-Electrogeräte GmbH, Munich,
Germany / München, Deutschland
In-house design / Werksdesign:
Heiko Thielen
www.siemens-hausgeraete.de

With a functional design, this 90-cm wide
range cooker qualifies as a professional
cooking appliance for the home. The
minimalist form is in keeping with the
Siemens portal concept, ensuring continuity
when combined with other appliances. Five
gas burners provide up to 3,400 watts of
heat, and the large 103-litre capacity oven
features innovative gas top heat as well as a
rotary spit. The mechanical timer focuses on
the essentials.

Mit einer funktionalen Gestaltung zeigt
sich dieser 90 cm breite Range Cooker
als professionelles Kochgerät für den
Heimbereich. Die minimalistische Form
nimmt das Siemens Portal-Design auf
und gewährleistet so in der Kombination
mit anderen Geräten ein einheitliches
Erscheinungsbild. Fünf Gasbrenner liefern
eine Leistung von bis zu 3.400 Watt. Der
103 Liter große Ofen bietet die innovative
Gas-Oberhitze und einen zuschaltbaren
Drehspieß. Der mechanische Timer ist auf
das Wesentliche reduziert.

**Siemens SK 76 M 530 EU
Built-In Dishwasher /
Einbau-Geschirrspüler**

Siemens-Electrogeräte GmbH, Munich,
Germany / München, Deutschland
In-house design / Werksdesign:
Wolfgang Kaczmarek
www.siemens-hausgeraete.de

The built-in dishwasher with elegant
stainless steel design fits into a 45 cm high
mounting recess in tall cupboards or as
an option directly under the worktop. The
brushed stainless steel front is harmoniously
complemented by a stylish, round handle
bar. Centred control panels in the front
display provide for the control of various
dishwashing programmes such as the
ecoProgramm with a water consumption of
only seven litres. The IntensiveZone in the
lower basket is designed for extremely dirty
dishes.

Der Einbau-Geschirrspüler in seiner eleganten Edelstahl-Ausführung eignet sich
für eine 45 cm hohe Einbaunische inmit-
ten von Hochschränken oder wahlweise
direkt unter der Arbeitsplatte. Die gebürstete Edelstahlfront wird von einer form-
schönen, runden Griffleiste harmonisch
ergänzt. Im Frontdisplay ermöglichen
mittenbetont angeordnete Bedientasten
verschiedene Spülprogramme anzusteuern
wie beispielsweise das ecoProgramm mit
nur sieben Litern Wasserverbrauch. Für
stark verschmutztes Geschirr ist die IntensiveZone im Unterkorb vorgesehen.

Siemens EL 75261 MX
Gas and Induction Hob/
Gas- und Induktionskochstelle

Siemens-Electrogeräte GmbH, Munich,
Germany/München, Deutschland
In-house design/Werksdesign:
Heiko Thielen
www.siemens-hausgeraete.de

The innovative combination of a gas burner
with an energy-efficient induction plate
gives this hob its enhanced value. The two
elements are proportionately arranged on
easy-to-clean Ceran glass. Simple knobs
allow for intuitive use and underscore the
functional orientation of the design. The
front edges of the hob are bevelled, while the
side edges feature delicate metal profiles.

Die innovative Kombination eines Gas-
brenners mit einer energieeffizienten
Induktionsplatte definiert den gehobenen
Gebrauchswert dieser Kochstelle. In ausgewogenen Proportionen wurden die
einzelnen Elemente auf dem leicht zu rei-
nigenden Ceranglas angeordnet. Die intuitive Bedienung erfolgt mittels schlichter
Drehknöpfe und betont das funktional
ausgerichtete Erscheinungsbild. An der
vorderen Seite wurden die Kanten dezent
abgeschrägt, während an den Seiten filigrane Metallprofile einen visuellen Reiz
setzen.

Siemens ER 74233 MX
Gas Hob/Gaskochstelle

Siemens-Electrogeräte GmbH, Munich,
Germany/München, Deutschland
In-house design/Werksdesign:
Heiko Thielen
www.siemens-hausgeraete.de

A classy contrast between black glass
and polished metal informs the overall
appearance of this gas hob designed for
the Chinese market. Minimalist contours
accentuate the two square burners.
Enamelled grates made of 4-mm thick steel
are flush with stainless steel plates that are
harmoniously integrated into the hob. Two
convenient cylinder switches in stainless
steel look continue the contrast to the
elegant base surface. The black tempered-
glass is easy to clean.

Ein edel anmutender Kontrast zwischen
schwarzem Glas und poliertem Metall
prägt das Gesamtbild dieser Gaskochstelle
für den chinesischen Markt. Die minimalistische Linienführung betont die beiden
quadratisch ausgerichteten Kochstellen.
Emaillierte Topfträger aus 4 mm dickem
Stahl fügen sich flächenbündig in harmonisch eingelassene Edelstahlschilder
ein. Zwei komfortable Zylinderschalter
im Edelstahl-Look führen den Kontrast
zur eleganten Grundfläche fort, wobei das
schwarze, gehärtete Glas leicht zu reinigen ist.

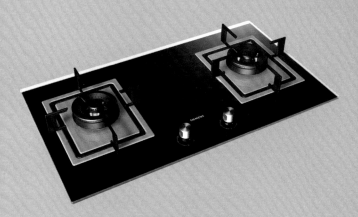

Siemens ER 75 K 253 MX
Gas Hob/Gaskochstelle

Siemens-Electrogeräte GmbH, Munich,
Germany/München, Deutschland
In-house design/Werksdesign:
Heiko Thielen
www.siemens-hausgeraete.de

This high-grade stainless steel gas hob
was designed for the Chinese market and
allows for quick heat-up with two 4-kW gas
burners. The burners ignite immediately upon
turning the knob, thanks to auto-ignition
technology, dispensing with the need to
hold down the knobs to start the flame. The
control panel, set apart on dark glass, has
an integrated timer that can be used to turn
the burners off at precise times. The hob also
features the Interlink function by which a
compatible cooker hood can be automatically
operated.

Diese hochwertige Edelstahl-Gaskochstelle
wurde für den chinesischen Markt konzipiert und erlaubt mit zwei 4 kW starken
Gasbrennern eine möglichst schnelle
Erhitzung. Mithilfe der Auto-Ignition-
Funktion entfällt das lange Drücken der
Schalter, die Brenner zünden automatisch.
Im durch dunkles Glas abgesetzten Steuerungsbereich wurde ein Timer integriert,
der ein minutengenaues Ausschalten der
Kochstellen ermöglicht. Zudem kann
über die Interlink-Funktion gleichzeitig
eine gerätekompatible Dunstabzugshaube
gesteuert werden.

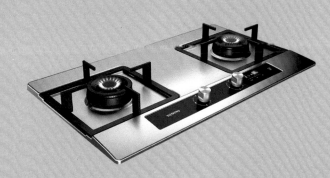

Siemens HB 86 P 582,
HB 36 D 582, HW 290582
Compact Appliances Product Line/
Kompaktgeräte-Produktlinie

Siemens-Electrogeräte GmbH, Munich,
Germany/München, Deutschland
In-house design/Werksdesign:
Frank Rieser, Gerd E. Wilsdorf
www.siemens-hausgeraete.de

The studioLine product line adapts the
design principles to the dimensions of
contemporary compact appliances. The
elegant combination of black, matt shiny
glass surfaces with select metal applications
gives these appliances an appealing, classy
touch. Stringently designed control elements,
accentuated by light blue keys on the left
and right as well as a knob in the centre,
allow for an intuitive operation of the many
functions. The front of the appliance blends
in well with the overall appearance thanks
to elaborately designed material transitions.
Special technical features and a revised
control concept meet the brand's innovative
standard of successfully interpreting the
interplay between high-quality materials,
technical innovation, and clear design.

Bei der studioLine-Produktlinie orien-
tierten sich die Gestaltungsprinzipien an
den Maßen zeitgemäßer Kompaktgeräte.
Die elegant anmutende Kombination
schwarzer, matt glänzender Glasflächen
mit sparsam eingesetzten Metallapplikationen wirkt gleichermaßen ansprechend
wie hochwertig. Stringent gestaltete
Bedienelemente erlauben eine intuitive
Handhabung der vielfältigen Funktionen,
auffallend heben sich dabei hellblau
abgesetzte Tasten links und rechts außen
sowie ein mittig integrierter Drehschalter
hervor. Prägend für das Erscheinungsbild
der Gerätefront sind zudem gut auf die
gesamte Formensprache abgestimmte, aufwendig gestaltete Materialübergänge. Die
technische Sonderausstattung sowie das
überarbeitete Bedienkonzept unterstützen
den innovativen Anspruch der Marke,
die sich einer Interpretation des Zusam-
menspiels von hochwertigen Materialien,
technischer Innovation und gestalterischer
Klarheit verpflichtet fühlt.

Siemens HB 78 A 4580,
HB 36 A 4580
Built-In Cooker / Einbauherd

Siemens-Electrogeräte GmbH, Munich,
Germany / München, Deutschland
In-house design / Werksdesign:
Frank Rieser, Gerd E. Wilsdorf
www.siemens-hausgeraete.de

As innovative built-in cookers, these universal ovens of the studioLine product line offers up to 13 different heating modes. Next to conventional programmes like top and bottom heat, these cookers can also be used for defrosting food, keeping it warm, or gently cooking it. The "hydroBacken" (hydro baking) mode was conceived as a special programme for yeast dough products, using the rising moisture in the oven. The design focuses on distinctive details, underlining the sophisticated combination of black, shiny glass surfaces and sparsely used metal applications. Control elements with an appealing design allow for intuitive simple handling of the wide range of functions. The elegant appearance of the front is defined by precise material transitions.

Als innovative Einbauherde bieten diese Universalbacköfen der studioLine-Produktlinie bis zu 13 unterschiedliche Heizarten. Neben konventionellen Programmen wie Ober- und Unterhitze lassen sich in diesen Herden auch Speisen auftauen, warmhalten oder sanft garen. Als spezielles Programm für Hefeteigwaren wurde das „hydroBacken" konzipiert, bei dem die aufsteigende Feuchtigkeit im Backraum genutzt wird. Die Gestaltung mit markanten Details unterstreicht die edle Kombination von schwarzen, glänzenden Glasflächen und sparsam eingesetzten Metallapplikationen. Ansprechend gestaltete Bedienelemente erlauben eine intuitiv einfache Handhabung der vielfältigen Funktionen. Das elegante Erscheinungsbild der Gerätefront wird durch präzise abgestimmte Materialübergänge definiert.

Siemens KG 39 FS 50
Fridge-Freezer/
Kühl-Gefrier-Kombination

Siemens-Electrogeräte GmbH, Munich,
Germany/München, Deutschland
In-house design/Werksdesign:
Max Eicher, Christoph Becke
www.siemens-hausgeraete.de

A black glass door panel contributes to the distinctive overall appearance of this energy-efficient fridge-freezer. Fully integrated lateral aluminium handles underscore the minimalist design of the appliance. This model stands out for its spacious zero-degree zone that offers excellent storage conditions for fish, meat and vegetables. Three fully extendable drawers provide exceptional accessibility. The glass and metal combination of the exterior is continued in the interior as well.

Eine Glas-Türfront in Schwarz prägt das markante Gesamtbild dieser energiesparenden Kühl-Gefrier-Kombination. Vollintegrierte seitliche Aluminium-Griffleisten unterstreichen die puristische Formensprache des Gerätes, das sich durch eine großzügige Nullgradzone auszeichnet, die sehr gute Lagerbedingungen für Fisch, Fleisch und Gemüse bietet. Durch drei Schubladen auf Vollauszügen ist das Kühlgut komfortabel zu erreichen. Mittels einer Kombination von Glas und Metall wird die Formensprache auch im Innenraum konsequent fortgeführt.

Siemens KG 36 NS 50/-51,
KG 36 NS 20/-21, KG 36 NS 90
Fridge-Freezer/
Kühl-Gefrier-Kombination

Siemens-Electrogeräte GmbH, Munich,
Germany/München, Deutschland
In-house design/Werksdesign:
Max Eicher, Christoph Becke
www.siemens-hausgeraete.de

Shiny glass door panels in black, white or titanium grey emphasise the elegant design of this high-grade fridge-freezer. Complementing the frameless glass front panels, fully integrated lateral aluminium handles underscore the minimalist style of these models. The interior features three different temperature zones, each of which is easily accessible by means of spacious drawers. Glare-free LED lighting on the side ensures perfect visibility. The select mix of glass and metal on the exterior is continued in the interior. As an optional feature, the control panel can be integrated into the glass door.

Glänzende Glas-Türfronten in Schwarz, Weiß oder Titan-Grau prägen das elegant anmutende Gestaltungskonzept dieser hochwertigen Kühl-Gefrier-Kombination. In Ergänzung zu den rahmenlosen Glasfronten unterstreichen vollintegrierte seitliche Aluminium-Griffleisten die betont reduzierte Formensprache der Geräte. Im Innenraum stehen drei unterschiedliche Temperaturzonen zur Verfügung, die jeweils durch großzügige Auszugsschalen leicht zugänglich sind. Für eine gute Übersicht über das Kühlgut sorgt eine blendfreie LED-Beleuchtung an der Seite. Der hochwertige Materialmix aus Glas und Metall findet im Innenraum eine konsequente Fortführung. Als zusätzliche Ausstattungsoption kann die Gerätesteuerung auf Wunsch in die Glastür integriert werden.

Siemens KI 42 FP 60, GI 38 NP 60
Fridge/Freezer/
Kühlgerät/Gefriergerät

Siemens-Electrogeräte GmbH, Munich,
Germany/München, Deutschland
In-house design/Werksdesign:
Max Eicher, Christoph Becke
www.siemens-hausgeraete.de

Behind an individual kitchen front the fully
integrated appliances of the coolConcept
series conceal a high degree of technical
perfection and comfortable use. Drawers in
all temperature zones ensure optimal access.
A continuously height-adjustable glass
shelf provides maximum interior flexibility.
Continuously height-adjustable door trays
allow customisation of the inside of the
refrigerator door. Glare-free lateral LED
lighting ensures perfect visibility. The freezer
has large drawers for convenient storage.
The space-saving compressor at the base of
the appliance provides maximum cooling
volume. This fridge/freezer meets class A++
requirements for energy efficiency.

Die vollintegrierten Geräte der cool-
Concept-Reihe halten hinter der individuellen Küchenfront ein hohes Maß an
technischer Perfektion und komfortabler
Nutzung bereit. Im Kühlschrank sorgen
Auszugsschalen in allen Temperaturzonen für einen optimalen Zugriff auf die
Lebensmittel. Ein stufenlos höhenver-
stellbarer Glasfachboden erweitert die
flexible Nutzung des Innenraums. Zudem
ermöglichen die stufenlos höhenverstellbaren Türabsteller eine bedarfsgerechte
Strukturierung der Kühlschrank-Innentür.
Blendfreie LED-Seitenlichter erleichtern
die Orientierung. Auch im Gefrierschrank
bieten große Schalen viel Stauraum. Das
platzsparende Aggregat im Gerätesockel
sorgt für ein maximales Kühlvolumen,
wobei das Gerät energiesparend der Klasse
A++ entspricht.

EEBK 6550.8BCX
Built-In Oven/Einbau-Backofen

Küppersbusch Hausgeräte AG, Gelsenkirchen, Germany/Deutschland
Design: Keicheldesign (Klaus Keichel),
Düsseldorf, Germany/Deutschland
www.kueppersbusch-hausgeraete.de
www.keichel-design.de

This built-in oven holds an innovative electronic control system behind the emotionally appealing front, which is kept in elegant black. At the touch of a fingertip individual programme functions can comfortably be selected. The user-friendly oven electronics offers six heating programmes and five functions for fully automatic baking and roasting. The ökotherm catalytic technology completes the modern functionality of this product.

Eine emotional ansprechende Geräte-front in elegantem Schwarz birgt bei diesem Einbau-Backofen eine innovative Steuerungselektronik. Per Fingertipp können die einzelnen Programmfunk-tionen komfortabel angewählt werden. Dabei ermöglicht die benutzerfreundliche Backofen-Elektronik den Zugriff auf sechs Beheizungsprogramme und fünf Funktio-nen zum vollautomatischen Backen und Braten. Die ökotherm-Katalysator-Techno-logie rundet die zeitgemäße Funktionalität dieses Produktes sinnvoll ab.

EDG 6550.0BCX
Built-in Steamer/Einbau-Dampfgarer

Küppersbusch Hausgeräte AG, Gelsenkirchen, Germany/Deutschland
Design: Keicheldesign (Klaus Keichel),
Düsseldorf, Germany/Deutschland
www.kueppersbusch-hausgeraete.de
www.keichel-design.de

This built-in steamer combines a black glass front with a black chrome handle bar. Beside the refined design its technology also meets high standards. By means of electronic controls fully automatic cooking programmes are comfortably selected. An external steam generator ensures precise steam supply and optimal climate during the preparation process. The easy-to-clean interior made of stainless steel is based on a functional concept as it has been equipped with a removable water tank.

Dieser Einbau-Dampfgarer kombiniert eine schwarze Glasfront mit einer Griff-leiste aus schwarzem Chrom. Neben der edlen Gestaltung entspricht auch die Technik einem hohen Standard. Mittels einer elektronischen Bedienung lassen sich vollautomatische Garprogramme komfortabel auswählen. Durch die externe Dampferzeugung erfolgt die Dampfzu-fuhr präzise und sorgt für ein optimales Klima bei der Zubereitung. Funktional durchdacht wurde der leicht zu reinigende Edelstahl-Innenraum mit einem heraus-nehmbaren Wasserbehälter ausgestattet.

EMWK 6550.0BC
Built-In Compact Oven/
Einbau-Kompaktbackofen

Küppersbusch Hausgeräte AG,
Gelsenkirchen, Germany/Deutschland
Design: Keicheldesign (Klaus Keichel),
Düsseldorf, Germany/Deutschland
www.kueppersbusch-hausgeraete.de
www.keichel-design.de

A black glass front with a black chrome handle bar stresses the superior serviceability of this combined solution. The innovative compact oven with integrated microwave displays an elegant aesthetics with horizontally aligned lines. The six oven and six microwave oven functions are operated by a fully electronic sensor touch control. There are also an integrated grill function and automatic baking and roasting programmes, which expediently complete the functionality of this built-in device.

Eine schwarze Glasfront mit einer Griff-leiste aus schwarzem Chrom unterstreicht den gehobenen Gebrauchswert dieser Kombilösung. Der innovative Kompakt-backofen mit integrierter Mikrowelle zeigt eine elegante Ästhetik mit horizontal ausgerichteter Linienführung. Seine sechs Backofen- und sechs Mikrowellenfunktio-nen können durch eine vollelektronische Sensor-Touch-Bedienung gesteuert wer-den. Zudem runden eine integrierte Grill-funktion sowie automatische Gar- und Backprogramme die Funktionalität des Einbaugeräts sinnvoll ab.

AEG MCC3880E MicroCombi oven/
MicroCombi-Backofen
AEG PE451M Automatic Coffee
Maker/Kaffeeautomat

Electrolux Home Products Corporation
N.V., Zaventem, Belgium/Belgien
In-house design/Werksdesign
www.electrolux.de

The appliances of this compact product range
have been newly interpreted and adjusted
to a rather slim furniture niche of 45 cm.
A stringently elaborate design concept
unites an automatic coffee maker and a
MicroCombi oven, among others, in a formal
style underlining their design identity. The
elegant and characteristic design additionally
supports the visual effect of the high-grade
materials. The satin-finished fronts of the
appliance can be harmoniously and flexibly
integrated into various kitchen arrangements.
Numerous cooking and baking functions
and technically high-quality equipment
grant high practical value and user-friendly
product benefits.

In einer Neuinterpretation wurden die
Geräte dieser Kompakt-Baureihe auf die
vergleichsweise schmale Möbelnische
von 45 cm abgestimmt. Ein stringent
durchdachtes Gestaltungskonzept vereint
unter anderem einen Kaffeeautomaten
und einen MicroCombi-Backofen in einer
Formensprache und unterstreicht ihre formale Identität. Die elegante und charakteristische Gestaltung unterstützt zudem
die visuelle Wirkung der hochwertigen
Materialien. Die satinierten Gerätefronten
lassen sich harmonisch und flexibel in
unterschiedliche Kücheneinrichtungen
integrieren. Zahlreiche Koch- und Back-
funktionen und eine technisch hochwertige Ausstattung ermöglichen einen hohen
Gebrauchswert mit nutzerfreundlichen
Produktvorteilen.

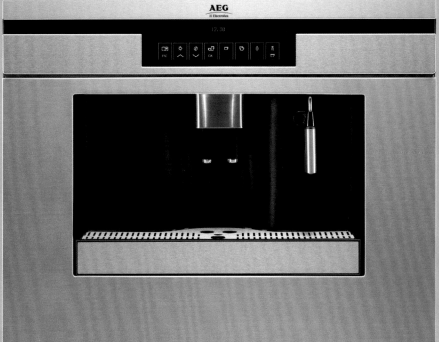

AEG HK953400FB
Induction Hob / Induktionskochmulde

Electrolux Home Products Corporation
N.V., Zaventem, Belgium / Belgien
In-house design / Werksdesign
www.electrolux.de

A minimalist look characterises the exquisite appearance of this modern induction hob of the MaxiSense product range. The glass surface, which can be flush integrated, is kept in reserved black. Reduced graphic elements emphasise the innovative induction technology in a visually appealing manner. A horizontally aligned arrangement allows frontal access to the three cooking zones. A comfortable slider function ensures that the powerful hob can be quickly, intuitively and reliably controlled. The position of the three touch-sensitive operator zones corresponds to the respectively assigned cooking zone.

Eine minimalistische Gestaltung prägt das edel anmutende Erscheinungsbild dieser zeitgemäßen Induktionskochmulde der MaxiSense-Baureihe. Die flächenbündig einbaubare Glasoberfläche ist in dezentem Schwarz gehalten. Reduziert eingesetzte, grafische Elemente heben dabei die innovative Induktionstechnologie visuell ansprechend hervor. Eine horizontal ausgerichtete Anordnung erlaubt dem Benutzer einen frontalen Zugang zu den drei Kochzonen. Mittels einer komfortablen Slider-Funktion erschließt sich die Bedienung der leistungsstarken Kochmulde schnell, intuitiv und sicher. Die Position der drei berührungsempfindlichen Bedienzonen entspricht der Position der jeweils zugeordneten Kochzone.

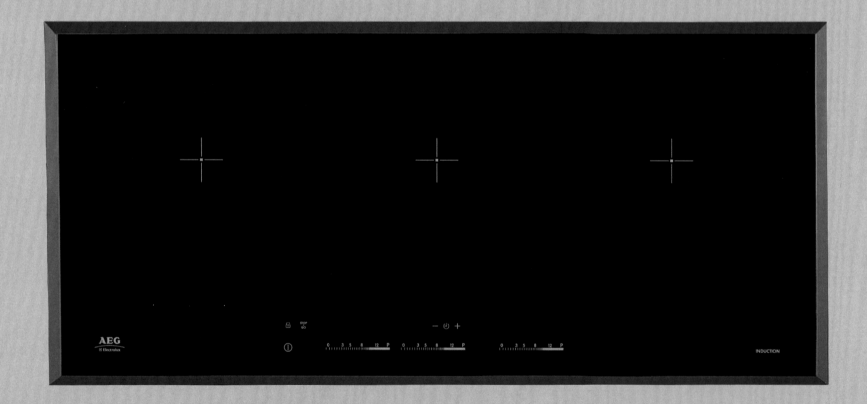

Doro 90 S
Cooker Hood / Dunstabzugshaube

Oranier Heiz- und Kochtechnik GmbH,
Gladenbach, Germany / Deutschland
In-house design / Werksdesign:
Thomas Tete
www.oranier.com

Aesthetics and functionality are characteristic features of this cooker hood, allowing free movement of the head. The whole surface is made of black glass giving the hood its particularly elegant look. The almost invisible rim exhaust ensures effective vapour extraction. Hidden air deflectors allow for optimum air guide and simple cleaning of the hood interior. An easily operable service opening with bevelled edges facilitates surface and filter cleaning. The exhaust air performance is controllable in four steps via touch control sensors. A 7-segment display informs on the respectively set performance level and reminds of filter cleaning. Four warm light power LEDs guarantee optimal lighting of the cooking area.

Ästhetik und Funktionalität zeichnen diese Kopffrei-Dunstabzugshaube aus. Die gesamte Oberfläche besteht aus schwarzem Glas, welches der Haube ihre besondere Eleganz verleiht. Für einen effektiven Wrasenabzug sorgt die fast unsichtbare Randabsaugung. Versteckte Luftleitbleche ermöglichen eine optimale Luftführung und eine einfache Reinigung des Geräteinneren. Eine leicht handhabbare Serviceöffnung mit Facettenschliff vereinfacht die Oberflächen- und Filterreinigung. Die Abluftleistung ist in vier Stufen über Touch-Control-Sensoren steuerbar, wobei eine 7-Segment-Anzeige über die jeweils eingestellte Leistungsstufe informiert und an die Filterreinigung erinnert. Für eine optimale Ausleuchtung der Kochfläche sorgen vier Warmlicht-Power-LEDs.

AEG HK854400XB
Induction Hob / Induktionskochmulde

Electrolux Home Products Corporation
N.V., Zaventem, Belgium / Belgien
In-house design / Werksdesign
www.electrolux.de

This wide separate hob features an induction heater including a power function. The induction hob is so efficient that one litre of cold water needs only two minutes to boil. The characteristic OptiFit hob frame with its large-scale frame part at the front defines the appearance of the elegant hob. The contemporary appliance can be flexibly incorporated into various kitchen arrangements. By means of the integrated OptiFix fastening the hob is safely inserted into the worktop section without requiring any additional installation of fixation parts. The XL product range includes different frame dimensions, which are available according to placement options.

Diese breite Autark-Kochmulde wurde mit einer Induktionsbeheizung inklusive Power-Funktion ausgestattet. Die Induktionskochmulde ist so leistungsstark, dass ein Liter kaltes Wasser bereits nach circa zwei Minuten kocht. Der charakteristische OptiFit Muldenrahmen mit seinem großformatigen Rahmenteil in der Front prägt das Erscheinungsbild der eleganten Kochmulde. Das zeitgemäße Gerät lässt sich flexibel in unterschiedliche Kücheneinrichtungen einfügen. Mittels der integrierten OptiFix-Befestigung wird die Kochmulde sicher in den Arbeitsplattenausschnitt eingesetzt, ohne dass eine zusätzliche Montage von Fixierungsteilen notwendig wird. Die XL-Baureihe umfasst verschiedene Rahmenabmessungen, welche – je nach Platzierungsmöglichkeit – zur Auswahl stehen.

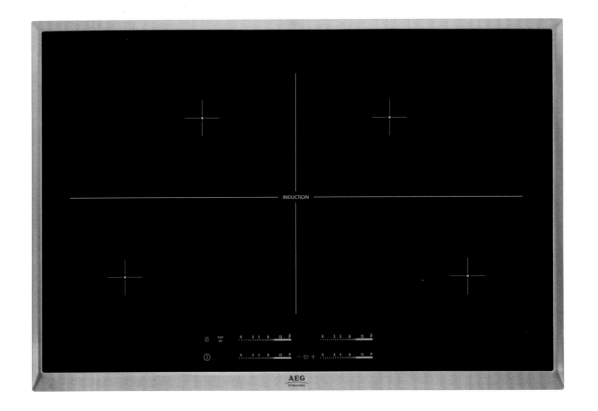

C49 C62 NO
Steam Oven / Dampfgarbackofen

Constructa-Neff Vertriebs GmbH,
Munich, Germany / München,
Deutschland
In-house design / Werksdesign:
Thomas Knöller
www.neff.de

The striking lines of this steam oven are emphasised by the visual effect of the straight-lined, strictly divided stainless steel frame. Slightly bevelled transitions add an interesting touch to the shape of the stainless steel surfaces. The exquisitely polished metal contrasts the black coloured glass front. The clearly formal appearance is emotionally enhanced by filigree, round operator buttons. The innovative combination of steam and hot air accounts for the high practical value allowing a particularly gentle preparation of food. Furthermore, the concurrently rotating door handle and the gently lowerable door are particularly expedient. Both design features have been developed according to ergonomic needs.

Mit einer markanten Linienführung wird bei diesem Dampfgarbackofen die visuelle Wirkung des geradlinigen, strikt unterteilten Edelstahlrahmens hervorgehoben. Leicht abgeschrägte Übergänge setzen bei der Gestaltung der Edelstahlflächen einen interessanten Akzent. Das edel polierte Metall bildet einen Kontrast zur schwarz getönten Glasfront. Emotional aufgewertet wird das betont formale Erscheinungsbild durch die filigran wirkenden, runden Bedienknöpfe. Der hohe Gebrauchswert des Geräts beruht auf der innovativen Kombination von Dampf und Heißluft, wodurch Nahrungsmittel besonders schonend zubereitet werden können. Von komfortablem Nutzen sind zudem der mitdrehende Türgriff sowie die sanft versenkbare Tür, beide Gestaltungsdetails wurden konsequent nach ergonomischen Gesichtspunkten konzipiert.

BM 275 Microwave Oven/
Mikrowellen-Backofen
CM 250 Fully Automatic Espresso
Machine/Espresso-Vollautomat
BS 254 Steam Oven/Dampfbackofen

Gaggenau Hausgeräte GmbH, Munich,
Germany/München, Deutschland
In-house design/Werksdesign:
Sven Baacke, Sören Strayle
www.gaggenau.com

The design of the 200 series of anthracite built-in appliances is determined by strictly concentrating on the essential, which goes beyond a merely functional kitchen appearance. The anthracite-coloured full glass fronts thereby underline a creative simplicity, which allows the combination of appliances with living space. The control module with full graphics display and rotary knobs characterises the puristic line management of this series. Thus, it obtains an independent elegance that successfully integrates the high functionality of the appliances into the living space. Beside a microwave oven, a fully automatic espresso machine and a steam oven, the built-in series includes warming drawers and ovens.

Das Design der Einbaugeräte-Serie 200 in Anthrazit wird bestimmt durch eine strikte Konzentration auf das Wesentliche, die über eine rein funktionale Küchenanmutung hinausgeht. Die anthrazitfarbenen Vollglas-fronten unterstreichen dabei eine gestalterische Schlichtheit, die es ermöglicht, Geräte und Wohnraum miteinander zu verbinden. Das Bedienmodul mit Vollgrafik-Display und Drehknöpfen prägt die puristische Lini-enführung der Serie. Diese erhält dadurch eine ganz eigenständige Eleganz, die die hohe Funktionalität der Geräte wie selbst-verständlich in den Lebensraum integriert. Die Einbaugeräte-Serie umfasst neben einem Mikrowellen-Backofen, einem Espresso-Vollautomaten und einem Dampfbackofen auch Wärmeschubladen und Backöfen.

AT 400 101
Table Ventilation / Tischlüftung

Gaggenau Hausgeräte GmbH, Munich,
Germany / München, Deutschland
In-house design / Werksdesign:
Sandor Klunker
www.gaggenau.com

This discreet stainless steel table ventilation was conceived as a professional cooking zone extraction system for private households. It is mounted directly onto the worktop behind the hob. The second worktop level it provides can be used for placing ingredients or plates; a matted glass cover and a wooden chopping board are available as accessories. An integrated surface illumination lights the hob without producing any glares. The ventilation works efficiently and silently in both recirculation air and exhaust air mode and is available in the widths 106 and 136 cm.

Diese dezente Edelstahl-Tischlüftung wurde als professionelle Kochstellen-Absaugung für den Privathaushalt konzipiert. Sie wird direkt auf der Arbeitsplatte hinter dem Kochfeld montiert. Auf der dadurch entstehenden zweiten Arbeitsebene lassen sich Zutaten bereitstellen oder Teller anrichten, eine mattierte Glasabdeckung sowie ein Holz-Schneidebrett sind als Zubehör erhältlich. Eine integrierte Flächenbeleuchtung leuchtet das Kochfeld blendfrei aus. Die Lüftung arbeitet effizient und leise im Umluft- oder Abluftbetrieb und ist in den Breiten 106 und 136 cm verfügbar.

RC 289 202
Vario Kälte-Serie 200
Refrigerators and Freezers / Kühl- und Gefriergeräte

Gaggenau Hausgeräte GmbH, Munich,
Germany / München, Deutschland
In-house design / Werksdesign:
Sebastian Knöll
www.gaggenau.com

With their modular, fully integrable refrigerators and freezers this product range provides storage capacities in a small space. Thanks to fully extractable trays and drawers access to the chilled goods is facilitated. In addition, transparent materials and a glare-free LED lighting concept allow free insight. The design concept is based on an appealing material mix. White plastic and aluminium are the dominating materials inside.
A step tray with integrated features for the accommodation of Gastronorm containers and the space-saving storage of chilled goods of different heights complete the equipment.

Mit ihren modularen, voll integrierbaren Kühl- und Gefriergeräten bietet diese Produktreihe Lagerkapazitäten auf kleinem Raum. Dank voll ausziehbarer Tablare und Schubladen wird der Zugriff auf das Kühlgut erleichtert, zudem ermöglichen transparente Materialien und ein blendfreies LED-Lichtkonzept einen guten Einblick. Das Gestaltungskonzept basiert auf einem ansprechenden Materialmix, im Innenraum dominieren weißer Kunststoff und Aluminium. Ein Stufentablar mit integrierten Vorrichtungen zur Lagerung von Gastronorm-Behältern sowie zur platzsparenden Aufbewahrung von unterschiedlich hohem Kühlgut komplettiert die Ausstattung.

RW 424 260 Wine Cooler Cabinet / Weinklimaschrank

Gaggenau Hausgeräte GmbH, Munich,
Germany / München, Deutschland
In-house design / Werksdesign:
Sebastian Knöll
www.gaggenau.com

This wine cooler cabinet was developed for storing and presenting precious wines. Its glass door is embraced by a stainless steel frame. The bottles are stored on fully extendable trays made of all-natural beech wood and aluminium. This material combination is visually attractive and prevents odours and flavours being transmitted. A special light can be switched on for presentation. Trays made of glass and wood, top elements and a humidor complete the presentation concept.

Für die Lagerung und Präsentation edler Weine wurde dieser Weinklimaschrank konzipiert. Seine Glastür wird von einem Edelstahlrahmen umfasst. Die Flaschen lagern auf voll ausziehbaren Ablagen aus unbehandeltem Buchenholz und Aluminium. Diese Materialkombination ist visuell ansprechend und verhindert Geruchs- oder Geschmacksübertragungen. Zur Präsentation kann ein Speziallicht zugeschaltet werden. Abstellflächen aus Glas und Holz, Aufsätze und ein Humidor runden das Präsentationskonzept ab.

CI 490 112 Induction Hob / Induktionskochfeld

Gaggenau Hausgeräte GmbH, Munich, Germany / München, Deutschland
In-house design / Werksdesign:
Sören Strayle
www.gaggenau.com

This induction hob allows easy access due to four cooking zones placed side by side. With regard to a depth of only 35 cm matching table ventilation is advisable. All graphic elements of the hob are reduced to the essential when they are switched off. They only show the four cooking zones and the main switch. The minimalist look enhances the digital operational concept with the centrally positioned stainless steel control knob. It combines the handling of a classic knob with cutting-edge technology.

Dieses Induktionskochfeld ermöglicht durch vier nebeneinander angeordnete Kochzonen einen komfortablen Zugriff. Mittels einer Tiefe von nur 35 cm empfiehlt sich die Kombination mit einer passenden Tischlüftung. Alle grafischen Elemente des Kochfeldes sind im ausgeschalteten Zustand auf das Wesentliche reduziert und zeigen nur die vier Kochzonen und den Hauptschalter an. Das puristische Erscheinungsbild hebt das digitale Bedienkonzept mit dem zentral positionierten Edelstahl-Bedienknebel hervor. Dieser kombiniert die Handhabung eines klassischen Knebels mit modernster Technologie.

CI 491 102 Induction Hob / Induktionskochfeld

Gaggenau Hausgeräte GmbH, Munich, Germany / München, Deutschland
In-house design / Werksdesign:
Sören Strayle
www.gaggenau.com

This induction hob can be flush integrated and harmoniously blends into the worktop. A minimalist look reduces the switched-off hob to just a few graphic elements that visualise the five cooking zones and the main switch. As soon as the digital control panel is activated all indicating and operating elements arranged around the centrally positioned stainless steel control knob light up. Now, by simply moving and turning the control knob, which is magnetically fastened, a cooking zone can be selected and set. Thus, the interface combines classic elements and state-of-the-art technology.

Flächenbündig integrierbar fügt sich dieses Induktionskochfeld harmonisch in die Arbeitsplatte ein. Eine minimalistische Gestaltung reduziert das ausgeschaltete Kochfeld auf nur wenige grafische Elemente, welche die fünf Kochzonen und den Hauptschalter visualisieren. Sobald das digitale Bedienfeld aktiviert wird, leuchten um den zentral positionierten Edelstahl-Bedienknebel herum alle Anzeige- und Bedienelemente auf. Nun kann mit einer einfachen Auslenkung und Drehung des magnetisch fixierten Bedienknebels eine Kochzone ausgewählt und geregelt werden. Das Interface vereint somit klassische Elemente und modernste Technik.

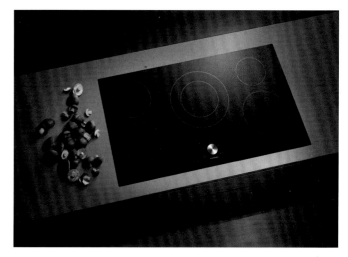

KB220 GN410 GN340 GN880 Gaggenau Gastronorm-System

Gaggenau Hausgeräte GmbH, Munich, Germany / München, Deutschland
In-house design / Werksdesign:
Sebastian Knöll
www.gaggenau.com

The professional Gastronorm system is a range of containers of different materials. Optionally, the high-quality vessels of hygienic stainless steel are available perforated or non-perforated. They are suitable for steam cooking, storage in the refrigerator or serving dishes. All elements are dishwasher-safe and they are available with matching covers. In addition, a roasting tray made of cast aluminium with special coating was developed for the multifunctional use on induction hobs and in ovens.

Das professionelle Gastronorm-System ist ein Sortiment von Behältern aus unterschiedlichen Materialien. Die hochwertigen Gefäße aus hygienischem Edelstahl sind wahlweise gelocht oder ungelocht erhältlich. Sie eignen sich für das Garen im Dampf, für die Lagerung im Kühlschrank oder zum Servieren von Speisen. Alle Elemente sind spülmaschinenfest und mit entsprechenden Abdeckungen erhältlich. Ein Bräter aus Aluminium-Druckguss mit Spezialbeschichtung wurde zudem für den multifunktionalen Einsatz auf Induktionskochfeldern und in Backöfen konzipiert.

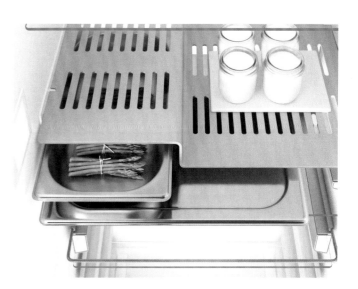

Combi Line
Induction Hob and Teppan Yaki Grill/
Induktionskochfeld und Teppan Yaki-Grill

Jaksch Küchentechnik GmbH,
Bodenkirchen, Germany/Deutschland
In-house design/Werksdesign:
Christian Jaksch, Adolf Jaksch
www.jaksch-kuechentechnik.com

As an innovative combination this hob connects cooking and grilling areas without any joints. The integration of intuitively controllable operating elements underneath a common glass surface brings about perfect harmony of colour, material and form. The puristic appearance of the grilling area, adjacent to the right side, is highlighted by its lines. This patented conception does not only simplify planning and mounting but first of all, it facilitates use and cleaning, irrespective of whether the appliance is mounted overlying or flush.

In Form einer innovativen Kombination bietet dieses Kochfeld eine fugenlose Verbindung von Koch- und Grillbereich. Durch die Integration der intuitiv steuerbaren Bedienelemente unter einer gemeinsamen Glasoberfläche ergibt sich eine hohe Ausgewogenheit von Farbe, Material und Form. Puristisch in ihrer Anmutung hebt sich die rechts angrenzende Grillfläche durch ihre Linienführung hervor. Diese patentierte Konzeption vereinfacht nicht nur die Planung und Montage, sondern erleichtert vor allem den Gebrauch und die Reinigung; unabhängig davon, ob das Gerät aufliegend oder flächenbündig eingebaut ist.

O-Touch Gas Hob/Gaskochfeld

Ningbo Fotile Kitchen Ware Co., Ltd.,
Cixi, Ningbo, China
In-house design/Werksdesign
www.fotile.com

This rimless ceramic hob with two gas burners follows a minimalist design. The newly formed burners are a particularly striking element in this material mix. They include five nozzles and five chambers that can be controlled in an even combustion process and with continuous performance without any air exhaust. In addition, the removable caps are easy to clean. By means of a safety ignition pin, which is water-repellent and stain-resistant, it is easy to ignite the burners in a modern and comfortable way.

Dieses rahmenlose Glaskeramikfeld mit zwei Gasbrennern folgt einem minimalistischen Gestaltungskonzept. Im edel anmutenden Materialmix fallen vor allem die neuartig geformten Brenner als reizvolles Element auf. Sie umfassen fünf Düsen und fünf Kammern, die sich bei gleichmäßiger Verbrennung und dauerhafter Leistung ohne Luftabzug regeln lassen. Die abnehmbaren Kappen sind zudem leicht zu reinigen. Ein Sicherheitszündungsstift, der dauerhaft wasser- und schmutzabweisend ist, macht das Anzünden zeitgemäß komfortabel.

JZ-JYJ Gas Hob/Gaskochfeld

Ningbo Oulin Kitchen Utensils Co. Ltd.,
Ningbo, China
In-house design/Werksdesign:
JianSheng Zheng
www.oulin.com

Unobtrusively this elegant gas hob can be integrated flush with the kitchen worktop. Contrasting the matt black glass ceramic, the cast-iron burners, made up of three curved elements, are characteristic of the independent appearance. With regard to functionality the hob offers interesting feature details: by means of a touch panel various control options can be addressed. A timer and safety shut-off complete the high ease of use.

Flächenbündig lässt sich dieses edel wirkende Gaskochfeld dezent in die Küchenarbeitsplatte integrieren. Im Kontrast zur mattschwarzen Glaskeramik prägen die gusseisernen Brenner, gebildet aus drei geschwungenen Elementen, das eigenständige Erscheinungsbild. Auch funktional bietet das Kochfeld interessante Ausstattungsdetails: Per Touchpanel lassen sich vielseitige Steuerungsmöglichkeiten abrufen. Der hohe Bedienkomfort wird durch eine Zeitautomatik und eine Sicherheitsabschaltung vervollständigt.

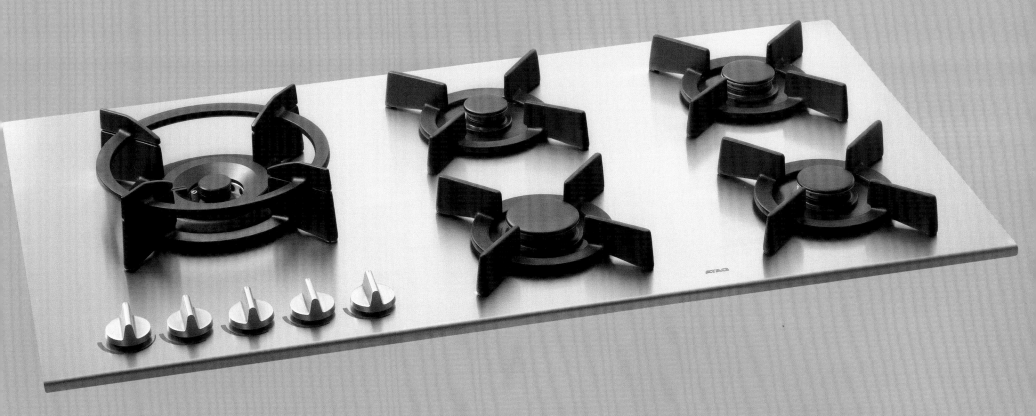

HG9711MX
Magna design
Gas Hob / Gaskochfeld

ATAG Nederland BV, Duiven, NL
In-house design / Werksdesign
Design: VanBerlo, Eindhoven, NL
www.atag.nl
www.vanberlo.nl

Puristically designed burner components mounted on a massive stainless steel surface give this gas hob an identity of its own. The robust and high-grade appliance has a 1.5 mm thick stainless steel base with precision-welded edges. Thus, the generous gas hob protrudes from the kitchen counter. The well-fashioned burners are forged from one piece, which facilitates cleaning. High quality is also provided by the cast-iron pan supports that are enhanced with dishwasher-safe enamel. Solid metal knobs allow for a user-friendly control of the desired burn performance, with a minimalist design underscoring the overall quality of the product. The wok burner, set apart on the left side of the hob, is well suited for large pans, while the four other burners on the right are sufficiently spaced apart to provide for convenient cooking.

Dieses Gaskochfeld erlangt durch die Montage puristischer Brennelemente auf einer massiven Edelstahlfläche einen eigenständigen Charakter. Der robuste und zudem hochwertige Eindruck basiert auf der 1,5 mm dicken Edelstahlplatte mit ihren präzisionsgeschweißten Rändern, wodurch sich das großzügige Gaskochfeld aus der Arbeitsplatte erhebt. Die markant ausgearbeiteten Brenner sind aus einem Stück gefertigt, was die Handhabung beim Saubermachen vereinfacht. Von ebenso hoher Qualität sind die Topfträger aus Gusseisen, welche mit einer spülmaschinenfesten Emaillierung veredelt wurden. Solide Metallknebel erlauben eine nutzerfreundliche Steuerung der gewünschten Brennleistung, wobei die minimalistische Ausgestaltung den Qualitätsanspruch des Produktes unterstreicht. Die Positionierung des Wokbrenners an der linken Seite ergibt viel Platz für größere Töpfe. Auch die vier übrigen Brenner rechts bieten einen großen Mittenabstand für genügend Stellraum.

Kitchen Furniture Concept/ Küchenmöbelkonzept

Alno AG, Pfullendorf,
Germany / Deutschland;
Robert Bosch Hausgeräte GmbH,
Munich, Germany / München,
Deutschland;
Schott AG, Mainz, Germany /
Deutschland
www.alno.de

With the ALNOSTAR SATINA glass kitchen a kitchen furniture concept was created that significantly contributes to a uniform appearance of kitchen appliances and furniture elements. In collaboration with Bosch Home Appliances and with Schott AG, a comfortable kitchen system was designed. Equipment features visualise a high standard of quality at the same time offering enhanced functionality. For the attractive and durable surfaces an especially matt glass with a striking effect was selected. The matt transparency of the dark glass surface unfolds a charming depth effect, particularly at the uniquely ground glass edges. These high-end glass fronts made of SCHOTT SatinPlus® are integrated into the handleless furniture as well as in the appliance fronts and form an overall minimalist look. Recessed handles with matching colours underscore the consistent discreetness of the flush-fitting kitchen units.

Die Glasküche ALNOSTAR SATINA wurde als ein Küchenmöbelkonzept entwickelt, das maßgeblich zu einem einheitlichen Gesamtbild von Küchengeräten und Möbelelementen beiträgt. In Kooperation mit Bosch Hausgeräte und der Schott AG wurde ein wohnlich anmutendes Küchensystem mit Ausstattungsdetails versehen, die Hochwertigkeit visualisieren und zugleich eine gehobene Funktionalität bieten. Ein auffallend mattes Spezialglas wurde für die Fertigung der attraktiven und unempfindlichen Oberflächen ausgewählt. Die matte Transparenz der dunklen Glasflächen entfaltet insbesondere an den Kanten mit Spezialschliff eine reizvolle Tiefenwirkung. Diese hochwertigen Glasfronten aus dem Material SCHOTT SatinPlus® kommen sowohl an den grifflosen Möbeln wie auch an den Gerätefronten zum Einsatz und prägen insgesamt ein puristisches Erscheinungsbild. Farblich angepasste Griffmulden unterstreichen die zurückhaltende Durchgängigkeit der flächenbündigen Küchenzeilen.

Bellevue HOT
Cooker Hood and Warming Bridge /
Dunstabzug und Wärmebrücke

Edel-Stahl Büchele,
Hard, Austria / Österreich
In-house design / Werksdesign:
Roman Büchele, Peter Büchele
www.buechele.com

This warming bridge is a high-quality feature supplement for semi-professional consumer kitchens. Bellevue HOT is a retractable cooker hood, which was combined with a heat-retaining zone. For integration into individual kitchens the upper cover can be manufactured of the same material as the worktop so that it is almost invisible after retraction. Thanks to its slim design the warming bridge displays reticence and elegance when it is lifted. The flow-optimised shape of the suction area harmoniously integrates into the otherwise straight-lined style. The appliance meets the criteria of a passive house as the circulated air is cleaned by a two-stage filter and directly discharged into the room – thus no space heating gets lost. According to the standard the fan is compactly integrated into the appliance. To save space in the substructure an external fan can be used optionally in a secondary room or in the basement. A further very well-conceived design detail is a slate on the back that can be written on with chalk.

Eine hochwertige Ausstattungsergänzung für die semiprofessionelle Küche im Privatbereich stellt diese Wärmebrücke dar. Bellevue HOT ist ein versenkbarer Dunstabzug, der zudem mit einer Warmhaltezone kombiniert wurde. In der individuellen Kücheneinpassung kann die obere Abdeckung aus dem gleichen Material gefertigt werden wie die Arbeitsplatte und ist dadurch im versenkten Zustand fast unsichtbar. Hochgefahren wirkt die Wärmebrücke durch ihre schlanke Formgebung zurückhaltend und elegant. Die strömungsoptimierte Gestaltung des Saugbereiches ist dabei harmonisch in die ansonsten geradlinige Formensprache eingepasst. Das Gerät entspricht den Kriterien eines Passivhauses, da die umgewälzte Luft durch einen zweistufigen Filter gereinigt und wieder direkt im Raum ausgeblasen wird – somit geht keine Raumwärme verloren. Serienmäßig ist der Ventilator kompakt in das Gerät integriert. Um Platz im Unterbau zu sparen, kann optional auch ein externer Lüfter im Nebenraum oder Keller zur Anwendung kommen. Ein weiteres durchdachtes Gestaltungsdetail ist außerdem eine an der Rückseite angebrachte und mit Kreide beschreibbare Schiefertafel.

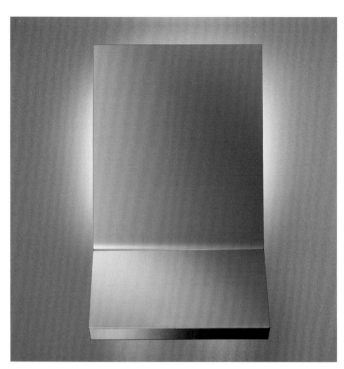

Rialto
Cooker Hood/Dunstabzugshaube

Falmec S.p.A., Vittorio Veneto,
Italy/Italien
Design: Alessandro Antoniazzi,
Vittore Niolu
www.falmec.com

This cooker hood combines a minimalist design with user-friendly functionality. Refined lines shape this hood into an elegant silhouette. The lower section is curved forward creating adequate capture area and easy access to controls. The combination of different stainless steel finishings attracts the attention of the viewer. Low energy consumption completes the contemporary image of the Rialto.

Diese Dunstabzugshaube vereint eine minimalistische Gestaltung mit benutzerfreundlicher Funktionalität. Die verfeinerte Linienführung verleiht ihr eine elegante Silhouette. Der untere Bereich ist nach vorn gewölbt und bildet so einen bedarfsgerechten Abzugsbereich und leichten Zugang zu den Bedienelementen. Die Kombination unterschiedlicher Edelstahloberflächen weckt die Aufmerksamkeit des Betrachters. Rialto weist zudem einen geringen Energieverbrauch auf.

Prestige
Cooker Hood/Dunstabzugshaube

Falmec S.p.A., Vittorio Veneto,
Italy/Italien
Design: Emo Design
(Francesco Costacurta, Lukasz Bertoli),
Fregona (Treviso), Italy/Italien
www.falmec.com
www.emo-design.it

The innovative combination of glass and stainless steel gives this cooker hood a unique appearance. This is further enhanced by the ornamental light concept. Elegantly shaped glass panels are illuminated by LEDs at the top of the hood while further LEDs ensure sufficient visibility of the cooker surface. A high-performance motor protected by stainless steel filters efficiently and silently extracts the cooking vapours.

Die innovative Kombination von Glas und Edelstahl verleiht dieser Dunstabzugshaube ein einzigartiges Erscheinungsbild, das durch das dekorative Lichtkonzept noch aufgewertet wird. Elegant geformte Glasblenden werden durch LEDs am oberen Rand der Haube beleuchtet, und zusätzliche LEDs sorgen für ein gut ausgeleuchtetes Kochfeld. Ein leise laufender, durch Edelstahlfilter geschützter Hochleistungsmotor sorgt für raschen und effektiven Dunstabzug.

CBNes 5167
**Fridge-Freezer/
Kühl-Gefrier-Kombination**

Liebherr-Hausgeräte GmbH,
Ochsenhausen, Germany/Deutschland
Design: PRODESIGN Brüssing, Neu-Ulm,
Germany/Deutschland
www.liebherr.com
www.prodesign-ulm.de

An electronic LCD display in the full-surface stainless steel door provides a visual accent emphasising the high functionality of this fridge-freezer with BioFresh-Plus. It features a clearly laid out menu navigation and a modern, easy-to-use touch system. The floor-mounted appliance is 75 cm wide providing plenty of space. The interior is lit by innovative LED light columns. Both BioFresh safes can be used as dry or hydro safe. The door features a SoftSystem soft-closing damping and an automatic closing system.

Ein elektronisches LCD-Display in der vollflächigen Edelstahltür setzt einen visuellen Akzent, der die hohe Funktionalität dieser Kühl-Gefrier-Kombination mit BioFresh-Plus betont. Es ermöglicht eine übersichtliche Menüführung bei zeitgemäßem Touch-Bedienkomfort. Das Standgerät bietet mit 75 cm Breite viel Stauraum, wobei der Innenraum mit innovativen LED-Lichtsäulen ausgeleuchtet wird. Beide BioFresh-Safes können als Dry- oder Hydro-Safe genutzt werden. Die Tür ist mit einer SoftSystem-Schließdämpfung und einer Schließautomatik ausgestattet.

DA 6290 W
Cooker Hood / Dunstabzugshaube

Miele & Cie. KG, Gütersloh,
Germany / Deutschland
In-house design / Werksdesign
www.miele.de

This wall hood represents an innovative design idea: it features a striking multicoloured LED glass edge lighting. The very slim stainless steel canopy gives the hood an elegant and delicate appearance. The gently rounded, puristic front edge incorporates the control panel as well as the glass edge lighting element. From among four preset light colours users may select their favourite colour. The colours can be programmed to change every minute or every quarter of an hour.

Eine innovative Gestaltungsidee verkörpert diese Wandhaube, auffallend ist dabei eine mehrfarbige LED-Glaskantenbeleuchtung. Der sehr flache Haubenkörper aus Edelstahl lässt das Erscheinungsbild elegant und filigran wirken. In die sanft gerundete, puristische Vorderkante wurden die Bedienleiste und die Glaskantenbeleuchtung integriert. Dabei kann aus vier voreingestellten Lichtfarben ein Favorit ausgewählt werden, zudem ist ein minütlicher sowie ein viertelstündlicher Farbwechsel programmierbar.

PT 7186
Professional Tumble Dryer / Gewerblicher Wäschetrockner

Miele & Cie. KG, Gütersloh,
Germany / Deutschland
In-house design / Werksdesign
www.miele.de

This stainless steel dryer is designed for professional use. It features a functional body and a clearly structured, maintenance-friendly interior. The large door is equipped with a second glass to protect against high temperatures that sits flush with the door and is easy to clean. The concealed recess, which runs around the door, allows users to open the door from whatever angle is most convenient for them. The large-volume drum is easy to load and unload.

Dieser Edelstahl-Trockner ist für den gewerblichen Einsatz konzipiert. Neben seinem funktionalen Korpus ist auch der Innenaufbau klar strukturiert und kundendienstfreundlich durchdacht. Die großen Türen haben zwei Gläser, ein wäscheabweisendes und ein türbündiges, das vor hohen Temperaturen schützt und zudem gut zu reinigen ist. Durch Greifen in die umlaufende Fase ist es möglich, die Tür an der ergonomisch günstigsten Stelle zu öffnen. Die großvolumige Trommel ist komfortabel zu befüllen und zu entladen.

PW 6080
Professional Washing Machine / Gewerbliche Waschmaschine

Miele & Cie. KG, Gütersloh,
Germany / Deutschland
In-house design / Werksdesign
www.miele.de

This model series has been designed for the professional use in laundries, hospitals and health care facilities. A plain stainless steel front enhances distinct lines. The internal componentry was structured service-friendly. The doors featuring a second protective glass are easy to operate and meet all safety requirements. In comparison with the previous generation, these models save 30 per cent water and 16 per cent electricity. In addition, the patented honeycomb drum forms a film of water to gently clean the clothes.

Diese Baureihe wurde für die gewerbliche Nutzung in Wäschereien, Kranken- und Pflegeeinrichtungen konzipiert. Eine schlichte Edelstahlfront unterstreicht die klare Linienführung, wobei der Innenaufbau kundendienstfreundlich gestaltet wurde. Die mit einem zweiten Schutzglas versehenen Türen lassen sich leicht bedienen und erfüllen alle Sicherheitsauflagen. Im Vergleich zur vorherigen Generation werden 30 Prozent Wasser und 16 Prozent Strom eingespart. Zudem bildet sich auf der patentierten Schontrommel ein textilschonender Wasserfilm.

Lissotis
Washing Machine / Waschmaschine

Vestel White Goods,
Manisa, Turkey / Türkei
Design: MG Design (Seyman Cay,
Melih Gürleyik), Istanbul, Turkey / Türkei
www.vestel.com.tr
www.mg-design.org

The elegant front panel of the Lissotis washing machine expresses its suitability for housing space. The combination of a shining black body and a polished stainless steel porthole frame emphasise its visual conciseness. The user-friendly design underlines the core controls and contributes to a minimalist overall impression. With regard to ergonomics the control of the front-loading washing machine is conveniently integrated so that the user can comfortably start the appliance. For all technical purposes this washing machine offers interesting product advantages: an advanced twin jet technology achieves optimised energy consumption with A+++ rated energy class and A rated class for improved washing efficiency. In addition, with a 12-minute wash cycle the floor-mounted appliance belongs to the particularly fast washing machines.

Eine elegante Gerätefront verleiht der Waschmaschine Lissotis ein wohnraumgeeignetes Erscheinungsbild. Die Kombination aus einem glänzend schwarzen Korpus und einer Bullaugeneinrahmung aus poliertem Edelstahl geben ihr visuelle Prägnanz. Die nutzerfreundliche Gestaltung hebt die wesentlichen Bedienelemente hervor und trägt zu einem minimalistischen Gesamteindruck bei. Die Steuerung der Frontlader-Waschmaschine wurde ergonomisch sinnvoll platziert, dadurch kann der Benutzer das Gerät bequem einschalten. Auch technisch gesehen bietet die Maschine interessante Produktvorteile: Eine weiterentwickelte Twin-Jet-Technologie erreicht einen optimierten Energieverbrauch der Effizienzklassse A+++ bei einer verbesserten Wascheffizienz der Klasse A. Darüber hinaus gehört das Gerät mit einem nur zwölf Minuten dauernden Waschgang zu den besonders schnellen Waschmaschinen.

Aramides
Washing Machine / Waschmaschine

Vestel White Goods,
Manisa, Turkey / Türkei
Design: MG Design (Seyman Cay,
Melih Gürleyik), Istanbul, Turkey / Türkei
www.vestel.com.tr
www.mg-design.org

The striking colours give this washing
machine a high-quality appearance; it
can harmoniously be integrated in homely
surroundings. A matt stainless steel
frame around the dark viewing window
aesthetically enhances the black front panel.
By means of its characteristic control panel
the Aramides washing machine permits user-
friendly operation. Behind the continuous
control panel there is an illuminated LCD
operator panel informing about the particular
programme status and other additional
functions. The generous opening with a
diameter of 33 cm allows comfortable
loading of the washing drum. Thanks to
an optimised twin jet technology, not only
water, detergent and energy consumption
are considerably reduced but the washing
performance is also improved. Therefore, with
regard to energy consumption energy class
A+++ is achieved, the washing efficiency
being A. An innovative feature is also a high-
speed wash cycle that only takes 12 minutes.

In ihrer markanten Farbgebung wirkt
diese Waschmaschine hochwertig und
sie lässt sich harmonisch in ein wohnliches Umfeld integrieren. Die schwarze
Gerätefront wird durch einen mattierten
Edelstahlrahmen rund um das dunkle
Sichtfenster ästhetisch aufgewertet. Mithilfe ihres charakteristischen Kontrollfelds
erlaubt die Waschmaschine Aramides eine
nutzerfreundliche Handhabung. Hinter
der durchgehenden Bedienfront befindet
sich ein beleuchtetes LCD-Bedienfeld,
welches über den jeweiligen Programmstatus sowie weitere Zusatzfunktionen
informiert. Die großzügige Öffnung mit
einem Durchmesser von 33 cm ermöglicht
eine komfortable Befüllung der Waschtrommel. Dank einer optimierten Twin-
Jet-Technologie wird nicht nur der Was-
ser-, Waschmittel- und Energieverbrauch
deutlich verringert, sondern auch bessere
Waschergebnisse erzielt. Deshalb wird
beim Energieverbrauch die Effizienzklas-
se A+++ und bei der Wascheffizienz die
Klasse A erreicht. Ein innovativer Aspekt
ist auch ein nur zwölf Minuten dauernder
Schnellwaschgang.

Cube 90 CN
Stainless Steel Sink/
Spülstein aus Edelstahl

Teka Küchentechnik GmbH, Haiger,
Germany/Deutschland
In-house design/Werksdesign
www.teka.com

The design of this sink plays with geometric forms. The two basins differ slightly in size but share the same refined edges and drain design. Well thought-out ergonomics allow Cube to be mounted at a user-customised height, independent of other kitchen furniture. The sink can be installed on the furniture, a height-reduced base cabinet, and between two base cabinets, or directly to the kitchen wall. Optional accessories include a stainless steel colander bowl, a wooden chopping board and a glass chopping board.

Die Gestaltung dieses Spülsteins spielt mit geometrischen Formen. In dezenter Variation fallen die beiden Spülbecken unterschiedlich groß aus, gemeinsam ist ihnen der edel ausgeformte Ablaufrand. Ergonomisch durchdacht lässt sich Cube auf eine nutzergerechte Höhe einbauen, und zwar unabhängig vom Küchenmöbel. Der Spülstein kann sowohl auf das Möbel, einen höhenreduzierten Unterschrank, zwischen zwei Unterschränken als auch direkt an der Küchenwand montiert werden. Als optionales Zubehör sind ein Edelstahl-Siebeinsatz, ein Holzschneidebrett sowie ein Glasschneidebrett erhältlich.

S8201 Stainless Steel Sink/
Edelstahlspüle

Ningbo Oulin Kitchen Utensils Co. Ltd.,
Ningbo, China
In-house design/Werksdesign:
Lin Lin, Ailian Dai
www.oulin.com

A special surface treatment gives this compact stainless steel sink an elegant and high-quality appearance. The basic structure of the bowls has an angular-shaped design, and the strikingly harmonious roundness of the inner surfaces of the bowls in particular creates an eye-catching look. This independent stylistic language was made possible by innovative manufacturing procedures that have especially been developed for this product series. Each part of the naturally shaped bowls is easy to reach and therefore easy to clean. The division in two separate bowls allows using the sink more flexibly. A rotatable tap and further accessories consistently adapt to the overall appearance.

Eine spezielle Oberflächenbehandlung verleiht dieser kompakten Edelstahlspüle eine edle und hochwertige Anmutung. Die in ihrer Grundstruktur eckig konstruierten Becken wurden vor allem durch die auffallend harmonischen Abrundungen der Beckeninnenflächen visuell interessant gestaltet. Ermöglicht wird diese eigenständige Formensprache durch innovative Fertigungsprozesse, die eigens für diese Produktreihe entwickelt wurden. Die organisch anmutende Beckenform ist überall gut zu erreichen und infolgedessen einfach zu reinigen. Die Unterteilung in zwei separate Becken erlaubt zudem eine flexiblere Nutzung der Spüle. Eine drehbare Armatur und weiteres Zubehör passen sich dem ansprechenden Gesamtbild konsistent an.

Blancoalaros 6 S
Kitchen Sink / Haushaltsspüle

Blanco GmbH + Co KG, Oberderdingen,
Germany / Deutschland
In-house design / Werksdesign
Design: Formteam, Schorndorf,
Germany / Deutschland
www.blanco.de
www.formteam.de

This kitchen sink with its symmetric design offers high convenience and formal generosity. Two flanking drainboards create a wing-like geometry. The centric XL bowl features an elegant overflow and a recessed tap ledge. In combination with a retractable mixer tap the bowl can be discreetly covered by the two chopping boards and contributes to a perfectly tidy workspace. The puristically shaped tap ledge is integrated into the convenient intermediate level underlining the general accent of a linear design language. That way, additional accessories can be placed like the Alaros structured stainless steel tray for extra drain space even over the filled bowl or the Carrier for convenient steam cooking.

Diese Spüle mit ihrem symmetrischen Aufbau bietet hohen Komfort und eine formale Großzügigkeit, zwei beidseitig angeordnete Tropfflächen verleihen ihr eine flügelartige Geometrie. Das mittige XL-Becken wurde mit einem eleganten Überlauf und einer tiefer liegenden Batteriebank ausgestattet. In Verbindung mit einer absenkbaren Küchenarmatur kann das Becken mit den beiden Schneidebrettern dezent abgedeckt werden und schafft damit einen rundum aufgeräumten Arbeitsbereich. Die puristisch geformte Batteriebank ist in die funktionale Zwischenebene des Beckens eingebunden und unterstreicht die betont geradlinige Formensprache. So lassen sich weitere Zubehörelemente platzieren, wie ein Alaros-Strukturtableau für zusätzliche Abtropffläche auch über dem befüllten Becken oder ein Carrier zum komfortablen Dampfgaren.

Twin Line
Kitchen Tap and Water Filter/
Küchenarmatur und Wasserfilter

Duratex – Deca,
São Paulo, Brazil / Brasilien
In-house design / Werksdesign:
Ana Orlovitz, Luiz Morales
www.deca.com.br

By an integrated drinking water filter this modern kitchen tap provides an innovative additional benefit. It articulates a minimalist design vocabulary, which is stringently continued in spite of the water filter that is integrated into the tap. The design objective, a combination of filter and tap, was realised in a compact and reduced way. The water dispenser was strikingly divided in two parts. The upper filigree tap serves to fill drinking glasses and the lower tap with a larger opening was conceived to admit washing-up water. Both water outlets are structurally connected with each other and yet to be operated independently. A specially developed mechanics allows comfortable opening and closing of both taps. Thus, for example, the valve of the upper tap is simply opened by a turn to the side. Before the water flows, it is reliably cleaned of odours, residues and chlorine by means of the certified Carbon Block system, which was newly developed for this product solution.

Mit einem eingebauten Trinkwasserfilter bietet diese zeitgemäße Küchenarmatur einen innovativen Zusatznutzen. Sie zeigt eine minimalistische Formensprache, welche trotz des im Hahn integrierten Wasserfilters stringent fortgeführt wurde. Das gestalterische Ziel, eine Kombination von Filter und Wasserhahn, wurde dabei kompakt und zurückhaltend umgesetzt. Einen auffallenden Gestaltungsakzent setzt hingegen der zweigeteilte Wasserspender, wobei der obere, filigrane Hahn zum Befüllen von Trinkgläsern dient und der untere Hahn mit einer größeren Öffnung für das Einlassen von Spülwasser konzipiert wurde. Beide Wasserausfälle sind strukturell miteinander verbunden und dennoch unabhängig voneinander zu bedienen. Eine speziell entwickelte Mechanik ermöglicht das komfortable Öffnen und Schließen der beiden Wasserhähne. So wird beispielsweise das Ventil des oberen Hahns einfach durch eine Seitwärtsdrehung geöffnet. Vor dem Austritt wird das Wasser mittels des zertifizierten Carbon-Block-Systems, das für diese Produktlösung neu konzipiert wurde, zuverlässig von Gerüchen, Schadstoffen und Chlor gereinigt.

Still One
Water Drinking Faucet /
Trinkwasserhahn

Shengtai Brassware Co., Ltd.,
Chang Hua, Taiwan
In-house design / Werksdesign:
JUSTIME Design Team
www.justime.com

This stylish faucet displays harmoniously
curved lines. The appealing elegance of Still
One matches its reliable functionality. With
its space-saving dimensions the faucet can
be flexibly integrated in various kitchens.
Lead-free brass and stainless steel preserve
drinking water quality. The easily operated
stainless steel water valve promises long
durability.

Dieser stilvolle Wasserhahn zeigt eine
harmonisch geschwungene Linienführung.
Still One vereint eine gute Funktionalität
mit einer ansprechenden Eleganz. Platzsparend in seinen Ausmaßen lässt sich der
Wasserhahn flexibel in unterschiedliche
Küchen integrieren. Dabei stellen blei-
freies Messing und Edelstahl die Trink-
qualität des Wassers sicher. Das leicht zu
bedienende Wasserventil aus Edelstahl
verspricht zudem eine lange Haltbarkeit.

**Dynapro
Concealed Slide System /
Unterflur-Führungs-System**

Grass GmbH & Co. KG,
Reinheim, Germany / Deutschland
In-house design / Werksdesign:
Jürgen Ahlfeld
Design: Studio Ambrozus
(Stefan Ambrozus),
Cologne, Germany / Köln, Deutschland
www.grass.at
www.studioambrozus.de

This concealed slide system is exceptionally synchronised so that the slides move without any disturbing noise or resistance. Even under high loads of up to 60 kg the reliable running performance is unchanged and the pull-out forces remain low. Since Dynapro features an integrated, three-dimensional adjustment facility, the whole drawer can be adjusted vertically and horizontally as well as in its tilt angle. All adjustments are tool-free, readily accessible and easy to handle. It takes just a few simple steps to achieve optimal alignment. Dynapro features the Soft-close damping system and can be combined with the Tipmatic-Plus and Sensomatic opening systems.

Dieses Unterflur-Führungs-System verfügt über eine außergewöhnliche Synchronisation, sodass sich die Führungsschienen frei von störenden Geräuschen und Widerständen bewegen. Auch unter einer hohen Belastung von bis zu 60 kg sind die Laufeigenschaften unverändert gut und die Auszugskräfte bleiben gering. Da Dynapro mit einer integrierten, dreidimensionalen Verstellmöglichkeit versehen wurde, lässt sich der gesamte Schubkasten sowohl vertikal, horizontal als auch in seiner Neigung variieren. Dabei sind alle Verstellungen werkzeugfrei zu bedienen, bequem zu greifen und einfach zu handhaben. Mit wenigen Handgriffen lassen sich so optimale Fugenbilder erzielen. Dynapro ist mit dem Dämpfungs-System Soft-close ausgestattet und kann optional mit den Öffnungs-Systemen Tipmatic-Plus und Sensomatic kombiniert werden.

ProM
Coffee Grinder / Kaffeemühle

MAHLKÖNIG GmbH & Co. KG,
Hamburg, Germany / Deutschland
Design: Carsten Gollnick –
Product Design, Berlin,
Germany / Deutschland
www.mahlkoenig.de
www.gollnick-design.de

The independent stylistic language of this coffee grinder stresses its professional functionality. For the preparation of espresso the coffee beans are ground in individual portions; filter coffee is dispensed directly in a storage bin. ProM features a storage hopper with a capacity of 250 grammes, precisely operating grinding discs, and manual turning knobs to set the degree of grinding and the automatic timer. In addition to the automatic start function the hands-free operation confirms the user-friendly impression.

Die eigenständige Formensprache dieser Kaffeemühle unterstreicht ihre professionelle Funktionalität. Für die Espressozubereitung werden die Bohnen portionsweise gemahlen, Filterkaffee wird direkt in einen Vorratsbehälter dosiert. Ausgestattet wurde ProM mit einem 250-Gramm-Bohnenvorratsbehälter, präzise arbeitenden Mahlscheiben sowie manuellen Drehknöpfen zur Einstellung von Mahlgrad und Zeitautomatik. Neben der automatischen Startfunktion ist zudem die Freihandnutzung anwenderfreundlich.

15/19 Bar 3-in-1
Coffee Centre / Kaffee-Center

South Asia International (HK) Ltd.,
Hong Kong
In-house design / Werksdesign:
Raymond Hoi Tak Lam
www.sai.com.hk

With rounded edges and harmonious lines this coffee centre stresses the stainless steel front in contrast to the black casing. The classy appearance visualises the professional functionality of the combined device that optionally prepares espresso, cappuccino or coffee. With a performance of 15/19 bar the Italian pump system meets a high quality level. Multifunctional programmes can be addressed by shapely press buttons.

Mit abgerundeten Ecken betont die harmonische Linienführung dieses Kaffee-Centers die Edelstahlfront im Kontrast zum schwarzen Gehäuse. Das edle Erscheinungsbild visualisiert die professionelle Funktionalität des Kombigeräts, mit welchem sich wahlweise Espresso, Cappuccino und Kaffee zubereiten lassen. Mit einer Leistung von 15 bzw. 19 Bar erreicht das italienische Pumpsystem einen hohen Qualitätsstandard. Multifunktionale Programme lassen sich über ansprechend gestaltete Drucktasten komfortabel anwählen.

Melitta Caffeo Solo
Fully Automatic Coffee Maker/ Kaffeevollautomat

Melitta Haushaltsprodukte GmbH & Co. KG, Minden, Germany / Deutschland
Design: Industrie Design
(Florian Seiffert, Ute Sickinger), Wiesbaden, Germany / Deutschland
www.melitta.de

Concentration on the basics accounts for the compact appearance of this fully automatic coffee maker. Its reduced operating elements were arranged in smallest dimensions allowing simple and intuitive handling. With three different models – white, black or silver front – Melitta Caffeo Solo offers high functionality. The water volume can be continuously adjusted to the respective cup size. Among others the coffee strength as well as the coffee temperature is adjustable.

Die Konzentration auf das Wesentliche prägt das kompakte Erscheinungsbild dieses Kaffeevollautomaten. Seine reduzierten Bedienungselemente wurden in kleinsten Abmessungen angeordnet und ermöglichen eine intuitive Handhabung. In drei unterschiedlichen Ausführungen, mit weißer, schwarzer oder silberner Front, bietet Melitta Caffeo Solo eine hohe Funktionalität. Die Wassermenge lässt sich stufenlos der jeweiligen Tassengröße anpassen, außerdem sind unter anderem die Kaffeestärke sowie die Kaffeetemperatur einstellbar.

Melitta c35
Fully Automatic Espresso Machine/ Espresso-Vollautomat

Melitta SystemService GmbH & Co. KG, Minden, Germany/Deutschland
Design: Carsten Gollnick
Product Design|Interior Design
(Carsten Gollnick), Berlin, Germany/ Deutschland
www.melitta.de/mss
www.gollnick-design.de

This fully automatic espresso machine with touchscreen was developed for the use in restaurants. Consequently the design concept focused on the front of the device and the operating areas were elaborated in a sophisticated way. A small width and vertical lines give the device a slim and elegant impression. Its reduced appearance highlights the core functions. Matt stainless steel, black-coated safety glass and high-quality synthetic components visualise the professional standard.

Dieser Espresso-Vollautomat mit Touchscreen wurde für den Einsatz in der Gastronomie entwickelt. Folglich hat sich das Gestaltungskonzept auf die Gerätefront fokussiert und die Bedienungsbereiche differenziert ausgearbeitet. Eine geringe Breite und vertikale Linien lassen das Gerät schmal und elegant wirken, wobei seine reduzierte Anmutung die Kernfunktionen in den Vordergrund stellt. Matter Edelstahl, schwarz beschichtetes Sicherheitsglas und hochwertige Kunststoffkomponenten visualisieren den professionellen Anspruch.

SKS-996
Kitchen Scales/Küchenwaage

Transtek Electronics Co., Ltd.,
Zhongshan, China
In-house design/Werksdesign:
Wilson Ma
www.transtek.cn

All the different types of this contemporary kitchen scales feature a remarkably slim device height. This creates a filigree impression while the design requirements of this product series are visually enhanced by an exquisitely brushed metal surface. At the back of the round or rectangular stainless steel body there are hooks inviting to mount the scales to the wall as a decorative kitchen accessory. The weighing result is indicated accurate to within a gramme on the LCD display up to a maximum of 5 kg.

Die unterschiedlichen Ausführungen dieser zeitgemäßen Küchenwaage zeigen alle eine auffallend geringe Gerätehöhe. Somit entsteht eine filigrane Anmutung, während der Designanspruch der Produktserie durch eine edel gebürstete Metalloberfläche visuell unterstützt wird. Auf der Rückseite des runden oder rechteckigen Edelstahlkorpus befinden sich Haken, die dazu einladen, die Waage als dekoratives Küchenaccessoire an die Wand zu hängen. Bis maximal 5 kg wird das Wiegeergebnis grammgenau auf dem LCD-Display angezeigt.

Kenwood FP970 Multipro Excel
Food Processor / Küchenmaschine

De'Longhi Deutschland GmbH,
Seligenstadt, Germany / Deutschland
In-house design / Werksdesign:
Robin Ferraby
www.kenwoodworld.com

Premium materials give this high-performance food processor not only a robust but also an appealing appearance. The combination of thick-walled glass and stainless steel guarantees long durability. A powerful 1,200-watt motor is controlled by a dual speed system with variably adjustable speed levels. Large processor bowls grant flexible use and are available in three different sizes up to a maximum filling capacity of 4 litres. Additionally, there is a glass mix liquidiser with a capacity of 1.5 litres.

Hochwertige Materialien lassen diese leistungsstarke Küchenmaschine nicht nur robust, sondern auch ansprechend erscheinen. Die Kombination aus dickwandigem Glas und Edelstahl gewährleistet eine lange Haltbarkeit. Ein kraftvoller 1.200-Watt-Motor wird über ein duales Geschwindigkeitssystem kontrolliert, wobei die Geschwindigkeitsstufen variabel einstellbar sind. Große Arbeitsbehälter in drei verschiedenen Größen mit einer maximalen Füllmenge von bis zu 4 Litern sowie ein Glas-Mixaufsatz mit 1,5 Litern Fassungsvermögen bieten flexible Kapazitäten.

Kenwood MG700 Excel Pro 2000
Meat Grinder / Fleischwolf

De'Longhi Deutschland GmbH,
Seligenstadt, Germany / Deutschland
In-house design / Werksdesign:
Robin Ferraby
www.kenwoodworld.com

A robust metal casing made of brushed aluminium covers this high-performance meat grinder and gives a professional impression. The compact floor-mounted appliance has been configured with regard to its functionality and offers comfortable handling. It allows quick grinding of up to 3 kg of meat per minute. Apart from the usual types of meat it is also possible to process chicken, duck, fish, venison, nuts and vegetables for the preparation of pâtés, terrines and noodle stuffing.

Ein robustes Metallgehäuse aus gebürstetem Aluminium umgibt diesen leistungsfähigen Fleischwolf und vermittelt ein professionelles Erscheinungsbild. Das kompakte Standgerät ist ganz auf seine Funktionalität ausgerichtet und bietet eine komfortable Handhabung. Es ermöglicht eine schnelle Verarbeitung von bis zu 3 kg Fleisch pro Minute. Außer den gängigen Fleischsorten können auch Huhn, Ente, Fisch, Wild, Nüsse und Gemüse verarbeitet und damit Pâtés, Terrinen sowie Nudelfüllungen zubereitet werden.

Kenwood KM070 Cooking Chef
Food Processor / Küchenmaschine

De'Longhi Deutschland GmbH,
Seligenstadt, Germany / Deutschland
In-house design / Werksdesign:
Darren Mullen
www.kenwoodworld.com

This functionally designed kitchen machine made of die-cast aluminium represents a powerful and robust product solution allowing simultaneous cooking and stirring. Here the combination of a traditional kitchen machine and a modern induction hob is an innovative feature that ensures particularly energy-saving and quick heating of the food. Matching accessories and the automatic stirring function of the kitchen machine expediently complement the application options of this high-quality appliance.

Diese funktional gestaltete Küchenmaschine aus Druckguss-Aluminium ist eine leistungsstarke und robuste Produktlösung, die ein gleichzeitiges Kochen und Rühren ermöglicht. Innovativ ist dabei die Kombination aus herkömmlicher Küchenmaschine und zeitgemäßer Induktionskochplatte, denn diese macht ein besonders energiesparendes und schnelles Erhitzen der Speisen möglich. Passendes Zubehör sowie die automatische Rührfunktion der Küchenmaschine ergänzen die Anwendungsbereiche dieses hochwertigen Gerätes sinnvoll.

MCM4200
Compact Kitchen Machine/
Kompakt-Küchenmaschine

BSH Bosch und Siemens Hausgeräte
GmbH, Munich, Germany/München,
Deutschland
In-house design/Werksdesign:
Tobias Krüger, Helmut Kaiser,
Karline Wichert
www.bsh-group.de

This comprehensive compact kitchen
machine combines a space-saving design
concept with a high degree of functionality. In discreet white, the appliance blends
in well with its surroundings, while the
single-button operation with LED backlight allows for continuous adjustment of
the desired operating speed. The kitchen
machine has a high-performance 800-
watt motor and an easy-to-clean surface.
Particularly convenient is the wide range
of accessories, which meet even professional requirements. A high degree of safety
is ensured by the halt mechanism and
the secure lid of the mixing vessel, while
strong suction feet guarantee stability
during operation.

Diese umfangreiche Kompakt-Küchenmaschine verbindet ein platzsparendes
Gestaltungskonzept mit einem hohen Maß
an Funktionalität. Eine dezente Farbgebung in Weiß unterstützt den flexiblen
Einsatz, wobei die Einknebel-Bedienung
mit LED-Beleuchtung eine stufenlose
Einstellung der erwünschten Arbeitsge-
schwindigkeit erlaubt. Die Küchenmaschine wurde mit einem leistungsstarken
800-Watt-Motor und einer pflegeleichten
Oberfläche ausgestattet. Als besonders
komfortabel erweist sich das umfangreiche Zubehör, mit welchem auch professionelle Ansprüche erfüllt werden sollen.
Ein hohes Maß an Sicherheit ermöglichen die Schüssel-Arretierung und die
Deckelsicherung des Mixbechers, zudem
garantieren kräftige Saugfüße eine große
Standfestigkeit.

**Kenwood HB710/714 Triblade
Hand Blender/Stabmixer**

De'Longhi Deutschland GmbH,
Seligenstadt, Germany/Deutschland
In-house design/Werksdesign
www.kenwoodworld.com

This 700-watt hand blender features an innovative three-winged knife. The stringent design especially enhances two details: the light-dark colour contrast harmoniously corresponds with the curved contours of the handle. Due to the continuation of the gripping surface the brand name is framed in an eye-catching way. The blender can be similarly used at home and in professional kitchens thus offering many possible applications and comfortable handling. It features an extensive package of component parts including a masher with extra wide foot, an egg whip and a shaker.

Dieser 700-Watt-Stabmixer ist ausgestattet mit einem innovativen 3-Flügel-Messer. Eine stringente Gestaltung hebt vor allem zwei Details hervor: Ein Farbkontrast von Hell und Dunkel korrespondiert harmonisch mit den geschwungenen Konturen des Griffs. Durch die Fortsetzung der Grifffläche wird der Markenname aufmerksamkeitsstark umrahmt. Gleichermaßen in Heim- und Profiküchen einsetzbar, bietet der Mixer vielseitige Einsatzmöglichkeiten, eine komfortable Handhabung sowie ein umfangreiches Zubehörpaket inklusive eines Pürierstabs mit extrabreitem Fuß, eines Schneebesens sowie eines Mixbechers.

**SCF870
Steamer and Blender/
Dampfgarer und Mixer**

Royal Philips Electronics, Eindhoven, NL
In-house design/Werksdesign:
Stefano Marzano + Design Team
www.philips.com/design

As a combined steamer and blender, this kitchen appliance offers an innovative functionality designed in particular for the fresh and hygienic preparation of healthy baby and children's food. Featuring the colours white and light green, the appliance has a natural and appealing look, while its more functional form rounds off the classic overall appearance. An intuitive knob allows to switch between the steam and blend functions.

Als kombinierter Dampfgarer und Mixer bietet dieses praktische Küchengerät eine innovative Funktionalität und soll vor allem der frischen und hygienischen Zubereitung gesunder Baby- und Kindernahrung dienen. Durch seine Farbgebung in Weiß und Hellgrün wirkt das Gerät natürlich und emotional ansprechend, seine rein funktional ausgerichtete Formgebung rundet das zeitlose Gesamtbild harmonisch ab. Ein intuitiv zu bedienender Drehknopf erlaubt die Wahl zwischen den beiden Gerätefunktionen.

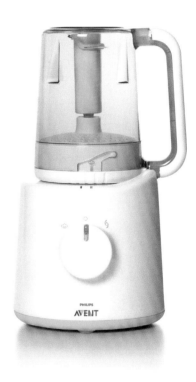

**Robust Collection
Kitchen Appliances/Küchengeräte**

Royal Philips Electronics, Eindhoven, NL
In-house design/Werksdesign:
Stefano Marzano + Design Team
www.philips.com/design

This product line was created with the goal to design a robust and user-friendly range of kitchen appliances. The design is informed by a harmonious material mix of anthracite-coloured plastic and matt polished stainless steel. The discreet form and the high-quality selection of materials provide for a long life cycle. The five kitchen appliances offer comfortable use and were designed according to ergonomic principles.

Mit der Zielsetzung, eine zugleich robuste wie nutzerfreundliche Kollektion von Küchengeräten zu konzipieren, entstand diese Produktlinie. Das Gestaltungskonzept wird durch einen harmonischen Materialmix aus anthrazitfarbenem Kunststoff und matt poliertem Edelstahl geprägt. Sowohl die dezent ausgerichtete Formgebung wie auch die hochwertige Materialauswahl visualisieren ein hohes Maß an Langlebigkeit. Die fünf Küchengeräte bieten eine komfortable Handhabung und wurden nach ergonomischen Gesichtspunkten gefertigt.

Edgeware Mandoline Elite
Mandoline Slicer / Küchenhobel

Smith's Edge, Hot Springs, USA
In-house design / Werksdesign
www.smithsedge.com

The Edgeware Mandoline Elite is a high-performance mandoline slicer made from cast aluminium. Its patent-pending functions offer comfortable handling, while the simple turn of a knob allows for the continuous adjustment of the cutting depth, from paper-thin to 9.5 mm. The selected setting stays in place without the need for an additional lock mechanism. V-shaped cutting edges made from German Solingen steel easily cut precise slices and allow for the slicing of even the most delicate and soft fruits and vegetables.

Edgeware Mandoline Elite ist ein leistungs-starker Küchenhobel aus gegossenem Aluminium. Seine zum Patent angemel-deten Funktionen bieten eine komforta-ble Handhabung, wobei die Schnitttiefe durch eine einfache Drehung des Knopfes stufenlos von hauchdünn bis zu 9,5 mm eingestellt werden kann. Die gewählte Einstellung bleibt dabei ohne Verriegelung bestehen. V-förmige Klingen, gefertigt aus Solinger Stahl, schneiden präzise Scheiben und erlauben sogar die Verarbeitung von zartem, weichem Obst oder Gemüse.

**KE0701 Electronic Kettle/
Elektronischer Wasserkocher**

Crastal Enterprise Group Co. Limited,
Shenzhen, China
In-house design/Werksdesign:
George Mohan Zhang, Xiaohong Li
www.crastal.com

This electronic kettle unites high usability and a discreet style. Elegant lines visually enhance the interaction of high-quality materials. A matt polished stainless steel ring gives the lid a prominent position above the elegantly manufactured plastic material of the other parts of the appliance. The casing is optionally kept in black or white and features a slim viewing window on the left side indicating the water fill level. In addition, it is colour illuminated during operation so that cold water is shown in blue and hot water in red. The easy-to-read LED display at the upper handle bar shows the exact water temperature and is an asset when preparing tea. The push buttons can be quickly and intuitively operated making the use of this kettle very easy and comfortable.

Dieser elektronische Wasserkocher vereint einen hohen Gebrauchswert mit einer dezenten Formensprache. Durch eine elegante Linienführung wird insbesondere das Zusammenspiel der hochwertigen Materialien visuell unterstützt. Der Deckel setzt sich durch einen matt polierten Edelstahlring vom elegant verarbeiteten Kunststoff des übrigen Gerätekorpus ab. Das wahlweise in Schwarz oder Weiß gehaltene Gehäuse verfügt an der linken Seite über ein schmales Sichtfenster, welches den Wasserfüllstand anzeigt. Darüber hinaus wird es während des Betriebs farblich illuminiert, sodass kaltes Wasser mit Blau und heißes Wasser mit Rot markiert wird. Das gut lesbare LED-Display in der oberen Griffleiste zeigt die exakte Temperatur des Wassers an, was bei der Zubereitung von Tee nützlich ist. Schnell und intuitiv zu bedienende Drucktasten machen die Anwendung des Wasserkochers komfortabel und nutzerorientiert.

Personal Warm & Cool Mist Humidifier/Luftbefeuchter

South Asia International (HK) Ltd.,
Hong Kong
In-house design/Werksdesign:
Raymond Hoi Tak Lam
www.sai.com.hk

The sturdy body of this device made of synthetic material hides a humidifier that optionally nebulises warm or cool damp air. The neutral white and light blue colouring allows inconspicuous use at home or in the office. Whenever the need arises the user will obtain optimum humidity of ambient air, which is beneficial to the respiratory system, skin and also to furniture. The water tank was built for continuous operation and is easy to refill and clean.

In diesem kompakten Gerätekorpus aus Kunststoff verbirgt sich ein Luftbefeuchter, der optional warme oder kalte Feuchtluft ausgibt. Die neutrale Farbgebung in Weiß und Hellblau ermöglicht einen unauffälligen Einsatz in privaten oder gewerblichen Räumen. Somit kann der Benutzer, wo immer Bedarf besteht, eine für Atemwege, Haut und Möbel optimale Raumluftfeuchtigkeit erzielen. Der leicht zu befüllende Wassertank wurde für einen dauerhaften Betrieb konstruiert und lässt sich unkompliziert reinigen.

ZTD95 EAST V Sterilizer

Ningbo Oulin Kitchen Utensils Co. Ltd.,
Ningbo, China
In-house design/Werksdesign:
Qi Dong, Hao Chen
www.oulin.com

This sterilizer combines innovative technology with an elegant appearance. The compact built-in unit features two spacious drawer compartments that can be used flexibly. The appliance disinfects with ozone and ultraviolet radiation; in addition, a PTC system is used for drying the dishes. The overall appearance is characterised by the elegantly coloured glass surfaces. Minimalist recessed aluminium grips that are flush integrated, form a charming contrast to the black drawer front. The LED display was elaborated in filigree design and allows intuitive operation by means of a touch sensor technology. Inside the appliance there are detachable grid inserts, which facilitate thorough cleaning.

Dieser Sterilizer verbindet eine innovative Technologie mit einem eleganten Erscheinungsbild. Das kompakte Einbaugerät bietet zwei geräumige Schubladenfächer, die flexibel genutzt werden können. Desinfiziert wird sowohl mittels Ozon als auch durch ultraviolette Bestrahlung, zudem wird ein PTC-System zum Trocknen des Geschirrs eingesetzt. Das Gesamtbild wird von den elegant getönten Glasoberflächen geprägt. Minimalistische Griffmulden aus Aluminium, welche flächenbündig integriert wurden, bilden dabei einen reizvollen Kontrast zur schwarzen Schubladenfront. Das filigran ausgearbeitete LED-Display ermöglicht eine intuitive Bedienung per Touch-Sensorik. Im Geräteinneren erleichtern herausnehmbare Gittereinsätze eine gründliche Reinigung.

Feller Guss-Sortiment
Schalter und Steckdosen/
Switches and Sockets

Feller AG, Horgen, Switzerland/Schweiz
In-house design/Werksdesign:
Cornelia Högger
www.feller.ch

An unconventional choice of material
gives the robust switches and sockets of
this range an extravagant appearance. The
shining aluminium surface stands out from
all surroundings and is supposed to attract
attention. The ball-polished structure of the
material surface communicates a coarse-
grained appearance. Its timeless aesthetics
makes it suitable for the use in commercial
and private rooms. Distinct lines and design
details such as clearly visible screws add a
playful air.

Eine unkonventionelle Materialwahl
verleiht den robusten Schaltern und
Steckdosen dieser Serie ein extravagantes
Erscheinungsbild. Die glänzende Aluguss-
oberfläche soll eine hohe Aufmerksamkeit
erzielen und sticht aus jedem Umfeld
hervor. Kugelpoliert wirkt die Struktur
der Materialoberfläche grobkörnig und
eignet sich in ihrer zeitlosen Ästhetik für
den Einsatz in gewerblichen wie auch privaten Räumen. Eine klare Linienführung
und Gestaltungsdetails wie gut sichtbare
Schrauben verleihen einen verspielten
Akzent.

ModKat Litter Box/Katzentoilette

ModProducts, New York, USA
Design: ModProducts (Rich Williams,
Brett Teper), New York, USA
www.modproducts.net

This interesting litter box is aesthetically
enhanced by a harmonious form and
design concept. The box can individually
be chosen in five pleasing colours, so that
it corresponds with different interiors. The
top entry lid allows for a fully enclosed box
design that is intended to offer cats more
privacy. In addition, the top entry acts as
a litter catcher so the litter stays inside
the box. There are further well-conceived
design details like a non-skid surface
and an oversized entryway. Thanks to the
removable lid and a functionally advanced
scoop the timeless product can be easily and
thoroughly cleaned. After use the scoop can
be stored at the rim of the box.

Diese interessante Katzentoilette wird
durch ein harmonisches Form- und Farbkonzept ästhetisch aufgewertet. In fünf
gefälligen Farben erhältlich, lässt sich
das Behältnis passend zur jeweiligen
Raumausstattung individuell auswählen.
Der Deckel mit Öffnung gibt dem Gefäß
eine geschlossene Form, die Katzen mehr
Privatsphäre bieten soll. Zusätzlich ist die
Öffnung so gestaltet, dass die Fäkalien in
der Box bleiben. Weitere, gut durchdachte
Gestaltungsdetails sind eine rutschfeste
Oberfläche und eine große Einstiegsluke.
Das zeitlose Produkt lässt sich durch den
abnehmbaren Deckel und eine funktional
ausgereifte Kelle komfortabel und gründ-
lich reinigen. Nach dem Gebrauch kann
die Kelle am Gefäßrand befestigt werden.

WM05
Food Waste Treatment System /
Lebensmittel–Abfallaufbereiter

Woongjin Coway Co., Ltd., Seoul, Korea
In-house design / Werksdesign:
Hun-Jung Choi, Jin-Gyu Seo
www.coway.co.kr

Organic food waste is dried in this modern
waste treatment system and then ground to
odourless powder. The substance resembles
coffee powder and can be reused as rich
fertiliser for flowers in pots or beds. The
innovative food waste treatment system
needs approximately three hours to converse
the waste thereby reducing the food waste
up to 1/10. Moreover, a powerful filter
eliminates the odours produced during
the drying process. The two-colour device
features a childproof lock that automatically
stops the disintegration process as soon as
the feeder lid or the receiver is opened.

Organische Lebensmittelreste werden
in diesem zeitgemäßen Abfallsystem
getrocknet und zu einem geruchlosen Pul-
ver zermahlen. Die Kaffeepulver ähnelnde
Substanz kann anschließend als gehalt-
reiches Düngemittel für Blumentöpfe
oder Beete wiederverwertet werden. Der
innovative Lebensmittel-Abfallaufbereiter
benötigt für die Abfallumwandlung etwa
drei Stunden, wobei die Lebensmittelreste
bis zu 1/10 verkleinert werden. Zudem
werden die beim Trocknungsprozess entstehenden Gerüche mittels eines leistungsstarken Filters beseitigt. Das zweifarbig
gestaltete Gerät verfügt über eine Kinder-
sicherung, die den Zerkleinerungsprozess
automatisch stoppt, sobald die Füllklappe
oder die Auffangschublade geöffnet werden.

VSH–05B
Vaporizing sterilization
humidifier / Dampfluftbefeuchter
mit Sterilisationsfunktion

Tong Yang Magic Co., Ltd., Seoul, Korea
In-house design / Werksdesign:
Jong Yoon Yu, Seung Ho Kim
www.magic.co.kr

Featuring aesthetic and discreet lines,
this humidifier blends in well with its
surroundings. With drastically streamlined
dimensions, this narrow, compact machine is
30 per cent smaller than comparable product
solutions. A high-performance air filter
cleans the ambient air with water, providing
for the lasting sterilization of the indoor
air. This significantly improves the quality
of the air, while water particles from the
natural vaporization process also humidify
the ambient air up to an optimal humidity of
between 40 and 60 per cent. The propagation
of bacteria is prevented with the use of
residual chlorine. For hygienic operation,
the device needs to be cleaned only once a
week. Maintenance is extremely reduced by
allowing for the removal of dust particles
and harmful gases without a filter change.

Mit seiner ästhetischen und zugleich
dezenten Linienführung fügt sich dieser
Luftbefeuchter harmonisch in das jeweilige Umfeld ein. Das schmale Kompakt-
gerät wurde in seinen Ausmaßen so stark
reduziert, dass es um 30 Prozent kleiner
ist als vergleichbare Produktlösungen.
Ausgestattet mit einem leistungsfähigen
Luftfilter reinigt der Luftbefeuchter die
Raumluft mit Wasser. Eine dauerhafte Sterilisationsfunktion soll dabei die Innen-
raumluft entscheidend verbessern, zudem
feuchten Partikel aus der natürlichen
Verdampfung die Raumluft auf eine optimale Luftfeuchtigkeit zwischen 40 und 60
Prozent an. Das Problem der möglichen
Vermehrung von Bakterien wurde mit
Restchlor gelöst, für einen hygienischen
Betrieb braucht das Gerät nur einmal in
der Woche gereinigt zu werden. Der Wartungsaufwand wurde auf ein Minimum
begrenzt, da Flugstaub und Schadgase
ohne Austausch der Filter entfernt werden
können.

Hackman Outdoor
Cooking Range/Kochserie

Fiskars Home, Hackman Cookware and
Cutlery, Helsinki, Finland/Finnland
Design: Pentagon Design Ltd.
(Sauli Suomela, Arni Aromaa), Helsinki,
Finland/Finnland
www.hackman.fi
www.pentagondesign.fi

This fold-out trolley cart has been conceived
as an outdoor range with accessories to
prepare, transport and serve dishes in the
open air. But it can also be used at home
all year round. Hard anodised aluminium
and contrasting colours create a dynamic
impression. The manifold accessories
range from a large steel spatula to storage
containers and dressing bottles made of
plastics to a pan with a lid that can also be
used as a tray.

Als Outdoor-Serie wurde dieser ausklappbare Handwagen samt Zubehör für die
Zubereitung, den Transport und das Servieren von Gerichten im Freien konzipiert,
er kann jedoch ganzjährig auch im Haus
eingesetzt werden. Hart eloxiertes Aluminium und kontrastreiche Farben erzeugen
ein dynamisches Erscheinungsbild. Die
vielfältigen Zubehör-Komponenten reichen vom großen Pfannenwender aus
Stahl über Aufbewahrungsdosen und
Sauce-Flaschen aus Kunststoff bis hin zu
einer Pfanne mit einem Deckel, der auch
als Servierbrett einsetzbar ist.

Profi EcoPerfect
Floor Wiper/Bodenwischer

Leifheit AG, Nassau/Lahn,
Germany/Deutschland
In-house design/Werksdesign
www.leifheit.com

The design concept of this floor wiper unites functionality and sustainability. Therefore, the Profi EcoPerfect is made of recycled or renewable materials. A robust bamboo stick that is complemented by elements made of plastic material dominates its appearance. The base plate with a wipe width of 42 cm can be easily opened by a foot pedal. Thanks to this design feature it is no longer necessary to put your hands in dirty water because the Profi EcoPerfect can be comfortably wrung in the wipe press.

Das Gestaltungskonzept dieses Bodenwischers verbindet Funktionalität mit einem Nachhaltigkeitsanspruch. Daher besteht der Profi EcoPerfect aus Materialien, die aus recycelten oder nachwachsenden Rohstoffen stammen. Sein Erscheinungsbild wird von einem stabilen Bambusstiel dominiert, der mit Kunststoffelementen ergänzt wird. Die Bodenplatte mit einer Wischtuchbreite von 42 cm lässt sich komfortabel über ein Fußpedal öffnen. Auf diese Weise geraten die Hände nicht mehr ins Schmutzwasser, denn der Bodenwischer Profi EcoPerfect kann bequem in der Wischtuchpresse ausgepresst werden.

BSGL5Pro1
Vacuum Cleaner/Staubsauger

BSH Bosch und Siemens Hausgeräte GmbH, Munich, Germany/München, Deutschland
In-house design/Werksdesign:
Jörg Schröter, Helmut Kaiser
www.bsh-group.de

This visually appealing compact vacuum cleaner comes with a particularly long vacuum cord. Four jointed metal castors and a 360-degree ball joint ensure good mobility. With an operating radius of 15 metres it is also suitable for professional use. Efficient impact protection is provided by the lateral AirBumper Protection System with its buffering air cushions. The Long-Life Compressor motor and the Air Flow Control System ensure maximum vacuum performance and clean air output. Further added value is provided by the noise-optimised roll nozzle, the robust fabric hose and the wide range of accessories.

Dieser visuell ansprechende Kompaktstaubsauger wurde mit einem besonders langen Staubsaugerkabel ausgestattet. Darüber hinaus ermöglichen vier Echtmetall-Lenkrollen und ein 360-Grad-Kugelgelenk eine gute Beweglichkeit. Mit einem Aktionsradius von 15 Metern wird das Gerät auch professionellen Ansprüchen gerecht. Für einen effizienten Aufprallschutz sorgt das seitliche AirBumper Protection System mit seinen abfedernden Luftpolstern. Der Long-Life Compressor-Motor sowie das Air Flow Control System gewähren eine maximierte Saugleistung bei sauberer Ausblasluft. Als weitere Gestaltungsdetails erhöhen die geräuschoptimierte Rollendüse, der robuste Gewebeschlauch und das umfangreiche Zubehör den Gebrauchswert.

Vacuum Cleaner Accessory/ Staubsauger-Zubehör

Vorwerk Elektrowerke GmbH & Co. KG,
Wuppertal, Germany/Deutschland
In-house design/Werksdesign:
Uwe Kemker
www.vorwerk.de

This functional vacuum cleaner accessory can be widely used. Its flexibly applicable components follow a consistent colour concept featuring a striking change of matt and glossy surfaces. This soft nozzle ensures high functionality as its bristles are arranged like a fan. They can be varied as needed and adapted to different working areas. The soft nozzle is complemented by a flexo nozzle, vario nozzle, drill dust nozzle, crevice nozzle, and a telescopic tube.

Dieses funktional gestaltete Staubsauger-Zubehör findet einen breiten Anwendungsbereich. Seine flexibel einsetzbaren Bestandteile folgen einem einheitlichen Farbkonzept, wobei der Wechsel zwischen mattierten und glänzenden Oberflächen auffällt. Eine hohe Funktionalität bietet diese Softdüse durch ihre fächerartig angeordneten Borsten, welche bedarfsgerecht in der Länge variieren und sich so unterschiedlichen Arbeitsbereichen anpassen. Die Softdüse wird ergänzt durch eine Flexodüse, eine Variodüse, eine Bohrstaubdüse, eine Fugendüse sowie ein Teleskoprohr.

BGS6Pro1
Vacuum Cleaner/Staubsauger

BSH Bosch und Siemens Hausgeräte
GmbH, Munich, Germany/München,
Deutschland
In-house design/Werksdesign:
Daniel Dockner, Helmut Kaiser
www.bsh-group.de

This bagless vacuum cleaner is compact-built and follows an appealing colour concept. The form and function of its rounded body and accessories are of an individual design. The strong vacuum performance can even pick up sawdust, sand or straw. The RobustAir System with its Long-Life Compressor motor, optimised airflow and intelligent cleaning system provides maximum effectiveness and clean air output. As soon as the performance wanes, the filter-cleaning mechanism is automatically activated. Four robust metal castors, a scratch-resistant titanium finish and a highly durable fabric hose make this vacuum cleaner suitable for home and for professional use.

Dieser beutellose Staubsauger wurde kompakt konstruiert und folgt einem ansprechenden Farbkonzept. Sowohl der abgerundete Korpus als auch die Zubehorteile sind formal wie funktional eigenständig gestaltet. Eine starke Saugleistung nimmt selbst Sägespäne, Sand oder Stroh zuverlässig auf. Das RobustAir System, bestehend aus einem Long-Life Compressor-Motor, einer optimierten Luftführung und einem intelligenten Reinigungssystem, sorgt für maximale Effektivität bei sauberer Ausblasluft. Sobald die Leistung abnimmt, wird automatisch die Filterreinigung aktiviert. Vier robuste Echtmetall-Lenkrollen, eine kratzunempfindliche Titanium-Lackierung und ein Gewebeschlauch für höchste Beanspruchung sollen auch professionellen Anforderungen gerecht werden.

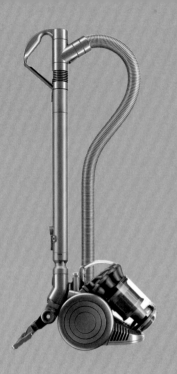

Dyson City DC26 Allergy
Vacuum Cleaner / Staubsauger

Dyson GmbH, Cologne,
Germany / Köln, Deutschland
In-house design / Werksdesign:
James Dyson
www.dyson.de

With its eye-catching colours the Dyson City DC26 Allergy is a compact cylinder vacuum cleaner that has been developed for small-spaced living conditions. Even though it fits on a sheet of DIN A4 paper it still delivers the performance of a full-size vacuum cleaner. During the minimisation process all 275 parts of the appliance were analysed and advanced with regard to size, weight, functionality and robustness. Furthermore, the patented Root Cyclone technology was compressed ensuring very high power output and low energy consumption.

Als kompakter Bodenstaubsauger wurde der farblich auffallende Dyson City DC26 Allergy für kleine Wohnverhältnisse entwickelt. Er passt auf ein DIN-A4-Blatt und verfügt dennoch über die Leistungsstärke eines großen Staubsaugers. Im Prozess der Minimierung wurden alle 275 Teile des Geräts analysiert und unter besonderer Berücksichtigung von Größe, Gewicht, Funktionalität und Robustheit neu entwickelt. Auch die patentierte Root Cyclone-Technologie wurde komprimiert und gewährleistet eine sehr hohe Leistungskraft bei geringem Energieverbrauch.

BSGL51300
Vacuum Cleaner / Staubsauger

BSH Bosch und Siemens Hausgeräte GmbH, Munich, Germany / München, Deutschland
In-house design / Werksdesign:
Jörg Schröter, Helmut Kaiser
www.bsh-group.de

This vacuum cleaner was designed to be user-friendly, compact and visually appealing. Its distinctive look supports the professional functionality of the appliance. High mobility is provided by four jointed castors and the patented 360-degree ball joint that can turn in all directions. An extra-long vacuum cord moreover allows for an operating radius of 15 metres. The laterally integrated AirBumper Protection System with buffering air cushions guarantees efficient and streak-free impact protection. An energy-efficient and quiet Long-Life Compressor motor and the Air Flow Control System ensure maximum performance and clean air output.

Nutzerfreundlich kompakt und visuell ansprechend wurde dieser Staubsauger gestaltet. Sein prägnantes Erscheinungsbild unterstützt die professionelle Funktionalität des Geräts. Für eine hohe Beweglichkeit sorgen vier Lenkrollen und das patentierte 360-Grad-Kugelgelenk, welches sich in alle Richtungen drehen lässt. Ein auffallend langes Staubsaugerkabel ermöglicht darüber hinaus, einen Aktionsradius von 15 Metern problemlos zu reinigen. Das seitlich integrierte AirBumper Protection System mit abfedernden Luftpolstern garantiert einen effizienten und streifenfreien Aufprallschutz. Bei niedrigem Energieeinsatz sorgen ein leiser Long-Life Compressor-Motor sowie das Air Flow Control System für maximale Leistung und saubere Ausblasluft.

VC-PS300X
Vacuum Cleaner / Staubsauger

Toshiba Home Appliances Corporation,
Tokyo, Japan
In-house design / Werksdesign:
Takashi Gumisawa,
Tomoyoshi Nakamura
www.toshiba.co.jp/living

This compact vacuum cleaner was designed with regard to the confined apartment conditions in Japan. The objective was to obtain a particularly space-saving housing structure. In addition, importance was attached to comparatively high manoeuvrability. Centrally arranged wheels of a remarkable large diameter strikingly emphasise the shape of the device and permit fast changes of direction and rotations. Furthermore, the harmoniously rounded housing contours cushion undesired collisions with furniture. An appealing material mix of plastics and stainless steel visually enhance distinctive design elements such as the stable handle bar. The housing structure was designed by reducing the large-size appliances that are customary in this sector of industry. The high-capacity canister vacuum cleaner features an innovative motor suspension reducing the emerging vibrations by 90 per cent and the noise development of the exhaust air to 47 decibel.

Bei diesem kompakten Staubsauger wurden die engen Wohnverhältnisse in Japan berücksichtigt und eine besonders platzsparende Gehäusestruktur angestrebt. Zudem wurde auf eine vergleichsweise hohe Wendigkeit Wert gelegt. Demzufolge prägen zentral angeordnete Räder mit einem auffallend großen Durchmesser die aufmerksamkeitsstarke Formensprache des Geräts. Die großen Räder machen schnelle Richtungswechsel und Drehungen möglich, zudem dämpfen die harmonisch abgerundeten Gehäusekonturen unerwünschte Kollisionen mit Möbelstücken. Im reizvollen Materialmix aus Kunststoff und Edelstahl werden markante Gestaltungselemente wie die stabile Griffleiste visuell hervorgehoben. Hinsichtlich der Gerätestruktur wurden die branchenüblichen Ausführungen großformatiger Geräte aufgegriffen und komprimiert. Der leistungsfähige Bodenstaubsauger verfügt über eine innovative Motoraufhängung, wodurch die Vibrationen um 90 Prozent und die Geräuschentwicklung der Abluft auf 47 Dezibel reduziert werden konnten.

TA-FVX83
Cordless Iron /
Schnurloses Bügeleisen

Toshiba Home Appliances Corporation,
Tokyo, Japan
In-house design / Werksdesign:
Satoshi Uchida
www.toshiba.co.jp/living

A striking colour design showcases the modern comfortable user-friendliness of this cordless iron. The blue or magenta casing of acrylic glass has a translucent appearance and provides an insight into the interior of the device. The harmoniously rounded shape conveys a feeling of dynamics and underlines its outstanding gliding ability that facilitates the ironing procedure. Without a cord the iron can be moved quickly and flexibly over textiles. Additional functional details like a powerful steam jet smooth even persistent wrinkles in one step. To eliminate the development of odours of damp clothes the device was equipped with a disinfection and deodorising function that neutralises unpleasant odours. Besides, an open handle improves the grip and handling of the iron.

Mit einem auffallenden Farbkonzept inszeniert dieses schnurlose Bügeleisen seine zeitgemäß komfortable Bedienfreundlichkeit. Das Plexiglasgehäuse in Blau und Magenta wirkt transparent und erlaubt Einblicke ins Geräteinnere. Die harmonisch abgerundete Formgebung vermittelt ein Gefühl von Dynamik und unterstreicht die außerordentliche Gleitfähigkeit, die den Bügelvorgang erleichtert. Schnurlos lässt sich das Bügeleisen schnell und flexibel über die Textilien führen. Weitere funktionelle Details wie ein kraftvoller Dampfstrahl glätten dabei auch hartnäckige Falten in einem Arbeitsschritt. Um die Geruchsbildung feuchter Kleidung zu beseitigen, wurde das Gerät mit einer Desinfektions- und Deodorantfunktion ausgestattet, die unangenehme Gerüche neutralisiert. Ein offener Griff verbessert zudem die Griffigkeit und Handhabung des Bügeleisens.

Sensixx B10L
Steam Station / Dampfstation

BSH Bosch und Siemens Hausgeräte GmbH, Munich, Germany / München, Deutschland
In-house design / Werksdesign: Stephanie Porsche, Helmut Kaiser
www.bsh-group.de

This steam station is well balanced with regard to design and functionality, conveying lightness while supporting the high quality standard of the brand. The user-friendly control panel is enhanced with a faceted design. The continuously adjustable steam pressure and the ergonomic design of the compact iron allow for vertical and horizontal use. The Advanced Steam System ensures smooth gliding action and improves steam distribution by means of optimised outlets. The long steam hose can be conveniently stored in an integrated storage compartment, while the automatic switch-off function provides additional safety.

Ausgewogen hinsichtlich Gestaltung und Funktionalität zeigt sich diese Dampfstation. Die formale Gliederung visualisiert Leichtigkeit und unterstützt den hohen Qualitätsanspruch der Marke. Das übersichtlich angeordnete Bedienfeld mit beleuchteten Funktionselementen wird durch eine Facettierung hervorgehoben. Der stufenlos regelbare Dampfdruck und die ergonomische Gestaltung des Kompaktbügeleisens ermöglichen einen sowohl vertikalen als auch horizontalen Einsatz. Schnelles Gleiten garantiert das Advanced Steam System, welches die Dampfverteilung mittels optimierter Austrittsöffnungen verbessert. Für zusätzliche Sicherheit sorgt die Abschaltautomatik. Nach Gebrauch kann der lange Dampfschlauch in einem integrierten Aufbewahrungsfach verstaut werden.

Vaärenta (VWP-KS300G)
Water Purifier / Wasserreiniger

GS SHOP, Seoul, Korea
Design: HaA Design
(Kyoung Boo Hwang, Matt Day),
Emeryville, USA
www.gsshop.com
www.haadesign.com

Vaärenta is a water purifier suited perfectly for the preparation of Asian dishes and beverages. The compact structure of the device addresses the lack of space in traditional Asian kitchens. The minimalist design of this water purifier features harmonious forms: an elongated, anthracite body covered by a shiny white ceramic lid. The swivel faucet allows for the flexible filling of small and large cooking pots, cups and other containers. Instead of the typical cylindrical stream of water, a special nozzle generates a tubular water jet that injects additional carbonic acid to the water. Special light effects serve not only to distinguish between cold and hot water but also to indicate whether carbonic acid is optimally introduced into the water. Moreover, built-in weight sensors activate the dispenser as soon as a container is placed beneath it, allowing for comfortable use with only one hand.

Vaärenta ist ein Wasserreiniger, der speziell auf die Zubereitung von asiatischen Speisen und Getränken zugeschnitten ist. Die kompakte Gerätestruktur berücksichtigt dabei die oftmals engen Platzverhältnisse in traditionellen asiatischen Küchen. Puristisch gestaltet zeigt der Wasserreiniger eine harmonische Formensprache, wobei der längliche, anthrazitfarbene Korpus von einem weiß glänzenden Keramikdeckel abgeschlossen wird. Der schwenkbare Wasserhahn erlaubt das flexible Befüllen von kleinen und großen Kochtöpfen, Tassen und sonstigen Behältnissen. Anstelle eines typischen zylinderförmigen Wasserstromes erzeugt eine Spezialdüse einen röhrenförmigen Wasserstrom, um das Wasser besser mit Kohlensäure zu versetzen. Spezielle Lichteffekte dienen nicht nur der Unterscheidung zwischen kaltem und heißem Wasser, sondern zeigen auch an, ob Kohlensäure optimal dem Wasser beigemischt wird. Zudem aktivieren eingebaute Gewichtssensoren die Wasserzufuhr, sobald ein Behälter gezielt platziert wird und ermöglichen so eine komfortable Bedienung mit nur einer Hand.

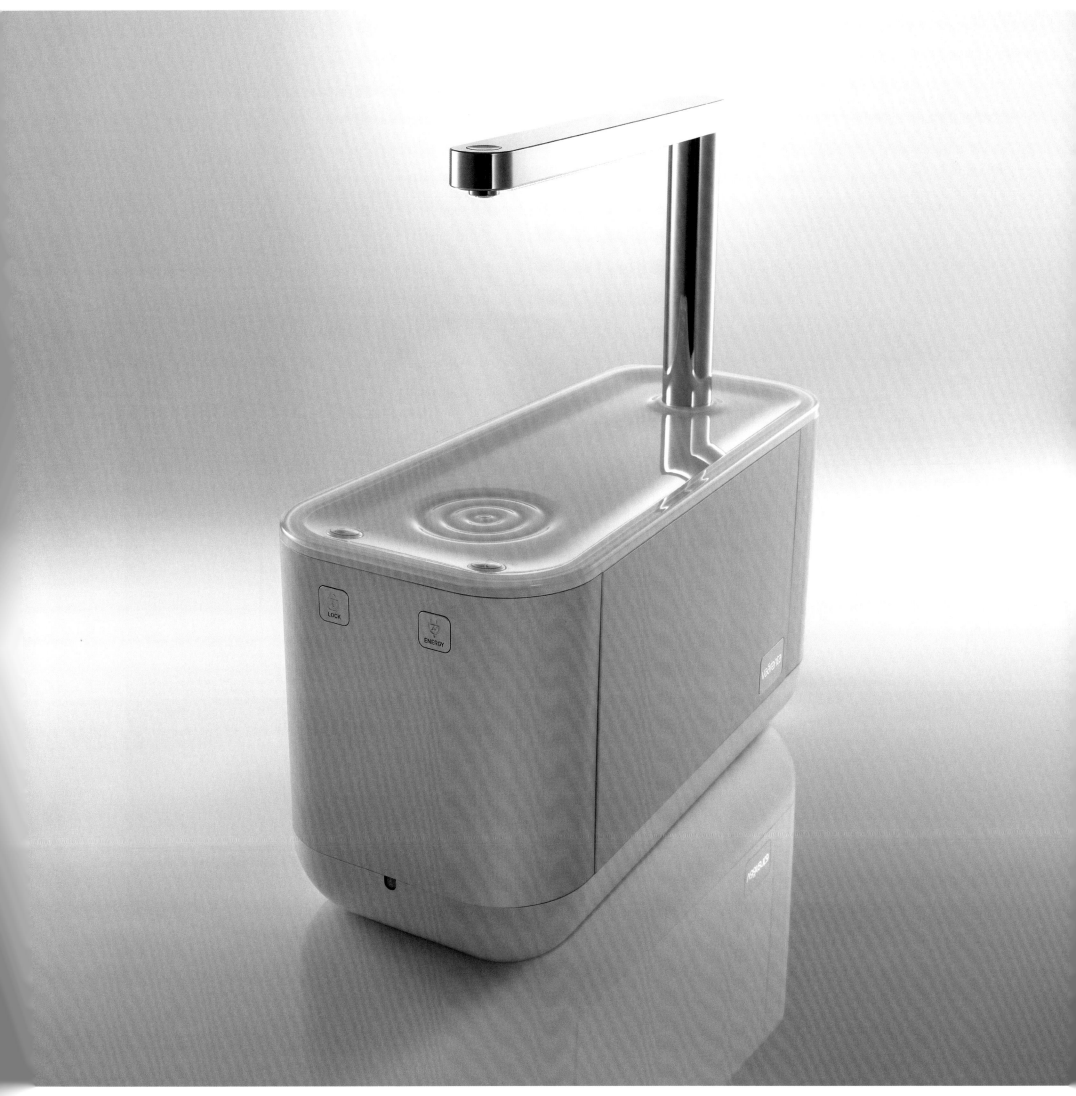

KGN36S53, KGN36S56, KGN36S55
Fridge-Freezer /
Kühl-Gefrier-Kombination

Robert Bosch Hausgeräte GmbH, Munich,
Germany / München, Deutschland
In-house design / Werksdesign:
Ralph Staud, Thomas Tischer
www.bosch-home.com

A frameless glass front informs the attractive
look of this fridge-freezer of the ColorGlass
range that follows the trend to merge kitchen
and living areas. Recessed handles, which are
laterally integrated into metallic profiles, ensure
that nothing distracts from the flat glass surface
of the front. The unit is available in the colours
black, quartz or red. In the interior, glare-free
LED lighting, mirror-finished applications and
telescopic shelves enhance the value of the
appliance.

Eine rahmenlose Glasfront prägt das
ansprechende Erscheinungsbild dieser Kühl-
Gefrier-Kombination der ColorGlass-Reihe,
welche dem Trend zur Verschmelzung von
Küche und Wohnraum gerecht wird. Dezente
Griffe wurden seitlich in Echtmetallprofile
integriert, wodurch nichts von der flächenbündigen Glasoberfläche ablenkt. Erhältlich
ist die Geräteserie in den Farben Schwarz,
Quarzsand und Rot. Im Innenraum unterstreichen eine blendfreie LED-Beleuchtung,
hochglanzgebürstete Applikationen und
Teleskopauszüge die Wertigkeit des Gerätes.

SKE63M05EU
Built-In Dishwasher /
Einbau-Geschirrspüler

Robert Bosch Hausgeräte GmbH, Munich,
Germany / München, Deutschland
In-house design / Werksdesign:
Thomas Ott, Robert Sachon
www.bosch-home.com

The compact built-in dishwasher that was
especially developed for the standard recess
height of 45 cm, features a puristic stainless
steel front. It can be installed below the worktop
or in a kitchen island without pedestal as well
as in a tall cabinet, which offers ergonomic
advantages. In spite of its compact structure,
the dishwasher provides enough space to hold
six standard place settings. The ActiveWater
hydraulic system ensures good cleaning results
and low consumption.

Der speziell für die Standardnischenhöhe
45 cm entwickelte kompakte Einbau-
Geschirrspüler wurde mit einer puristischen
Edelstahlfront versehen. Neben dem ergonomisch vorteilhaften Einbau in einem Hoch-
schrank kann das Gerät auch in einer Nische
unterhalb der Arbeitsfläche oder in einer
sockellosen Kücheninsel eingebaut werden.
Trotz seiner kompakten Bauform bietet der
Geschirrspüler genügend Platz für sechs
Maßgedecke. Das ActiveWater-Hydraulik-
System garantiert gute Reinigungsergebnisse
und niedrige Verbrauchswerte.

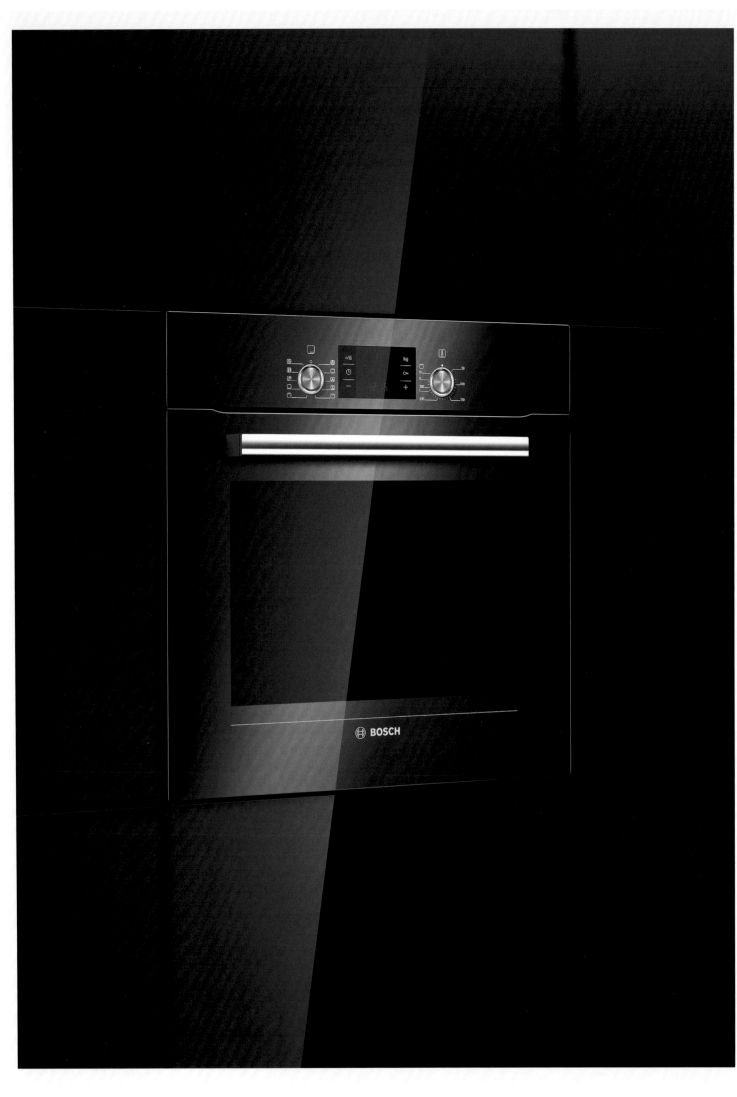

Robert Bosch Hausgeräte GmbH, Munich,
Germany / München, Deutschland
In-house design / Werksdesign:
Robert Sachon, Ulrich Goss,
Bernd Kretschmer
www.bosch-home.com

The premium built-in ovens of this product
series reflect the concept of open kitchens. They
can be harmoniously integrated in a homely
kitchen environment. The glass surface, which
is available in the popular colours white, black
or brown, contrasts with the aesthetically
designed metal elements. A nice brushed finish
additionally enhances these control elements.
Due to the use of modern touch technology all
secondary control elements discreetly blend in
with the background.

Die hochwertigen Einbau-Backöfen dieser Produktserie nehmen das Konzept der
offenen Küche auf und lassen sich harmonisch in ein wohnliches Küchenumfeld
integrieren. Eine optional in den Trendfarben Weiß, Schwarz und Braun erhältliche
Glasoberfläche kontrastiert mit ästhetisch
ausgestalteten Metallelementen. Diese
Bedienelemente werden zudem durch eine
feine Bürstung hervorgehoben. Durch den
Einsatz moderner Touch-Technologie treten
alle sekundären Bedienelemente dezent in
den Hintergrund.

HCE854450
Free-Standing Electric Cooker/
Elektro-Standherd

Robert Bosch Hausgeräte GmbH, Munich,
Germany/München, Deutschland
In-house design/Werksdesign:
Robert Sachon, Alexander Marsch
www.bosch-home.com

By using high-quality materials this free-
standing cooker was interpreted in a new
impressive style. It features state-of-the-art
induction technology, which generates the
heat in the cookware itself thus saving energy.
The glass ceramic cooking surface is durable,
robust and easy to clean. Apart from stainless
steel, much glass has been used at the front
of the appliance in order to visually enhance
the insight into the spacious oven cavity. Flush
retractable control elements and a solid metal
handle underline the value of the appliance.

Die gestalterische Neuinterpretation dieses
Standherds mit zeitgemäßer Induktionstechnologie, bei der die Wärme energieeffizient
direkt im Kochgeschirr erzeugt wird, besticht
durch den Einsatz hochwertiger Materialien.
Die Glaskeramik-Oberfläche der Herdplatte
ist langlebig, robust und gut zu reinigen. An
der Gerätefront wurde neben Edelstahl viel
Glas eingesetzt, um den großzügigen Einblick
in den Backraum visuell zu unterstreichen.
Flächenbündig versenkbare Bedienelemente
sowie ein Vollmetallgriff betonen die Wertigkeit des Gerätes.

Siemens ED 895 RB 90 EU
piano a filo
Gas Hob / Gas-Kochstelle

Siemens-Electrogeräte GmbH, Munich,
Germany / München, Deutschland
In-house design / Werksdesign:
Jörn Ludwig
Design: BSH Bosch und Siemens
Hausgeräte GmbH (Elena Leinmüller),
Munich, Germany / München, Deutschland
www.siemens-hausgeraete.de
www.bsh-group.de

The flush gas hob stands out by its clear design. Thanks to a special frame it is possible to integrate it in stainless steel worktops. In addition, the burner rating of the five cooking zones also meets superior demands.

Die flächenbündige Gas-Kochstelle zeichnet sich durch eine klare Gestaltung und einen speziellen Rahmen aus, wodurch ein planer Einbau in Edelstahlarbeitsplatten möglich wird. Zudem wird die Brennerleistung der fünf Brenner auch gehobenen Ansprüchen gerecht.

Siemens SK 26 E 201 EU
Compact Dishwasher /
Kompakt-Geschirrspüler

Siemens-Electrogeräte GmbH, Munich,
Germany / München, Deutschland
In-house design / Werksdesign:
Wolfgang Kaczmarek
www.siemens-hausgeraete.de

This compact dishwasher provides large interior space. The front display at the base facilitates programme control by means of a rotary knob. Among others the low-noise dishwasher features energy- and time-saving programmes.

Dieser Kompakt-Geschirrspüler bietet einen großen Innenraum. Ein an der Gerätebasis befindliches Frontdisplay erleichtert die Programmsteuerung per Drehknopf. Die geräuscharme Spülmaschine verfügt unter anderem über energie- und zeitsparende Programme.

Siemens SK 26 E 800 EU
Compact Dishwasher /
Kompakt-Geschirrspüler

Siemens-Electrogeräte GmbH, Munich,
Germany / München, Deutschland
In-house design / Werksdesign:
Wolfgang Kaczmarek
www.siemens-hausgeraete.de

With its silver finish this compact dishwasher has a modern distinguished appearance. Its large interior is easy to load and permits water- and energy-saving operation. The unobtrusively illuminated display indicates the particular programme status.

Mit seiner silbernen Oberfläche wirkt dieser Kompakt-Geschirrspüler zeitgemäß und edel. Sein großer Innenraum lässt sich einfach beladen und erlaubt einen wasser- und stromsparenden Betrieb. Das dezent beleuchtete Display zeigt den jeweiligen Programmstatus an.

Siemens KI 38 CP 60
Fridge-Freezer /
Kühl-Gefrier-Kombination

Siemens-Electrogeräte GmbH, Munich,
Germany / München, Deutschland
In-house design / Werksdesign:
Max Eicher, Christoph Becke
www.siemens-hausgeraete.de

This built-in appliance is an energy-efficient
fridge-freezer of the coolConcept series that
can be perfectly integrated in any kitchen
unit. It features an amazing clearly structured
storage space. The model includes a "basement"
compartment, a separate cooling zone and a
spacious freezer compartment, which together
offer optimal storage conditions.

Dieses perfekt in die Küchenzeile zu integrie-
rende Einbaugerät ist eine energiesparsame
Kühl-Gefrier-Kombination der coolConcept-
Reihe und überrascht durch einen übersichtlich strukturierten Stauraum, wobei unter
anderem ein Kellerfach, eine separate Kühl-
zone und ein geräumiges Gefrierfach gute
Lagerbedingungen bieten.

Siemens KI 39 FP 60
Fridge-Freezer /
Kühl-Gefrier-Kombination

Siemens-Electrogeräte GmbH, Munich,
Germany / München, Deutschland
In-house design / Werksdesign:
Max Eicher, Christoph Becke
www.siemens-hausgeraete.de

This fridge-freezer combines an elegant look
with user-friendly features. The space-saving
base-mounted compressor ensures energy-
efficient cooling performance that meets
class A++ requirements. In the interior, the
refrigerator contents can be conveniently stored
in drawers, on a height-adjustable glass shelf, or
in the spacious zero-degree zone.

Diese Kühl-Gefrier-Kombination verbindet
ein elegantes Erscheinungsbild mit nutzerfreundlichen Ausstattungsmerkmalen. Das
platzsparende Sockelaggregat sorgt für eine
energiesparsame Kühlleistung der Geräteklas-
se A++. Im Innenraum lässt sich das Kühlgut
übersichtlich in Auszugsschalen, auf einem
stufenlos höhenverstellbaren Glasfachboden
sowie in einem großzügigen Nullgradbereich
verstauen.

HG9711CB
Gas Hob/Gaskochfeld

ATAG Nederland BV, Duiven, NL
In-house design/Werksdesign
Design: VanBerlo (Marnix Oosterwelder),
Eindhoven, NL
www.atag.nl
www.vanberlo.nl

A flat base and cast-iron pan supports spanning the entire hob give this gas hob an architectural feel. The Easy Flame Control system increases the user comfort: the burners ignite immediately when operated, no need to keep the knob pressed.

Eine flache Grundfläche sowie gusseiserne Topfträger über die gesamte Breite der Mulde verleihen diesem Gaskochfeld eine architektonische Anmutung. Das Easy Flame Control-System erhöht die Nutzerfreundlichkeit: Die Brenner zünden sofort, ohne dass die Knebel eingedrückt gehalten werden müssen.

HI7271S
Induction Hob/Induktionskochfeld

ATAG Nederland BV, Duiven, NL
In-house design/Werksdesign:
Iris Hogervorst
Design: Willemien Brand, Voorburg, NL
www.atag.nl
www.willemienbrand.nl

This induction hob follows a clear graphical design concept and offers ample space for different-sized pots. Circular slider pads (Iris Slide Control) allow for easy and intuitive operation. The feedback is strikingly visualised with red LED lights.

Dieses Induktionskochfeld folgt einem klaren, grafischen Gestaltungskonzept, welches umfangreichen Platz für verschiedene Töpfe bietet. Die intuitive Steuerung über kreisförmige Sliderpads (Iris Slide Control) wird analog zur angewählten Leistung durch rote LEDs markant visualisiert.

QHA93
Gas Hob/Gaskochfeld

Industrial Design Center of Haier Group,
Qingdao, China
In-house design/Werksdesign: Lian Zhen,
Zhu Yuntao, Chi Shasha, Zhang Anchao,
Jin Le
www.haier.com

Visually captivating due to its sweeping lines, this gas hob also features a technical innovation: both burners are equipped with a temperature sensor that automatically extinguishes the flame when it senses that a pot is overheated.

Dieses mit seiner geschwungenen Linienführung ansprechend gestaltete Gaskochfeld birgt eine technische Innovation: Beide Brenner wurden mit einem Temperatursensor ausgestattet, der die Flamme automatisch herunterregelt, sobald der Kochtopf überhitzt.

Belling BI60i Eco Induction Oven
Built-In Oven / Einbau-Backofen

Glen Dimplex Home Appliances,
Liverpool, GB
In-house design / Werksdesign:
Ian Johnstone
www.gdha.com

This built-in oven uses induction technology in a new way. The striking glass and stainless steel front visually emphasises its innovative ambition. Compared to traditional ovens with A rated energy class it consumes 50 per cent less energy. The induction plate integrated in the spacious oven cavity is likewise suitable for slow cooking, roasting, grilling, steaming, fan cooking or baking. The scope of delivery includes a special cast iron pot as well as a steaming and roasting trivet.

Dieser Einbau-Backofen nutzt die Induktionstechnologie auf neuartige Art und Weise, seine markante Glas- und Edelstahlfront unterstützt den innovativen Anspruch visuell. Im Vergleich zu herkömmlichen Backöfen der Energieklasse A verbraucht er 50 Prozent weniger Energie. Die im geräumigen Innenraum integrierte Induktionsplatte eignet sich gleichermaßen zum Garen, Braten, Grillen, Dünsten, Umluftbacken oder Überbacken. Zum Lieferumfang gehören ein spezieller gusseiserner Topf sowie Dünst- und Bratuntersetzer.

AEG HK955420FB
Induction Hob / Induktionskochmulde

Electrolux Home Products Corporation
N.V., Zaventem, Belgium / Belgien
In-house design / Werksdesign
www.electrolux.de

This spacious induction hob of the MaxiSense product range features five cooking zones, which are easy to operate via a centrally positioned slider function. The reduced graphic design characterises the appearance and wants to visually enhance the innovative induction technology.

Diese großzügige Induktionskochmulde der MaxiSense-Baureihe bietet fünf Kochzonen, welche mit einer zentral positionierten Slider-Funktion einfach bedient werden können. Die reduzierte Grafik prägt das Erscheinungsbild und will die innovative Induktionstechnologie visuell unterstreichen.

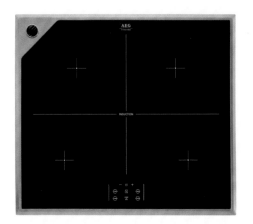

AEG HM634400MB
Ceran Hob / Ceran-Kochmulde

Electrolux Home Products Corporation
N.V., Zaventem, Belgium / Belgien
In-house design / Werksdesign
www.electrolux.de

This Ceran hob has been equipped with innovative heating technologies as well as user and installation advantages. Its design concept focuses on the graphically visualised function display and the different frame designs.

Diese Ceran-Kochmulde wurde mit innovativen Beheizungstechnologien sowie Bedien- und Einbauvorteilen ausgestattet. Ihr Gestaltungskonzept konzentriert sich auf die grafisch visualisierten Funktionsanzeigen und das in unterschiedlichen Varianten erhältliche Rahmendesign.

Built-In Cooker Product Range /
Einbauherd-Produktreihe

Electrolux Home Products Corporation
N.V., Zaventem, Belgium / Belgien
In-house design / Werksdesign
www.electrolux.de

A slightly curved handle bar and the functional design of the operating panel with integrated control elements and indicators underline the characteristic appearance of these built-in cookers. The matching Ceran hobs follow this stylistic language.

Das charakteristische Erscheinungsbild dieser Einbauherde wird durch eine funktionale Gestaltung der Bedienblende mit integrierten Bedien- und Anzeigeelementen sowie eine leicht geschwungene Griffleiste geprägt. Dieser Formensprache folgen auch dazu passende Ceran-Kochmulden.

**AI 280 120 Island Hood /
Insel-Abzugshaube**

Gaggenau Hausgeräte GmbH, Munich,
Germany / München, Deutschland
In-house design / Werksdesign:
Sandor Klunker
www.gaggenau.com

A large radius gives this island hood its
distinctive form at the same time visualising its
essential functional feature. Due to a special
ventilation duct escaping cooking fumes are
effectively extracted already at a low power
level even at the leading edges.

Ein großer Radius gibt dieser Insel-Abzugshaube ihre prägnante Form und visualisiert
zugleich ihr wesentliches Funktionselement.
Aufgrund einer speziellen Luftführung wird
ausbrechender Kochdunst selbst an den Vor-
derkanten bereits auf einer niedrigen Leistungsstufe effektiv abgezogen.

**RS 295 130
Fridge-Freezer /
Kühl-Gefrier-Kombination**

Gaggenau Hausgeräte GmbH, Munich,
Germany / München, Deutschland
In-house design / Werksdesign:
Sebastian Knöll
www.gaggenau.com

Due to its monolithic character, this fridge-
freezer renders a sculptural impression. An easy-
to-clean touch interface controls ice and water
dispensers and the three temperature zones in
the interior where a stepped shelf board allows
for space-saving storage.

Diese Kühl-Gefrier-Kombination wirkt durch
ihren monolithischen Charakter skulptural.
Ein reinigungsfreundliches Touch-Interface
steuert den Eis- und Wasserspender sowie
die drei Temperaturzonen im Innenraum, wo
ein Stufentablar eine platzsparende Lagerung
ermöglicht.

**Backofen-Serie 200 Aluminium
Built-In Ovens / Einbau-Backöfen**

Gaggenau Hausgeräte GmbH, Munich,
Germany / München, Deutschland
In-house design / Werksdesign:
Sven Baacke
www.gaggenau.com

The design vocabulary of this built-in appliance
series is characterised by multiple-glazed,
aluminium-backed doors. A special feature is the
user-friendly LCD function display module at the
top or the bottom of the panel-free door.

Die Formensprache dieser Einbaugeräte-Serie
wird von mehrfach verglasten, mit Aluminium hinterlegten Türen geprägt. Einen Akzent
auf den blendenlosen Türen setzt das einfach
zu handhabende Bedienmodul mit LCD-
Funktionsdisplay am oberen bzw. unteren
Türrand.

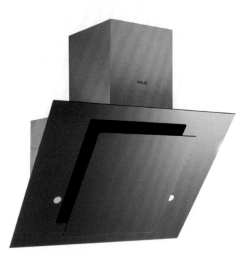

CXW-200-F05 Cooker Hood/
Dunstabzugshaube

Ningbo Oulin Kitchen Utensils Co. Ltd.,
Ningbo, China
In-house design/Werksdesign:
Sheng Sun, Qi Dong
www.oulin.com

The innovative shape of this cooker hood permits an almost flush integration of the low-energy outlet. A material mix of stainless steel and aluminium creates charming contrasts. The programme symbols have been laser engraved.

Eine innovative Formgebung ermöglicht bei dieser Dunstabzugshaube eine fast flächenbündige Integration des energiesparsamen Abzugs. Ein Materialmix aus Edelstahl und Aluminium schafft reizvolle Kontraste, wobei die Programmsymbole per Laser eingraviert wurden.

DGC 5080 XL
Combi Steam Oven/
Kombi-Dampfgarer

Miele & Cie. KG,
Gütersloh, Germany/Deutschland
In-house design/Werksdesign
www.miele.de

This combi steam oven with a useable volume of 39 litres hides a special feature behind the control panel. With a gentle touch of the sensor button the lift panel swings upwards and reveals the view onto the water tank and thermometer. The relocation of the water tank allows the enlargement of the cooking chamber across almost the whole width of the appliance.

Dieser Kombi-Dampfgarer mit einem Nutzvolumen von 39 Litern verbirgt hinter der Bedienblende eine Besonderheit: Eine leichte Berührung der Sensortaste lässt die Liftblende nach oben schwingen und gibt die Sicht auf Wassertank und Thermometer frei. Die Verlagerung des Wassertanks ermöglicht die Verbreiterung des Garraums auf nahezu die gesamte Gerätebreite.

FD1541TS Electric Double Oven/
Doppelstöckiger Backofen

LG Electronics Inc., Seoul, Korea
In-house design/Werksdesign:
Soo-Yeon Kim, Na-Jung Cho,
Kyoung-Ha Lee
www.lge.com

The electric double oven increases the use value of this essential kitchen appliance and allows for the energy-efficient use of a small baking cavity. The robust body made from matt polished stainless steel accentuates the prominent, intuitive dual control & display, which emphasises the comfortable usability of this oven.

Der doppelstöckige Backofen erweitert den Gebrauchswert dieses Küchengeräts und erlaubt optional die energieeffiziente Nutzung eines kleinen Backraums. Der robuste Gerätekorpus aus matt poliertem Edelstahl betont das markante, intuitiv zu bedienende Steuerungs- und Anzeigeelement, das auch die leichte Bedienbarkeit dieses Ofens unterstreicht.

Volcano
Built-In Microwave Oven/ Einbau-Mikrowellenofen

Foshan Shunde Midea Microwave and Electrical Appliances Manufacturing Co., Ltd., Shunde District, Foshan, Guangdong, China
In-house design/Werksdesign: Midea MWO Design Team
www.midea.com.cn

The gloss effect of a polished metal front benefits a distinct design concept with a discreetly illuminated control panel. The elegant overall appearance of this built-in microwave oven is enhanced by the special effect of the darkly oxidised aluminium buttons.

Ein klares Gestaltungskonzept mit einem dezent ausgeleuchteten Bedienfeld nutzt hier vor allem den Glanzeffekt der polierten Metallfront. Aufgewertet wird das elegante Gesamtbild des Einbau-Mikrowellenofens durch die Wirkung dunkel oxidierter Aluminiumknöpfe.

Water Zone Preparing
Fittings and Sinks/ Armaturen und Becken

Aloys F. Dornbracht GmbH & Co. KG Armaturenfabrik,
Iserlohn, Germany/Deutschland
Design: Sieger Design GmbH & Co. KG (Michael Sieger),
Sassenberg, Germany/Deutschland
www.dornbracht.com
www.sieger-design.com

With specially configured fittings and sinks, the Water Zones concept enables various water-related tasks to be separated, also for domestic kitchens. The Water Zone Preparing is well equipped for everything concerning preparation.

Mit speziell konfigurierten Armaturen und Becken ermöglicht das Water Zones-Konzept die Trennung wasserbezogener Arbeitsprozesse, auch für Privatküchen. Die Water Zone Preparing ist für alles gut ausgestattet, was mit der Vorbereitung zu tun hat.

ORGA-LINE
Foil Cutter/Folienschneider

Julius Blum GmbH,
Höchst, Austria/Österreich
Design: Form Orange Produktentwicklung (Wolfgang Held),
Hard, Austria/Österreich
www.blum.com
www.form-orange.com

With this simple foil cutter plastic wraps can be used and conveniently stored as required. During cutting, the wrap is stretched onto both sides of the unit, which reliably prevents the foil from clinging.

Mit Hilfe dieses schlichten Folienschneiders lässt sich Frischhaltefolie komfortabel verstauen und bedarfsgerecht handhaben. Während des Schneidevorgangs wird die Folie an beiden Seiten gespannt, was das Verkleben der Folie zuverlässig verhindert.

O-Touch Sterilizer

Ningbo Fotile Kitchen Ware Co., Ltd.,
Cixi, Ningbo, China
In-house design / Werksdesign
www.fotile.com

The aesthetic appearance of this sterilizer is characterised by a shining glass front in black. Contrasting are the angular stainless steel handle bars. A patented technology enables the appliance to fight automatically against bacteria and odours.

Das ästhetische Erscheinungsbild dieses Sterilizers wird von einer glänzenden Glasfront in Schwarz geprägt. Im Kontrast dazu stehen die eckigen Griffleisten aus Edelstahl. Eine patentierte Technologie ermöglicht eine automatische Bakterien- und Geruchsbekämpfung.

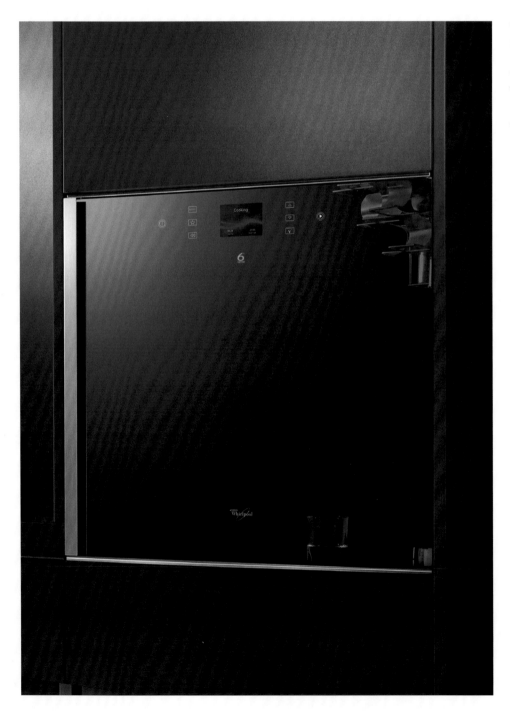

Whirlpool Glamour Oven
Built-In Oven / Einbau-Backofen

Whirlpool Corporation,
Varese, Italy / Italien
In-house design / Werksdesign
www.whirlpool.com

This elegant built-in oven follows a minimalist design. A touch control and a display that is only visible when the appliance is used have been integrated in the full glass door, which is laterally opened. Up to three dishes can be prepared simultaneously and energy-efficiently.

Dieser elegante Einbau-Backofen zeigt eine minimalistische Anmutung. In der seitlich zu öffnenden Vollglastür wurden ein Touch-Bedienfeld und ein Bildschirm integriert, der nur im Betrieb sichtbar ist. Es können bis zu drei Speisen gleichzeitig und energieeffizient zubereitet werden.

Seamless Canvas
Kitchen Surface / Küchenoberfläche

LG Hausys, Design Center, Seoul, Korea
In-house design / Werksdesign:
Gaye Kim, Hwayeon Lee
www.lghausys.com

This futuristic material enables the individual design of kitchen surfaces and follows a stringent design concept based on flowing lines and seamless surfaces. The surfaces of the units thus blend seamlessly into one another. This is made possible with HI-MACS acrylic solid surface – a highly flexible material that offers pleasant tactile qualities, versatile usability and impressive light transparency.

Dieses futuristisch anmutende Material zur individuellen Gestaltung von Küchenoberflächen folgt einem stringenten Gestaltungskonzept der fließenden Linien und nahtlosen Flächen. Entsprechend gehen die Arbeitsflächen fließend ineinander über. Ermöglicht wird dies durch den Einsatz des acrylgebundenen Mineralwerkstoffs HI-MACS. Das hochflexible Material bietet haptisch angenehme Eigenschaften, eine vielfältige Nutzbarkeit und eine effektvolle Lichtdurchlässigkeit.

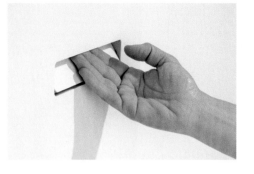

next125
Hidden Recessed Grip/
Flächenbündige Eingriffschale

Schüller Möbelwerk KG,
Herrieden, Germany/Deutschland
In-house design/Werksdesign:
Theo Albrecht, Thomas Pfister
www.next125.de
www.schueller.de

This flush hidden recessed grip supports the homogeneity of contemporary kitchen fronts and reduces the surfaces of cabinets and drawers to their effects of material and form. Made of coloured solid laminate it unobtrusively fits into the front without protrusion. Solely a subtle joint provides orientation. Thus, shape follows pure function – quick access, safe in the hand and hygienically closed. The material is easy to maintain and promises long service life.

Diese flächenbündige Eingriffschale unterstützt die Homogenität zeitgemäßer Küchenfronten und reduziert die Schrank- und Schubladenoberflächen auf ihre Material- und Formwirkung. Gefertigt aus durchgefärbtem Schichtstoff fügt sie sich dezent und ohne Überstände in die Front ein, einzig eine feine Fuge gibt Orientierung. Somit folgt die Form der reinen Funktion – schnell im Zugriff, sicher in der Hand und hygienisch geschlossen. Das Material ist pflegeleicht und verspricht eine lange Lebensdauer.

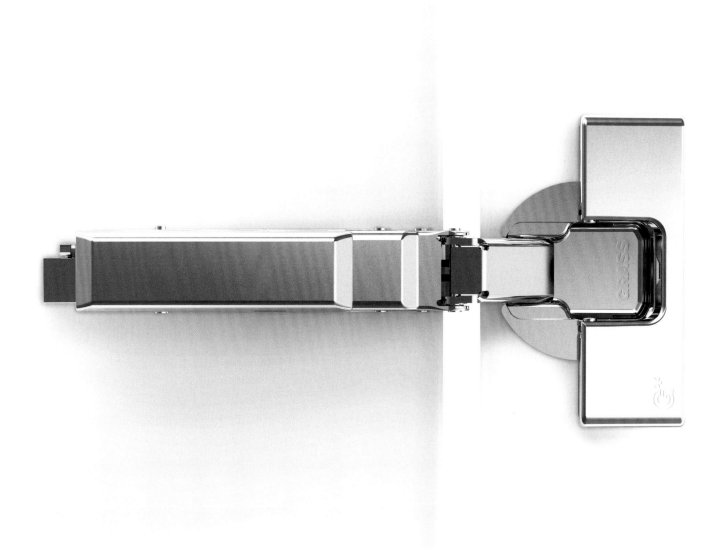

**Tiomos
Hinge System /
Scharnier-System**

Grass GmbH & Co. KG,
Reinheim, Germany / Deutschland
Design: Studio Ambrozus
(Stefan Ambrozus),
Cologne, Germany / Köln, Deutschland
www.grass.at
www.studioambrozus.de

All function details of the Tiomos hinge system have been redeveloped and implemented in a distinct style. A user-friendly detail is the stepwise adjustment of the Soft-close closing damper whose damping technology has been integrated invisibly into the hinge. In each phase of movement the closing process is smooth and without any abrupt transition. Apart from its high stability values, the kinematics of the hinge has the advantage that it is very easy to open furniture doors.

Sämtliche Funktionsdetails des Scharnier-Systems Tiomos wurden neu entwickelt und in einer prägnanten Formensprache umgesetzt. Ein nutzerfreundliches Detail ist die stufenweise regulierbare Schließdämpfung Soft-close, deren Dämpfungstechnologie unsichtbar im Scharnier integriert ist. Der Schließvorgang erfolgt in jeder Bewegungsphase gleichmäßig und übergangslos. Neben den hohen Stabilitätswerten bietet die Kinematik des Scharniers den Vorteil, dass ein sehr leichtes Öffnen der Möbeltüren möglich wird.

allure
Filter Coffee Maker /
Filterkaffeemaschine

Russell Hobbs Deutschland GmbH,
Nuremberg, Germany/Nürnberg,
Deutschland
In-house design/Werksdesign:
Luke Bradshaw
www.russell-hobbs.de
www.russellhobbs.com

The monolithic overall picture of this coffee
maker places the essential design elements in
the foreground. Geometric forms with heavily
chamfered edges as well as a black border
are characteristic elements of the appliance,
whereas the controls are deliberately kept
simple.

Das monolithische Gesamtbild dieser Kaffeemaschine lässt die wesentlichen Gestaltungselemente in den Vordergrund treten. Geometrische Formen mit stark abgeschrägten
Kanten und eine schwarze Einfassung prägen
das Gerät, dessen Bedienelemente betont
puristisch gehalten sind.

KM 5005
Filter Coffee Maker/
Filterkaffeemaschine

Krups GmbH, Offenbach/Main,
Germany/Deutschland
Design: Dahlström Design AB
(Björn Dahlström),
Stockholm, Sweden/Schweden
www.krups.de
www.groupeseb.com
www.dahlstromdesign.se

In a remarkably minimalist way the control panel of this premium filter coffee maker is reduced to only two press buttons. Brushed stainless steel harmoniously matches a black housing whose curved lines reflect the stylistic language of the coffee pot.

Auffallend minimalistisch reduziert sich das Bedienfeld dieser Premium-Filterkaffeemaschine auf nur zwei Druckknöpfe. Gebürsteter Edelstahl fügt sich harmonisch in ein schwarzes Gehäuse ein, dessen gebogene Linienführung die Formensprache der Kaffeekanne widerspiegelt.

KM 5065
Filter Coffee Maker/
Filterkaffeemaschine

Krups GmbH, Offenbach/Main,
Germany/Deutschland
Design: Dahlström Design AB
(Björn Dahlström),
Stockholm, Sweden/Schweden
www.krups.de
www.groupeseb.com
www.dahlstromdesign.se

In this premium filter coffee maker the design language of the stainless steel housing is harmoniously continued to the shape of the glass jug. The ergonomically tilted control panel with LCD display ensures free access to all functions.

Bei dieser Premium-Filterkaffeemaschine mit patentierter Brühtechnologie wird die Formensprache des Edelstahlgehäuses in der Gestaltung der Glaskanne harmonisch fortgeführt. Das ergonomisch angewinkelte Bedienfeld mit LCD-Display bietet einen leichten Zugang zu allen Funktionen.

KM 5055
Filter Coffee Maker/
Filterkaffeemaschine

Krups GmbH, Offenbach/Main,
Germany/Deutschland
Design: Dahlström Design AB
(Björn Dahlström),
Stockholm, Sweden/Schweden
www.krups.de
www.groupeseb.com
www.dahlstromdesign.se

As premium version this filter coffee maker displays an aesthetic appearance matching its user-friendly functionality. The brushed stainless steel control panel dominates the contrasting black housing and visualises multiple programme options.

Als Premiumausführung zeigt diese Filterkaffeemaschine ein ästhetisches Erscheinungsbild, passend zur nutzerfreundlichen Funktionalität: Das Bedienfeld aus gebürstetem Edelstahl dominiert im Kontrast zum schwarzen Gehäuse und visualisiert vielfältige Programmoptionen.

Circolo
Coffee Maker/
Kaffeemaschine

WIK Elektrogeräte,
Essen, Germany/Deutschland
Design: Multiple SA (Pierre Struzka),
La Chaux-de-Fonds, Switzerland/Schweiz
www.wik-service.de
www.multiple-desgin.ch

This coffee maker catches the eye with its unconventional outer contours and organic curves. Emotionally appealing colours complement the persistent implementation of the 360-degree design. The user's attention is drawn to the centrally arranged control panel, which is framed by bright red and black body components. Thanks to its circular design, Circolo blends well with most room interiors, kitchen or not.

Eine unkonventionelle Außenkontur mit organisch anmutenden Rundungen lässt diese Kaffeemaschine auffallen. Die formal konsequente Umsetzung der 360-Grad-Gestaltung wird zudem durch ein emotional ansprechendes Farbkonzept unterstützt. Die Aufmerksamkeit richtet sich auf die zentral angeordneten Bedienelemente, welche durch leuchtend rote und schwarze Korpuselemente eingerahmt sind. Durch die kreisförmige Gestaltung fügt sich Circolo in beinahe jede Umgebung, ob Küche oder Wohnraum, gut ein.

Soup–Server
Soup Dispenser / Suppenautomat

Vendinova, Den Bosch, NL
Design: VanBerlo, Eindhoven, NL
www.vendinova.com
www.vanberlo.nl

The fully automatic Soup-Server was developed for the preparation of fresh soup in the commercial and public sector. The design is based on the idea to visualise the richness and quality of fresh soup. High-quality materials and a distinctive form create a unique identity for the IT-driven appliance, which handles stock and consumption data automatically.

Der vollautomatische Soup-Server wurde für die Zubereitung von frischer Suppe für gewerbliche Zwecke und öffentliche Veranstaltungen entwickelt. Grundlage für die Gestaltung war die Absicht zu zeigen, wie reichhaltig und qualitätsvoll frische Suppen sein können. Der Einsatz von hochwertigen Materialien und die prägnante Form machen das IT-gesteuerte Gerät einzigartig. Vorrats- und Verbrauchsdaten werden automatisch erfasst.

GBF-835
Body Fat Scales/
Körperfettwaage

Transtek Electronics Co., Ltd.,
Zhongshan, China
In-house design/Werksdesign:
Bin Wang
www.transtek.cn

The elegant appearance of these filigree body fat scales is based on the material selection. Correspondingly, the black-tinted glass forms an attractive contrast to the metallic sensors. A blue shining LED display indicates respective data.

Die edle Anmutung dieser filigranen Körper-fettwaage beruht auf der Materialauswahl. Entsprechend bildet das schwarz getönte Glas einen reizvollen Kontrast zu den metall-farbenen Sensoren. Ein blau leuchtendes LED-Display zeigt die jeweiligen Werte an.

MFQ4080
Hand Mixer/Handrührer

BSH Bosch und Siemens Hausgeräte GmbH, Munich, Germany/München, Deutschland
In-house design/Werksdesign:
Tobias Krüger, Helmut Kaiser
Design: Hyve (Gerd Schwarz), Munich, Germany/München, Deutschland
www.bsh-group.de
www.hyve.de

With an elegant form, this hand mixer offers a wide range of uses. The ergonomically optimised handle can be held comfortably in the hand. The state-of-the-art motor is quiet yet powerful, with six speeds to choose from. The clever eject lock offers the convenience of changing accessories quickly.

Elegant in seiner Formensprache erlaubt dieser Handrührer einen breiten Einsatzbe-reich. Der nach ergonomischen Gesichts-punkten optimierte Griff liegt angenehm in der Hand. Kraftvoll und auffallend leise arbeitet der zeitgemäße Motor, wobei sechs Geschwindigkeitsstufen zur Auswahl stehen. Der durchdachte Eject-Verschluss bietet die komfortable Möglichkeit, Zubehör schnell zu wechseln.

Sudster™ Kitchen Cleaning Tools/ Küchen-Reinigungstools

Chef'n Corp, Seattle, USA
In-house design/Werksdesign: Chef'n
In-house Design Team (Adam Jossem,
Jonah Griffith, Matt Krus, Dave Hull,
David Holcomb)
www.chefn.com

The design idea behind this set of cleaning tools for various purposes is to combine the cleaning of dishes with a certain fun factor. Next to ergonomically designed round handles, trendy colour accents are employed.

Die Gestaltungsidee dieser auf unterschiedliche Gebrauchsvorgänge abgestimmten Reinigungstools ist es, Geschirrreinigung mit einem Spaßfaktor zu verbinden. Neben ergonomisch konzipierten, runden Griffen werden trendige Farbakzente genutzt.

Tefal Vitacuisine Compact Steamer/Dampfgarer

SAS SEB, Selongey, France/Frankreich
In-house design/Werksdesign:
Reiner Guillaume
www.groupeseb.com

This steamer attracts attention due to its colouring and rounded forms. Green handles are a highlight, while other design elements remain unobtrusive. Thanks to the Vitamin+ function vitamins are better preserved. In a creative way the food products can be cooked in aroma-preserving bowls or in a sauce in cooking trays. Thanks to its compact structure the appliance can be conveniently stored in small spaces with the bowls placed upside down on the base plate.

Mit seiner Farbgebung und den gerundeten Formen zieht dieser Dampfgarer die Aufmerksamkeit auf sich. Grüne Griffe setzen einen besonderen Akzent, während andere Designelemente unauffällig bleiben. Dank der Vitamin+ Funktion bleiben mehr Vitamine erhalten. Auf kreative Weise wird das Essen in den aromaschonenden Behältern zubereitet oder aber in einer Soße mit verschiedenen Kocheinsätzen. Aufgrund der kompakten Bauweise lässt sich das Gerät auch auf kleinem Raum gut unterbringen. Die Behälter werden dabei umgekehrt auf die Bodenplatte gestellt.

I WASH Washing Machine/ Waschmaschine

Industrial Design Center of Haier Group,
Qingdao, China
In-house design/Werksdesign: Kong Zhi,
Jiang Chunhui, Jiang Song, Li Weiyi,
Suzuki Kiyoshi
www.haier.com

The compact design of this top-loading washing machine offers a unique feature. A flexible fold-up lid on top of the discreet white body conceals an electronic touch control unit as well as the access to the wash drum.

Mit ihrer kompakten Gestaltung bietet diese Waschmaschine einen unkonventionellen Aufbau. Der Toplader mit einem dezent anmutenden Korpus in Weiß verbirgt hinter einer flexibel aufklappbaren Abdeckung ein elektronisches Touch-Kontrollfeld sowie den Zugang zur Waschtrommel.

Water Purifier and Ice Maker /
Wasserreiniger und Eisbereiter

Woongjin Coway Co., Ltd., Seoul, Korea
In-house design / Werksdesign:
Hun-Jung Choi, Dae-Hoo Kim
www.coway.co.kr

The elegant body of this water purifier displays a superior appearance. The mix of matt and high-gloss surfaces shapes the slim silhouette with harmoniously rounded edges. The electronic control panel intuitively reveals itself and differentiates manifold options for the withdrawal of water and ice. A multi-filter removes heavy metals and bacteria from the water, which are harmful to health. The treated water can be optionally taken in a tempered, cold or frozen condition.

Der elegante Korpus dieses Wasserreinigers prägt das ästhetisch hochwertige Erscheinungsbild. Der Mix aus matten und hochglänzenden Oberflächen formt eine schlanke Silhouette mit harmonisch abgerundeten Ecken. Das elektronische Bedienfeld erschließt sich intuitiv und zeigt vielfältige Optionen zur Wasser- und Eisentnahme. Ein Multifilter entfernt gesundheitsschädliche Schwermetalle und Bakterien aus dem Wasser, welches wahlweise temperiert, kalt oder gefroren entnommen werden kann.

Woongjin Coway Co., Ltd., Seoul, Korea
In-house design / Werksdesign:
Hun-Jung Choi, Jong-Keon Jeon
www.coway.co.kr

With its strikingly compact and puristic design
this water purifier discreetly integrates into
its environment. The elliptically curved front
gives a transparent impression due to its bright
materials illustrating the value of purified water.
The control panel for optional cold or warm
water is comfortably accessible; each button
is illuminated in a specific colour indicating its
function. The abstract design of this light effect
reminds of drops of water.

Auffallend kompakt und puristisch fügt sich
dieser Wasserreiniger dezent in seine Umgebung ein. Die elliptisch geschwungene Front
vermittelt durch ihre hellen Materialien eine
transparente Anmutung und symbolisiert den
Wert des gereinigten Wassers. Das Bedienfeld
gestaltet den Zugang zu wahlweise kaltem
oder warmem Wasser komfortabel, wobei
jede Taste ihre Funktion durch die Beleuchtung in einer spezifischen Farbe anzeigt. In
ihrer abstakten Formgebung erinnern diese
Lichteffekte an Wassertropfen.

P-09CR
Water Filtration System/
Wasserfilter-System

Woongjin Coway Co., Ltd., Seoul, Korea
In-house design/Werksdesign:
Hun-Jung Choi, Jong-Keon Jeon
www.coway.co.kr

This discreet, space-saving water filtration
system can be easily installed under the sink. A
smooth, white frame incorporates the light grey
body. The compact appliance is smaller than
comparable products. There is no need to fix
it at the wall for installation. The five variably
usable filters are easy to replace, and the dual
filter arrangement allows users to choose the
combination of the filters according to their
needs.

Dieses diskret anmutende Wasserfilter-
System lässt sich platzsparend und unkompliziert direkt unter der Spüle anbringen.
Sein Korpus in Hellgrau wird von einem
glatten, weißen Rahmen umfasst. Das kompakte Gerät ist kleiner als Vergleichsprodukte
und muss für die Installation nicht extra an
der Wand befestigt werden. Die fünf variabel
einsetzbaren Filter sind leicht auszutauschen,
wobei die Doppelfilteranordnung dem
Benutzer erlaubt, die Kombination der Filter
bedarfsgerecht zu wählen.

CHP-09B
Water Purifier / Wasserreiniger

Woongjin Coway Co., Ltd., Seoul, Korea
In-house design / Werksdesign:
Hun-Jung Choi, So-Young Jung
www.coway.co.kr

Independent of existing water connections
the unobtrusive water purifier with integrated
water tank supplies offices, hospitals or
classrooms with drinking water. The system of
the eco-friendly water dispenser disposes of
PET bottles and features an innovative RO filter
system that economises the use of water as a
precious resource. The compact stationary unit
harmoniously fits into any room thanks to its
slim shape. It is available in different colours.

Dieser dezent anmutende Wasserreiniger mit
eingebautem Wassertank bietet, unabhängig von vorhandenen Wasseranschlüssen,
Trinkwasser in Büros, Krankenhäusern oder
Klassenzimmern. Als umweltschonender
Wasserspender verzichtet das System auf
PET-Flaschen und verfügt über ein innovatives RO-Filtersystem, welches mit der
kostbaren Ressource Wasser sparsam umgeht.
Das kompakte Standgerät passt sich aufgrund
seiner schmalen Form jedem Raum harmonisch an und ist in unterschiedlichen Farben
erhältlich.

Massimo Iosa Ghini

Prof. Danny Venlet

Lyndon Neri

Tableware
Functional timelessness

Tableware
Zweckmäßige Zeitlosigkeit

There is a discernible tendency to less playful and deliberately simple approaches with clean, reduced structures.

In the past years, design in the "Tableware" category has again turned to less playful and deliberately simple approaches with clean, reduced structures. The design concepts give the impression of being timeless and functional without appearing too slick or cool. Particular attention is paid to the appropriate and attractive integration of the manufacturer logo or brand name on the product, with the aim for immediate identity recognition and a seamless integration into the whole. With ecological awareness still on the rise, the sector makes increasing use of natural materials, whereby their combination with synthetic materials is commonplace and no longer perceived as a contradiction to the back-to-nature orientation. In all, the products appear extremely coherent and meet high standards with regard to materials, functionality and aesthetic quality.

Es ist eine Tendenz zu weniger verspielten, bewusst einfach gestalteten Produkten mit klaren, eher reduzierten Strukturen erkennbar.

In der Kategorie „Tableware" ist nach der zunehmenden Hinwendung zu aktuell geltenden Trends in den letzten Jahren inzwischen wieder eine Tendenz zu weniger verspielten, bewusst einfach gestalteten Produkten mit klaren, eher reduzierten Strukturen erkennbar. Dadurch erwecken die Entwürfe den Eindruck, zeitlos und funktional zu sein, ohne dabei unterkühlt zu wirken. Der adäquaten und ansprechenden gestalterischen Umsetzung des Herstellerlogos oder Markennamens auf dem Produkt wird besondere Aufmerksamkeit geschenkt, schließlich soll es auf den ersten Blick der Identität Ausdruck verleihen und sich harmonisch in das Gesamtbild einfügen. Aufgrund des weiter wachsenden ökologischen Bewusstseins werden zunehmend Materialien natürlichen Ursprungs eingesetzt, wobei deren Kombination mit künstlich hergestellten Stoffen ebenfalls als gängiges Element der Gestaltung etabliert ist und nicht mehr als Widerspruch zur Rückbesinnung auf Natürlichkeit erscheint. Insgesamt wirken die Produkte äußerst stimmig und werden höchsten Ansprüchen an Material, Funktionalität und ästhetischer Qualität gerecht.

Magisso Cake Server / Tortenheber

Magisso Ltd.,
Helsinki, Finland / Finnland
In-house design / Werksdesign:
Maria Kivijärvi
www.magisso.com

This cake server has two functions: slicing a piece of cake and serving it onto the plate. The characteristic shape of the product presents an accomplished response to the design challenge of combining a knife with tongs. The cake server yields consistent portions in the shape of the elegant curves and requires only little pressure to press through a cake. For this, the bottom edges of the stainless steel utensil are sharpened as blades. Lifting a piece of cake is also very easy: only slight pressure on the server tongs suffice. The mirrored steel lends the product its classic elegance. Forged from one piece, the end product adheres to a minimalist approach in table culture and features user-friendly functionality.

Dieser Tortenheber verbindet zwei Funktionen in einem Servier-Utensil: Die Nutzer können damit zunächst ein Kuchen- oder Tortenstück ausschneiden, um es gleich anschließend auf die Teller der jeweiligen Gäste zu heben. Die charakteristische Formgebung des Produkts gibt dabei eine gelungene gestalterische Antwort auf die Kombinierbarkeit von Messer und Zange. Die elegante Linienführung des Tortenhebers bildet die Form für eine gleichmäßige Portionierung des Kuchens, wobei das Küchenutensil nur mit einem leichten Druck durch den Kuchen oder die Torte geführt werden muss. Um dies zu ermöglichen, wurde das aus Edelstahl gefertigte Kuchenbesteck an seinen unteren Kanten zu einer klingenartigen Schneidfläche verjüngt. Auch die weitere Handhabung erschließt sich intuitiv: Um das Kuchenstück anzuheben, genügt bereits ein leichtes Zusammendrücken der Servierzange. Das hochglänzende Material verleiht dem Produkt eine klassische Eleganz. Die aus einem Stück gefertigte Produktkreation folgt der Maxime einer puristischen Tischkultur und visualisiert darüber hinaus eine nutzerfreundliche Funktionalität.

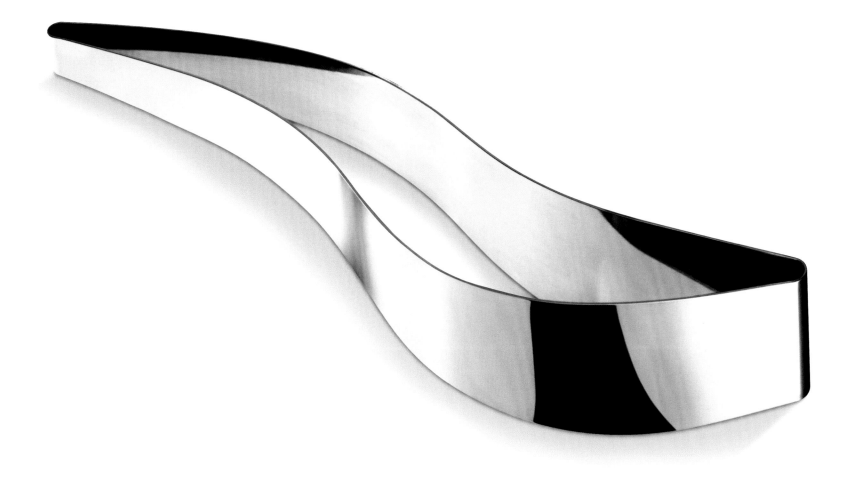

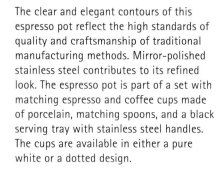

**Giannina Espresso Pot /
Espressokanne**

Carlo Giannini S.p.A.,
Cellatica (Brescia), Italy / Italien
Design: Feiz Design Studio
(Feiz Khodi), Amsterdam, NL
www.giannini.it
www.feizdesign.com

The clear and elegant contours of this espresso pot reflect the high standards of quality and craftsmanship of traditional manufacturing methods. Mirror-polished stainless steel contributes to its refined look. The espresso pot is part of a set with matching espresso and coffee cups made of porcelain, matching spoons, and a black serving tray with stainless steel handles. The cups are available in either a pure white or a dotted design.

Die klare und elegant geschwungene Formensprache dieser Espressokanne unterstreicht den hohen Qualitätsanspruch einer Manufakturfertigung. Auf Hochglanz polierter Edelstahl rundet ihre edle Anmutung harmonisch ab. Diese Espressokanne ist Teil einer Serie mit passenden Espresso- und Kaffeetassen aus Porzellan, den dazu passenden Löffeln sowie einem schwarzen Serviertablett mit Tragegriffen aus Edelstahl. Die Tassen sind optional in Reinweiß oder mit einem Pünktchendekor erhältlich.

Balance
Bowl / Schale

Auerhahn Bestecke GmbH,
Altensteig, Germany / Deutschland
Design: Jens Borstelmann,
Hannover, Germany / Deutschland
www.auerhahn-bestecke.de

A characteristic feature of the Balance bowl is a slightly offset balance point that is arranged excentrically creating a dynamic asymmetry. A precisely outlined rim brings both outer sides of the double bowl together in a curved arch. In addition, the upper and lower parts are formed in differently pronounced shapes giving an elegant volume to the oblong design. The clear lining is enhanced by striking effects: the highly polished stainless steel reflects the surrounding area in the surfaces. These reflections emphasise the exciting curvatures of the bowls.

Ein charakteristisches Merkmal der Schale Balance ist ein leicht verschobener, außermittig angelegter Schwerpunkt, durch den eine dynamische Asymmetrie entsteht. Ein präzise gezogener Rand führt die beiden Außenflächen der Doppelschale schwungvoll zusammen. Hinzu kommen unterschiedlich stark geformte Ober- und Unterseiten, die der länglichen Form ein elegant anmutendes Volumen verleihen. Die klare Linienführung wird durch augenfällige Effekte unterstrichen: Im hochglanzpolierten Edelstahl spiegelt sich die Umgebung auf den Oberflächen wider, die Reflexionen heben die spannungsvollen Krümmungen der Schalen hervor.

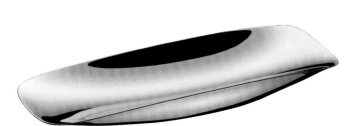

Moon

Barazzoni S.p.A.,
Invorio (Novara), Italy / Italien
Design: Claudio Bellini Design+Design
(Claudio Bellini),
Milan, Italy / Mailand, Italien
www.barazzoni.it
www.claudiobellini.com

Clear lines and a high-quality material lend this minimalist accessory its elegant style. Usable as a fruit bowl, tray, or design object, the product features a polished stainless steel surface that reflects the colours and forms of its surroundings. The product series is available in five different forms: two rectangular, two round, and one square version. While the upper surface is level, the bottom side is slightly curved, adding a further touch of sophistication to the object.

Eine klare Linienführung und hochwertiges Material geben diesem puristischen Accessoire seine elegante Anmutung. Vielfältig nutzbar als Obstschale, Tablett oder Designobjekt, spiegelt seine polierte Edelstahloberfläche die Farben und Formen der Umgebung reizvoll wider. Die Produktserie ist in fünf unterschiedlichen Formen – zwei rechteckigen, zwei runden und einer quadratischen Ausführung – erhältlich. Während die obere Fläche plan ist, wurde die Unterseite dezent gebogen, was das Produktprofil filigraner erscheinen lässt.

ID+IM Design Lab., Kaist, Deajon, Korea
In-house design/Werksdesign:
Prof. Sangmin Bae
http://idim.kaist.ac.kr

This interactive tumbler was designed for
the benefit of a Korean charity project,
with sales proceeds going to educational
programmes for underprivileged children.
The prominent LED light on the side of the
thermal tumbler indicates the temperature
of the beverage within, with blue indicating
a cold beverage, red a hot beverage such as
coffee, and orange a warm beverage such
as tea. A temperature sensor on the bottom
controls the colour of the LED display. The
tumbler has a tight silicone lid that allows
for convenient use on the go. The bottom of
the tumbler features a white, heart-shaped
area that can be written on by hand and
used as a message card. This heart – the logo
of the tumbler – has a strong black-and-
white contrast. When the person drinking
lifts the tumbler, the logo becomes visible
to the person sitting in front of them, which
then serves to stimulate conversation and
communicate the social project behind the
tumbler.

Als interaktiver Becher wurde dieses
Produkt zur Unterstützung eines koreanischen Wohltätigkeitsprojekts konzipiert – die Verkaufserlöse kommen der
Bildungsförderung bedürftiger Kinder
zugute. Das auffallende, farbige LED-Licht
an der Seite des Thermobechers informiert über die jeweilige Temperatur des
Getränks, wobei Blau für kalte Getränke,
Rot für heiße Getränke wie Kaffee und
Orange für temperierte Getränke wie Tee
steht. Ein temperaturempfindlicher Sensor
am Gefäßboden steuert die Farbgebung
der LED-Anzeige. Das Trinkgefäß ist mit
einem Silikondeckel dicht verschlossen
und ermöglicht somit auch unterwegs die
komfortable Nutzung. Eine magnetische
Münze haftet am Becherboden und kann
als Grußemblem Verwendung finden,
indem die Freifläche in Herzform individuell beschriftet wird. Das Farbkonzept
setzt die Positionierung des Herz-Symbols
mittels eines Schwarz-Weiß-Kontrastes
wirkungsvoll in Szene. Da das Herz erst
beim Trinken sichtbar wird, sorgt es beim
Gegenüber für Aufmerksamkeit und kommuniziert zugleich das soziale Engagement.

Tkaro
Water Bottle / Wasserflasche

Design: Tkaro Inc. (Kai Fejer),
Toronto, Canada / Kanada
www.tkaro.com

This water bottle designed for on-the-go use consists of a glass bottle enclosed in a protective stainless steel casing. The clarity of its aesthetic form reflects the purity of the resource water. All materials were carefully selected to be durable, dishwasher-safe and recyclable. With this invention, the producer wishes to reduce the demand for plastic bottles and to thereby make a contribution to the environment.

Als tragbare Wasserflasche für unterwegs ist diese Glasflasche mit einer schützenden Edelstahl-Ummantelung versehen. Die ästhetische Klarheit der Formensprache soll die Reinheit der Ressource Wasser widerspiegeln. Konzipiert für einen langfristigen Gebrauch, wurde bei der Materialwahl neben der Haltbarkeit und Spülmaschinentauglichkeit auch auf die Recyclingfähigkeit des Produkts geachtet. Mit der Intention, den Bedarf an Plastikflaschen zu mindern, möchte der Hersteller einen Beitrag für den Umweltschutz leisten.

Coffee To Go
Thermal Mug / Thermobecher

ASA Selection GmbH,
Höhr-Grenzhausen,
Germany / Deutschland
In-house design / Werksdesign:
Aleks Samek
www.asa-selection.de

The keep-it-simple look of this thermal mug intends to highlight its functionality. The main asset of the porcelain mug is that it keeps cold liquids cold and hot liquids hot, without burning fingers. This is made possible thanks to an insulating air layer encased between an innovative porcelain double wall. A high-quality, tight-fitting lid made of flexible silicone ensures safe, leakproof handling. Available in 12 designs, the mug offers a high degree of comfort, whether at home or on the go.

Das minimalistische Erscheinungsbild dieses Thermobechers soll sich seiner Funktionalität unterordnen. In diesem Porzellanbecher bleibt Kaltes kühl und Heißes dauerhaft heiß, ohne dass man sich die Finger verbrennt. Möglich wird dies durch eine isolierende Luftschicht, welche zwischen der innovativen Porzellan-Doppelwandung eingeschlossen ist. Zudem schließt ein hochwertiger Deckel aus flexiblem Silikon die Becheröffnung hygienisch und dicht ab. Erhältlich in zwölf Dekoren, bietet der Thermobecher ein hohes Maß an Komfort für unterwegs und zu Hause.

elementBottle
Drinking Bottle / Trinkflasche

alfi GmbH, Wertheim,
Germany / Deutschland
Design: Pearl Creative,
Storti & Rummel GbR
(Tim Storti, Thomas Rummel),
Ludwigsburg, Germany / Deutschland
www.alfi.de
www.pearlcreative.com

With the use of recycled stainless steel for this drinking bottle, the designers encourage the reuse of materials all the while offering a stylish look. Made of eco-friendly materials, the sustainability of the elementBottle is furthermore enhanced by its sustainable robustness and its high-quality steel that is non-reactive with fruit acids. The bottle can be easily cleaned thanks to a large opening and is available in different sizes and colour designs.

Mit der Verwendung von recyceltem Edelstahl nutzen die Gestalter dieser Trinkflasche den Mehrweggedanken und wecken durch ein betont modisches Erscheinungsbild Aufmerksamkeit. Die elementBottle ist schadstofffrei, die Nachhaltigkeit des Produkts manifestiert sich in formstabiler Robustheit, wobei der hochwertige Edelstahl prinzipiell nicht auf Fruchtsäuren reagiert. Die Flasche lässt sich zudem durch ihre große Öffnung leicht reinigen, sie ist in unterschiedlichen Größen und vielfältigen Farbausführungen erhältlich.

Delice
Dinnerware / Geschirr

Dibbern GmbH,
Bargteheide, Germany / Deutschland
Design: Bodo Sperlein, London, GB
www.dibbern.de

The deep plates and bowls of the Delice chinaware series feature a soft, elegantly curved design. The harmonious lines of the plates flow evenly from the discreet base to the pronounced plate rim. The transparent shimmer gives the series a classic, timeless appeal. The specially smooth and harmonious surface is obtained by a traditional manufacturing procedure, in which plates and bowls are turned but not isostatically pressed. Dibbern only uses lead-free glazing.

Die tiefen Teller und Schalen der Porzellanserie Delice vermitteln mit ihrer sanft geschwungenen Formensprache eine zurückhaltende Eleganz. Die harmonische Linienführung der Teller zieht sich gleichmäßig filigran vom dezenten Fuß bis hin zum prägnanten Tellerrand. Klassisch und zeitlos wirkt die Ästhetik des transparent schimmernden Porzellans. Die besonders glatte und ebenmäßige Oberfläche entsteht durch das traditionelle Herstellungsverfahren, bei dem die Teller und Schalen gedreht und nicht isostatisch gepresst werden. Dibbern verwendet ausschließlich bleifreie Glasuren.

400 each
Glass Set / Glasserie

h concept co., ltd., Tokyo, Japan
Design: Studio in the Air
(Masato Yamamoto),
Ebikon, Switzerland / Schweiz
www.h-concept.jp
studio.intheair.ch

The allure of this glass set consists of each glass being able to hold exactly 400 ml. With very different heights and widths, the glasses are at first perceived as differing substantially. The surprise effect then lies in discovering their commonality. The set's wide array of forms also allows for a multitude of uses. As such the glasses can be used to serve beverages as well as desserts. They are moreover stackable for easy and attractive storage.

Der konzeptionelle Reiz dieser Glasserie beruht auf dem Überraschungseffekt, dass in jedes Glas genau 400 ml passen. Die sehr unterschiedlichen Glasformen lassen diese Gemeinsamkeit zunächst nicht vermuten – zu stark variieren Höhe und Breite und dadurch auch die subjektiv wahrgenommene Größe der Gläser. Die Auswahlmöglichkeit erweitert zudem den Einsatzbereich. Es lassen sich in den Gläsern wahlweise Getränke oder Desserts servieren. Zusätzlich lassen sie sich nach dem Gebrauch platzsparend stapeln.

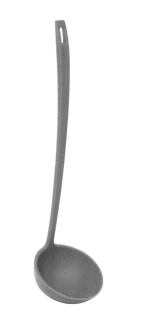

Tate otama
Ladle / Schöpfkelle

h concept co., ltd., Tokyo, Japan
Design: Mikiya Kobayashi, Tokyo, Japan
www.h-concept.jp
www.mikiyakobayashi.com

This unique ladle cannot only be stacked onto each other; it can also stand upright. The slightly flattened rear base of the ladles allows for this unusual positioning without minimising the quantity of soup the utensil can hold. The motivation behind this design was to create a kitchen utensil that is optimised for the limited space available in urban dwellings.

Diese ungewöhnliche Schöpfkelle lässt sich nicht nur stapeln, sondern zudem vertikal aufstellen. Ein dezent abgeflachter Boden auf der Rückseite der Kelle ermöglicht diese ungewohnte Positionierung, ohne dabei die Füllmenge der Kellen zu mindern. Das funktionale Gestaltungskonzept folgt damit der Intention, Küchenutensilien für die begrenzten Stellflächen urbaner Haushalte zu entwerfen.

OXO Soft Works POP Containers
Food Storage Containers/
Aufbewahrungsboxen

OXO, New York, USA
Design: Form Co., Ltd.
(Tamotsu Matsumoto, Makiko Kida),
Chiba, Japan
www.oxo.com
www.form.co.jp

These dry food storage containers can be recycled and were developed according to ergonomic principles. A button in the middle of the lids serves as the lock mechanism. With a simple push on the button, the button pops up and can be used as a handle to pull the lid open. The container can be closed by pressing the button down again. These airtight containers are suitable for long-term storage. They are available in different sizes and can be conveniently stacked.

Diese recyclebaren Aufbewahrungsboxen für getrocknete Lebensmittel wurden nach ergonomischen Gesichtspunkten entwickelt. Um einen möglichst leichtgängigen Schließmechanismus zu erreichen, haben die Deckel einen zentralen Knopf, der im geöffneten Zustand zudem als Haltegriff dient. Zum Schließen wird der Knopf mit leichtem Druck wieder nach unten gepresst. Die luftdichten Gefäße ermöglichen eine dauerhafte Lagerung. In unterschiedlichen Größen erhältlich, lassen sich die Boxen flexibel stapeln.

OXO Good Grips TOP Containers
Food Storage Containers/
Aufbewahrungsboxen

OXO, New York, USA
In-house design/Werksdesign:
Dean DiPietro
Design: Input Creative Group
(Tim Kennedy, Sherwood Forlee),
Leonia, USA
www.oxo.com

These food storage containers are airtight and watertight thanks to their unique lid design. The lids can be easily opened and closed with one simple motion; just lift up the outer frame to open and push down to close. The outer frame clearly indicates when the container is sealed. The clear lids make contents visible from every angle. The product series can be conveniently stacked and is suitable for freezing. All parts are microwave- and dishwasher-safe, and BPA-free.

Diese Aufbewahrungsbehälter für Nahrungsmittel sind luft- und wasserdicht dank ihrer besonderen Deckelgestaltung. Mit einer einfachen Bewegung lassen sich die Deckel leicht öffnen und schließen. Zum Öffnen muss der äußere Rand nur angehoben und zum Schließen heruntergedrückt werden. Der äußere Rand zeigt eindeutig an, wenn der Behälter dicht verschlossen ist. Durch die durchsichtigen Deckel ist der Inhalt immer klar zu erkennen. Die Produktreihe kann bequem gestapelt werden und eignet sich zur Verwendung in der Tiefkühltruhe. Alle Teile sind mikrowellen- und spülmaschinengeeignet sowie BPA-frei.

BENTO Lunch Box

Pacific Market International,
Shanghai, China
In-house design/Werksdesign:
Flying Lu
www.aladdin-pmi.com/eu

The compact and well thought-out BENTO Lunch Box meets high standards with regard to both form and function. The double wall foam insulation keeps meals warm or cold for up to five hours. A removable divider allows to separate the content and users can add one, two or more containers through the unique stackable design. In this way even hot/cold combinations such as soup and salad can be taken on the go. The box is leakproof and microwave-safe.

Kompakt und durchdacht präsentiert sich die BENTO Lunch Box. Das innovative Produkt erfüllt formal wie funktional hohe Anforderungen. Die Doppelwand-Schaumisolierung hält Speisen bis zu fünf Stunden warm oder kalt. Ein optional einsetzbarer Teiler separiert den Inhalt, zudem lassen sich ein, zwei oder mehr Behälter unkompliziert zu einer Einheit verbinden. Selbst Heiß/Kalt-Kombinationen, wie beispielsweise Salat und Suppe, können so gleichzeitig transportiert werden. Die Box ist auslaufsicher und mikrowellengeeignet.

Collapsible Salad Spinner/
Zusammenklappbare Salatschleuder

Progressive International, Kent, USA
In-house design / Werksdesign:
Progressive International Design Team
www.progressiveintl.com

This collapsible salad spinner allows for space-saving storage when not in use. A transparent, hard shell plastic and a green silicone ring are the core materials of the folding mechanism. The white colander and white lid contrast nicely with the transparent green bowl. In keeping with this colour scheme, the colour green is also used for the pull-cord mechanism.

Diese zusammenklappbare Salatschleuder lässt sich nach ihrem Gebrauch platzsparend verstauen. Ein Materialmix aus einem transparenten Hartschalen-Kunststoff und einem grünen Silikonring bildet die Grundlage dieses Klappmechanismus. Das Farbkonzept setzt das weiße Sieb und den weißen Deckel in einen dezenten Kontrast zur transparent grünen Schüssel. Als weiterer wirkungsvoller Akzent wurde bei der Gestaltung der Kurbel die Trendfarbe Grün erneut eingesetzt.

Foldable Colander / Faltbarer Seiher

RÖSLE GmbH & Co. KG,
Marktoberdorf, Germany / Deutschland
In-house design / Werksdesign:
Thomas Amann
www.roesle.de

This colander can also be used as a steam insert and takes up very little space: the handles and base – made of stainless steel – ensure a secure grip and stability, and the central part – made of silicone – can be folded flat after use. The innovative mix of materials is heat-resistant and dishwasher-safe. The product is available in the diameters 20 cm and 24 cm and in the colours black, red, green, orange, violet and yellow.

Dieser Seiher, der auch als Dämpfeinsatz verwendet werden kann, wurde besonders platzsparend konstruiert: Während Griffe und Boden aus Edelstahl für sicheren Halt und Stabilität sorgen, lässt sich das Mittelteil aus Silikon nach dem Gebrauch flach zusammenfalten. Der innovative Materialmix ist hitzebeständig und lässt sich gut in der Spülmaschine reinigen. Die Produktserie ist in den Durchmessern 20 cm und 24 cm, jeweils in den Farben Schwarz, Rot, Grün, Orange, Violett und Gelb, erhältlich.

concept pro
Cookware / Kochgeschirr

Norbert Woll GmbH,
Saarbrücken, Germany / Deutschland
Design: Ralph Krämer,
Büro für Gestaltung,
Saarbrücken, Germany / Deutschland
www.woll-cookware.com
www.ralph-kraemer.com

The concept pro cookware is based on an innovative multi-layer technology comprised of two stainless steel layers that are sheathed seamlessly around three aluminium layers. This combination of materials conducts heat evenly to the bottom and sides. The lid allows for multifunctional handling: it can stay on top, be in a raised position for safe pouring, or rest sideways to let condensed water drip off.

Das Kochgeschirr concept pro wurde auf Basis einer innovativen Mehrschicht-Technologie entwickelt und besteht aus zwei Edelstahllagen, die drei Aluminium-lagen fugenlos umschließen. Die Kombination dieser Materialien leitet die Wärme gleichmäßig in Boden und Seitenwände. Der multifunktionale Deckel bietet eine flexible Bedienbarkeit, indem er wahlweise aufliegend, in einer erhöhten Position zum sicheren Abgießen oder in einer seitlichen Parkposition zum Abtropfen des Kondens-wassers benutzt werden kann.

Neo Glass
Cookware / Kochgeschirr

Berghoff Worldwide,
Heusden-Zolder, Belgium / Belgien
In-house design / Werksdesign:
Frederik Aerts
www.berghoffworldwide.com

This cookware series offers a perfect blend of aesthetics and well thought-out functionality. The first eye-catcher of the stainless steel pot is its user-friendly integration of the handles on the sides and on the lid. This unconventional construction allows to open and close the lid with a simple twist. The lid can also be fixed in place in a slightly open position to prevent contents from boiling over or to pour liquids out of the pot. Moreover, while attractive, the glass lid also functions to reduce the loss of nutrients with users less apt to open a pot frequently when they can look into it. The handles do not conduct heat, thereby ensuring safe and comfortable handling.

Eine harmonische Formensprache wurde bei dieser Kochgeschirr-Serie mit einer gut durchdachten Funktionalität kombiniert. Die nutzerfreundliche Integration der Griffe, welche am Edelstahltopf und am Topfdeckel seitlich angebracht sind, fällt auf. Diese unkonventionelle Konstruktion bietet den Vorteil, dass der Deckel mit einer leichten Drehbewegung geöffnet und wieder verschlossen werden kann. Zudem kann er in einer leicht geöffneten Position arretiert werden, wodurch die Speisen nicht mehr überkochen und zudem eine sinnvolle Ausgussrinne entsteht. Darüber hinaus sorgen die nicht leitenden Griffe für eine sichere und komfortable Handhabung. Ein ansprechendes Gestaltungselement ist der gläserne Deckel, der den Nährstoffver-lust durch häufiges Öffnen mindert.

Vital
Knife Series/Messerserie

Fa. Gehring GmbH,
Solingen, Germany/Deutschland
In-house design/Werksdesign:
Volker Gehring
www.gehring-schneidwaren.de

This knife series features puristic grips and was developed for the emerging trend kitchen. The shapes of the blades inspired by tradition and the Far East are made of high-grade Damascus steel. With their ergonomic and extraordinary grips they give a highly aesthetic impression and offer supreme edge-holding abilities. The grip is made of rustproof stainless steel (18/10) and is bonded with the Damascus steel blade by an advanced welding technique. The very durable, sharp edge made of high-alloyed carbon steel (VG 10) is ice-hardened. On both exterior sides rustproof and flexible Damascus steel is applied with 32 layers each. These outer layers protect the knife from cracking and corrosion. If the layers of both outer sides and the core material are added the blade consists of 65 layers.

Diese Messerserie mit ihren puristischen Griffen wurde für die junge Trendküche entwickelt. Die fernöstlichen sowie tradtionellen Klingenformen aus hochwertigem Damaststahl bieten in Kombination mit dem ergonomisch gestalteten und ausgefallen anmutenden Griff ein Höchstmaß an Ästhetik und Schnitthaltigkeit.

Der Griff besteht aus rostfreiem Edelstahl (18/10) und wird durch moderne Schweißtechnik mit der Damaststahl-Klinge verbunden. Die sehr harte, scharfe Schneide aus einem hochlegierten Kohlenstoffstahl (VG 10) ist eisgehärtet. Auf beiden Außenseiten ist ein rostbeständiger und flexibler Damaststahl mit jeweils 32 Lagen aufgebracht. Diese Außenlagen schützen das Messer vor Bruch und Korrosion. Zählt man die Lagen beider Außenseiten und das Kernmaterial zusammen, so besteht die Klinge aus 65 Lagen.

K2
Small Kitchen Knife/
Kleines Kochmesser

Robert Herder GmbH & Co. KG,
Solingen, Germany/Deutschland
In-house design/Werksdesign:
Giselheid Herder-Scholz,
Tomoyuki Takada
www.windmuehlenmesser.de

This small kitchen knife offers outstanding cutting performance. Its blade – 12 cm long and slightly curved – allows for easy use. K2 has a traditional thin-ground blade that has been manually refined for maximum sharpness. In short, this is a handy, all-purpose knife that cuts vegetables and meat smoothly and precisely. The knife is available in three attractive handle choices: plum wood, black POM plastic or white acrylic plastic.

Mit seiner 12 cm langen Klinge bietet dieses kleine Kochmesser gute Schnitteigenschaften. Der sanfte Bogen der Klinge ermöglicht eine leichtgängige Handhabung, wobei sich K2 für alle Arbeiten auf dem Brett eignet. Das Kochmesser schneidet Gemüse oder Fleisch glatt und präzise. Die Klinge ist traditionell dünn geschliffen und in Handarbeit auf höchste Schärfe veredelt. Das handliche Messer ist in den drei attraktiven Griffvarianten Pflaumenholz, schwarzem POM-Kunststoff und weißem Acryl-Kunststoff erhältlich.

Jack – der Maronischreck
Chestnut Cutter/Maroni-Ritzer

Take2 Designagentur GmbH & Co. KG,
Rosenheim, Germany/Deutschland
In-house design/Werksdesign:
Markus Roling, Matthias Quaas
www.take2-design.de

This chestnut cutter is an innovative tool with a specially serrated blade for the perforation of chestnuts (scoring chestnuts is recommended prior to roasting). Much more precise than conventional knives, this device allows moving the blade over the rounded side of the chestnut with the necessary pressure so as to score the shell without ruining the fruit. The cutter is made entirely of stainless steel, is dishwasher-safe, and is housed in an attractive wooden casing.

Dieser Maroni-Ritzer ist ein neuartiges Werkzeug mit speziell gezahnter Klinge zur Perforierung von Esskastanien. Das Einritzen der Schale empfiehlt sich vor dem Rösten. Im Vergleich zur Verwendung herkömmlicher Messer arbeitet dieses Produkt präziser. Die Klinge wird mit dem nötigen Druck über die bauchige Seite der Marone geführt und prägt so eine Perforation in die Schale, ohne dabei die Frucht zu verletzen. Vollständig aus Edelstahl gefertigt, ist der Maroni-Ritzer spülmaschinenfest und in einer Holzschachtel sicher verpackt.

Clongs
Kitchen Utensil / Küchenutensil

Dreamfarm, Brisbane,
Australia / Australien
In-house design / Werksdesign:
Dreamfarm
www.dreamfarm.com.au

This kitchen utensil has transformed everyday-use tongs: an innovative locking mechanism allows the Clongs to be locked or unlocked with one hand. The utensil moreover features an unconventional and unique design as a kink in the handle allows the Clongs to be put down during cooking without the ends touching or dirtying the counter surface. This kink also gives the Clongs a distinctive edge and a playful note.

Dieses Gerät vermittelt der herkömmlichen Küchenzange eine neue Dimension: Ein innovativer Schließmechanismus macht es möglich, dass Clongs mit einer Hand verriegelt und geöffnet wird. In seiner Form ist dieses Gerät ungewöhnlich und einzigartig gestaltet. Mit seinem besonderen Knick im Griff kann Clongs beim Kochen abgelegt werden, ohne dass die Enden die Tischplatte berühren und verschmutzen. Dieser Knick verleiht Clongs zudem eine markante und gleichzeitig spielerische Anmutung.

ToddlerTable
Baby Cutlery / Kinderbesteck

ToddlerCompany,
Hellerup, Denmark / Dänemark
Design: Josefine Bentzen,
Frederiksberg, Denmark / Dänemark
www.toddler.dk
www.josefinebentzen.com

The ToddlerTable flatware is designed to adapt to the way in which a baby holds onto objects. The utensils are short, thick and round to fill the entire palm of the child's hand. This makes it easier for the child to control its knife, fork or spoon until its motor skills are fully developed. All three utensils are child safe and available in a variety of trend colours.

Die Formgebung des ToddlerTable-Bestecks ist speziell der besonderen Art und Weise angepasst, in der Kleinkinder nach Gegenständen greifen. Um die Handfläche vollständig auszufüllen, wurden die Besteckteile kurz, dick und rund gestaltet. Dies vereinfacht es für das Kind, sein Messer, seine Gabel oder seinen Löffel unter Kontrolle zu halten, bis die motorische Koordination voll entwickelt ist. Die drei Besteckteile sind in all ihren Ausführungen kindersicher und in vielen Trendfarben erhältlich.

Bud
Cutlery/Besteck

Robert Welch Designs Ltd.,
Chipping Campden, GB
In-house design/Werksdesign:
Kit De Bretton Gordon
www.welch.co.uk

This slender-handled cutlery reflects the organic beauty of nature with the stem-like handle tapering, and gently curving into the palm of the hand giving a comfortable grip. The eye is drawn to a deep v-ridge in the metal, as though the metal has burst open and from this natural extension, the tines of the fork, the bowl of the spoon and blade of the knife appear like newly formed buds. As the spoons and forks are made from 18/10 stainless steel, the knives are forged from a single ingot of hardened stainless steel for a fine cutting edge.

Mit seinen schlanken Griffen, die sich wie Blumenstängel verjüngen, spiegelt dieses Besteck die natürliche Schönheit der Natur wider. Der Griff schmiegt sich sanft in die Hand und gibt einen guten Halt. Der Blick wird von der V-förmigen Kerbe im Metall angezogen, die so wirkt, als wäre das Metall dort aufgebrochen. In dieser natürlichen Ausdehnung erscheinen die Zinken der Gabeln, die Rundung des Löffels und die Messerschneide wie aufbrechende Knospen. Die Löffel und die Gabeln bestehen aus 18/10 Edelstahl, die Messer aus einem einzigen Block gehärteten Edelstahls, sodass die Klinge besonders scharf ist.

Mulberry Taster Spoons/Probierlöffel

Studio William Welch Ltd.,
Stratford-upon-Avon, Warwickshire, GB
In-house design/Werksdesign:
William Welch, Martin Drury
www.studiowilliam.com

These innovative taster spoons stand out for their unusual striking design and are suitable for professional use in restaurant kitchens. The spoon bowls come in various forms, including bowls with separate compartments, designed to stimulate the different taste receptors of the tongue allowing diners to savour the taste. The spoons can also be used to serve food in a creative way.

Durch eine ungewöhnliche Formensprache fallen diese innovativen Probierlöffel auf. Das aufmerksamkeitsstarke Gestaltungskonzept strebt vor allem den professionellen Einsatz in Restaurants an. Die unterschiedlich geformten und teilweise zweigeteilten Schöpfteile der Löffel wurden so konzipiert, dass sie die auf der Zunge befindlichen Rezeptoren gezielt stimulieren – der Genuss der Speisen wird dadurch geschmacklich intensiviert. Zudem lassen sich die Speisen mithilfe dieser Löffel auf kreative Weise servieren.

Bread Bag Bunny
Food Bag Clip / Brotbeutel-Clip

Mint Forest Corp., Seoul, Korea
In-house design / Werksdesign:
Sung Hyun Kim
www.mintforest.net

These reusable clips for bread bags offer a new kind of closing mechanism. Their unconventional shape, suggesting bunny ears, encourages playfulness. The set is offered in an array of six trendy colours that give the product an emotional added value. The good functionality of the Bread Bag Bunny is based on its simple clip mechanism: as the bunny ears arch outward, the lock component glides easily onto the plastic bag when pressing the thumb on the round contact surface. This one-step procedure will prevent the bag from slipping out of the lock. For an airtight lock, the top of the bag can be wrapped once more around a bunny ear and into the lock. These clips can be used for all kinds of bags and are suitable for sealing solid foods, from trail mix to potato chips and tortillas.

Dieser wiederverwendbare Clip-Verschluss für Pausenbrottüten repräsentiert eine neue Art der Verschlusstechnik. Mit seiner unkonventionellen Formgebung erinnert er an Hasenohren, was zu einem spielerischen Umgang mit dem Clip animiert. Darüber hinaus spricht das sympathisch wirkende Farbkonzept mit seinen sechs Trendfarben die Emotionen des Benutzers an. Die gute Funktionalität beruht beim Bread Bag Bunny auf einer einfachen Klemmmechanik: Dank ihrer Abrundungen führen die Hasenohren die jeweilige Plastiktüte leichtgängig in den Clip-Verschluss, während eine runde Kontaktplatte am unteren Teil des Verschlusses das Einklemmen der Plastiktüte mit nur einem Daumendruck ermöglicht. Dabei soll das gerade Einschieben verhindern, dass die Tüte aus dem Verschluss rutscht. Nach diesem ersten Einschieben der Tüte in die Verschlussvorrichtung wird ihre Öffnung noch einmal um ein Hasenohr gewickelt. Das zweite Einklemmen bewirkt einen zusätzlichen, luftdichten Verschluss der Pausenbrottüte. Diese Verschlüsse können für jede Art von Tüten verwendet werden und eignen sich zum Verschließen von festen Nahrungsmitteln, vom Müsli über Kartoffelchips bis hin zu Tortillas.

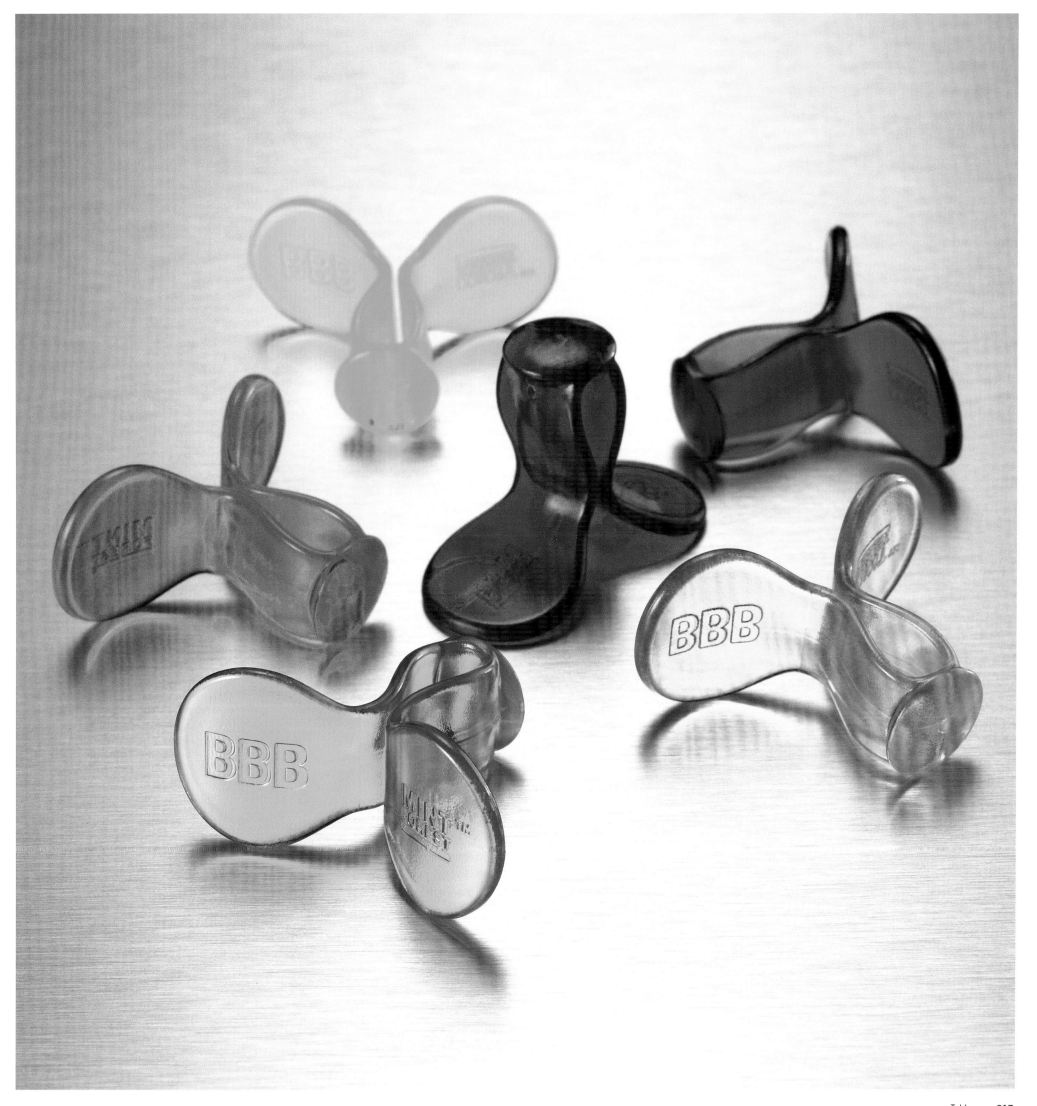

Table Clocks / Tischuhren

Takata Lemnos Inc.,
Takaoka City, Toyama Prefecture, Japan
Design: Kanaé Design Labo
(Kanaé Tsukamoto), Tokyo, Japan
www.lemnos.jp
www.kanaedesignlabo.com

These clearly designed table clocks are meant to be placed on office desks, living room shelves, consoles or even windowsills. The surface of the clocks is very smooth as it is made of porcelain. The idea was to pick up impressions of nature and develop forms that conjoin with porcelain. An arrangement of several pieces appears as a work of art.

Diese schnörkellos gestalteten Tischuhren eignen sich für Büroschreibtische, Wohnzimmerregale, Konsolen oder auch Fensterbänke. Ihre Oberfläche ist sehr glatt, da sie aus Porzellan gefertigt ist. Die Idee dabei war, Impressionen der Natur aufzugreifen und Formen zu schaffen, die eine Verbindung mit Porzellan eingehen sollten. Ein Arrangement mehrerer dieser Uhren wirkt wie ein Kunstwerk.

Dolly
Salt and Pepper Shaker/
Salz- und Pfefferstreuer

Normann Copenhagen,
Copenhagen, Denmark/
Kopenhagen, Dänemark
Design: Ross McBride
www.normann-copenhagen.com

The Dolly salt and pepper shaker, with its round, feminine design, is humorous and likable. Made from one piece of porcelain, it houses two separate compartments for salt and pepper. A slightly flattened bottom serves as the structural base, which is hardly perceived as such as the unit seems to teeter. The organic curves of the set are interrupted only by the discreet shake holes on the sides, with the fill openings of the shaker concealed on the bottom.

Humorvoll und sympathisch wirkt der Salz- und Pfefferstreuer Dolly mit seiner runden, femininen Formensprache. In einem Stück aus Porzellan gefertigt, beherbergt er zwei getrennte Kammern für Salz und Pfeffer. Eine sanft abgeflachte Unterseite bildet eine Standfläche, die als solche kaum wahrgenommen wird. Das Gebilde scheint zu wippen. Die organisch abgerundete Gestaltung wird nur durch die dezenten Streuöffnungen an der Seite unterbrochen, während die Befüllöffnungen des Gewürzbehälters an der Unterseite verborgen bleiben.

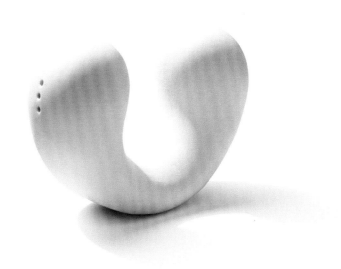

Y-Grinder
Salt and Pepper Mill/
Salz- und Pfeffermühle

Joseph Joseph Ltd., London, GB
Design: DesignWright (Adrian Wright, Jeremy Wright), London, GB
www.josephjoseph.com
www.designwright.co.uk

This salt and pepper mill stands out for its sleek design and its strong colour contrasts. Its ergonomic design features a double chamber that allows for the separate grinding of salt and pepper. The high-quality ceramic grinder can be set to grind from fine to coarse, is rust-free, and comes with a ten-year guarantee. The mill is suitable for all kinds of spices and seasonings, including rock salt.

Eine schlichte Gestaltung lässt diese Salz- und Pfeffermühle vor allem durch ihr kontraststarkes Farbkonzept auffallen. Das nach ergonomischen Gesichtspunkten konzipierte Gefäß verbirgt eine Doppelkammer, die es ermöglicht, Salz und Pfeffer in einer Mühle aufzubewahren und getrennt voneinander zu mahlen. Das hochwertige Keramik-Mahlwerk kann optional von fein bis grob eingestellt werden, ist nicht rostend und bietet eine Garantie von zehn Jahren. Die Mühle ist für alle Arten von Gewürzen, Steinsalz eingeschlossen, einsetzbar.

ONLINE
Pot Pad / Topfunterlage

Tescoma s.r.o.,
Zlin, Czech Republic /
Tschechische Republik
In-house design / Werksdesign:
Petr Tesak
www.tescoma.cz

This expandable pot pad offers an innovative and elegant way to place hot pots and pans on tables and counters. The pad is made from high-quality wood and comprises three segments that can be easily unfolded – single-handedly – to increase or decrease the pad in size. In this way, it can be adapted to round, oval, square or rectangular pot bases and is thus suitable for all kinds of pots, pans, as well as roasting pans or baking sheets.

Eine elegante Produktlösung stellt diese innovativ zusammenlegbare Topfunterlage dar. Aus hochwertigem Holz gefertigt, umfasst sie drei einzelne Elemente. Dank flexibler Ausklapp-Möglichkeiten kann die Topfunterlage schnell vergrößert bzw. verkleinert werden. Mit nur einer Hand lässt sie sich an runde, ovale, quadratische sowie rechteckige Topfböden anpassen. Das Produkt ist universell für Töpfe, Bratpfannen sowie Bräter oder Backbleche verschiedener Größen geeignet.

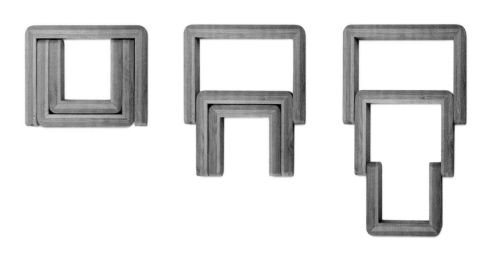

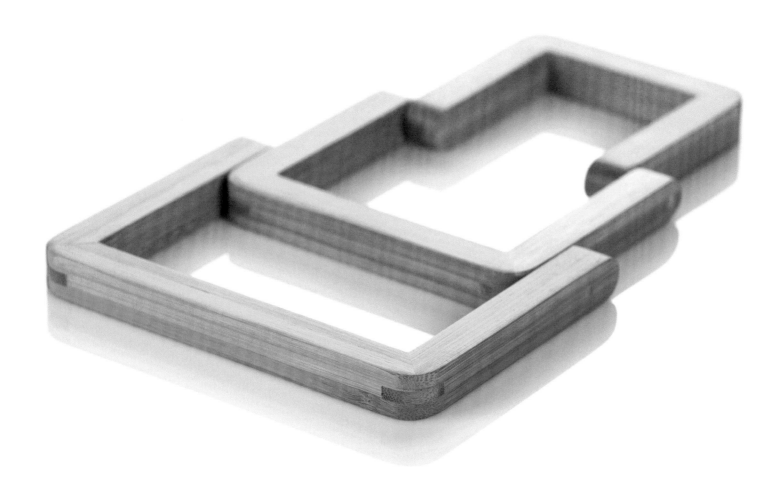

Finger Dip

Design: studio AMeBE
(Alessandra Mantovani e Eleonora
Barbareschi), Varese, Italy / Italien
Production / Produktion: ALGAM Spa,
Novate Milanese, Italy / Italien
www.studioamebe.com
www.algam.com

When silverware is nowhere in sight, Finger Dip comes to the rescue to allow for sanitary eating with the hands. By pulling the three latex caps over the tips of the thumb, index and middle finger, users can enjoy snacks when on the go without having to wash hands before or afterwards. The single-use product is certified food safe and is available in triple sets of different colours.

Wenn kein Besteck zur Hand ist, dient Finger Dip als essenzielles Werkzeug, um hygienisch mit den Händen zu essen. Die drei Einweg-Fingerhütchen aus Latex werden über Daumen, Zeigefinger und Mittelfinger gezogen, um damit unterwegs, beispielsweise auf Reisen oder Events, Snacks genießen zu können, ohne sich vorab oder anschließend die Hände waschen zu müssen. Das Einwegprodukt wurde auf Lebensmittelverträglichkeit überprüft und ist, im Dreierset verpackt, in unterschiedlichen Farben erhältlich.

Advent Calendar / Adventskalender
Spice Calendar with Recipes / Gewürzkalender mit Rezepten

Design: Clormann Design GmbH
(Marc Clormann),
Gilching, Germany / Deutschland
Production / Produktion:
Hauff Druck Art GmbH,
Kaufering, Germany / Deutschland
www.clormanndesign.de
www.hauff-medien.de

This elegant gift box contains an unusually conceived Advent calendar. The 24 little boxes contain precious spices in small, numbered glasses, each with an instruction leaflet, which gives a recipe for each day in the Advent and interesting information on the origin and application of the spices. Under the motto "Kein Genuss ist vorübergehend..." ("No pleasure is temporary..."), the Advent calendar is supposed to stimulate people to use it forever. After the Advent season the small glasses can be refilled at discretion.

Diese elegante Geschenkbox beinhaltet einen ungewöhnlich konzipierten Adventskalender. In den 24 kleinen Schachteln werden edle Gewürze in kleinen nummerierten Gläschen mit je einem Beipackzettel aufbewahrt. Dieser enthält neben einem Rezeptvorschlag für jeden Adventstag auch interessante Informationen zu Herkunft und Verwendung der Gewürze. Unter dem Motto „Kein Genuss ist vorübergehend..." soll der Adventskalender zum dauerhaften Gebrauch anregen. Die Gläschen können nach der Adventszeit nach Belieben nachgefüllt werden.

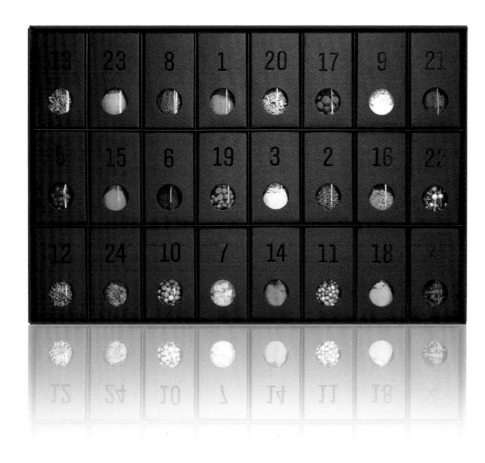

Glassware Series / Gläserserie

Kahve Dünyasi, Istanbul, Turkey / Türkei
Design: Ypsilon Tasarim (Yesim Bakirküre),
Istanbul, Turkey / Türkei
www.kahvedunyasi.com
www.ypsilontasarim.com

These water and affogato glass creations were designed for use in gastronomy and are part of a eight-pieces series. The design concept of the glasses is based on the idea of supporting the memorability of each beverage by creating a characteristic glass for each one. Therefore, every beverage owning its specific "body" will be remembered with its glass.

Diese Wasser- und Affogato-Glaskreationen wurden für den Gebrauch in der Gastronomie entworfen und gehören zu einer achtteiligen Gläserserie. Das Gestaltungskonzept der Gläser basiert auf der Idee, durch die Gestaltung eines charakteristischen Glases für jedes einzelne Getränk dessen Einprägsamkeit zu unterstützen. Somit wird jedes Getränk, das seinen eigenen „Körper" besitzt, gemeinsam mit seinem Glas in Erinnerung gebracht.

Ferrarelle Platinum Edition
Glass Bottle / Glasflasche

Hangar Design Group,
Milan, Italy / Mailand, Italien
In-house design / Werksdesign
www.hangar.it

The design of this glass bottle symbolises the very essence of water. The transparency of the glass is disrupted only by a discreet silkscreen label, the bright red graphics of which correspond to the same-coloured bottle cap. The spirited relief line on the bottleneck gives the bottle its unique tactile appeal. Able to hold 750 ml, the bottle is suitable for elegant dining and emphasises the quality of the brand.

Die Gestaltung dieser Glasflasche soll die kostbare Essenz des Wassers symbolisieren. Die Transparenz des Glases wird nur durch eine minimalistische Siebdruck-Etikettierung unterbrochen, wobei der hellrote Markenschriftzug mit einer gleichfarbigen Verschlusskappe harmonisch korrespondiert. Die schwungvolle Linienführung des Reliefs am Flaschenhals gibt der ästhetischen Flaschenform einen besonderen haptischen Reiz. Die 750 ml fassende Glasflasche dient dem stilvollen Servieren am Tisch und unterstreicht den Anspruch der Marke.

Family Bowl
Dinnerware / Geschirr

JIA Inc., Hong Kong
Design: designschneider,
Berlin, Germany / Deutschland

A harmonious combination of bamboo and porcelain create the elegant profile of this dinnerware. The materials are joined by means of innovative production methods in which carbonised wood is bent around porcelain bowls. A slanted rim lends the bowls their special character.

Eine harmonische Verbindung von Bambus und Porzellan prägt die elegante Silhouette dieses Geschirrs. Mittels innovativer Herstellungsverfahren wird karbonisiertes Holz um Porzellanschalen gebogen. Ein abgeschrägter Rand gibt den Schüsseln einen besonderen Charakter.

Hands On
Salad Bowl / Salatschale

Joseph Joseph Ltd., London, GB
Design: Pengelly Design Ltd.
(Simon Pengelly), London, GB
www.josephjoseph.com
www.pengellydesign.com

This salad bowl stands out for its different-coloured salad servers, which are integrated into the sides of the bowl. Made from melamine, this product offers an attractive solution for both indoor and outdoor use.

Ein interessantes Gestaltungsmerkmal dieser Salatschale ist das farblich abgesetzte Salatbesteck, welches in die Kontur der Schale integriert wurde. Hergestellt aus Melamin bietet dieses Produkt eine ansprechende Lösung für den Indoor- und Outdoor-Gebrauch.

The Buzbox
Ice Cube Tray / Eiswürfelbehälter

Raaya Design, San Francisco, USA
Design: Raaya Design (Rupa Chaturvedi),
San Francisco, USA
www.raayadesign.com

This ice cube tray is designed in striking colours. The two-part unit is made of a solid plastic water container and a flexible silicone lid with square separators. In this way, the tray doesn't have to be turned around to remove ice cubes.

Dieser Eiswürfelbehälter ist in auffälligen Farben gestaltet. Das zweiteilige Gefäß besteht aus einem festen Wasserbehälter aus Kunststoff und einem flexiblen Silikondeckel mit quadratischen Unterteilungen. So muss der Behälter nicht umgedreht werden, um die Eiswürfel herauszunehmen.

Travel Press
Coffee Maker / Kaffeezubereiter

Bodum AG,
Triengen, Switzerland / Schweiz
In-house design / Werksdesign:
Bodum Design Group
www.bodum.com

This coffee mug comes in two versions, each for a different use: the Travel Press has a built-in coffee press for those who prefer freshly made coffee on the way, while the Travel Mug is designed to take already brewed coffee. Both models are made from stainless steel and are vacuum-insulated. The reliably sealed lids have a closable drink-through opening. The non-skid silicone band is available in different colours.

Die beiden Ausführungen dieses Kaffeebechers decken unterschiedliche Wünsche ab: Im Travel Press mit eingebauter Kaffeepresse lässt sich Kaffee auch unterwegs frisch zubereiten, während bereits fertig gebrühter Kaffee im Travel Mug bequem mit auf den Weg genommen werden kann. Beide Modelle sind aus rostfreiem Stahl und mit einer Vakuumisolierung ausgestattet. Die zuverlässig abdichtenden Deckel haben eine verschließbare Trinköffnung. Das rutschfeste Silikonband ist in verschiedenen Farben erhältlich.

Lufthansa Starter Box/
Lufthansa Vorspeisenbox

LSG Sky Chefs Catering Logistics GmbH,
Neu-Isenburg, Germany/Deutschland
In-house design/Werksdesign:
Volker Klag, Daniel Knies
www.lsgskychefs.com

The starter box is made of high-quality plastic and was developed for the Lufthansa Business Class in line with the "Special Moment" concept. As a universal reusable box it features the basis for extraordinary culinary experiences. In cooperation with international star chefs various menu creations can be presented in individually developed disposable inlays in ever changing variations. In addition to the optimisation of functional and logistic aspects, Lufthansa's brand values like innovation and quality are realised by the design language of the product. A bento box that originates in the Asian region is yet interpreted in a modern way and communicates Lufthansa's cosmopolitan understanding.

Die Vorspeisenbox aus hochwertigem Kunststoff wurde für die Lufthansa Business Class im Rahmen der „Special Moments" entwickelt. Als universelle Mehrwegbox bietet sie den Rahmen für außergewöhnliche kulinarische Erlebnisse. In Zusammenarbeit mit internationalen Spitzenköchen können die jeweiligen Menükreationen in einem individuell entwickelten Einweg-Inlay immer wieder neu präsentiert werden. Neben der Optimierung funktionaler und logistischer Aspekte setzt der Entwurf die Markenwerte von Lufthansa, wie Innovation und Qualität, produktsprachlich um. Eine aus dem asiatischen Raum stammende, aber modern interpretierte Bentobox vermittelt das kosmopolitische Verständnis von Lufthansa.

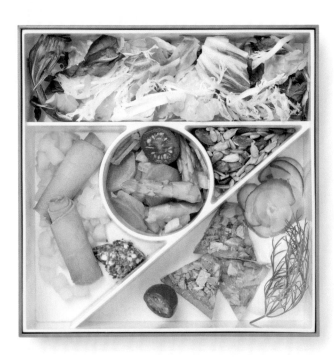

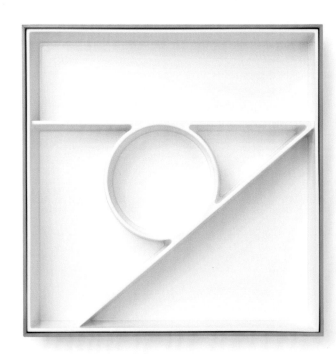

Fiskars
Rolling Pin / Nudelholz

Fiskars
Design: HEIBERG industrial design
(Jakob Heiberg), Gentofte,
Denmark / Dänemark
www.fiskars.com
www.heiberg-id.com

The ergonomic design of this rolling pin features
handles that bend 70 degrees upwards. Orange
handle ends set a strong contrast to the
predominant black. Made of glass-reinforced
nylon and Teflon-coated aluminium, this durable
kitchen utensil is dishwasher-safe.

Bei dieser ergonomisch durchdachten
Gestaltung wurden die beiden Griffe des
Nudelholzes um 70 Grad nach oben gebogen.
Die orangefarbigen Griffabschlüsse bilden
dabei einen starken Kontrast zu dem ansonsten vorherrschenden Schwarz. Das aus
glasfaserverstärktem Nylon und teflon-
beschichtetem Aluminium hergestellte
Küchenutensil ist spülmaschinentauglich.

setdown4
Trivet / Topfrost

cap. GmbH, Hüllhorst,
Germany / Deutschland
In-house design / Werksdesign:
Freimut Stehling
www.cap-direct.de

If required the delicate construction of
individual metal rods is extended to create a
large utility space. After use this trivet can be
pushed together and permits convenient and
space-saving storage.

Bei Bedarf wird das filigrane Konstrukt aus
einzelnen Metallstäben zu einer Aufstellfläche
auseinandergezogen. Komfortabel und platzsparend lässt sich dieser Topfrost nach seinem
Gebrauch wieder zusammenschieben.

Enjoy
Kitchen Tools / Küchenhelfer

Tefal, Groupe SEB,
Rumilly, France / Frankreich
Design: Sebastian Bergne Ltd.
(Sebastian Bergne), London, GB
www.tefal.fr
www.sebastianbergne.com

The slightly bent handle fits ergonomically
into the hand, while the design of the scoops
is inspired by the shape of a leaf. These kitchen
tools are made of 95 per cent recycled PET
plastic. The heat-resistant material allows
bright colours without staining.

Der leicht gebogene Griff fügt sich ergonomisch in die Hand. Die Form der Pfannenwender und Löffel sind von der Form eines
Blattes inspiriert. Diese Küchenhelfer sind
zu 95 Prozent aus wiederverwertbarem PET-
Kunststoff hergestellt. Das hitzebeständige
Material ist auch bei hellen Farbtönen
fleckenabweisend.

Ceramic Knife / Keramikmesser

Mastrad, Paris, France / Frankreich
In-house design / Werksdesign:
Lucas Bignon
www.mastrad.fr

This aesthetic ceramic knife was designed with a swivel handle for blade protection. Zirconium ceramic is nearly as hard as a diamond and offers an exceptional cutting quality without oxidising. The non-slip handle is ergonomically designed to fit well in the hand.

Dieses ästhetisch anmutende Keramikmesser wurde mit einem schwenkbaren Griff zum Schutz der Klinge versehen. Zirkoniumkeramik ist fast so hart wie ein Diamant und bietet eine herausragende Schneidequalität ohne zu oxidieren. Der rutschfeste Griff liegt ergonomisch gut in der Hand.

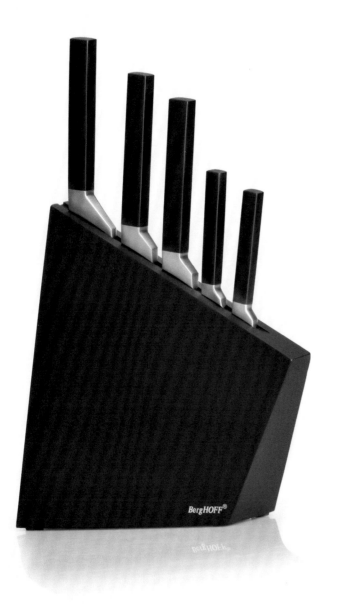

Cubo
Knives and Knife Block /
Messer und Messerblock

Berghoff Worldwide,
Heusden-Zolder, Belgium / Belgien
In-house design / Werksdesign:
Leen Lisens
www.berghoffworldwide.com

This compact and sturdy knife set offers the five most frequently used types of knives. The knives, comprised of satin-finish blades and matt black handles, are housed in an attractive narrow knife block.

Als kompakte Produktlösung reduziert sich dieses Messerset auf die fünf gebräuchlichsten Ausführungen und bietet eine robuste Qualität. Die Kombination von mattierten Klingen und mattschwarzen Griffen wird von einem schmalen Messerblock ansprechend ergänzt.

Zakiyah
Scissors Series / Scherenserie

Scherenfabrik Paul GmbH,
Harsefeld, Germany / Deutschland
Design: Ina-Marie von Mohl,
Hamburg, Germany / Deutschland
www.inamariemohl.com
www.scheren-paul.de

The lively curves of this scissors series were inspired by traditional calligraphy. The inner surfaces of the grips are ergonomically designed and the fillet between the blades consists of a smooth radius for the forefinger. Characteristic for these five scissors is also the contrast between the precision-sharp blades and the voluptuous, soft handles. All scissors sizes have one small and one large handle hole, which is unusual in particular for small scissors.

Inspiriert durch traditionelle Schriftzeichen entstand die schwungvolle Formensprache dieser Scherenserie. Die Radien in den Innenflächen sind ergonomisch angepasst, während sich an der Außenseite des Stegs ein weicher Radius für den Zeigefinger befindet. Charakteristisch für diese fünf Scheren ist zudem der Kontrast zwischen den scharfen Klingen und den geschwungenen, weichen Griffen. Alle Scherengrößen haben ein kleines und ein großes Auge, was insbesondere für kleine Scheren unkonventionell ist.

Prof. Carlos Hinrichsen

Prof. Ron Nabarro

Wolfgang K. Meyer-Hayoz

Bathrooms, spa and air-conditioning
Holistic yet systematic

Bad, Wellness und Klimatechnik
Ganzheitliche Gestaltungslösungen mit System

The integration of different functions leads to the reduction of an often incoherent design language.

Wellness is increasingly becoming an all-embracing design experience that integrates different sectors such as bathrooms and air-conditioning into one. Apart from new, unusual material combinations with sophisticated details, this trend has brought forth comprehensive system solutions for a wide range of functions. This results in a simplification of what was formerly a diverse, manifold, and often incoherent design language. At the same time, it paved the way for new, holistic solutions that also affect other areas. Home intelligence, for example, which is currently making waves, covers aspects such as water management and energy and light control. Design in the "Bathrooms, spa and air-conditioning" sector thus continues to pursue an exciting development process that continually challenges itself to find appropriate design solutions.

Die Integration verschiedener Funktionen führt zur Reduktion einer oft unstimmigen Formensprache.

Mehr und mehr wird „Wellness" zu einem gestalterischen Gesamterlebnis, welches verschiedene Bestandteile wie „Baden" und „Klimatechnik" in sich vereint. Neben neuen, ungewöhnlichen Materialkombinationen mit raffinierten Details entstehen zunehmend umfassende Systemlösungen, die mehrere unterschiedliche Funktionen integrieren. Dadurch ergibt sich in dieser Kategorie die Reduktion einer ehemals vielfältigen, facettenreichen, aber oft auch unstimmigen Formensprache. Gleichzeitig wird der Weg für neue, ganzheitliche Lösungen frei, die auch andere Bereiche betreffen – Hausintelligenz lautet das aktuelle Stichwort, welches Elemente wie Wassermanagement sowie Energie- und Lichtsteuerung umfasst. Es scheint, als unterliege das Design im Bereich „Bad, Wellness und Klimatechnik" weiterhin einem spannenden Entwicklungsprozess, der immer wieder neue Ansprüche an eine angemessene gestalterische Umsetzung stellt.

Neorest
Bathtub / Badewanne

Toto Ltd., Tokyo, Japan
In-house design / Werksdesign:
Ken Igarashi, Mitsuya Obara
www.toto.co.jp

Made of transparent epoxy resin crystal this built-in bathtub displays an aesthetically curved design language with a streamlined appearance. LED lights have been embedded below the haptically pleasing and seamless surface; they integrate an appealing and at the same time energy-efficient light concept. This is achieved by the innovative crystal material, which produces an organically soft, translucent impression in contrast to other materials.

Aus lichtdurchlässigem Epoxidharz-Kristall gefertigt, zeigt diese Einbaubadewanne eine ästhetisch geschwungene Formensprache mit einer stromlinienförmigen Anmutung. Unter der haptisch angenehmen, komplett nahtlosen Oberfläche wurden LED-Leuchten eingelassen, die ein ansprechendes und zugleich energieeffizientes Lichtkonzept integrieren. Möglich wird dies durch das innovative Kristallmaterial, das im Gegensatz zu anderen Materialien einen organisch weichen, transparenten Eindruck erzeugt.

HUG Soft Bathtub / Badewanne

Whitespa, Pyeongtaek City,
Gyunggi-do, Korea
In-house design / Werksdesign

The interior surface of this bathtub features an unusually soft material. The organic shape of the free-standing tub reflects the comfortable qualities of its innovative coating. Aside from a pleasing feel to the touch, the material of the coating adapts ergonomically to the contours of the body. Skid-free, the coating also serves to prevent falls or to absorb the shock of falls. It is also antibacterial, heat-retaining, and durable.

Im Innenraum dieser Badewanne wurde ein ungewohnt weiches Material verwendet. Die organisch anmutende Formensprache der freistehenden Wanne unterstützt die komfortablen Eigenschaften dieser innovativen Badewannenbeschichtung. Neben seiner angenehmen Haptik passt sich das Material dem liegenden Körper ergonomisch vorteilhaft an. Zudem ist es rutschfest, verhindert entsprechend Unfälle und federt eventuelle Stürze ab. Die Beschichtung wirkt antibakteriell, speichert die Wasserwärme und ist langlebig.

La Belle
Bathtub / Badewanne

Villeroy & Boch AG,
Mettlach, Germany / Deutschland
Design: .molldesign,
Schwäbisch Gmünd,
Germany / Deutschland
www.villeroy-boch.com
www.molldesign.de

As a reinterpretation of the sensuous
Romantic period, the free-standing La Belle
bathtub translates classical forms into a new
design: delicate lines and a gentle sweeping
movement set the scene for warm harmony
and fine elegance – either as an individual
piece or as part of the matching sanitary
ware and furniture collection. At the same
time, the curves and length of the inside
of the bathtub create generous, ergonomic
bathing comfort. High-quality Quaryl® makes
this design possible: the bathtub consists of
two perfectly matched parts with clear-cut
edges. The outer panel is self-supporting
without the need for any reinforcement. All
this means that the easy-to-install design
can be made of just one recyclable material:
Quaryl®. La Belle is also available as a built-
in variant.

Die freistehende Badewanne La Belle
übersetzt als Neuinterpretation der sinnlichen Romantik-Epoche klassische Formen
in eine neue Designsprache: Filigrane
Linien und sanfter Schwung inszenieren
warme Harmonie und feine Eleganz – als
Einzelstück oder als Teil einer passenden
Sanitär- und Möbelkollektion. Gleichzeitig
schaffen Rundung und Länge des Wanne-
ninnenraums großzügigen, ergonomischen
Badekomfort. Die Formgebung ist durch
die Fertigung aus hochwertigem Quaryl®
möglich: Die Badewanne besteht aus zwei,
mit klaren Abschlusskanten perfekt aufeinander passenden Teilen, das äußere
Paneel ist ohne weitere Verstärkungs-
materialien selbsttragend – so kommt
die leicht installierbare Konstruktion
mit nur einem, recycelbarem Material,
dem Quaryl®, aus. La Belle ist auch als
Einbauvariante erhältlich.

Ellipso Duo Oval
Bathtub/Badewanne

Franz Kaldewei GmbH & Co. KG,
Ahlen, Germany/Deutschland
Design: Phoenix Design GmbH + Co.KG
(Andreas Haug), Stuttgart,
Germany/Deutschland
www.kaldewei.com
www.phoenixdesign.com

A soft elliptical inner contour promises
security and comfort. The rounded shoulder
section and carefully calibrated side walls
create a generous space, in which to lean
back and relax, either alone or with a partner.
The Ellipso Duo Oval takes the luxurious
feeling one step further with an outer
shape that mirrors the inner ellipse. As free-
standing option the moulded panel surrounds
the ellipse like a second skin, enhancing the
beautiful outer shape.

Eine weiche und elliptische Innenform
verspricht Geborgenheit und Komfort.
Die rund angeformte Schulterpartie und
präzise verlaufende Seitenwände schaffen
dabei großzügig Raum, der zum entspannten Baden sowohl allein als auch
zu zweit einlädt. Die Ellipso Duo Oval
unterstreicht das Gefühl von Luxus und
Extravaganz noch zusätzlich, da sich bei
ihr die innere elliptische Form auch in der
Außenform widerspiegelt. Mit der elliptischen Wannenverkleidung, die sich wie
eine zweite Haut um die Wanne schließt,
wird die Außenform der freistehenden
Badewanne noch stärker zur Geltung
gebracht.

Losanga Element Free
Washbasin / Waschbecken

Gruppo Sanitari Italia S.p.A.,
Gallese, Italy / Italien
In-house design / Werksdesign
www.gsisanitari.it

This unconventional washbasin has a
monolithic look thanks to a combination of
straight and rounded contours. The spacious
basin can be installed with wall waste or
as free-standing unit with floor waste. It is
available in two versions. In the version with
a shelf for tap fitting, the washbasin includes
an overflow and an integrated tap. In the
version without shelf for tap fitting, it is
mounted with external fittings.

Das monolithische Erscheinungsbild
dieses Waschbeckens wirkt durch die
Kombination von geraden und abgerundeten Konturen unkonventionell. Das
großzügig dimensionierte Becken lässt
sich freistehend mit Bodenablauf wie auch
an der Wand mit Wandablauf platzieren.
Es ist in zwei unterschiedlichen Ausführungen erhältlich, zum einen mit einer
integrierten Armatur und einem Überlauf,
zum anderen für eine Kombination mit
passenden Armaturen.

Free Loft
Shower Partition/Duschwand

Duscholux AG,
Thun, Switzerland/Schweiz
Design: designaffairs GmbH,
Munich, Germany/
München, Deutschland
www.duscholux.ch
www.designaffairs.com

The minimalist design of this shower
partition works with the transparency of
its large glass surfaces. The shower can be
freely accessed from the right and left sides.
Free Loft consists of two staggered glass
panes that are connected to each other
with a high-quality aluminium profile. From
inside the shower, the area where the panes
connect serves as a spacious shelf, while
outside the shower, that space is used for
a towel rack. The user-friendly functional
elements enhance the overall aesthetics of
the shower partition.

Das puristische Gestaltungskonzept
dieser Duschwand nutzt die transparente
Wirkung ihrer großzügigen Glasflächen.
Der Zugang zur Dusche bleibt rechts wie
links offen. Free Loft besteht aus zwei
versetzten Glasplatten, welche in der Mitte durch hochwertige Aluminiumprofile
miteinander verbunden sind. Durch diese
Konstruktion entsteht im Nassbereich ein
großzügiges Ablagesystem für hohen Ord-
nungsanspruch. An der Außenseite wird
der entstandene Überhang für eine über
die komplette Front laufende Handtuch-
stange genutzt. Die nutzerfreundlichen
Funktionsdetails dienen zudem der
visuellen Aufwertung der eleganten
Duschwand.

Raindance Showerpipe 240
Shower System / Duschsystem

Hansgrohe AG, Schiltach,
Germany / Deutschland
Design: Phoenix Design GmbH + Co. KG
(Andreas Haug, Tom Schönherr),
Stuttgart, Germany / Deutschland
www.hansgrohe.com
www.phoenixdesign.com

The Raindance Showerpipe 240 shower
system employs elegant lines and quality-
finished materials. Flush-to-the-wall
mounting of the control elements contributes
to the system's functional and minimalist
design. The user-friendly overhead and
hand shower units, together with the slim
shower pipe, present a visually pleasing,
coherent ensemble. The thermostat for
concealed installation allows the user to
easily and comfortably adjust the flow rate
and temperature of the water as well as to
switch between overhead and hand shower.
The compact arrangement of the various
elements leaves ample room for the user
beneath the high overhead shower, which
measures 240 mm in diameter. Optional
EcoSmart technology reduces the shower's
water consumption to approximately nine
litres per minute, which is significantly less
than the average amount of water used
during a shower.

Das Duschsystem Raindance Showerpipe 240 folgt einem minimalistischen
Gestaltungskonzept und nutzt neben einer
eleganten Linienführung die hochwertige Wirkung veredelter Materialien. Ihre
puristische Ästhetik wird durch die Unter-
putzmontage der wandbündigen Bedienelemente funktional schlüssig umgesetzt.
Das nutzerfreundliche Ensemble aus
Kopf- und Handbrause bildet, verbunden
durch die wasserführende, schlanke
Brausenstange, visuell eine gestalterische
Einheit. Ein hinter der Wand montierter
Thermostat ermöglicht die komfortable
Einstellung von Wassermenge und Temperatur sowie die Umstellung von Kopf-
und Handbrause. Die kompakte Anordnung der einzelnen Elemente eröffnet
viel Bewegungsfreiraum unter der weit
auskragenden Kopfbrause mit einem
Durchmesser von 240 mm. Eine Modell-
variante mit EcoSmart-Technologie
erlaubt einen sparsamen Umgang mit
Wasser, da der Verbrauch von etwa neun
Litern pro Minute deutlich unter dem
einer durchschnittlichen Brause liegt.

Sunrise
Electronic Basin Faucet /
Elektronische Waschbecken-Armatur

Xiamen Renshui Industries Co. Ltd.,
Xiamen, China
In-house design / Werksdesign:
Stefano Ollino, Pingli Dong, Kai Lin

The innovative use of an electronic control adds to the elegance of this unconventional basin faucet. The unit stands out for its horizontal orientation as well as for the interesting contrast between the black coating and the stainless steel body. The water tap and nozzle form a tubular core, from which two square surfaces wing off to the sides. The right surface holds a touch control panel that allows for easy and intuitive use. The electronic controls, which also include a light-emitting memory system, allow for precise adjustment of water temperature and quantity. This high-end product solution blends easily into any modern bathroom décor.

Der innovative Einsatz einer elektronischen Steuerung verleiht dieser unkonventionellen Waschbecken-Armatur eine auffallend elegante Formensprache. Ihre horizontale Ausrichtung prägt das eigenständige Erscheinungsbild, wobei der Kontrast zwischen einer schwarzen Beschichtung und einem Edelstahlkorpus herausgestellt wird. Wasserhahn und -düse bilden eine röhrenförmige Verdickung, an deren Seiten sich zwei quadratische Flächen gleich Flügeln abspreizen. Auf der rechten Fläche befindet sich das Touch-Bedienfeld, welches eine intuitiv einfache Handhabung ermöglicht. Die Wassertemperatur und -menge lassen sich durch die elektronische Steuerung präzise einstellen, zudem wurde diese durch ein lichtemittierendes Memory-System nutzerfreundlich ergänzt. Die ästhetisch hochwertige Produktlösung kann flexibel in jedes moderne Badambiente integriert werden.

Smarts Single Cold Tap 010300
Tap / Armatur

ABM Building Materials Technology
Co. Ltd., Foshan, Guangdong, China
In-house design / Werksdesign:
Xiaoping Tang
www.abm365.com

The unique design of this bathroom fixture
contributes a new aesthetic dimension to
the usual bathroom experience. The fixture's
rectangular contours build on and enhance
the simple shape of the angled valve. The
shiny chrome coating, subjected to a special
treatment, provides extra durability and
enhanced aesthetic value to the user-friendly
tap. The mixing tap is ergonomically designed
to be comfortably operated with only one
hand. Black markings on the side set a nice
contrast to the chrome surface and allow for
an intuitive, easy adjustment of the water
temperature. Thanks to its neutral style, this
discreet fixture goes well with all kinds of
washbasins.

Um dem tagtäglichen Gebrauch sanitärer
Anlagen eine neue Ästhetik zu geben,
kreiert das interessante Gestaltungskonzept
dieser Armatur eine harmonische Formensprache. In Anlehnung an den schlichten
Strukturaufbau eines Eckventils wurde
bewusst eine rechtwinklige Kontur aufgegriffen und durch eine zurückhaltende
Linienführung ästhetisch aufgewertet. Die
glänzende Chrombeschichtung wurde mit
einem speziellen, Haltbarkeit gewährlei-
stenden Verfahren so veredelt, dass sie die
Wertigkeit der nutzerfreundlichen Armatur
visuell unterstützt. Die Mischbatterie
wurde ergonomisch sinnvoll konzipiert
und ist mit nur einer Hand komfortabel
bedienbar. Schwarze Markierungen an der
Seite setzen sich kontrastreich von der
Chromoberfläche ab und ermöglichen eine
intuitiv einfache Einstellung der Wassertemperatur. Die dezente Armatur lässt sich
stilistisch neutral mit Waschbeckenformen
aller Art kombinieren.

Smarts Single Cold Tap 010310
Tap / Armatur

ABM Building Materials Technology
Co. Ltd., Foshan, Guangdong, China
In-house design / Werksdesign:
Xiaoping Tang
www.abm365.com

This wall fixture has a sleek and compact
structure. Specific elements are employed
to further enhance the minimalist effect.
The laterally attached mixing tap protrudes
from the contour of the rest of the tap. Its
rectangular orientation stands in distinct
contrast to the otherwise harmoniously
curved lines. The water jet is integrated
nearly invisibly in the short front part of
the tap. A shiny surface underscores the
elegant form and reflects the colours of
the surrounding environment. A special
treatment applied to the chrome coating
prevents tarnishing. Designed according
to ergonomic principles, the fixture can be
comfortably operated with one hand. Its
discreet appearance allows for the flexible
integration with different room interiors.

Bei der Gestaltung dieser Wandarmatur
wurde eine möglichst schlichte und
kompakte Struktur angestrebt. Einzelne
Gestaltungsdetails werden betont minimalistisch eingesetzt. Prägnant ragt die
seitlich angebrachte Mischbatterie aus
der Kontur der Armatur heraus. Ihre
rechtwinklige Ausrichtung steht in auf-
fallendem Kontrast zur ansonsten harmonisch abgerundeten Linienführung. Die
Wasserdüse wurde hingegen fast unsichtbar in den kurzen, vorderen Teil der
Armatur integriert. Eine hochglänzende
Oberfläche betont das elegant wirkende
Gebilde und spiegelt die Farben der Umgebung reizvoll wider. Um das Anlaufen
der Chrombeschichtung zu verhindern,
wurde im Fertigungsprozess ein spezielles Veredelungsverfahren zum Einsatz gebracht. Die nach ergonomischen Gesichtspunkten konzipierte Armatur lässt sich
bequem mit einer Hand bedienen. Ein
zurückhaltendes Erscheinungsbild ermöglicht eine flexible Kombination mit
unterschiedlichen Raumausstattungen.

Smarts Angle Valve 010330
Tap / Armatur

ABM Building Materials Technology
Co. Ltd., Foshan, Guangdong, China
In-house design / Werksdesign:
Xiaoping Tang
www.abm365.com

This fixture comes with a particularly minimalist design dedicated to making the everyday use of the product comfortable and visually appealing. The tap can be optionally used as a washing machine hook-up, in which case the water nozzle is replaced with a special valve in the short front part of the tap. The mixing tap protrudes laterally at a right angle from the otherwise harmoniously curved lines of the tap. This allows to use the fixture comfortably with one hand. A high-gloss chrome surface – specially treated to resist tarnishing over the long term – enhances the overall effect of the quality production. The fixture's discreet appearance allows for its flexible use in a variety of different interiors.

Diese Armatur verkörpert ein betont minimalistisches Gestaltungskonzept, welches den täglichen Gebrauch komfortabel und visuell ansprechend gestalten möchte. Als bedarfsgerecht einsetzbarer Wasseranschluss lässt sich an diese Armatur problemlos eine Waschmaschine anschließen. Dazu wurde anstelle der Wasserdüse ein Spezialventil in den kurzen, vorderen Teil des Hahns integriert. Die seitlich angebrachte Mischbatterie ragt rechtwinklig aus der ansonsten harmonisch abgerundeten Linienführung der Armatur heraus. Diese Anordnung kommt der ergonomischen Zielsetzung, die Armatur bequem mit einer Hand bedienbar zu machen, entgegen. Eine hochglänzende Chromoberfläche unterstützt die Wirkung der detailgenauen Verarbeitung, wobei ein spezielles Veredelungsverfahren das Anlaufen der Chrombeschichtung auch langfristig verhindert. Das zurückhaltende Erscheinungsbild ermöglicht einen flexiblen Einsatz in unterschiedlichen Interieurs.

Smarts Angle Valve 010370
Tap / Armatur

ABM Building Materials Technology
Co. Ltd., Foshan, Guangdong, China
In-house design / Werksdesign:
Xiaoping Tang
www.abm365.com

Minimalist design principles give this shower wall fixture its distinctive look and provide for comfortable everyday use. A high-gloss chrome surface – specially treated to resist tarnishing over the long term – enhances the effect of the fixture's quality production. All functional elements of this tap are in keeping with a clean design approach that aims for harmonious proportions. The connection valve for the hand shower is conveniently positioned on the bottom of the tap. Two mixing taps protrude laterally at a right angle from the otherwise harmoniously curved lines of the tap. This demonstrates the successful implementation of an ergonomic concept that strives for ease of use.

Minimalistische Gestaltungsprinzipien prägen das Erscheinungsbild dieser Wandarmatur, die den täglichen Gebrauch komfortabel und ästhetisch gestalten soll. Eine Beschichtung aus glänzendem Chrom unterstreicht die Wertigkeit der präzisen Verarbeitung, wobei ein spezielles Veredelungsverfahren auch langfristig das Anlaufen der Chrombeschichtung verhindert. Alle Funktionselemente dieser Armatur folgen einer klaren Formensprache, die auf harmonische Proportionen abzielt. Bedarfsgerecht wurde das Anschlussventil für die Handbrause an der Unterseite positioniert. Zwei seitlich angebrachte Mischbatterien ragen rechtwinklig aus der ansonsten abgerundeten Linienführung der Armatur heraus. Hier zeigt sich die konsequente Umsetzung einer ergonomisch durchdachten Konzeption zugunsten einer komfortablen Bedienbarkeit.

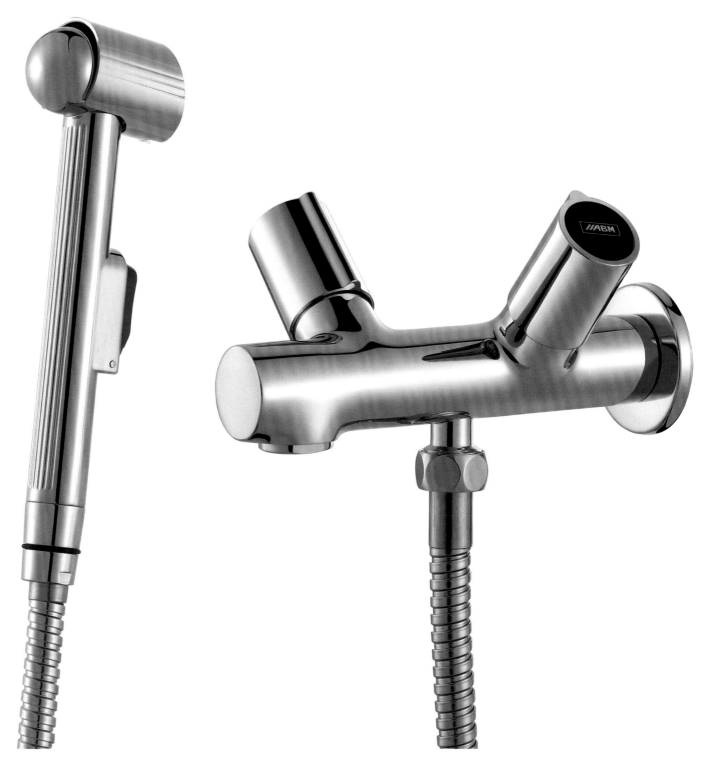

Duo
Basin Faucet /
Waschbecken-Armatur

ISMA, Hangzhou City, China
In-house design / Werksdesign:
Christian Laudet, Gia-Dinh To

The design of this unconventional basin faucet was inspired by dualism. A symmetrical empty space in the tap spout and mixer, combined with a distinctive colour scheme in a choice of anthracite, chrome or white, gives the faucet a sculptural presence. The design goal was to suggest a harmony between metal, water and air. When the tap is turned on, the water jets out in two separate streams, which then merge into one as they pass through an aerator nozzle. The elegant "obsidian" model in anthracite offers a pronounced contrast to the white washbasin. Duo comes equipped with a user-friendly mounting system that allows for effortless DIY installation by hand. A water-saving flow regulator contributes to the faucet's high use value.

Inspiriert durch das Prinzip der Dualität entstand das Gestaltungskonzept dieser unkonventionellen Waschbecken-Armatur. Eine symmetrische Freilassung im Handgriff und in der Hahnmündung erweckt eine skulpturale Anmutung, welche durch die prägnante Farbgebung in Anthrazit, Chrom oder Weiß visuell unterstrichen wird. Gestalterisches Ziel war es, eine Harmonie zwischen Metall, Wasser und Luft zu suggerieren. Durch die charakteristische Formensprache strömt das Wasser in zwei voneinander getrennten Linien, um im vorderen Teil der Armatur mittels eines Luftsprudlers zu einem sanften Strahl zu verschmelzen. In der eleganten „Obsidian"-Ausführung in Anthrazit wird ein markanter Kontrast zum weißen Waschbecken angestrebt. Duo wurde mit einem benutzerfreundlichen Befestigungssystem versehen, welches sich einfach und mühelos von Hand betätigen lässt. Die zeitgemäße Ausstattung mit einem wassersparenden Strahlregler rundet den hohen Gebrauchswert ab.

arwa–Lb® LumiTouch & LumiTouchfree Electronic Washbasin Faucet / Elektronischer Waschtischmischer

Similor AG, Laufen,
Switzerland / Schweiz
Design: Jürg Heuberger,
Laufen Bathrooms, Laufen,
Switzerland / Schweiz
www.similorgroup.com
www.laufen.ch

This electronic mixer stands out for its clean, discreet design. The front and back ends round off harmoniously to create a well-balanced whole. The low-contact LumiTouch offers a choice of three pre-set temperature levels, while a circle on the tap changes colours to indicate which temperature level is in use. The LumiTouchfree tap is equipped with a self-closing mechanism to reduce water and energy consumption.

Dezent und klar in seiner Formensprache präsentiert sich dieser elektronische Mischer. Gestaltet mit ausgewogenen Proportionen spiegeln sich die abgerundeten Enden der vorderen und hinteren Kontur. Mit drei voreingestellten Temperaturstufen ermöglicht die berührungsarme LumiTouch-Elektronik eine komfortable Bedienung, wobei die jeweils ausgewählte Temperatur durch einen farbig illuminierten Kreis angezeigt wird. Der LumiTouchfree-Wasserhahn wurde zudem mit einer Selbstschlussautomatik ausgestattet, die den Wasser- und Energieverbrauch reduziert.

Runtal Splash
Decorative Radiator/Designheizkörper

Zehnder Group Vaux Andigny S.A.S.,
Vaux-Andigny, France / Frankreich
Design: Christian Ghion,
Paris, France / Frankreich
www.zehndergroup.com
www.christianghion.com

Thanks to a specific material combination, it was possible to devise an independent and artistically inspired design for this radiator. Runtal Splash consists of two components: a decoratively designed front and a supporting structure made of expanded natural graphite. The surface is made of Corian, a material, which was particularly developed for this purpose. The style presents a three-dimensional theme, whose concentric circles are reminiscent of waves that form when a drop hits the water surface. The heating elements are electrically operated and embedded in the graphite layer. The radiator ensures quick and even distribution of heat. It provides a heating performance of 750 watts and can be adjusted via a programmable remote control. According to space conditions the flatly designed radiator can be installed either horizontally or vertically. As an architectural element it sets visual priorities.

Die eigenständige, künstlerisch inspirierte Gestaltung dieses Heizkörpers wurde durch eine besondere Materialkombination ermöglicht: Runtal Splash besteht aus zwei Bestandteilen, einer dekorativ formbaren Front und einer Unterkonstruktion aus expandiertem Naturgraphit. Das für diese Zwecke entwickelte Oberflächenmaterial Corian ermöglicht dabei die Formensprache eines plastischen Motivs, dessen konzentrische Kreise an die Wellenbildung eines aufschlagenden Wassertropfens erinnern. Die in die Graphitschicht eingebetteten, elektrisch betriebenen Heizelemente sorgen für eine schnelle und gleichmäßige Verteilung der Wärme. Der Heizkörper bietet eine Wärmeleistung von 750 Watt und kann über ein programmierbares Steuergerät extern geregelt werden. Je nach Platzgegebenheiten lässt sich der flach konstruierte Heizkörper wahlweise horizontal oder vertikal ausgerichtet anbringen und setzt visuell einen klaren, architekturorientierten Akzent.

Conforto
Seat Heater / Sitzheizkörper

C + C Innovative Products OG,
Nussbach, Austria / Österreich
In-house design / Werksdesign:
Christian Mayr
www.meinheizkoerper.at

This innovative seat heater has two uses: it serves both as a heater and as a comfortable seating unit. With a range of surface design options, the device can be readily adapted to suit the ambience of any room. As a wall unit, it has a straight appearance and a clear design language. Reduced to the essentials, the focus is on select features, such as a towel holder and discreet coat hooks. Depending on the heating technology in place, the Conforto can either be equipped with an infrared heating plate or connected to a conventional hot-water heating system.

Eine innovative Idee vereint in diesem Sitzheizkörper einen doppelten Nutzen: einerseits eine Heizfunktion und andererseits eine komfortable Sitzgelegenheit. Der in seiner Oberflächenausführung individuell gestaltbare Heizkörper lässt sich stilistisch dem jeweiligen Raumambiente anpassen. Das wandebene Objekt zeichnet sich durch ein geradliniges Erscheinungsbild und eine klare Formensprache aus. Die Reduktion auf das Wesentliche führt zur Konzentration auf wenige Gestaltungsdetails wie einen Handtuchhalter oder dezente Garderobenhaken. Abhängig von der Heiztechnik vor Ort, kann der Conforto entweder mit einer Infrarotwärmeplatte ausgestattet sein oder an die herkömmliche Warmwasserheizung angeschlossen werden.

Stile
Flat-Panel Heater / Flächenheizkörper

C + C Innovative Products OG,
Nussbach, Austria / Österreich
In-house design / Werksdesign:
Christian Mayr
www.meinheizkoerper.at

Clear lines underscore the remarkably flat build of this wall heater. Mineral surfaces permit individual designs that integrate well into a wide range of rooms and interiors. The heater's ceramic surfaces require a minimum mounting height of only 43 mm and offer long-lasting corrosion and scratch resistance. Optionally the Stile can either be equipped with an infrared heating plate or connected to a conventional hot-water heating system.

Eine klare Linienführung unterstreicht die auffallend flache Bauweise dieses Wandheizkörpers. Mineralische Oberflächen erlauben eine individuelle Gestaltung, die sich harmonisch in jeden beliebigen Raum eingliedern lässt. Zudem ermöglichen keramische Oberflächen eine minimale Aufbauhöhe von nur 43 mm und bieten eine dauerhafte Säure- und Kratzbeständigkeit. Der Stile kann optional elektrisch mit einer Infrarotwärmeplatte ausgestattet sein oder an die herkömmliche Warmwasserheizung angeschlossen werden.

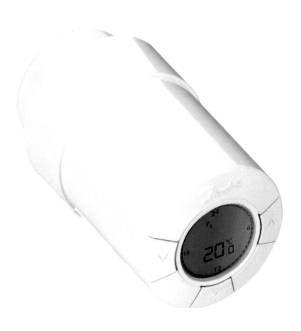

living eco
Radiator Thermostat/
Heizungsthermostat

Danfoss A/S, Vejle,
Denmark/Dänemark
In-house design/Werksdesign:
Anders Ostergaard Clausen,
Michael Qvortrup
www.danfoss.com

The programmable electronic thermostat has a remarkable compact design. Its unobtrusive appearance is reduced to an illuminated display visualising sophisticated functionality. Due to an improved control of the room climate, energy consumption is reduced – the temperature is lowered when no one is present in the room. The thermostat is adaptive as it registers the respective heating-up time and automatically lowers the heating function as soon as the room is aired.

Dieses programmierbare, elektronische Thermostat wurde auffallend kompakt gestaltet. Sein zurückhaltendes Erscheinungsbild reduziert sich auf ein beleuchtetes Display, welches eine ausgefeilte Funktionalität visualisiert. Mittels einer verbesserten Regulierung des Raumklimas und einer Temperaturabsenkung bei Nichtanwesenheit wird ein reduzierter Energieverbrauch erreicht. Das Thermostat ist lernfähig, indem es die jeweils benötigte Aufheizzeit registriert und die Heizung automatisch herunterfährt, sobald gelüftet wird.

living connect
Radiator Thermostat/
Heizungsthermostat

Danfoss A/S, Vejle,
Denmark/Dänemark
In-house design/Werksdesign:
Anders Ostergaard Clausen,
Michael Qvortrup
www.danfoss.com

This adaptive thermostat works independently or in a network by being wirelessly linked to the intelligent Danfoss Link regulation system. The temperature can thus be regulated individually in each room or uniformly for the whole living area. The thermostat with a compact design features an illuminated display; it notices how fast the heater heats up the living area and determines the heating time accordingly. If the thermostat registers a drop in temperature when a room is aired it turns the heater down.

Dieses lernfähige Thermostat arbeitet sowohl allein als auch vernetzt, indem es drahtlos mit dem intelligenten Regelsystem Danfoss Link verknüpft wird. Damit lässt sich die Temperatur optional raumweise oder für den gesamten Wohnbereich einheitlich einstellen. Das kompakt gestaltete Thermostat mit beleuchtetem Display erkennt selbsttätig, wie schnell die Heizkörper den Wohnbereich erwärmen und legt entsprechend den Zeitpunkt des Heizens fest. Registriert das Thermostat beim Lüften einen Temperaturabfall, regelt es die Heizung herunter.

Central Control Display/
Zentrale Regeleinheit

Danfoss A/S, Vejle,
Denmark/Dänemark
In-house design/Werksdesign:
Michael Qvortrup, Henning Guld
www.danfoss.com

As a result of a puristically functional design principle this control unit is reduced to a display flush with the wall. Integrated in a white frame it harmoniously blends into the different living ambiences. As a central control unit, the display allows access to all system data and adjustments. It is possible to call up service reports, temperature display, etc. Thanks to a wireless, portable display, controlling is comfortable; internet-based remote monitoring and remote adjustment are possible as well.

Im Rahmen eines puristisch funktionalen Gestaltungsprinzips reduziert sich diese Regeleinheit auf ein wandebenes Display. Integriert in einen weißen Rahmen fügt es sich harmonisch in das jeweilige Wohnambiente ein. Als zentrale Regeleinheit ermöglicht das Display den Zugang zu allen Systemdaten und -einstellungen, es können Serviceberichte, Temperaturanzeigen usw. abgerufen werden. Dank einer drahtlosen, portablen Anzeige erfolgt eine komfortable Steuerung, internetgestützt ist zudem eine Fernüberwachung und Ferneinstellung möglich.

evohome
Individual Room Control System / Einzelraumregelungssystem

Honeywell Technologies Sàrl,
Rolle, Switzerland / Schweiz
Design: Shore Design
(James McLusky), Edinburgh, GB
www.honeywell.com
www.shore-design.co.uk

This individual room control system can be used with most heating systems and offers eight individually adjustable temperature zones and time programmes. In addition to excellent energy efficiency, the product provides state-of-the-art user comfort via a wireless communication system. The ergonomic device can be used as either a table or wall unit and is available in the colours brilliant black, metallic silver and brilliant white. With a sleek design and balanced proportions, the control system blends in effortlessly with its surrounding environment.

Dieses Einzelraumregelungssystem unterstützt die gängigen Heizungssysteme und bietet acht individuell wählbare Temperaturzonen und Zeitprogramme. Neben einer nachhaltigen Energieeffizienz war ein zeitgemäßer Bedienkomfort per kabelloser Kommunikation für die Produktentwicklung zielgebend. Das ergonomisch gestaltete Bediengerät ist als Tisch- und Wandgerät wahlweise in den Farben Brillantschwarz, Metallicsilber und Brillantweiß erhältlich. Mit einer klaren Formensprache und ausgewogenen Abmessungen passt es sich der Umgebung harmonisch an.

Room Sensor / Raumsensor

Danfoss A/S, Vejle,
Denmark / Dänemark
In-house design / Werksdesign:
Michael Qvortrup
Design: 3PART A/S (Simon Skafdrup),
Århus, Denmark / Dänemark
www.danfoss.com
www.3part.com

This unobtrusively designed room sensor indicates the current room temperature thus facilitating the setting of an individually desired heater performance. The square-shaped sensor can be mounted discretely on the wall. The neutral white colouring enhances the harmonious integration into different room designs. Only the circular display in the centre is set apart from the plain style. By means of a radio control, the room sensor can be adjusted according to different needs.

Dieser dezent gestaltete Raumsensor zeigt die aktuelle Temperatur im Raum an und erleichtert somit die Regelung der individuell gewünschten Heizungsleistung. Der quadratische Sensor lässt sich unauffällig an die Wand montieren, eine neutrale Farbgebung in Weiß trägt zur harmonischen Integration in unterschiedliche Raumgestaltungen bei. Einzig das kreisrunde Display in der Mitte hebt sich aus der schlichten Formensprache hervor. Eine Funksteuerung ermöglicht es zudem, den Raumsensor bedarfsgerecht zu programmieren.

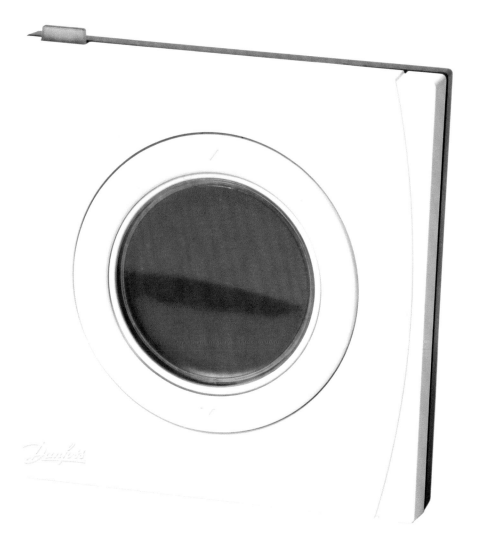

**Kessel Design Covers /
Kessel Design–Roste
Bathroom Drain Covers /
Abdeckungen für Badabläufe**

Kessel AG, Lenting,
Germany / Deutschland
In-house design / Werksdesign:
Mark Jung
www.kessel.de

This product series was designed to satisfy
the demand for increased individualism
in bathrooms. The different designs of the
bathroom drain covers range from geometric
patterns to playful arrangements of circular
and elliptical slots. The quality-finished
stainless steel covers ensure durability and
meet a high manufacturing standard. The
Lock & Lift system is optionally available
to facilitate easy removal of the covers for
maintenance.

Dem Wunsch nach mehr Individualität im
Bad möchte diese Produktserie entsprechen.
Die unterschiedlichen Abdeckungen für
Badabläufe nutzen sowohl eine streng
geometrische Symmetrie der Ablauf-
schlitze als auch eine spielerische Anordnung von punkt- und ellipsenförmigen
Ausstanzungen. Die hochwertige Ausführung in Edelstahl unterstreicht den
Qualitätsanspruch und garantiert Langlebigkeit. Optional sind die Roste mit
dem Lock & Lift-System erhältlich, das
als Rost-Entnahmehilfe die Reinigung
des Ablaufes erleichtert.

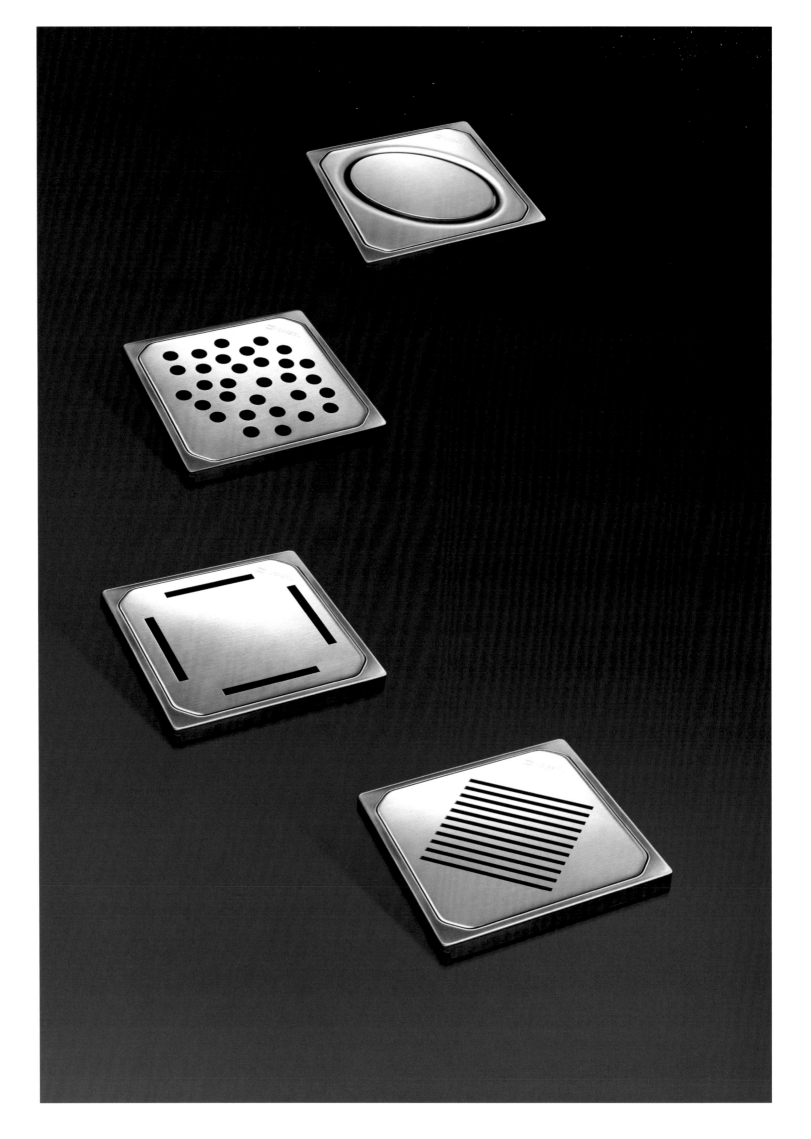

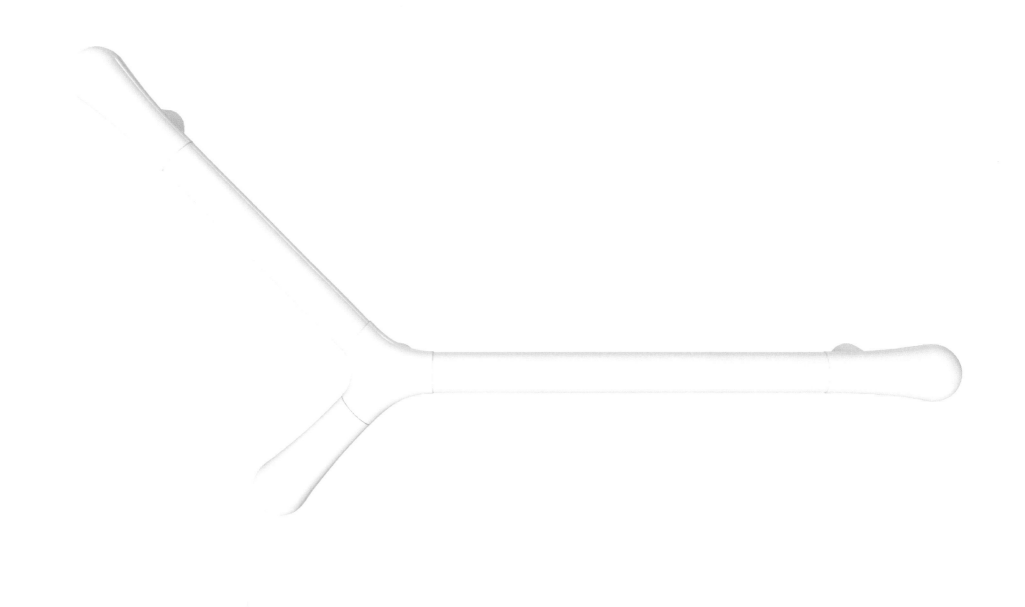

I-Zecure
Holding Bar / Haltegriff

Bathroom Design Co., Ltd.,
Bangkok, Thailand
In-house design / Werksdesign
www.bathroomtomorrow.com

This series of differently shaped holding bars was designed to increase safety in bathrooms. The use of innovative materials, slip-free surfaces, and harmoniously rounded corners and edges reduces the risk of accidents and offers a high degree of stability. Each of the four product versions can support up to 200 kg. I-Zecure also offers an innovative sensor technology that can recognise accidents and activate calls for help via SMS or radio frequency. The neutral white colour scheme allows for flexible use in traditional as well as contemporary bathroom interiors. The harmonious lines evoke the image of tree branches and make for an attractive appearance that appeals to the emotions and instils a sense of trust.

Dieses System unterschiedlich geformter Haltegriffe soll die Sicherheit in Badezimmern erhöhen. Ihre innovative Materialität reduziert die Unfallgefahr und bietet zugleich ein hohes Maß an Stabilität. Bei der Fertigung wurde auf eine rutschfeste Oberfläche sowie harmonisch abgerundete Ecken und Kanten großer Wert gelegt. Alle vier unterschiedlichen Ausführungen der Produktserie können mit einem Maximalgewicht von über 200 kg belastet werden. Zudem umfasst I-Zecure eine innovative Sicherheitstechnologie, die mittels Sensoren einen Unfall registriert und einen SOS-Notruf per SMS oder Funk aktiviert. Die neutrale Farbgebung in Weiß ermöglicht einen stilistisch flexiblen Einsatz in klassischen wie auch zeitgemäßen Badezimmereinrichtungen. Die harmonische Linienführung ähnelt abstrahierten Baumästen und schafft ein emotional ansprechendes Erscheinungsbild, das Vertrauen erweckt.

**Swissdent
Short Head Toothbrush/
Kurzkopfzahnbürste**

Swissdent Cosmetics AG,
Zürich, Switzerland/Schweiz
In-house design/Werksdesign:
Magdalena Basinska, Andreas Michaelis,
Vaclav Velkoborsky
Production/Produktion:
Bürstenfabrik Ebnat-Kappel AG
www.swissdent.com

The balanced curves of this toothbrush evoke
the shape of a precision dental instrument.
In accordance with ergonomic principles,
the brush neck has been kept short, as a
short distance between the hand and the
mouth reduces the lever effect, minimising
the pressure that needs to be applied on
the brush. The small brush head allows for
comfortable access to the back molars, and
the concave cut of its bristles facilitates the
removal of plaque from between the teeth.

Die ausgewogene Linienführung dieser
Zahnbürste wurde einem zahnmedizini-
schen Instrument nachempfunden. Eine
ergonomische Ausrichtung führte zur Entwicklung eines kurzen Zahnbürstenhalses,
da der geringe Abstand zwischen Hand
und Mund die Hebelarmwirkung mindert
und somit weniger Druck auf die Bürste
ausgeübt werden muss. Der kleine Kopf
ist von funktionalem Nutzen, da er den
Zugang zu den hintersten Backenzähnen
erleichtert. Zudem entfernt der konkave
Schnitt der Borsten Plaque auch in den
Zahnzwischenräumen.

**Interdental Set
Oral Hygiene Product/
Mundhygiene-Produkt**

Bürstenfabrik Ebnat-Kappel AG,
Ebnat-Kappel, Switzerland/Schweiz
In-house design/Werksdesign:
Lucy Buonanno, Daniel Lutz
www.ebnat.ch

Consisting of seven pieces this innovative
interdental set serves as oral hygiene
supplement. Constant application of the
interdental brushes and the tongue cleaner
is supported by the ready-to-hand storage in
compactly designed supports. The grip, which
is shaped according to ergonomic aspects,
allows better access to the backmost tongue
and teeth area. A distinct colour concept
additionally serves the simple distinction
of the four different top pieces that can be
quickly and easily exchanged.

Bestehend aus sieben Teilen dient dieses
innovative Interdental-Set der ergänzenden
Mundhygiene. Die regelmäßige Anwendung
der Interdental-Bürsten und des Zungen-
reinigers wird durch die griffbereite Aufbewahrung im kompakten Halter unterstützt. Der nach ergonomischen Gesichtspunkten geformte Griff ermöglicht einen
besseren Zugang zum hinteren Zungen-
und Zahnbereich. Ein klares Farbkonzept
dient zudem der einfachen Unterscheidung
der vier verschiedenen Aufsätze, die sich
einfach und schnell auswechseln lassen.

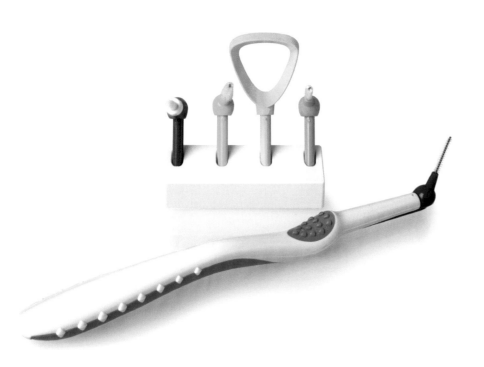

DotPot
Toddler Toilet / Kleinkind-Toilette

BabyMatters, Lier, Belgium / Belgien
In-house design / Werksdesign
www.babymatters.com
www.dotbaby.eu

This toddler toilet has a long usage life given its variable uses. Made from recyclable materials, the DotPot serves as a potty, with the carrying handle functioning to support the child's back. When the child passes to the next development phase, the removable seat frame serves as a toilet trainer, with the upside-down pot serving as a footstool and step for children up to 40 kg. Anti-slip nubs on the bottom of the pot provide for good stability.

Das Gestaltungskonzept dieser Kleinkind-Toilette erlaubt eine lange Nutzung, da sie variabel einsetzbar ist. Der aus recycelbarem Material hergestellte DotPot dient zunächst als Töpfchen, wobei der Tragegriff den Rücken des Kindes stützt. Die herausnehmbare Sitzschale eignet sich im weiteren Entwicklungsprozess als Toilettentrainer, der umgedrehte Topf als Fußbank und Trittbrett für Kinder bis zu 40 kg. Dabei gewähren die rutschfesten Noppen an der Unterseite des Topfes eine gute Standfestigkeit.

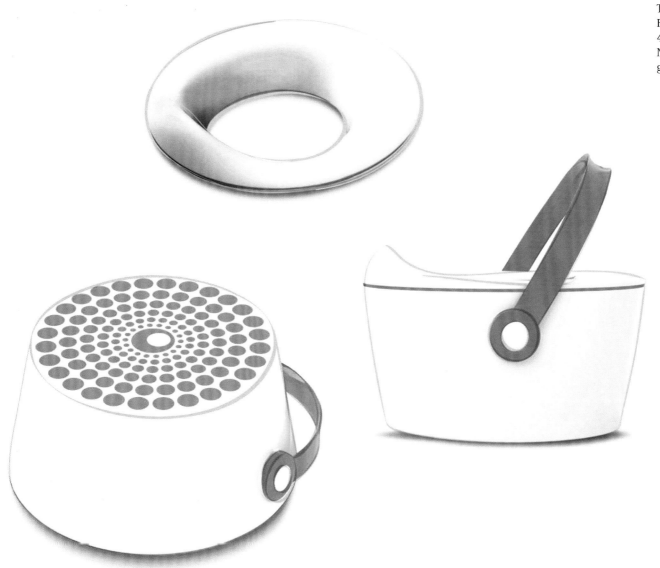

Aito
Sauna Head Support/
Sauna-Kopfstütze

Silgmann Ges.m.b.H. & Co. KG,
Mondsee, Austria/Österreich
In-house design/Werksdesign:
Michael Kogelnik
www.silgmann.com

The importance of healthy breathing was taken into consideration in the design of this ergonomic head support for the sauna. Comfortable inhalation and exhalation while lying down is facilitated by a raised head support. The unique form of Aito is designed to adapt to people of different ages, genders and sizes. The use of three-dimensionally shaped wood veneer meets high functional standards. The head support is stackable, allowing for efficient storage and transport.

Bei der Entwicklung dieser ergonomisch durchdachten Kopfstütze für den Sauna-bereich waren unterschiedliche Zielset-zungen ausschlaggebend. Zum einen wurde Aito so gestaltet, dass das Atmen im Liegen durch die Anhebung des Kopfes erleichtert wird. Denn entspanntes Ein- und Ausatmen in einer heißen Umgebung wie einer Sauna ist aus gesundheitlichen Gründen wichtig. Entsprechend entstand eine eigenständige Formensprache, die auf Menschen unterschiedlichen Alters, Geschlechts oder Größe ausgerichtet wurde. Die Verwendung von dreidimen-sional verformtem Holzfurnier entspricht den hohen funktionalen Anforderungen. Zudem ist die Kopfstütze stapelbar und kann deshalb platzsparend gelagert und transportiert werden.

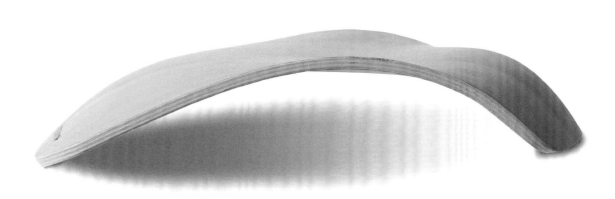

Tylö Scandinavia
Sauna Heater/Saunaofen

Tylö, Halmstad, Sweden/Schweden
Design: Propeller AB (Olle Gyllang,
Karl Forsberg), Stockholm,
Sweden/Schweden
www.tylo.com
www.propeller.se

Tylö Scandinavia is a modern sauna heater that reinterprets the traditional northern style. Its cast-iron grill, the core component, picks up the curved design of an amphitheatre. The white housing with its rounded edges and raised sides communicates a rather unadorned appearance. At the front of the grill there is a removable bowl, which may be filled with water, herbs or aromatic essences to enrich the ambient air.

Tylö Scandinavia ist ein zeitgemäßer Sau-naofen, der den traditionellen nordischen Stil gestalterisch neu interpretiert. Sein gusseiserner Grill, die zentrale Kompo-nente des Ofens, greift die bogenförmige Formensprache eines Amphitheaters auf. Vergleichsweise schlicht wirkt hingegen das weiße Gehäuse mit seinen abgerunde-ten Ecken und den hochgezogenen Seiten. An der Vorderseite des Grills befindet sich eine abnehmbare Schale, durch welche optional Wasser, Kräuter oder aromatische Essenzen die Raumluft anreichern.

PowerSpa
Lounger / Liegemöbel

Invora Innovation Group,
Invora GmbH, Karlsruhe,
Germany / Deutschland
In-house design / Werksdesign:
Volker Rathert, Raphael Krauss
www.powerspa.eu

PowerSpa is a lounger that lets people experience medical wellness not only in the professional field, but also in the privacy of their own homes. A distinctive design accentuates the structure of the materials used. Wood composites and microfibre covers provide a tactile appeal and users can customise their lounger with a wide choice of textiles and colours. The functional components of the lounger are integrated into the overlying functional unit, which forms a harmonious whole by embedding in the body and allows the technology to be hidden.

PowerSpa ist ein Liegemöbel, das Medical Wellness nicht nur im professionellen Bereich, sondern auch im Privathaushalt erlebbar macht. Eine klare Gestaltung betont die Struktur der verwendeten Materialien. Holzwerkstoffe und Mikrofaserbezüge laden zur Berührung ein, wobei alle Oberflächen aus einer Vielzahl von Textilien und Farben individuell zusammengestellt werden können. Die funktionalen Elemente wurden in die aufliegende Funktionseinheit integriert, welche durch das Einbetten in den Korpus ein harmonisches Ganzes bildet und die Technik unsichtbar werden lässt.

AP-1210AH
Air Purifier / Luftreiniger

Woongjin Coway Co., Ltd., Seoul, Korea
In-house design / Werksdesign:
Hun-jung Choi, Sang-hwa Lee
www.coway.co.kr

This air purifier has been conceived with regard to the numerous pathogenic agents and other harmful dust particles that may occur in the urban environment. It has an integrated humidifier function. When used as a humidifier it uses a rotating disk that absorbs the water and sends the moist air with the air that has been cleaned through the HEPA and other filters. The humidifying quantity matches with most ultrasonic humidifiers. The water tank is easy to detach from the rear by a simple handle mechanism. For the front cover decoration, a hairline effect was given to the mould and a special resin was injected to give a subtle shine. On the bottom it has a pollution indicator.

Dieser Luftreiniger wurde konzipiert im Hinblick auf die zahlreichen Krankheitskeime sowie sonstige schädliche Staubpartikel, die in der städtischen Umgebung auftreten können. Er verfügt über eine integrierte Befeuchtungsvorrichtung. Wird er als Befeuchter verwendet, kommt eine Drehscheibe zum Einsatz, die das Wasser absorbiert und die Feuchtigkeit in die Luft abgibt, die durch den Schwebstofffilter HEPA und weitere Filter gereinigt wurde. Die Menge an befeuchteter Luft entspricht der Leistung der meisten Ultraschall-Befeuchter. Mit einem einfachen Griffmechanismus lässt sich der Wassertank an der Rückseite leicht abnehmen. Zur Verzierung der Vorderseite wurden haarfeine Strukturen in die Form eingearbeitet. Außerdem wurde ein spezielles Harz eingespritzt, um einen dezenten Glanzeffekt zu erzeugen. Unten am Gerät befindet sich eine Schadstoffanzeige.

Woongjin Coway Co., Ltd., Seoul, Korea
In-house design / Werksdesign:
Hun-Jung Choi, Mi-Youn Kyung
www.coway.co.kr

This battery-run water softener with rounded contours has a friendly aesthetics. Its shiny, bright white surface symbolises the purity of the water. The ecologically designed product filters heavy metals and pollutants out of the water by means of ion exchange. Other user-friendly aspects, such as easy cleaning and maintenance, were also considered in the unit's development. The manufacturing process is both low cost and ecological. LED control elements on the front of the unit reliably indicate the filter status and remaining life of the battery. A bright orange line runs around the sides of the unit, lending the product a certain posture and stability. A recessed notch in this line allows the user to easily open the front lid. An ion resin storage tank minimises the required maintenance.

Die Gestaltung dieses batteriebetriebenen Wasserenthärters schafft mit organisch abgerundeten Konturen eine freundliche Anmutung. Seine glänzende Oberfläche in strahlendem Weiß symbolisiert die Reinheit des gereinigten Wassers. Das umweltfreundlich konzipierte Produkt filtert mittels Ionenharz Schwermetalle und Verunreinigungen aus dem Wasser. Weitere nutzerfreundliche Aspekte wie eine einfache Reinigung und eine bequeme Wartung wurden bei der Konzeption berücksichtigt. Beim Fertigungsprozess wurden die Kosten sowie die Belastung für die Umwelt gering gehalten. Die Bedienelemente an der Vorderseite zeigen per Lichtkennzeichnung den Filterstatus und den Zustand der Batterie zuverlässig an. Die Linie an der Seite des Gerätes wird durch ein helles Orange visuell hervorgehoben und lässt das Produkt schlank und stabil wirken. Durch eine dortige Einkerbung lässt sich der vordere Deckel leicht öffnen. Zudem verringert ein Ionenharz-Vorratstank den Wartungsaufwand.

BADU Jet vogue
Counter Swim Unit /
Gegenstrom-Schwimmanlage

Speck Pumpen
Verkaufsgesellschaft GmbH,
Neunkirchen am Sand,
Germany / Deutschland
Design: Cölln.Company Design Agentur
(Roland Cölln), Wuppertal,
Germany / Deutschland
www.speck-pumps.com
www.coellncompany.de

This compact counter swim unit provides both enhanced functionality and exceptional design. A round stainless steel ring encircles the main body of the unit, which holds the water nozzle and the control panel. In addition to its use as a counter swim unit, the BADU Jet vogue provides mood lighting for the pool by means of an integrated LED light.

Grundlegende Zielsetzung bei der Entwicklung dieser kompakten Gegenstrom-Schwimmanlage war es, ihre gehobene Funktionalität durch ein eigenständiges Erscheinungsbild zu visualisieren. Markant hebt sich ein kreisrunder Edelstahlring um den Korpus mit der zentral positionierten Wasserdüse und den Bedienelementen hervor. Die BADU Jet vogue bietet zudem weiteren Nutzen, indem eine integrierte LED-Leuchte die stimmungsvolle Beleuchtung des Pools ermöglicht.

Vitocal 300-G
Water/Water Heat Pump/
Wasser/Wasser-Wärmepumpe

Viessmann Werke, Allendorf/Eder,
Germany/Deutschland
Design: Phoenix Design GmbH + Co.KG,
Stuttgart, Germany/Deutschland
www.viessmann.com
www.phoenixdesign.com

The design of the Vitocal 300-G heat pump
employs a less-is-more aesthetics that
reflects the pump's capacity to generate
economical and eco-friendly heat. The
clearly structured body in Vitosilver has
an unobtrusive yet strong presence and
blends in effortlessly with its surrounding
environment. The pump is subtly accented
with elements in Vitorange to draw attention
to the compact control unit.

Das Erscheinungsbild der Wärmepumpe
Vitocal 300-G folgt der Gestaltungsmaxime „Weniger ist mehr" und unterstreicht die Gerätefunktion, wirtschaftlich
und umweltverträglich Wärme zu erzeugen.
Dabei zielt die puristische Formensprache
auf die hochwertige Anmutung eines
Wärmetresors ab. Der klar gegliederte
Korpus in Vitosilber fügt sich unaufdring-
lich und dennoch eigenständig in das
räumliche Umfeld ein. In Kombination
mit der Akzentfarbe Vitorange wird
die Aufmerksamkeit auf das kompakte
Bedienelement gelenkt.

Vitodens 300-W
Wall-Mounted Gas-Fired Condensing
Boiler/Gas-Brennwert-Wandgerät

Viessmann Werke, Allendorf/Eder,
Germany/Deutschland
Design: Phoenix Design GmbH + Co.KG,
Stuttgart, Germany/Deutschland
www.viessmann.com
www.phoenixdesign.com

With a minimalist design, this wall-mounted
gas-fired condensing boiler blends in
seamlessly with its environment. The discreet,
compact casing in neutral white is nicely
offset by the sleek, high-gloss control panel
in black. The condensing boiler provides
state-of-the-art energy efficiency as well as
clean combustion.

Reduziert auf eine puristische Formensprache ermöglicht dieses Gas-Brennwert-
Wandgerät eine gute Integrationsfähigkeit
in das Wohnumfeld. Unterstützt wird
dies durch eine kompakte Bauweise und
eine Farbgebung in neutralem Weiß. Das
dezente Gehäuse wird spannungsvoll
unterbrochen durch den schwarzen
Bedienbereich, wobei dessen Hochglanz-
Finish einen kontrastreichen Akzent
setzt und den hohen Qualitätsanspruch
unterstreichen soll. Der Brennwert Kessel
garantiert eine zeitgemäße Energieeffizienz
sowie eine saubere Verbrennung.

geoTHERM
Air/Brine Heat Exchanger Module/
Luft/Sole-Wärmetauschermodul

Vaillant GmbH, Remscheid,
Germany/Deutschland
In-house design/Werksdesign
Design: Vistapark, Wuppertal,
Germany/Deutschland
www.vaillant.de
www.vistapark.de

The independent design concept of this air/brine heat exchanger module merges high technical requirements with a corporate image to become a harmonious entity. Innovative technology is concealed behind the compactly built, white appliance front with visually conspicuous fins. So the efficient geoTHERM air heat pump integrated system consists of two vital components that smoothly complement each other with regard to their function. Thereby the externally positioned air/brine heat exchanger module extracts heat from the ambient air at first. Then an internally installed brine heat pump utilises the extracted heat for energy-saving heating and environment-friendly hot-water preparation by compressing it. The relative low noise development of this efficient heat exchanger is particularly user-friendly. In addition, it is easy to install and allowance was made for robustness and longevity when it was configured.

Das eigenständige Gestaltungskonzept dieses Luft/Sole-Wärmetauschermoduls fügt die hohen technischen Anforderungen und ein herstellertypisches Erscheinungsbild zu einem harmonischen Ganzen. Hinter der kompakt konstruierten, weißen Gerätefront mit ihren visuell prägnanten Lamellen verbirgt sich eine innovative Technologie. So besteht der effiziente Luftwärmepumpen-Verbund geoTHERM aus zwei wesentlichen Bestandteilen, die sich hinsichtlich ihrer Funktionalität reibungslos ergänzen. Dabei entzieht zunächst das außen stehende Luft/Sole-Wärmetauschermodul der Umgebungsluft die Wärme. Danach nutzt eine innen installierte Sole-Wärmepumpe die gewonnene Wärme durch Kompression zum energiesparenden Heizen und zur umweltgerechten Warmwasserbereitung. Als besonders nutzerfreundlich erweist sich bei diesem effizienten Wärmetauscher die vergleichsweise geringe Geräuschentwicklung. Darüber hinaus wurde das Produkt robust und langlebig ausgelegt und ist einfach zu installieren.

zeoTHERM
Zeolite Gas Heat Pump/
Zeolith-Gas-Wärmepumpe

Vaillant GmbH, Remscheid,
Germany/Deutschland
In-house design/Werksdesign
Design: Vistapark, Wuppertal,
Germany/Deutschland
www.vaillant.de
www.vistapark.de

zeoTHERM is a gas-powered heat pump that hides groundbreaking technological innovations in the field of hybrid heating technology. The innovation of the unobtrusively designed compact appliance is based on a freely repeatable physical process around the mineral zeolite. This material resembles ceramics and is non-toxic and non-combustible. This matter can take up water at the same time releasing large quantities of heat. If the water-saturated stones are heated they release the water as steam. In connection with an efficient condensing technology and the coupling of free environmental energy through flat-plate solar collectors, energy savings of approximately 25 per cent are reached in comparison to traditional condensing technology.

zeoTHERM ist eine gasbetriebene Wärmepumpe, die wegweisende technologische Neuerungen im Bereich der hybriden Heiztechnik birgt. Die Innovation des dezent gestalteten Kompaktgeräts basiert auf einem beliebig wiederholbaren physikalischen Prozess um das Mineral Zeolith, ein keramikähnliches Material, das ungiftig und nicht brennbar ist. Dieser Stoff kann Wasser aufnehmen und gibt währenddessen eine große Menge Wärme ab. Heizt man die mit Wasser gesättigten Minerale dann wieder auf, geben sie das Wasser als Dampf frei. In Verbindung mit effizienter Brennwerttechnik und Einkopplung kostenloser Umweltenergie durch Solar-Flachkollektoren wird eine Energieeinsparung von etwa 25 Prozent im Vergleich zur herkömmlichen Brennwerttechnik erreicht.

miniVED
Electric Instantaneous Water
Heater/Elektro-Durchlauferhitzer

Vaillant GmbH, Remscheid,
Germany/Deutschland
In-house design/Werksdesign
www.vaillant.de

The independent design of this instantaneous water heater elegantly and harmoniously blends in with various living environments and visualises corporate design elements, which are emphasised by striking lines. The miniVED is suitable for living areas where hot water is needed at irregular intervals. It provides energy-efficient hot-water comfort due to the continuous-flow principle. In comparison to electric hot-water storage tanks, power savings of approximately 65 per cent are possible.

Die gestalterische Eigenständigkeit dieses Durchlauferhitzers fügt sich elegant und harmonisch in das jeweilige Wohnumfeld ein und visualisiert markentypische Gestaltungselemente, hervorgehoben durch eine markante Linienführung. Der miniVED empfiehlt sich für die Wohnbereiche, in denen warmes Wasser nur unregelmäßig benötigt wird. Dabei ermöglicht er durch das Durchlaufprinzip einen energieeffizienten Warmwasserkomfort, im Vergleich zu Elektro-Warmwasserspeichern wird rund 65 Prozent Strom eingespart.

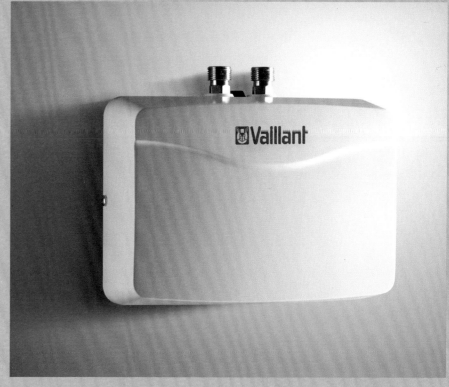

TECEsquare
WC Flushing
Activator/WC-Betätigung

TECE GmbH, Emsdetten,
Germany/Deutschland
Design: Nexus Product Design
(Ulli Finkeldey, Kai Uetrecht),
Bielefeld, Germany/Deutschland
www.tece.de
www.nexusproductdesign.de

With its puristically designed stainless steel
activating panel, this WC flushing activator
integrates flat into the wall. The middle of
the three horizontally aligned belts consists
of a dual flush button that allows the user
to choose different water amounts. With
a timeless appearance, the design concept
makes use of balanced proportions and
provides comfortable and easy operation.
The panel features a soil-resisting coating
to avoid undesired fingerprints.

Diese wandeben integrierte WC-Betätigung
reduziert sich in ihrer Form auf eine puristisch anmutende Betätigungsplatte aus
Edelstahl. Das mittlere der drei horizontal
ausgerichteten Bänder verbirgt dabei die
Ansteuerung der WC-Spülung, wobei zwei
unterschiedliche Wassermengen zur Auswahl stehen. Mit dem Ziel einer formalen
Langlebigkeit nutzt die Gestaltung eine
ausgewogen proportionierte Formensprache,
welche die komfortable und einfache
Bedienbarkeit visuell unterstützt. Die
Platte ist ausgestattet mit einer schmutzabweisenden Beschichtung zur Vermeidung hässlicher Fingerabdrücke.

Oreck ProShield
Air Purifier/Luftreiniger

Oreck Corporation, Nashville, USA
Design: Product Ventures Ltd.
(Javier Verdura, Edmund Farmer),
Fairfield, USA
www.oreck.com
www.productventures.com

This remarkably designed air purifier was
developed to allow for both vertical and
horizontal positioning. The form of the black
body, with its rounded back and prominent
slats, underscores the enhanced functionality
of the device. Innovative UV technology
destroys viruses, while the six-level cleaning
system filters out minute particles. The
device ensures fast, effective, and energy-
efficient air purification.

Dieser markant gestaltete Luftreiniger
wurde flexibel konstruiert, sodass eine
senkrechte wie auch waagrechte Aufstellung möglich ist. Der schwarze Korpus
unterstreicht mit seiner abgerundeten
Rückseite und den auffälligen Lamellen
die gehobene Funktionalität des Geräts.
Eine innovative UV-Technologie zerstört
Viren. Zudem eignet sich das sechsstufige
Reinigungssystem für das Ausfiltern win-
ziger Luftpartikel. Das Gerät gewährleistet
eine schnelle und effektive Luftreinigung
bei niedrigem Stromverbrauch.

ECA 100 ipro
Small Room Fan/Kleinraumventilator

Maico Elektroapparate-Fabrik GmbH,
Villingen-Schwenningen,
Germany/Deutschland
Design: Weinberg & Ruf
(Martin Ruf, Andreas Weinberg),
Filderstadt, Germany/Deutschland
www.maico-ventilatoren.com
www.weinberg-ruf.de

This small room fan blends in well with
any room ambience thanks to a concealed
front. The spherical curve of the housing
follows a linear aesthetics and provides a
contemporary look. Two buttons behind the
housing allow the user to set the switch-on
delay and the overrun time. The energy-
efficient device offers two performance
levels: a low-noise comfort level (78 m³/h)
and a high-performance power level (92 m³/h).

Dank seiner geschlossenen Abdeckung
fügt sich dieser Kleinraumventilator
dezent ins Raumambiente ein. Die sphä-
rische Krümmung der Abdeckung visualisiert eine ästhetische Linienführung und
sorgt für ein zeitgemäßes Erscheinungsbild. Dahinter befinden sich zwei Tasten,
über welche die Einschaltverzögerung
sowie die Nachlaufzeit eingestellt werden
können. Das energiesparsame Gerät bietet optional zwei Betriebsstufen, eine
geräuscharme Komfortstufe (78 m³/h) und
eine leistungsstarke Powerstufe (92 m³/h).

FiWoo
Air Conditioner / Klimaanlage

Industrial Design Center of Haier Group,
Qingdao, China
In-house design / Werksdesign:
Tao Sha, Juno, Jin Yong
www.haier.com

The clean design of this compact air conditioner focuses on select details. The sleek, shiny body conceals the functional elements, while a digital control panel behind black glass displays the room temperature and the on/off modes. The main body features a matt decorative motif that gives the unit a certain Asian aesthetics and an emotional appeal.

Ein zurückhaltendes Gestaltungskonzept konzentriert sich bei dieser kompakten Klimaanlage auf die Betonung weniger Details. Der schlichte, hochglänzende Korpus verdeckt dabei die funktionalen Elemente und lenkt die Aufmerksamkeit auf eine digitale Bedienleiste hinter schwarzem Glas, wo die Raumtemperatur und der jeweilige Gerätemodus angezeigt werden. Ein asiatisch anmutendes Dekor mit einer mattierten Beschichtung ergänzt das reduzierte Erscheinungsbild durch einen emotional ansprechenden Akzent.

Heatstrip
Infrared Radiant Heater / Infrarot-Heizstrahler

Moonich GmbH,
Sauerlach bei München,
Germany / Deutschland
In-house design / Werksdesign:
Lars Keussen
www.moonich.de

A clear-cut design enhances the aesthetic value of this discreet infrared radiant heater. Its innovative technology generates heat without emitting red light that many find disturbing. The ribbed, slightly curved surface is designed to ensure optimal heat distribution. A thermal separation inside the device allows the front surface to reach temperatures up to 400 degrees centigrade, while the back surface heats up to only about 90 degrees centigrade. The remote control with Enocean technology can be easily integrated into modern HVAC systems.

Eine klare Formensprache wertet diesen dezenten Infrarot-Heizstrahler ästhetisch auf. Seine innovative Technologie wärmt, ohne dabei störendes Rotlicht abzugeben. Die gerippte, leicht gewölbte Oberfläche wurde so konzipiert, dass sich die Wärme gleichmäßig verteilt. Eine thermische Trennung im Gerät ermöglicht es, auf der Oberfläche Temperaturen von bis zu 400 Grad zu erreichen, während sich die Rückseite nur auf ca. 90 Grad erhitzt. Die Funksteuerung mit Enocean-Technologie lässt sich problemlos in die zeitgemäße Haustechnik integrieren.

Zero-Otto
Radiator / Heizkörper

Antrax IT S.r.l., Resana, Italy / Italien
Design: LuccheseDesign
(Francesco Lucchese),
Milan, Italy / Mailand, Italien
www.antrax.it
www.francescolucchese.com

The unconventional design of this radiator speaks to the emotions. Its organic curves are accentuated with a consistent colour scheme. Made from aluminium, the circular construct with its high-gloss surface makes a stylish addition to any contemporary bathroom interior. Apart from its heating function, Zero-Otto also offers the option to emit scents thanks to a discreetly integrated unit with perfume essences.

Emotional ansprechend wirkt die unkonventionelle Gestaltung dieses Heizkörpers. Seine organisch anmutenden Rundungen werden von einem stringenten Farbkonzept visuell unterstützt. Aus Aluminium gefertigt setzt das Ringgebilde mit einer hochglänzenden Oberfläche einen trendbewussten Akzent und ergänzt die zeitgemäße Badezimmerausstattung. Zero-Otto bietet zusätzlich zur Heizfunktion die Möglichkeit einer Raumbeduftung, indem ein dezenter Behälter für Parfumessenzen in die gestalterische Einheit integriert wurde.

Hitachi PAM Air Conditioner S Series
(S • SC • SX)/JT Series
Air Conditioner/Klimaanlage

Hitachi Appliances, Inc., Tokyo, Japan
Design: Hitachi, Ltd., Design Division
(Kunihito Kawamura, Syunji Fujimori),
Tokyo, Japan
www.hitachi.com

This room air conditioner with integrated energy efficiency function allows for the targeted air conditioning of specific room areas in response to user's location. Cutting-edge technology distributes an "ion mist" formed from microscopic particles of ionised water, which will contribute to suppressing activities of pollen allergens clinging to fabric. Stainless steel elements within the unit prevent the formation of bacteria. A minimalist design with high-quality details serves to underscore the technical qualities of the product. Thanks to its unobtrusive form and discreet colour, the system blends easily into a wide range of home interiors. The sleek front of the device features only a few horizontal divisions and concludes with a high-quality, bevelled metallic panel.

Diese Raumklimaanlage mit integrierter Energiesparfunktion erlaubt eine gezielte Raumtemperatursteuerung, die sich am Aufenthaltsort einer Person im Raum orientiert. Eine zeitgemäße Technologie versprüht einen Ionen-Nebel, gebildet aus mikroskopischen Partikeln ionisierten Wassers. Dieses Verfahren soll neben der Luftkühlung dazu beitragen, Allergene in der Raumluft zu reduzieren. Darüber hinaus wird die Bildung von Bakterien innerhalb des Gerätes durch integrierte Edelstahlelemente verhindert. Eine reduzierte Formensprache mit hochwertigen Details soll die technischen Eigenschaften des Produktes betonen. Dank des unaufdringlichen Geräteaufbaus lässt sich das System dezent und farblich neutral in unterschiedliche Wohnwelten integrieren. Die Gerätefront wurde klar und zurückhaltend mit nur wenigen horizontalen Fugen gegliedert und durch eine hochwertige Metallfase abgeschlossen, welche die kompakte Konstruktion visuell unterstreicht.

FeelFN
Air Conditioner / Klimaanlage

Industrial Design Center of Haier Group,
Qingdao, China
In-house design / Werksdesign:
Luo Yaocheng, Juno, Jin Yong,
Jiang Chuanli
www.haier.com

This air conditioner, designed as a standing device, is characterised by its tall and narrow build. A sleek front with soft, rounded edges contrasts nicely with the air fins that occupy an inconspicuous place on the side of the unit. The sophisticated functionality of the air conditioner is also echoed by the visual dialogue between the white lower front and the black control panel on top. When the unit is not in operation, the dark control panel has a shiny surface similar to rest of the front. Only when the unit is on do additional air fins and the red digital temperature display become visible on the control panel. The device offers two performance levels: one low-noise mode and another mode providing a faster cooling performance.

Eine schmale und hoch aufragende Bauweise prägt das unkonventionelle Erscheinungsbild dieser Klimaanlage, welche als Standgerät konzipiert wurde. Ihre prägnante Formensprache wird durch sanft abgerundete Ecken harmonisch ergänzt, wobei die Lüftungslamellen an der Seite die puristisch gestaltete Gerätefront visuell unterbrechen. Das in sich geschlossene Gesamtbild hebt durch einen farblich markanten Kontrast zwischen der weißen Front und dem schwarzen Bedienfeld die hohe Funktionalität der Klimaanlage hervor. Das dunkle Bedienfeld hat dabei eine ähnlich glänzende Oberflächenbeschichtung wie die übrige Gerätefront. Erst im eingeschalteten Modus werden im oberen Teil des Bedienfelds zusätzliche Lamellen sowie eine rote Digitalanzeige mit Informationen zur Raumtemperatur sichtbar. Das Gerät bietet zwei Leistungsstufen, wodurch optional eine geräuscharme oder eine schnelle Temperaturregelung erfolgt.

BetteSpa
Bath / Badewanne

Bette GmbH & Co. KG,
Delbrück, Germany / Deutschland
Design: Jochen Schmiddem,
Berlin, Germany / Deutschland
www.bette.de
www.schmiddem-design.de

As a real two-seater bath, BetteSpa's exceptional size (170 cm length and 120 cm width) not only offers plenty of space to bath in – even next to each other – but also stresses the luxury of a large bath. The ergonomically inclined back profile provides comfortable bathing.

Als echte Zweisitzer-Wanne bietet die BetteSpa durch ihre außergewöhnliche Größe von 170 cm Länge und 120 cm Breite viel Platz für das Badevergnügen – auch nebeneinander – und unterstreicht den Luxus eines großen Bades. Dabei sorgt das ergonomisch abgeschrägte Rückenprofil für hohen Liegekomfort.

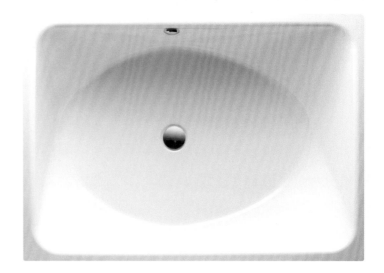

Wash Mug
Free-Standing Washbasin/
Freistehender Waschtisch

LG Hausys, Design Center, Seoul, Korea
In-house design/Werksdesign: Gaye Kim
www.lghausys.com

This washbasin with a sculptural feel was designed especially for commercial bathrooms. Its design replicates the contours of a mug, with the "handle" on the right shaped to create a surface to put personal items such as mobile phones or cosmetics. Once an item is placed on it, the surface lights up to attract attention and to keep the user from forgetting their items when they leave. Once the items are removed, a sensor turns off the light automatically.

Speziell für gewerbliche Sanitäranlagen eignet sich dieser skulptural anmutende Waschtisch. Seine Formensprache lehnt sich an die Kontur eines Bechers an, wobei der stilisierte Henkel an der rechten Seite eine halbkugelförmige Ablagefläche für persönliche Dinge wie Mobiltelefone oder Kosmetik schafft. Sobald die Ablage genutzt wird, leuchtet die Halbkugel auf, um die Aufmerksamkeit zu stärken und zu verhindern, dass etwas vergessen wird. Ein Sensor schaltet die Beleuchtung automatisch wieder aus, wenn die Schale geleert wird.

Pasa, Pasa XP
Shower Enclosures / Duschkabinen

Kermi GmbH,
Plattling, Germany / Deutschland
In-house design / Werksdesign
www.kermi.de

Pasa, clean and frameless, and Pasa XP, with integrated panel profile, are two trendsetting series in the fittings/shower cabin segment, whose form language embraces superior functionality and ergonomic comfort. The smooth organic design of the fittings gives particular benefits: they are easy to clean, as all internal surfaces are completely seamless; easy to raise/lower; and feature 180-degree pendulum doors. The ergonomic design of the grab handles, comfort accessories and a unique level of pre-assembly meet every requirement for contemporary bathroom fittings.

Pasa, puristisch und rahmenlos, und Pasa XP, mit integriertem Wandprofil, sind zwei zukunftsweisende Beschlags-Duschkabinen-Serien, deren Formensprache anspruchsvolle Funktionalität und ergonomischen Komfort vereint. Die dezente, organisch anmutende Gestaltung der Beschläge bietet besondere Vorteile: Sie sind aufgrund der vollkommen nahtlosen Innenflächen gut zu reinigen, verfügen über eine Hebe-Senk-Funktion und 180-Grad-Pendeltüren. Die ergonomische Gestaltung der Bügelgriffe, Komfort-Accessoires und ein hoher Vormontagegrad erfüllen alle Forderungen an eine zeitgemäße Badausstattung.

Cher
Bathroom Furniture/
Badezimmermöbel

Kolpa d.d., Metlika, Slovenia/Slowenien
Design: Grafik in fanatik d.o.o.
(Primoz Tomsic, Aljosa Podbrscek),
Nova Gorica, Slovenia/Slowenien
www.kolpa.si
www.gif.si

This elegant bathroom furniture series was designed for boats, mobile homes, and small living spaces. With a depth of only 22.5 cm, the cabinets have multiple uses. The interiors contain glass shelves as well as a fold-out washbasin. LED lighting, discreet doors, and high-quality materials such as mirrored fronts make for appealing, homelike bathroom furniture with high functionality.

Diese Möbelserie wurde für die elegante Badausstattung in den Bereichen Nautik und Wohnmobile sowie für kleinere Wohnbereiche konzipiert. Mit einer Tiefe von nur 22,5 cm bieten die Badezimmerschränke vielseitige Anwendungsmöglichkeiten. Im Innenraum wurde zusätzlich zu den Ablageflächen aus Glas ein ausklappbares Waschbecken in den Schrank integriert. Eine LED-Beleuchtung, gedämpfte Türen und hochwertige Materialien wie eine verspiegelte Front schaffen ein wohnlich wirkendes Badezimmer-Interieur von hoher Funktionalität.

BA14 Digital Bidet

Woongjin Coway Co., Ltd., Seoul, Korea
In-house design / Werksdesign:
Hun-Jung Choi, Seung-Woo Kim
www.coway.co.kr

The innovative design of this electronic bidet combines user comfort with a purely functional aesthetics. The shiny surfaces of the recyclable materials suggest hygiene and technical progress. An innovative technology ensures that all water used is sterilised. A user-friendly control panel next to the seat rounds off the ergonomics of the product.

Das innovative Gestaltungskonzept dieses elektronischen Bidets unterstreicht den Nutzungskomfort mit einer rein funktional ausgerichteten Formensprache. Mit ihren glänzenden Oberflächen suggerieren die recycelbaren Materialien Hygiene und technischen Fortschritt. Die innovative Funktionsweise sorgt dafür, dass ausschließlich entkeimtes Wasser zum Einsatz kommt. Eine bedienungsfreundliche Steuerungsleiste rechts neben der Sitzfläche rundet das ergonomisch durchdachte Produkt sinnvoll ab.

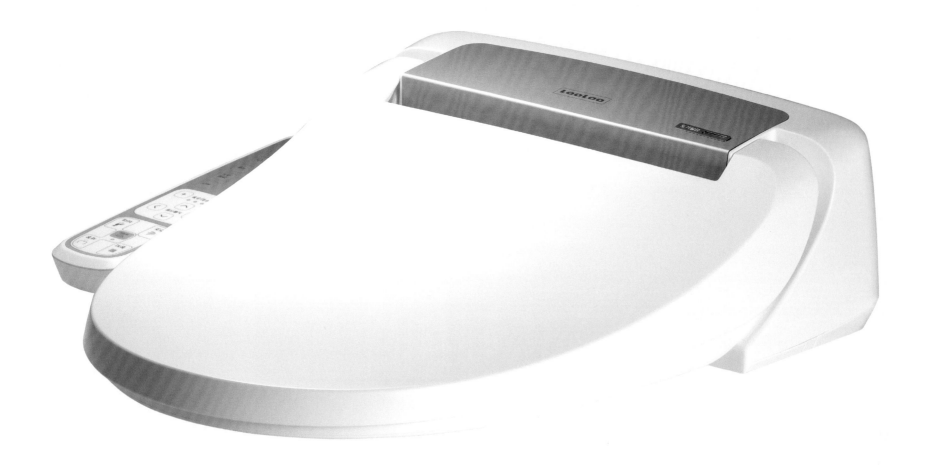

Rêve Bidet

Kohler Europe, Cheltenham, GB
In-house design / Werksdesign
www.kohler.com

The streamlined contours of this bidet provide a high degree of user comfort and lend the unit its minimalist elegance. Pronounced geometric lines und softly rounded edges make for a harmonious whole, which integrates well into the comprehensive Rêve bathroom collection. The bidet is available as a wall- or floor-mounted unit, in either white or igneous black.

Stromlinienförmige Konturen verleihen diesem Bidet eine minimalistische Eleganz, dem Nutzer bietet es ein hohes Maß an Komfort. Mit seiner markant geometrischen Linienführung und sanft abgerundeten Kanten entsteht die Anmutung von Harmonie, proportional ausgewogen fügt sich das Erscheinungsbild des Bidets in das Gesamtbild der umfassenden Badserie Rêve ein. Das Bidet ist in zwei Ausführungen zur Wand- oder Bodenmontage erhältlich, die Badserie ist in den Farben Weiß oder Igneous Black wählbar.

Inventio
Shower Tap/Duscharmatur

Daelim Trading Co., Ltd., Seoul, Korea
In-house design/Werksdesign:
Kwi Hoon Ha, Pil Gon Kim, Hyunsoo Choi
www.dltc.co.kr

Innovation and elegant design characterise
this digitally controlled shower tap. The touch-
sensitive, flush-to-the-wall control unit allows
for intuitive and easy use. Divided into two
square surfaces, the right side features the
on/off button and the left the wide range of
functions. The unconventional design plays with
the contrast between the black glass surface
and the matt polished metal surface and uses
LED light effects.

Der innovative Ansatz einer digitalen Steuerung prägt das elegante Erscheinungsbild
dieser wandebenen Duscharmatur, wobei sich
der Gebrauch des berührungsempfindlichen
Bedienfelds intuitiv einfach erschließt. Unterteilt in zwei quadratische Flächen, befindet
sich rechts der An/Aus-Schalter und links
der differenzierte Steuerungsbereich. Das
unkonventionelle Gestaltungskonzept spielt
mit dem Kontrast zwischen einer schwarzen
Glasfläche und einer matt polierten Metalloberfläche und nutzt zudem LED-Lichteffekte.

i-soft
Water Softener / Wasserenthärter

JUDO Wasseraufbereitung GmbH,
Winnenden, Germany / Deutschland
In-house design / Werksdesign:
Ralf Söcknick
Design: kienledesign (Rudi Kienle),
Leinzell, Germany / Deutschland
www.judo.eu
www.kienledesign.de

With its intelligent water management, the fully automatic water softener JUDO i-soft provides soft water around the clock. The water quality can be determined at the push of a button and adjusted to the respective requirements. A timeless design allows the appliance to integrate harmoniously into any surrounding.

Der vollautomatische Wasserenthärter JUDO i-soft sorgt mit intelligentem Wassermanagement rund um die Uhr für weiches Wasser. Die Wasserqualität wird per Knopfdruck eingestellt und passt sich an die Anforderungen an. Mit einer zeitlosen Gestaltung integriert sich das Gerät harmonisch in jede Umgebung.

Methven Shower Infusions
Dispenser / Spender

Methven Ltd.,
Auckland, New Zealand / Neuseeland
In-house design / Werksdesign:
Kent Sneddon
www.methven.com

This easy-to-install dispenser infuses essential oils and natural extracts into the shower water, which provides full-body moisturising and aromatherapy while you shower. Thanks to a sleek design, the dispenser integrates well into most showers. The system uses recyclable refill cartridges.

Dieser einfach anzubringende Spender führt dem Duschwasser ätherische Öle und natürliche Extrakte zu. So wirken beim Duschen rückfettende Duftstoffe auf den ganzen Körper ein. Aufgrund seiner glatten Form fügt sich der Spender gut in die meisten Duschen ein. Zum Nachfüllen werden wiederverwertbare Einsätze angeboten.

Axor Citterio Overhead Shower 3jet /
Axor Citterio Kopfbrause 3jet

Hansgrohe AG,
Schiltach, Germany / Deutschland
Design: Antonio Citterio and Partners
(Antonio Citterio),
Milan, Italy / Mailand, Italien
www.hansgrohe.com
www.antoniocitterioandpartners.it

Enhanced functionality and a compact aesthetics make for the distinctive appearance of this robust overhead shower. A prominent adjustment handle on the side of the shower head allows for easy switching between the three different spray modes.

Die Kombination aus einer gehobenen Funktionalität und kompakten Ästhetik prägt das eigenständige Erscheinungsbild dieser robusten Kopfbrause. Prägnant wirkt der seitliche Verstellgriff, welcher eine direkte Einstellung der drei verschiedenen Strahlarten erlaubt.

Ceramic Tower
TCH 7590 EB
Heater/Heizstrahler

De'Longhi Appliances,
Treviso, Italy/Italien
In-house design/Werksdesign:
Mauro Cereser, Amedeo Comarella
www.delonghi.it

Striking lines are characteristic of the look of
this ceramic heater. Like a tower the slim, black
body of the appliance rises from a circular
base element. Its high functionality is achieved
by an advanced technology. A blue shining
display allows easy and comfortable handling.
The combination of different material finishes
follows a harmonious design concept, which
picks up Italian style elements.

Eine markante Linienführung prägt das
Erscheinungsbild dieses Keramikheizstrahlers.
Turmförmig ragt der schlanke, schwarze
Gerätekorpus aus einem kreisrunden Fußelement hervor. Seine hohe Funktionalität
erreicht das Gerät durch eine weiterentwickelte Technologie, ein blau leuchtendes
Display ermöglicht eine einfache und komfortable Handhabung. Die Kombination der
unterschiedlichen Materialoberflächen folgt
einem harmonischen Gestaltungskonzept, das
italienische Stilelemente aufgreift.

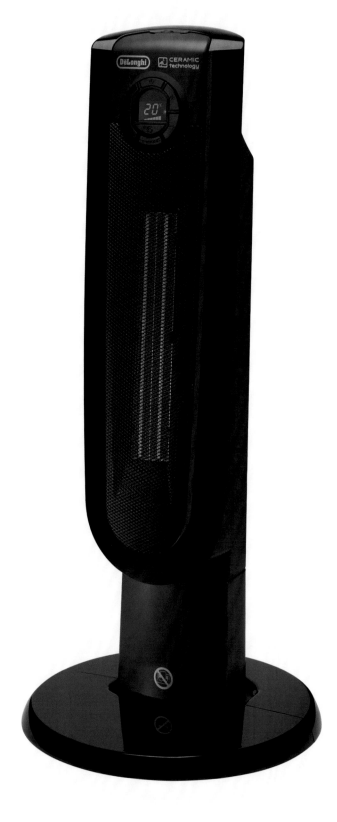

Axor Citterio Single-Lever Basin Mixer/ Axor Citterio Einhebel-Waschtischmischer

Hansgrohe AG,
Schiltach, Germany/Deutschland
Design: Antonio Citterio and Partners
(Antonio Citterio),
Milan, Italy/Mailand, Italien
www.hansgrohe.com
www.antoniocitterioandpartners.it

A dynamic tension between shiny surfaces and precision edges characterises the appearance of this single-lever mixer. A classic tall spout harmoniously unites with a joystick handle protruding laterally from the fixture.

Ein Spannungsverhältnis von glänzenden Flächen und präzisen Kanten prägt das Erscheinungsbild dieser Einhebel-Armatur. Stilistisch stimmig wird ein klassisch anmutender, hoher Auslauf mit einem Joystick-Griff verbunden, der markant seitlich aus der Armatur ragt.

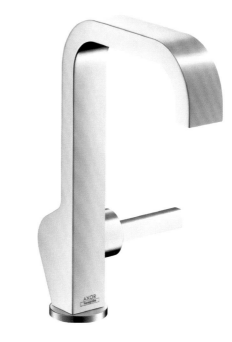

**Radian
Tap/Armatur**

V.R. Union Co., Ltd., Samutsakorn, Thailand
In-house design/Werksdesign:
Pisanu Hathaipantalux,
Phichit Hathaipantalux
www.vrh.co.th

The flowing contours of this compact tap create a dynamic tension that is further enhanced whenever the water valve is turned on or off. A minimalist elegance informs the overall appeal of this tap that offers outstanding user comfort.

Die fließenden Konturen dieser kompakten Armatur sollen eine spannungsreiche Dynamik erzeugen, die durch das Öffnen und Schließen des Wasserventils verstärkt wird. Die puristische Eleganz des Gesamtbilds wird von einer komfortablen Bedienbarkeit ergänzt.

Farca Single-Lever Basin Mixer/ Einhebel-Waschtischmischer

Vanguardia Europea,
Stanza, Guadalajara, Mexico/Mexiko
Design: Ezequielfarca (Ezequiel Farca,
Valeria Tamayo),
Mexico City, Mexico/Mexiko
www.stanza.com.mx
www.ezequielfarca.com

This single-lever mixer with a geometric aesthetics is forged from a single piece of metal. A horizontal tall spout releases a remarkably narrow, elegant water jet. The discreetly offset tap lever controls the water flow by means of an innovative water supply mechanism.

Mit einer geometrisch anmutenden Form wurde diese Einhebel-Armatur aus einem einzigen Metallteil geschmiedet, wobei ein hoher, horizontaler Auslauf einen auffallend schmalen, eleganten Wasserstrahl freisetzt. Ein dezent seitlich angebrachter Bedienhebel nutzt einen innovativen Mechanismus für die Wasserzufuhr.

Illiana
Bath Mixer / Badarmatur

Daelim Trading Co., Ltd., Seoul, Korea
In-house design / Werksdesign:
Kwi Hoon Ha, Pil Gon Kim, Hyunsoo Choi
www.dltc.co.kr

A clear and independent design language characterises this innovative bath mixer, featuring efficiently arranged control elements and a concealed spout. The space-saving unit made of shiny chrome offers a high degree of user comfort and functionality and has a fairly flat profile when in the off mode. When the water is turned on, a square spout flips forward and releases a dynamic gush of water into the tub.

Eine klare und eigenständige Formensprache prägt diese innovative Badarmatur, welche neben den flach angeordneten Bedienelementen einen versteckt platzierten Wasserauslauf umfasst. Die platzsparende Konstruktion aus glänzendem Chrom bietet ein hohes Maß an Bedienkomfort und Funktionalität, wobei die Armatur im geschlossenen Modus eine weitgehend plane Struktur zeigt. Erst mit dem Öffnen der Wasserzufuhr klappt ein rechteckiger Wasserhahn nach vorne und leitet einen dynamisch wirkenden Wasserschwall ins Becken.

Inspirit
Basin Mixer / Waschtischarmatur

Gustav Schmiedl GmbH & Co KG,
Hall in Tirol, Austria / Österreich
In-house design / Werksdesign:
Oliver Anker
www.schmiedl.eu

The aesthetics of this basin mixer is
characterised by rectilinear lines, which join
together at right angles to form a puristic
impression. Only a filigree in pin grip visually
interrupts the stringent geometry of the slim-
shaped chrome body.

Die Ästhetik dieser Waschtischarmatur ist
von geraden Linien geprägt, die sich rechtwinklig zu einem puristischen Gesamtbild
zusammenfügen. Lediglich ein filigraner Pin-
Griff unterbricht visuell die stringente Geometrie des flach gestalteten Chrom-Korpus.

HighTech-iqua senso
Sanitary Faucet / Sanitärarmatur

Aquis Sanitär AG,
Rebstein, Switzerland / Schweiz
Design: Pearl Creative,
Storti & Rummel GbR
(Tim Storti, Christian Rummel),
Ludwigsburg, Germany / Deutschland
www.aquis.ch
www.pearlcreative.com

An architecturally conceived design concept
interprets the classic two-grip structure and
gives this electronic faucet an interesting
cosmopolitan appearance. Its innovative
raindrop aerator allows water savings of
up to 70 per cent.

Ein architektonisch ausgerichtetes Gestaltungskonzept interpretiert die klassische
Zweigriff-Struktur und verleiht dieser
elektronischen Armatur eine interessante
kosmopolitische Anmutung. Ihr innovativer
Raindrop-Strahlregler ermöglicht eine
Wassereinsparung von bis zu 70 Prozent.

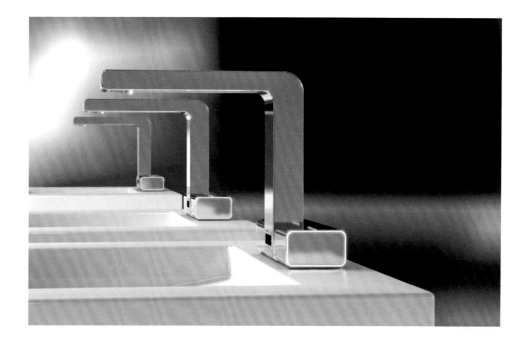

Virage
Faucet Collection / Armatur-Serie

Brizo, Indianapolis, USA
In-house design / Werksdesign: Judd Lord
www.brizo.com

The unconventional style of this faucet
collection was inspired by the traditional art
of smithery. Its characteristic lines create
intertwined arcing spouts whose lateral
alignment gives the faucet a dynamic
expression.

Inspiriert vom traditionellen Schmiedehand-
werk ist die unkonventionelle Formensprache
dieser Armatur-Serie. Ihre prägnante Linienführung kreiert in sich verdrehte Bögen,
deren seitliche Ausrichtung der Armatur
Dynamik verleiht.

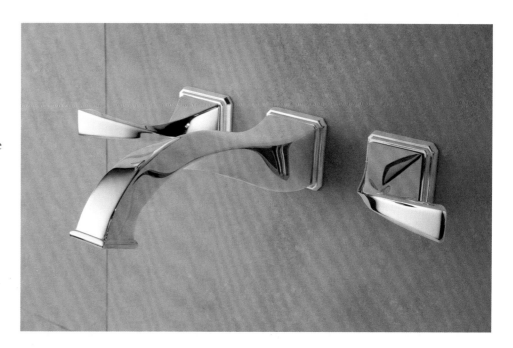

Daikin Emura
Air Conditioner / Klimaanlage

Daikin Europe N.V.,
Oostende, Belgium / Belgien
Design: Design 3 Produktdesign
(Wolfgang Wagner, Wanjo Koch),
Hamburg, Germany / Deutschland
www.daikineurope.com
www.design3.de

This wall-mounted air conditioner meets most exigent energy efficiency requirements and delivers both high functionality and an elegant aesthetics. The sleek, two-dimensional front rounds off harmoniously at the sides. The unobtrusive ventilation slots are discreetly placed on the top: when in use, the slightly opened unit reveals barely visible slots. As a result, this air conditioner blends in with every interior. The casing is available in matt white or in finely structured aluminium.

Diese wandmontierte Klimaanlage erfüllt strengste Energiespar-Anforderungen und unterstreicht ihre hohe Funktionalität durch ein elegantes Erscheinungsbild. Die schlichte, zweidimensional geformte Front ist an den Seiten harmonisch abgerundet. Dezent verdeckte Ventilationsöffnungen wurden an der Oberseite versteckt angeordnet und sind kaum sichtbar, sobald sich das Gerät im Betrieb leicht öffnet. Deshalb fügt sich diese Klimaanlage in jede Umgebung gut ein. Das Gehäuse ist wahlweise in Mattweiß oder in fein strukturiertem Aluminium erhältlich.

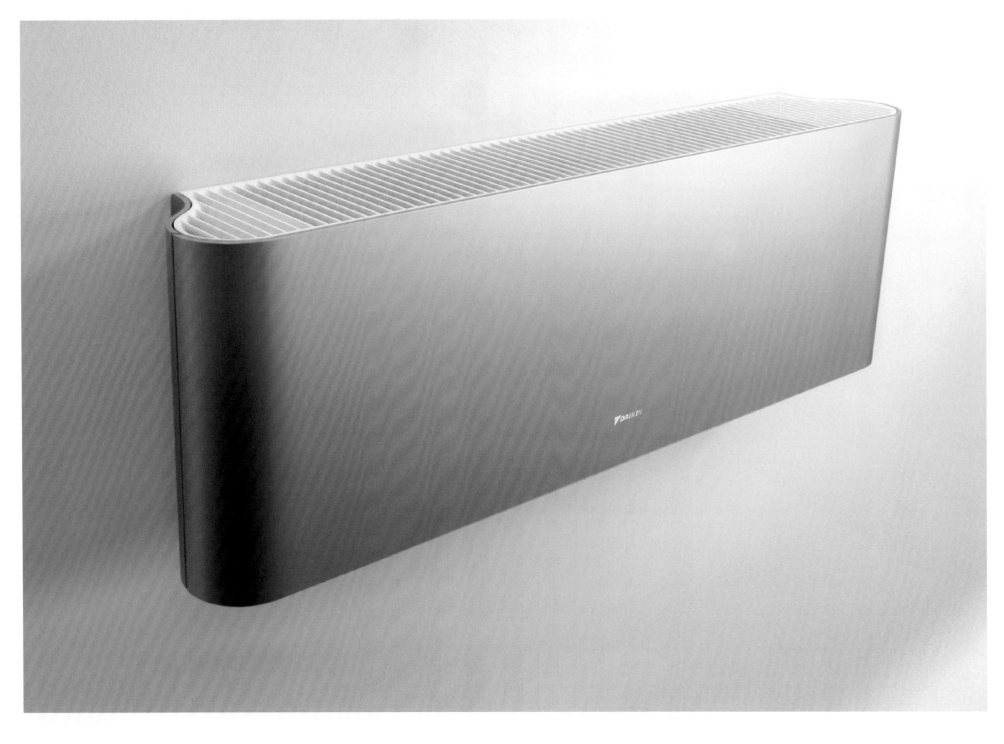

Portable Twin Fan
Fan / Ventilator

Hugogate Limited, Hong Kong
In-house design / Werksdesign:
David Koo
www.hugogate.com

This fan can be placed horizontally or upright
and is suitable for indoor as well as outdoor use.
Its compact appearance is characterised by the
double fans. A touch control panel is located on
the side of the waterproof casing.

Dieser Ventilator kann im Hoch- und Quer-
format platziert werden, zudem eignet er
sich für den In- und Outdoor-Einsatz. Sein
kompaktes Erscheinungsbild wird durch
die beiden Lüfter geprägt, an der Seite des
wasserdichten Gehäuses befindet sich eine
Touch-Bedienleiste.

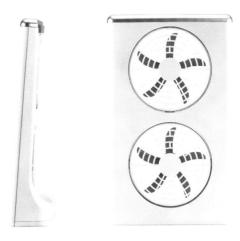

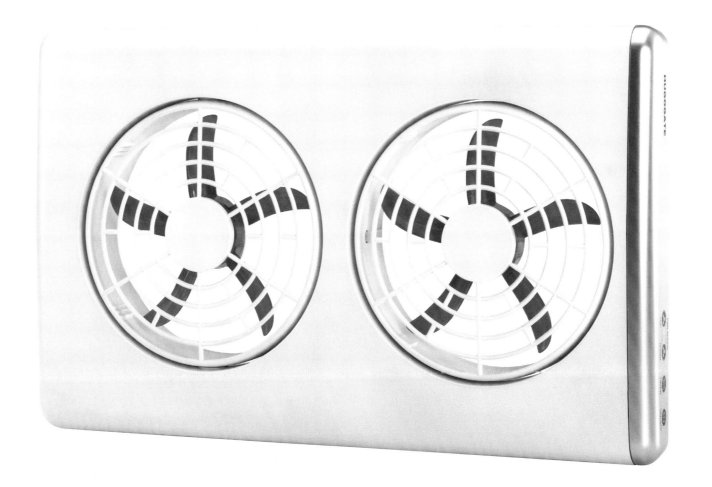

Dr. Mark Breitenberg

Tony K. M. Chang

Robert Stadler

Lighting and lamps
Progress with a wide range of contrasts

Licht und Leuchten
Fortschrittlichkeit in facettenreichen Kontrasten

With intelligent control mechanisms and advanced technology, light is increasingly becoming a communicative element.

The marked diversity in the "Lighting and lamps" sector presents a rich form language in which rigorous geometry meets an organic, flowing design. The broad array of selected materials is testimony to the wide range of demands addressed, while the quality perception of the products is very high. The increasing market presence of LED technology allows for a more matter-of-course and coherent integration of these lights in the design concepts. Nevertheless, the classic light bulb has not become entirely extinct; its characteristic shape is even playfully echoed in some concepts. With intelligent control mechanisms and advanced technology, light is increasingly becoming a communicative element. The design potential in this sector is still very large and varied, with much promise for the future.

Durch intelligente Steuerungsmechanismen und fortschrittliche Technologie wird Licht immer mehr zu einem kommunikativen Element der Architektur.

Die ausgeprägte Vielfalt im Bereich „Licht und Leuchten" zeigt eine kontrastreiche Formensprache, in der einer streng geometrischen Reduktion eine organische Lyrik entgegengesetzt wird. Die Auswahl der verarbeiteten Materialien ist breit gefächert und lässt erkennen, dass die Gestaltung unterschiedlichsten Ansprüchen gerecht werden soll. Dabei ist das Qualitätsempfinden bei den Produkten sehr hoch. Die weiter fortschreitende Etablierung der LED-Technologie sorgt für eine immer selbstverständlichere und stimmigere Integration in die Entwürfe. Dennoch scheint die klassische Glühbirne nicht ganz von der Bildfläche zu verschwinden, ihre charakteristische Form wird sogar mit einem Augenzwinkern in einigen Konzepten aufgegriffen. Durch intelligente Steuerungsmechanismen und fortschrittliche Technologie wird Licht immer mehr zu einem kommunikativen Element der Architektur. Das gestalterische Potenzial in diesem Bereich ist nach wie vor sehr groß und abwechslungsreich und lässt für die Zukunft noch einiges erwarten.

Stadium
Spotlight / Strahler

Havells Sylvania, Newhaven, GB
In-house design / Werksdesign:
Tony Lawrence, Shane Alce
www.havells-sylvania.com

The design of this energy-saving spotlight focused on enhanced accent and display lighting. The flexible spotlight with its powerful LED assembly can be used in demanding situations, in terms of illumination, such as museums, galleries, or upmarket sales and exhibition surfaces. The slim metal housing has a height of only 30 mm and contains 16 LEDs as well as a control gear, an LED lens, and LED cooling unit. Stadium excels with high colour rendering, zero UV/IR radiation, and a large energy saving potential. The spotlight can be comfortably mounted to a ceiling rail and allows for need-based illumination of the selected surroundings. With 16 one-watt LEDs, the spotlight guarantees consistent and reliable room illumination and energy conservation which previous lighting technologies like low-voltage halogen and metal halide lamps were not able to achieve.

Eine verbesserte Möglichkeit der Akzent- und Verkaufsflächenbeleuchtung stand im Mittelpunkt der Gestaltung dieses energiesparenden Strahlers. Mit seiner leistungsstarken LED-Ausstattung kann der flexible Strahler in anspruchsvollen Beleuchtungssituationen eingesetzt werden, wie sie beispielsweise in Museen, Galerien oder gehobenen Verkaufs- und Ausstellungsflächen anzutreffen sind. In dem schmalen Metallgehäuse von nur 30 mm Höhe befinden sich 16 LEDs, zudem verbergen sich darin sowohl ein Vorschaltgerät als auch eine LED-Linse sowie ein LED-Kühler. Stadium zeichnet sich durch eine hohe Farbwiedergabe, einen vollständigen UV/IR-Stopp und ein großes Energieeinsparungspotenzial aus. Die komfortable Montage auf einer Deckenschiene ermöglicht die bedarfsgerechte Ausrichtung auf den bevorzugt auszuleuchtenden Bereich. Mit einer hohen Lichtleistung von 16 x 1 Watt gewährt der Strahler eine kontinuierlich zuverlässige Raumbeleuchtung bei einer Energieersparnis, die bisherigen Lampentechnologien wie Niedervolthalogen- und Metalldampflampen vorbehalten waren.

Xinua
Wall Lamp/Wandleuchte

Sigllicht GmbH, Munich,
Germany/München, Deutschland
In-house design/Werksdesign:
Klaus Sigl
Design: Rüdiger Goth, Munich,
Germany/München, Deutschland
www.sigllicht.de

The emotionally appealing appearance of Xinua recreates the design concept of an unfolded die; it includes six versions with different numbers of points. Flamboyant colours underscore the visual effect of this playful wall creation – the square-shaped light objects allow a large variety of colour mixtures. The single dice pips are milled into the light-dispersing material, which is centrally backlit by colour-changing RGB LEDs. The different versions of the lamp series can be individually positioned or combined in a set to form random patterns. Furthermore, Xinua can be flexibly mounted to the wall or ceiling; it is suitable for hiding undesired lamp connections. Thanks to an especially developed LED electronics, each lamp can be connected to an individual 230-volt connection or to a light outlet by means of integrated connecting rods. A technically mature electronic system synchronises the dices with each other and allows for various static and colour-dynamic programme processes to be selected by a laterally arranged rotary switch or a remote control obtainable on order.

Das emotional ansprechende Erscheinungs-bild von Xinua greift die Gestaltungsidee eines aufgeklappten Spielwürfels auf und umfasst sechs Ausführungen mit unter-schiedlicher Punkteanzahl. Grelle Farben unterstreichen die visuelle Wirkung der spielerischen Wandgestaltung – die qua-dratischen Lichtobjekte erlauben eine große Vielfalt von Farbmischungen. In das lichtstreuende Material werden die einzelnen Würfelaugen eingefräst und zentrisch durch farbveränderliche RGB-LEDs hinterleuchtet. Die unterschiedlichen Ausführungen der Leuchten-Serie können einzeln positioniert oder im Set zu belie-bigen Mustern kombiniert werden. Xinua lässt sich zudem flexibel an Wand oder Decke montieren und eignet sich auch zum Kaschieren unerwünschter Lampen-anschlüsse. Durch eine eigens entwickelte LED-Elektronik kann jede Leuchte an einen eigenen 230-Volt-Anschluss oder mittels integrierter Verbindungsstangen an nur einen Lichtauslass angeschlossen werden. Eine ausgereifte Elektronik synchronisiert die Würfel untereinander und lässt ver-schiedene statische und farbdynamische Programmabläufe zu, die mittels eines seit-lich angeordneten Drehschalters oder einer separat zu bestellenden Fernbedienung auswählbar sind.

Doride
Floor Lamp/Stehleuchte

Artemide S.p.A.,
Pregnana Milanese, Italy/Italien
Design: Karim Rashid, New York, USA
www.artemide.com
www.karimrashid.com

The delicate and elegantly curved silhouette of this floor lamp reminds of a roughly outlined brushstroke or a water wave that rears up vertically. In a harmonious way the rod merges seamlessly with the lampshade. Thus, a zoomorphic design language is created, which describes the design concept as "digital nature". The unobtrusive elegance underlines the high functionality of this floor lamp with its timeless appearance. A joint at the vertical axis allows the diffuser to rotate by 350 degrees and it thus ensures precise adjustment of the light. A formally striking anti-dazzle screen covers the fluorescent light source and ensures convenient dazzle-free light distribution in any position. Optionally direct or indirect room lighting can be chosen.

Die filigrane und elegant geschwungene Silhouette dieser Stehleuchte erinnert an einen skizzenhaften Pinselstrich oder an eine sich senkrecht aufbäumende Wasserwelle. Der Stab geht harmonisch und nahtlos in den Leuchtenschirm über. So entsteht eine zoomorphische Formensprache, die das Gestaltungskonzept als „digitale Natur" beschreibt. Die zurückhaltend anmutende Eleganz unterstreicht dabei die hohe Funktionalität dieser zeitlos wirkenden Stehleuchte. Ein Gelenk an der vertikalen Achse erlaubt eine Drehung des Leuchtenkopfes um 350 Grad und ermöglicht so eine genaue Ausrichtung des Lichts. Ein formal auffälliges Blendschutzgitter verdeckt die Leuchtstofflampe und gewährleistet eine angenehme, blendfreie Lichtverteilung in jeder beliebigen Position. Optional ist zwischen einer direkten und indirekten Raumausleuchtung zu wählen.

Cosmic Leaf
Pendant Lamp/Pendelleuchte

Artemide S.p.A.,
Pregnana Milanese, Italy/Italien
Design: Ross Lovegrove, London, GB
www.artemide.com
www.rosslovegrove.com

The design of this pendant lamp has a mystic appearance. It seems to be a self-contained sculpture detached from its environment and to emanate from another world because of its unusual design language. Like the scales of a reptile its surface is structured in such detail that a fascinating overall picture created from light and shadow is produced. The gently curved lamp body made of transparent methacrylate reflects the direct light diffusing it generously into the room. Inside the conspicuous lamp a chrome-plated steel structure and an illumination unit of painted metal are concealed. The striking lighting fixture is mounted to a chrome-plated steel frame. The illumination unit is made of lacquered metal and incorporates a modern LED light source, which illuminates the body from above. It provides strong, warm light and ensures low power consumption.

Die Gestaltung dieser Pendelleuchte strahlt eine mystische Anmutung aus. Sie wirkt wie eine vom Interieur losgelöste, eigenständige Skulptur und erweckt in ihrer unkonventionellen Formensprache den Eindruck, aus einer anderen Welt zu stammen. Gleich den Schuppen eines Reptils ist die Oberfläche so detailliert strukturiert, dass im eingeschalteten Modus ein faszinierendes, aus Licht und Schatten erzeugtes Gesamtbild entsteht. Der sanft geschwungene Leuchtenkorpus aus transparentem, strukturiertem Methacrylat reflektiert das direkte Licht und streut es weit in den Raum. Der markante Leuchtenkörper ist an einem Gestell aus verchromtem Stahl befestigt. Die Beleuchtungseinheit aus lackiertem Metall beherbergt eine zeitgemäße LED-Lichtquelle, die den Körper von oben anstrahlt und für kräftiges, warmes Licht bei geringem Stromverbrauch sorgt.

Cover
Recessed Wall Lamp/
Wandeinbauleuchte

Artemide Megalit SAS,
Saint Florent sur Cher, France/Frankreich
Design: Format Design Studio
(Luca Turrini), Imola (Bologna),
Italy/Italien
www.artemide.com
www.formatdesignstudio.it

These elegant lamps can be harmoniously flush integrated into the wall enhancing the interior architecture by a high-contrast light concept. With geometric forms an illuminated and a black lamp surface join together to become an artistic unit that is reminiscent of a light well. The lighting fixture is available in two versions and offers the choice between a diffuse and an asymmetrical lighting. Its glass surface ensures reliable protection against dust and can be removed by means of special vacuum cups. Energy-saving light sources like fluorescent lamps or LEDs are hidden behind. According to requirements Cover can be installed horizontally or vertically. Five different sizes allow flexible adaptation to the particular room dimensions. The low thickness of 60 mm provides for easy installation in plaster walls or, in combination with a special housing for installation, in solid walls as well.

Harmonisch und flächenbündig lassen sich diese eleganten Leuchten in die Wand integrieren und unterstreichen die Raumarchitektur mit einem kontrastreichen Lichtkonzept. In geometrischen Formen fügen sich eine beleuchtete und eine schwarze Leuchtenoberfläche zu einer gestalterischen Einheit, die an einen Lichtschacht erinnert. Der Leuchtenkörper ist in zwei Ausführungen erhältlich und ermöglicht die Auswahl zwischen einer diffusen oder asymmetrischen Beleuchtung. Seine Glasoberfläche gewährleistet einen zuverlässigen Staubschutz und kann mithilfe von speziellen Saugnäpfen abgenommen werden. Dahinter verbirgt sich eine energiesparende Bestückung mit Leuchtstofflampen oder LEDs. Cover kann je nach Wunsch horizontal oder senkrecht eingebaut werden, fünf unterschiedliche Größen ermöglichen dabei eine flexible Anpassung an die jeweiligen Raummaße. Die geringe Tiefe von 60 mm erlaubt einen unkomplizierten Einbau in Gipswände oder mitsamt einem speziellen Einbaugehäuse auch in Massivwände.

Cadmo
Floor Lamp/Stehleuchte

Artemide S.p.A., Pregnana Milanese,
Italy/Italien
Design: Karim Rashid, New York, USA
www.artemide.com
www.karimrashid.com

Designed with harmoniously balanced
proportions, Cadmo is a floor lamp in the
style of a veil or a monastic quiet insular
robe. The discreetly contoured line forms
a light with an elegant and distinctive
impression. The slim silhouette of the
stainless steel lampshade opens up towards
the top, revealing an aperture of light on
the side with varying width. In this way,
the light is completely shaded to one side
while at the same time a soft indirect light is
reflected upwards and towards the opposite
side. Due to the specific form of the light
aperture, the diffuse light is emitted with
varying intensity alongside the vertical
opening. The interior of the slim Cadmo lamp
has a combination of different halogen light
sources which provides illumination with
interesting changes of intensity. Separate
switching allows for individual control of
each halogen lamp.

Mit ihren harmonisch ausgewogenen
Proportionen wirkt die Stehleuchte
Cadmo wie ein Schleier oder ein stilles
klösterliches Gewand. Die zurückhaltend gestalteten Konturen formen ein
Licht mit unverwechselbarem, elegantem
Charakter. Die schlanke Silhouette des
Lampenschirms aus Edelstahl öffnet sich
nach oben hin und gibt an der Seite eine
Lichtöffnung von unterschiedlicher Größe
frei. So ist das Licht auf der einen Seite
vollkommen abgeschirmt, während gleichzeitig ein warmes, indirektes Licht nach
oben und auf die gegenüberliegende Seite
reflektiert wird. Aufgrund der besonderen
Form der Lichtöffnung wird gestreutes
Licht mit unterschiedlicher Intensität entlang der Längsöffnung erzeugt. Im Inneren der schlanken Leuchte Cadmo befindet
sich eine Kombination aus verschiedenen
Halogen-Lichtquellen, die für eine in ihrer
Intensität abwechslungsreiche Beleuchtung sorgen. Die einzelnen Halogenlampen sind durch getrennte Schalter separat
regelbar.

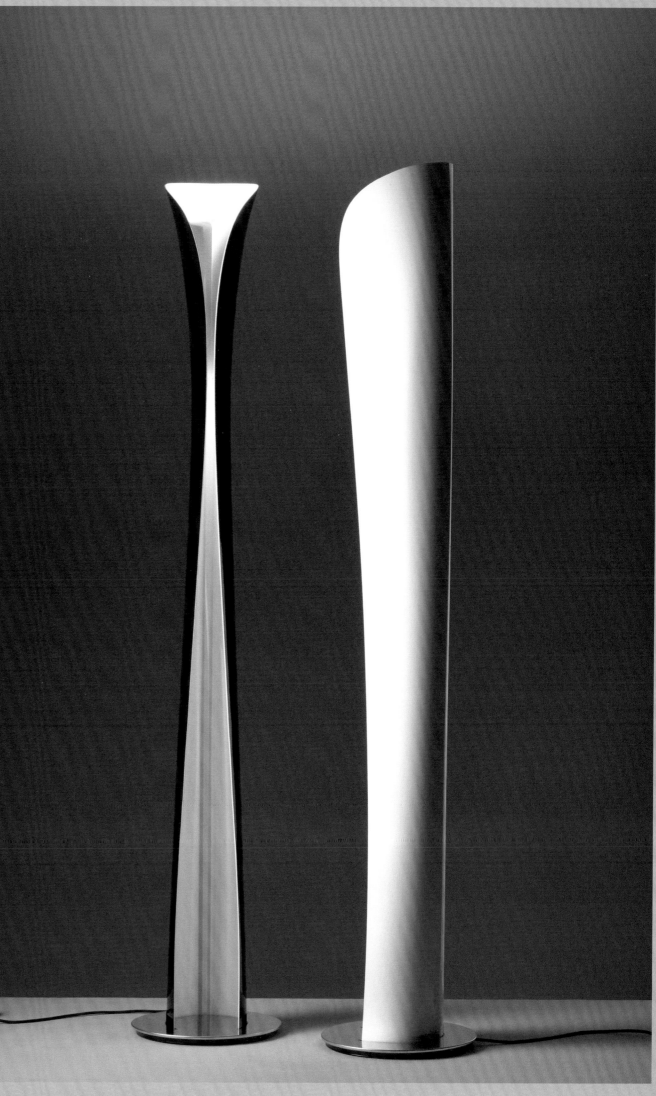

senses EYES
Light Series / Leuchtenserie

senses, interactive lights,
Steinel Solutions AG,
Einsiedeln, Switzerland / Schweiz
Design: Oliver Haefeli
(The Lateral Company),
Zürich, Switzerland / Schweiz
www.spirit-of-senses.ch

The senses EYES light series features aesthetic, high-quality light objects that engage playfully with the fascinating power and changeability of light. With a form language that thrives on opposites, the design contrasts a square light body with a cable-like supporting element. A measured bend in the otherwise static cable creates a stable support base and provides for a slim overall profile. The product series is available in different heights as either a floor lamp or a table lamp. A minimalist glass cube conceals innovative, interactive LED technology by which users can – touch-free and with the movement of only one hand – compose their preferred light ambience, bringing partial to full lighting as well as light and shade variations into play. In this way, users become virtual light composers as they orchestrate their own, individual room lighting.

Die Leuchtenserie senses EYES umfasst eine Reihe von ästhetisch hochwertigen Lichtobjekten, die mit der faszinierenden Kraft und Veränderlichkeit des Lichts spielerisch umgehen. Ihre Formensprache lebt von Gegensätzen und kombiniert einen würfelförmigen Leuchtkörper mit einem kabelgleichen Stützelement. Durch eine dezente Biegung des ansonsten statischen Kabels entsteht eine stabile Standfläche, welche die Silhouette der Leuchte auf ein Minimum reduziert. Die Produktserie ist in unterschiedlichen Höhen als Steh- oder Tischleuchte erhältlich. Ein puristischer Glaswürfel verbirgt eine innovative LED-Technologie, die interaktiv den Zugriff auf eine partielle oder vollständige Beleuchtung des Glaskörpers ermöglicht: Berührungsfrei, nur durch die Bewegung einer Hand, können immer neue Lichtkompositionen aus hell und dunkel, aus Licht und Schatten geschaffen werden. Der Benutzer wird auf diese Weise zum Lichtarrangeur und kann die Raumausleuchtung nach Belieben akzentuieren.

QLD-203
LED Table Lamp / LED-Tischleuchte

Qisda Corporation, Taipei, Taiwan
Design: Qisda/QisDesign, Taipei, Taiwan
www.qisda.com
www.qisdesign.com

In the style of classical elegance of a piano, the design concept of this LED light fixture reflects the high demands of contemporary home décor. The appearance of the table lamp is both formal and functionally harmonious. Similar to a piano keyboard, the lamp consists of independent units, each of which can work solo or in harmony, and which visually remind the viewer of 12 piano keys. By gently tilting the individual elements, illumination according to individual preferences can be realised with single units or all of them lit up. Front and back side of the luminary emit light in different intensities; whereas one side provides enough light for reading, the other rather provides just enough light for ambient illumination.

In Anlehnung an die klassische Eleganz eines Klaviers spiegelt das Gestaltungs-konzept dieser LED-Leuchtvorrichtung die hohen Ansprüche einer zeitgemäßen Wohnkultur wider. Das Erscheinungsbild der Tischleuchte wirkt dabei formal wie auch funktional stimmig. Gleich einer Klaviatur besteht das Beleuchtungsfeld aus voneinander unabhängigen Einheiten, die einzeln angesteuert werden können und visuell an zwölf Klaviertasten erinnern. Eine individuell gewünschte Beleuchtung wird komfortabel durch ein leichtes Kippen der Elemente aktiviert, wobei diese sowohl einzeln als auch gemeinsam illuminiert werden können. Die beiden Seiten des Leuchtkörpers strahlen jeweils eine unterschiedlich starke Lichtintensität aus. Während die eine Seite eine helle, lesetaugliche Beleuchtung bietet, eignet sich die andere Seite für eine eher gedämpfte Raumbeleuchtung.

To Be Touched
Light Switch/Lichtschalter

Royal Philips Electronics, Eindhoven, NL
In-house design/Werksdesign:
Stefano Marzano + Design Team
www.philips.com/design

The distinctive appearance of this light switch is characterised by a dynamic wheel-shaped control module. Intuitively this colour-changing wheel operates different light parameters including lightness, colour spectrum and saturation as well as colour temperature. A simulation at the switch visualises the respective selection – this projection facilitates operation. LEDs illuminate the innovative light wheel, which is activated when the touch-sensitive buttons are operated.

Ein dynamisches, kreisrundes Steuermodul prägt das markante Erscheinungsbild dieses Lichtschalters. Intuitiv lassen sich mit dem farblich veränderlichen Rad verschiedene Lichtparameter wie Helligkeit, Farbspektrum, -sättigung und -temperatur regeln. Eine Simulation am Lichtschalter selbst visualisiert die jeweilige Einstellung und erleichtert per Vorausschau die Bedienung. Das innovative Leuchtrad wird von LEDs illuminiert und reagiert auf die Betätigung der berührungsempfindlichen Schaltknöpfe.

Novallure
LED Candle and Lustre/
LED-Kerze und -Leuchter

Royal Philips Electronics, Eindhoven, NL
In-house design/Werksdesign:
Stefano Marzano + Design Team
www.philips.com/design

These innovative B35 LED lamps present a user-oriented reinterpretation of traditional electric bulbs. By a classic look the changeover to LED technology is supposed to take place in a simpler way. Users have the choice between two different versions. The light quality as well is deliberately configured to obtain the impression of an incandescent candle lamp. Due to its long lifetime this sustainable product solution reduces energy consumption thus improving one's personal carbon footprint.

Diese innovativen B35-LED-Lampen stellen eine nutzerorientierte Neuinterpretation herkömmlicher Glühbirnen dar. Mit einer klassischen Formensprache soll der Umstieg auf die LED-Technologie vereinfacht werden. Dem Verbraucher stehen dabei zwei unterschiedliche Ausführungen zur Auswahl. Auch die Lichtqualität ist bewusst der einer weißglühenden Kerzenbirne nachempfunden. Aufgrund ihrer langen Lebenszeit reduziert die nachhaltige Produktlösung den Energieverbrauch und verbessert somit auch die persönliche Klimabilanz.

Kreaton
Modular Lamp/Modulare Lampe

NTT Design S.r.l., Milan,
Italy/Mailand, Italien
In-house design/Werksdesign:
Sergio Nava
www.kreaton.it

Kreaton is a modular lamp system with a playful design component prompting interaction with the user. Shape and colour of the luminary can be varied, according to individual preferences, with flexible components. In this way, the user can create abstract fantasy structures but also concrete objects like hearts or houses. The lamp system consists of a bright standard base made of transparent polycarbonate and coloured modules in three different sizes.

Kreaton ist ein modulares Lampensystem mit einer spielerischen Gestaltungskomponente, welche die Interaktion mit dem Benutzer anregt. Über flexibel zusammenstellbare Einzelteile können Form und Farbe des Leuchtkörpers nach eigenen Wünschen variiert werden. So lassen sich abstrakte Phantasiegebilde, aber auch Gegenständliches wie Herzen oder Häuser kreieren. Das Lampensystem besteht aus einer hellen Standardunterseite aus transparentem Polycarbonat und farbigen Modulen in drei unterschiedlichen Größen.

Piani Lungo
Pendant Lamp / Pendelleuchte

K.B. Form GmbH, Rellingen,
Germany / Deutschland
Design: Kai Byok
www.kbform.com

This timeless pendant lamp was conceived for the dining or extended living area. Its geometrical belt, 50 mm wide and 8 mm thin, has been milled from solid aluminium and polished by hand. The reflecting surface is interrupted by four filigree copper cables leading up to the canopy, providing the power supply. Floating seemingly weightless, the lamp brightly illuminates the surface underneath with ten anti-glare LED reflectors.

Diese zeitlose Pendelleuchte wurde für den Esstisch oder den erweiterten Wohnbereich konzipiert. Ihre 50 mm breite und 8 mm dünne Bandgeometrie ist aus massivem Aluminium gefräst und von Hand hochglanzveredelt. Die spiegelnde Oberfläche wird von vier filigranen Kupfergeflechtseilen unterbrochen, welche die Stromversorgung zum optional erhältlichen Baldachin sicherstellen. Scheinbar schwerelos schwebend, gewährt die Leuchte mittels zehn LED-Reflektoren eine lichtstarke und blendfreie Ausleuchtung der darunter liegenden Fläche.

Nastrino
Table Lamp / Tischleuchte

K.B. Form GmbH, Rellingen,
Germany / Deutschland
Design: Kai Byok
www.kbform.com

Discreetly sanded aluminium profiles give this table lamp with its balanced proportions an independent character. The filigree profiles lead to a vertical foot element which, like the entire construction, does without any visible screws. The optional clamping foot also mirrors the straight-lined design vocabulary. The slim upper arm accommodates the LED technology with up to three anti-glare illumination zones. While the upper joint is held by resilient friction, the lower one is enforced with a hidden spring.

Dezent geschliffene Aluminiumprofile geben dieser ausgewogen proportionierten Tischleuchte einen eigenständigen Charakter. Die filigran anmutenden Profile münden in einem vertikalen Fußelement, welches, wie die gesamte Konstruktion, ohne sichtbare Schrauben auskommt. Auch der optionale Klemmfuß folgt einer geradlinigen Formensprache. In den schmalen Armen findet eine LED-Technik mit bis zu drei blendfreien Leuchtzonen Platz. Während das obere Gelenk per Reibung Halt findet, ist das untere mit einer verdeckten Federtechnik verstärkt.

Mood Flame
Tea Light Holder / Teelichthalter

Royal VKB, Zoetermeer, NL
Design: Jan Hoekstra, Genk,
Belgium / Belgien
www.royalvkb.com
www.janhoekstra.com

Mood Flame is an emotionally appealing tea light holder whose design concept utilises an interplay of colours and transparent material. Made of silicone, a delightful translucent light effect is brought about with the respective lamp shade colour. A minimalist line management creates a large reflexion surface, optionally in the colours cherry red, green, taupe or white. Mood Flame is designed for use with white standard tea lights with a diameter of 39 mm and is heat- and fire-resistant.

Mood Flame ist ein emotional ansprechender Teelichthalter, dessen Gestaltungskonzept das Zusammenspiel von Farben und transparentem Material nutzt. Aus Silikon gefertigt, entsteht ein reizvoll durchscheinender Lichteffekt in der jeweiligen Lampenschirmfarbe. Eine minimalistische Linienführung kreiert eine große Reflexionsfläche, die wahlweise in den Farben Kirschrot, Grün, Taupe oder Weiß leuchtet. Mood Flame ist für den Gebrauch mit weißen Standardteelichtern im Durchmesser von 39 mm bestimmt und zudem hitze- und feuerbeständig.

LUXCR111
Energy-Saving Lamp/
Energiesparlampe

Dais Electric Co., Ltd., Shanghai, China
In-house design/Werksdesign:
Peijun Dai
www.dais.com.cn

Clear structures and the use of high-grade materials are the design attributes of this energy-saving lamp. A funnel-shaped line management results in an attractive design language, visually underlining the high degree of functionality of this eco-friendly lamp with its multifaceted reflector surface. As a further development of conventional compact fluorescent lamps, this product solution provides constant bright illumination from the very beginning, eliminating the need for preheating after turning on the luminary. Its patented technology is based on the fluorescent component parts, which are effectively protected. Even frequent turning on and off does not reduce the life cycle of this robust lamp. An innovative tube which has the patented upside-down design form in its interior allows for a wide angle of high illumination.

Klare Strukturen und der Einsatz hochwertiger Materialien sind die gestalterischen Attribute dieser Energiesparlampe. Eine trichterförmige Linienführung führt zu einer attraktiven Formensprache, wobei die hohe Funktionalität der umweltfreundlichen Lampe durch eine facettenreiche Reflektorfläche visuell unterstrichen wird. Als Weiterentwicklung herkömmlicher Kompaktleuchtstofflampen bietet diese Produktlösung eine konstant helle Ausleuchtung von Beginn an, ohne dass nach dem Einschalten ein Vorglühen notwendig ist. Ihre patentierte Technologie beruht auf den fluoreszierenden Bestandteilen, die effektiv geschützt sind. Selbst häufiges An- und Ausschalten beeinträchtigt nicht die Lebensdauer der robusten Lampe. Eine innovative, patentierte Röhrenform ermöglicht einen breiten Strahlungswinkel mit hoher Beleuchtungsstärke.

Nature
LED Lightbulb/LED-Glühbirne

Advanced-Connectek Inc.,
Taipei, Taiwan
Design: Process Design AG Taiwan Branch,
Taipei, Taiwan
www.justledliting.com
www.acon.com

The basic design concept behind the new development of this LED light bulb is a combination of a classic iconic design vocabulary with sophisticated LED technology. With reduced outline and balanced proportion, the elegant bulb can be harmoniously blended into different interiors without any additional lampshade. The unconventional contours, symbolise a high functional value and the state-of-the-art energy saving technology. The innovative LED bulb meets the expectations of a reliable dimmable illumination with surroundings in 360 degrees. The patented T-Tech is capable of saving up to 90 percent energy, compared to incandescent bulbs. Additional attributes of this LED lamp are a prolonged life cycle, a compact light construction, and the use of environmental-friendly materials.

Die grundlegende Gestaltungsidee zur Neuentwicklung dieser LED-Glühbirne ist die Verbindung einer klassischen, ikonenhaften Formensprache mit den gehobenen Anforderungen einer LED-Technologie. Puristisch und ausgewogen in ihren Proportionen, lässt sich die elegante Glühbirne auch ohne zusätzlichen Lampenschirm in unterschiedliche Interieurs harmonisch einfügen. Eine unkonventionelle Kontur symbolisiert dabei den hohen Gebrauchsnutzen sowie den technischen Fortschritt eines zeitgemäßen Energiesparens. Die innovative LED-Glühbirne erfüllt dabei die Erwartungen an eine stufenlos dimmbare Lichtquelle, die einen vollen 360-Grad-Umkreis zuverlässig ausleuchtet. Ihre patentierte Lichtführung T-Tech ermöglicht im Vergleich zu herkömmlichen Glühbirnen eine 90-prozentige Energieeinsparung. Eine verlängerte Lebensdauer dank kompaktem, leichtem Aufbau sowie der Einsatz gesundheitlich unbedenklicher Materialien sind weitere stimmige Aspekte dieser LED-Glühbirne.

Douala
Pendant, Ceiling and Wall Luminaires/
Pendel-, Decken- und Wandleuchten

RZB-Leuchten, Bamberg,
Germany/Deutschland
In-house design/Werksdesign:
Helmut Heinrich
www.rzb.de

Douala, a product range of pendant, ceiling
and wall luminaires, unites two different
light technologies in one hybrid luminaire:
a mouth-blown opal glass distributes
the light of two ring lamps in the room.
In the middle of the glass, a reflector
directs the light of a bright LED module
downwards as a focused spotlight. The two
complementary illumination systems can
be operated together or independent from
each other. The stainless steel base with
its clear visual language and the precisely
integrated opal glass body combine to create
a unity with a harmonious design. Due
to their slim construction, the lamps can
either be mounted as a seemingly floating
pendant luminaire, or directly to the wall
or ceiling. The evenly distributed intensity
of illumination guarantees a high degree of
viewing comfort. The lamps are available
in a diameter of either 400 or 500 mm.
The luminaire is an architectural element
whose design is reduced to the body of the
luminaire.

Douala, eine Produktserie von zeitlos
gestalteten Pendel-, Decken- und Wandleuchten, vereint zwei unterschiedliche
Lichttechniken in einer Hybridleuchte:
Zum einen verteilt ein mundgeblasenes
Opalglas das Licht zweier Ringlampen frei
im Raum. Darüber hinaus befindet sich
in der Mitte des Glases ein Reflektor, der
das Licht eines hellen LED-Moduls als
fokussiertes Spotlight nach unten lenkt.
Die beiden sich ergänzenden Beleuch-
tungssysteme sind wahlweise zusammen
oder unabhängig voneinander ein- und
ausschaltbar. In ihrer klaren Formensprache bildet die runde Edelstahleinfassung
mit dem passgenau integrierten, opalen
Glaskörper eine harmonische gestalterische Einheit. Aufgrund ihrer flachen
Bauart lassen sich die Leuchten wahlweise
filigran schwebend oder unmittelbar auf
Wand oder Decke montieren. Dank ihrer
gleichmäßigen Beleuchtungsstärke bieten
sie einen hohen Sehkomfort und sind in
zwei Größen mit einem Durchmesser von
400 oder 500 mm erhältlich. Die Leuchte
ist ein architektonisches Element, das sich
in seiner Gestalt auf den Leuchtenkörper
reduziert.

Areno
Wall and Ceiling Luminaires/
Wand- und Deckenleuchte

RZB-Leuchten, Bamberg,
Germany/Deutschland
In-house design/Werksdesign:
Helmut Heinrich
www.rzb.de

This wall and ceiling luminaires is
characterised by a factual and functionally
oriented design. It reinterpets a classic
form and functionality and is particularly
suitable for use in commercial or private
spaces. Whereas the previous classic bulbous
form was defined by the round shape of the
lightbulb, the change to contemporary lamps
allows for a minimalist and slim shape. The
flat luminary made of glass contains three
3.6-watt mains voltage LEDs providing
comprehensive illumination of the room.
The base made of die-cast aluminium,
shockproof crystal glass coated on the
inside, and a newly designed glass fixture
altogether result in an overall high-grade
appearance of this classic luminaire. The
technically sophisticated luminaire with the
measurements 215 x 142 x 85 mm provides
a degree of protection IP 65 and guarantees
long-lasting, maintenance-free operation.

Eine funktional ausgerichtete Gestaltung
prägt die sachliche Anmutung dieser
Wand- und Deckenleuchte. Sie interpretiert eine klassische Form und Funktionalität neu und eignet sich vor allem für
den Einsatz in gewerblichen oder privaten
Nutzräumen. Da die bisherige, klassisch
bauchige Form durch die runde Kontur
der Glühlampe geprägt war, wird mit dem
Wechsel zu einer zeitgemäßen Leuchtmit-
telbestückung eine minimalistisch flache
Form ermöglicht. Im Inneren des nun
flachen, gläsernen Leuchtkörpers befinden
sich drei 3,6-Watt-Netzspannungs-LEDs,
die für eine flächendeckende Ausleuchtung des Raums sorgen. Eine Armatur aus
Alu-Druckguss führt in Verbindung mit
einem stoßfesten, innen beschichteten
Kristallglas sowie einer neu gestalteten
Glasfixierung zu einem hochwertigen
Gesamtbild des Leuchtenklassikers. Die
technisch ausgereifte Leuchte in den
Maßen 215 x 142 x 85 mm erreicht eine
Schutzart von IP 65 und gewährt einen
langfristig wartungsfreien Betrieb.

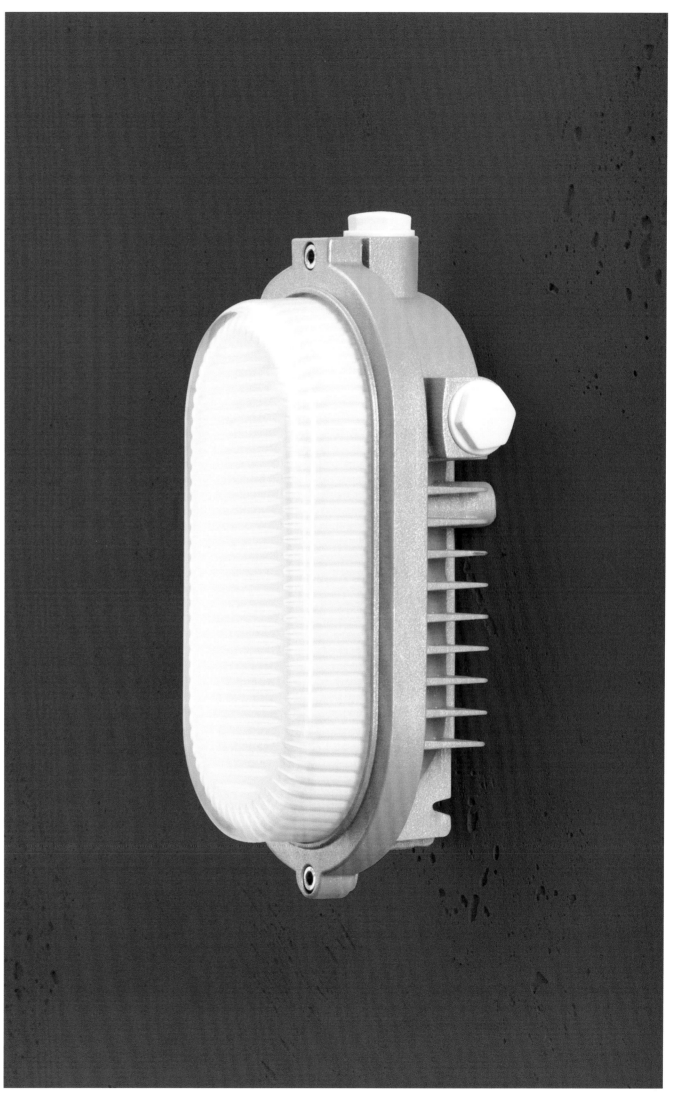

Lavano
Wall Lamp / Wandleuchte

RZB-Leuchten, Bamberg,
Germany / Deutschland
In-house design / Werksdesign:
Helmut Heinrich
www.rzb.de

With a unique elegance, the Lavano wall lamp is a visually appealing light object that adapts readily into an architecturally oriented interior. A clean and timeless form language divides the lamp body into three tall, narrow strips, the outer two of which are illuminated. Between the two outer strips, a mirroring metal profile serves to counterbalance the adjoining light surfaces. An elliptical curve of the lamp front underscores the detail-oriented design. The two diffusers generate a bright and shiny light that distributes evenly outwards and that ensures a high degree of visual comfort. A selection of high-quality materials, a modular construction system and energy-efficient LED lights provide for a long product life. The light-intensive lamp series is available in two sizes, whereby the base of the fixture can be used for further light types.

Mit ihrer eigenständigen Eleganz empfiehlt sich die Wandleuchte Lavano als visuell ansprechendes Lichtobjekt, welches sich einem architekturorientierten Interieur harmonisch anpasst. Eine klare und zeitlose Formensprache unterteilt den Korpus in drei schmale Rechtecke, von denen die beiden äußeren illuminiert werden. In der Mitte des Leuchtkörpers befindet sich eine spiegelnde Metallblende, welche die angrenzenden Lichtflächen proportional ausgewogen unterbricht. Eine ellipsenförmige Wölbung der Frontpartie unterstreicht die detailbetonte Gestaltung. Die Konstruktion der beiden Diffusoren schafft einen brillant funkelnden Lichteffekt, der gleichmäßig in die Breite streut und einen hohen Sehkomfort sichert. Eine Auswahl hochwertiger Materialien, eine Verarbeitung im Baukastensystem sowie eine energieeffiziente LED-Ausrüstung sind für eine lange Lebensdauer konzipiert. Die lichtstarke Leuchtenserie ist in zwei Größen erhältlich, wobei die Armatur eine Plattform für weitere Leuchtentypen bildet.

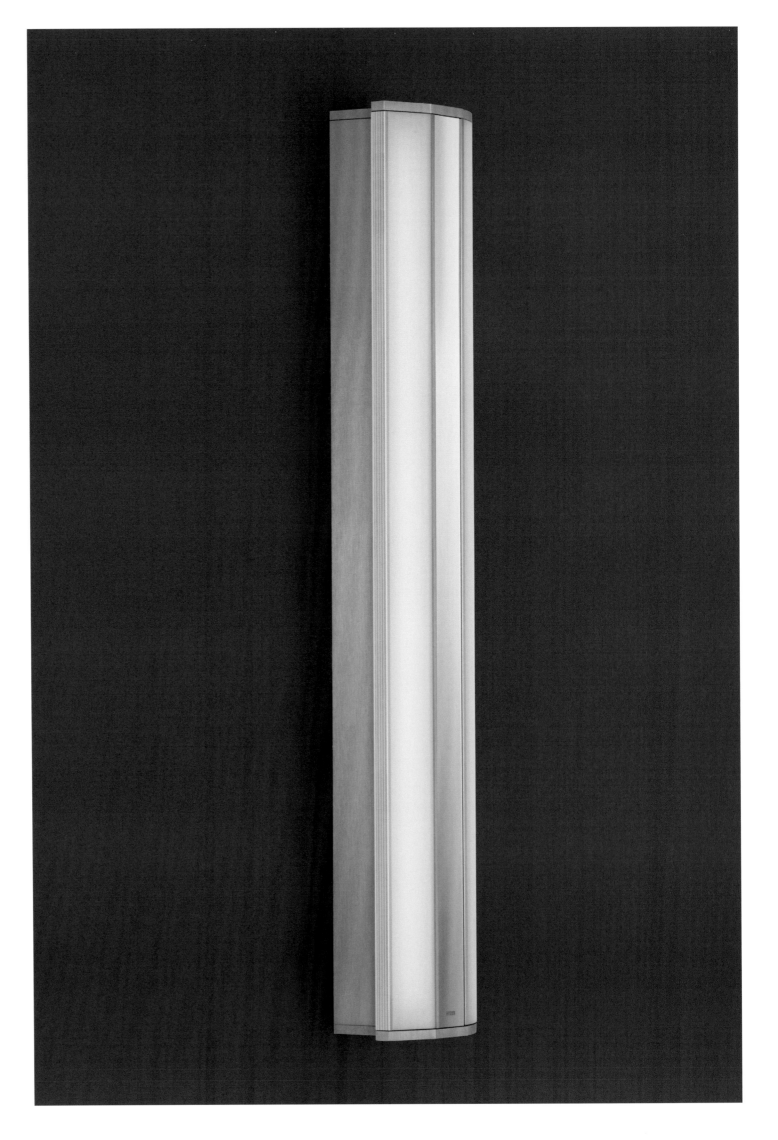

Calla
Multifunctional Street Lighting/
Multifunktionale Straßenbeleuchtung

Daelim Industrial Co. Ltd., Seoul, Korea
In-house design/Werksdesign:
Sung Soo Bae
Design: Taewon Lighting Co. Ltd. (Jung
Ho Lim, Sang Sung Kim), Seoul, Korea
www.taewon.co.kr

Calla is an outdoor lamp that uses a light
source of CDM 150W. It is installed along
pedestrian roads in residential complexes
or parks and features aesthetic beauty and
brightness to pedestrians. The exterior of
Calla basically consists of the head area,
which emits light; pillar with embedded
electric wires; fixture that is embedded with
a CCTV and location receiver; and a base that
can support the ground surface and outdoor
lamp.

Die Außenleuchte Calla verwendet die
Lichtquelle CDM mit 150 Watt. Sie eignet
sich für die Beleuchtung von Fußgän-
gerwegen in Wohnanlagen oder Parks,
indem sie ästhetischen Reiz mit fußgän-
gerfreundlicher Helligkeit verbindet. Ihr
Äußeres besteht im Wesentlichen aus dem
Kopfbereich mit der Lichtquelle, der Säule
mit der integrierten Verkabelung, einer
Halterung mit integriertem CCTV-System
und Standortempfänger sowie der Basis
für die Verankerung der Außenleuchte
im Boden.

LIM – Light in Motion
Multifunction LED Light/
Multifunktions-LED-Leuchte

Haworth GmbH, Ahlen,
Germany/Deutschland
In-house design/Werksdesign:
Ralph Reddig
Design: Pablo Designs,
San Francisco, USA
www.haworth.com
www.pablodesigns.com

The design of this light strives for a reduced
and, at the same time, striking design
language. A distinctive black housing is
the expression of this functionally self-
contained creation. Strikingly slim aluminium
profiles are combined with each other in a
deliberately plain way by means of magnets.
In this way, the multifunction LED light can
be flexibly placed on the worktop. Innovative
LED technology allows for a large number of
application options and always guarantees
precisely accurate illumination. This light
blends harmoniously into different interiors
and can be flexibly used as individual object
or in combination with several other lights.
LIM meets contemporary and environmental
standards as it is made of recycled
aluminium. The multifunction LEDs have a
life cycle of up to 50,000 hours.

Die Gestaltung dieser Leuchte strebt eine
reduzierte und zugleich prägnante Formensprache an. Ein markantes, schwarzes
Gehäuse ist der Ausdruck dieser auch
funktional eigenständigen Kreation.
Auffallend schmale Aluminiumprofile
werden durch den Einsatz von Magneten
auf bewusst einfach wirkende Weise miteinander verbunden. Dadurch kann diese
Multifunktions-LED-Leuchte ganz flexibel eingesetzt werden. Eine innovative
LED-Technologie ermöglicht vielseitige
Anwendungsmöglichkeiten und gewährt
eine stets punktgenaue Ausleuchtung.
Diese Leuchte fügt sich harmonisch in
unterschiedliche Raumausstattungen ein
und kann sowohl freistehend als auch im
Verbund mit mehreren flexibel eingesetzt
werden. Sie erfüllt zeitgemäße Umwelt-
kriterien, denn in ihrem Fertigungsprozess
kommt recyceltes Aluminium zum Einsatz, darüber hinaus spenden langlebige
Multifunktions-LEDs bis zu 50.000
Stunden Licht.

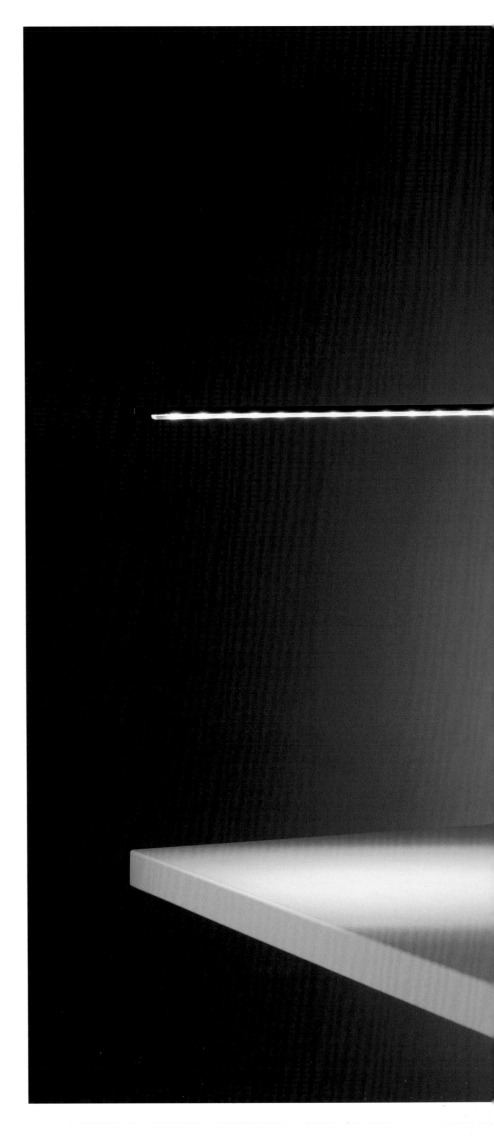

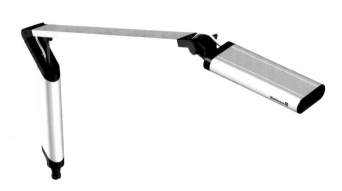

Minela
LED Task Luminaire /
LED-Arbeitsplatzleuchte

Herbert Waldmann GmbH & Co. KG,
Villingen-Schwenningen,
Germany / Deutschland
Design: Weinberg & Ruf, Filderstadt,
Germany / Deutschland
www.waldmann.com
www.weinberg-ruf.de

This energy-saving LED task luminaire combines distinctive design with a high degree of flexibility. Thanks to a gas pressure spring, Minela can be easily positioned, and the lamp head can be adjusted in three directions. All metal parts are made of white powder-coated aluminium profiles; the joints are made of glass fibre reinforced plastic component parts. High-performance LEDs with innovative reflector technology provide bright large surface illumination.

Diese energiesparsame LED-Arbeitsplatzleuchte verbindet eine prägnante Gestaltung mit einem hohen Maß an Flexibilität. Minela ist über eine Gasdruckfeder-Zugentlastung einfach positionierbar, wobei der Leuchtenkopf in drei Richtungen verstellbar ist. Alle Metallteile sind aus weißen, pulverbeschichteten Aluminiumprofilen gefertigt, zudem übernehmen glasfaserverstärkte Kunststoffteile die Funktion der Gelenke. Für eine großflächige Ausleuchtung kommen Hochleistungs-LEDs mit einer innovativen Reflektortechnik zum Einsatz.

Pipe
LED Table Lamp / LED-Tischleuchte

Advanced-Connectek Inc.,
Taipei, Taiwan
Design: Process Design AG Taiwan Branch,
Taipei, Taiwan
www.justledliting.com
www.acon.com

The Pipe table lamp with simple design vocabulary and appealing aesthetics represents innovative LED technology. In the shape of a plain tube, the lamp consists of a static base element and a detachable luminary element. In this way, the patented table lamp can be used as a wireless flashlight. An electronic management system can sense to light up automatically during a power cut by delivering up to two hours of emergency lighting. Pipe is charged by a flexible solar panel outdoor.

Die Tischleuchte Pipe verkörpert mit ihrer schlichten Formensprache und ihrer ansprechenden Ästhetik eine innovative LED-Technologie. In Form eines einfachen Rohrs besteht die Leuchte aus einem statischen Fuß- und einem abnehmbaren Leuchtelement. Deshalb ist die patentierte Tischleuchte auch als kabellose Stablampe einsetzbar. Ein elektronisches Management registriert eine mögliche Stromunterbrechung und liefert bis zu zwei Stunden stromunabhängiges Licht als Notbeleuchtung. Pipe wird durch ein flexibles Solarpanel geladen.

Infinity
Desk Light / Schreibtischleuchte

Unilux, Savigny-sur-Orge,
France / Frankreich
Design: 360 Design Industriel Design
Global (Patrick Jouffret),
Toulon, France / Frankreich
www.unilux.fr
www.agence-360.com

Infinity introduces an innovative technology through a geometrical environment coming from a simple metal sheet, which is folded and articulated between two pure discs. This French made lamp offers not only a pure and contemporary design, but also real visual comfort, thanks to its four power LEDs equipped with lenses, and its fitted dimmer switch, allowing to choose the desired light intensity. Infinity is particularly eco-friendly due to the long service life of the LEDs.

Infinity führt eine innovative Technologie durch eine „geometrische" Umgebung ein, die aus einem einfachen, gefalteten Metallblatt resultiert, das zwischen zwei makellosen Scheiben beweglich angebracht ist. Zusätzlich zu ihrer schlichten, modern anmutenden Gestaltung bietet diese in Frankreich hergestellte Leuchte mit ihren vier Power-LEDs einen hohen Sehkomfort. Ihr Touch-Schalter mit Dimmer ermöglicht die Wahl der Lichtstärke. Dank der langen Lebensdauer ihrer LEDs ist Infinity besonders umweltfreundlich.

Young w094
Desk Light / Schreibtischleuchte

Wästberg, Helsingborg,
Sweden / Schweden
Design: Michael Young Ltd.
(Michael Young), Hong Kong
www.wastberg.com
www.michael-young.com

A star-shaped arm is the distinctive feature of this desk light. This unconventional form language is made possible by a manufacturing technique borrowed from the bicycle industry offering a fresh approach to the design of desk light typologies: the arm of the light is made of extruded, i.e., pressed out as one piece, aluminium material. The flexible, adjustable arm can be turned in six positions around its 360-degree axis.

Ein sternenförmiger Schaft ist prägendes Merkmal dieser Schreibtischleuchte. Möglich wird diese unkonventionelle Formensprache durch ein Herstellungsverfahren, das aus der Fahrradindustrie stammt und eine neue Herangehensweise an die Typologie von Schreibtischleuchten erlaubt: Der Arm der Leuchte wird extrudiert, d. h. als Formstück aus thermoplastischem Material gepresst. Der flexible, verstellbare Schaft kann in sechs Positionen um die 360-Grad-Achse gedreht werden.

Athene
LED System Light /
LED-Systemleuchte

Less'n'more GmbH, Pulheim,
Germany / Deutschland
In-house design / Werksdesign:
Kai Steffens
www.less-n-more.com

Based on a growing number of puristically designed components the Athene light system offers options to create different luminaires. Materials of a cool and unemotional impression give it the appearance of a stringent simplicity, which is a consistent result of its function. The combination of the patent-protected focus system, the flexibly adjustable shaft, and a textile coating available in different colours, wants to employ the LED light technology for both the commercial sector and private homes in a visually attractive way.

Aufbauend auf einer wachsenden Anzahl puristisch gestalteter Komponenten bietet das Lichtsystem Athene die Möglichkeit der Realisierung unterschiedlicher Leuchten. Kühl und sachlich wirkende Materialien verleihen ihm die Anmutung einer stringenten Einfachheit, die sich konsequent aus der Funktion ergibt. Die Kombination aus patentrechtlich geschütztem Fokussystem, der flexibel einstellbaren Welle sowie den farblich wählbaren Textilummantelungen möchte die LED-Lichttechnologie nicht nur im Objektbereich, sondern auch im privaten Wohnbereich visuell attraktiv einsetzen.

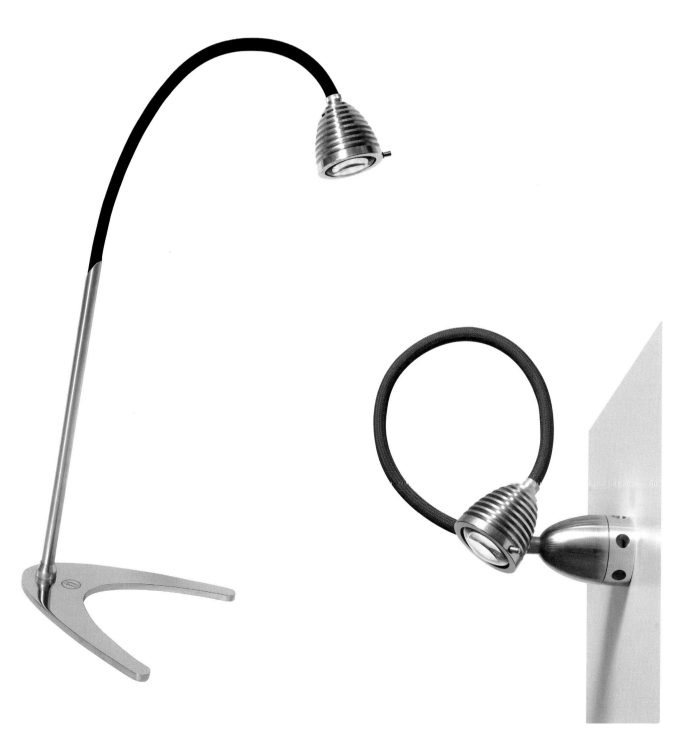

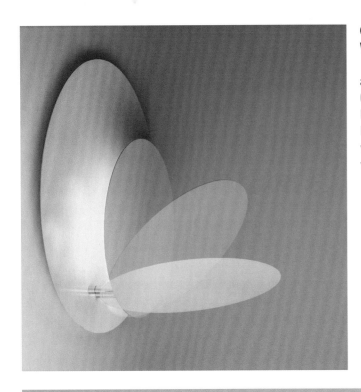

GUAU
Wall Lamp/Wandleuchte

arturo alvarez, Calor Color S.L., Vedra
(A Coruña), Spain/Spanien
Design: El Ultimo Grito (Roberto Feo,
Rosario Hurtado), London, GB
www.arturo-alvarez.com
www.eugstudio.com

The GUAU wall lamp is an emotionally
appealing combination of atmospheric and
direct light. In closed mode, the diffuse light
illuminating the wall is reminiscent of a
lunar eclipse, thanks to a circular interior
cover. When opening it up to 90 degrees,
the intensity of spatial illumination can
be determined according to individual
preferences. Thanks to a double twist from
left to right, the light beam of the compact
fluorescent lamp can be directed towards the
desired space.

Die Wandleuchte GUAU bietet eine emotional ansprechende Kombination aus
atmosphärischem und direktem Licht. Im
geschlossenen Modus erinnert das diffuse,
wandgerichtete Licht dank einer kreisrunden Abblendscheibe an eine Mond-
finsternis. Mit dem Öffnen dieses Innen-
zirkels bis zu 90 Grad wird die Intensität
der Raumausleuchtung bedarfsgerecht
bestimmt. Dank einer möglichen Doppel-
drehung von links nach rechts kann der
Lichtstrahl der Kompakt-Leuchtstofflampe
zudem in die gewünschte Richtung
gelenkt werden.

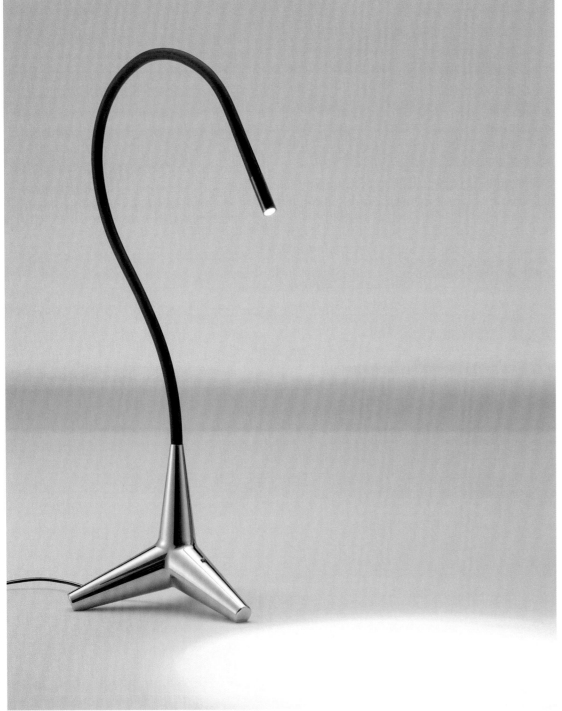

Yamagiwa Stem Ray Light
Desk Light/Schreibtischleuchte

Yamagiwa Corporation, Tokyo, Japan
Design: Studio Conran
(Tristram Keech), London, GB
www.yamagiwa.co.jp
www.conran.com

The Yamagiwa Stem Ray Light allows many
kinds of lighting, a flexible, rubberised stem
targets light in any direction. The LED doesn't
generate heat, so the light source is recessed
20 mm into the stem to eliminate glare and
provide soft, yet focussed illumination. In
contrast to the stem, the chrome-plated,
die-cast tripod base, inspired by concrete
coastal defence forms, provides stability and
poise. The base houses a rechargeable battery
source so the lamp can be uniquely cable-
free for up to 1.5 hours.

Die Leuchte Yamagiwa Stem Ray bietet viele Beleuchtungsarten. Dank eines
beweglichen Ständers mit Gummiumman-
telung kann das Licht in alle Richtungen
scheinen. Die LED-Technik erzeugt keine
Wärme, deshalb ist die Lichtquelle 20 mm
tief in den Ständer eingelassen, sodass
sie nicht blendet, sondern eine sanfte und
gleichzeitig gezielte Beleuchtung ermöglicht. Mit dem Ständer kontrastierend
bietet der verchromte, druckgegossene
Dreifuß Stabilität und Halt. Er ist inspiriert von den Beton-Tetrapoden, die als
Küstenbefestigung dienen. Der Fuß birgt
einen wiederaufladbaren Akku, sodass
die Leuchte auf einzigartige Weise bis zu
1,5 Stunden ohne Kabel auskommt.

LED2
LED Floor Lamp/LED-Stehleuchte

Tunto Design, Järvenpää,
Finland/Finnland
In-house design/Werksdesign:
Mikko Kärkkäinen
www.tunto.com

This minimalist LED floor lamp combines the effect of an expressive form language with the texture of a natural wood grain. Available in oak, walnut or birch, and in several different stains, the lamp integrates readily into a diverse range of interiors. The interplay of horizontal and vertical lines leads to the light surface, which bears nine energy-efficient LED diodes. A barely visible, touch-sensitive switch is integrated into the lamp's flat body.

Diese puristische LED-Stehleuchte kombiniert die Wirkung einer ausdrucksvollen Formensprache mit einer natürlichen Holzmaserung. Erhältlich in unterschiedlich eingefärbter Eiche, Walnuss oder Birke passt sie sich der jeweiligen Einrichtung flexibel an. Das Zusammenspiel von horizontalen und vertikalen Linien mündet in einer mit neun Leuchtdioden bestückten Lichtfläche, deren LED-Technologie eine energiearme Nutzung ermöglicht. Ein berührungsempfindlicher Schalter ist kaum sichtbar in den flachen Korpus integriert.

BPL StudyLite
Desk Light/Schreibtischleuchte

BPL Technovision Pvt Ltd, Bangalore,
India/Indien
Design: Studio ABD, Bangalore,
India/Indien
www.studylite.in
www.studioabd.in

To present a solution to the problem of frequent power cuts, this desk light was developed which can be operated either with rechargeable batteries or on the mains. In case of a power cut, the batteries guarantee mains-independent illumination up to six hours; subsequently, they can be recharged with a solar panel. The unconventional design of the light is characterised by a distinctive ring with embedded LEDs reminiscent of a halo. The elements of the flexible swan neck have been formed by spherical elements leading down to a circular foot. Available in different signal colours like red and yellow, BPL StudyLite co-created with optometry experts provides eye-friendly illumination without the generation of heat, UV- or IR radiation.

Um dem Problem häufiger Stromausfälle lösungsorientiert zu begegnen, wurde diese strom- wie batteriebetriebene Schreibtischleuchte entwickelt. Im Störungsfall gewähren die Batterien einen stromunabhängigen Weiterbetrieb von bis zu sechs Stunden, danach lassen sie sich durch Solarenergie wieder aufladen. Die unkonventionelle Anmutung der Leuchte ist von kreisrunden LEDs geprägt, die in Anlehnung an einen Heiligenschein in einen prägnanten Leuchtring integriert sind. Auch die Glieder des flexibel biegsamen Halses bestehen aus kugelförmigen Elementen und führen zu einem runden Fuß. Erhältlich in unterschiedlichen Signalfarben wie Rot und Gelb, bietet die in Zusammenarbeit mit Augenoptikern entwickelte BPL StudyLite ein augenfreundliches Licht ohne Hitzeentwicklung, UV- oder IR-Abstrahlung.

Gera Light System 6/
Gera Lichtsystem 6

Gera Leuchten GmbH, St. Gangloff,
Germany/Deutschland
Design: Thomas Ritt Industrial Design,
Warendorf, Germany/Deutschland
www.gera-leuchten.de

The Gera Light System 6 is an innovative lighting concept whose futuristic design is conceived for creative applications in commercial areas. A comprehensive selection of different pendulum or wall lights can be individually combined with differently illuminated furniture elements. Next to a light railing, lighted door or mirror frames, high-grade glass shelves, elegant shining furniture shelves and shelf systems are available. Moreover, an innovation with well-conceived functionality is the flexibly plannable, stable light shelf, which is created by means of a profile component system of aluminium profiles and various illuminants. With the ScanAndLight technology, LED light colours can be synchronised using sensors and programmable microelectronics according to individual preferences. The system can also automatically adapt to light conditions depending on season or weather.

Das Gera Lichtsystem 6 versteht sich als ein innovatives Leuchtenkonzept, dessen futuristisch anmutendes Gestaltungskonzept unter anderem auf den kreativen Einsatz in gewerblichen Bereichen abzielt. Eine umfassende Auswahl verschiedener Pendel- oder Wandleuchten kann mit unterschiedlich illuminierten Möbelelementen individuell zusammengestellt werden. Neben einer Lichtreling, einem Tür- oder Spiegelrahmen oder hochwertigen Glasablagen sind auch edel leuchtende Möbelfachböden erhältlich. Eine Innovation mit durchdachter Funktionalität ist zudem das flexibel planbare, stabile Lichtregal, das sich mithilfe eines Profilbaukastens aus Aluminiumprofilen und diversen Leuchtmitteltypen erstellen lässt. Aufgrund der ScanAndLight-Technologie können beispielsweise LEDs mithilfe von Sensoren und programmierbarer Mikroelektronik hinsichtlich ihrer Lichtfarben aufeinander abgestimmt werden und sich interaktiv auf die individuellen Wünsche oder automatisch auf jahreszeit- oder wetterbedingte Lichtgegebenheiten einstellen.

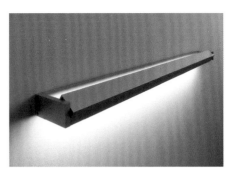

JEP
LED Pendant Luminaire/
LED-Pendelleuchte

Spectral Lichttechnik GmbH,
Freiburg, Germany/Deutschland
In-house design/Werksdesign:
Markus Kocks
www.spectral-online.de

Like a sheet of paper held aloft by the wind, the JEP pendant luminaire seems to float in space. In an emotive way light emitting diodes evenly illuminate the generous surface of the lampshade. At the same time they visually underline the geometric form of the luminaire. As the LED technology is so flexible, it was possible to realise a slight curvature giving the luminaire the impression of weightlessness, and overcome the hitherto existing restrictions with regard to form and functionality of common illuminants. A discreet frame elegantly surrounds the floating light panel. The integral foamed housing of the luminaire, which is made of reusable plastic and produced in an unusual manufacturing process, and an innovative anti-glare technology provide the technical basis for this well-balanced light concept, which combines standard illumination with the demands for sustainability and the options of a modern LED technology.

Gleich einem vom Wind empor gehobenen Blatt Papier scheint die Pendelleuchte JEP im Raum zu schweben. Die großzügige Fläche des Lampenschirms wird mit Leuchtdioden stimmungsvoll und gleichmäßig illuminiert, wodurch die geometrische Formensprache der Lampe visuell unterstützt wird. Die Flexibilität der LED-Technologie ermöglicht die Umsetzung einer leichten Wölbung, welche der Leuchte den Eindruck von Schwerelosigkeit verleiht und die bisherigen Einschränkungen hinsichtlich Form und Funktionalität herkömmlicher Leuchtmittel überwindet. Ein dezenter Rahmen fasst die schwebende Lichtfläche elegant ein. Die technische Basis für das stimmige Lichtkonzept liefern ein für Leuchten ungewöhnliches Fertigungsverfahren in Form eines geschäumten Integralgehäuses aus recycelbarem Kunststoff sowie ein innovativer Blendschutz, der eine normgerechte Ausleuchtung mit dem Anspruch an Nachhaltigkeit sowie den Möglichkeiten einer zeitgemäßen LED-Technologie verbindet.

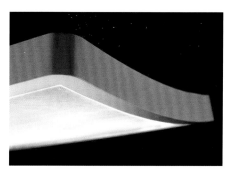

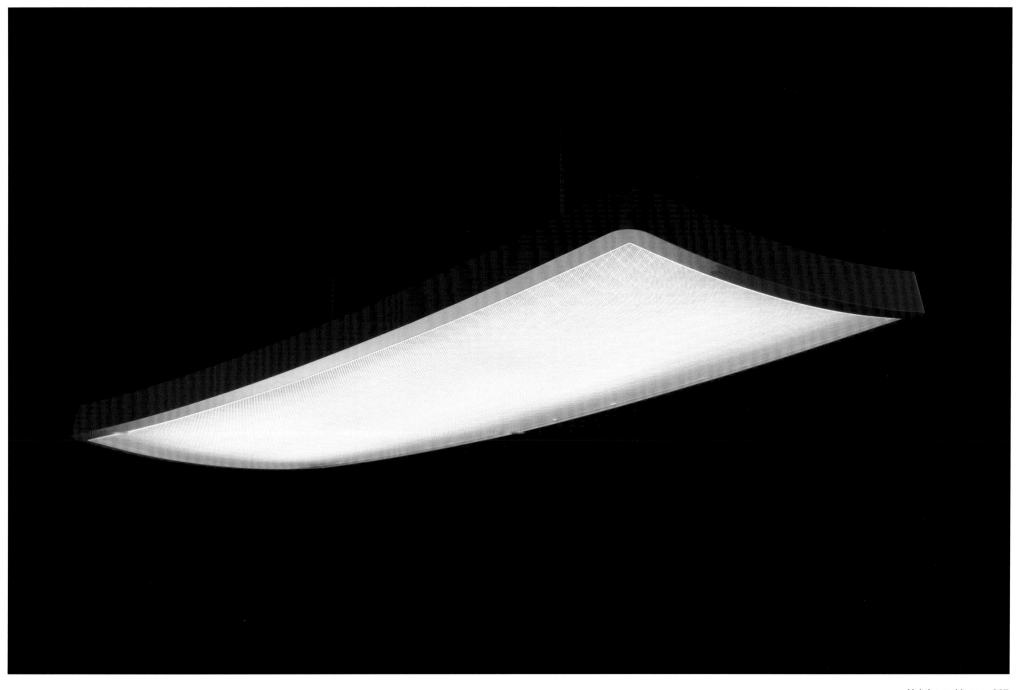

Neximo
LED Office Luminaire/
LED-Office-Leuchte

TRILUX GmbH & Co. KG, Arnsberg,
Germany/Deutschland
Design: designaffairs GmbH
(Michael Lanz, Ina Jade Seng), Munich,
Germany/München, Deutschland
www.trilux.de
www.designaffairs.com

The LED office luminaire Neximo with
its unconventional and elegant design
vocabulary represents a self-contained
light concept: the LEDs are harmoniously
combined in the organic form of the
luminaire, creating a dynamic overall
impression. The flat body contains compact
special lenses providing precise and direct
illumination of the workplace. In addition,
the filigree luminaire also lights the room
indirectly. Designed in discreet black
(optionally also available in white), the
suspended luminaire seems to float in the
room, in particular when turned on.

Mit ihrer unkonventionellen und elegant
anmutenden Formensprache stellt die
LED-Office-Leuchte Neximo ein eigenständiges Lichtkonzept dar: In Form
organisch anmutender Ornamente sind
die LEDs harmonisch miteinander verbunden und tragen zu einem dynamischen
Gesamtbild bei. Im flachen Korpus verbergen sich kompakte Speziallinsen, die für
eine exakte und direkte Ausleuchtung des
Arbeitsbereichs sorgen. Ergänzend ver-
sorgt der filigran wirkende Leuchtkörper
den Raum mit indirektem Licht. Gestaltet
in dezentem Schwarz (wahlweise auch in
Weiß erhältlich), erweckt die Hängeleuchte
insbesondere im eingeschalteten Modus
den Eindruck, im Raum zu schweben.

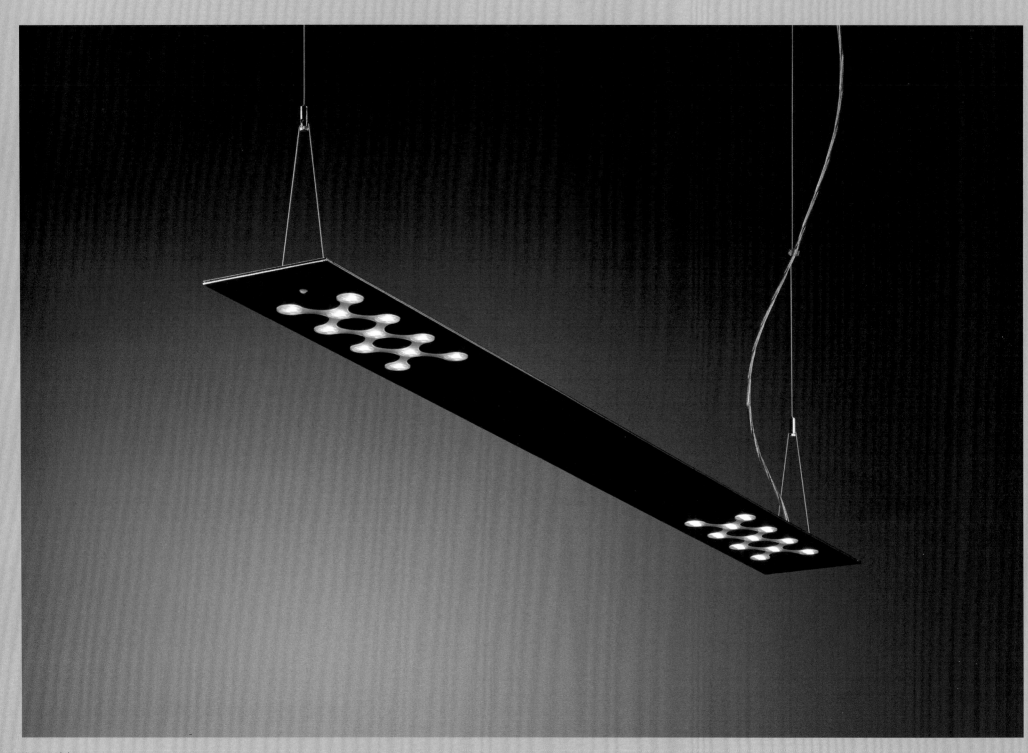

Hope
Pendant Lamp / Pendelleuchte

Luceplan Spa,
Milan, Italy / Mailand, Italien
Design: Francisco Gomez Paz, Paolo
Rizzatto, Milan, Italy / Mailand, Italien
www.luceplan.com
www.gomezpaz.com
www.paolorizzatto.it

The design of the Hope pendant lamp is inspired by the blue diamond of the same name. Effective light reflexions are reminiscent of the fascination of traditional glass chandeliers. By contrast, Hope presents a high-tech, modern version made of innovative materials. The lampshade is composed of a series of delicate plastic Fresnel lenses, which are coated with a prism-treated polycarbonate film. Being lighter than glass their refractive power therefore equals that of glass. The lenses reduce the strong impact of the light source and multiply it infinitely so that a festive sparkle is produced. This optical effect also works with the light switched off as the geometric nature of the thin lenses captures and refracts both daylight and interior light. The delicate, three-dimensional load-bearing frame made of curved steel and a variable number of transparent arms to which the lenses are attached support the lightness of the overall impression.

Die Gestaltung der Pendelleuchte Hope ist vom gleichnamigen blauen Diamanten inspiriert. Effektvolle Lichtreflexionen erinnern an die Faszination traditioneller Kronleuchter aus Glas. Doch im Unterschied dazu stellt Hope eine hochtechnologische, zeitgemäße Ausführung mit innovativen Materialien dar. Den Lampenschirm bildet eine Reihe filigraner Fresnel-Linsen aus Kunststoff, die mit einer prismenbehandelten Polycarbonatfolie beschichtet sind. Dadurch kommt deren Brechungsvermögen dem von Glas gleich, ohne dessen Gewicht zu haben. Die Linsen dämpfen das starke Licht der Leuchtquelle und multiplizieren es mannigfaltig, sodass ein festliches Funkeln entsteht. Dieser optische Effekt funktioniert auch bei ausgeschalteter Leuchte, da die Geometrie der dünnen Linsen gleichsam das natürliche Tages- und Raumlicht einfängt und bricht. Die Leichtigkeit des Gesamteindrucks wird mithilfe der grazilen, dreidimensionalen Trägerstruktur aus gebogenem Stahl und einer variablen Anzahl von transparenten Armen, auf denen die Linsen befestigt sind, unterstützt.

Occhio Più
Spotlight Series / Strahlerserie

Axelmeiselicht GmbH, Munich,
Germany / München, Deutschland
In-house design / Werksdesign:
Axel Meise, Christoph Kügler
www.occhio.de

Occhio Più is an innovative, multifunctional spotlight series for the commercial use and private homes. Its modular concept unites high design quality and well-conceived detail solutions. High quality basic materials and first class optical components ensure an exceptional quality experience. The spotlight heads are available in chrome, matt chrome, or in a white and black complete coating; they are adapted to the prevailing colours and surfaces of the architecture and the interior design. Più's design follows the Occhio Sento line. In addition to common halogen and metal halide light sources, the latest LED technology is employed. Thanks to an in-house system the LED chip is replaceable so it will always be possible to keep its technology up-to-date.

Occhio Più ist eine innovative, multifunktionale Strahlerserie für den Wohn- und Objektbereich. Ihr modulares Konzept vereint hohe Designqualität mit modernster Lichttechnologie und kombiniert Funktionalität mit durchdachten Detaillösungen. Hochwertige Grundmaterialien und erstklassige optische Komponenten ermöglichen ein außergewöhnliches Qualitätserlebnis. Die Strahlerköpfe, die in Chrom, Chrom matt, weißer und schwarzer Glanzlackierung erhältlich sind, sind abgestimmt auf die vorherrschenden Farben und Oberflächen der Architektur und Raumgestaltung. Gestalterisch orientiert sich Più an der Occhio Sento Linie. Lichttechnisch wird neben den bisher gewohnten Leuchtmitteln Halogen und Metalldampf die neueste LED-Technologie eingesetzt. Durch ein selbst entwickeltes System ist der LED-Chip austauschbar und kann dadurch immer auf den aktuellen Technologiestand gebracht werden.

Ahn (安) Series
Lighting / Beleuchtung

Samsung C & T Corporation,
Seoul, Korea
In-house design / Werksdesign:
Heung Jun Ahn
Design: Taewon Lighting
(Seunghyun Shin), Seoul, Korea
www.samsung.com

The dynamic flexibility of these ceiling lights is based on their innovative materiality. Similar to a luminous piece of wrapping cloth, the planar luminaries show an emotionally appealing materiality, referring to the design language of traditional Korean wrapping cloth. Available in different forms and sizes, the individual luminary elements can be combined to versatile ceiling installations. They can be installed flush with the adjacent surface or on top of it. The flexible material also allows for the individual use of attractive colour and light effects. According to the angle of view, the appearance of the ceiling light is varying, and the charming play of shadows at the ceiling renders the impression of a floating piece of cloth made of light. In standard mode, the calming light flows harmoniously from the outside towards the centre of the luminary, thus illuminating the room homogeneously and glare-free.

Die dynamische Wandelbarkeit dieser Deckenleuchten beruht auf ihrer innovativen Materialität. Gleich einem leuchtenden Tuch weisen die planen Leuchtkörper eine emotional ansprechende Stofflichkeit auf und zitieren damit die Formensprache der traditionellen, koreanischen Einschlagtücher. In unterschiedlichen Formen und Größen erhältlich, lassen sich die einzelnen Leuchtelemente zu vielfältigen Deckeninstallationen zusammenstellen. Sie können je nach Bedarf flächenbündig oder bauchig gewölbt installiert werden. Das flexible Material ermöglicht zudem den individuellen Einsatz von attraktiven Farb- und Lichteffekten. Je nach Blickwinkel differenziert sich das Erscheinungsbild der Deckenleuchte, im reizvollen Schattenspiel zur Decke entsteht der Eindruck, als ob dort ein Stofftuch aus Licht schweben würde. Das beruhigend wirkende Licht fließt im Standardmodus harmonisch von der Außenseite in Richtung Lichtobjektmitte und leuchtet den Raum gleichsam homogen und blendfrei aus.

Velas
Pendant Lamp / Pendelleuchte

Sattler Objektlicht, Heiningen,
Germany / Deutschland
In-house design / Werksdesign:
Jürgen Beckert
www.sattler-objektlicht.de

A transparent modular construction and a sophisticated functionality distinguish the form language of this pendant lamp. Made from a single piece of acryl glass, the light fixture hovers, seemingly weightlessly, from above. Visible technics gives the lamp a unique touch, as the cables are milled directly into the translucent structure. Two energy-efficient fluorescent tubes combined with satined diffusers make for glare-free light, and the combination of direct and indirect light creates a comfortable atmosphere.

Eine transparente Bauweise sowie eine ausgefeilte Funktionalität prägen die Formensprache dieser Pendelleuchte. Schwerelos schwebend mutet das aus einem Stück gefertigte Leuchtengehäuse aus Acryl an. Die Kabelführung wurde ins Gestell eingefräst, die sichtbare Beleuchtungstechnik verleiht der Leuchte einen individuellen Reiz. Zwei energieeffiziente Leuchtstofflampen sind durch satinierte Diffusoren augenfreundlich abgeblendet, das sowohl direkte als auch indirekte Licht schafft eine angenehme Atmosphäre.

Circolo
Light Series / Leuchtenserie

Sattler Objektlicht, Heiningen,
Germany / Deutschland
In-house design / Werksdesign:
Ulrich Sattler
www.sattler-objektlicht.de

The design concept of this light series is built around the circle as a simple, basic form. A reduced form language and high-quality materials are the unifying characteristics of these versatile lamps, available in pendant, wall, corner and recessed models. A wide selection of sizes, from 0.7 to 2.3 metres, allows for use in large commercial spaces as well as in private homes. Whether as a stand-alone item or in combination with other lighting – Circolo creates a space for exploration. In addition, the LED components are optionally available with RGB colour control.

Ausgehend von einem Kreis als schlichter Grundform entstand das Gestaltungskonzept dieser Leuchtenserie. Eine reduziert anmutende Formensprache und hochwertige Materialien vereinen die vielseitigen Pendel-, Wand-, Eck- und Einbauleuchten. Die Größenvielfalt zwischen 0,7 und 2,3 Meter erlaubt den Einsatz in gewerblichen Großobjekten sowie in Privathaushalten. Ob als Solitär oder in Kombination mit anderen Leuchten – Circolo schafft einen kreativen Spielraum, wobei die LED-Ausstattung auf Wunsch auch mit RGB-Farbsteuerung erhältlich ist.

Acousticlight
Light Series / Leuchtenserie

Sattler Objektlicht, Heiningen,
Germany / Deutschland
In-house design / Werksdesign:
Ulrich Sattler
www.sattler-objektlicht.de

The lights of this innovative product series combine homogeneous, soft light with noise-absorbing technology. Acousticlight comprises recessed, surface-mounted, or pendant lamps, as well as complete light ceilings. The distinctive frame casing is made from zinc- and powder-coated metal and holds energy-efficient fluorescent lamps inside. An effective reduction of the reverberation time provides acoustic control even in large rooms.

Die Leuchten dieser innovativen Produktserie verbinden ein homogenes, weiches Licht mit einer schallabsorbierenden Technologie. Acousticlight umfasst sowohl Einbau-, Anbau- oder Pendelleuchten wie auch komplette Lichtdecken. Das markante Rahmengehäuse aus verzinktem Metall ist pulverbeschichtet, wobei sich im Inneren des Leuchtkörpers energiesparsame Leuchtstofflampen befinden. Dank einer wirksamen Reduzierung der Nachhallzeit können selbst große Räume akustisch kontrolliert werden.

Natural Sky
Lighting System /
Beleuchtungssystem

Zumtobel Lighting GmbH, Dornbirn,
Austria / Österreich
Design: dai design (Florin Baeriswyl),
Zürich, Switzerland / Schweiz
www.zumtobel.com
www.dai.ch

Deliberately avoiding homogeneous
illumination, Natural Sky emits light in a
non-uniform way to create the impression
of a natural sky with light and shadow. A
control system integrated into the individual
lamp modules allows for a smooth change of
colour temperature and intensity. This change
of light has a positive effect on people's
well-being and reduces energy consumption.
Translucent side panels supply additional
lighting. The lamp is covered with a sound-
absorbing textile for noise reduction.

Eine homogene Ausleuchtung bewusst
vermeidend, nutzt Natural Sky eine
ungleichmäßige Lichtemission, um den
Eindruck eines natürlichen Himmels mit
Licht und Schatten zu schaffen. Eine
in den einzelnen Lampenmodulen integrierte Steuerung ermöglicht eine sanfte
Veränderung von Farbtemperatur und
-intensität, wobei sich der Lichtwech-
sel positiv auf das Wohlempfinden der
Menschen und nicht zuletzt auf den
Energieverbrauch auswirkt. Ein seitlicher
Lichtaustritt unterstützt das markante
Erscheinungsbild dieser zugleich schallabsorbierenden Leuchte.

ino
Ceiling Light / Deckenleuchte

GROSSMANN Leuchten GmbH & Co.
KG, Ense, Germany / Deutschland
In-house design / Werksdesign: Nadine
Klassen, Simone Maria Phoebe Jasinski
www.grossmann-leuchten.de

The design of this aesthetic ceiling light
focuses on its minimalist line management
visually underlining the efficient illumination
quality. The purist construction of two
identically formed stainless steel panels,
each one with a centrically arranged radius,
presents a momentum of tension. The
reflexion of the stainless steel front panel
results in an additional, indirect ceiling
illumination, and the interior luminary made
of high-grade acrylic glass provides an all-
around, homogeneous illumination of the room.

Gestalterischer Schwerpunkt dieser
ästhetischen Deckenleuchte ist ihre minimalistische Linienführung, welche die
effiziente Beleuchtungsqualität visuell
unterstreicht. Die puristische Bauart der
zwei identisch geformten Edelstahlblen-
den mit ihren zentrisch ausgerichteten
Radien stellt ein Spannungsmoment dar.
Die Reflexion der vorderen Edelstahl-
blende bewirkt eine zusätzliche, indirekte
Deckenbeleuchtung, wobei der innenliegende Lichtkörper aus hochwertigem
Acrylglas für eine rundum homogene
Raumausleuchtung sorgt.

como IvyLight
Wall Lamp / Wandleuchte

IP44 Schmalhorst GmbH & Co. KG,
Rheda-Wiedenbrück,
Germany / Deutschland
In-house design / Werksdesign
www.ip44.de

With its reserved cubic form, this wall lamp
blends flexibly into different architectural
surroundings. The corpus with its balanced
proportions is lathed from solid aluminium
and milled from one piece. The purist LED
lamp is available in the surface finishings
aluminium brushed, anodised, or in bronze
noir colour shade. Special lens optics
provide a focused and efficient outdoor light
illuminating facades upwards and downwards
in an appealing way.

Mit ihrer zurückhaltenden Quaderform
passt sich diese Wandleuchte flexibel
unterschiedlichen architektonischen
Umgebungen an. Der Korpus mit seinen
ausgewogenen Proportionen wird aus
Aluminium gedreht und aus einem Stück
gefräst. Wahlweise ist die puristisch wirkende LED-Leuchte in den Oberflächen
Aluminium gebürstet, eloxiert oder im
Farbton Bronze Noir erhältlich. Eine spezielle Linsenoptik spendet ein fokussiertes und effizientes Außenlicht, welches
Fassaden reizvoll nach oben und unten
ausleuchtet.

One Eighty Suspension
Suspension Lamp / Hängeleuchte

Serien Raumleuchten GmbH, Rodgau,
Germany / Deutschland
Design: Yaacov Kaufman, Tel Aviv, Israel
www.serien.com

This suspension lamp with its reduced design vocabulary is a contemporary interpretation of a classic spotlight. The elegantly curved lampshade has the form of an inverted funnel and is available in finely honed aluminium or with a white finish contrasting the stainless steel ring. One Eighty Suspension is manufactured with two different shade sizes and can be easily and steplessly adjusted in height, thanks to a special winding mechanism in the canopy.

Als zeitgemäße Interpretation eines klassischen Strahlers zeigt diese Hängeleuchte eine reduzierte Formensprache. Der elegant geschwungene Lampenschirm öffnet sich trichterförmig nach unten und ist entweder aus veredelt geschliffenem Aluminium oder kontrastierend zum Edelstahlring weiß lackiert erhältlich. One Eighty Suspension wird in zwei unterschiedlichen Schirmgrößen gefertigt und kann über einen speziellen Wickelmechanismus im Baldachin leicht und stufenlos in der Höhe verstellt werden.

Dezall Lamptops
Lighting Accessory /
Beleuchtungsaccessoire

Creality AB, Stockholm,
Sweden / Schweden
In-house design / Werksdesign:
Karin Ljungren
www.dezall.se

With balanced proportions and a large number of variants, this canopy adapt harmoniously to different types of pendant lamps. A patented suspension system enables the user to attach the lamptop tightly to the ceiling without the use of tools. The robust material is durable, and the visual language of the lamptops is reminiscent of the harmonic contours of musical instruments. The lamptops are available in different colours and with either glossy or matt surface structure.

Mit ausgewogenen Proportionen und vielfältigen Varianten passt dieser Lampen-Baldachin auf harmonische Weise zu unterschiedlichen Hängelampen. Dank eines patentierten Aufhängungssystems kann der Nutzer den Baldachin ohne den Einsatz von Werkzeugen sicher an der Decke befestigen. Das robuste Material ist langlebig, und die Formensprache der Baldachine erinnert an die harmonischen Konturen von Musikinstrumenten. Die Baldachine sind in verschiedenen Farben erhältlich, mit glänzender oder matter Oberfläche.

CableCup
Ceiling Cup for Pendant Lamps /
Deckenkappe für Hängeleuchten

CableCup AB, Uddevalla,
Sweden / Schweden
In-house design / Werksdesign:
Lars Wettre, Jonas Forsman
www.cablecup.com

CableCup is a smoothly designed and user-friendly ceiling cup for pendant lamps. The white cap made of a soft material can be turned inside out, allowing for a free view of the cables when mounting. A cord grip for setting the required cable length is included in the product. Once the ceiling cup is flipped back to its standard shape after mounting, it adapts – regardless of the length of the ceiling hook – seamlessly onto the ceiling, even if these are uneven.

CableCup ist eine dezent gestaltete und komfortabel zu handhabende Deckenkappe für Hängeleuchten. Die weiße Kappe aus weichem Material lässt sich beim Montieren einfach umstülpen, sodass beim Anschließen der Stromkabel freie Sicht bleibt. Eine Klemme zum Bestimmen der notwendigen Kabellänge ist bereits im Produktset enthalten. Sobald die Deckenkappe nach der Montage zurückgeklappt wird, schmiegt sie sich – unabhängig von der Länge des Deckenhakens – selbst an unebene Zimmerdecken passgenau an.

JellyFish
Mood Lamp / Stimmungslicht

Yantouch, Hsin-Chu, Taiwan
In-house design / Werksdesign:
Ken Ouyang, Nick Lee
www.yantouch.com

The design concept of this atmospheric luminary was inspired by colourful ocean jellyfish. Its softly rounded contours show a glossy, organic surface upon which emotionally appealing colour effects can be activated. The square-shaped touch panel is visually highlighted on the front surface. With the tip of a finger, the individually preferred play of colours can be selected from a spectrum of 16 million colour combinations.

Inspiriert von einer farbenprächtigen Qualle im Meer entstand das Gestaltungskonzept dieses atmosphärisch wirkenden Leuchtkörpers. Seine sanft abgerundeten Konturen bieten eine glänzende, organisch anmutende Oberfläche, auf der emotional ansprechende Farbeffekte aktiviert werden können. Das quadratische Touch-Bedienfeld hebt sich auf der vorderen Objektfläche visuell ab. Dort lässt sich per Fingertipp das individuell gewünschte Farbspiel aus einem Spektrum von 16 Millionen Farbkombinationen auswählen.

Geena
Recessed Light / Einbauleuchte

Tal, Pittem, Belgium / Belgien
In-house design / Werksdesign
www.tal.be

The design of this interactive recessed light was inspired by the Warp drive, a fictitious technology used in the television series "Star Trek". When turned off, Geena appears plain and unostentatious; the only thing visible is a small circular mirror in a white housing. When turned on, an optical effect comes about, directing the viewer's attention to a tunnel-like reflexion. The spot, now lit up in red, creates a three-dimensional room atmosphere reminiscent of a look into the universe.

Die Inspiration zu dieser interaktiven Einbauleuchte stammt von der fiktiven Technologie des Warp-Antriebs aus der Fernsehserie „Star Trek". Im ausgeschalteten Modus wirkt Geena schlicht, es ist nur ein kleiner runder Spiegel in einem weißen Gehäuse sichtbar. Sobald die Leuchte eingeschaltet wird, entsteht ein optischer Effekt, der den Blick in eine tunnelartige Spiegelung lenkt. Der nun rot leuchtende Spot erzeugt durch diverse Lichtpunkte eine dreidimensionale Raumwirkung, die einem Blick in den Weltraum ähnelt.

LED Brite Strip Combo /
LED-Leuchtstreifenkombination

Lei Yueh Enterprise Co., Ltd.,
Taipei, Taiwan
In-house design / Werksdesign:
Yuan Lin, Shih Hao Lo
www.leiyueh.com

The flexible LED Brite Strip Combo is an effective, low-maintenance solution guaranteeing low energy consumption. Its design minimises the number of component parts used and utilises waterproof, transparent plastics. The economical, chip-based LED illumination generates less heat and plays with the aesthetic appeal of numerous light dots. A striking colour concept enhances the effect of these futuristic light elements.

Die flexible LED-Leuchtstreifenkombination stellt eine effektive und wartungsarme Lösung für einen sparsamen Energieverbrauch dar. Ihre Gestaltung minimiert die Anzahl der verwendeten Einzelteile und nutzt einen wasserdichten, transparenten Kunststoff. Die sparsame LED Beleuchtung auf Chipbasis erzeugt weniger Hitze und spielt mit dem ästhetischen Reiz diverser Lichtpunkte. Ein plakatives Farbkonzept verstärkt die Wirkung dieser futuristisch anmutenden Lichtelemente.

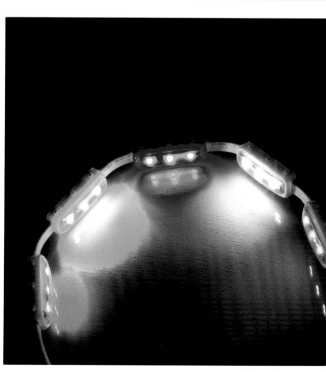

Innosol Kubo
Table and Bright Light Therapy Lamp/
Tisch- und Lichttherapieleuchte

Innojok Oy, Helsinki, Finland/Finnland
Design: Prof. h.c. Eero Aarnio
www.innojok.fi
www.innolux.fi

This innovative lamp creation has two functions: a decorative table lamp and a bright light therapy lamp. Its visual form language combines three different-sized cubes to create a coherent whole. The lamp allows for flexible placement in rooms and sets a distinctive, geometric accent. When using the transparent light body for therapeutic purposes, the lamp emits a vitality-enhancing bright light of 10,000 lux.

Diese innovative Leuchtenkreation bietet zwei unterschiedliche Anwendungsbereiche: Sie ist als dekorative Tischleuchte und als Leuchte für die Lichttherapie nutzbar. Ihre bildliche Formensprache kombiniert drei unterschiedlich große Würfel miteinander und bildet ein eigenständiges Objekt. Die Leuchte kann flexibel im Raum platziert werden und setzt einen geometrisch prägnanten Akzent. Für therapeutische Zwecke strahlt der transparente Lichtkörper ein vitalitätssteigerndes helles Licht von 10.000 Lux aus.

iPro
Spotlight/Strahler

iGuzzini illuminazione,
Recanati, Italy/Italien
Design: Mario Cucinella,
Bologna, Italy/Italien
www.iguzzini.com
www.mcarchitects.it

The iPro spotlight was developed for the striking illumination of facades. Its unobtrusively designed housing features lighting technology, which meets the most diverse illumination requirements by using super spot, spot, flood or asymmetrical lateral and longitudinal optics. Evenly designed high-precision light cones aesthetically enhance the facades and underline horizontal and vertical structural elements. The spot itself seems to disappear in the facade. It is available in grey and white. Numerous accessories increase the functionality of the dazzle-free compact fluorescent lamp and make it possible to enlarge or focus the light cone. Furthermore, special colour effects can be created by means of colour filters.

Der Strahler iPro dient der wirkungsvollen Beleuchtung von Fassaden. Sein dezent gestaltetes Gehäuse beinhaltet eine Lichttechnologie, die per Super-Spot, Spot, Flood oder asymmetrische Quer- und Längsoptiken unterschiedlichen Beleuchtungsanforderungen gerecht wird. Gleichmäßige Lichtkegel von hoher Präzision werten Fassaden ästhetisch auf und betonen horizontale und vertikale Bauelemente. Der Strahler selbst, erhältlich in Grau und Weiß, scheint dabei in der Fassade zu verschwinden. Zahlreiche Zubehörteile erhöhen die Funktionalität der blendfreien Kompaktleuchtstofflampe und ermöglichen die Vergrößerung bzw. Fokussierung des Lichtkegels. Mittels Farbfilter lassen sich darüber hinaus besondere Farbeffekte kreieren.

Arzy
Wall Lamp/Wandleuchte

Wever & Ducré,
Roeselare, Belgium / Belgien
Design: Frank Janssens,
Zoersel, Belgium / Belgien
www.wever-ducre.com

The design concept of this distinctive wall fixture pays homage to the 1950s architecture. Rectangular, overlapping profiles comprise the independent form language of this lamp which emanates a sculptural and fascinating look. A concealed LED light source, emitting a cold or a warm light colour, as per customer's choice, engages in a play of light and shadow. The intricate light body is also suitable for outdoor use and is available in white, chrome and Corten steel.

Das Designkonzept dieser charakteristischen Wandleuchte ist eine Hommage an die Architektur der 1950er Jahre. Rechteckige, sich überlappende Profile bilden die eigenständige Formensprache dieser Leuchte, die skulptural und faszinierend wirkt. Eine verdeckte LED-Lichtquelle, in einer kalten oder einer warmen Lichtfarbe erhältlich (auf Kundenwunsch), ergibt ein Schauspiel von Licht und Schatten. Die komplexe Leuchte ist auch für den Außenbereich geeignet und ist in Weiß, Chrom und Cortenstahl verfügbar.

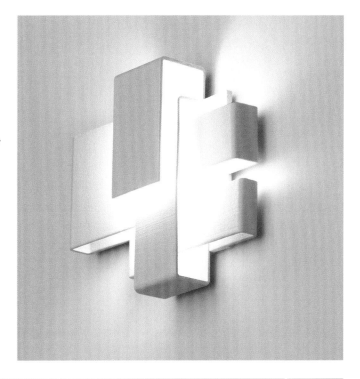

Blacklight
Pendant Lamp / Pendelleuchte

iGuzzini illuminazione, Recanati,
Italy / Italien
Design: Studio & Partners
(Fritze Torsten), Milan, Italy / Mailand,
Italien
www.iguzzini.com
www.studioandpartners.com

The Blacklight pendant lamp is characterised by an elegant and purist design vocabulary. It was conceived as a glare-free lamp for direct and indirect lighting of offices and other workspaces. The seamless body is made from a single block of solid aluminium, showing a clear line management and lightness with a depth of just 50 mm. The two colour versions white and black underline the elegance of the lamp. Blacklight offers flexible luminance control. Due to the innovative secondary reflector system, the installed illuminants are not directly visible from below, providing glare-free illumination of computer workstations as well.

Eine elegante und puristische Formensprache zeichnet die Pendelleuchte Blacklight aus. Sie wurde mit ihrer blendfreien Lichtqualität für die direkte und indirekte Beleuchtung von Büros und sonstigen Arbeitsbereichen konzipiert. Eine klare Linienführung charakterisiert den nahtlosen, aus einem einzigen Aluminiumblock gefertigten Korpus, wobei seine geringe Tiefe von 50 mm Leichtigkeit vermittelt. Die für die zwei Ausführungen gewählten Farben Weiß und Schwarz unterstreichen die Eleganz der Leuchte. Blacklight bietet eine flexible Kontrolle der Leuchtdichte. Das innovative Sekundär-Reflektorsystem, aufgrund dessen die installierten Leuchtmittel nicht von unten einsehbar sind, schließt auch an Bildschirmarbeitsplätzen jegliche Blendung aus.

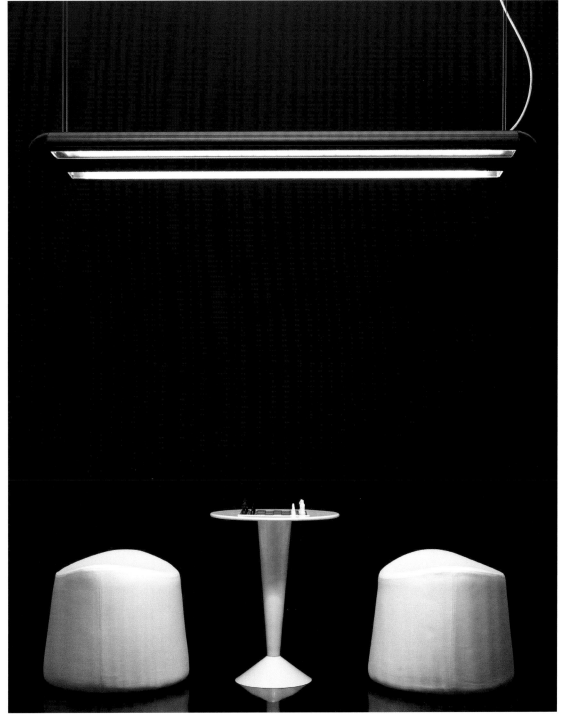

UFO
Lighting / Beleuchtung

WOOREE Lighting, Ansan, Korea
In-house design / Werksdesign:
Eunhee Nam
www.wooree.co.kr

The design concept of this ceiling light with its clear design language evokes associations of a UFO. In contrast to the plain white luminary, the viewer's attention is directed to an illuminated colour ring. The light combines innovative LED technology with the use of specific energy-saving lamps, and thus the advantages of a conventional lamp with those of a contemporary low energy consumption product. To bring about different room effects, a large number of colour rings are available. In the respective colour spectrum, the LED light source emits a smooth natural light. The UFO spot does not need any heat sinks and is therefore very lightweight. A special spring allows for an adjustment of the mounting height according to specific preferences. With its low energy consumption, the ceiling light is eco-friendly, does not produce any UV- or IR radiation, and does neither contain any substances harmful to health.

Das Gestaltungskonzept dieser Deckenleuchte ruft mit seiner klaren Formensprache Assoziationen an ein UFO hervor. Im Kontrast zum schlichten weißen Leuchtkörper wird die Aufmerksamkeit auf einen leuchtenden Farbring gelenkt. Die Leuchte verbindet eine innovative LED-Technologie mit dem Einsatz spezifischer Energiesparlampen und kombiniert somit die Gebrauchsvorteile einer konventionellen Lampe mit denen eines zeitgemäßen Niedrigenergie-Produkts. Um unterschiedliche Raumwirkungen zu erzielen, steht eine Vielzahl von Farbringen zur Verfügung. Im jeweiligen Farbspektrum erstrahlt die LED-Lichtquelle in einem sanften, natürlichen Licht. Der UFO-Spot kommt ohne Kühlkörper aus und weist daher nur ein geringes Eigengewicht auf. Eine spezielle Feder ermöglicht es, die Montagehöhe bedarfsgerecht anzupassen. Aufgrund ihres geringen Energiebedarfs ist die Deckenleuchte umweltfreundlich, erzeugt keine UV- oder IR-Abstrahlung und enthält zudem keinerlei gesundheitsschädliche Substanzen.

Nachteule
Reading Light/Leselicht

LeuchtKraft GmbH,
Stuttgart, Germany/Deutschland
In-house design/Werksdesign:
Anja Schaepertoens, Dawid Kulesz,
Andreas Rueping
www.leuchtkraft-gmbh.de

Nachteule was specially developed and designed to be easily clipped to any pair of glasses. It has an ultra-compact form and a light weight of only eight grammes. The ball-joint design ensures complete swivel rotation and its universally fixable clip provides secure grip. Its functional appearance and neutral colouring characterise a product that has been thoroughly thought through in terms of ergonomic design. The latest LED technology combined with a lithium battery illuminates the reader's field of vision with up to 40 hours of light.

Die Nachteule wurde speziell zur Befestigung an einer Brille entwickelt und gestaltet, aufgrund ihrer sehr kompakten Form wiegt sie nur acht Gramm. Die Gestaltung mit einem Kugelgelenk ermöglicht eine vollständige Drehbewegung, und ein universal einsetzbarer Clip erlaubt eine sichere Handhabung. Die funktionale Anmutung sowie eine neutrale Farbgebung prägen ein Produkt, das vor allem ergonomische Gesichtspunkte berücksichtigt. Zur Beleuchtung des individuellen Sichtfeldes wird eine zeitgemäße LED-Technologie genutzt, wobei eine Lithiumbatterie bis zu 40 Stunden Licht bietet.

perelin
Luminous Objects/Leuchtobjekte

markusjbecker, Berlin,
Germany/Dcutschland
In-house design/Werksdesign:
Markus Becker
www.markusjbecker.de

These three-dimensional, self-supporting luminous objects are characterised by a harmonious design language. They are made of a glossy electroluminescent foil. Its filigree appearance combines with a high degree of flexibility. The energy-efficient lights use a distinctively coloured surface as essential design feature. In the style of a curved piece of paper, they show a clearly defined cut. The properties of the indirect light additionally highlight the contrast between front and rear of the lights.

Eine harmonische Formensprache prägt diese dreidimensional ausgerichteten und statisch selbsttragenden Leuchtobjekte. Sie sind aus einer glänzenden Elektrolumineszenz-Leuchtfolie gefertigt, und ihre filigrane Anmutung verbindet sich mit einem hohen Maß an Flexibilität. Die energiesparsamen Leuchten nutzen eine farblich markante Oberfläche als wesentliches Gestaltungsmerkmal. In Anlehnung an in sich gedrehtes Papier folgen diese einem klar definierten Zuschnitt. Mit der Eigenschaft des indirekten Lichts wird zudem der Kontrast zwischen Vorder- und Rückseite herausgestellt.

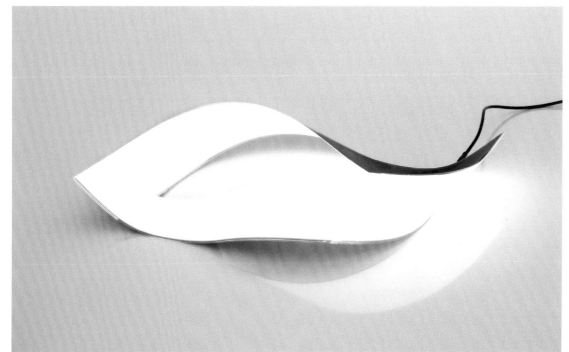

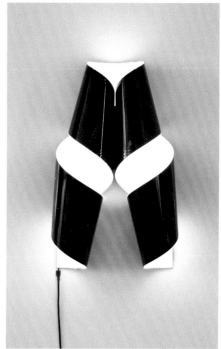

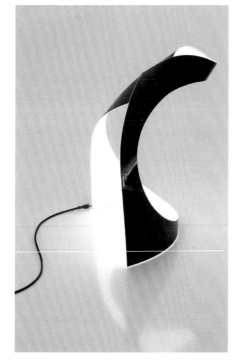

LED LENSER M7
LED Torch Light / LED-Taschenlampe

Zweibrüder Optoelectronics GmbH,
Solingen, Germany / Deutschland
In-house design / Werksdesign:
Rainer Opolka, Andre Kunzendorf
www.zweibrueder.com

A clearly structured design vocabulary underlines the high degree of functionality of this LED torch light discreetly designed in black. The Smart Light Technology, operated by a microcontroller, offers seven light functions for different applications. In addition, the push-button switch allows access to an energy-saving function as well as stepless dimming, a stroboscope- and blinking mode, and an SOS function. The user can choose between constant invariable, electronically controlled, and constantly decreasing light intensity.

Eine klar strukturierte Formensprache unterstreicht die hohe Funktionalität dieser dezent in Schwarz gestalteten LED-Taschenlampe. Die per Microcontroller gesteuerte Smart Light Technology bietet sieben Lichtfunktionen für unterschiedliche Anwendungen. Zudem gewährt der Tastschalter den Zugriff auf eine Stromsparfunktion, einen Stroboskop- und Blinkmodus, eine SOS-Funktion sowie ein stufenloses Dimmen. Optional kann der Anwender zwischen gleich bleibender, elektronisch geregelter oder konstant abfallender Lichtleistung wählen.

LED LENSER M1/M5
LED Torch Light / LED-Taschenlampe

Zweibrüder Optoelectronics GmbH,
Solingen, Germany / Deutschland
In-house design / Werksdesign:
Rainer Opolka
www.zweibrueder.com

This series of torch lights combines matter-of-fact aesthetics with a high degree of user comfort. The compact housing with its ergonomic grip fits well in the hand and has a very low weight. The titanium-coloured ring at the lamp head creates a distinctive contrast to the black housing. The two powerful pocket models are operated with a high-capacity lithium battery and/or with a standard AA battery. Various light settings allow for flexible, user-friendly handling and effective, need-based illumination in different surroundings.

Bei dieser Taschenlampen-Serie verbindet sich eine sachliche Ästhetik mit einem hohen Bedienkomfort. Das in seinen Ausmaßen kompakte Gehäuse bietet eine ergonomisch sinnvolle Grifffläche und liegt dank seines geringen Gewichts leicht in der Hand. Mit einem titanfarbenen Ring am Lampenkopf setzt das funktional ausgerichtete Gestaltungskonzept einen kontrastreichen Akzent zum schwarzen Gehäuse. Die beiden lichtstarken Pocket-Modelle werden mit einer Hochleistungs-Lithium-Batterie bzw. mit einer handelsüblichen AA-Batterie betrieben. Verschiedene Lichtprogramme ermöglichen eine flexible, benutzerfreundliche Handhabung und eine effektive und bedarfsgerechte Ausleuchtung in unterschiedlichen Umgebungen.

LED LENSER H14
LED Head Lamp / LED-Kopflampe

Zweibrüder Optoelectronics GmbH,
Solingen, Germany / Deutschland
In-house design / Werksdesign:
Rainer Opolka, Andre Kunzendorf
www.zweibrueder.com

The distinctive feature of this LED head lamp is its outstanding luminance. Its appearance is additionally enhanced by a striking design vocabulary in black and blue. The flexible fastening system allows to use the lamp head on a headband or a belt. Optionally, the lamp can also be fixed on a bicycle handlebar with a special fastening system. The lamp can be steplessly focused and swivelled and features different light modes such as dim light, stroboscope, SOS, or continuously variable dimming.

Ihre hohe Leuchtkraft ist das prägende Attribut dieser LED-Kopflampe, deren Erscheinungsbild durch eine markante Formensprache in Schwarz und Blau aufgewertet wird. Mithilfe eines flexiblen Befestigungssystems kann der Lampen-kopf wahlweise als Stirnband oder am Gürtel getragen werden. Darüber hinaus besteht die Möglichkeit, die Lampe mit einer speziellen Halterung am Fahrrad zu befestigen. Stufenlos fokussierbar und schwenkbar, bietet die kompakte Lampe verschiedene Lichtmodi wie Abblendlicht, Stroboskop, SOS oder gedimmtes Licht.

LED LENSER P5R/M7R
LED Torch Light / LED-Taschenlampe

Zweibrüder Optoelectronics GmbH,
Solingen, Germany / Deutschland
In-house design / Werksdesign:
Rainer Opolka
www.zweibrueder.com

The rechargeable torch lights P5R and M7R and their accessories pursue a stringent design concept visually underlining the high quality of this devices with a detailed line management. The different surface structures of the matt black housing are distinctly highlighted, and a red adapter creates an eye-catching accent. The powerful torch lights are charged in a magnetic fixture so that the rechargeable batteries do not have to be taken out. Thanks to the microcontroller-based Smart Light Technology, several light programmes with different functions like dim light, continuously variable dimming, stroboscope and SOS can be selected.

Die akkubetriebenen Taschenlampen P5R und M7R folgen mitsamt ihrem Zubehör einem stringenten Gestaltungskonzept, welches die Hochwertigkeit der Lampen durch eine detailgenaue Linienführung visuell unterstreicht. Prägnant heben sich die unterschiedlichen Oberflächenstruk-turen des mattschwarzen Gehäuses hervor, ein roter Adapter setzt einen aufmerksam-keitsstarken Akzent. Der Ladevorgang der lichtstarken Taschenlampen erfolgt über eine Magnethalterung, sodass das lästige Entnehmen der Akkus entfällt. Dank der per Microcontroller gesteuerten Smart Light Technology stehen für den bedarfs-gerechten Einsatz diverse Programme mit unterschiedlichen Lichtfunktionen wie Abblendlicht, stufenloses Dimmen, Stro-boskop oder SOS zur Verfügung.

**Light Attendant
Lighting Concept/
Beleuchtungskonzept**

der Kluth: GmbH,
Hilden, Germany/Deutschland
In-house design/Werksdesign:
Manfred Kluth
www.derkluth.de

Light Attendant was developed as a pleasant, safe and energy-efficient lighting concept for long passageways such as tunnels and hallways. A light strip installed flush with the ceiling emits coloured basic lighting that suffices for orientation and that changes colour over the course of the day. The different colour spectrums are employed specifically to enhance the well-being of those passing through the passageway. For example, green is emitted for a calming effect, orange for a stimulating effect, blue for a relaxing effect, and yellow for an inspiring effect. As soon as a person enters the detection area of this innovative ceiling light, an additional bright white light is activated that follows and accompanies the person along their path. In this way,

the person is always in a well-lit sector. This new technology also affords up to 80 per cent energy savings. If there is more than one person in the passageway, the system provides lighting to each person independently.

Als energiesparsames Beleuchtungskonzept wurde Light Attendant speziell für eine angenehme und sichere Ausleuchtung von langen Durchgangsbereichen, beispielsweise Tunneln oder Fluren, entwickelt. Eine flächenbündig in die Decke eingebaute Lichtleiste strahlt eine farbige Grundbeleuchtung aus, die zur Orientierung ausreicht und im Laufe des Tages ihre Farbe wechselt. Dabei werden die einzelnen Farbspektren gezielt zur

Steigerung des Wohlbefindens eingesetzt – Grün wirkt beispielsweise beruhigend, Orange anregend, Blau entspannend und Gelb inspirierend. Sobald eine Person in den Erfassungsbereich der innovativen Deckenbeleuchtung eintritt, wird zusätzlich eine helle weiße Beleuchtung aktiviert, die der Bewegungsrichtung der Person folgt und sie somit begleitet. Entsprechend befindet sich die Person stets in einem gut ausgeleuchteten Bereich, trotzdem werden bis zu 80 Prozent der herkömmlichen Energiekosten eingespart. Befinden sich weitere Personen im Durchgangsbereich, begleitet das helle Extralicht jede Person unabhängig voneinander.

onLED
Visual Information System / Visuelles Informations-System

der Kluth: GmbH,
Hilden, Germany / Deutschland
In-house design / Werksdesign:
Manfred Kluth
www.derkluth.de

onLED is a visual information system that targets and plays with human comprehension and its selective perception. The system is designed to serve as a complementary information medium for sophisticated displays and exhibits in contexts such as trade show booths or store windows. The function-oriented appearance of the information surface remains minimalist and discreet, without diverting too much attention away from the exhibit pieces. A transparent structure made of delicate tubes shows images, text, or films by means of innovative LED technology. The light motifs are designed to be easily recognisable, especially from a distance or in the dark.

The information medium is meant to attract attention and arouse curiosity. The closer the viewer moves to the information medium, the more he or she will perceive the actual exhibits positioned behind onLED.

onLED ist ein visuelles Informations-System, welches die menschliche Wahrnehmung und dessen selektive Auffassungsgabe gezielt nutzt. Das System wurde konzipiert, um in anspruchsvollen Ausstellungssituationen, wie beispielsweise auf Messeständen oder in einem Schaufenster, eine ergänzende Information zu den gezeigten Exponaten zu präsentieren. Das funktional ausgerichtete Erschei-

nungsbild der Infowand bleibt dabei puristisch dezent, ohne von den Exponaten abzulenken. In einer transparenten, sichtdurchlässigen Konstruktion aus filigranen Rohren werden mittels einer innovativen LED-Technik leuchtende Bilder, Texte oder Filme gezeigt. Dabei ist die Illumination so gestaltet, dass die Licht-Motive vor allem aus der Distanz oder in der Dunkelheit präzise wahrzunehmen sind. Das Informations-System soll somit Aufmerksamkeit und Neugier erregen. Je mehr sich der Betrachter dem Informations-System nähert, desto deutlicher werden jedoch die hinter onLED positionierten Exponate wahrgenommen.

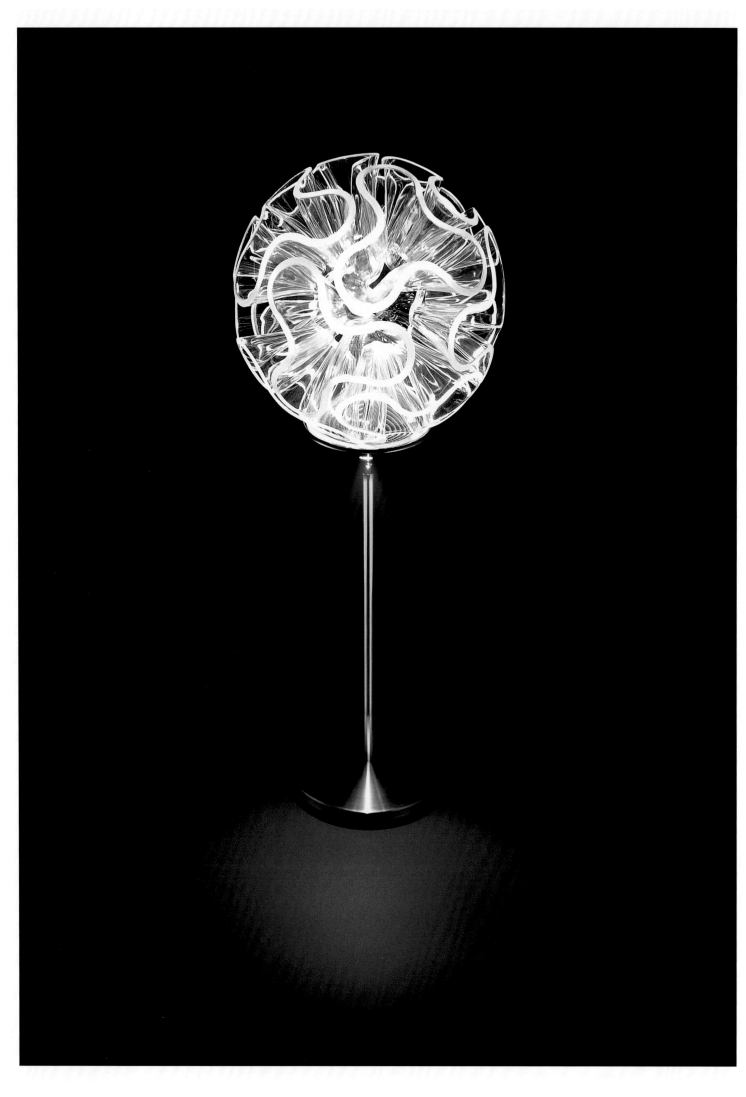

Qisda Corporation, Taipei, Taiwan
Design: Qisda/QisDesign, Taipei, Taiwan
www.qisda.com
www.qisdesign.com

Inspired by nature, the light concept of this LED table lamp imitates the way corals reflect the light from underwater. The light emitted by a multi-diffuser also emulates a hydrangea in full blossom. The light of each diffuser interacts with that of the other ones, creating a transparent light effect, a visually appealing interplay of light and shadow. In addition, the QLD-104 serves as reading lamp.

Inspiriert von der Natur, imitiert das Licht-konzept dieser LED-Tischleuchte die Art und Weise, wie Korallen das Licht unter Wasser reflektieren. Das durch einen Mehrfachdiffu-sor ausgestrahlte Licht wirkt darüber hinaus wie eine in voller Blüte stehende Hortensie. Jeder einzelne Diffusor interagiert dabei mit den anderen und erzeugt einen transparent wirkenden Lichteffekt. Dabei entsteht ein visuell reizvolles Spiel aus Licht und Schatten. Ergänzend ist die Leuchte QLD-104 mit einer Lesefunktion ausgestattet.

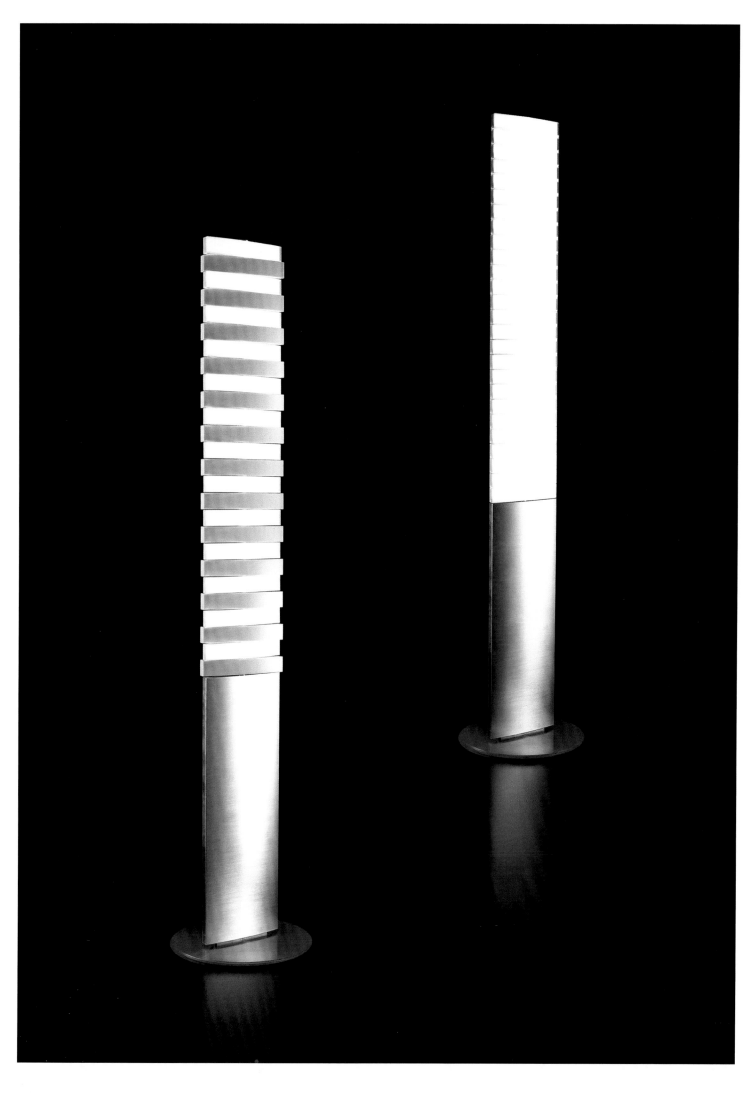

QLD-202
LED Floor Lamp/LED-Stehleuchte

Qisda Corporation, Taipei, Taiwan
Design: Qisda/QisDesign, Taipei, Taiwan
www.qisda.com
www.qisdesign.com

The design language of this aesthetic and
appealing floor lamp is sculptural and elegant.
Its slim silhouette is subdivided into a refined
metal base and 26 luminary elements, which
can be activated individually. Inspired by the
classical elegance of a piano, the elements in
piano key form can be turned down by slightly
tilting them. In this way, the intensity of the
room illumination can be adjusted according to
individual preferences.

Skulptural und elegant wirkt die Formensprache dieser ästhetisch ansprechenden
Stehleuchte. Ihre schmale Silhouette unterteilt sich in einen veredelten Metallfuß und
26 einzeln aktivierbare Leuchtelemente.
Inspiriert von der klassischen Eleganz eines
Klaviers lassen sich die Leuchtkörper in
Tastenform bereits durch leichtes Kippen
illuminieren. Auf diese Weise kann die Intensität der Raumbeleuchtung den individuellen
Wünschen angepasst werden.

Lamina
Pendant Lamp / Pendelleuchte

Philipp Glass, Kriens,
Switzerland / Schweiz
In-house design / Werksdesign:
Philipp Glass
www.philippglass.eu

The design of this object-like pendant lamp
is inspired by floral forms. The elegant, self-
supporting structure holds twelve harmoniously
curved lamella, which, placed laterally, reflect
the light in a unique way.

Eine florale Formensprache verleiht dieser
objekthaft anmutenden Pendelleuchte
Prägnanz. Die elegante, selbsttragende
Konstruktion umfasst zwölf harmonisch
geschwungene Lamellen, die das Licht auf
reizvolle Weise seitlich reflektieren.

Air
Table Lamp / Tischleuchte

LZF Lamps, Chiva, Spain / Spanien
Design: Ray Power, Barcelona,
Spain / Spanien
www.lzf-lamps.com

The clear design of this table lamp underlines
the effect of the natural wood grain. The idea to
combine curved surfaces to a three-dimensional
figure resulted in an appealing and zestful visual
language of this lamp. It is manufactured from
thin sheets of veneer and available as table or
wall lamp in different colours.

Eine klare Gestaltung unterstreicht bei dieser
Tischleuchte die Wirkung der natürlichen
Holzmaserung. Entstanden aus der Idee,
Flächen zu einer dreidimensionalen Figur
zu formen, bildet sich eine ansprechend
schwungvolle Linienführung heraus. Gefertigt aus einem dünnen Furnierblatt, ist Air
als Tisch- oder Wandleuchte sowie in verschiedenen Farben erhältlich.

A' 650 Magni
Table Lamp/Tischleuchte

Andersen Lighting GmbH, Hildesheim,
Germany/Deutschland
In-house design/Werksdesign:
Henrik Andersen
www.andersen-lighting.com

A minimalist design, exclusive materials, and an
energy-efficient advanced technology are united
in the A' 650 Magni table lamp. This design
object gives each room its individual language.
A' 650 Magni fills the room with light to be
chosen from three natural tones. The light can
be projected to the wall in the form of a light
circle. The table lamp is controlled by the C' 712
Cube remote control. The cube changes lightness
and tone of the luminaire by tilting movements
of the hand.

Eine minimalistische Gestaltung, exklusive
Materialien sowie eine energieeffiziente und
zukunftsweisende Technologie vereinen sich
in der Tischleuchte A' 650 Magni. Sie ist ein
Designobjekt, welches dem Raum eine individuelle Sprache verleiht. Das Licht der A' 650
Magni erfüllt den Raum mit einem von drei
wählbaren, natürlichen Farbtönen, welche
durch Projektion als Lichtkreis an die Wand
gestrahlt werden können. Die Tischleuchte
wird mit dem Fernsteuerelement C' 712 Cube
bedient. Der Quader liegt dabei in der Hand
und verändert per Kippbewegung die Helligkeit und den Farbton der Leuchte.

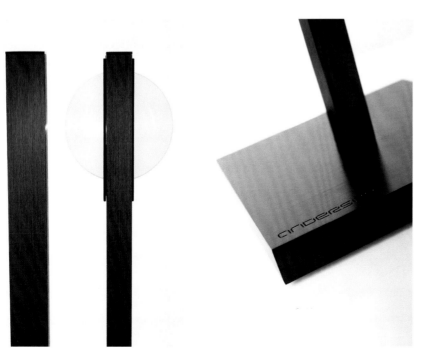

Robin Edman

Dr. Thomas Lockwood

Manuel Alvarez Fuentes

Gardens
Ergonomic functionality

Garten
Ergonomische Funktionalität

Ergonomics, aesthetics, and user-friendliness of intelligent concepts achieve a remarkable quality.

The emphasis in the "Gardens" category is currently placed less on spectacular innovations and more on intelligent functionality and high quality. The materials used provide high weather resistance and durability. Careful manufacturing procedures contribute considerably to the perceived product comfort. Especially in the tools sector, the ergonomics, aesthetics, and user-friendliness of intelligent concepts achieve a remarkable quality and are setting the course for the future. Maximum safety of the products in their daily use continues to play an essential role in these people-oriented design solutions.

Ergonomie, Ästhetik und Benutzerfreundlichkeit erreichen durch sorgfältig durchdachte Konzepte eine bemerkenswerte Qualität.

In der Kategorie „Garten" wird bei der Gestaltung derzeit nicht so sehr auf spektakuläre Innovationen als vielmehr auf intelligente Funktionalität und hohe Qualitätsanmutung gesetzt. Die verwendeten Materialien zeichnen sich durch besondere Widerstandsfähigkeit sowie Langlebigkeit bei allen erdenklichen Witterungsverhältnissen aus. Ihre sorgsame Verarbeitung trägt erheblich zum wahrgenommenen Produktkomfort bei. Gerade im Bereich der Werkzeuge erreichen Ergonomie, Ästhetik und Benutzerfreundlichkeit durch sorgfältig durchdachte Konzepte eine bemerkenswerte Qualität und weisen den Weg in die Zukunft. Die maximale Sicherheit bei der Benutzung der Produkte im alltäglichen Gebrauch spielt weiterhin eine essenzielle Rolle und spiegelt die größtmögliche Ausrichtung der Gestaltungslösungen auf den Menschen wider.

Wave
Hammock / Hängematte

Royal Botania, Nijlen, Belgium / Belgien
In-house design / Werksdesign:
Kris Van Puyvelde
Design: Wave
(Erik Nyberg, Gustav Ström),
Stockholm, Sweden / Schweden
www.royalbotania.com
www.wave.st

Wave is an exclusive and inviting outdoor furniture with a sculptural shape. Hovering halfway between heaven and earth its rounded form, based on one foot only, communicates a flowing impression. Wave gives the feeling of security in a defined natural space. Gently enwrapped you can swing slowly or just enjoy the calmness. As the stand is rotatable by 360 degrees it can always be aligned with the sun without effort. Wave's headlining and the well-upholstered lounge area are covered with a perforated, slightly transparent plastic fabric, which screens people lying underneath to 86 per cent against solar radiation. A robust construction of electropolished stainless steel withstands the impacts of adverse weather conditions. This outdoor furniture is therefore user-friendly and easy to clean.

Wave ist ein skulptural gestaltetes, einladendes und exklusives Outdoor-Möbel. Schwebend auf halbem Weg zwischen Himmel und Erde vermittelt seine runde Form, auf nur einer einzigen Stütze stehend, einen fließenden Eindruck. Wave bietet das Gefühl der Geborgenheit in einem festgelegten, natürlichen Raum – sanft umhüllt kann man langsam schaukeln oder nur die Ruhe genießen. Da der Standfuß um 360 Grad gedreht werden kann, lässt er sich stets gut zur Sonne ausrichten. Sowohl der Himmel wie auch der gut gepolsterte Liegebereich von Wave sind mit einem perforierten und leicht transparenten Kunststoffgewebe bespannt, welches den Darunterliegenden zu 86 Prozent vor Sonneneinstrahlung schützt. Eine robuste Konstruktion aus einem elektropolierten Edelstahl widersteht auch starken Einwirkungen von Wind und Wetter und verleiht diesem Outdoor-Möbel nutzer- wie reinigungsfreundliche Eigenschaften.

Mini Spa
Wellness Oasis / Wellness-Oase

Terramanus Landschaftsarchitektur,
Bonn-Bad Godesberg,
Germany / Deutschland
In-house design / Werksdesign:
Manuel Sauer
www.terramanus.de

The Mini Spa is an urban wellness oasis especially for the small sites of approx. 120 sqm of terraced houses. Its design is to be the advancement of the classic water basin, from a simple decorative element to a useable reflecting pool for bathing according to the standards of modern swimming pool construction. Thus, the ordinary swimming pool turns into an adequate, individual design element of modern landscape gardening. The Mini Spa is feasible even in very small outdoor areas thus accounting for the development of urban planning towards smaller properties. Intentionally no tropical woods but regional products are used. Thanks to the splinter-free finishing of all wood surfaces and edges the Mini Spa is realised for perfect bathing pleasure, as it is inoffensive to the skin.

Das Mini-Spa ist eine urbane Wellness-Oase speziell für ein kleines Reihenhausgrundstück von etwa 120 qm. Seine Gestaltung versteht sich als eine Weiterentwicklung des klassischen Wasserbeckens vom einfachen Zierelement hin zu einem „beschwimmbaren Zierbecken" nach den Standards des modernen Schwimmbadbaus. So wird der gewöhnliche Swimmingpool zum vollwertigen, individuellen Gestaltungselement der modernen Gartenarchitektur. Das Mini-Spa ist selbst in sehr kleinen Außenräumen realisierbar und berücksichtigt dadurch die Entwicklung des Städtebaus zu immer kleineren Grundstücken. Es werden bewusst regionale Produkte und kein Tropenholz verwendet. Durch eine splitterfreie Nachbearbeitung aller Holzoberflächen und Kanten ist das Mini-Spa hautfreundlich und steht für einen ungetrübten Badespaß.

Axis
Outdoor Furniture/
Outdoor-Möbel

Gloster Furniture Ltd., Bristol, GB
Design: Mark Gabbertas, London, GB
www.gloster.com
www.gabbertas.com

The Axis range comprises dining and low chairs, occasional tables and three sizes of dining table, including an extendable version seating up to 12 people. There is a sable lacquered option to certain pieces. Axis represents a new design aesthetic for outdoor teak furniture, but also meets the specific and extreme constructional demands of this typology, including the ability to be flat packed. The design of the lead item, the dining chair, is based on a trapezoid, and this slender frame section is achievable as the result of the natural strength of this structure. This is balanced by the considered use of generous solid teak sections for the back and seat, which convey comfort, strength, solidarity and quality. This angularity is carried through to the tables where it allows perfectly for maximum legroom.

Die Axis-Kollektion umfasst Ess- und niedrige Stühle, Beistelltische und drei unterschiedlich große Esstische einschließlich einer ausziehbaren Version mit Platz für bis zu 12 Personen. Einige Möbelstücke sind als lackierte Alternative auch in der Farbe Sable erhältlich. Axis repräsentiert eine neue Designästhetik für Outdoor-Möbel aus Teakholz und erfüllt gleichzeitig die besonderen und extremen Konstruktionsanforderungen dieses Produkttyps. Dies schließt auch die Möglichkeit ein, die Möbel als Flatpack zu versenden. Die Gestaltung des zentralen Möbelstücks, des Ess-Stuhls, basiert auf einem Trapez. Die schlanke Rahmenkonstruktion ist aufgrund der natürlichen Festigkeit dieser Konstruktion möglich. Dies wird durch den wohldurchdachten Einsatz großzügiger Abschnitte aus massivem Teakholz für die Lehne und die Sitzfläche ausbalanciert, die Komfort, Solidität und Qualität vermitteln. Die Winkligkeit setzt sich in den Tischen fort und lässt maximale Beinfreiheit zu.

Magnus
Garden Furniture / Gartenmöbel

Heinz Kettler GmbH & Co. KG,
Ense, Germany / Deutschland
Design: Formmodul
(Guido Franzke, Detlef Fischer),
Sassenberg, Germany / Deutschland
www.kettler.net
www.formmodul.de

The innovative combination of two typical outdoor components is in the focus of the design of this garden furniture. It thus follows the interior design colour trend. The Magnus garden furniture range combines the two components teakwood and plastic. The FSC-certified teakwood originates from managed forests. The employed Kettalux resin is a two-component material whose outer layer consists of high-quality resin and the internal core of recycled material. By using these materials, this garden furniture range is long lasting, fully weatherproof, and 100 per cent recyclable. The range includes a chair, an armchair, and tables in three different sizes.

Die innovative Kombination zweier typischer Outdoor-Werkstoffe steht im Mittelpunkt der Gestaltung dieser Gartenmöbel und nimmt damit einen Farbtrend aus dem Interior Design auf. Die Gartenmöbel-Serie Magnus verbindet in einer geradlinig anmutenden Formensprache die beiden Werkstoffe Teakholz und Kunststoff, wobei das FSC-zertifizierte Teakholz aus kontrolliertem Anbau stammt. Bei dem eingesetzten Kunststoff Kettalux handelt es sich um ein Komponenten-Material, bei dem die Außenschicht aus hochwertigem Kunststoff besteht und der innen liegende Kern aus Recycling-Material. Durch diesen Materialmix ist die Gartenmöbel-Serie sehr langlebig, sie besitzt gute Außeneigenschaften und ist zu 100 Prozent recycelbar. Diese Serie umfasst einen Stuhl, einen Sessel sowie drei Tischgrößen.

Liberty
Stacking Chair / Stapelsessel

solpuri GmbH, Munich, Germany /
München, Deutschland
Design: karsten weigel | design
(Karsten Weigel), Hamburg,
Germany / Deutschland
www.solpuri.com
www.karsten-weigel.de

The elegant design language of this stacking chair collection is defined by straight lines and accentuated edges. The style of Liberty establishes a symbiosis with the traditional teakwood material. Timeless elegance unites with the contrast between warm, smooth wood and the angularity of the line management.

Die elegant anmutende Formensprache dieser Kollektion von Stapelsesseln ist durch gerade Linien und akzentuierte Kanten definiert. Die Gestaltung von Liberty geht eine Symbiose mit dem traditionellen Material Teakholz ein. Eine zeitlose Eleganz verbindet sich dabei mit dem Gegensatz des warmen, weichen Holzes und der Kantigkeit in der Linienführung.

Flip No.1
Folding Table / Klapptisch

Weishäupl Möbelwerkstätten GmbH,
Stephanskirchen, Germany / Deutschland
Design: Archicult (Roland Breunig, Sven
Unger), Zell am Main,
Germany / Deutschland
www.weishaeupl.de
www.archicult.de

The elegant look of the Flip No.1 folding table is based on the combination of two high-grade materials. It is used in pretentious environments and there, with its distinct look, it appears to be robust and delicate at the same time. Seating and matching benches of the same style are available as well as various surface finishes. For outdoor use Flip No.1 features a weatherproof board made of teakwood combined with satin stainless steel. For indoor use it comes with a board of solid oak and stainless steel legs.

Die elegante Anmutung des Klapptischs Flip No.1 basiert auf der Kombination zweier hochwertiger Materialien. Er findet Einsatz in anspruchsvollen Umgebungen, wo er mit seiner klaren Formensprache robust und filigran zugleich wirkt. In der gleichen Formensprache sind eine Bestuhlung wie auch passende Bänke erhältlich und es stehen verschiedene Oberflächen wie Ausführungen zur Auswahl. Für den Außenbereich ist Flip No.1 beispielsweise mit einer wetterfesten Teakholzplatte und gebürstetem Edelstahl gestaltet, für den Innenbereich mit einer Tischplatte aus massiver Eiche mit Edelstahlfüßen.

Tuli
Outdoor Lighting Concept/
Beleuchtungskonzept für draußen

Techmar B.V., Haaksbergen, NL
Design: D'Andrea & Evers Design,
Enter, NL
www.tuli.nl
www.de-design.nl

Tuli is a modular 12-volt outdoor lighting
concept. Its design offers convenient options
to combine outdoor and indoor living. The
modular design concept allows the users
to create their own individual lamps. Tuli
is available in five different versions: Floor
lamp, table lamp, wall-mounted lamp,
pendant lamp and disc lamp. It is also
possible to choose frames and lampshades in
different colours and patterns. The result is
a modern range of lamps with a conspicuous
look and nicely designed details.

Tuli ist ein 12-Volt-Beleuchtungskonzept
für den Außenbereich. Es bietet eine gute
Möglichkeit, das Leben drinnen und
draußen miteinander zu verbinden. Durch
das Baukastenprinzip kann der Nutzer
eine vollständige, eigene Lampe gestalten.
Tuli gibt es in fünf verschiedenen Versionen: Steh-, Tisch-, Wand-, Hängelampe
und Scheibenleuchte. Erhältlich ist zudem
eine Auswahl an Gestellen und Lampen-
schirmen in unterschiedlichen Farben
und Designs. So entsteht eine zeitgemäße
Leuchtenserie in ungewöhnlicher Form
mit ansprechend gestalteten Details.

Pan
Chair / Stuhl

Garpa Garten &
Park Einrichtungen GmbH,
Escheburg, Germany / Deutschland
Design: Christian Hoisl, Munich,
Germany / München, Deutschland;
Alessandro Andreucci,
Macerata, Italy / Italien
www.garpa.de
www.garpa.com

With its transparent looks the Pan chair expediently blends in with the living environment of gardens. A brushed stainless steel frame and delicately curved skids harmoniously unite with a permanently elastic plastic fibre in the seat and armrest. The distinctive lacing threaded through decorative eyes in the frame adapts to the contours of the body. The fibre of the stackable chair is made of UV- and frost-resistant synthetic material ensuring permanent use.

Der Stuhl Pan fügt sich mit seiner transparenten Formensprache gut in die Wohnwelt Garten ein. Ein gebürstetes Edelstahlgestell mit filigran geschwungenen Kufen ist auf stimmige Weise mit einer dauerelastischen Kunststoff-Faser in der Sitz- und Rückenlehne vereint. Die markante Schnürung des stapelbaren Stuhls, die durch dekorative Ösen im Rahmen geführt ist, passt sich bequem der Körperkontur an. Das Material ist ein langlebiger, UV- und frostbeständiger Kunststoff, der einen dauerhaften Gebrauch erlaubt.

Flat
Outdoor Furniture / Outdoor-Möbel

Gandia Blasco, Ontinyent
(Valencia), Spain / Spanien
Design: Mario Ruiz Design, S.L.
(Mario Ruiz), Barcelona, Spain / Spanien
www.gandiablasco.com
www.marioruiz.es

Characterised by the basic material polypropylene and a coloured aluminium frame this elegant outdoor furniture collection comprises coaches, seating furniture and tables. The connection between frame and corpus as well as the profiles and glides are characterised by a subtle curvature giving them their distinctive look. The armrests of all seating elements are of different length thus ensuring enhanced seating comfort. The transition from the armrests to the body is the same for all pieces of furniture. This range comes with upholstered parts and cushions.

Der farbige Aluminiumrahmen und der Werkstoff Polypropylen sind auffällige Merkmale dieser eleganten Möbelkollektion für den Außenbereich. Sie umfasst Sofas, Stühle und Tische. Die Verbindung zwischen Rahmen und Korpus sowie die Konturen und Kufen zeichnen sich durch eine fein geschwungene Linie aus, was ihnen ihr charakteristisches Aussehen verleiht. Die Armlehnen aller Sitzmöbel sind unterschiedlich lang und gewährleisten somit mehr Sitzkomfort. Die Verbindung der Armlehnen zum Korpus ist bei allen Sitzmöbeln gleich. Die Kollektion gibt es als gepolsterte Ausführung mit Kissen.

Baya
Nesting Place / Nisthaus

Garpa Garten &
Park Einrichtungen GmbH, Escheburg,
Germany / Deutschland
Design: Hadi Teherani AG
(Hadi Teherani),
Hamburg, Germany / Deutschland
www.garpa.de
www.garpa.com

Baya is a garden object whose design goes beyond the mere purpose. The nests of the African weaver birds (Ploceus baya) served as inspiration for the spindle-shaped form, which remotely reminds of elegant reed and grass shapes. The employed materials comprise refined, weatherproof plantation teakwood and high-grade stainless steel. The multi-part nesting place can be disassembled and thus completely cleaned inside. For soft surfaces a ground spike is available, for hard grounds a floor plate.

Baya ist ein objekthaftes Garten-Accessoire, dessen Gestaltung über den puren Zweck hinausgeht. Als Inspiration für seine spindelartige Form, die entfernt an elegante Schilfe und Gräser erinnert, dienten die Nester der afrikanischen Webervögel (Ploceus baya). Die eingesetzten Materialien sind ein edles, wetterfestes Plantagenteakholz sowie hochwertiger Edelstahl. Das mehrteilige Nisthaus ist demontierbar und kann dadurch vollständig von innen gereinigt werden. Eine Aufstellung für weiche Untergründe bietet ein Erdspieß, für härtere Böden ist eine Bodenplatte erhältlich.

The Spíritree
Urn and Planter /
Urne und Pflanzgefäß

The Spíritree Forest Company,
San Juan, Puerto Rico
In-house design / Werksdesign:
José Fernando Vázquez-Pérez /
URBANA, CSP
www.thespiritree.com

As a link between conventional funeral commemoration and ecological protection and restoration, the Spíritree is a biodegradable cinerary urn that transforms into a living memorial in the form of a tree. The two-piece container is composed of an organic bottom shell and a chemically inert, weathering ceramic cover. The bottom shell holds the cremated remains within its internal concavity, and is meant to be planted on the ground. The porous ceramic cover protects the cremated remains from dispersion, while allowing water absorption and promoting biodegradation. Additionally, the container features a central cavity designed to receive a tree seedling or sapling. When planted along with the Spíritree, the growing plant gradually feeds itself from the decomposing biodegradable bottom shell and the calcium-rich cremated remains. In due time, the protective ceramic shell is broken by the growing tree, which becomes the actual living memorial to the loved one's memory.

Spíritree verbindet das herkömmliche Totengedenken mit Umweltschutz und Erneuerung. Es handelt sich um eine biologisch abbaubare Urne, die sich in einen Baum und damit in eine lebendige Gedenkstätte verwandelt. Der zweiteilige Behälter besteht aus einer organischen Bodenschale und einer chemisch neutralen Witterungsabdeckung aus Keramik. Die Bodenschale enthält die eingeäscherten sterblichen Überreste und kann in den Boden eingesetzt werden. Dank der porösen Keramikabdeckung werden die Überreste nicht verstreut, während gleichzeitig jedoch Wasser aufgenommen werden kann und der biologische Abbau gefördert wird. Außerdem hat der Behälter in der Mitte eine Aushöhlung, die einen Keimling oder einen jungen Baum aufnehmen kann. Wenn die wachsende Pflanze in den Spíritree eingepflanzt wird, kann sie sich selbst von der biologisch abbaubaren Bodenschale sowie den sterblichen Überresten ernähren, die reich an Kalzium sind. Wenn die Zeit gekommen ist, sprengt der wachsende Baum die schützende Keramikschicht und wird so zu einer wirklichen, lebendigen Gedenkstätte für einen geliebten Menschen.

Lechuza Balconera
Planter / Pflanzbehälter

geobra Brandstätter GmbH & Co. KG,
Zirndorf, Germany / Deutschland
In-house design / Werksdesign
www.lechuza.com

The Balconera combines innovative functionality with longevity and lightness. With widths of 50 and 80 cm this planter is generously dimensioned and there are many ways to put plants in the container. An integrated subirrigation system considerably facilitates the care of balcony plants. A robust form of high-grade plastic with structural design makes the Balconera impervious to impacts, wind and weather. The wicker look gives it a Mediterranean charm and lightness so that this planter harmonises well with other modern outdoor furniture.

Der Balconera verbindet eine innovative Funktionalität mit Langlebigkeit und Leichtigkeit. Großzügig dimensioniert in den Maßen 50 und 80 cm, kann dieser Pflanzbehälter vielseitig bepflanzt werden, wobei ein integriertes Erd-Bewässerungssystem die Pflege der Balkonpflanzen erheblich erleichtert. Dank einer robusten Gestaltung aus einem hochwertigen Kunststoff in Struk-turdesign ist der Balconera gegen Stöße, Wind und Wetter unempfindlich. Einen mediterranen Charme sowie Leichtigkeit verleiht ihm die Flechtoptik, durch die dieser Pflanzbehälter gut mit anderen zeitgemäßen Outdoor-Möbeln harmoniert.

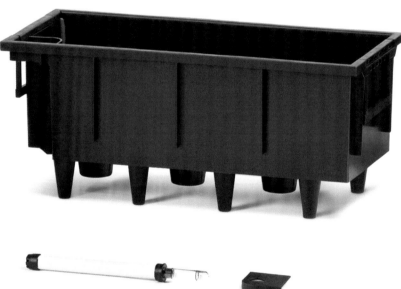

Compost Mixer / Komposter

KETER, Herzliya, Israel
Design: d-vision (Eran Messalem,
Tal Shwartz)
www.keter.com/products/
dynamic-composter

This dynamic composter combines innovative composting methods with an aesthetically and eye-catching design. Equipped with a specially developed gear mechanism (and safety ratchet) the composter makes the composting process much easier and quicker. Other well thought aspects of design are internal mixing fins, which break up compost lumps while the drum is rotating. Adjustable aeration vents allow control of the air circulation and the extraction of compost tea. Due to its design the dynamic composter reduces the usual composting process time allowing two to three compost cycles each season. This composter is made of recycled material. It can be reground and used for the manufacture of new products.

Dieser dynamische Komposter verbindet Innovationen im Kompostierverfahren mit einer ästhetischen und auffälligen Gestaltung. Ausgestattet mit einem speziell entwickelten Getriebemechanismus (einschließlich Sicherheitssperrvorrichtung), erleichtert und beschleunigt dieses Gerät das Kompostieren. Weitere gut durchdachte Gestaltungsaspekte sind die innen liegenden Mischflügel, welche die Kompoststücke zerkleinern, während sich die Trommel dreht. Mit den einstellbaren Belüftungsleitungen wird die Luftzufuhr geregelt sowie die Extraktion von Komposttee ermöglicht. Aufgrund seiner Gestaltung verringert sich mit dem dynamischen Komposter die übliche Kompostierzeit und ermöglicht zwei bis drei Kompostierzyklen pro Saison. Dieser Komposter ist aus erneuerbarem Material hergestellt und kann wieder vermahlen und für die Herstellung neuer Produkte verwendet werden.

Fiskars QuikFit
Locking System / Arretierungssystem

Fiskars, Slupsk, Poland / Polen
In-house design / Werksdesign:
Fiskars R&D, Billnäs
www.fiskars.com

The QuikFit mechanism ensures effortless change of heads (rakes, cultivators, hoes, weeders, edgers, brooms, etc.). The functional design with integral slider allows easy and comfortable connection with one movement. At the sound of a "click" the exchanged head is automatically attached to the shaft and the device is immediately ready for use.

Der QuikFit-Mechanismus ermöglicht ein leichtes Wechseln von Geräteköpfen (Rechen, Krümmer, Hacken, Unkraut-stecher, Rasenkantenstecher, Besen usw.). Die funktionale Gestaltung mit einem integrierten Schieber ermöglicht ein schnelles wie einfaches Verbinden in einer Bewegung. Beim Aufsetzen eines neuen Kopfes ist dieser automatisch mit dem Stiel verbunden, wenn ein „Klick" zu hören ist. Das Gerät ist dann sofort einsatzbereit.

ErgoPlus+
Gel-Padded Handle / Gel-Griff

Fiskars, Slupsk, Poland / Polen
In-house design / Werksdesign:
Fiskars R&D, Billnäs
www.fiskars.com

According to an elaborate concept the ergonomic Fiskars spades, shovels and forks are equipped with an innovative gel-padded handle. It features an aluminium/gel core, which absorbs shocks and lies comfortably in the hand. The large D-handle is ergonomically shaped and fits any hand size with or without gloves.

Nach einem durchdachten Konzept sind die ergonomischen Fiskars Spaten, Schaufeln und Gabeln mit einem innovativen Gel-Griff ausgestattet. Der Griff verfügt über einen Aluminium-Gel-Kern, der Stöße abfedert und dabei sehr komfortabel in der Hand liegt. Der große D-Griff ist für alle Handgrößen, mit oder ohne Handschuh, passend gestaltet und ergonomisch geformt.

Isio 2
Shrub Shear / Strauchschere

Robert Bosch GmbH,
Leinfelden-Echterdingen,
Germany / Deutschland
Design: Teams Design
(Hans-Peter Aglassinger),
Esslingen, Germany / Deutschland
www.bosch.com
www.teams-design.de

The Isio 2 shrub shear is a garden tool, which makes it easy to create little green works of art and well-trimmed lawn edges. As in particular its ergonomics has been optimised, it is compact and handy. A powerful 3.6-volt lithium-ion battery provides a runtime of 50 minutes with a charging time of only 3.5 hours. It is ready for use without memory effect. An innovative anti-blocking system ensures continuous cutting even for thicker branches and long blades of grass.

Die Strauchschere Isio 2 ist ein Gartengerät, das durch seine Gestaltung die Schaffung kleiner grüner Kunstwerke sowie gepflegter Rasenkanten erleichtert. Sie ist kompakt und handlich, da insbesondere die Ergonomie optimiert wurde. Ein leistungsstarker 3,6-Volt-Lithium-Ionen-Akku bietet eine Laufzeit von 50 Minuten und ist ohne Memoryeffekt bei einer Ladedauer von nur 3,5 Stunden einsatzbereit. Ein innovatives Anti-blockier-System ermöglicht ein kontinuierliches Schneiden auch bei dickeren Ästen und hohen Grashalmen.

VIKING GE 450
Garden Shredder / Gartenhäcksler

Viking GmbH, Langkampfen/Kufstein,
Austria / Österreich
In-house design / Werksdesign:
Stefan Pendl, Georg Duregger
Design: Busse Design + Engineering
(Martin Hannig), Elchingen,
Germany / Deutschland
www.viking-garden.com
www.busse-design.com

This electric multi garden shredder is equipped with an optimised twin-chamber system and two separate funnels. It can thus process both hard and soft shredding material. A straight feed chute for softer material features a large feed opening allowing comfortable processing of even large quantities of bulky soft material. A backwards-folding branch feed supports the feeding of stronger branches. The innovative "One Click/One Turn" safety switch is directly integrated into the closure screw.

Dieser elektrische Multi-Gartenhäcksler ist mit einem optimierten Zwei-Kammer-System und zwei getrennten Einfüllöffnungen ausgestattet und kann daher hartes wie auch weiches Häckselmaterial verarbeiten. Ein gerader Trichter für weicheres Material verfügt über eine große Einfüllöffnung und ermöglicht so ein bequemes Beschicken mit großen Mengen von Häckselmaterial, eine nach hinten ausklappbare Astzuführung unterstützt das Zuführen von stärkeren Ästen. Eine Innovation ist ein nutzerfreundlicher „One Click/One Turn"-Sicherheitsschalter, der direkt in die Verschluss-Schraube integriert ist.

Gardena Pipeline
Water Connectors / Wassersteckdosen

Gardena GmbH, Ulm,
Germany / Deutschland
Design: Attivo Creative Resource S.r.l.
(Aleks Tatic, Alessandro Cereda,
Marco Picco), Milan, Italy /
Mailand, Italien
www.gardena.com
www.attivocreative.com

This system of water connectors and water plugs for garden pipelines allows comfortable water tapping, similar to drawing electricity from the mains. An innovative connection box and a regulating and shut off valve facilitate water distribution through the sprinkler system. All connectors of this range feature a robust pop-up ball cover. A broad rim inhibits grass ingrowth. The filter prevents the connector shaft to be soiled; it can be removed for cleaning.

Dieses System von Wassersteckdosen und Wassersteckern für die Garten-Pipeline erlaubt ein einfaches Wasserzapfen ähnlich der Entnahme von Strom aus der Steckdose. Eine innovative Anschlussdose sowie eine Regulier- und Absperrdose erleichtern die Wasserverteilung mit dem Sprinklersystem. Alle Dosen dieser Reihe sind mit einem versenkbaren und robusten Kugeldeckel gestaltet, ein breiter Rand verhindert das Einwachsen von Gras. Ein zum Reinigen entnehmbares Sieb vermeidet ein Verschmutzen des Dosenschachtes.

ErgoCut
Hedge Trimmers / Heckenscheren

Gardena GmbH,
Ulm, Germany / Deutschland
Design: Attivo Creative Resource S.r.l.
(Aleks Tatic, Alessandro Cereda,
Ivàn Colominas, Marco Picco),
Milan, Italy / Mailand, Italien
www.gardena.com
www.attivocreative.com

For sideways hedge cutting the ErgoCut hedge trimmers have been equipped with an ergonomic, hedge cutting head that can be rotated at right angles. So neither has the cutting person to distort his or her body nor has the work process to be adjusted. The user is always in an ideal cutting position beside the hedge. As the weight of the hedge trimmers is well balanced they always lie comfortably and securely in the hand. As the blade geometry was also optimised, efficient cutting results are guaranteed.

Für das seitliche Schneiden an der Hecke wurden die ErgoCut-Heckenscheren mit einem ergonomisch gestalteten, rechtwinklig drehbaren Heckenscherenkopf ausgestattet. Dadurch wird bei dieser Einsatzsituation weder der Körper des Schneidenden verdreht, noch muss während des Arbeitsverlaufs umgegriffen werden. Der Anwender steht immer in idealer Schneidposition neben der Hecke und die Heckenscheren liegen mit ihrem gut ausbalancierten Gewicht in jeder Griffposition bequem und sicher in der Hand. Mit einer ebenfalls optimierten Messergeometrie bieten sie dabei gute Schneidergebnisse.

CST 2018-Li
Accu Chainsaw / Akku-Kettensäge

Gardena GmbH,
Ulm, Germany / Deutschland
Design: Attivo Creative Resource S.r.l.
(Aleks Tatic, Marco Picco),
Milan, Italy / Mailand, Italien
www.gardena.com
www.attivocreative.com

With its ergonomic comfort handles and haptically pleasing soft plastics material this battery-operated chainsaw lies comfortably in the hand. A powerful lithium replacement battery provides persistent cutting of even thick and hard wood. Therefore, this chainsaw is suitable for both wood care and the safe and adequate cutting of firewood. The replacement battery can be recharged at any time without memory effect. The chain tension is set without tools.

Mit ihren ergonomisch gestalteten Komfortgriffen und haptisch angenehmen Weichkunststoffkomponenten liegt diese akkubetriebene Kettensäge gut in der Hand. Ein leistungsfähiger Lithium-Wechselakku erlaubt das ausdauernde Schneiden auch von dickem und hartem Holz, weshalb diese Kettensäge für die Gehölzpflege ebenso wie für das sichere und feuerungsgerechte Zuschneiden von Brennholz eingesetzt werden kann. Der Wechselakku ist jederzeit ohne Memoryeffekt nachladbar, die Kettenspannung erfolgt werkzeuglos.

T 100, T 200, T 380
Turbo-Driven Pop-Up Sprinklers / Turbinen-Versenkregner

Gardena GmbH,
Ulm, Germany / Deutschland
Design: Attivo Creative Resource S.r.l.
(Aleks Tatic, Christian Eisenegger,
Marco Picco), Milan, Italy /
Mailand, Italien
www.gardena.com
www.attivocreative.com

The T 100, T 200 and T 380 turbo-driven pop-up sprinklers ensure even distribution of water individually or in combination with a sprinkler system irrigation conduit. Thanks to its functional and ergonomic design the required spray and water range can be set quickly and intuitively. All other settings can be changed comfortably by hand without the need for special tools. The turbo-driven gear is sand-proof allowing trouble-free functional reliability.

Die Turbinen-Versenkregner T 100, T 200 und T 380 ermöglichen – jeder für sich oder in Kombination an einem Sprinklersystem-Bewässerungsstrang – eine gleichmäßige Verteilung des Wassers. Durch eine funktionale wie ergonomische Gestaltung kann sowohl die gewünschte Beregnungsbreite als auch die Wurfweite des Wassers intuitiv und schnell eingestellt werden. Alle anderen Einstellungen lassen sich ohne Spezialwerkzeug komfortabel von Hand durchführen. Für eine störungsfreie Funktionssicherheit sind die Turbinengetriebe sandgeschützt.

Automower 260 ACX
Automatic Robotic Lawnmower /
Automatischer Roboter-Rasenmäher

Husqvarna AB, Huskvarna,
Sweden / Schweden
In-house design / Werksdesign:
Andreas Johansson, Rajinder Mehra
www.husqvarna.se

This automatic robotic lawnmower is suitable for lawns up to 3,000 sqm. It tackles uneven and complex lawns. To manage larger lawns or more complex shapes it is supplied with a large installation package. An anti-theft alarm as well as a backlit keypad and display provide comfort and security. Equipped with an intelligent technology this lawnmower features many interactive functions: built-in sensors using ultrasonic technology help to avoid hard collisions. When more power is needed the lawnmower always finds its way back to the charging station all by itself.

Dieser automatische Roboter-Rasenmäher eignet sich für Rasengrößen bis zu 3.000 qm. Er bewältigt unebene und schwierige Rasenstücke. Für die Bearbeitung von größeren Rasenflächen und komplizierten Formationen ist er mit einem großen Installationspaket ausgestattet. Er hat eine Diebstahl-Warneinrichtung sowie eine beleuchtete Tastatur mit Display, was zu einer größeren Sicherheit beiträgt. Aufgrund einer intelligenten Technologie verfügt dieser Rasenmäher über viele interaktive Funktionen: Eingebaute Sensoren mit Ultraschall-Technologie verhindern größere Zusammenstöße. Wird der Akku schwach, findet er seinen Weg zur Ladestation alleine.

Revolve L
Folding Bucket / Falteimer

W I L Langenberg GmbH,
Hückeswagen, Germany / Deutschland
Design: General Ocean Industry Limited,
Jiangmen Folding Bucket Factory
(He Tingzhi), Guangdong, China
www.foldingbucket.com
www.go2wil.de

The Revolve L is a folding bucket that can be stowed away in its cover thus saving space. This functional design allows using it in the household and garden. It is made of polyester and thanks to its internal PVC coating it is waterproof. A well-conceived metal handle with rubber insert provides for easy and convenient handling. The Revolve L comes in black, blue and red. It is delivered with cover; its maximum capacity is 11 litres.

Der Revolve L ist ein faltbarer Eimer, der bei Bedarf platzsparend in seiner Hülle verstaut werden kann. Derart funktional gestaltet, findet er Einsatz in Haushalt und Garten. Er besteht aus Polyester und ist aufgrund seiner Innenbeschichtung aus PVC wasserdicht. Ein durchdachter Metallbügel mit Gummieinsatz ermöglicht ein einfaches und angenehmes Tragen. Der Revolve L ist in Schwarz, Blau und Rot erhältlich und wird inklusive der Hülle geliefert, sein maximales Fassungsvermögen beträgt elf Liter.

Aqua Jet Eco P1900E-00
Fountain Pump / Wasserspielpumpe

Heissner GmbH, Lauterbach,
Germany / Deutschland
Design: Fritsch & Freunde
(Harald Jürgen Fritsch),
Neuhof, Germany / Deutschland
www.heissner.de
www.fritschundfreunde.de

The design of this fountain pump emulates the look of a large gravel. Like a stone that has been rounded by eroding watercourses the organic form smoothly adapts to the underwater world. Thanks to an innovative body-pump concept, the housing can be equipped with different motors providing for attractive water games in the garden pond. The well-conceived concept integrates three water games: cascade, bell and spring as well as options to connect the pumps with rock fountains, pond figures and small brooks.

Die Gestaltung dieser Wasserspielpumpe orientiert sich an der Anmutung eines großen Bachkiesels. Wie ein durch das Wasser rund gespülter Stein schmiegt sich die organische Form der Unterwasserwelt an. Ein innovatives Body-Pump-Konzept erlaubt es, den Gehäusekorpus mit unterschiedlichen Motoren zu bestücken, wodurch attraktive Wasserspiele im Gartenteich möglich werden. Dazu integriert das durchdachte Konzept die drei Wasserspiele Kaskade, Glocke und Quell sowie die Anschlussmöglichkeiten von Quellsteinen, Teichfiguren und kleinen Bachläufen.

HT 440 Basic Cut
Hedge Trimmer / Heckenschere

AL-KO Geräte GmbH,
Kötz, Germany / Deutschland
Design: Blankdesign (Stefan Blank),
Weißenhorn, Germany / Deutschland
www.al-ko.de

The HT 440 Basic Cut hedge trimmer by
AL-KO guarantees cleanly trimmed hedges
thanks to its permanently sharp blade.
An impact guard protects the blade when
cutting along the ground or walls. Ergonomic
control elements prevent fatigue during use.
The integrated level ensures straight hedge
trimming. A provided blade cover, which can
be mounted to the wall, permits space-saving
storage.

Die AL-KO Heckenschere HT 440 Basic
Cut gewährleistet dank ihres dauerhaft
scharfen Messers einen sauberen Heckenschnitt. Durch den Anschlagschutz wird
das Messer bei Schnitten entlang an
Boden und Wänden geschützt. Ergonomisch geformte Bedienelemente ermöglichen ein ermüdungsfreies Arbeiten. Die
integrierte Wasserwaage unterstützt einen
geraden Heckenschnitt. Der mitgelieferte
Schutzköcher mit Wandhalter-Funktion
dient einer platzsparenden Aufbewahrung.

Lazy Lounge
Lounge System

Stern GmbH & Co. KG,
Affalterbach, Germany / Deutschland
Design: Doser + Zimprich
(Wolf Doser, Yvonne Zimprich),
Stuttgart, Germany / Deutschland
www.stern-moebel.de
www.doser-zimprich.de

As a modular and individually adaptable lounge system Lazy Lounge offers comfortable recreation inside and outside the house. A distinctive look is obtained by separating the contrasting forms of the base frame and the seat shell.

Als ein modulares und individuell arrangierbares Lounge-System bietet Lazy Lounge dem Nutzer komfortable Entspannung im In- und Outdoor-Bereich. Die Anmutung ist durch die kontrastierende formale Trennung von Untergestell und Sitzschale geprägt.

Single
Lounger / Relaxsessel

Stern GmbH & Co. KG,
Affalterbach, Germany / Deutschland
Design: Doser + Zimprich
(Wolf Doser, Yvonne Zimprich)
Stuttgart, Germany / Deutschland
www.stern-moebel.de
www.doser-zimprich.de

The design language of the Single lounger is characterised by an interplay of visual lightness and weight. The generously dimensioned back serves both as rest and screen. It defines this lounger as a cosy retreat for hot summer days.

Ein Wechselspiel aus visueller Leichtigkeit und Schwere prägt die Formensprache von Single. Der großzügig dimensionierte Rücken dient sowohl als Lehne wie auch als Paravent und definiert diesen Relaxsessel als einen behaglichen Rückzugsort für heiße Sommertage.

Cocoon
Outdoor Oasis / Outdoor-Oase

Cubist Outdoor Residences Ltd., Berlin,
Germany / Deutschland
In-house design / Werksdesign
www.cubist.ee

This luxurious outdoor bed offers the comfort and safe feeling of homely relaxation also outside the house. It integrates lighting and two comfortable divan beds; there are many options for installing additional equipment like for example a fridge or a modern multimedia station.

Dieses luxuriöse Outdoor-Bett bietet den Komfort und die Geborgenheit der häuslichen Entspannung auch im Freien. Es integriert eine Beleuchtung sowie zwei bequeme Liegen und kann optional vielfältig ausgestattet werden, etwa mit einem Kühlschrank oder einer zeitgemäßen Multimediastation.

OXO Good Grips
Hand Pruners and Hedge Shears/
Handgarten- und Heckenscheren

OXO, New York, USA
Design: Smart Design, New York, USA
www.oxo.com
www.smartdesignworldwide.com

These hand pruners and hedge shears are
functionally well thought out. Both tools
feature a user-friendly design; they are well
balanced and weighted for increased control
and accuracy. They are easy to use even by those
with less strength or smaller hands.

Diese Handgarten- und Heckenscheren sind
funktional ausgereift. Beide Geräte sind
nutzerfreundlich gestaltet, für eine bessere
Kontrolle und präzises Schneiden wurde ihr
Gewicht gut ausbalanciert. Sie sind auch für
diejenigen leicht zu bedienen, die weniger
Kraft oder kleine Hände haben.

SmartCut
Ratchet Secateurs/Ratschenschere

Gardena GmbH, Ulm,
Germany/Deutschland
Design: Attivo Creative Resource S.r.l.
(Aleks Tatic, Marco Picco, Silvina Iglesias),
Milan, Italy/Mailand, Italien
www.gardena.com
www.attivocreative.com

The ratchet secateurs can be used in many
cutting situations. On the basis of an innovative
ratchet function, which can be optionally
activated, the user no longer has to expend
additional energy on stronger branches or
hard wood.

Für eine Vielzahl von Schneidsituationen
kann diese Ratschenschere eingesetzt werden. Auf der Grundlage einer innovativen,
zuschaltbaren Ratschenfunktion muss der
Nutzer auch bei dickeren Ästen oder hartem
Holz keine zusätzliche Kraft aufwenden.

Manhattan
Gas Barbecue Grill/Gasgrill

Enders Colsman AG, Werdohl,
Germany/Deutschland
Design: cube DESIGN,
Pleuger & Schmidt GbR,
Krefeld, Germany/Deutschland
www.enders-colsman.de
www.cube-design.de

Thanks to its versatile functionality, premium
equipment, and its sophisticated appearance this
gas barbecue grill provides a delightful outdoor
experience. Even heat distribution on the grill
grate always ensures excellent barbecue food.

Mit einer vielseitigen Funktionalität und
hochwertigen Ausstattung bietet dieser
edel anmutende Gasgrill ein genussvolles
Outdoor-Erlebnis. Eine gleichmäßige Hitze-
verteilung auf dem Grillrost ermöglicht ein
stets gutes Grillergebnis.

Jorge Pensi

Shashi Caan

Prof. Werner Aisslinger

Architecture and interior design
Permanence and stability through clear structures

Architektur und Interior Design
Dauerhaftigkeit und Stabilität durch klare Strukturen

Striving for timelessness is expressed in less playful, more clearly structured forms and discreet colours.

In weniger verspielten, klar strukturierten Formen und dezenten Farben findet das Streben nach Zeitlosigkeit Ausdruck.

Hardly a design discipline shapes living spaces and the experiences made therein as much as the "Architecture and interior design" sector. Human interactions are here given concrete forms through both the perceived and the actual design quality. Economic considerations and a growing ecological awareness influence the selection of the materials, and therewith the overall aesthetics, while technological progress calls for flexible design concepts. In an effort to evoke a timelessness that goes beyond short-lived trends, the sector displays clearly structured and less playful forms as well as discreet colours. In unstable times such as these, the designers are reverting to solid, high-quality, but little innovative concepts that convey the feeling of safety and durability.

Kaum eine gestalterische Disziplin vermag es, Lebensräume und darin gemachte Erfahrungen derart zu prägen wie der Bereich „Architektur und Interior Design". Menschlichen Interaktionen werden hier sowohl durch die empfundene als auch durch die tatsächliche Designqualität konkrete Formen verliehen. Wirtschaftliche Überlegungen und ein wachsendes ökologisches Bewusstsein beeinflussen die Auswahl der Materialien und damit die gesamte Ästhetik, während der technologische Fortschritt nach flexiblen Gestaltungskonzepten verlangt. In weniger verspielten, klar strukturierten Formen und dezenten Farben findet das Streben nach Zeitlosigkeit abseits kurzlebiger Trends Ausdruck. In instabilen Zeiten besinnen sich die Designer auf solide, qualitativ hochwertige, aber wenig innovative Entwürfe, die ein Gefühl von Sicherheit und dauerhaftem Wert vermitteln.

Pircher Oberland Spa, Dobbiaco
(Bolzano), Italy / Italien
Design: Studio Bestetti Associati
(Gianfranco Bestetti), Segrate (Milano),
Italy / Italien
www.pircher.eu/planit
www.bestettiassociati.com

An innovative architectural system forms
the basis for Planit. Modules of three
different sizes provide for a combination in
accordance with individual requirements.
By means of element construction private
residential buildings, public institutions,
offices, showrooms and shops are thus
developed. This module system extends the
idea of prefabricated houses as it allows
detailed projected architectures and adapts
to individual needs and topographies. When
choosing the materials only those are used
that meet high quality standards and are
justifiable from an ecological point of
view. A wooden structure forms the basis
of this concept, which mainly consists in a
wood panel structure with soft wood fibre
insulation.

Planit basiert auf einem innovativen
architektonischen System, wobei Module in drei unterschiedlichen Größen
eine Kombination nach individuellen
Ansprüchen erlauben. In Elementbau-
weise entstehen Eigenheime, öffentliche
Einrichtungen, Büros, Showrooms und
Shops. Dieses Modulsystem erweitert das
Prinzip des Fertigbauhauses, da es detail-
lierte, geplante Architekturen ermöglicht
und sich den individuellen Ansprüchen
sowie der Topographie anpassen kann. Bei
der Auswahl der Materialien werden nur
solche eingesetzt, die hohen Qualitäts-
standards entsprechen und die ökologisch
vertretbar sind. Die Basis dieses Konzepts
bildet eine Holzstruktur, die vorwiegend
als Holzständerbauweise mit einer Holz-
weichfaserdämmung ausgeführt wird.

Midrash Building

Design: Isay Weinfeld, Domingos Pascali, Elena Scarabotolo, Marcelo Alvarenga, Fausto Natsui, Adriana Zampieri, São Paulo, Brazil / Brasilien
www.isayweinfeld.com

The Midrash Building was designed to house a study centre for the Congregação Judaica do Brasil (Jewish Congregation of Brazil). The centre is devoted to debates, discussions and the teaching of various themes around Jewish traditions in literature, arts or history. On the facade, a fibreglass mesh made up of Hebrew letters in different layers, sizes, and tones of white overlaps the brickwork, extending from the first floor to the top, and to the limit of the neighbouring lots. In order to communicate what this building is about, letters always form the word "Midrash", which means, "to draw sense".

Das Midrash Building wurde als ein Studienzentrum der jüdischen Gemeinde in Brasilien (Congregação Judaica do Brasil) konzipiert. In Debatten, Diskussionen und Lehre beschäftigt sich das Zentrum mit Themen jüdischer Traditionen in Literatur, Kunst oder Geschichte. Auf dem Mauerwerk der Fassade ist ein hervorstehendes Gewebe aus Glasfasern angebracht, das aus hebräischen Buchstaben in verschiedenen Ebenen, Größen und Weißtönen besteht und vom ersten Stockwerk bis zum Dach und den angrenzenden Nachbarngrundstücken reicht. Die Buchstaben bilden immer wieder das Wort „Midrash", das so viel bedeutet wie „einen Sinn finden". Sie zeigen damit auf, worum es in diesem Gebäude geht.

SL 82
Folding Glass Door /
Glas-Faltwand

Solarlux Aluminium Systeme GmbH,
Bissendorf, Germany / Deutschland
In-house design / Werksdesign:
Werner Helmich
www.solarlux.com

This folding glass door looks to be completely made of glass. It features a reduced and slim design language and creates interesting perspectives for contemporary architecture. Flush inserted glass and the control of the comfort lock evenly integrated into the glass surface are characteristic of this folding door. Thermally-insulated sections combined with low-E glass provide modern high-level heat insulation. Featuring a functionally mature and high-quality stainless steel track technology this folding door is suitable for realising large space openings without thresholds, which interconnect the inner and the outer world.

Diese Glas-Faltwand wirkt, als bestünde sie vollständig aus Glas. Sie ist gestaltet mit einer reduzierten und schlank anmutenden Formensprache und schafft interessante Perspektiven für die zeitgenössische Architektur. Flächenbündig eingelegte Gläser sowie eine eben in die Glasfläche eingelassene Bedienung der Komfortverriegelung prägen das Erscheinungsbild dieser Glas-Faltwand. Wärmegedämmte Profile kombiniert mit Wärmeschutzglas bieten einen zeitgemäß hohen Wärmeschutz. Ausgestattet mit einer funktional durchdachten und hochwertigen Edelstahl-Lauftechnik, können mit dieser Glas-Faltwand großflächige, schwellenlose Raumöffnungen realisiert werden, die Innen- und Außenwelt miteinander verbinden.

Artificial Alabaster Stone / Künstlicher Alabasterstein

Rong Jih Enterprise Co., Ltd., Taichung County, Taiwan
In-house design / Werksdesign:
Ching-Liang Chu
www.rongjih.com.tw

This artificial stone lets the light shine through and thus offers new ways of lighting. The stone is made by hand of alabaster, it softens the light source and gives the light in the city a new kind of expression. The procedure of a non-kiln burnt process reduces pollution, and also the use of recycled materials makes this product an eco-friendly one. The malleability and workability of the light penetrating stone material helps to satisfy the needs, and even caters to the unconventional imaginations and sketches of designers. It is also a demonstration of workmanship as the simulation of rare stone (grain) can only be done by the hands of highly experienced masters.

Dieser künstliche Stein ist lichtdurchlässig und bietet damit neue Möglichkeiten der Beleuchtung. Mit der Hand wird der Stein aus Alabaster geformt. Er dämpft die Lichtquelle ab und verleiht dem Licht in der Stadt einen neuen Ausdruck. Das Produktionsverfahren ohne herkömmlichen Brennofen reduziert die Verschmutzung, weshalb er, in Verbindung mit dem Einsatz von Recycling-Materialien, umweltfreundlich ist. Da das lichtdurchlässige Steinmaterial formbar und gut zu verarbeiten ist, spricht es unterschiedliche Bedürfnisse an, bis hin zu ungewöhnlichen Vorstellungen und Entwürfen von Designern. Das Material stellt schließlich auch eine besondere Demonstration handwerklicher Leistung dar, denn nur besonders erfahrenen Meistern gelingt die Imitation seltener Steine.

astec b.1000
Sliding Door Fitting / Schiebetürbeschlag

astec gmbh, Albstadt,
Germany / Deutschland
In-house design / Werksdesign
www.astec-design.de

As the roller guide tracks of this sliding door fitting remain unnoticed at first sight, the clarity and simplicity of rooms can be identified more easily. That way, there is a multitude of new options to design, divide and use rooms. Without frames and fittings the doors silently slide across the room with no apparent effort. Customised to individual specifications, narrow, shallow roller guide tracks integrated in the floor bear weights up to 300 kg per metre.

Da die Führungsnuten dieses Schiebetürbeschlages auf den ersten Blick nicht sichtbar sind, können Räume in ihrer Klarheit und Einfachheit wahrgenommen werden. Damit bieten sich vielfältige neue Möglichkeiten der Raumplanung, Raumunterteilung und Raumnutzung. Ohne Rahmen und Beschläge gleiten die Türen mit nur geringem Kraftaufwand leise durch den Raum. Nach individuellen Maßvorgaben in den Boden integrierte, schmal und flach gestaltete Rollenschienen tragen dabei Gewichte bis zu 300 kg pro Meter.

iMotion 2301
Sliding Door Drive / Schiebetürantrieb

Tormax, Landert Motoren AG, Bülach,
Switzerland / Schweiz
In-house design / Werksdesign
www.tormax.com

This generation of iMotion has an innovative design featuring a 32-bit control unit and a corresponding operating unit. It can be used for sliding doors as well as swing, folding, and revolving doors. It is suitable for both indoor and outdoor use. As the drives are operated by brushless and gearless synchronous motors the components are long-lasting and require little maintenance. The control automatically configures itself, permanently monitors itself and optimises itself during operation, for example if the temperature changes. The iMotion 2301 sliding door drive is characterised by low-noise and dynamic leaf movements, minimal maintenance, and a high degree of safety. With a distinct and puristic design, iMotion doors blend in well with the architecture of a building.

Im Mittelpunkt der innovativen Gestaltung der iMotion-Generation stehen eine 32-Bit-Steuerung sowie eine darauf abgestimmte Bedieneinheit. Diese können für Schiebe-, Drehflügel-, Falt- und Karusselltüren, im Außen- wie auch im Innenbereich einheitlich verwendet werden. Da die Antriebe mit bürsten- und getriebelosen Synchronmotoren arbeiten, sind die Komponenten langlebig und wartungsarm. Die Steuerung konfiguriert sich selbst, überwacht sich permanent und optimiert sich im Betrieb, beispielsweise bei Temperaturänderungen. Der Schiebetürantrieb iMotion 2301 zeichnet sich durch geräuscharme und dynamische Türflügelbewegungen und geringen Aufwand im Unterhalt sowie ein hohes Maß an Sicherheit aus. Klar und puristisch gestaltet, passen sich iMotion-Türen gut der Gebäudearchitektur an.

Clear View Window – SL
Window/Fenster

LG Hausys, Design Center, Seoul, Korea
In-house design/Werksdesign:
Hwayeon Lee, Joon Baek, Dongwoo
Shin, Jongbong Woo
www.lghausys.com

The Clear View Window allows a better view to the outside; nature and city are pleasantly framed. The clear surface coating attracts the sunlight providing a luxurious depth and glow in the profile. The black metal frame of the glazing stays in the background; it gives the window a modern look and makes it appear to be slimmer and modern. By using coextrusion the surface treatment of the PVC material for the Clear View Window series was improved. The colour design of the frame gives it a modern look and makes the PVC window an attractive product. Both features create multiple design options for the PVC window. In addition, it is no longer necessary to wrap the PVC parts in decorative vinyl to adapt the design to the surrounding area. This also contributes to energy saving.

Das Clear View Window ermöglicht einen besseren Blick ins Freie, Natur wie Stadt werden auf ansprechende Weise „gerahmt". Die klare Oberflächenbeschichtung zieht das Sonnenlicht förmlich an. Sie verleiht dem Profil eine große Tiefe und einen besonderen Glanz. Der schwarze Metallrahmen der Verglasung hält sich im Hintergrund, dadurch wirkt das Fenster modern und auch schmaler, als es tatsächlich ist. Für die Fensterserie SL wurde die Oberflächenbehandlung des Ausgangsmaterials PVC durch ein Koextrusionsverfahren verbessert. Die farbliche Gestaltung des Rahmens gibt dem Ganzen ein modernes Aussehen. Dadurch wird das PVC-Fenster zu einem ansprechenden Produkt. Diese beiden Merkmale eröffnen dem PVC-Fenster vielfältige Gestaltungsmöglichkeiten. Außerdem entfällt auf diese Weise die Verkleidung der PVC-Teile mit dekorativem Vinyl, um das Design an die Umgebung anzupassen. Damit wird auch ein Beitrag zur Energieeinsparung geleistet.

Hidden Frame Window / Fenster

LG Hausys Ltd., Seoul, Korea
In-house design / Werksdesign:
Ju Yeon Won, Dongwoo Shin
Design: Hwayeon Lee, Joon Baek Baek,
Seoul, Korea
www.lghausys.com

The individual lifestyle in South Korea favours a generous view from the living room. This plain window presents some aesthetic options for minimising the visual weight of the frame that is bound to obscure the view. By renouncing unessential details, the window is user-friendly and easy to clean, and its frame meets general needs for more visual simplicity and a reduced visual presence. The window is thus enhanced in terms of quality. Aligned sliding frames give the product a uniform look. Another contribution to the upmarket visual and aesthetic quality looked for in interior design is the use of mirror glass and a screen-printing technique.

Der individuelle Lebensstil in Südkorea bevorzugt einen großzügigen Ausblick aus dem Wohnzimmer. Dieses schlichte Fenster präsentiert ästhetische Möglich-keiten, um das einschränkende optische Gewicht des Rahmens zu reduzieren. Durch den Verzicht auf unwesentliche Details ist es einfach zu nutzen und zu reinigen. Der Fensterrahmen kommt dem allgemeinen Bedürfnis nach größerer visueller Schlichtheit und reduzierter visueller Präsenz entgegen. Damit wird das Fenster qualitativ aufgewertet. Darauf abgestimmte Gleitrahmen verleihen dem Produkt ein einheitliches Aussehen. Der Einsatz von Spiegelglas und Siebdruck-verfahren stellt einen weiteren Beitrag zu der gehobenen gestalterischen und ästhe-tischen Qualität dar, die in der Innen-architektur gewünscht wird.

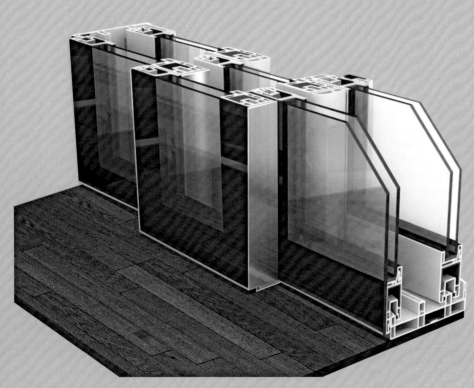

Live
Window / Fenster

Giorgio Senatore,
Ercolano (Napoli), Italy / Italien
In-house design / Werksdesign:
Angelo Senatore
www.giorgiosenatore.it
www.finestralive.it

The Live window, which was designed with a sliding and lifting opening, allows seamless glazing and thus creates a distinct and reduced architecture. This also applies to windows with two or three sashes, which usually have to be interrupted by vertical connection profiles. With 66 mm, the visible interior frame features minimal dimensions and the external view provides a pure glass view. This innovative concept could be implemented by using a mineral alloy that differs from the material used for the wooden sashes. The width of the connection of the sashes is thus reduced to merely 17 mm, the connection being invisible from both inside and outside. The miniaturisation is accompanied by the development of a corresponding weather-resistant central locking.

Das Fenster Live, gestaltet mit einer schiebenden und einer hebenden Öffnung, ermöglicht eine durchgehende Verglasung und somit eine klare und reduzierte Architektur – auch bei Fenstern, die aus zwei oder drei Flügeln bestehen und die deshalb in der Regel durch vertikale Kupplungsprofile unterbrochen werden müssen. Der sichtbare Innenrahmen hat minimale Ausmaße von 66 mm, die Außensicht bietet eine reine Glasansicht. Möglich wurde dieses innovative Konzept durch den Einsatz einer Mineral-Legierung, die sich von den für die Holzflügel verwendeten Materialien unterscheidet. Auf diese Weise reduziert sich die Breite der Verkuppelung der Flügel auf nur 17 mm und die Kuppelung bleibt innen und außen unsichtbar. Diese Miniaturisierung wird ergänzt von der Entwicklung einer entsprechenden witterungsbeständigen Zentralverriegelung.

WiVinci
Windows/Fenster

W. Hofer Schreinerei AG, Rothrist,
Switzerland/Schweiz
In-house design/Werksdesign:
Willy Hofer
www.qualitaetsschreiner.ch

The concept of the WiVinci window opens up new perspectives for architecture and interior design. Equipped with invisible fittings, it is interpreted as a "frameless window". This window frame can be smoothly integrated, flush with the wall, into any setting, for the window sash and frame are on the same plane and merge to become a visual unit. The option of unifying the colour of the wall with that of the window, and vice versa, is another interesting aspect. The window can be used in wet areas and is very easy to clean, demonstrating further important advantages of the concept. As WiVinci's whole surface is completely made of glass, labour-intensive cleaning of the frame proves unnecessary.

Das Konzept der Fenster WiVinci eröffnet der Architektur und Innenarchitektur neue Möglichkeiten. Interpretiert als ein „rahmenloses Fenster" ist es mit nicht sichtbaren Beschlägen gestaltet. Der Fensterrahmen lässt sich fließend und mauerbündig in ein Objekt integrieren, wobei Fensterflügel und Rahmen sich auf einer Ebene befinden und zu einer visuellen Einheit verschmelzen. Ein interessanter Aspekt dieser Fenster ist die Möglichkeit, die Farbe der Wände mit dem Fenster zu vereinen und umgekehrt. Wichtige Vorteile sind die Einsatzmöglichkeit der Fenster in Nasszonen sowie ihre Reinigungsfreundlichkeit. Dadurch, dass die Fenster ganzflächig aus Glas sind, entfällt das mühselige Reinigen des Rahmens.

UNISASH Arx view
Universal Window Sash/
Universalfensterrahmen

Kovinoplastika Lož d.d., Stari trg pri
Ložu, Slovenia/Slowenien
In-house design/Werksdesign:
Aleksander Vukovič
Design: Gigodesign d.o.o., Miha Klinar,
Ljubljana, Slovenia/Slowenien
www.unisash.eu
www.gigodesign.com

In the field of construction elements a
universal window sash is in the centre of
this interesting concept. It can be built
into a PVC, wood or aluminium frame. The
concept features harmoniously distinct
lines offering a variety of architectural
advantages and considerable savings in
the production process and resources. The
principle of a variably installable universal
window frame leads to a considerably higher
glazing and noticeably narrower window
profiles. Thus, there is an increase in thermal
insulation as well as an increase in light
and solar energy transmittance. This system
integrates very well into the architecture,
as it can be installed without any visible
connection parts. It thus forms a smooth and
harmonised surface for indoor and outdoor
use. Individualisation of glass screen-printing
offers further architectural options.

Im Mittelpunkt dieses interessanten Konzepts im Bereich der Bauelemente steht
ein Universalfensterrahmen, der sowohl in
einen PVC- wie auch in Holz- oder Aluminiumrahmen eingebaut werden kann.
Das Konzept bietet mit seiner harmonisch
klaren Linienführung eine Vielzahl architektonischer Vorteile sowie erhebliche
Einsparungen im Produktionsprozess und
bei den Ressourcen. Das Prinzip eines
variabel einsetzbaren Universalfenster-
rahmens führt zu einer deutlich erhöhten
Verglasung der Fenster sowie wesentlich
engeren Fensterprofilen. Die Fenster sind
damit besser wärmegedämmt und sie
haben eine verbesserte Durchlässigkeit
für die Licht- und Sonnenenergie. In die
Architektur integriert sich dieses System
sehr gut, da es ohne sichtbare Anschluss-
stücke eingebaut werden kann und eine
plane und harmonisierte Oberfläche im
Innen- und Außenbereich entsteht. Weitere architektonische Möglichkeiten bietet
eine Individualisierung im Bereich des
Siebdrucks.

**SmartHandle 3062
Digital Door Fitting/
Digitaler Türbeschlag**

SimonsVoss Technologies AG,
Unterföhring, Germany/Deutschland
Design: Ergon3 (Peter Trautwein),
Munich, Germany/München,
Deutschland
www.simons-voss.de
www.ergon3.de

This digital door fitting combines intelligent access control with an ergonomic design. The elegant, flat housing hides an innovative technology. In the digital locking and access control system 3060, the door fitting communicates with identification media via RFID. It controls the access of up to 64,000 users with regard to time and space. With this innovative door fitting, mounting features an interesting aspect: it can be quickly and easily installed without wiring and there is no need to drill through the door leaf or change it otherwise. Essentially, mounting simply means that a screw is tightened. A functional principle, for which the patent is pending, guarantees a stable and secure position. In addition, this locking system is operated by batteries allowing for a lifespan of more than ten years.

Eine intelligente Zutrittskontrollfunktionalität kombiniert dieser digitale Türbeschlag mit einer ergonomischen Gestaltung. Das elegant anmutende, flache Gehäuse birgt eine innovative Technologie, denn der Türbeschlag kommuniziert im digitalen Schließ- und Zutrittskontrollsystem 3060 über RFID mit Identifikationsmedien und steuert den Zutritt für bis zu 64.000 Benutzer nach Ort und Zeit. Ein interessanter Aspekt dieses innovativen digitalen Türbeschlags ist die Möglichkeit einer schnellen und einfachen Montage ohne Verkabelung und ohne das Türblatt durchbohren oder anderweitig verändern zu müssen. Der Montageaufwand reduziert sich im Wesentlichen auf das Anziehen einer Schraube. Ein zum Patent angemeldetes Funktionsprinzip sichert einen dauerhaften und festen Sitz. Dieses Schließsystem arbeitet zudem mit Batterien, die eine Lebensdauer von mehr als zehn Jahren gewährleisten.

Digital SmartRelay 3063/ Digitales SmartRelais 3063

SimonsVoss Technologies AG,
Unterföhring, Germany/Deutschland
Design: Ergon3 (Peter Trautwein),
Munich, Germany/München,
Deutschland
www.simons-voss.de
www.ergon3.de

The distinct and elegant style of this digital access control is combined with intelligent technology. The well-proportioned housing can be integrated inconspicuously into any architectural environment, for instance into a classic old building or a modern office building. A transponder with access authorisation at the SmartRelay is an interesting feature. If it is activated a green LED lights up at the upper side of the housing. Barriers, gates, automatic doors, revolving doors and lifts or alarm systems can thus be easily integrated into the digital locking and access control system 3060 and operated by the transponder. The SmartRelay can be easily and quickly mounted without using any wiring.

Ihre klare und elegant anmutende Formensprache verbindet diese digitale Zutrittskontrolle mit einer intelligenten Technologie. Das ausgewogen proportionierte Gehäuse gliedert sich unauffällig in die architektonische Umgebung ein, beispielsweise in einen klassischen Altbau oder aber ein modernes Bürogebäude.

Ein interessantes innovatives Ausstattungsmerkmal dieser Zutrittskontrolle ist ein zutrittsberechtigter Transponder am SmartRelais: Wird dieser betätigt, leuchtet eine grüne LED an der Oberseite des Gehäuses auf. Schranken, Tore, Automatik- und Drehtüren sowie Aufzüge oder Alarmanlagen können auf diese Weise gut in das digitale Schließ- und Zutrittskontrollsystem 3060 integriert und mit dem Transponder bedient werden. Ohne jegliche Verkabelung lässt sich das SmartRelais unkompliziert und schnell montieren.

AY-B4663, AY-B1663, AY-B3663
Fingerprint Readers/Fingerabdruck-Lesegeräte

Rosslare Enterprises Ltd., Hong Kong
In-house design/Werksdesign:
Gvishi Itzhak
www.rosslaresecurity.com

This innovative line of swipe fingerprint readers comes in three compact and aesthetic designs which are combined in one clear form language. Each of the biometric readers uses the Mifare Smart Card Fingerprint Swipe Sensor MOC, a user-friendly Match-on-Card (MOC) technology. This technology allows readers to use a Swipe type biometric sensor to check for a 1:1 verification of fingerprint data and a biometric template stored in a Mifare card (as opposed to the controller's database). When the verification is confirmed, the reader transmits the card ID to the Access Control panel.

Diese neue Reihe von Fingerabdruck-Lesegeräten gibt es in drei kompakten und ästhetischen Versionen, die alle eine klare Formensprache verbindet. In allen diesen biometrischen Lesegeräten kommt der MOC-Sensor für Mifare Smart Cards zum Ablesen von Fingerabdruckdaten zum Einsatz, eine nutzerfreundliche Match-on-Card (MOC)-Technologie. Mithilfe dieser Technologie können Lesegeräte einen biometrischen Swipe-Sensor verwenden, um einen 1:1-Abgleich der Fingerabdruckdaten mit den biometrischen Daten vorzunehmen, die auf einer Mifare Card gespeichert sind (im Unterschied zur Speicherung in einer Datenbank). Wenn der Abgleich zu einem positiven Ergebnis führt, vermittelt das Lesegerät die Karten-ID an die Einheit für die Zugangssteuerung.

Ezon SHS-6020
Digital Door Lock/
Digitales Türschloss

Seoul Commtech Co., Ltd., Seoul, Korea
In-house design/Werksdesign:
Jae Hoon Kim, Jeong Hoon Ha
www.scommtech.com

Thanks to an innovative and user-friendly safety system this digitally controlled locking device offers a high degree of comfort and security. The system is operated by entering a password or using an RFID or other available cards. During normal operation an action is confirmed by LED displays and acoustic signals. If a wrong password or an unregistered card is entered five times an alarm goes off and the electronic system is switched off for a predetermined time set by the operator. By means of an automatic locking function the door is then automatically locked. The safety is additionally enhanced by an alarm signal, which automatically starts in case of fire; at the same time the locking system is activated.

Diese digitale elektronisch gesteuerte Sperrvorrichtung bietet mit einem innovativen und nutzerfreundlichen Sicherheitssystem ein hohes Maß an Komfort und Sicherheit. Das System wird mittels einer Passworteingabe mit einer RFID-Karte oder auch mit anderen verfügbaren Karten bedient. Im Normalbetrieb wird durch LED-Anzeigen und akustische Signale die Durchführung bestätigt. Nach fünfmaliger fehlerhafter Passwort- oder Karteneingabe ertönt ein Warnsignal und die Elektronik wird für eine bestimmte Zeitspanne, die individuell vom Betreiber festgesetzt werden kann, ausgeschaltet. Mittels einer automatischen Verschließfunktion wird die Tür dann automatisch verschlossen. Die Sicherheit wird darüber hinaus durch ein bei Feuer automatisch ertönendes Warnsignal erhöht, wobei sich zugleich das Schließsystem öffnet.

ALR Vitraplan
Sectional Door/Sectionaltor

Hörmann KG VKG, Steinhagen,
Germany/Deutschland
In-house design/Werksdesign:
Thomas Hörmann, Martin J. Hörmann
www.hoermann.com

Flush glazing hides the frame structure, which is usually visible in doors that are glazed over a large area, and which interrupts the distinct overall impression. By its design this door gives an elegant appearance and is perceived as a closed and uniform surface. Beyond its purpose of being the closure of a hall it can be incorporated as a design element in the architectural concept of a building. It becomes an integral part of the facade design and is suitable for representative residential or commercial buildings. The glazing is available in the colours grey and brown. An interesting combination of reflection and transparency creates a fascinating effect.

Eine flächenbündige Verglasung verdeckt hier die bei anderen großflächig verglasten Toren sichtbare und damit den klaren Gesamteindruck unterbrechende Rahmenkonstruktion. Durch diese Gestaltung wirkt dieses Tor elegant und ist als geschlossene und einheitliche Fläche wahrnehmbar. Über seine reine Funktion als Hallenabschluss hinaus, lässt es sich auf diese Weise als Gestaltungselement in den architektonischen Entwurf des Gebäudes einbeziehen. Es wird ein integraler Bestandteil der Fassadengestaltung und eignet sich für repräsentative Privat- oder Gewerbebauten. Die Verglasung ist in den Farben Grau und Braun erhältlich, mit einer interessanten Kombination von Spiegelung und Durchsicht entsteht dabei ein spannender Effekt.

ASR 40
Sectional Door / Sectionaltor

Hörmann KG VKG, Steinhagen,
Germany / Deutschland
In-house design / Werksdesign:
Martin J. Hörmann, Ken Maher
www.hoermann.com

The ASR 40 sectional door was developed for commercial buildings with elaborate architecture. At first sight the door is not recognised as such, which is an interesting design aspect offering architects and designers new options. A frame structure with very slim profiles of 65 mm is in the focus. Vertically and horizontally they feature the same width giving them an elegant appearance. The transitions of the single door slats are invisible so that this industrial door seems to be one sole facade element. It seamlessly integrates into facades with large-scale glazing. Its functional design, moreover, meets high standards with regard to robustness, longevity and heat insulation.

Das Sectionaltor ASR 40 wurde für architektonisch anspruchsvolle gewerbliche Bauten entwickelt. Ein interessanter Aspekt seiner Gestaltung ist, dass es zunächst nicht als Tor erkennbar ist und sich der Architektur und Planung dadurch neue Möglichkeiten bieten. Im Mittelpunkt steht eine Rahmenkonstruktion, bei der die Profile mit 65 mm sehr schmal sind. Sie sind vertikal wie horizontal gleich breit gestaltet, wodurch eine elegante Anmutung entsteht. Die Übergänge der einzelnen Torlamellen sind unsichtbar, weshalb dieses Industrietor wie ein einziges Fassadenelement wirkt und sich nahtlos in großflächig verglaste Fassaden integrieren lässt. In seiner funktionalen Gestaltung erfüllt es zudem hohe Anforderungen hinsichtlich Robustheit, Langlebigkeit und Wärmedämmung.

MOD. 07_S
Handle / Griff

Heyerdesign GmbH & Co. KG,
Frankenberg / Eder,
Germany / Deutschland
In-house design / Werksdesign
www.heyerdesign.de

The door handle is made of solid stainless steel and nestles comfortably and soft to the touch in the gripping hand. With its puristic and timeless appearance it pleasingly complements contemporary architecture. All stainless steel elements are rotated and milled. The fitting is also available in different rosette forms or as a window handle.

Der Türgriff besteht aus massivem Edelstahl und schmiegt sich haptisch angenehm in die Hand des Greifenden. Mit seiner puristischen und zeitlosen Form ergänzt er sehr gut zeitgenössische Architektur. Sämtliche Edelstahlelemente werden bei der Herstellung gefräst und gedreht. Der Beschlag ist auch mit anderen Rosettenformen und als Fensterolive lieferbar.

Pado Door Pullers / Türzieher

Pado, Cambé (Paraná), Brazil / Brasilien
Design: BMW Group DesignworksUSA,
Newbury Park, USA
www.pado.com.br
www.designworksusa.com

These elegantly designed door pullers are targeted at premium and contemporary architectural applications. In the range of five door pullers, each shows its own distinctive architectural character, yet sharing a strong family feel. A strong use of contrasting metal finishes; contrasting texture and grain with bright polished surfaces creates a visual depth that reinforces the concept of solidity and geometric form.

Diese elegant gestalteten Türzieher sind für den hochwertigen und modernen Einsatz in der Architektur gedacht. In dieser Serie von fünf Türziehern zeigt jeder seinen eigenen unverwechselbaren architektonischen Stil, wobei alle etwas Verbindendes haben. Der intensive Einsatz ganz unterschiedlicher Metallausführungen und kontrastreicher Stoffe sowie von Texturen mit hell polierten Oberflächen erzeugt eine optische Tiefe, die das Konzept von Solidität und geometrischen Formen unterstreicht.

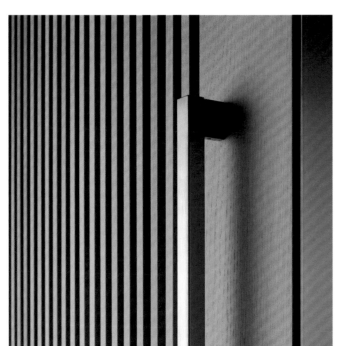

IP-Door
Front Door / Eingangstür

IP-Company GmbH, Visbek,
Germany / Deutschland
Design: CP-Architektur (Christian Prasser), Vienna, Austria / Wien, Österreich
www.schmidt-visbek.de
www.cp-architektur.com

IP-Door is a wooden front door system that has been conceptualised as a module for individualised architecture. It enables planners to integrate a door which is consistent with their concepts by using different wooden surfaces, fittings, and accessories. The main feature is the flush-fitting design of the doors – from door panels with smoothly embedded lateral glazing to the door fittings. The system offers the installation version ip-55 with a classic doorframe and the model ip-0 with a frameless doorframe.

IP-Door ist ein Holzhaustüren-System, das sich als Baustein für eine individuelle Architektur versteht. Es ermöglicht dem Planenden, durch unterschiedliche Holzoberflächen, Beschläge und Zubehör eine Tür schlüssig in sein Konzept zu integrieren. Übergeordnetes Gestaltungsmerkmal ist die durchgängige Flächenbündigkeit der Tür vom Türblatt über die Anbindung an die Seitenverglasung bis hin zu den Beschlägen. Das System bietet die Einbauvariante ip-55 mit einem klassischen Türstock sowie die Variante ip-0 mit rahmenlosem Türstock.

Space 35
Front Door / Haustür

KeraTür GmbH & Co. KG, Raesfeld,
Germany / Deutschland
In-house design / Werksdesign:
Werner Kemming
www.keratuer.de

The DoorFace system facilitates the
innovative integration of front entryways
into the architecture of a building. It is suited
for both the new construction sector and
old-building refurbishment. With this system,
frontally attached facade elements generally
conceal the classic doorframe construction
of the building's front door. Thus, the door
entrance becomes an inseparable part of
the facade itself and stands out impressively
against traditional front doors and windows.
Almost any material can be used for this
thermally separated system. The overall
construction achieves very good insulation
values (UD as of 0.45 W/m^{2}K) and thus lies
far below the requirements for low-energy
houses. The basic material shown here is
concrete, which – due to its minimalist style
– is becoming more and more significant for
modern-day architecture

Das System DoorFace ermöglicht eine
integrative Einbindung von Hauseingän-
gen in die Gebäudearchitektur, sowohl im
Neubausektor als auch in der Altbausanie-
rung. Vorgesetzte Fassadenelemente ver-
decken bei diesem System grundsätzlich
die klassische Blendrahmenkonstruktion
der Haustür. Dadurch wird der Hausein-
gang zum untrennbaren Bestandteil der
Fassade selbst und er hebt sich eindrucksvoll von herkömmlichen Haustüren ab. In
diesem thermisch getrennten System können nahezu alle Werkstoffe zum Einsatz
kommen. Die Gesamtkonstruktion erzielt
sehr gute Wärmedämmwerte (UD ab 0,45
W/m^{2}K) und bleibt damit weit unter den
Passivhaus-Anforderungen. Der hier
gezeigte Werkstoff Beton gewinnt durch
seine puristische Formensprache in der
modernen Architektur eine immer größere
Bedeutung.

Blow
Door/Tür

Albed Delmonte S.r.l., Nova Milanese,
Italy/Italien
Design: Karim Rashid, New York, USA
www.albed.it
www.karimrashid.com

Blow follows the idea of eliminating the presence of a handle by making a door become a straightforward transition point leading from one space to another. These doors differ from the traditional concept and thus are focused on the future. Blow is distinctive for its interesting handle design: the concept is of semi-elliptical decoration placed vertically on one side of the door. This system of opening/closing is rounded in the central part and thin at the ends, to interrupt the linear presence of the panel shaping in the form of a wave.

Blow orientiert sich an der Idee, den Türgriff überflüssig zu machen, indem eine Tür als geradliniger Übergang verstanden wird, der von einem Raum in den anderen führt. Diese Türen heben sich von dem traditionellen Konzept ab und richten den Blick auf die Zukunft. Blow zeichnet sich durch sein interessantes Türgriffkonzept aus: Der Entwurf beruht auf einer halbelliptischen Verzierung, die in vertikaler Position an einer der Türseiten angebracht wurde. Dieses System zum Öffnen und Schließen ist im Mittelteil abgerundet und wird zu den Enden hin schlanker, um so die lineare Form der Türfüllung in Form einer Welle zu unterbrechen.

Ring
Door/Tür

Albed Delmonte S.r.l., Nova Milanese,
Italy/Italien
Design: Karim Rashid, New York, USA
www.albed.it
www.karimrashid.com

Karim Rashid said the Albed collection arose from the "idea of eliminating the presence of a handle by making the door become a straightforward transition point leading from one space to another. These doors differ from the traditional concept and thus are focused on the future." Ring is intended to function without a doorframe and the entire concept is thus very original. Thanks to the absence of a handle, which has been made integral within the door by an ingenious opening system, the door appears to be characterised by lines that are pure and soft. Where usually one sees the handle there is a circular hole inside which is a metal ring: when pulled, this enables one to close/open the door.

Karim Rashid sagt, der Ausgangspunkt für die Albed-Kollektion sei die „Idee gewesen, ohne Tür auszukommen und die Tür zu einem direkten Übergangsmedium von einem Raum zum nächsten zu machen. Diese Türen unterscheiden sich vom herkömmlichen Konzept und weisen somit in die Zukunft." Ring beruht auf einer originellen Idee: Diese Tür soll ohne Türrahmen funktionieren. Da es keinen richtigen Türgriff gibt, sondern ein ins Innere der Tür verlegtes Öffnungssystem, zeichnet sich die Tür durch eine klare und weiche Linienführung aus. Dort, wo gewöhnlich ein Türgriff ist, ist jetzt ein rundes Loch zu sehen, in dessen Innern sich ein Metallring befindet. Wird er gezogen, öffnet oder schließt sich die Tür.

Mellon Town Residential Building
Bamboo Lobby Interior Design

Gemdale Shenzhen Company,
Shenzhen, China
Design: One Plus Partnership Limited
(Ajax Ling Kit Law, Virginia Lung),
Hong Kong
www.onepluspartnership.com

Chinese culture provides the framework
for this lobby in a residential building in
Shenzhen. Bamboo is the plant that is
symbolically representative for Chinese
culture and was therefore chosen as the
inspirational material for this project. The
bamboo lobby (tower 11) has been inspired
by the linear form of the bamboo plant
and is imbued with a striking green colour.
The circular bamboo stalks have been
transformed to create a special lighting
system as well as mailboxes.

Die chinesische Kultur bildet den Rahmen
dieser Eingangshalle eines Wohnhauses in
Shenzhen. Bambus ist die Pflanze, die als
Symbol für chinesische Kultur steht. Deshalb wurde es als Ausgangsmaterial für
dieses Projekt gewählt. Die Bambus-Ein-
gangshalle (Turm 11) orientiert sich an der
linearen Form der Bambuspflanze und ist
in auffälligem Grün gestaltet. Der runden
Bambusstäbe wurden zu einer besonderen
Beleuchtungsanlage und zu Briefkästen
umgeformt.

ArtMe – individual design for the building envelope

Trimo, d.d., Trebnje,
Slovenia / Slowenien
In-house design / Werksdesign:
Dr. Viktor Zaletelj
Design: Gorenje Design Studio, d.o.o.
(David Cugelj, Saša Hribernik, Rok
Jenko), Velenje, Slovenia / Slowenien
Technology development / Technolo-
gische Entwicklung: University of
Ljubljana, Faculty of Mechanical
Engineering (Dr. Aleš Petek), Ljubljana,
Slovenia / Slowenien
www.trimo.si
www.gorenjedesignstudio.com
www.fs.uni-lj.si

ArtMe is a unique high-tech solution that provides an answer to modern trends of individuality and creative design. It offers a fully functional facade envelope solution, enhanced by custom designs, allowing literally unlimited shapes, patterns and visual effects to be reproduced for individual expression on facade envelope design. The power of ArtMe comes from a 3D continuously formed steel sheet surface, where the observed effect changes for each little alteration of the environment. The main innovation of this surface lies in the development of a forming technology resulting in a precoated steel sheet surface of facade elements without any rear support. No additional material is needed, leaving the surface clean and smooth to the touch. Additional benefit comes when taking into account the cleaning and self-cleaning properties of the homogeneous surface, as well as the ergonomics of handling. ArtMe is not just a facade, it is about 100 per cent individual expression on a facade envelope; it creates a story, highly sensitive to the emotions.

ArtMe ist eine einzigartige Hightech-Lösung, die eine Antwort auf moderne Bestrebungen nach Individualität und kreativen Formen gibt. Sie bietet eine Gesamtlösung für die vollfunktionale Ummantelung einer Fassade, die durch kundenindividuelles Design noch betont wird. Sie erlaubt es, geradezu zahllose Formen, Muster und optische Effekte zu entwerfen, die bei der Gestaltung einer Fassadenummantelung zu einem ganz individuellen und ausdrucksvollen Ergebnis führen. Die besondere Stärke von ArtMe beruht auf einer Strangguss-Stahlblechoberfläche, auf der sich der beobachtete Effekt bei jeder kleinen Änderung in der Umgebung ebenfalls ändert. Die Hauptneuerung dieser Oberfläche besteht in der Entwicklung eines Formgebungsverfahrens, bei dem vorbeschichtete Stahlblechoberflächen von Fassadenelementen ohne Rückenstütze hergestellt werden. Es wird kein zusätzliches Material benötigt, sodass sich die Oberfläche sauber und glatt anfühlt. Zusätzlicher Nutzen wird deutlich, wenn die Reinigungs- und Selbstreinigungseigenschaften der gleichförmigen Oberfläche und die ergonomische Handhabung mit berücksichtigt werden. ArtMe ist nicht einfach eine Fassade, sie ist ganz und gar individueller Ausdruck auf einer Fassadenummantelung. Sie erfindet eine Geschichte, die auf intensive Weise die Gefühle anspricht.

Agrob Buchtal, Schwarzenfeld,
Germany / Deutschland
In-house design / Werksdesign:
Adelheid Bannach, Elio Majdpour,
Elke Habermann
www.agrob-buchtal.de

The design of this tile concept for walls and
floors is inspired by the rhythm of natural
slate structures. The ceramic tiles interpret
motion in the surface in an imaginative way.
Based on the delicate diagonal structures
of the glazed wall tile dynamics is further
enhanced by two other decorative elements.
The model Twig shows the movement of
natural branches reduced to their basic
geometry. The version Slope (photo) in
contrast is based on the interplay of different
textures. Form and material are the core
values that constitute the basis of these
decorative versions. "Discreet appeals"
combine to form a visually and haptically
expressive design.

Die Gestaltung dieses Fliesenkonzeptes für
Wand und Boden ist inspiriert vom Rhyth-
mus natürlicher Schieferstrukturen. Das
Thema der Bewegung in der Fläche wurde
dabei phantasievoll keramisch umgesetzt.
Ausgehend von zarten Schrägstrukturen
der glasierten Wandfliese wird die Dynamik zusätzlich mit zwei Dekorelementen
weiter ausgeführt. Das Modell Twig zeigt
die Bewegung natürlicher Äste, die auf
ihre Grundgeometrie reduziert sind, die
Ausführung Slope (Bild) basiert hingegen
auf dem Wechselspiel unterschiedlicher
Texturen. Die Kernwerte Form und Material bilden die Grundlage der Dekorvari-
anten und „leise Reize" verbinden sich zu
einer visuell und haptisch ausdrucksvollen
Formensprache.

Lavestido velvetYstone
Porcelain Stoneware Range /
Feinsteinzeugserie

V&B Fliesen GmbH, Merzig,
Germany / Deutschland
In-house design / Werksdesign:
Stephan Gerhart
www.villeroy-boch.com

The design of this porcelain stoneware range for walls and floors was inspired by nature. Based on an innovative technology the relief surface offers an independent style. The new finishing method, velvetYstone, gives the polished surfaces a haptically soft character, even in the deeper parts of the relief. The method involves an interplay between the matt and glossy surfaces and produces an optical depth effect.

Die Gestaltung dieser Feinsteinzeugserie für Wand und Boden wurde von der Natur inspiriert. Auf der Grundlage einer innovativen Technologie entstand eine in ihrer Formensprache eigenständige reliefierte Oberfläche. Mittels des neuen Veredelungsverfahrens, velvetYstone, erhalten die anpolierten Oberflächen, selbst in der Reliefvertiefung, einen fühlbar samtweichen Charakter. Das Verfahren bewirkt zudem ein Wechselspiel der matten und glänzenden Oberflächen, wodurch eine optische Tiefenwirkung entsteht.

La Diva
Décor Tiles / Dekorfliesen

V&B Fliesen GmbH, Merzig,
Germany / Deutschland
In-house design / Werksdesign:
Claudia Becker
www.villeroy-boch.com

La Diva is a room concept citing craftsmanship from various countries and eras and uniting them in one style. The décors and borders feature reliefs in several designs. Pure manufacturing processes and industrial fabrication are combined to form an independent type of production. This innovative manufacturing process makes every tile unique. Plasticity is created by a relief, which is refined by gold hues in order to make it look "used".

La Diva ist ein Raumkonzept, das Handwerkskünste aus verschiedenen Ländern und Epochen zitiert und in einer Formensprache vereint. Die Dekore und Bordüren tragen Reliefs in mehreren Dessins. Zur Herstellung werden reine Manufakturabläufe und industrielle Fertigung zu einer eigenständigen Produktionsart kombiniert. Dieser innovative Herstellungsprozess lässt jede der Fliesen zu einem Unikat werden. Plastizität wird durch ein Relief erzeugt, das mit Goldtönen in einer „used" wirkenden Oberfläche veredelt wird.

La Diva
Mosaic and Floor / Mosaik und Boden

V&B Fliesen GmbH, Merzig,
Germany / Deutschland
In-house design / Werksdesign:
Claudia Becker
www.villeroy-boch.com

The mosaic is congruent with the style of the wall tile design. It is meticulously set by hand and refined with real gold foil. In order to produce the mosaic, pure manufacturing processes and industrial fabrication are combined to one production process - an interesting aspect of the overall concept. A module of 30 x 30 cm forms the ornamental motif in Tulipe Noire and Gold. A decorated porcelain stoneware tile was developed as floor covering. The pattern of the floor tile is created by the interplay of matt and silky-matt areas that move in and out of the foreground, depending on the lighting.

Das Mosaik La Diva ist übereinstimmend mit der Formensprache der Wandfliesendessins. Es wird aufwendig von Hand gesetzt und veredelt mit echtem Blattgold. Ein interessanter Aspekt des Gesamtkonzeptes ist, dass für die Herstellung des Mosaiks reine Manufakturabläufe und industrielle Fertigung zu einem Herstellungsprozess vereint werden. Das ornamentale Motiv in Tulipe Noire und Gold ist in einem Modul von 30 x 30 cm aufgebaut. Als Bodenbelag wurde eine dekorierte Feinsteinzeugfliese entwickelt. Das Muster der Bodenfliese wird erzeugt durch den Wechsel von matten und seidenmatt glänzenden Flächen, die je nach Beleuchtung stärker oder schwächer zum Vorschein kommen.

Code
Wall Tile / Wandfliese

Calvert Plastics Ltd., Lower Hutt,
New Zealand / Neuseeland
In-house design / Werksdesign:
Jonathan Mountfort
Design: Last Paddock Design
(Natasha Perkins), Paekakariki,
New Zealand / Neuseeland
Distribution / Vertrieb:
Woven Image Ltd.
tiles@calvert-plastics.com

A three-dimensional form gives this acoustic tile a fascinating appearance. The designers decided in favour of this shape to reinforce the acoustic advantages of the carrier material in the room. This tile needs no further treatment; it can be printed and proves lightweight and durable at the same time. It has a felt-like appearance achieved through industrial needle punching. The tile is made of soft material that has been manufactured from 60 per cent recycled materials and has a pleasing, aesthetic feel and look.

Ihre dreidimensionale Form verleiht dieser Fliese eine interessante Anmutung. Die Gestaltung wählte diese Form, um die akustischen Vorteile des Trägermaterials im Raum zu verstärken. Die Fliese benötigt keine Weiterbearbeitung, sie ist bedruckbar, leichtgewichtig und langlebig. Ihr filzähnliches Aussehen erhält sie durch eine industrielle Nadelstanzung. Die Fliese besteht zu 60 Prozent aus recycelten Materialien. Sie fühlt sich angenehm an und sieht ästhetisch aus.

Vegas
Tile Collection / Fliesen-Kollektion

VitrA Tiles, Istanbul, Turkey / Türkei
In-house design / Werksdesign:
Huseyin Isler, Erden Gulkan
www.vitrakaro.com

The pulsating lights of Las Vegas seem to be reflected in the tiles of this collection. This impression is caused by an innovative metal surface. Its the three-dimensional microstructure communicates qualities like luxury and understatement. The collection offers a great choice of tiles and additionally matching decorative tiles with geometric patterns or superior damask themes. It is therefore used in private homes or in upmarket objects.

Die pulsierenden Lichter von Las Vegas scheinen sich in den Fliesen dieser Kollektion widerzuspiegeln. Diese Anmutung entsteht durch eine innovative Metalloberfläche, deren dreidimensionale Mikrostruktur die Attribute Luxus und Understatement kommuniziert. Die Kollektion bietet eine vielseitige Auswahl an Fliesen und zusätzlich passenden Dekorfliesen mit geometrischen Mustern oder edlen Damastmotiven. Sie findet deshalb Einsatz in der Privatwohnung wie auch im gehobenen Objektbereich.

Z:IN Floor
Flooring / Fußbodenbelag

LG Hausys, Design Center, Seoul, Korea
In-house design / Werksdesign:
Han Kyu Lee, Min A Lee
Design: Mendini Atelier Design Studio
(Alessandro Mendini), Milan, Italy /
Mailand, Italien
www.lghausys.com
www.ateliermendini.it

Z:IN is an organically designed flooring material whose modularity provides for interesting patterns and combinations. It differs from typical, square flooring through its versatility, thereby facilitating the opportunity to appreciate it time and again in varying constellations. The innovative technology combines both a size-reinforcing layer and a balancing layer below the durable chip layer of the homogeneous structure. This superb system promotes durability and overcomes the size-instability found in traditional homogenous flooring, thus minimising a gap in tiles caused by variations in temperature and humidity. Mendini's flooring tiles come in 36 refined colours and with five nature-symbolizing shapes. They can create over 13,000 unique spaces adaptable to the specific preferences of customers via the reconfiguration of the tiles like pieces of a jigsaw puzzle.

Z:IN ist ein organisch gestalteter Fußbodenbelag, dessen Modularität interessante Muster und Kombinationen erlaubt. Durch seine Vielseitigkeit und die Möglichkeit, ihn stets aufs Neue wahrnehmen zu können, unterscheidet er sich von einem typischen quadratischen Fußboden. Die innovative Technologie dieser besonderen Struktur verbindet eine verstärkte Schicht und eine ausbalancierende Schicht, die unter der stabilen Chipschicht liegen. Diese Struktur begünstigt Dauerhaftigkeit und beseitigt Unausgewogenheiten, wie sie bei herkömmlichen Bodenbelägen zu finden sind. So werden Spalten zwischen den Fliesen, die durch Temperaturschwankungen und Feuchtigkeit entstehen können, auf ein Minimum reduziert. Mendinis Bodenfliesen sind erhältlich in 36 Farben und fünf, die Natur symbolisierenden Formen. Mit den Fliesen lassen sich 13.000 unterschiedliche Formen bilden. Sie können immer wieder wie Puzzlestücke neu gruppiert und dadurch den verschiedensten Kundenwünschen angepasst werden.

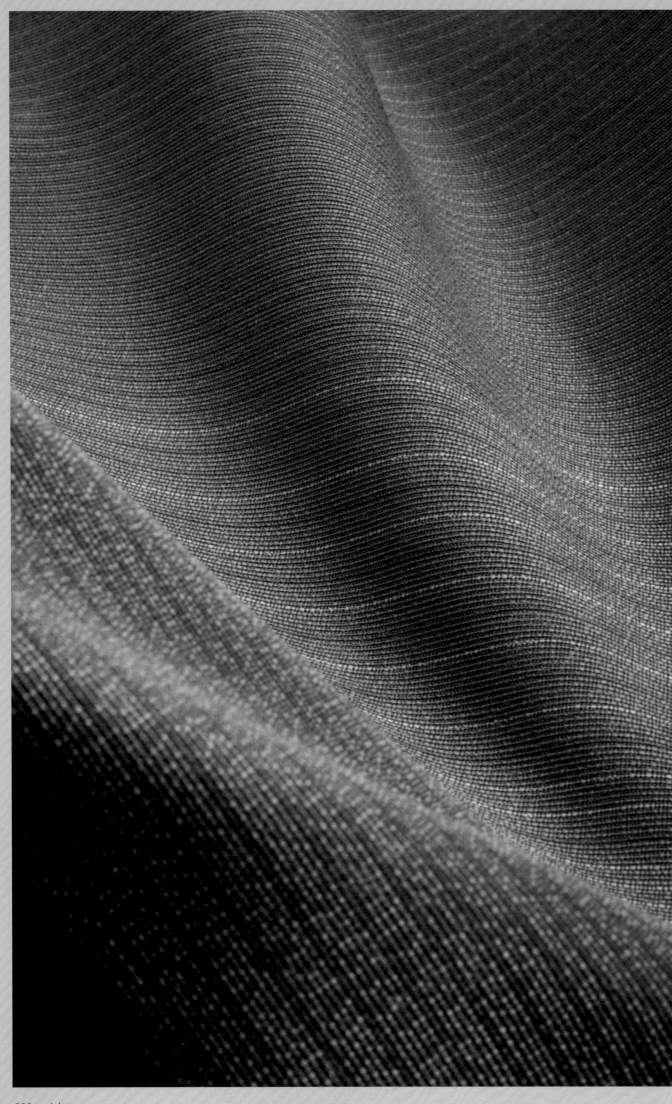

Textile Aircraft Interior Concept/ Textiles Flugzeug-Interior-Konzept

rohi Stoffe GmbH, Geretsried,
Germany/Deutschland
Anker Teppichboden Gebr. Schoeller
GmbH & Co. KG, Düren,
Germany/Deutschland
In-house design/Werksdesign
www.rohi.com
www.anker.eu

With their demands for a comfortable
and relaxing ambience, passengers of the
premium economy class are the target group
for this textile aircraft interior. The idea of
"contrast in harmony" formed the conceptual
basis for the creation of three independent
textile worlds. Although the range of textiles
is meant to illustrate the differences between
the individual cabin classes, it does so in a
restrained manner. The design dispenses with
the usual bold patterns and instead works
with a distinct, modern style that is realised
by means of subdued fabric structures and
novel interlacing techniques – aiming at
a subtle, multifaceted, and relaxing effect
on the passengers. The appearance of
the textiles changes with the perspective
of the viewers and interacts with their
perceptions: upon entering the cabin, a
harmonious overall picture is revealed, yet
when seated the passenger experiences the
interaction of individual textiles. Despite the
diversity of these textile worlds, the cabin
appears homogenous and evokes a uniform
atmosphere.

Für die Zielgruppe der Premium Economy
Class und deren Ansprüche an ein wohnliches und entspanntes Ambiente, wurde
diese textile Flugzeugausstattung gestaltet. Das Konzept „Contrast in Harmony"
besteht drei autarke Textilwelten, die die
Unterschiede der einzelnen Kabinenklas-
sen zwar deutlich machen, aber dennoch
zurückhaltend vermitteln sollen. Die
Gestaltung verzichtet auf die übliche pla-
kative Musterung und arbeitet mit einer
klaren und zeitgemäßen Formensprache,
die mit dezent anmutenden Gewebestruk-
turen und neuartigen Bindungstechniken
umgesetzt wird. Dies soll subtil, mehr-
schichtig und entspannend auf die Pas-
sagiere wirken. Das Erscheinungsbild der
Textilien verändert sich mit dem Blickwinkel des Betrachters und interagiert mit
seinen Wahrnehmungen: Beim Betreten
der Kabine ergibt sich ein harmonisches
Gesamtbild, vom Sitz aus soll der Passa-
gier jedoch individuelle, interagierende
Textilien erleben. Die Kabine erscheint
trotz der Unterschiedlichkeit in einer
einheitlichen Atmosphäre.

 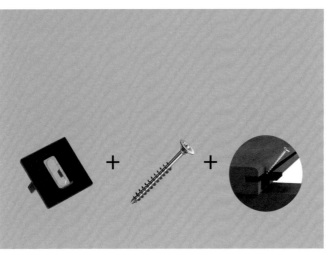 

HARDWOOD CLIP®

Archi Wood SPRL, Brussels,
Belgium / Brüssel, Belgien
In-house design / Werksdesign:
Marc Luypaert, Rob Pelc
www.hardwoodclip.com

HARDWOOD CLIP® is a simple and innovative invisible solution for installing deck boards. It is unique, because boards are screwed down to the joist. The HARDWOOD CLIP® "M" fastener with a 4-mm thick integrated spacer is designed to let wood boards both expand and contract and to guarantee automatic and even board spacing. Its simple square shape and the stainless steel insert in the moulded fastener provide exceptional resistance. The HARDWOOD CLIP® "M" fastening solution uses exclusive Spax® self-tapping screws made of stainless steel. This Spax® screw do not require pre-drilling. Its point separates wood fibres while ground serrations on the shank advance the screw with no splintering. The size of the head is designed to fit perfectly with the fastener.

HARDWOOD CLIP® ist eine einfache und innovative unsichtbare Lösung zur Befestigung von Brettern. Es ist außergewöhnlich, da die Bretter mit der Halterung verschraubt werden. Das Befestigungselement HARDWOOD CLIP® „M" mit einem 4 mm dicken integrierten Abstandshalter ist so gestaltet, dass Holzbretter sowohl größer als auch kleiner werden können und trotzdem gleichmäßige Zwischenräume bei den Brettern problemlos möglich sind. Die schlichte quadratische Form und der Einsatz aus Edelstahl sorgen für ungewöhnliche Festigkeit. Die HARDWOOD CLIP® „M"-Befestigungslösung verwendet besondere, selbstbohrende Spax®-Schrauben aus Edelstahl. Die Spax®-Schraube erfordert kein Vorbohren. Ihre Spitze trennt Holzfasern, wobei geschliffene Kerben am Schaft die Schraube splitterfrei vorantreiben. Die Kopfgröße ist so gestaltet, dass sie perfekt zum Befestigungselement passt.

Atmos
Wall Luminaires / Wandleuchten

Brick in the Wall NV, Waregem,
Belgium / Belgien
Design: Carl Devolder, Roeselare,
Belgium / Belgien
www.brickinthewall.eu

Atmos reveals itself by emitting a light beam out of the wall thus cutting through the architecture. The seamless plaster fitting can be installed as a wall-washer with the light beam at the top or the bottom. The creation of gently undulating waveforms gives the architect freedom on a high level. A specially designed printed circuit board for the new generation of the "Rebel" LED (Lumileds) with integrated driver allows easy installation. The use of coloured LEDs allows architects to personalise their project. Atmos can be directly installed on a solid wall or in gypsum by means of an optional plaster kit. For this luminaire, Brick in the Wall developed its own snow-white plaster Calcyt, which is an environmentally degradable product.

Atmos gibt sich zu erkennen, indem es einen Lichtstrahl quasi aus der Wand schickt, der die Architektur durchschneidet. Das nahtlose Gipsgehäuse kann als Wandfluter mit oben oder unten angebrachtem Lichtstrahl eingebaut werden. Es erzeugt sanft wogende Wellenformationen, die dem Architekten große Freiheit lassen. Mit einem besonders gestalteten gedruckten Schaltplan für die neue Generation von „Rebel"-LEDs (Lumileds) mit integriertem Treiber ist die Installation einfach. Durch den Einsatz farbiger LEDs kann der Architekt sein Projekt individuell gestalten. Atmos kann direkt an einer festen Wand angebracht werden oder in Gips mit Hilfe eines möglichen Gipseinbausatzes. Für diese Leuchte entwickelte Brick in the Wall seinen eigenen schneeweißen Calcyt-Gips, der umweltfreundlich abbaubar ist.

Prizeotel Hotel

Prizeotel, Bremen,
Germany / Deutschland
Design: Karim Rashid, New York, USA
www.prizeotel.com
www.karimrashid.com

The Prizeotel is a project by the designer Karim Rashid in "Designocrasy". It is an expression of elaborate design, which not only addresses the elite but is affordable for everyone. For the designer this concept had to be smart and economical and at the same time accommodating and inspiring. Prizeotel is a pleasurable experience, for which the consumer has to pay little. It offers travellers a special experience and is ground breaking for the budget hotel market. "Today, design must prove its worth. In an inhumanely built environment it is supposed to offer us more enjoyment, more humane and more qualitative and aesthetic conditions. We have to advance by means of design. It has

to improve and embellish our society. I have therefore tried, on a small scale, to create a spirit that makes it pleasant for people to stay at a budget hotel," says Karim Rashid with a view to this hotel.

Das Prizeotel ist ein Projekt des Designers Karim Rashid in „Designocrasy". Es ist Ausdruck eines ausgereiften Designs, das sich nicht nur an die Eliten wendet, sondern für alle gedacht ist. Für den Designer sollte das Konzept pfiffig und wirtschaftlich sein, gefällig und gleichzeitig anregend. Prizeotel ist eine vergnügliche Erfahrung, für die der Verbraucher wenig zahlt. Es bietet Reisenden ein spezielles

Erlebnis und ist wegweisend im Bereich der günstigen Hotels. „Heutzutage muss Design seinen Wert beweisen. Es soll uns in einer unmenschlich gebauten Umwelt mehr Vergnügen, mehr menschliche, qualitative und ästhetische Bedingungen bieten. Design muss uns weiterentwickeln und für eine Verschönerung und Verbesserung in der Gesellschaft sorgen. So habe ich in einem kleinen Rahmen versucht, einen Geist zu schaffen, der den Menschen das Leben in einem preisgünstigen Hotel angenehm gestaltet", sagt Karim Rashid mit Blick auf dieses Hotel.

**Enjoy the Variety / Leben sie Vielfalt
Trade Fair Stand / Messestand**

D. Lechner GmbH, Rothenburg ob der
Tauber, Germany / Deutschland
Design: Spatial Design, Munich,
Germany / München, Deutschland
Production / Produktion: Image
Production GmbH, Erkelenz,
Germany / Deutschland
www.lechner-ag.de
www.spatialdesign.de
www.image-construction.com

Following the slogan "Enjoy the Variety"
this trade fair stand transforms a formerly
abstract brand communication into three
easy-to-understand materials: wood,
stone and glass. By the imaginative and
associative realisation of a ship and a
stack of wooden boards, the particular
performance and competence of the
company had to be visualised. Like a huge
ship hull the stand rises up from the floor,
so to speak, and towers up to three levels,
which in a dramaturgical course end in the
glass arrangement at the top. The exhibits
are staged on artistic walls composed of
collages, which were directly printed on
glass. They visualise a shift of content from
the product to the application and to "human
being and life".

Mit dem Claim „Leben Sie Vielfalt" wurde mit diesem Messestand eine vormals
abstrakte Markenkommunikation in die
drei leicht verständlichen Werkstoffbe-
reiche Holz, Stein und Glas gegliedert. In
einer bildhaft-assoziativen Umsetzung
eines Schiffs sowie eines Plattenstapels
sollte dabei die besondere Leistungsfähigkeit und Kompetenz des Unternehmens
visualisiert werden. Wie ein riesiger
Schiffsrumpf wuchs der Stand gleichsam
aus dem Boden heraus und türmte sich
zu drei Ebenen auf, die in einem drama-
turgischen Parcours zur Spitze mit der
Glaskollektion führten. Die Exponate wurden durch Künstlerwände mit direkt auf
Glas gedruckten Collagen inszeniert. Diese
visualisierten einen inhaltlichen Shift
vom Produkt hin zur Anwendung und zu
„Mensch und Leben".

voestalpine Stahlwelt
Brand Museum / Markenmuseum

voestalpine AG, Linz,
Austria / Österreich
Design: KMS TEAM, Munich, Germany /
München, Deutschland; jangled nerves,
Stuttgart, Germany / Deutschland
www.voestalpine.com
www.kms-team.com

In order to familiarise visitors of the voestalpine Stahlwelt brand museum with the voestalpine steel group and the material of steel itself, a didactic concept involving exploration and knowledge has been realised by means of multimedia exhibition elements. The exhibition dramaturgy of the world of steel begins with the experience of steel and leads to information on processing, products, and the company. The adventure takes place in an abstracted "crucible", in which 80 chrome-plated steel spheres with a diameter of up to 2.50 metres are arranged in accordance with the molecular structure of iron. They are surrounded by a 700-sqm LED case with alternating light and colour effects. In an adjacent tower, knowledge is imparted as a vertical conveyor belt transports steel exhibits that illustrate the value creation chain of the material.

Um dem Besucher des Markenmuseums voestalpine Stahlwelt den Stahlkonzern voestalpine und auch den Werkstoff Stahl näherzubringen, wird hier ein didaktisches Konzept aus Erlebnis und Wissen mittels multimedialer Ausstellungselemente umgesetzt. Die Ausstellungsdramaturgie der Stahlwelt führt vom Erlebnis Stahl zum Wissen über Verarbeitung, Produkte und Konzern. Das Erlebnis findet in einem abstrahierten „Tiegel" statt, in dem 80 verchromte Stahlkugeln mit einem Durchmesser von bis zu 2,50 Meter entsprechend der Molekularstruktur von Eisen angeordnet und von einer 700 qm großen LED-Hülle mit wechselnden Licht- und Farbeffekten umgeben sind. In einem angegliederten „Turm" wird Wissen vermittelt, indem ein vertikales Förderband Stahlexponate transportiert, die die Wertschöpfungskette des Materials veranschaulichen.

Canyon.Home Showroom

Canyon Bicycles GmbH, Koblenz,
Germany / Deutschland
Design: KMS TEAM, Munich,
Germany / München, Deutschland
www.canyon.com
www.kms-team.com

The task involved creating an appealing brand home for the local seat of a bicycle manufacturer specialised in Internet sales – resulting in a base that communicates the philosophy of the company. Canyon.Home is a combination of company headquarters, development centre, production site, repair shop, logistics centre, and flagship store – a definition of the site, which was also to be reflected in its design. The basic idea for the conceptual design therefore formed a spatial interpretation of the Canyon appearance. The cursive dynamics of the brand's signature style became the formal principle of the layout, which is structured by single, monolithic elements. As a result, Canyon is presented in a stylised way, with both formal and semantic reference to the brand.

Für einen auf Internetvertrieb spezialisierten Fahrradhersteller sollte eine attraktive Markenheimat vor Ort entstehen, die die Philosophie des Unternehmens kommuniziert. Canyon.Home ist dabei eine Kombination aus Unternehmenszentrale, Entwicklungszentrum, Produktionsstandort, Reparaturwerkstatt, Auslieferungszentrum und Flagship-Store – eine Definition des Ortes, die sich auch in der Gestaltung widerspiegelt. Die Grundidee für die Konzeption des Showrooms bildete deshalb eine räumliche Interpretation des Canyon-Erscheinungsbildes. Die kursive Dynamik des Namenszugs wurde zum Formprinzip des durch einzelne monolithische Elemente strukturierten Raums. Daraus ergibt sich ein stilisiert dargestellter Canyon, der sowohl formal als auch semantisch auf die Marke verweist.

T-Gallery
Exhibition Room / Ausstellungsraum

Deutsche Telekom AG, Bonn,
Germany / Deutschland
In-house design / Werksdesign:
Deutsche Telekom Product Design
www.telekom.de

The T-Gallery is Deutsche Telekom's central "future forum", where the visions of the digital life of tomorrow can be experienced today. As a future forum, T-Gallery continually collaborates with international experts from all company departments, to design and describe the world of tomorrow together with external partners and specialists. The core team keeps a permanent eye on the latest trends and developments, and uses this information to create the vision of the future. In turn, the open, modular platform of the T-Gallery realises these visions as early-stage prototypes, where guests, partners, experts and customers can experience them hands-on. The concepts and prototypes are displayed in a circular room with a total area of 1,600 sqm (approx. 17,200 sqft). The natural link between digital contents and the analogue world was purposely integrated in the architecture and is reflected in the most minor details. The interior and furniture design adopt formal elements of the product design, helping intensify customers feeling of simplicity in future product experience.

Die T-Gallery ist das zentrale Zukunftsforum der Deutschen Telekom, in dem die Visionen des digitalen Lebens von morgen schon heute erlebbar sind. Einfachheit und Freude bei der Nutzung von Produkten und Services, das Nutzerlebnis und das Zusammenwachsen von Technologien, Endgeräten und Medien nehmen in der T-Gallery Gestalt an. Als Zukunftsforum arbeitet die T-Gallery kontinuierlich mit internationalen Experten aus allen Unternehmensbereichen zusammen, die gemeinsam mit externen Partnern und Spezialisten die Welt von morgen konzipieren und gestalten. Dargestellt werden die Konzepte und Prototypen in einem kreisförmigen Raum auf insgesamt 1.600 qm. Die natürliche Verbindung und Einfachheit der digitalen Inhalte mit der analogen Welt wurde konsequent in der Architektur umgesetzt und findet sich in den kleinsten Details wieder. Das Interior und Furniture Design nimmt formale Elemente des Product Designs auf und führt so zu einer stringenten Darstellung des zukünftigen Produkterlebnisses.

Zeiss Tower
Multimedia Brand Ambassador /
Multimedialer Markenbotschafter

Carl Zeiss Vision International GmbH,
Aalen
Trend Factory GmbH, Rottweil,
Germany / Deutschland
Design: Labor Weltenbau
(Elmar Gauggel), Stuttgart,
Germany / Deutschland
www.vision.zeiss.com
www.trendfactory.com
www.labor-weltenbau.de

As the key component of a shop system, this tower is meant to put customers in the mood for experiencing consultation. With a distinct and clearly laid-out structure, it offers multimedia recordings that can be enjoyed at the integrated monitor, where the client is given the opportunity to individually regulate the sound via loudspeakers or earphones, and on the Zeiss Cinemizer. The Zeiss Book to be leisurely paged through is another informational medium. So as to cater for the varying spatial situations within the shops, the key components of the tower have been designed in three versions. The tower is available as a stand-alone column, a fully functional and compact desktop variant, or as a counter solution. Each model consists of a full-value multimedia unit featuring appropriate marketing material and a storage compartment for additional documents.

In seiner Funktion als Kernelement eines Shop-Systems soll dieser Tower die Kunden auf das Beratungserlebnis einstimmen. In einer klaren und übersichtlichen Strukturierung bietet er Multimedia-Einspielungen am Monitor – der Ton kann wahlweise über Lautsprecher oder Kopfhörer empfangen werden – und über den mitgelieferten Zeiss Cinemizer. Ein weiteres Informationsmedium ist das Zeiss-Buch, welches hier in Ruhe durchgeblättert werden kann. Um den unterschiedlichen räumlichen Situationen der Shops zu entsprechen, wurden die Kernelemente des Towers in drei Versionen konzipiert. Der Tower ist verfügbar als freistehende Säule, als eine kompakt gestaltete Tisch- oder Thekenvariante sowie als funktionaler Couchtisch. Jede dieser Versionen stellt eine vollwertige Multimedia-Einheit dar, sie wird mit entsprechendem Marketing-Material ausgestattet und verfügt über Stauraum für weitere Unterlagen.

Maxoptical Mazara del Vallo
Centro di Eccellenza Zeiss
Interior Shop Design/
Innenarchitektur

Design: Labor Weltenbau
(Elmar Gauggel), Stuttgart,
Germany/Deutschland
www.maxoptical.it
www.vision.zeiss.com
www.trendfactory.com
www.labor-weltenbau.de

The interior design developed for an optician in Sicily had the objective of creating a completely new shopping experience. At impressively designed locations distinctly structured sales and lounge areas, high-tech measurement tools, and an eye spa invite to make an extravagant purchase of glasses. An oversized picture of Sophia Loren is the visual core element. She stands in a marble-framed archway and follows the visitor with her fascinating eyes throughout the whole sales area – as an emblem of Italy, she breathes atmosphere and spirit into the shop. The historic architecture of the sales room has been once again uncovered, and the colour white gives it a modern and timeless look. The shape of the furniture discreetly flows around the architectural elements of the rooms: the interior design immerses the space in a modern yet timeless atmosphere, which becomes the antagonist of historic vaulted ceilings, stucco, and capitals.

Das Ziel des Interior Designs war es, für einen Optiker in Sizilien ein völlig neues Kauferlebnis zu schaffen. In imposant gestalteten Räumlichkeiten laden klar strukturierte Verkaufsflächen, Lounge-bereiche, hochtechnische Vermessungs-instrumente und ein Augenspa zum luxuriösen Brillenkauf ein. Zentrales visuelles Element ist eine überlebensgroße Darstellung von Sophia Loren. Sie steht in einem mit Marmor umrahmten Torbo-gen und verfolgt den Betrachter mit ihren faszinierenden Augen über die gesamte Verkaufsfläche hinweg. Als Sinnbild Italiens verleiht sie dem Ladengeschäft Temperament. Die historische Architektur des Verkaufsraumes wurde wieder frei-gelegt und erhielt, durch die Farbe Weiß, eine moderne und zeitlose Anmutung. Die historische Architektur tauch die Räume in eine moderne und dennoch zeitlose Atmosphäre, die zum Gegenspieler von historischen Gewölbedecken, Stuck und Kapitellen wird.

PLATOON KUNSTHALLE
Temporary Architecture /
Temporäre Architektur

PLATOON KUNSTHALLE,
Seoul, Korea
In-house design / Werksdesign:
Christoph Frank, Tom Bueschemann
Design: GRAFT architects + Baik Jiwon
www.platoon.org
www.graftlab.com

PLATOON is an international communication organisation started out from Berlin in 2000 and is also based in Seoul since 2007. It uses the power of creative subcultures to move messages. Further, PLATOON has a network of almost 4,000 creatives from all around the world, which it taps on for various projects. One of its key projects is PLATOON KUNSTHALLE, an artistic and creative venue designed for mixed uses and constructed from stacked containers, set up in Seoul as a space for subculture in Asia. Its programmatic orientation towards cultural movements creates a dynamic space where new ideas are born and presented.

PLATOON ist eine internationale Kommunikationsorganisation, die 2000 in Berlin gegründet wurde und seit 2007 auch in Seoul einen Sitz in Asien hat. In ihren Projekten werden mit der Kraft kreativer subkultureller Konzepte Botschaften vermittelt. Zudem zählt das weltweite Netzwerk von Kreativen mit nahezu 4.000 Mitgliedern, die in verschiedenen Kooperationen ihr Know-how einsetzen, zu den wichtigsten Merkmalen der Organisation. Die PLATOON KUNSTHALLE ist eines der Schlüsselprojekte von PLATOON, ein kreativer Treffpunkt in Seoul für subkulturelle Strömungen in Asien, der für die unterschiedlichsten Nutzungen konzipiert wurde. Die innovative Architektur besteht ausschließlich aus gestapelten Cargo-Containern. Die programmatische Ausrichtung mit subkulturellen Inhalten kreiert einen dynamischen Ort, an dem neue Ideen geboren und präsentiert werden.

Nike Sportswear Store
Shop/Interior Design

Nike, Hilversum, NL
Design: Day Creative Business Partners
B.V. (Gesina Roters, Louk de Sévaux,
Mette Hoekstra), Amsterdam, NL
www.nike.com
www.day.nu

In order to present a new collection of Nike Sportswear, a collection, which is based on timeless sports apparel and shoes, this pilot flagship store in the city of Paris should clearly communicate the brands image. The brief required the target to include sportswear retail designs from the US as well as designs of exhibits and guerrilla stores. The store, located in an old bookstore in the Paris district Le Marais, offered the unique opportunity to mix classic Parisian beauty, wear and tear, and performance equipment. Including the ambience of the location relevant historic details and finishes of the building were combined with strong and iconic fixtures and designs. These distinctive features were integrated harmoniously in the overall concept. By delicately balancing the various original characteristics of the building with new design elements, a highly distinctive, charismatic environment was created. The French design duo Antoine + Manuel have been roped in to design the in-store graphics, which are changed out regularly so that the building gets a new shot of life every now and then.

Für die Präsentation einer neuen Nike Sportbekleidungskollektion, einer Kollektion mit zeitloser Sportbekleidung und -schuhen, sollte dieser Pilot-Flagship-Store in Paris das Markenprofil deutlich kommunizieren. Der Auftrag lautete, das Sortiment solle Sportbekleidung aus den USA sowie Design aus Ausstellungen sowie aus Guerilla Stores bieten. Der Laden, eine ehemalige Buchhandlung, liegt im Stadtteil Le Marais und offeriert eine einmalige Gelegenheit, um den klassischen Pariser Chic, Gammel-Look und Sportausrüstung miteinander zu verbinden. Unter Einbeziehung der Atmosphäre vor Ort wurden wesentliche historische Details und Gebäudebesonderheiten mit ausdrucksvollen und kulthaften Einrichtungsgegenständen kombiniert. Diese charakteristischen Aspekte wurden harmonisch in das Gesamtkonzept integriert. Durch die feinfühlige Verbindung verschiedener ursprünglicher Gebäudemerkmale mit neuen Designelementen entstand eine ganz eigene, charismatische Einkaufsumgebung. Das französische Design-Duo Antoine + Manuel wurde einbezogen, um In-Store-Grafiken zu gestalten. Diese werden in regelmäßigen Abständen ausgetauscht, sodass das Gebäude immer wieder von neuer Lebendigkeit durchdrungen wird

Bosch ConceptFrameSystem (KFS)/
Bosch KonzeptFrameSystem (KFS)
Product Display for Bosch Household
Appliances/Produktdisplay für Bosch
Haushaltsgeräte

Holzfurtner & Wöls GmbH, Bruckmühl,
Germany/Deutschland
Design: WengerWittmann GmbH
(Udo Wittmann, Stefan Knoblauch, Anja
Klose), Haar, Germany/Deutschland
www.das-schreinerhaus.de
www.wengerwittmann.de

This system is supposed to present the
appliances of a brand within a clearly defined
framework. It is flexible and adjustable so
that all appliances can be shown. Simple
change of the main bodies and fronts allows
the system to offer the option of showing
both single appliances and built-in units of
the different product ranges (refrigeration,
laundry, dish-washing and heating) in the
same framework thus providing consistent
presentation. Due to a surrounding socket
light, the display seems to float. It can
be used on all floor coverings. The clearly
defined shapes and colouring emphasise the
corporate design of the manufacturer.

Mit diesem System sollen in einem klar
definierten Rahmen die Geräte der Marke
präsentiert werden. Es ist flexibel und
anpassungsfähig gestaltet, um auf diese Weise alle Haushaltsgeräte zeigen zu
können. Durch ein unkompliziertes Wechseln der Korpusse und Fronten bietet das
System die Möglichkeit, sowohl Sologe-
räte als auch Einbaugeräte der einzelnen
Produktbereiche (Kühlen, Wäschepflege,
Spülen und Wärme) im selben Rahmen zu
zeigen, wobei ein durchgängiges Erscheinungsbild entsteht. Ein umlaufendes
Sockellicht lässt das Display, das auf allen
Bodenbelägen eingesetzt werden kann,
scheinbar schweben. Die klar definierte
Form- und Farbgebung dieses Rahmen-
systems unterstreicht das Corporate
Design des Herstellers.

Sanaa
Museum Display Case /
Museumsvitrine

Meyvaert Glass Engineering, Ghent,
Belgium / Gent, Belgien
Design: Concrete (Alexander Crolla,
Pieter Lesage), Antwerp,
Belgium / Antwerpen, Belgien
www.meyvaert.be
www.concrete.be

The modularity of the Sanaa display case offers museums and galleries a variety of different configurations to create an optimal solution for changing exhibitions. With its minimalistic elegance and high-quality finishing, it keeps the focus on the exhibit. Similar to premium museum cases, the sealed air inside is regulated by a gentle airflow and humidity absorptions packs. It can be safely transported as a flat package, and easily assembled and disassembled without the need for any tools. Sanaa, a modular display case with museum quality.

Das Baukastenprinzip der Sanaa-Vitrine bietet Museen und Galerien eine Reihe verschiedener Optionen und ermöglicht damit optimale Lösungen für wechselnde Ausstellungen. Wegen ihrer minimalistischen Eleganz und der hochwertigen Anmutung bleibt die Aufmerksamkeit auf das Ausstellungsstück gerichtet. Wie bei hochwertigen Museumsvitrinen wird bei Sanaa die eingeschlossene Luft durch eine sanfte Belüftung und den Einsatz von Trockenmittel reguliert. Als Flatpack ist sie sicher zu transportieren. Ohne Werkzeuge ist sie leicht auf- und abzubauen. Sanaa ist eine modulare Vitrine mit Museumsqualität.

Blox
Modular Furniture System /
Modulares Möbelsystem

Blox Systems, Antwerp,
Belgium / Antwerpen, Belgien
Design: Filip Van Ceulebroeck,
Alexander Crolla
www.bloxsystems.com
www.dpi.eu

This modular furniture system offers a multitude of creative and elegant solutions, which can adapt to the changing ideas of its users. Sophisticated technical options together with an individual design language define this system as a coherent tool for points of sale and exhibitions. It enables the user to spread out timely and spatially and with great ease. The multifunctional modularity of Blox allows the creation of complex architectural structures.

Dieses modulare Möbelsystem bietet eine Vielzahl kreativer und eleganter Lösungen, die sich den wechselnden Vorstellungen des Nutzers anpassen können. Durchdachte technische Möglichkeiten in Verbindung mit einer individuellen Formensprache definieren dieses System als ein stimmiges Werkzeug für Verkaufspunkte und Ausstellungen. Das System ermöglicht, sich rechtzeitig und räumlich mit einem hohen Maß an Bequemlichkeit auszubreiten. Die weitreichende Modularität von Blox erlaubt die Kreation komplizierter architektonischer Strukturen.

Presentation Leolux
IMM Cologne 2010
Trade Fair Stand / Messestand

Leolux Meubelfabriek, Venlo, NL
Design: Leolux Creative Team/Muller
van Tol (Bas van Tol), Amsterdam, NL
www.leolux.nl

With its generous dimensions of 900 sqm, this trade fair stand offers a multifaceted world of brand experience. In an abstract wood, visitors follow a winding forest path where they encounter impressive furniture presentations at various clearings. The styling additionally reinforces the colourful ambience thus created, with objects larger than life adding to the inviting impression.

Mit den großzügigen Ausmaßen von 900 qm bietet dieser Messestand eine facettenreiche Erlebniswelt der Marke. In einem abstrakt dargestellten Wald folgt der Besucher einem sich schlängelnden Waldweg und trifft an den Lichtungen auf stimmungsvolle Möbelpräsentationen. Das Styling soll das farbenfrohe Ambiente zusätzlich bekräftigen; überlebensgroße Objekte verstärken die einladende Wirkung.

Media Bus Shelter / Wartehäuschen

Hyundaicard, Seoul, Korea
Design: CA PLAN (Chae Jung Woo,
Ahn Seong Mo, Jung Seung Young, Kim
Ae Rin, Kim Yong Hak, Park Jong Ho,
Choo Ho Nam), Seoul, Korea
www.ca-plan.co.kr

This bus station is installed at Seoul Train Station Bus Transfer Center. With about 36,400 LEDs, integrated in two transparent glass panels, this public space system allows for an oversize media display. There are 12 bus shelters, which are eight metres wide and 2.5 metres high. Moving images and pictures connect the glass walls and ceilings of all bus shelters. In addition, this system can integrate location-specific information. Complex interactions between people and the infrastructure become possible by motion sensors, an urban bus information system (BIS), an infrared bus arrival sensor, and online networks.

Diese Bushaltestelle befindet sich am Seoul Train Station Bus Transfer Center. Mit etwa 36.400 LEDs, angebracht zwischen zwei transparenten Glasscheiben, ermöglicht diese Anlage für den öffentlichen Raum eine überdimensionale Medienanzeige. Es gibt zwölf Wartehäuschen, die acht Meter breit und 2,50 Meter hoch sind. Bewegte Bilder und Fotos verbinden die gläsernen Wände und Überdachungen aller Wartehäuschen. Außerdem kann dieses Mediensystem ortsbezogene Informationen aufnehmen. Durch Bewegungsmelder, ein städtisches Businformationssystem (BIS), einen Infrarotsensor für die Busankunft und Online-Netzwerke entstehen vielschichtige Interaktionen zwischen Mensch und Infrastruktur.

Tree
Bus Shelter / Fahrgastunterstand

Telekom Deutschland GmbH, Bonn,
Germany / Deutschland
Design: Barski Design GmbH,
Frankfurt / Main, Germany / Deutschland
www.telekom.de/oohm
www.barskidesign.com

By consistently implementing the leitmotif of a tree, the design of this bus shelter refers to the familiar image of an old village lime tree in public space. The bus shelter is a lightweight construction and very versatile. It mainly consists of a centre column and connecting glass panels. The centre column forms the interface between the shelter and the waiting passengers. It contains both the lighting in the roof and rear wall, as well as the passenger information system. In addition, it assumes a load-bearing function for the seating elements. The central column illuminates the shelter. Thanks to the satined glass, light shines evenly and gives the waiting passengers a comfortable feeling of security at night. With an optional intelligent light control system this surface can assume various functions: When a passenger approaches, the light shines brighter and it becomes darker again when the passenger moves away.

Die Gestaltung dieses Fahrgastunterstandes knüpft in einer konsequenten Umsetzung des Leitmotivs „Baum" an das vertraute Bild der alten Dorf-Linde im öffentlichen Raum an. In Leichtbauweise konstruiert und vielseitig variabel, besteht der Fahrgastunterstand im Wesentlichen aus einer zentralen Mittelsäule und verbindenden Glasflächen. Die Mittelsäule bildet die Schnittstelle zum wartenden Fahrgast, sie beinhaltet sowohl die Beleuchtung im Dach und in der Rückwand wie auch das Fahrgastinformationssystem, zusätzlich übernimmt sie eine tragende Funktion für Sitzelemente. Der Fahrgastunterstand wird durch die zentrale Mittelsäule ausgeleuchtet, wobei durch das satinierte Glas das Licht gleichmäßig strahlt und dem wartenden Fahrgast nachts ein sicheres und angenehmes Gefühl vermittelt. Optional kann diese Fläche durch eine intelligente Lichtsteuerung, verschiedene Funktionen übernehmen: wenn sich ein Fahrgast nähert, wird sie heller, wenn er sich entfernt wieder dunkler.

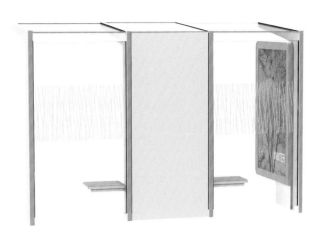

Bike-Pullway
Bicycle Ramp / Fahrradrampe

Neomerce, Incheon, Korea
In-house design / Werksdesign:
Seong Woo Jeon, Yong Rok Kim,
Jeong Sik Kim, Jeong Il Ju
www.bike-pullway.com
www.neomerce.co.kr

This bicycle ramp has been designed to solve the problems cyclists usually have when they have to overcome stairs. With the anti-skid Bike-Pullway, they are able to move their bicycle conveniently and safely along the stairs because it is slip-proof. In addition, the side rail has been rounded to prevent users from getting hurt. The dimensions of the ramp have been optimally configured so that pedestrians don't feel inconvenienced. Made of extruded aluminium that ensures solidity and durability, this ramp features a pure design language, thus differing from the conventional wood or welded stainless steel pipe.

Diese Fahrradrampe soll die Probleme lösen, mit denen sich Fahrradfahrer bei der Überwindung von Treppen konfrontiert sehen. Mit dem rutschsicheren Bike-Pullway lässt sich das Fahrrad bequem und sicher die Stufen entlang bewegen. Außerdem wurde die Seitenleiste abgerundet, damit die Nutzer sich nicht verletzen können. Die Größe der Rampe ist optimal gestaltet, sodass sich Fußgänger nicht gestört fühlen. Aus stranggepresstem Aluminium hergestellt, präsentiert sie sich in puristischer Gestaltung und unterscheidet sich dadurch von den üblichen Holzrohren oder den geschweißten Edelstahlrohren.

Bus Waiting Booth of
Ningbo South Business District
Bus Shelter / Wartehäuschen

Ningbo Yingzhou District City
Construction Investment & Development Co., Ltd., Ningbo, China
Design: Yang Design (Kim Wu,
Jamy Yang), Shanghai, China
www.nbyz.gov.cn
www.yang-design.com

The principle of this modular system for a bus shelter is divided into three units. It can be reduced or increased according to the size of the shelter. All components speak the same unostentatious design language. User-friendly details feature soft, flowing curves. Two upright benches provide for a temporary pause of the passengers and leave enough standing room for many others. Between the benches a city information center, an advertisement billboard and a bus schedule screen is integrated. Solar panels are installed on top to provide energy.

Das Baukastenprinzip dieses Wartehäuschens an einer Bushaltestelle ist in drei Einheiten unterteilt. Je nach Größe des Wartehäuschens kann das System verkleinert oder vergrößert werden. Die Elemente ähneln sich in ihrer schlichten Gestaltung. Benutzerfreundliche Details haben weiche, fließende Kurvenformen. Zwei aufrecht stehende Bänke laden die Wartenden zu einer kurzen Pause ein, lassen aber noch genügend Raum für viele Menschen, die im Stehen warten. Zwischen den Bänken befinden sich eine Tafel mit Informationen zur Stadt, eine Werbetafel und ein Busfahrplan. Als Energiequelle sind Solar-Panels auf dem Dach angebracht.

lightbox
Modular Container System/
Modulare Kleinbauten

Design: Aebi & Vincent Architekten SIA
AG, Bern, Switzerland/Schweiz
Production/Produktion: Tschannen
Metallbautechnik AG,
Ostermundigen, Switzerland/Schweiz
www.lightbox-system.ch

The lightbox is a functional and aesthetic answer to the problem of an increased use of public space by commercial and private interests. With its modular structure, the system provides containers of different sizes that are suited to the most varied purposes and convey an attractive appearance. By means of the frame profile, specially developed for this purpose, a stable, watertight box can be built with just one connecting part. Hinged and swing doors, which can be freely situated, are seamlessly integrated into this system. Later, the size and positioning of these openings may be easily adjusted according to changing needs. At night, the lightbox becomes a light sculpture discreetly shimmering in public space thanks to its translucent outer shell made of shock-resistant PET.

Die lightbox versteht sich als eine funktionale und ästhetische Antwort auf die Problematik der zunehmenden Beanspruchung des öffentlichen Raums durch private und kommerzielle Nutzungen. Das modular aufgebaute System schafft Behältnisse unterschiedlicher Größen, welche für verschiedenste Zwecke geeignet sind und dem jeweiligen Betreiber zu einem attraktiven Auftritt verhelfen sollen. Das eigens entwickelte Rahmenprofil erlaubt es, mit nur einem Verbindungsdetail eine stabile, wasserdichte Box zu errichten. Auch die frei platzierbaren Klapp- und Flügeltüren fügen sich nahtlos in dieses System ein. Die Größe und die Positionierung der Öffnungen können nachträglich sich ändernden Bedürfnissen angepasst werden. Nachts wird die lightbox dank ihrer transluzenten Außenhülle aus schlagresistentem PET zu einer dezent im öffentlichen Raum schimmernden Lichtskulptur.

Chemelot
Signage System/
Ausschilderungssystem

Chemelot, Geleen, NL
Design: VanBerlo, Eindhoven, NL
www.chemelot.com
www.vanberlo.nl

This signage system was designed for the Chemelot research campus. It sets out to offer easy-to-recognise orientation and to guide visitors comfortably to their destinations. The design maxim of "honesty" smoothly unites with the high-tech component of this down-to-earth research environment. The outer design is made of Corten steel and merges with the surrounding landscape while nevertheless serving as a distinctly noticeable signpost. The signage system thus succeeds in emphasising the identity of the campus in a subtle way.

Für den Forschungscampus Chemelot entwickelt, will dieses Ausschilderungssystem eine gut wahrnehmbare Orientierung bieten und den Besucher auf einfache Weise zum gewünschten Ziel führen. Die Gestaltungsmaxime der „Ehrlichkeit" in Material und Form passt zu der Hightech-Komponente der praktisch ausgerichteten Forschungsumgebung. Die Elemente aus Cortenstahl vermischen sich mit der umgebenden Landschaft, fungieren aber dennoch als klar erkennbare Wegzeichen. Auf diese Weise hebt das Ausschilderungssystem subtil die Campus-Identität hervor.

Audi Pylon

Audi AG, Ingolstadt,
Germany/Deutschland
Design: Mutabor Design GmbH,
Hamburg, Germany/Deutschland
www.audi.de
www.mutabor.de

The puristic style of this pylon by the Audi brand stringently communicates attributes like dynamics and progressiveness. Its asymmetrical design originates from the architectural idiom of the Audi terminal and sets out to visualise the lightweight aluminium construction as a consistent core competence of the brand. Being that this material is used in both the facade of the Audi terminal and the architectural concept for dealerships, it follows that the new Audi pylon likewise integrates aluminium.

Die puristische Formensprache dieses Pylonen für die Marke Audi kommuniziert stringent die Attribute Dynamik und Progressivität. Die asymmetrische Gestaltung wurde abgeleitet aus der Architektursprache des Audi Terminals und will den Aluminium-Leichtbau als eine durchgehende Kernkompetenz der Marke visualisieren. Das Material Aluminium findet sich sowohl in der Fassade der Audi Terminals wie auch in dem Architekturkonzept für die angesprochenen Händlerbetriebe wieder, folgerichtig wird es auch bei diesem Pylonen verwendet.

Scandium
Superstructure System/
Überbausystem

Expotechnik Heinz Soschinski GmbH,
Taunusstein, Germany/Deutschland
Design: Nose AG, Zürich,
Switzerland/Schweiz
www.expotechnik.com
www.nose.ch

This superstructure system features a distinct and unobtrusive design. It provides a coherent frame for presentations and unites efficiency with a high degree of functionality. Elegantly the superstructure system integrates all the communication elements and light technology. The carrier supporting structure allows widths of four to eight metres. In addition, freely projecting canopies can be installed measuring two metres in each direction. Perforated aluminium sheets and stretched cloth panels can be used as ceiling panels. As the Scandium superstructure system is configured for surface areas of 50 to 250 sqm it offers a very good long-range effect.

Dieses Überbausystem ist mit einer klaren und zurückhaltenden Formensprache gestaltet. Es bietet einen stimmigen Rahmen für Präsentationen und vereint Effizienz mit einem hohen Maß an Funktionalität. In das Überbausystem sind auf elegante Art und Weise sämtliche Kommunikationselemente sowie die Lichttechnik integriert. Die Träger-Stützenkonstruktion ermöglicht Spannweiten von vier bis acht Metern, frei auskragende Vordächer von zwei Metern in alle Richtungen sind möglich. Als Deckenfelder können perforierte Aluminiumbleche sowie gespannte Stoffsegel eingesetzt werden. Da das Überbausystem Scandium für Flächen von 50 bis 250 qm ausgelegt ist, bietet es eine sehr gute Fernwirkung.

All-Weather Shelter / Dauer-Zelt

Shelter and Roam, Mannheim,
Germany / Deutschland
In-house design / Werksdesign: Prof.
Sigmar Willnauer, Robert Franzheld
www.shelterandroam.de

All details of this tent have been thoroughly conceptualised and designed for difficult expeditions or for use in emergencies such as earthquakes. It reliably protects two to five people even in extreme weather conditions from −10 to +40 degrees centigrade and with ambient humidity of 100 per cent. The tent is manufactured from polypropylene and recycled honeycomb boards that feature good insulation properties and additionally increase protection. Functional zigzag folds facilitate transport to the site of operation as the tent is stackable and can be compressed thanks to its folding capacities. In addition, it is long-lasting and does not deteriorate through extended use or storage. Details such as a water-collecting roof and mosquito screens for windows are very advantageous. An attic in the roof of the tent is accessible from inside the tent and protects stocks and equipment. This tent can be set up without training or tools, thus proving to be a well-conceived asset in case of emergency.

Für den Einsatz bei Katastrophen wie Erdbeben oder bei schwierigen Expeditionen, wurde dieses bis ins Detail durchdachte Zelt gestaltet. Es schützt zwei bis fünf Personen zuverlässig auch bei extremen Witterungsbedingungen von −10 und +40 Grad sowie bei einer Luftfeuchtigkeit von 100 Prozent. Gefertigt ist es aus Polypropylen- und Recyclat-Wabenplatten, die gute Isolationseigenschaften besitzen und den Schutz zusätzlich erhöhen. Eine funktionale Zick-Zack-Faltung erleichtert den Transport zum Einsatzort, da das Zelt durch diese Faltung gut komprimiert und gestapelt werden kann. Es ist langlebig und verträgt eine lange Nutzung und Lagerung, ohne zu verschleißen. Details wie ein wassersammelndes Dach oder Moskitonetze an den Fenstern sind von großem Vorteil. Ein von innen zugänglicher Speicher im Dach des Zeltes schützt Vorräte und die Ausrüstung. Ideal für den Notfall ist die Tatsache, dass dieses Zelt ohne Training und Werkzeug aufgebaut werden kann.

**Crew 21
Container Programme/
Behälterprogramm**

Rosconi GmbH, Weilburg/Lahn,
Germany/Deutschland
Design: Ingenhoven Architects,
Düsseldorf, Germany/Deutschland,
www.rosconi.com
www.ingenhovenarchitects.com

Crew 21 is part of a container programme with clear-cut design. Its various dimensions and functions provide for a uniform solution to modern waste management. The basic modules in three different sizes are combined with diverse top elements. The design of containers and top elements harmonise with each other and feature high quality formats and finishes. The adapter rings of the top elements are made of ground stainless steel; the body is manufactured in stainless steel or RAL coated in white.

Crew 21 ist Teil eines klar gestalteten Behälterprogramms, das mit verschiedenen Dimensionen und Funktionen eine einheitliche Lösung zur zeitgemäßen Abfallentsorgung bietet. Die Grundmodule in drei verschiedenen Größen werden mit unterschiedlichen Behälteraufsätzen kombiniert. Diese Behälter und Aufsätze sind gestalterisch aufeinander abgestimmt und hochwertig in ihrer Ausführung sowie ihrem Finish. Die Aufsatzringe bestehen aus geschliffenem Edelstahl, der Korpus ist jeweils in Edelstahl oder Weiß beschichtet ausgeführt.

**Crew 1
Smokers Point/
Zigarettensäule**

Rosconi GmbH, Weilburg/Lahn,
Germany/Deutschland
Design: Ingenhoven Architects,
Düsseldorf, Germany/Deutschland
www.rosconi.com
www.ingenhovenarchitects.com

Crew is a modular system of functional steles that feature functional modules, which can be combined with each other, as there are waste bins, ashtrays, orientation and advertising billboards, as well as an optionally installable illumination. Special functional steles adapt to the specific local needs and offer a high degree of stability and safety. The elements can be mounted to the ground; the waste bins and ashtrays are secured against unauthorised access. The Crew 1 cigarette column for access areas of buildings features a hinged lid to avoid unpleasant odours and completes the range. The design of the surface finishes harmonises with the standalone container range. The frame components are coated in usual colours for outdoor products. The Smokers Point Crew 1 is also available with illumination.

Crew ist ein modulares System von Funktionsstelen mit den untereinander kombinierten Funktionsmodulen Abfallbehälter, Ascher, Orientierungs- und Werbetafeln sowie einer optional integrierbaren Beleuchtung. Spezielle Funktionsstelen passen sich den Bedürfnissen des Ortes an und bieten ein hohes Maß an Stabilität und Sicherheit. Die Elemente können am Boden befestigt werden, die Abfallbehälter und Ascher sind gegen unbefugten Zugriff gesichert. Das Programm wird durch die Zigarettensäule Crew 1 für Gebäudezugangsbereiche ergänzt, die mit einer Ascherwippe zur Vermeidung von Geruchsbelästigung ausgestattet ist. Die Oberflächen wurden gestalterisch abgestimmt auf das freistehende Behälterprogramm. Auch der Smokers Point Crew 1 ist optional beleuchtbar.

Crew 5
Functional Stele /
Funktionsstele

Rosconi GmbH, Weilburg/Lahn,
Germany / Deutschland
Design: Ingenhoven Architects,
Düsseldorf, Germany / Deutschland
www.rosconi.com
www.ingenhovenarchitects.com

The distinctly designed Crew 5 functional stele is in the focus of a modular system comprising functional elements that can be freely combined. It can take up waste bins, ashtrays, orientation and advertising billboards, and an optionally installable illumination. A high degree of safety is achieved by the option to permanently fix the elements to the ground. The waste bin and the ashtray are secured against unauthorised access. The surface look of the functional stele matches the standalone container range.

Die klar gestaltete Funktionsstele Crew 5 steht im Mittelpunkt eines modularen Systems von frei untereinander kombinierbaren Funktionsmodulen. Sie kann einen Abfallbehälter, Ascher, Orientierungs- und Werbetafeln sowie eine optional integrierbare Beleuchtung bergen. Ein hohes Maß an Sicherheit entsteht durch die Möglichkeit, die Elemente dauerhaft am Boden zu befestigen, die Abfallbehälter und Ascher sind gegen unbefugten Zugriff gesichert. Die Oberfläche der Funktionsstele ist gestalterisch abgestimmt auf das freistehende Behälterprogramm.

Crew 7
Umbrella Bag Stand /
Schirmtütenspender

Rosconi GmbH, Weilburg/Lahn,
Germany / Deutschland
Design: Ingenhoven Architects,
Düsseldorf, Germany / Deutschland
www.rosconi.com
www.ingenhovenarchitects.com

This well-conceived umbrella bag stand integrates a waste bin for used umbrella bags. It is part of a modular system of functional steles. They feature functional modules like waste bins, ashtrays, orientation and advertising billboards and an optional illumination, which can all be combined with each other. The elements as well as this umbrella bag dispenser can be mounted to the ground. Waste bin and ashtray are secured against unauthorised access. The surface design harmonises with the standalone container range. The frame components are coated in usual colours for outdoor products according to DB703 or they are RAL colour-coated.

Dieser gut durchdacht gestaltete Schirmtütenspender integriert einen Abfallbehälter für gebrauchte Schirmtüten. Er ist Teil eines modularen Systems von Funktionsstelen mit den untereinander kombinierten Funktionsmodulen Abfallbehälter, Ascher, Orientierungs- und Werbetafeln und optional integrierbarer Beleuchtung. Die Elemente wie auch dieser Schirmtütenspender können am Boden befestigt werden, Abfallbehälter und Ascher sind gegen unbefugten Zugriff gesichert. Die Oberflächen sind gestalterisch abgestimmt auf das freistehende Behälterprogramm, die Rahmenbauteile sind in der für Produkte des Außenbereichs üblichen Farb-Oberfläche nach DB703 oder in Farbe nach RAL beschichtet.

Schüco CTB
Solar Shading / Sonnenschutz

Schüco International KG, Bielefeld,
Germany / Deutschland
In-house design / Werksdesign
www.schueco.com

This solar shading can be completely integrated into a facade and is very wind stable, two characteristic features, which are of high interest to architects and designers. Even at a force 11 storm or a hurricane this wind stability is guaranteed. The aluminium slats of the solar shading are elastically and flexibly attached to stainless steel ropes. These slats feature a convex shape at the outside to improve shadowing and a concave form at the inside to optimise lighting conditions in the interior. Due to this form of slats only two per cent of the sunlight can pass into the room. With up to 35 per cent translucency it offers a high degree of transparency. The stable hangings can be easily rolled up and retracted invisibly into the facade.

Für Architektur und Planung ist besonders interessant, dass dieser Sonnenschutz sich vollständig in die Fassade integrieren lässt und durch eine sehr hohe Windstabilität überzeugt. Auch bei Windstärke 11 oder einem orkanartigen Sturm ist diese Windstabilität gewährleistet. Die Aluminiumlamellen des Sonnenschutzes sind biegsam und flexibel an Edelstahlseilen aufgehängt. Außen sind diese Lamellen konvex gestaltet, um die Abschattung zu verbessern, innen sind sie konkav geformt, um die Lichtverhältnisse im Innenbereich zu optimieren. Diese Lamellenform lässt nur zwei Prozent des Sonnenlichtes in den Raum hinein und bietet mit bis zu 35 Prozent Durchsicht ein hohes Maß an Transparenz. Der stabil gestaltete Behang ist leicht aufwickelbar und kann verdeckt in die Fassade eingefahren werden.

Shan
Cassette Awning/
Kassetten-Markise

Shadelab S.r.l.,
Motta di Livenza, Italy / Italien
Design: MARIO MAZZER
architect | designer,
Conegliano, Italy / Italien
www.shadelab.it
www.mariomazzer.it

This elegant cassette awning shades without affecting the lines and the decoration of the architecture. Designed with a compact size the awning can be extended forward to up to 400 cm. When closed it is a parallelepiped characterised by slight engraves on the surface, which optically lends lightness to the whole form. A special mechanism (Dynamic Tipping System) allows the smooth extension of the arms to ensure good coupling of the profiles during the closing phase. Shan is made of die-cast extruded aluminium and it is 100 per cent recyclable.

Diese elegante Kassetten-Markise spendet Schatten, ohne Linien oder Besonderheiten der Gebäudearchitektur zu stören. Bei einer kompakten Formgebung kann die Markise 400 cm nach vorn ausgefahren werden. In geschlossenem Zustand bildet sie ein Parallelepiped, das durch leichte Auskerbungen an der Oberfläche geprägt ist, was der gesamten Form Leichtigkeit verleiht. Ein besonderer Mechanismus (Dynamic Tipping System) gewährleistet ein möglichst ruhiges Ausfahren der Seitenstreben, sodass die Profile in der Schließphase gut einrasten können. Shan ist aus gepresstem Druckguss-Aluminium hergestellt, das zu 100 Prozent wiederverwertbar ist.

SunSquareAXIS
Motor-Driven Sunsail/
Automatisches Sonnensegel

SunSquare, Tulln, Austria / Österreich
Design: Gerald Wurz, Vienna,
Austria / Wien, Österreich
www.sunsquare.com

This rectangular-shaped sunsail opens up new options in contemporary architecture. The elegant sunsail was designed for long, slim ground plans up to 15 metres length. It offers sun protection of up to 70 sqm of covered space. Its range of use is expanded by the possibility to pull out the sunsail on both sides. The mechanics of the patented cable pull was integrated in 11 extruded aluminium profiles. The mechanics is self-explaining and functionally mature.

Dieses rechteckig gestaltete Sonnensegel eröffnet neue Möglichkeiten in der temporären Architektur. Konzipiert wurde das elegant anmutende Sonnensegel für lange, schlanke Grundrisse bis 15 Meter Länge, es bietet Sonnenschutz für bis zu 70 qm überspannte Flächen. Erweitert werden seine Einsatzbereiche auch durch die Möglichkeit, das Sonnensegel auf beiden Seiten ausfahren zu können. Die Mechanik des patentierten Seilzuges wurde in elf Aluminium-Strangpressprofilen integriert, wobei die komplexe Mechanik funktional durchdacht und selbsterklärend ist.

Luccotherm
Translucent Structural Element / Lichtdurchlässiges Bauelement

Luccon Lichtbeton GmbH, Klaus,
Austria / Österreich
In-house design / Werksdesign:
Jürgen Frei
Design: Ingo Gast, Graben-Neudorf,
Germany / Deutschland
www.luccon.com
www.ingogast.com

Designed with translucent concrete that is infused with commercial insulating material at its core, this innovative structural element can also be used for exterior walls. By means of light-wave-conductive fibres, light is guided through both the concrete and the insulation core so that it enters the building during daylight hours. At night, the light emanating from inside the building brightly illuminates the facade outside, with shadows and silhouettes becoming discernible through the concrete.

Gestaltet aus einem lichtdurchlässigen Beton mit einem im Kern eingegossenen handelsüblichen Isoliermaterial, kann dieses innovative Bauelement auch als Außenwand eingesetzt werden. Sowohl durch den Beton wie auch durch den Isolierkern wird mittels Lichtwellenleitern Licht geleitet. Das Ergebnis ist, dass tagsüber Tageslicht in das Gebäude eindringt. Nachts zeigt sich durch das Licht im Gebäude die Fassade nach außen hin hell erleuchtet, Schatten und Konturen sind dann durch den Beton erkennbar.

Bio Glass

Coverings Etc, Miami, USA
In-house design / Werksdesign:
Ofer Mizrahi
www.coveringsetc.com

The Bio Glass is made from 100 per cent recycled glass – from wine, beer, and water bottles – and is 100 per cent recyclable. Layers of compressed glass pieces, which are fused together through heat, create unique patterns through which light permeates. The solid surface seems to be lit from within. The innovative material is versatile in its application and can be used for flooring, countertops, partitions, facades, as well as other decorative surfaces. There are six colours of Bio Glass to choose from.

Das Bio Glass besteht zu 100 Prozent aus Recyclingglas, das von Wein-, Bier- und Wasserflaschen stammt, und ist zu 100 Prozent wiederverwertbar. Es wird aus blätterartigen Glasstücken hergestellt, die durch Wärme miteinander verschmolzen werden. Diese Schichten aus gepressten Glasstücken erzeugen ein einzigartiges, lichtdurchlässiges Muster. Es scheint, als ob die solide Oberfläche von innen erleuchtet wird. Das innovative Material lässt sich vielseitig verwenden. Es kann in Bodenbelägen, Arbeitsplatten, Raumteilern, Fassaden oder anderen dekorativen Oberflächen zum Einsatz kommen. Das Bio Glass wird in sechs Farben angeboten.

Tegalit Star Matt
Concrete Roof Tile / Dach-Stein

Monier Braas GmbH, Oberursel,
Germany / Deutschland
In-house design / Werksdesign:
Juergen Armbrust
www.braas.de

This concrete roof tile allows the creation
of individual designs. Its distinct lines and
a geometric top view of the roof allow
for generous roofscapes having their own
specific style. The cutting edge was optimised
by applying the soil-resisting micro mortar
layer not only to the surface but also to the
cutting edge itself. This property especially
accounts for a reduced greening process.

Eine individuelle Gestaltung ermöglicht
dieser Dach-Stein. Seine klare Linienführung und ein geometrisches Deckbild
ermöglichen großzügige Dachflächen mit
einer jeweils spezifischen Formensprache. Die Schnittkante wurde dahingehend
optimiert, dass die Mikromörtelschicht mit
ihrer schmutzabweisenden Wirkung nicht
nur auf die Oberfläche aufgebracht wird,
sondern auch auf die vordere Schnittkante. Diese Eigenschaft trägt wesentlich
zu einem reduzierten Begrünungsverhal-
ten bei.

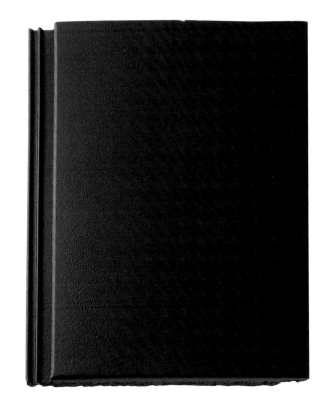

Rubin 13V
Clay Roof Tile / Dach-Ziegel

Monier Braas GmbH, Oberursel,
Germany / Deutschland
Design: Tegulas GmbH (Andreas Galiga),
Berg, Switzerland / Schweiz
www.braas.de
www.tegulas.ch

Consistent radiuses and transitions of these
clay roof tiles create harmony after they
have been laid. The split line and the shape
of the profile provide for an optimised
front edge, the stabilised geometry for
rectangularity. The detail-oriented shape at
the upper and lower side of the tile improves
its functionality. The tiles therefore offer high
weather tightness. They are stackable thus
saving space and ensure safe walkability.
Thanks to innovative V technology it is easy
to partition the roof with a head lap of
30 mm.

Gleichmäßige Radien und Übergänge
lassen bei diesen Dach-Ziegeln Harmonie
im eingedeckten Zustand entstehen. Der
Pressgratverlauf mit dem Ziegelprofil
sorgt für eine optimierte Sichtkante, die
stabilisierte Geometrie für Rechtwinklig-
keit. Die auf das Detail bedachte Gestaltung auf der Ober- und Unterseite der
Ziegel verbessert ihre Funktionalität.
So bieten sie eine hohe Regensicherheit,
sie lassen sich platzsparend stapeln und
sicher begehen. Dank innovativer V-Tech-
nologie ist eine leichte Dacheinteilung
möglich mit einem Verschiebebereich
von 30 mm.

EX-17
Digital Switch/Digitalschalter

Rosslare Enterprises Ltd., Hong Kong
In-house design/Werksdesign
www.rosslaresecurity.com

The EX-17 is a heavy-duty, time-controlled digital switch with non-sparking and non-magnetic qualities. Its elegantly designed, attractive case is made with architects and designers in mind. Being corrosion resistant, illuminated, and vandal-safe, the switch is suitable for both indoor and outdoor use. Following an innovative concept, it features solid-state piezoelectric switch technology that generates a dry-contact N.O. and N.C. relay pulse. This is achieved by the simple touch of a finger without any physical movement or moving parts. Among its well thought-out features are also a jumper selectable illumination status with light-dimming option as well as timed-operation and relay-toggle options. The EX-17 mounts directly to a standard US-size switchbox and is crafted to high manufacturing standards out of the finest materials under Rosslare's ISO 9001:2000 Certified Quality Standards.

EX-17 ist ein hochleistungsfähiger, zeit-gesteuerter Digitalschalter. Er ist funken-sicher und nicht magnetisch. Mit seinem elegant und attraktiv anmutenden Gehäu-se richtet er sich vor allem an Archi-tekten und Designer. Er ist rostbeständig, beleuchtet, vor mutwilligen Zerstörungen gesichert und somit für den Innen- und Außenbereich geeignet. Als Teil eines innovativen Konzepts verfügt der Schalter über eine piezoelektrische Schaltertechno-logie für Festkörper, die einen potenzial-freien Öffnungs- und Schließ-Relaisimpuls ermöglicht. Dies gelingt durch einfaches Berühren mit dem Finger, ohne weitere Bewegungen oder bewegliche Teile. Zum durchdachten Konzept zählen ein wähl-barer Beleuchtungsmodus mit Dimmfunk-tion, der über Jumper eingestellt wird, ein zeitlich festgelegter Betrieb sowie eine Umschaltfunktion am Relais. Der EX-17-Schalter passt in eine Schalterdose nach US-Standard. Er besteht aus hochwer-tigen, handgefertigten Materialien und entspricht damit den hohen Herstellungs-anforderungen gemäß den unter Rosslares ISO 9001:2000 zugelassenen Qualitäts-standards.

Safe-O-Tronic access
Electronic Locking System/
Elektronisches Schließsystem

Schulte-Schlagbaum AG, Velbert,
Germany/Deutschland
Design: piu products©
(Torsten Gratzki, Jens Deerberg),
Essen, Germany/Deutschland
www.sag-schlagbaum.com
www.piuproducts.com

This electronic locking system flexibly organises access to hall closets, safe-deposit boxes, and functional furniture. Due to the new slim construction of the housing, this product line can be mounted on almost any closet door. It is suitable for retrofitting or upgrading existing furniture with mechanical locks. The distinct, ergonomic design of this lock allows intuitive user operation, which is supported by audible and visual feedback.

Dieses elektronische Schließsystem organisiert auf flexible Art und Weise den Zugriff auf Garderobenschränke, Wertfächer und Funktionsmöbel. Durch eine neuartige schmale Konstruktion des Gehäuses können die Produkte auf nahezu jeder Schranktür angebracht werden, und sie eignen sich für das Nachrüsten bzw. „Upgraden" von Möbeln mit bestehenden mechanischen Verschlüssen. Die klare und ergonomische Gestaltung dieses Verschlusses ermöglicht eine intuitive Benutzerführung, die durch akustische und optische Feedbacks unterstützt wird.

OBID i-scan
RFID Gate Antennas/
RFID-Gate-Antennen

Feig Electronic GmbH, Weilburg,
Germany/Deutschland
Design: piu products©
(Torsten Gratzki, Jens Deerberg), Essen,
Germany/Deutschland
www.feig.de
www.piuproducts.com

The antennas of this product family are used as reliable anti-theft devices in libraries. Three versions, Gate, Clear Gate, and Crystal Gate have been developed, each of them featuring individual characteristics and matching the high demands of architects and planners. With consistently high electronic performance they become a characteristic element of style in modern as well as in more traditional libraries.

Die Antennen dieser Produktfamilie dienen als zuverlässige Diebstahlsicherungen in Bibliotheken. Mit den Modellen Gate, Clear Gate und Crystal Gate wurden drei verschiedene Varianten entwickelt, die jeweils individuelle Gestaltungsmerkmale aufweisen und den kritischen Anforderungen von Architekten und Planern standhalten können. Bei gleichbleibend hoher elektronischer Performance werden sie zu einem prägenden gestalterischen Element in modernen wie auch in eher klassischen Bibliotheken.

acciomatic
Pivot Barrier/Drehsperre

Gallenschütz GmbH, Bühl,
Germany/Deutschland
In-house design/Werksdesign:
Thomas Gallenschütz
www.gallenschuetz.com

The acciomatic pivot barrier provides access control, for example with card readers. The drive and locking unit is enclosed in a slim stainless steel case that laterally limits the passage. This is advantageous to the architecture, for the width of the installation is thereby minimised. Both barrier arms can move independently of each other allowing various functions like single access or emergency opening. A low-noise function combined with an unobtrusive look avoids any annoyance.

Die Drehsperre acciomatic dient der Zutrittskontrolle beispielsweise mit Kartenlesern. Die Antriebs- und Sperreinheit wird von einem flach gestalteten Edelstahlgehäuse aufgenommen, das den Durchgang seitlich begrenzt. Dies ist von Vorteil für die Architektur, da die Breite der Anlagen dadurch minimiert wird. Die beiden Arme können sich unabhängig voneinander bewegen, was verschiedene Funktionen wie Einzelzutritte oder Notöffnung zulässt. Durch ihren geräuscharmen Betrieb und ihre unaufdringliche Form werden Belästigungen vermieden.

Mainline B Series Adaptor System / Adaptersystem

Power and Data Corporation, Sydney, Australia / Australien
Design: 4design (Robbie Wells), Sydney, Australia / Australien
www.mainlinepower.com
www.4design.com.au

The B Series adaptor system is an integral part of a track-based, power distribution solution, which enables flexible access to power. Designed to fit with the Mainline power track distribution system, the series comprises a range of dedicated adaptors each suitable for a specific regional electrical standard, but designed from a common platform facilitating a global solution. This means that more than 75 per cent of the adaptor's components are the same across all regional variants, this reduces cost, turnaround time, inventories and environmental impact.

Das Adaptersystem der B-Serie ist ein wesentlicher Bestandteil einer schienenbasierten Stromverteilungslösung. Es ermöglicht flexiblen Zugriff auf Strom und wurde so konzipiert, dass es zum Mainline-Stromverteilungssystem passt. Die Serie umfasst eine Reihe von passenden Adaptern, die alle für einen regionalspezifischen elektrischen Standard geeignet sind, aber auf der Grundlage einer gemeinsamen Plattform gestaltet wurden und eine globale Lösung ermöglichen. Das heißt, dass die Bestandteile des Adapters zu mehr als 75 Prozent in allen regionalen Nebenformen identisch sind. Dies verringert Kosten und Warenbestände, die Zeitdauer für den Turnaround und die Wirkung auf die Umwelt.

Centronic MC441-II Hand Transmitter / Handsender

Becker-Antriebe GmbH, Sinn, Germany / Deutschland
Design: Busse Design + Engineering (Michael Tinius), Elchingen, Germany / Deutschland
www.becker-antriebe.com
www.busse-design.com

With this hand transmitter it is possible to control electric shutter drives, awnings and blinds in an intuitive way while sitting in an armchair. The organically shaped hand transmitter is reduced to its essential; it controls a single drive or a defined group. By a simple keystroke a memory timer function can be activated in certain receivers. Afterwards, shutters will automatically go up or down at this specified point of time. The time automatic is simply switched on or off by a sliding switch.

Mit diesem Handsender lassen sich elektrische Rollladen- und Sonnenschutz-Antriebe intuitiv vom Sessel aus bedienen. Der organisch und in einer Reduktion auf das Wesentliche gestaltete Handsender steuert dabei einen einzelnen Antrieb oder eine definierte Gruppe. Durch einfachen Tastendruck kann in bestimmten Empfängern eine Memory-Zeitschaltfunktion aktiviert werden. Rollläden fahren danach zu diesem Zeitpunkt automatisch auf oder ab. Die Zeitautomatik kann einfach per Schiebeschalter an- und ausgeschaltet werden.

Centronic TC445-II Timer / Zeitschaltuhr

Becker-Antriebe GmbH, Sinn, Germany / Deutschland
Design: Busse Design + Engineering (Michael Tinius), Elchingen, Germany / Deutschland
www.becker-antriebe.com
www.busse-design.com

Distinct lines and a soft, organic shape of the casing are characteristic features of this timer. Its transmitter includes five channels, each of which controls one drive or a defined group of drives. The text-based display menu allows intuitive handling.

Eine klare Linienführung und eine weiche, organische Formensprache des Gehäuses prägen die Anmutung dieser Zeitschaltuhr. Ihr Sender verfügt über fünf Kanäle, mit denen jeweils ein Antrieb oder eine definierte Gruppe von Antrieben gesteuert wird. Das textgestützte Display-Menu ermöglicht eine intuitive Bedienung.

**The USB Smart Surge Protector /
Überspannungsschutz**

Powertech Industrial Co., Ltd., Chung
Ho City, Taipei County, Taiwan
In-house design / Werksdesign:
Powertech ID Dept., Hui-Ju Chuang
www.power-tech.com.tw

Designed mainly for energy conservation,
this USB Smart Surge Protector provides
an easy and efficient way to manage surge
protector outlets and stop stand-by power
waste. To solve the problems of power
sensing technology, due to different current
consumption patterns between master
devices, the green USB Smart Surge solution
uses an innovative USB signal detecting
technology. For the detection of signals, the
wireless USB control element is connected
to a notebook. When the notebook is turned

on or off the USB control element wirelessly
turns on or off, the peripheral devices
connected to the notebook as well.

Der Überspannungsschutz USB Smart
Surge wurde vor allem für die Einspa-
rung von Energie konzipiert. Er bietet
aber auch eine einfache und wirkungs-
volle Möglichkeit, Anschlüsse mit einem
Überspannungsschutz zu überwachen
und Energieverschwendung im Stand-by-
Modus zu verhindern. Um das Problem

der Stromerfassung bei unterschiedlichen
Verbrauchsszenarien von Geräten zu
lösen, nutzt die umweltfreundliche USB
Smart Surge-Lösung eine innovative USB-
Signalerfassungstechnik. Das drahtlose
USB-Steuerelement wird für die USB-
Signalerfassung an ein Notebook ange-
schlossen. Wird das Notebook ein- oder
ausgeschaltet, schaltet die Signalerken-
nung auch die darüber angeschlossenen
Peripherie-Geräte kabellos ein oder aus.

Scenario Launcher
Remote Control / Fernbedienung

Somfy GmbH, Rottenburg am Neckar,
Germany / Deutschland
In-house design / Werksdesign:
Olivier Charleux
www.somfy.com

The Scenario Launcher is a remote control for controlling house automation. Thanks to an ergonomic cavity for the thumb the user can grip the device in spite of its rounded form and operate it reliably and comfortably even in the dark. Coloured rubber framings give the control an individual character and a good grip so it snugly nestles in the hand. The transmitter works with the io-homecontrol radio technology allowing the user to create two different control scenarios with the appropriate software.

Der Scenario Launcher ist eine Fernbedienung für die Regelung der Haustechnik. Eine ergonomisch gestaltete Vertiefung für den Daumen sorgt dafür, dass der Nutzer das Gerät trotz seiner runden Form gut greifen und selbst im Dunkeln zuverlässig und komfortabel betätigen kann. Farbliche, gummierte Umrahmungen verleihen der Steuerung einen individuellen Charakter sowie eine griffige Oberfläche und schmiegen sich gut in die Hand. Der Sender arbeitet mit der Funktechnologie io-homecontrol, für die der Nutzer zwei unterschiedliche Steuerungs-Szenarien mittels Software entwerfen kann.

Enzo
Switch / Schalter

Basalte bvba, Ghent, Belgium /
Gent, Belgien
In-house design / Werksdesign:
Klaas Arnout, Sandra Maes
www.basalte.be

Enzo is a multi-touch switch that is available in dual and quadruple variants. Its smoothly rounded retro design and the use of high-quality materials, including polished aluminium, glass, and leather, make it a timeless product with an exclusive touch. Despite its retro look, Enzo uses the latest technology and features highly sensitive touch sensors, a multi-touch function, and a temperature indicator. The entire housing is touch-sensitive – with a simple finger swipe across the housing or a touch on the edge, light is activated. The integrated, multicoloured LED backlight makes Enzo visible in the dark. It can also be used for status feedback. Enzo has been designed to work with home automation systems such as KNX.

Enzo ist ein Multitouch-Schalter, der als Zweifach- und Vierfach-Version erhältlich ist. Sein Retrolook mit weich abgerundeten Kanten und der Einsatz hochwertiger Materialien wie gebürstetes Aluminium, Glas und Leder lassen ihn zu einem zeitlosen und exklusiv anmutenden Produkt werden. Trotz dieses Retrolooks kommt bei Enzo allerneueste Technologie zum Einsatz. Er verfügt über hochempfindliche Berührungssensoren, eine Multitouch-Funktion sowie einen Temperaturmesser. Das ganze Gehäuse ist berührungsempfindlich. Wischt man nur mit dem Finger über die Oberfläche oder berührt sie an der Kante, wird die Beleuchtung dort aktiviert. Die integrierte, mehrfarbige LED-Hintergrundbeleuchtung macht Enzo im Dunkeln sichtbar und kann auch den Status anzeigen. Enzo wurde für die Anwendung in Gebäudeautomationssystemen wie KNX entwickelt.

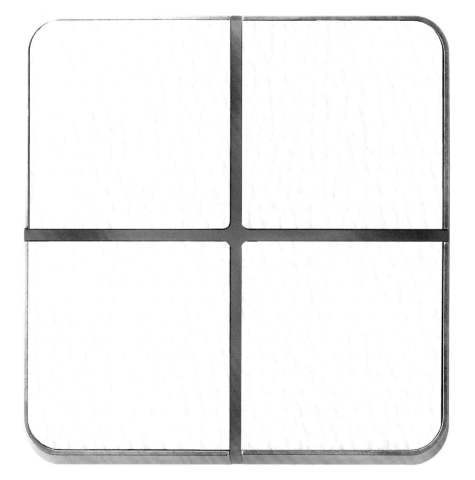

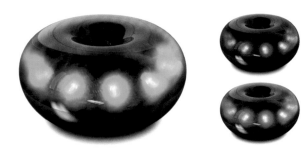

Flying Doughnut
Parking Guidance System /
Parkleitsystem

Versor d.o.o., Maribor,
Slovenia / Slowenien
In-house design / Werksdesign:
Primož Zajšek, Dejan Rojko
www.versor.si

The Flying Doughnut is a sensor unit that simplifies the detection and indication of free parking spaces in car parks. The units are installed above individual parking spaces and indicate whether the parking site is occupied or not. The rounded design allows equal distribution of high performance LEDs (green, red and blue) around the housing and offers good visibility from all directions. Its core feature is a conspicuous signal horn, which serves as an ultrasound amplifier that minimises power consumption.

Der Flying Doughnut ist eine Sensoreinheit, welche die Detektion und Angabe von freien Parkplätzen in Parkhäusern vereinfacht. Die Einheiten werden über den einzelnen Parkplatz installiert und zeigen an, ob der Parkplatz besetzt ist oder nicht. Eine runde Form ermöglicht eine gleichmäßige Verteilung von Hochleistungs-LEDs (grün, rot und blau) um das Gehäuse herum und bietet eine gute Sichtbarkeit aus allen Richtungen. Das Hauptmerkmal ist ein auffälliges Signalhorn, das als ein Ultraschallverstärker dient und den Energieeinsatz minimiert.

LCN-GT6D
Sensor Keypad / Sensor-Tastenfeld

Issendorff KG, Laatzen/Rethen,
Germany / Deutschland
In-house design / Werksdesign:
Issendorff Design
www.lcn.de

The sensor keypad LCN-GT6D is an operating element of the LCN building control system. Featuring an elegant and distinct glass surface with bevelled edges, it harmoniously blends in with modern living and business rooms. The six sensor keys can be individually customised by the user. To this end, a printed foil is inserted behind the glass front. The sensor keypad can be intuitively operated through gentle touch, with each key controlling three functions. The brilliant 2.4" (61 mm) OLED colour display features a wide viewing angle. Six symbols and up to four text lines can be presented. Moreover, the size of the characters can be doubled so that even people with impaired visual performance are able to read the display without difficulty.

Das Sensor-Tastenfeld LCN-GT6D ist ein Bedienelement für die LCN-Gebäudeleittechnik. Gestaltet mit einer elegant und klar anmutenden Glasoberfläche mit geschliffenen Kanten, fügt es sich harmonisch in moderne Wohn- und Geschäftsräume ein. Die sechs Sensortasten können individuell vom Anwender gestaltet werden. Dazu wird eine bedruckte Folie hinter die Glasscheibe geschoben. Dieses Sensor-Tastenfeld kann intuitiv durch eine sanfte Berührung bedient werden, mit jeder Taste lassen sich drei Funktionen steuern. Das brillante 2.4" (61 mm) OLED-Farbdisplay bietet einen besonders weiten Einblickwinkel. Hier können sechs Symbole und bis zu vier Textzeilen dargestellt werden. Die Zeichengröße lässt sich verdoppeln, so dass die Anzeige auch von in ihrer Sehleistung beeinträchtigten Personen gut abgelesen werden kann.

golf
Electrical Distribution Board / Elektrokleinverteiler

Hager Electro GmbH & Co. KG,
Blieskastel, Germany / Deutschland
Design: Hager WIN-co (Erwin van
Handenhoven), Illkirch-Graffenstaden
(Strasbourg), France / Frankreich
www.hager.de
www.wincodesign.com

The golf electrical distribution board features a particularly innovative and distinctive appearance within this product range and, as such, proves to be an aesthetic eye-catcher that integrates well into any living area. Due to its compact and sturdy construction, this electrical distribution board offers users clearly defined and intuitive applicability. Its formal language is the expression of a uniform design concept. An example par excellence for the new brand image of Hager.

Der Elektrokleinverteiler golf besitzt eine für diesen Produktbereich innovative und sehr klare Anmutung. Auf diese Weise wird er zu einem ästhetischen Blickfang, der sich gut in jeden Wohnbereich integrieren lässt. Er ist kompakt und robust, die Anwendung ist eindeutig und intuitiv. Seine Formensprache ist Ausdruck einer einheitlichen Gestaltungslinie. Der neue golf steht für das neue Markenimage von Hager.

Banksys Yomani
Payment Terminal / Bezahlterminal

Atos Worldline S.A./N.V., Brussels,
Belgium / Brüssel, Belgien
Design: VanBerlo, Eindhoven, NL
www.banksys.com
www.vanberlo.nl

The Yomani countertop payment terminal offers a high degree of security so as to prevent criminal acts in places where electronic money transactions are carried out. The designers attached great importance to the user-friendliness of the machine, which can be intuitively operated with a large full-colour display and illuminated card slots providing guidance through the payment process. Yomani's visual style is characterised by a compact mono-volume shape providing integrated protection of privacy. This specialised design also served to provide the elements for a contemporary style. The terminal can be operated with both swipe and chip cards and has been optionally prepared for non-contact card reading.

Das Bezahlterminal Yomani bietet ein hohes Maß an Sicherheit, um kriminelle Vorgänge bei elektronischen Geldtransaktionen zu vermeiden. Die Designer legten großen Wert auf die Benutzerfreundlichkeit des Geräts. Mit einem ganzfarbigen Display und beleuchteten Kartenschlitzen führt es nutzerfreundlich durch den Zahlungsvorgang. Yomanis Formensprache ist geprägt durch einen kompakten, monoformen Korpus, der integrierten Schutz für die Privatsphäre bietet. Durch diese Art der Gestaltung wurden zugleich Elemente für ein zeitgemäßes Styling geschaffen. Das Terminal eignet sich sowohl für magnetische Streifenkarten als auch für Chipkarten. Optional ist auch die Unterstützung kontaktloser Karten vorgesehen.

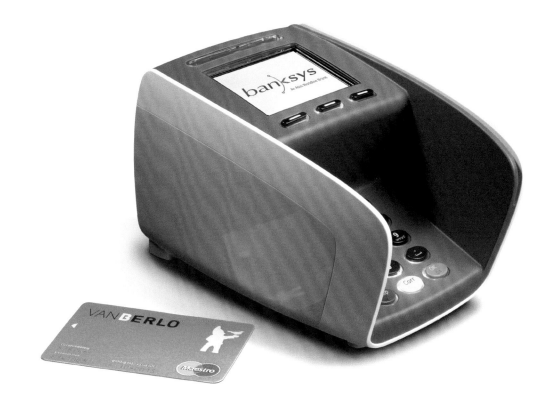

House Number / Hausnummer

Korn Produkte, Kassel,
Germany / Deutschland
In-house design / Werksdesign:
Jochen Korn
www.korn-produkte.de

The striking design of these house numbers shows visitors the way. Made of weatherproof and durable special concrete, these numbers become distinctive signs in the architecture. The precisely crafted typography of the house numbers follows the typeface of the Helvetica font and blends in well with contemporary architecture. Attached assembly instructions, an installation kit, and a drilling template make it easy to mount the numbers accurately.

Mit einer markanten Gestaltung weisen diese Hausnummern Gästen den Weg. Aus einem wetterfesten und sehr langlebigen Spezialbeton gefertigt, werden sie zu einem individuellen Zeichen in der Architektur. Die präzise gearbeiteten Nummern folgen dem Schriftbild der Helvetica und fügen sich gut in die zeitgenössische Architektur ein. Eine leicht verständliche Aufbauanleitung, ein Montageset sowie eine Bohrschablone ermöglichen eine problemlose Montage.

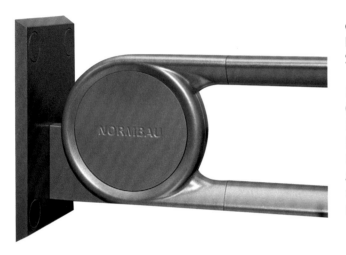

cavere
Lift-Up Support Rail / Stützklappgriff

Normbau, Renchen/Baden,
Germany / Deutschland
In-house design / Werksdesign:
Martin Homberg
Design: Arkitektfirmaet C. F. Møller,
Århus, Denmark / Dänemark
www.normbau-extranet.de
www.cfmoller.com

This aluminium lift-up support rail is part of a bathroom product range for disabled persons. The design focuses on a triangular profile, with propping and gripping likewise possible thanks to the ergonomic grip shape of the rail. This multifunctional instrument aids the user in moving from a wheelchair to the WC and back, serving as a supporting grip with safe arm support. A centrally arranged bearing bracket reinforces the grip and emphasises the revolving profile. Due to its functional form, it can be used in a wide variety of situations.

Dieser Stützklappgriff aus Aluminium ist Teil einer Badserie für gehandicapte Menschen. Durch das dreieckige Profil besitzt der Stützklappgriff eine ergonomische Griffkontur, damit werden Abstützen und Greifen gleichermaßen ermöglicht. So wird der Griff als Umsetzhilfe vom Rollstuhl auf das WC und auch als Stützgriff mit sicherer Armauflage genutzt. Mit einer mittig angeordneten Lagerkonsole ist der Griff kompakt und akzentuiert das umlaufende Profil. Die funktionale Gestaltung erlaubt die Nutzung in verschiedenen Bereichen.

Sitty
Foldable Seat / Klappsitz

Petrič d.o.o., Ajdovščina,
Slovenia / Slowenien
Design: Gigodesign d.o.o. (Miha Klinar,
Martin Šoštarič), Ljubljana,
Slovenia / Slowenien; Pirnar & Savšek,
Zagorje ob Savi, Slovenia / Slowenien
www.petric.si
www.gigodesign.com

Sitty is an interesting foldable seat, with a wooden board that is folded down to the seating position. After use automatically retracts into an upward position clearing the space again. The design is based on high technical standards. Furthermore, great importance was attached to the observance of safety standards and to protection against vandalism. Due to its ergonomic design this foldable seat is very comfortable and easy to handle.

Sitty ist ein interessanter Klappsitz, bei dem ein Holzbrett in die Sitzposition geklappt wird. Nach Gebrauch klappt es automatisch in die senkrechte Grundstellung zurück und schafft wieder freien Raum. Bei der Gestaltung wurden technische Qualitätsanforderungen berücksichtigt. Weiterhin wurde großer Wert auf die Einhaltung von Sicherheitsstandards und den Schutz vor Vandalismus gelegt. Aufgrund seiner ergonomischen Form ist der Sitz sehr bequem und außerdem einfach zu benutzen.

Select
Letterbox / Briefkasten

S. Siedle & Söhne, Furtwangen,
Germany / Deutschland
In-house design / Werksdesign:
Eberhard Meurer
www.siedle.de

The Select letterboxes are part of a series
conceived for the entrance area of a single-
family house. Displaying a distinctive design,
they are user-friendly and comfortable due
to their sandwich structure along with a solid
aluminium front, both of which integrate
well into the surrounding architecture.
An interesting aspect of the design is a
translucent body, which communicates
lightness and can be discreetly illuminated.
Additional features are offered by the models
Audio and Video.

Diese Briefkästen sind Teil einer Serie für
den Eingangsbereich des Einfamilien-
hauses. Klar gestaltet, sind sie mit ihrer
Sandwichbauweise sowie einer massiven
und langlebigen Aluminiumfront ebenso
nutzerfreundlich wie komfortabel und
fügen sich gut in die Architektur ein. Ein
interessanter Aspekt der Gestaltung ist ein
transluzenter Korpus, der den Briefkästen
Leichtigkeit verleiht und der auch dezent
beleuchtet werden kann. Die Modelle
Audio und Video bieten zusätzliche Funktionen.

**Geniax
Heating Pump System/
Heizungspumpensystem**

Wilo SE, Dortmund,
Germany/Deutschland
Design: Mehnert Corporate Design
GmbH & Co. KG (Jan Eickhoff,
Prof. Kurt Mehnert), Berlin,
Germany/Deutschland
www.wilo.com
www.mehnertdesign.de

This remotely operated heating pump system stands out due to its energy efficiency and heating cost savings at an average of 20 per cent. With Geniax, a pump replaces the conventional thermostat valve, and separate operating devices allow individual temperature and time profiles to be set in each room. The heating pump system conforms to high functional requirements and features a distinct and consistent design language that fosters high brand recognition.

Mit diesem dezentral arbeitenden Heizungspumpensystem kann eine Energieeffizienz und Heizkostenersparnis von durchschnittlich 20 Prozent erreicht werden. Dabei wird das herkömmliche Thermostatventil durch eine Pumpe ersetzt; über Bediengeräte in jedem Raum können verschiedene Temperatur- und Zeitprofile individuell eingestellt werden. Das Heizungspumpensystem entspricht hohen funktionalen Anforderungen, und seine klare, durchgängige Formensprache besitzt einen hohen Wiedererkennungswert.

**Tube
Bioethanol Fireplace/
Bioethanol-Feuerstelle**

Acquaefuoco wellness mood,
San Vendemiano, Italy/Italien
Design: MARIO MAZZER
architect | designer,
Conegliano, Italy/Italien
www.acquaefuoco-mood.it
www.mariomazzer.it

Tube is a bioethanol fireplace designed for the installation in public or private space. It can be considered a real design furniture complement because it neither requires a chimney nor any construction measures. It consists of a circular burner made of inox steel, which generates heat by using bioethanol, a denatured alcohol produced by fermenting sugars. These are derived from agricultural and forestry organic products. In the combustion process no fumes are released. Tube can be incorporated into an existing fireplace or mounted on the wall.

Tube ist eine Bioethanol-Feuerstelle, die an öffentlichen oder privaten Orten installiert werden kann. Sie ist eine echte Ergänzung zu Design-Möbeln, weil sie einen Kamin überflüssig macht und keine besonderen Baumaßnahmen erfordert. Die Feuerstelle besteht aus einem Rundbrenner aus Inox-Stahl, der mithilfe von Bioethanol, also denaturiertem Alkohol, Wärme erzeugt. Dieser Brennstoff wird bei der Fermentierung von Zuckerarten gebildet, die von organischen Produkten aus der Land- oder Forstwirtschaft stammen. Bei der Verbrennung bildet sich kein Rauch. Tube kann in eine bestehende Feuerstelle eingebaut oder an der Wand angebracht werden.

Skalar
Curtain Rod / Vorhangstange

MHZ Hachtel GmbH & Co. KG,
Leinfelden-Echterdingen,
Germany / Deutschland
In-house design / Werksdesign
www.mhz.de

The Skalar curtain rod features a very unconventional visual language. With its elliptical design, it produces a delicate and at the same time distinct impression in the room, where it automatically attracts a high degree of attention.

Die Vorhangstange Skalar zeigt eine sehr eigenwillige Formensprache. Mit ihrer elliptischen Gestaltung wirkt sie im Raum filigran und zugleich markant und zieht die Blicke auf sich.

Designa
Insect Screen / Fliegengitter

Hamstra, Almere, NL
In-house design / Werksdesign:
Mark de Haan, Arnoud Fransen
www.hamstrahorren.nl

The modular structure of the insect screen Designa allows for its effective use in window and door openings. It does not require any visually disturbing elements like fasteners, mesh seams, or any other visible construction elements, which is an innovative aspect of its clear design. The possibility of locking the fly screen in any desired position is a valuable advantage in daily use. Moreover, the spring drive can be adjusted and the mesh exchanged without disassembling the screen.

Mit seinem modularen Aufbau ermöglicht das Fliegengitter Designa einen vielseitigen Einsatz in Fenster- und Türöffnungen. Ein innovativer Aspekt seiner klaren Gestaltung ist die Tatsache, dass es ohne visuelle störende Teile wie Schrauben, Gazesäume oder andere sichtbare Konstruktionsteile auskommt. Ein im täglichen Gebrauch nützlicher Vorteil ist die Möglichkeit, dieses Insektengitter auf jeder gewünschten Position zu fixieren. Das Einstellen des Federmotors oder das Austauschen der Gaze kann ohne Demontierung geschehen.

Cupa
Stackable Chair / Stapelstuhl

Brune GmbH & Co. KG, Königswinter,
Germany / Deutschland
Design: X-Products / Prof. Matthias
Rexforth, Krefeld-Forstwald,
Germany / Deutschland
www.brune.de
www.xproducts-rexforth.de

The delicate structure of this stackable chair,
including its fine seat shell, communicates
high material transparency and complies
with today's demands on modern seating.
An intelligent, detailed solution for armrests,
linking devices, and writing tablets is
characteristic of this chair. The lightness of
its skid base and a materiality that exudes a
sense of value provide for stylish seating in
an architecture-based living environment.

Die filigrane Struktur dieses Stapelstuhls
sowie eine fein anmutende Schalenform
kommunizieren eine hohe Materialtrans-
parenz und entsprechen den ästhetischen
Anforderungen an modernes Sitzen.
Charakteristisch ist die intelligente Detail-
lösung für Armlehne, Reihenverbindung
und Schreibtablar. Mit seiner Leichtigkeit
der Kufenstruktur und einer hochwertig
anmutenden Materialität bietet dieser Sta-
pelstuhl stilvolles Sitzen in einem archi-
tekturaffinen Objekt.

LCTherm
Concrete Facade Element /
Betonfassadenelement

LCT GesmbH,
light & concrete technology,
St. Ruprecht a. d. Raab,
Austria / Österreich
In-house design / Werksdesign:
Oliver Fischer, Dornbirn,
Austria / Österreich

The design of this concrete facade unites the properties of prefabricated ferro-concrete with nature's inherent lighting. Thus, an element of innovative appearance is created that offers manifold architectural options. LCTherm is a self-supporting concrete facade element that is light permeable and offers outstanding heat insulation, which also makes it suitable for external wall areas. The single element dimensions of this concrete facade are variable and can reach up to 280 x 600 cm.

Die Gestaltung dieser Betonfassade vereint die Eigenschaften einer Stahlbetonfertigteilfassade mit dem Lichtspiel der Natur, wodurch ein Element mit einer innovativen Anmutung entsteht, das vielfältige architektonische Möglichkeiten bietet. LCTherm ist ein lichtdurchlässiges und selbsttragendes Betonfassadenelement, das gut wärmegedämmt ist und deshalb auch im Außenwandbereich Einsatz findet. Die Größe der einzelnen Elemente ist variabel, sie kann bis zu 280 x 600 cm betragen.

Arboris
Tree Protection Grilles /
Baumschutz-Roste

Humberg Metall- & Kunstguss GmbH,
Nottuln, Germany / Deutschland
Design: Tom Schrier, Enschede, NL
www.humberg-guss.de

These tree protection grilles offer manifold protection systems for trees and humans in the urban space. They feature a distinct and significant style that protects the root area of the trees from ground compaction caused by vehicles. At the same time they safeguard pedestrians by their slip resistant structure. Grooves that already form during the sand casting process are visible at the surface; they are part of an individual style and integrate harmoniously in the overall picture of the tree protection grilles.

Diese Baumschutz-Roste vereinen vielseitige Sicherheitsaspekte für Bäume und Menschen im urbanen Raum. Gestaltet mit einer klaren und hochwertigen Formensprache, schützen sie den Wurzelbereich der Stadtbäume vor Bodenverdichtungen durch Fahrzeuge. Ihre rutschhemmende Rillen-Struktur auf der Oberfläche, die bereits während des Sandgussprozesses entsteht, trägt gleichzeitig zum Schutz von Fußgängern bei und fügt sich harmonisch in das Gesamtbild der Baumschutz-Roste ein.

Gira Smoke Alarm Device Dual/VdS/
Gira Rauchwarnmelder Dual/VdS

Gira Giersiepen GmbH & Co. KG,
Radevormwald, Germany / Deutschland
Design: Phoenix Design GmbH + Co.KG,
Stuttgart, Germany / Deutschland
www.gira.de

This elegant smoke alarm device features two ways of detection offering a high degree of security. Small smoke particles are visually detected; additionally, heat sensors measure any change in temperature in the room. Diffused light is visually inspected by means of a processor-controlled signal analysis. The smoke alarm detects the heat development via an additional thermo-differential sensor. Both sensors continuously measure the optical and thermal values in the room environment. An intelligent monitoring module examines the values and detects any pollution in the room air. Thus, different kinds of fire like smouldering fire or liquidity fire can be reliably identified and registered quite fast. Moreover, the alarm behaviour in the area of use with unavoidable perturbations like kitchen vapours, dust or electric disturbing pulses can be better controlled.

Dieser elegant anmutende Rauchwarnmelder ist mit zwei Erkennungsverfahren ausgestattet und bietet ein hohes Maß an Sicherheit. Kleine Rauchpartikel werden optisch erfasst, zusätzlich messen Wärmesensoren Temperaturveränderungen im Raum. Die optische Überprüfung des Streulichts erfolgt mit einer prozessorgesteuerten Signalauswertung, die Wärmeentwicklung detektiert der Rauchwarnmelder über einen zusätzlichen Thermodifferentialsensor. Die beiden Sensoren messen fortlaufend die optischen und thermischen Werte in der räumlichen Umgebung, wobei ein intelligentes Überwachungsmodul die Werte prüft und Verschmutzungen in der Raumluft erkennt. Auf diese Weise können verschiedene Brandarten wie Schwelbrand oder Flüssigkeitsbrand schneller registriert und sicher erkannt werden. Auch lässt sich das Alarmverhalten in Einsatzbereichen mit unvermeidbaren Störeinflüssen wie Küchendämpfen, Staub oder elektrischen Störimpulsen besser kontrollieren.

AURORA C2010
Automatic Fire Sprinkler/
Automatische Sprinkleranlage

Industrial Technology Research
Institute, Hsinchu, Taiwan
In-house design/Werksdesign:
Jung-Huang Liao, Jia-Wei Jan
Design: Duckimage (Li-Hao Liu,
Hung Cheng), Hsinchu, Taiwan
www.itri.org.tw
www.duckimage.com.tw

To avoid panic in case of power failure, this
sprinkler uses liquid-driven illumination
technology that is integrated into the
automatic sprinkler at the ceiling. If the
automatic fire sprinkler is activated in case
of fire, the flowing water drives a turbine
blade for immediate power generation and
lighting of the LED, transforming it into
an emergency light and alarm system. The
device is moreover equipped with a laser
projector that additionally indicates escape
paths and emergency exits.

Um Panik bei einem Stromausfall zu vermeiden, nutzt dieser Sprinkler eine flüs-
sigkeitsbetriebene Beleuchtungstechnolo-
gie in der automatischen Sprinkleranlage
an der Decke. Wird die Sprinkleranlage
bei Feuer ausgelöst, treibt das ausströ-
mende Wasser ein Turbinenblatt zur
sofortigen Stromerzeugung und zum Einschalten der LED-Beleuchtung an, sodass
daraus eine Notbeleuchtungs- und Warn-
anlage wird. Ein Laserprojektor in dem
Sprinkler kennzeichnet darüber hinaus die
Fluchtwege und Notausgänge.

B1
Fire-Resistant Magnetic Frame/
Brandschutz-Magnetrahmen

Halbe-Rahmen GmbH, Kirchen,
Germany/Deutschland
In-house design/Werksdesign:
Heinrich Halbe
www.halbe-rahmen.de

In order to meet increasingly stringent
fire protection requirements in public
buildings, particular attention was paid to
self-explanatory handling as well as to the
precise manufacture of sustainable materials
when this fire-resistant magnetic frame
was designed. The magnetic frame meets
the requirements of the building material
class B1 for flame-resistance (according to
the DIN 4102-1 standard). For example, it
may be used as a picture frame in schools
or as building guidance system in manifold
variations. The frame features a neutral look,
and the different profiles, glass types, and
freely selectable formats allow for individual
creative freedom.

Um den steigenden Anforderungen an
einen vorbeugenden Brandschutz in
öffentlichen Gebäuden gerecht zu werden,
wurde bei der Gestaltung dieses Brand-
schutz-Magnetrahmens besonderer Wert
auf eine selbsterklärende Handhabung
sowie eine präzise Verarbeitung nachhaltiger Materialien gelegt. Der Magnetrah-
men erfüllt die Anforderungen der Bau-
stoffklasse B1/schwer entflammbar nach
DIN 4102-1 und kann beispielsweise als
Bilderrahmen in Schulen oder als Gebäu-
deleitsystem in vielfältigen Varianten eingesetzt werden. Durch seine neutrale Formensprache und seine unterschiedlichen
Profile, Glassorten und frei wählbaren
Formate schafft der Rahmen individuelle
Gestaltungsspielräume.

SIGNEO Bunte Wandfarbe 0,8 l
Wall Paint/Wandfarbe

J.W. Ostendorf GmbH & Co. KG,
Coesfeld, Germany/Deutschland
In-house design/Werksdesign
Design: Brand IQ GmbH, Coesfeld,
Germany/Deutschland
www.signeo.de
www.jwo.com

The creation of individualised colour schemes and the shaping of personal lifestyle were of focus when this innovative system was designed. Current colour harmonies were composed and the handling of the spraying unit was reinterpreted in order to appeal to a female target group in particular. The result is a user-friendly spraying system with a self-explanatory and ergonomically designed spray painting gun that can be effortlessly handled. A 0.8-litre paint can from the collection can be screwed directly onto the gun – "plug & spray", so to speak. The colour is cleanly applied to the wall as soon as the button of the spray gun is activated.

Eine individuelle Farbgestaltung und ein persönlicher Wohnstil standen im Mittelpunkt der Entwicklung dieses innovativen Systems. Um vor allem die weibliche Zielgruppe anzusprechen, wurden aktuelle Farbharmonien zusammengestellt und auch die Handhabung der Gebinde wurde gestalterisch neu überdacht. Das Ergebnis ist ein nutzerfreundliches Sprühsystem mit einer ergonomisch gestalteten Sprühpistole, die spielerisch leicht bedient werden kann. Ein 0,8-Liter-Gebinde der Kollektion kann direkt mit der Pistole im Sinne von „Plug & Spray" verschraubt werden; die Farbe wird sauber auf die Wand aufgetragen, sobald ein Knopf der Sprühpistole betätigt wird.

SIGNEO Buntlack 0,43 l
Coloured Gloss / Buntlack

J.W. Ostendorf GmbH & Co. KG,
Coesfeld, Germany / Deutschland
In-house design / Werksdesign
Design: Brand IQ GmbH, Coesfeld,
Germany / Deutschland
www.signeo.de
www.jwo.com

The individual design of a room using coloured gloss from the SIGNEO spraying system is accomplished with an innovative spray gun. From the product design to the packaging layout to the POS presentation – the overall concept of this painting system is directed towards a female target group. It is possible to screw the practical 0.43-litre paint can directly under the spray gun. The device is effortlessly handled – with the push of a button, colour is applied without paint overspray.

Die individuelle Raumgestaltung mit dem Buntlack des Sprühsystems SIGNEO geschieht mit einer innovativen Sprühpistole. Vom Produktdesign über die Verpackungsgestaltung bis hin zur Präsentation ist das Konzept dieses Farbensystems auf eine weibliche Zielgruppe ausgerichtet. Das praktische 0,43-Liter-Gebinde wird direkt unter die spielerisch leicht zu bedienende Sprühpistole geschraubt, dann kann die Farbe auf Knopfdruck schnell und sauber aufgetragen werden.

IdeenBotschaft of the advertising agency Grey Global Group Düsseldorf, Germany
IdeenBotschaft der Werbeagentur Grey Global Group Düsseldorf, Deutschland

Design: Claudia de Bruyn, Uta Cossmann
www.two-design.com
www.cossmann-jacobitz.com

The interior design is a spatial presentation of the new head office of the advertising agency Grey, the IdeenBotschaft, in the form of an imaginative, visionary society. The interaction of form, materiality and function creates animated spaces of beautiful and natural immediacy.

Die Innenarchitektur für die neue Repräsentanz der Werbeagentur Grey, die IdeenBotschaft, stellt die Agentur als eine „ideenreiche, visionäre Gemeinschaft" räumlich dar. In einem Wechselspiel von Form, Materialität und Funktion entstanden lebendige Räume von schön und selbstverständlich anmutender Präsenz.

While
Armchair / Sessel

Caprotti S.a.s., Muggiò (Milano),
Italy / Italien
Design: Marco Goffi, Milan,
Italy / Mailand, Italien
www.marcogoffi.com

An essential metal frame and a single cover of dense textile form the components of the While armchair. Its look features an exciting interplay of seating and back leaning. It is presented as a reinterpretation of a typical piece of furniture, for it does not adopt any new materials but combines the traditional ones in an innovative way.

Ein essenzieller Metallrahmen und eine einzige Bespannung aus dichtem Gewebe bilden die Komponenten des Sessels While. Seine Gestaltung birgt ein spannungsreiches Zusammenspiel zwischen Sitzen und Zurücklehnen und versteht sich als eine neue Interpretation eines typischen Möbelstücks, indem sie nicht nach neuen Werkstoffen sucht, sondern herkömmliche Materialien auf innovative Art und Weise kombiniert.

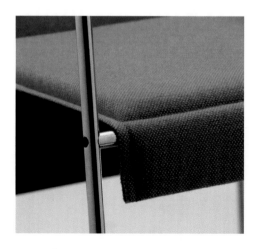

DLW Linoleum – Lino Art
Flooring / Bodenbelag

Armstrong DLW GmbH,
Bietigheim-Bissingen,
Germany / Deutschland
In-house design / Werksdesign
www.armstrong.com

An essential aspect of the design of this collection is the combination of classic DLW linoleum with real metal granulate. It gives the floorings a vintage look and a shimmering elegance that is modified in different ways according to the respective model. Along with a washed-out retro stripe design and contrasting chip flooring the colour world of the Lino Art collection includes 18 matching black, grey and brown hues in six colour ranges.

Ein wesentlicher Aspekt der Gestaltung dieser Kollektion ist die Kombination von klassischem DLW Linoleum mit Echtmetall-Granulat. Die Bodenbeläge erhalten dadurch eine hochwertige Anmutung und sie schimmern auf eine elegante Art und Weise, die, je nach Ausführung, unterschiedlich modifiziert wird. Gemeinsam mit einem verwaschen anmutenden Retro-Streifendesign sowie einem kontrastierenden Chipbelag umfasst die Farbwelt der Lino Art-Kollektion 18 aufeinander abgestimmte Schwarz-, Grau- und Brauntöne in sechs Farbreihen.

Modular Window / Fenster

LG Hausys Ltd., Seoul, Korea
In-house design / Werksdesign:
Dongwoo Shin, Hyung Geun Kim
Design: Kang Hyo Lee, Seoul, Korea
www.lghausys.com

This modular window opposes the traditional notion of a typical window. It adapts to the constantly changing preferences and lifestyles by fulfilling personal wishes and creating individualised living spaces. The window functions can be expanded by choosing various different modules. This includes ventilation, energy-saving and storage options. The combination of window modules provides for a dynamic design inside and outside of a building and imbues the living environment with life. The adaptation of size, colour, and configuration according to individual needs assures a cosy, private space.

Dieses modular gestaltete Fenster möchte der traditionellen Vorstellung von der Form eines Fensters etwas entgegensetzen. Es kann den sich verändernden Vorlieben und Lebensgewohnheiten angepasst werden, mit ihm werden individuelle Wünsche erfüllt und persönliche Wohnräume geschaffen. Mit der Wahl einzelner Module lassen sich die Fensterfunktionen erweitern. Dazu gehören Belüftung und Aufbewahrungsmöglichkeiten sowie Energieeinsparung. In der dynamischen Gestaltung der Innen- wie auch der Außenseite eines Gebäudes beleben die Fenstermodule den Wohnraum. Größe, Farbe und Anordnung können individuell gewählt werden, was einen gemütlichen, privaten Raum schafft.

Programma IT 150
Door Handle / Türgriff

PBA S.p.A., Tezze sul Brenta (Vicenza),
Italy / Italien
In-house design / Werksdesign:
Luciano Masiero
www.pba.it

In the case of this door handle, that which
cannot be seen is in fact the point of focus: the
clear, subtle design of the handle highlights the
disappearing door rosette. Here, form reveals
function.

Bei diesem Türgriff steht das, was nicht vor-
handen ist, im Mittelpunkt: Die klare, reduzierte Ausführung lenkt die Aufmerksamkeit
auf die verschwindende Türrosette. Die Form
zeigt die Funktion.

Chorwo
Door / Tür

Lueb und Wolters GmbH & Co. KG,
Borken/Westfalen, Germany / Deutschland
In-house design / Werksdesign:
Hendrik Rohkämper
www.luebwolters.de

The distinct style of this door is enhanced by the
integration of concealed ribbons into the very
slim cladding with a width of only 18 mm. Thus
flush mounting of the frame on the ribbon side
or the opposite side is possible.

Die klare Formensprache dieser Tür wird
dadurch erreicht, dass bei einer sehr
schmalen Bekleidungsbreite von nur 18 mm
verdeckt liegende Bänder eingebaut wurden.
Damit wird ein wandbündiger Einbau der
Zarge auf der Band- oder Bandgegenseite
ermöglicht.

Meandre
Bicycle Rack/Radständer

mmcité a.s., Bilovice,
Czech Republic/Tschechische Republik
In-house design/Werksdesign:
David Karasek, Radek Hegmon
www.mmcite.com

The Meandre bicycle rack combines an elegant style language and the option to be used from both sides. A rubber band spans wheels of different dimensions; continuous pipes protect the bicycle from theft.

Die Möglichkeit, ihn von beiden Seiten nutzen zu können, verbindet der Radständer Meandre mit einer elegant anmutenden Formensprache. Ein Gummiband umspannt Räder verschiedener Abmessungen, durchgehende Rohre sichern das Fahrrad vor Diebstahl.

DA-PIN-0902
Bollard/Poller

Design Dada Associates, Inc., Seoul, Korea
In-house design/Werksdesign: Seok Hoon Park, Kwan Joong Jeon, Jin Sup Kim
www.dada-da.com

With its simple and concise form, this bollard presents itself as an expressive and significant element in urban space. The inner core consists of a highly resilient urethane bar, which aids in absorbing sudden shocks if a vehicle drives against the pole. In spite of its reduced and slim shape tapering towards the top, the bollard makes a solid impression.

In seiner prägnanten Schlichtheit präsentiert sich dieser Poller als ein aussagekräftiges Element im städtischen Raum. Sein innerer Kern ist ein Stab aus Urethan, ein sehr nachgiebiges Material, das plötzliche Stöße abfedert, wenn ein Fahrzeug dagegen fährt. Trotz der zurückhaltenden, schlanken Form, die sich nach oben kegelförmig verjüngt, wirkt der Poller stabil.

kPark
Precast Concrete Garage /
Beton-Fertigteil-Garage

Beton Kemmler GmbH, Tübingen-Hirschau,
Germany / Deutschland
In-house design / Werksdesign:
Dr. Marc Kemmler, Martin Heimrich
Design: Schmutz & Partner
(Prof. Eduard Schmutz, Matthias Mayer),
Stuttgart, Germany / Deutschland
www.beton-kemmler.de
www.schmutz-partner.de

With its transparent design this variable garage
system featuring a green covered roof and back
wall surface can be easily adapted to garden
and area formations. By its haptic properties
the surface quality of the concrete underlines
the monolithic appearance of this system. An
essential advantage of kPark is the reduction
of ground sealing; it dispenses with gutters
and rainwater downpipes. As electric cables are
integrated into walls and ceilings, the interior
displays a calm appearance as well.

Mit seiner transparenten Gestaltung lässt sich
dieses variable Garagensystem mit begrünter
Dach- und Rückwandfläche gut an die Gar-
ten- und Geländeformation anpassen. Die
Oberflächenqualität des Betons unterstreicht
durch ihre Haptik die monolithische Anmutung dieses Systems. Ein wesentlicher Vorteil
von kPark ist, dass die Flächenversiegelung
reduziert wird und keine Dachrinnen und
Regenfallrohre mehr nötig sind. Die Wände
und Decken mit integrierten Elektrozulei-
tungen schaffen ein ruhiges Erscheinungsbild
auch im Inneren.

Hydra Linearis
Rod Grating / Dränagerinne

Richard Brink GmbH & Co. KG,
Schloß Holte-Stukenbrock,
Germany / Deutschland
In-house design / Werksdesign:
Stefan Brink
www.richard-brink.de

Hydra Linearis is a straight-lined, longitudinal rod grating which can be placed on all drainage channels and gutters. The bottom parts of the gutter are constructed such in a way that the grating is solely held in place from underneath. Consequently, only the longitudinal rods can be seen after the gratings have been fitted. The innovation ensures safe drainage of surface water.

Hydra Linearis ist ein geradlinig gestalteter Längsstabrost, der auf allen Formen von Entwässerungsrinnen bzw. Dränagerinnen aufgebracht werden kann. Die Rinnenunterteile werden dabei so gebaut, dass der Rost nur im unteren Bereich eingefasst wird. Im eingebauten Zustand sind daher nur die Längsstäbe zu sehen, diese ermöglichen einen sicheren Abfluss von Oberflächenwasser.

Solbeam
Solar Plant Colonnade /
Säulen-Solaranlage

GS Engineering & Construction,
Seoul, Korea
In-house design / Werksdesign:
Eun Young Kim, Joon Won Suh
www.gsconst.co.kr

The solar plant colonnade Solbeam is an ecological sculpture powered by solar and rainwater energy. Shaped like a colonnade, it can be installed in residential units or public space. At certain intervals, the stored rainwater is sprayed.

Die Säulen-Solaranlage Solbeam ist eine ökologische Skulptur, die mit Sonnen- und Regenwasserenergie betrieben wird. Solbeam hat die Form einer Säulenanlage und kann in Wohneinheiten oder im öffentlichen Raum aufgestellt werden. Das gespeicherte Regenwasser wird in bestimmten Abständen versprüht.

Wicked
City Light Advertising Unit/
City-Light-Posteranlage

EUROmodul d.o.o., Viskovo,
Croatia / Kroatien
In-house design / Werksdesign:
Karlo Babic
www.euromodul.hr

Wicked is a two-sided City Light advertising
unit mounted on a pillar in combination with a
bench. The pillar and the city light display can
also be installed without additional equipment.
LED lights in the middle of the pillar create a
lively nightlife scene.

Wicked ist eine doppelseitige City-Light-Pos-
teranlage, die aus einer Säule und einer Bank
besteht. Die Säule und die City-Light-Vitrine
können ohne weiteres Zubehör aufgestellt
werden. LED-Leuchten in der Mitte der Säule
schaffen eine ansprechende Nachtszenerie.

Assessment criteria

- Degree of innovation
- Functionality
- Formal quality
- Ergonomics
- Durability
- Symbolic and emotional content
- Product peripherals
- Self-explanatory quality
- Ecological soundness

Beurteilungskriterien

- Innovationsgrad
- Funktionalität
- Formale Qualität
- Ergonomie
- Langlebigkeit
- Symbolischer und emotionaler Gehalt
- Produktperipherie
- Selbsterklärungsqualität
- Ökologische Verträglichkeit

The jurors of the "red dot award: product design"
International orientation and objectivity

Die Juroren des red dot award: product design
Internationalität und Objektivität

All members of the "red dot award: product design" jury are appointed on the basis of independence and impartiality. They are independent designers, academics in design faculties, representatives of international design institutions, and design journalists. The jury is international in its composition, which changes every year. These conditions assure a maximum of objectivity. The members of this year's jury are presented in alphabetical order in the following pages.

In die Jury des red dot award: product design wird als Mitglied nur berufen, wer gänzlich unabhängig und unparteiisch ist. Dies sind selbstständig arbeitende Designer, Hochschullehrer der Designfakultäten, Repräsentanten internationaler Designinstitutionen und Designfachjournalisten. Die Jury ist international besetzt und wechselt in jedem Jahr ihre Zusammensetzung. Unter diesen Voraussetzungen ist ein Höchstmaß an Objektivität gewährleistet. Auf den folgenden Seiten werden die Jurymitglieder des diesjährigen Wettbewerbs in alphabetischer Reihenfolge vorgestellt.

"The red dot design award is the 'global hub' of worldwide design competitiveness."

„Der red dot design award ist der ‚global hub' des weltweiten Wettbewerbs im Design."

Prof. Werner Aisslinger

Professor Werner Aisslinger was born in 1964. After studying design at HdK, Berlin, he worked for Jasper Morrison and Ron Arad in London and in the Studio De Lucchi in Milan. In 1993, he founded Studio Aisslinger in Berlin, focusing on product development, conceptual design and brand architecture. His clients include vitra, interlübke, Cappellini, Jaguar, Bertelsmann and ZDF. From 1994 he was a visiting lecturer at HdK, Berlin, as well as the Lahti Design Institute in Finland, and from 1998 to 2005 was a professor of product design at the Hochschule für Gestaltung in Karlsruhe. His works have won numerous awards, among others in the Design Plus Award, the Compasso d'Oro Selection, the Blueprint 100% Design Award and the red dot design award, and are part of collections at the Vitra Design Museum, Weil am Rhein, the Centre Georges Pompidou in Paris and the Museum of Modern Art in New York, among others. Since 2006 Aisslinger has been on the board of curators for the Raymond Loewy Foundation and has acted as juror in the Lucky Strike Design Award.

Professor Werner Aisslinger, 1964 geboren, arbeitete nach seinem Designstudium an der Hochschule der Künste Berlin bei Jasper Morrison und Ron Arad in London sowie im Studio De Lucchi in Mailand. 1993 gründete er in Berlin das Studio Aisslinger mit den Schwerpunkten Produktentwicklung, Designkonzeption und Brand Architecture und arbeitet u. a. für vitra, interlübke, Cappellini, Jaguar, Bertelsmann und ZDF. Ab 1994 war er als Gastdozent an der HdK in Berlin sowie am finnischen Lahti Design Institute tätig, und 1998–2005 hatte er eine Professur für Produktdesign an der Hochschule für Gestaltung, Karlsruhe, inne. Seine Arbeiten wurden vielfach ausgezeichnet, u. a. beim Design Plus Award, Compasso d'Oro Selection, Blueprint 100% Design Award und red dot design award, und in Sammlungen wie die des Vitra Design Museums, Weil am Rhein, des Centre Georges Pompidou in Paris oder des Museum of Modern Art in New York aufgenommen. Seit 2006 ist Aisslinger Kuratoriumsmitglied der Raymond Loewy Foundation und in der Jury des Lucky Strike Design Award.

Professor Werner Aisslinger supported the expert jury in the category "Architecture and interior design" as well as "Offices", and expressed his delight at the design quality that he encountered in this categories: "The design quality of established brands continues to be high with a tendency toward an ever stronger focus on product design – a tendency that is most pleasing for the design world," the renowned designer said. "Besides that, there are new manufacturers, start-ups and unknown brands who, we are happy to see, are up to competing with the established brands in the red dot design award. However, in terms of technical realisation, the level of conceptual innovation and, above all, the standard of design, they often still lack originality."

What current trends do you see in the category "Architecture and interior design"?
Architecture today follows an ever more complex approach, and the resulting aesthetics are influenced by issues such as energy efficiency, self-sufficiency, sustainability, the life cycle of elements, and the interrelation with infrastructure – therefore architects today are operating in an exciting and ever more complex domain. In interior design, formal approaches dominate; the integration of new worlds of materials and the virtuoso use of light and projectors or screens is particularly interesting.

What trends do you see in the category "Offices"?
The office furniture industry is facing tremendous cost pressure, yet in part it displays astonishing creativity – in particular in terms of surfaces, materials and the reduction of obvious engineering, for instance in "seat machines". Also interesting is the tendency, particularly in the area of swivel chairs, to no longer conform to all existing DIN norms when designing a chair, but to rather archetypically create a basic chair with a reduced range of functions.

Professor Werner Aisslinger unterstützte die Expertenjury in den Bereichen „Architektur und Interior Design" sowie „Büro". Dabei äußerte er sich über die Designqualität in diesen Kategorien erfreut: „Die Designqualität der etablierten Marken ist gleichbleibend hoch, mit Tendenz zu einem immer größeren Fokus auf das Produktdesign – alles in allem eine erfreuliche Tendenz für die Designwelt", so der renommierte Designer. „Daneben gibt es natürlich neue Hersteller, Start-ups und unbekannte Marken, die sich erfreulicherweise mit den bekannten Brands beim red dot design award messen wollen. Bei der technischen Umsetzung, dem konzeptionellen Innovationsgrad und vor allem beim Designniveau lassen sie eine Eigenständigkeit aber oft noch vermissen."

Welche aktuellen Trends sehen Sie im Bereich „Architektur und Interior Design"?
Architektur wird heute immer komplexer gedacht, und die entstehende Ästhetik ist mehr durch Themen wie Energieeffizienz, Autarkheit, Nachhaltigkeit, Lebenszyklen von Komponenten und dem Zusammenwirken mit der Infrastruktur beeinflusst – die Architekten bewegen sich deshalb zurzeit in einem spannenden und komplexer werdenden Umfeld. Beim Interior Design herrschen formale Herangehensweisen vor; interessant sind die Einbindung neuer Materialwelten und der teilweise virtuose Umgang mit Licht und Projektionen oder Screens.

Welche Trends sind in der Kategorie „Büro" erkennbar?
Die Büromöbelbranche steht unter einem harten Kostendruck und zeigt sich teilweise dennoch erstaunlich kreativ – besonders im Umgang mit Oberflächen, Materialien und der Reduktion von sichtbarem Engineering, z. B. bei „Sitzmaschinen". Interessant ist auch die Tendenz, besonders im Drehstuhlbereich, nicht mehr den alle DIN-Normen der Welt erfüllenden Stuhl zu kreieren, sondern eher archetypisch einen Basisstuhl mit reduziertem Funktionsspektrum zu entwerfen.

"I see design as one of the disciplines that address and impact survival and are capable conveying social meaning through products."

„Ich verstehe Design als eine der Disziplinen, die sich mit dem Überleben befassen und in der Lage sind, durch Produkte sozial Bedeutsames zu schaffen."

Manuel Alvarez Fuentes

Manuel Alvarez Fuentes studied industrial design at Universidad Iberoamericana, Mexico City, where he later served as director of the design department. In 1975, he received a Master of Design from the Royal College of Art, London. He has almost 40 years experience as a practising designer in the fields of product design, furniture and interior design, packaging design, signage, and visual communications. Since 1992, Manuel Alvarez Fuentes has been director (senior partner) of Diseño Corporativo (diCorp), a design consultancy office in Querétaro, Mexico. He acts as consultant and advisor for numerous companies and institutions as well as a board member of various designers' associations; for example, he was a member of the Icsid Board of Directors 1999–2001, vice president of the National Chamber of Industry of Mexico, Querétaro, 2007–2008, and director of the Innovation and Design Award, Querétaro, 2007.

Manuel Alvarez Fuentes studierte Industriedesign an der Universidad Iberoamericana, Mexiko-Stadt, wo er später die Leitung des Fachbereichs Design übernahm, und erhielt 1975 zudem einen Master of Design des Royal College of Art, London. Er verfügt über nahezu 40 Jahre Erfahrung als praktizierender Designer in Bereichen wie Produkt- und Möbelgestaltung, Interior Design, Verpackungsdesign, Leitsystemen und visueller Kommunikation. Seit 1992 ist er Direktor (Senior-Partner) der Diseño Corporativo (diCorp), einem Beratungsunternehmen für Produktgestaltung in Querétaro, Mexiko. Manuel Alvarez Fuentes ist als Berater und Experte für zahlreiche Unternehmen und Institutionen sowie als Vorstandsmitglied in verschiedenen Designverbänden tätig, z. B. im Icsid-Vorstand 1999–2001, als Vizepräsident der mexikanischen Industrie- und Handelskammer im Bundesstaat Querétaro 2007–2008 und als Direktor des Innovation and Design Award, Querétaro, 2007.

Manuel Alvarez Fuentes, who acted as juror in the categories "Sport, games and leisure" as well as "Gardens", mentioned right after the adjudication process how he was fascinated by the innovations and design developments of this year: "I can mention that in the product design of this year's red dot design award I was able to see innovations that will impact the industry and the market. Take, for instance, innovative products manufactured with the proper selection of materials and finishes, some of which become so important that one cannot be surprised by the enormous contribution they make to other design fields. In my opinion, this is one of the major concerns for an exceptional manufacture and product performance."

What, in your opinion, is the significance of design quality in the industries judged by you?
Design quality in all industries means, for any given product, not only delivering a great product appearance but also going deeper with innovation and having excellent manufacturing. The significance of high design quality in products within the two categories "Sport, games and leisure" and "Gardens" means clear functionality, optimal interaction with users, unsurpassed manufacture with an incomparable selection of materials and finishes, as well as a sustainable approach towards product fabrication and usage. red dot design award entries have shown a high level of design quality among a great variety of products.

What current trends do you see in the category "Sport, games and leisure"?
A trend that stands out in most of the products in this category is undoubtedly the overall image that is rendered by the products; image becomes relevant above other factors. The appearance of products in this category creates magic and basically conveys the purpose of all design efforts and decisions.

Manuel Alvarez Fuentes, der die Kategorien „Freizeit, Sport und Spiel" sowie „Garten" bewertete, äußerte sich im Anschluss an die Jurierung begeistert von den Innovationen und Entwicklungen im Design in diesem Jahr: „Im diesjährigen red dot design award habe ich Innovationen gesehen, die die Branche und den Markt stark beeinflussen werden. Mit der angemessenen Auswahl an Materialien und Finishes hergestellt, werden einige von ihnen derart wichtig werden, dass man von ihrem enormen Beitrag, den sie auch für andere Designbereiche leisten, nicht überrascht sein wird. Meiner Meinung nach ist dies eines der wichtigsten Ergebnisse einer außergewöhnlichen Herstellungs- und Produktleistung."

Wie würden Sie den Stellenwert von Designqualität in den von Ihnen beurteilten Branchen einschätzen?
Designqualität bedeutet in allen Branchen und für jedes Produkt, nicht nur eine großartige Anmutung zu bieten, sondern in Innovation und exzellenter Fertigung tiefer zu gehen. Der Stellenwert von Designqualität in den Produkten der Kategorien „Freizeit, Sport und Spiel" und „Garten" betrifft klare Funktionalität, optimale Interaktion mit dem Anwender, unübertroffene Fertigung mit einer nicht vergleichbaren Auswahl an Materialien und Finishes sowie einen nachhaltigen Ansatz in Bezug auf die Produktherstellung und Anwendung. Die Einreichungen zum red dot design award haben ein hohes Maß an Designqualität in einer großen Bandbreite von Produkten gezeigt.

Welche Trends sehen Sie derzeit in der Kategorie „Freizeit, Sport und Spiel"?
Ein Trend, der bei den meisten Produkten in dieser Kategorie hervorsticht, ist zweifellos das von diesen Produkten vermittelte Gesamtimage; das Image steht über allen anderen Faktoren. Die Anmut der Produkte in dieser Kategorie besitzt Magie und vermittelt im Grunde den Sinn und Zweck aller gestalterischen Bemühungen und Entscheidungen.

"The red dot design award is ... the design competition that demonstrates the increasing value of design in business."

„Der red dot design award ist ... der Designwettbewerb, der den steigenden Wert von Design in Unternehmen aufzeigt."

Dr. Mark Breitenberg

Dr. Mark Breitenberg studied English literature at the University of California, San Diego, and holds a PhD in literature and critical theory. He worked in the film industry as an independent writer, producer, and story analyst for Bedford Falls, Columbia Pictures, Disney and other companies, before holding teaching positions at Swarthmore College in Pennsylvania and Otis College of Art and Design in Los Angeles. He was then Chair of Liberal Arts and Sciences at the Art Center College of Design in Pasadena, and from 2004 to 2007 he was Dean of Undergraduate Education and later became Dean of Humanities and Design Sciences until 2009. Since then he has been Provost at California College of the Arts (CCA) in San Francisco. In addition, Mark Breitenberg is the author of many books and published articles, and at present he is President of Icsid; he serves among many others on the advisory board and is an adjunct faculty member at the Tecnológico de Monterrey, Graduate School of Design in Mexico.

Dr. Mark Breitenberg studierte englische Literatur an der Universität von Kalifornien, San Diego, und trägt einen Doktortitel in Literatur und Kritischer Theorie. Er arbeitete in der Filmindustrie als unabhängiger Autor, Produzent und Storyberater für Bedford Falls, Columbia Pictures, Disney und andere Firmen, bevor er in lehrender Position am Swarthmore College in Pennsylvania und dem Otis College of Art and Design in Los Angeles tätig war. Daraufhin war Breitenberg Ordinarius der Liberal Arts and Sciences am Art Center College of Design in Pasadena, von 2004 bis 2007 Dekan im Bereich Undergraduate Education und später, bis 2009, Dekan der Humanities and Design Sciences. Seitdem ist er Direktor des California College of the Arts (CCA) in San Francisco. Zudem ist Mark Breitenberg, Autor vieler Bücher und publizierter Artikel, der derzeitige Präsident des Icsid; er dient unter vielem anderen im Beirat und ist außerordentliches Fakultätsmitglied am Tecnológico de Monterrey, der Graduate School of Design in Mexiko.

Dr. Mark Breitenberg, who this year was a first-time member of the red dot jury, judged the products in the categories "Living rooms and bedrooms" as well as "Lighting and lamps". The expert design theoretician, who defines design as "the ability to identify and solve a truly human need," pointed out that the entries to the "red dot award: product design" showed a heightened awareness of sustainability and concern with energy-saving products.

What is, in your opinion, the significance of design quality in the industries judged by you?
The significance is that industry and consumers increasingly understand the value of good design as a competitive edge, so quality becomes more important.

How important is design quality in the global market?
Over the last ten years or so, the importance of design quality has increased dramatically as consumers have become more design literate. The success of the red dot competitions is a testament to the growing importance of design quality in the global market.

What current trends do you see in the field of "Living rooms and bedrooms"?
For the most part, the entrants represented interpretations of established or iconic designs from before.

What current trends do you see in the category "Lighting and lamps"?
Only a few of the entrants were breaking new ground in this category. Certainly there was more attention to energy-saving products.

Do you see a clear development in design emerging this year, for example with regards to choice of materials and manufacturing techniques, or possibly regarding surprising innovations?
I did not see surprising innovations, but in general there was more attention to sustainability in most of the products.

Dr. Mark Breitenberg, in diesem Jahr erstmals Mitglied der red dot-Jury, bewertete die Kategorien „Wohnen und Schlafen" sowie „Licht und Leuchten". Der fachkundige Designtheoretiker, der Design als „die Fähigkeit, zutiefst menschliche Bedürfnisse zu erkennen und zu erfüllen" definiert, nahm unter den Einreichungen zum red dot award: product design insbesondere eine erhöhte Aufmerksamkeit hinsichtlich nachhaltiger und energiesparender Produkte wahr.

Wie würden Sie den Stellenwert von Designqualität in den von Ihnen beurteilten Branchen einschätzen?
Der Stellenwert ist der, dass sowohl die Industrie als auch die Konsumenten den Wert guten Designs zunehmend als Wettbewerbsvorteil verstehen, sodass Qualität immer wichtiger wird.

Wie wichtig ist Designqualität im globalen Markt?
Etwa während der letzten zehn Jahre hat sich die Bedeutung der Designqualität dramatisch erhöht, da die Konsumenten designkundiger geworden sind. Der Erfolg der red dot-Wettbewerbe ist ein Beleg für die wachsende Designqualität im globalen Markt.

Welche Trends sehen Sie derzeit im Bereich „Wohnen und Schlafen"?
Größtenteils stellen die Einreichungen Interpretationen bereits etablierter Gestaltungen und Designikonen dar.

Welche Trends sehen Sie derzeit in der Kategorie „Licht und Leuchten"?
Nur ein Teil der Einreichungen in dieser Kategorie betritt neuen Boden. Gewiss lag ein größeres Augenmerk auf energiesparenden Produkten.

Sehen Sie eine sich in diesem Jahr klar abzeichnende Entwicklung im Design, zum Beispiel in Hinsicht auf Materialwahl oder Herstellungstechniken, oder womöglich gar überraschende Innovationen?
Ich habe keine überraschenden Innovationen gesehen, aber im Allgemeinen zeigten die meisten der Produkte eine erhöhte Aufmerksamkeit in Bezug auf die Nachhaltigkeit.

"Design is ... an intention made manifest."

„Design ist ... eine manifestierte Intention."

Shashi Caan

Shashi Caan received a BFA (Hons) in environmental design at the Edinburgh College of Art, Great Britain, as well as two Master's degrees (in industrial design and architecture) at the Pratt Institute, New York. Subsequently, she worked in architecture and design agencies such as Gensler Associates, New York, and was design director of the New York office of Skidmore, Owings & Merrill Architects. In 2002, Shashi Caan was appointed chairwoman of the interior design degree programme at the Parsons School of Design and founded her own agency, Shashi Caan Collective, with herself as managing director. Highly engaged in research seeking further development of design and design education, among others with New York's Columbia University where she is currently leading a research effort exploring design education, Shashi Caan serves on the boards of a number of professional associations and is the current President of IFI (International Federation of Interior Architects/Designers).

Shashi Caan erhielt einen Bachelor of Fine Arts (Hons) in Environmental Design am Edinburgh College of Art, Großbritannien, sowie zwei Masterabschlüsse (Industrial Design und Architektur) am Pratt Institute, New York, USA. Im Anschluss arbeitete sie in Architektur- und Designbüros wie Gensler Associates, New York, und war Design Director des New Yorker Büros von Skidmore, Owings & Merrill Architects. 2002 wurde sie zur Vorsitzenden des Studiengangs Interior Design an der Parsons School of Design ernannt und gründete ihr eigenes Büro, Shashi Caan Collective, dessen Geschäftsführerin sie ist. Shashi Caan beschäftigt sich intensiv mit Forschungsprojekten zur weiteren Entwicklung der Bereiche Produktgestaltung und Designausbildung u. a. an der New Yorker Columbia University, wo sie derzeit Forschungsarbeiten im Bereich Design Education leitet. Shashi Caan ist Ausschussmitglied verschiedener professioneller Verbände und gegenwärtig Präsidentin der IFI (International Federation of Interior Architects/Designers).

Shashi Caan supported this year's jury of experts in the categories "Architecture and interior design" and "Offices". After the process of judging, which lasted several days, the prolific designer and architect defined the red dot design award as "an important endorsement of design quality and innovation while simultaneously acknowledging design talent and accomplishment."

What, in your opinion, is the significance of design quality in the industries judged by you?
While all design affects human beings, interior design shapes human behaviour and life experiences. Quality – both literal and perceived – intrinsically shapes the quality of human interactions.

How important is design quality in the global market?
Design quality is very important. It helps to elevate quality of life for people worldwide.

What current trends do you see in the realm of "Architecture and interior design"?
Cultural change, driven primarily by the global economy, and ecological concerns continue to have an impact on materiality and aesthetics. Technological advancement strives for innovation. Combined, these factors ask for change in processes and behaviours that have an impact on the architectural design thinking.

What trends do you see in the category "Offices"?
Greater product flexibility, which allows for a multitude of work activity, continues to be tantamount. The ability to produce bespoke solutions using standardised components remains an important design criterion.

Do you see a clear development in design emerging this year, for example with regards to the choice of materials and manufacturing techniques?
The use of fewer components applied to a greater variety of solutions is one driver for redesign and renovation of facilities. This fosters the streamlining of products and enhancement of activities.

Shashi Caan unterstützte die Expertenjury in diesem Jahr in den Bereichen „Architektur und Interior Design" sowie „Büro". Am Ende des mehrtägigen Auswahlprozesses definierte die engagierte Designerin und Architektin den red dot design award als „eine wichtige Bestätigung für Designqualität und Innovation und als gleichzeitige Anerkennung von Designtalenten und -errungenschaften."

Wie würden Sie den Stellenwert von Designqualität in den von Ihnen beurteilten Branchen einschätzen?
Während alle Gestaltung den Menschen berührt, prägt Interior Design das menschliche Verhalten und Erleben. Und Qualität – im wörtlichen wie im wahrgenommen Sinne – prägt die Qualität der menschlichen Interaktion an sich.

Wie wichtig ist Designqualität im globalen Markt?
Designqualität ist sehr wichtig. Sie unterstützt die Menschen weltweit, ihre Lebensqualität anzuheben.

Welche aktuellen Trends sehen Sie im Bereich „Architektur und Interior Design"?
Die primär durch die globale Wirtschaft und ökologische Fragen vorangetriebene Kulturveränderung beeinflusst die Materialität und Ästhetik nach wie vor. Technologischer Fortschritt strebt nach Innovation. Zusammen fordern diese Faktoren die Veränderung von Prozessen sowie des Verhaltens, die sich auf das architektonische Gestaltungsdenken auswirken.

Welche Trends sehen Sie in der Kategorie „Büro"?
Größere Produktflexibilität, die eine Vielzahl von Arbeitsaktivitäten ermöglicht, ist weiterhin wichtig. Auch die Fähigkeit, maßgeschneiderte Lösungen mit standardisierten Komponenten zu schaffen, bleibt ein wichtiges Gestaltungskriterium.

Sehen Sie eine sich in diesem Jahr klar abzeichnende Entwicklung im Design, zum Beispiel in Bezug auf Materialwahl oder Herstellungstechnik?
Der Einsatz von weniger Komponenten für eine größere Vielfalt an Lösungen ist eine der Antriebskräfte für die Um- und Neugestaltung von Infrastrukturen. Das fördert die Optimierung der Produkte und die Steigerung von Aktivität.

"The red dot design award is a symbol of advanced living and a platform to generate innovations and solutions to people's everyday lives."

„Der red dot design award ist Symbol einer fortschrittlichen Lebensweise und eine Plattform zur Generierung von Innovationen und Lösungen für das Alltagsleben der Menschen."

Tony K. M. Chang

Tony K. M. Chang, born in 1946, studied architecture at Chung Yuan Christian University in Chung Li, Taiwan. He is currently chief executive officer of the Taiwan Design Center and editor-in-chief of DESIGN magazine. Chang has made tremendous contributions to industrial design, both in his home country and in the Asia-Pacific region. As an expert in design management and design promotion, he has served as a consultant for governments and in the corporate sector for decades. From 2005 until 2007 and again since 2009, he has been an executive board member of the International Council of Societies of Industrial Design and is now masterminding the 2011 IDA Congress in Taipei. In 2008, he was elected founding chairman of the Taiwan Design Alliance, a consortium of government-supported and private design entities aimed at promoting Taiwanese design. Tony K. M. Chang has been invited to lecture in Europe, the United States, and Asia, and he often serves as a juror in prestigious international design competitions.

Tony K. M. Chang, 1946 geboren, studierte Architektur an der Chung Yuan Christian University in Chung Li, Taiwan. Er ist derzeit Chief Executive Officer des Taiwan Design Centers und Chefredakteur des Magazins „DESIGN". Chang hat im Bereich Industriedesign Erhebliches geleistet, sowohl in seinem Heimatland als auch im gesamten Asien-Pazifik-Raum. Als Experte in Designmanagement und Designförderung ist er seit Jahrzehnten als Berater in Regierungs- und Unternehmenskreisen tätig. Zwischen 2005 und 2007 war er und ist seit 2009 erneut Vorstandsmitglied des International Council of Societies of Industrial Design und ist jetzt federführend in der Planung des IDA Congress 2011 in Taipei. Im Jahr 2008 wurde er zum Founding Chairman der Taiwan Design Alliance gewählt, einem Konsortium staatlich geförderter und privater Designorgane mit dem Ziel der Förderung taiwanesischen Designs. Tony K. M. Chang erhielt Einladungen zu Vorträgen in Europa, den USA und Asien und fungiert oft als Juror in hochangesiedelten internationalen Designwettbewerben.

For Tony K. M. Chang, who adjudicated the entries from the categories "Living rooms and bedrooms" as well as "Lighting and lamps", the significance of design quality in these industry branches cannot be evaluated highly enough. He also emphasises in particular that the task of designers has naturally included taking into account aspects of sustainability and ecological soundness in their designs.

What, in your opinion, is the significance of design quality in the industries judged by you?
The quality of design plays a crucial role. In addition to outward appearance, a designer should also attach importance to product safety and functionality. There are also issues of environmental protection and energy conservation which require attention. Design should stress recyclability with an ideal of "cradle to cradle design."

How important is design quality in the global market?
As far as the global market is concerned, a designer should control quality with the intention of furthering convenience in people's lives. He or she should refrain from generating more entanglements and unnecessary repercussions with the design.

What current trends do you see in the category "Lighting and lamps"?
Regarding home furnishing designs, I see more innovative materials being applied, with increased consideration being granted to energy conservation, carbon reduction, and greenness. Cutting-edge technology and innovative design are always favoured by modern users. Energy conservation is also a focal point in the latest home furnishing designs.

What are the challenges that the design industry is facing and what do you think solutions to these challenges could look like?
An important issue in modern design is how to integrate innovative materials and new technology. This process should start from simplicity and advance to complexity. It should also avoid "design just for design's sake" and be user-oriented with the intention of offering solutions.

Für Tony K. M. Chang, der die Einreichungen in den Bereichen „Wohnen und Schlafen" sowie „Licht und Leuchten" beurteilte, kann der Stellenwert der Designqualität in diesen Branchen nicht hoch genug eingeschätzt werden. Besonders hebt er dabei auch die Aufgabe der Designer hervor, die Nachhaltigkeit und Umweltverträglichkeit ihrer Entwürfe zu berücksichtigen.

Wie würden Sie den Stellenwert der Designqualität in den von Ihnen beurteilten Branchen einschätzen?
Die Designqualität spielt eine entscheidende Rolle. Neben der rein äußerlichen Gestaltung sollten Designer auch der Sicherheit und Funktionalität eines Produktes Bedeutung beimessen. Auch die Punkte Umweltschutz und Energiesparen fordern Beachtung. Design sollte Recycelfähigkeit im Sinne des Ideals „Von der Wiege zur Wiege" für sich beanspruchen.

Wie wichtig ist Designqualität im globalen Markt?
Was den globalen Markt anbelangt, sollten Designer Qualität mit dem Ziel kontrollieren, das Leben der Menschen noch angenehmer zu gestalten. Sie sollten von noch mehr Verknüpfung und unnötigem Nachhall in ihren Gestaltungen Abstand nehmen.

Welche derzeitigen Trends sehen Sie in der Kategorie „Licht und Leuchten"?
Im Bereich Wohnungseinrichtung sehe ich in den Gestaltungen den Einsatz von mehr innovativen Materialien mit größerem Bedacht auf Energieeffizienz, CO_2-Einsparung und Ökologie. Moderne Nutzer favorisieren stets neuste Technologie und innovative Gestaltung. Energiesparen ist auch eines der zentralen Themen bei den neuesten Gestaltungen der Wohnungseinrichtung.

Vor welchen Herausforderungen steht die Designbranche Ihrer Meinung nach, und wie könnte ein Lösungsansatz dafür aussehen?
Ein wichtiges Thema im modernen Design ist die Frage, wie innovative Materialien und neue Technologien integriert werden können. Dieser Prozess sollte sich von Schlichtheit ausgehend zur Komplexität entwickeln. Er sollte „Gestaltungen um der Gestaltung willen" vermeiden und stattdessen benutzergerecht sein, mit dem Ziel, Lösungen zu bieten.

Sebastian Conran

Sebastian Conran's career began in 1977 working as a designer for The Clash, designing record sleeves, posters, stage sets, and clothing. In 1979, he joined leading branding consultancy Wolff Olins, and in 1981 he became Head of Merchandise Design at Mothercare, before setting up his own design studio in 1986. With specific focus on innovative merchandise development and user experience design, Sebastian Conran Associates is known for ingenious and elegant design solutions. The studio's work has received many design and innovation awards as well as dozens of patents in a variety of industries. Sebastian Conran is also visiting Professor of Design Against Crime at Central Saint Martins College of Art and Design; Leader of the UK Home Office "Design and Technology Alliance against Crime"; Chairman of the "Creative Industries Knowledge Transfer Network" for the Technology Strategy Board; founding Trustee of the Design Museum; and Member of the Design Council.

Sebastian Conran begann seine Karriere 1977 als Designer für The Clash, für die er Plattencover, Poster, Bühnenbilder und Bekleidung entwarf. 1979 wechselte er zur führenden Markenberatung Wolff Olins und wurde 1981 Leiter des Bereichs Merchandise Design bei Mothercare, bevor er 1986 sein eigenes Designstudio gründete. Mit seinem besonderen Schwerpunkt auf der Entwicklung innovativer Handelswaren und der Gestaltung von Benutzererfahrung ist Sebastian Conran Associates bekannt für ausgeklügelte und elegante Designlösungen. Das Studio erhielt für seine Arbeit zahlreiche Design- und Innovationspreise und Dutzende Patente in verschiedenen Branchen. Sebastian Conran ist darüber hinaus Gastprofessor für „Design Against Crime" am Central Saint Martins College of Art and Design, Leiter der Expertengruppe „Design and Technology Alliance against Crime" des britischen Innenministeriums, Vorsitzender des „Creative Industries Knowledge Transfer Network" für das Technology Strategy Board, mitbegründender Verwalter des „Design Museum" und Mitglied des Design Council.

Sebastian Conran, jury member in the category "Households and kitchens", in his concluding remarks about this year's product submissions to the red dot design award makes a surprising observation about the influence of the Internet on the significance of design quality in an international comparison. In the designer's own words: "Now the Internet makes us more aware of everything available; it is design quality that will give the edge rather than price, as this will erode profitability to zero."

What is, in your opinion, the significance of design quality in the industries judged by you?
As kitchens have become part of the living space and domestic cooking equipment is on show, their appearance is especially important. When you use them their performance becomes more important. When you clean them their functionality and usability are key. But when you buy them, it is brand, design and quality against cost.

What current trends do you see in the category "Households and kitchens"?
Functional innovation, differentiation and homogenisation combined with a bit of domestic sculpture to counteract the tendency towards generic Teutonic rationalism.

Do you see a clear development in design emerging this year, for example with regards to choice of materials and manufacturing techniques, or possibly regarding surprising innovations?
Definitely there are some tendencies towards subtle playfulness, but largely due to economic constraints there are inevitably more incremental innovations rather than quantum leaps of creativity.

Sebastian Conran, Jury-Mitglied in der Kategorie „Haushalt und Küche", zieht in seinem Fazit der diesjährigen Einreichungen zum red dot design award bemerkenswerte Rückschlüsse vom Internet auf den Stellenwert der Designqualität im internationalen Vergleich. So präzisiert der erfolgreiche Designexperte: „Heutzutage bietet sich uns dank Internet ein größeres Bewusstsein dessen, was es auf dem Markt gibt; den Wettbewerbsvorteil bringt dabei die Designqualität und nicht der Preis, da Letzterer die Profitabilität gegen null treibt."

Wie würden Sie den Stellenwert von Designqualität in den von Ihnen beurteilten Branchen einschätzen?
Da sich Küchen zu einem Teil des Wohnbereichs gewandelt haben und die heimische Kochausrüstung dadurch besonders hervortritt, ist ihre Anmutung überaus wichtig. Im Einsatz wird ihre Leistungsfähigkeit wichtiger, beim Reinigen sind ihre Funktionalität und Gebrauchstauglichkeit entscheidend. Beim Kauf aber stehen Marke, Gestaltung und Qualität dem Preis gegenüber.

Welche aktuellen Trends sehen Sie in der Kategorie „Haushalt und Küche"?
Funktionale Innovation, Differenzierung und Homogenisierung verbunden mit einem Hauch häuslicher Skulptur, um der Tendenz zum allgemeinen teutonischen Rationalismus entgegenzuwirken.

Sehen Sie eine sich in diesem Jahr klar abzeichnende Entwicklung im Design, beispielsweise bezüglich Materialwahl und Herstellungstechnik, oder womöglich gar überraschende Innovationen?
Es gibt eindeutig einige Tendenzen zu subtiler Verspieltheit, doch aufgrund der ökonomischen Zwänge zeigen sich die Innovationen größtenteils eher schrittweise denn als Quantensprünge der Kreativität.

"Design is ... the only cross-functional discipline spanning from micro to macro and truly focusing on the people's needs and desires."

„Design ist ... die einzige funktions-übergreifende Disziplin, die sich von Mikro bis Makro spannt und sich dabei wahrhaft mit den Bedürfnissen und Wünschen der Menschen auseinandersetzt."

Robin Edman

Robin Edman, born in 1956 and raised in Sweden, studied industrial design at Rhode Island School of Design in Providence, USA. After graduating in 1981, he started as an industrial designer and later advanced to Assistant Director of Industrial Design at AB Electrolux in Stockholm. In 1989, he moved to Columbus, Ohio (USA), as vice-president of industrial design for Frigidaire Company, where he also initiated and ran the Electrolux Global Concept Design Team for future forecasting of user needs. In 1997, Edman moved back to Stockholm as vice-president of Electrolux Global Design and was appointed chief executive of the Swedish Industrial Design Foundation (SVID) in 2001. From 2003 to 2007, Robin Edman was a board member of the International Council of Societies of Industrial Design, and from 2005 to 2007, he served as its treasurer.

Robin Edman, geboren 1956 und aufgewachsen in Schweden, studierte Industriedesign an der School of Design in Providence, Rhode Island, USA. Nach seinem Abschluss 1981 arbeitete er zunächst als Industrie-designer, später als Assistant Director für Industrie-design bei AB Electrolux in Stockholm. 1989 zog er nach Columbus, Ohio, USA, um bei der Frigidaire Company die Position des Vizepräsidenten für Industriedesign zu übernehmen sowie das Electrolux Global Concept Design Team zur Vorhersage der Verbraucherbedürfnisse ins Leben zu rufen. 1997 kehrte Edman als stellvertretender Geschäftsführer bei Electrolux Global Design nach Stock-holm zurück und wurde 2001 zum Geschäftsführer der Swedish Industrial Design Foundation (SVID) ernannt. Von 2003 bis 2007 war Robin Edman Mitglied im Vor-stand des International Council of Societies of Industrial Design, wobei er zwischen 2005 und 2007 das Amt des Schatzmeisters innehatte.

Robin Edman, a member of the international expert jury for many years now, judged the submissions in the categories "Gardens" and "Sport, games and leisure". This year he was fascinated above all by the broad scope and growing popularity of the red dot design award, which at the same time made it necessary "to focus on meanings and not just technical solutions. This will be a challenge for all of us," the highly active designer said, "to support, foster and develop the next steps to include our entire society."

What is, in your opinion, the significance of design quality in the industries judged by you?
It is becoming more and more important – even though in "Sport, games and leisure" and "Gardens" the level is already relatively high. This means that the winners will be the ones that truly understand the user's needs and desires.

How important is design quality in the global market?
With everything else being equal, this is what makes the difference. With things being unequal, this is what makes you incomparable!

What current trends do you see in the category "Sport, games and leisure"?
The feeling is that we see more technical materials, more technology transfer, more refined solutions, better functionality and a desire to make the users feel good.

What trends do you see in the category "Gardens"?
We have seen a lot of teak, composites and mesh, but it is in tools where the trends stand out – and some are just fantastic! Fit, feel and finish, but more than that: user focus and usability.

Robin Edman, langjähriges Mitglied der internationalen Exper-tenjury, bewertete die Einreichungen in den Kategorien „Garten" sowie „Freizeit, Sport und Spiel". In diesem Jahr begeisterten ihn dabei vor allem die Reichweite und die wachsende Popularität des red dot design award, die es gleichzeitig erforderlich mach-ten, „sich auf Bedeutung zu konzentrieren und nicht nur auf rein technische Lösungen. Dies wird eine Herausforderung für uns alle sein", so der engagierte Designer, „die nächsten Schritte zu fördern, zu unterstützen und zu entwickeln, um so unsere gesamte Gesellschaft einzubinden."

Wie würden Sie den Stellenwert von Designqualität in den von Ihnen beurteilten Branchen einschätzen?
Sie wird immer wichtiger – auch wenn das Niveau in „Freizeit, Sport und Spiel" sowie „Garten" bereits relativ hoch ist. Das bedeutet, dass die Gewinner diejenigen sein werden, die die Bedürfnisse und Wünsche der Benutzer wirklich verstehen.

Wie wichtig ist Designqualität auf dem globalen Markt?
Wenn alles andere gleichwertig ist, ist sie es, die den Unterschied macht. Und wenn es Unterschiede gibt, ist sie es, die einen unvergleichlich macht!

Welche Trends sehen Sie derzeit in der Kategorie „Freizeit, Sport und Spiel"?
Mein Gefühl ist, dass wir mehr technische Materialien vorfin-den, einen stärkeren technologischen Transfer, ausgereiftere Lösungen, eine höhere Funktionalität und schließlich das Bestre-ben, dem Nutzer ein gutes Gefühl zu geben.

Welche Trends sehen Sie in der Kategorie „Garten"?
Es gab viel Teak, Verbundstoffe und Gewebe, aber gerade bei den Werkzeugen gibt es herausragende Trends – und einige davon waren einfach fantastisch! Passform, Anmut und Ausführung, und mehr noch: Anwenderorientiertheit und Benutzerfreundlich-keit.

"The red dot design award is ... critique that rewards."

„Der red dot design award ist ... Kritik, die sich auszahlt."

Massimo Iosa Ghini

Massimo Iosa Ghini, born in 1959 in Bologna, Italy, studied architecture in Florence and graduated from the Polytechnic University in Milan. In 1985, he founded the Bolidismo movement, which draws from pop culture and uses massive, aerodynamic forms, and he also became a member of the Memphis Group led by Ettore Sottsass. During this time, he opened the Studio Iosa Ghini in Bologna and Milan and has since been designing products for leading international firms such as Cassina, Dornbracht, Mandarina Duck, Maserati, and Moroso. As an architect and designer, Iosa Ghini has developed furniture collections and objects as well as avant-garde buildings and interiors for retail chains, among them the Ferrari Stores in Europe, the United States, and Asia. Among his realised building projects are the Kröpcke tube station in Hanover, Germany, the shopping centre The Collection in Miami, and, in Italy, the IBM Executive Business Centre in Rome and the Casa Museo Giorgio Morandi in Bologna.

Massimo Iosa Ghini, 1959 in Bologna, Italien, geboren, studierte Architektur in Florenz und machte seinen Abschluss am Institut für Polytechnik in Mailand. 1985 gründete er die Boldismus-Bewegung, deren Stil sich an die Popkultur anlehnt und für wuchtige aerodynamische Formen steht, und wurde Mitglied der Memphis-Gruppe von Ettore Sottsass. In dieser Zeit eröffnete er das Studio Iosa Ghini in Bologna und Mailand und entwirft seither Produkte für führende internationale Unternehmen wie Cassina, Dornbracht, Mandarina Duck, Maserati und Moroso. Als Architekt und Designer entwickelte Iosa Ghini Möbelkollektionen und Objekte ebenso wie avantgardistische Bauwerke und Innenausstattungen für Handelsketten, darunter die Ferrari Stores in Europa, den USA und Asien. Zu seinen realisierten Bauprojekten zählen u. a. die U-Bahn-Station Kröpcke in Hannover, die Einkaufsmeile The Collection in Miami, USA, sowie in Italien das IBM Executive Business Centre in Rom und das Casa Museo Giorgio Morandi in Bologna.

Massimo Iosa Ghini took part in the evaluation and selection of products for the red dot design award for the first time this year, supporting the jury board in the category "Tableware". For the high-profile designer, who explores the intersections between design and architecture, good design doesn't happen by accident but is rather the result of precise consideration and research.

What, in your opinion, is the significance of design quality in the industry judged by you?
If we consider Western industries, I would say it is vital; the only way to avoid the turbulence of the global market is to differentiate from the masses and offer unbeatable value.

How important is design quality in the global market?
Design is thinking and reasoning – answers that are not casual but precise. Quality means care in researching real solutions, and I believe it is necessary to increase the range of available products with outstanding design quality, for simply stating that people want "quality" is banal.

What current trends do you see in the category "Tableware"?
In "Tableware" I saw an evolution towards simplification – less play and more consciousness.

Do you see a clear development in design emerging this year, for example with regards to the choice of materials and manufacturing techniques, or maybe even surprising innovations?
The most powerful evolution is the ability to mix the organic with the artificial, bringing together processes with natural and artificial materials, which can be separated again.

Massimo Iosa Ghini nahm zum ersten Mal an der Jurierung des red dot design award teil und unterstützte das Wettbewerbs-gremium in der Kategorie „Tableware". Für den profilierten Gestalter, der sowohl als Designer wie auch als Architekt tätig ist, entsteht gute Gestaltung nicht durch Zufall, sondern als ein Ergebnis präzisen Überlegens und Erforschens.

Wie würden Sie den Stellenwert von Designqualität in der von Ihnen beurteilten Branche einschätzen?
Ich würde sagen, sie ist für die westliche Wirtschaft zentral; die einzige Möglichkeit, sicher durch die Turbulenzen des globalen Marktes zu kommen, besteht darin, sich von der Masse abzuset-zen und einen unschlagbaren Wert anzubieten.

Wie wichtig ist Designqualität auf dem globalen Markt?
Design ist logisches Nachdenken und Abwägen; präzise statt beiläufige Antworten. Qualität bedeutet Sorgfalt bei der Suche nach tatsächlichen Lösungen, und ich glaube, auch das Ange-bot an Produkten mit herausragender Designqualität muss sich erweitern, da es schlicht banal ist, nur zu behaupten, dass die Menschen Qualität wollen.

Welche Trends sehen Sie derzeit in der Kategorie „Tableware"?
Bei „Tableware" sehe ich eine Entwicklung zur Vereinfachung – weniger Verspieltheit und mehr Bewusstheit.

Sehen Sie eine sich in diesem Jahr klar abzeichnende Entwicklung im Design, beispielsweise bezüglich Materialwahl oder Herstellungstechnik, oder womöglich gar überraschende Innovationen?
Die stärkste Entwicklung besteht in der Möglichkeit, Organisches mit Künstlichem zu mischen sowie in der Fertigung aus zugleich natürlichen und künstlichen Materialien, die aber auch wieder voneinander getrennt werden können.

"Design means a better world to live in for all people on this planet."

„Design bedeutet eine bessere Welt für alle Menschen dieses Planeten."

Prof. Renke He

Professor Renke He, born in 1958, was educated at Hunan University in civil engineering and architecture. From 1987 to 1988, he was a visiting scholar at the Industrial Design Department of the Royal Danish Academy of Fine Arts in Copenhagen and, from 1998 to 1999, at North Carolina State University's School of Design. Renke He is dean and professor of the School of Design at Hunan University in China and is also director of the Chinese Industrial Design Education Committee. Currently he holds the position of vice-chair of the China Industrial Design Association.

Professor Renke He wurde 1958 geboren und studierte an der Hunan University Bauingenieurwesen und Architektur. Von 1987 bis 1988 war er als Gastprofessor für Industrial Design an der Royal Danish Academy of Fine Arts in Kopenhagen tätig, und von 1998 bis 1999 hatte er eine Gastprofessur an der School of Design der North Carolina State University inne. Renke He ist Dekan und Professor an der Hunan University China, School of Design, sowie Direktor des Chinese Industrial Design Education Committee. Er ist zudem stellvertretender Vorsitzender der China Industrial Design Association.

This year Professor Renke He once again judged designs in the category "Households and kitchens". The acclaimed industry expert said that he was surprised again and again by the diversity of entries and by the extraordinarily innovative performance of individual products.

What, in your opinion, is the significance of design quality in the industry you judged?
In 2010, the significance of design quality is represented by detailed design in the products. Because household and kitchen items are mature products already, it is very hard to achieve truly great innovation in design. So designers have to concentrate on details, for example on LED lighting systems in refrigerators, to create new features that will attract the eyes of consumers.

How important is design quality in the global market?
This year red dot received a record number of entrants. This is an indication that the worldwide recession may present a good opportunity for the design industry to expand its professional arena, for design quality is now becoming one of the most important issues for companies to address if they want to be successful in the global market.

What current trends do you see in the category "Households and kitchens"?
Household and kitchen products are strongly connected with local cultures and lifestyles. In order to expand into the global market, designers must have a true understanding of cultures and lifestyles in the target marketplaces in order to meet the real needs of the local consumers. In the West, the dishwasher is a normal kitchen product, but in the East, especially in China, it is not useful because people use bowls instead of plates, so kitchen sterilizers are much more common than dishwashers.

Professor Renke He beurteilte in diesem Jahr erneut die Arbeiten der Kategorie „Haushalt und Küche". Immer wieder sei er dabei von der Vielfalt und der außergewöhnlichen Innovationsleistung einzelner Produkte überrascht worden, so der anerkannte Branchenkenner.

Wie würden Sie den Stellenwert von Designqualität in der von Ihnen beurteilten Branche einschätzen?
Im Jahr 2010 liegt der Stellenwert der Designqualität in der Gestaltung von Produktdetails. Weil Haushalts- und Küchenprodukte bereits voll ausgereift sind, ist es hier sehr schwierig, echte Designinnovationen zu kreieren; Designer müssen sich auf Details konzentrieren, z. B. auf LED-Beleuchtungssysteme in Kühlschränken, um neue Elemente zu schaffen, die die Aufmerksamkeit der Konsumenten auf sich ziehen.

Wie wichtig ist Designqualität auf dem globalen Markt?
In diesem Jahr hatte red dot so viele Einreichungen wie nie zuvor. Dies ist ein Anzeichen dafür, dass die weltweite Rezession eine gute Gelegenheit für die Designbranche sein könnte, ihren Wirkungsbereich auszuweiten, da Designqualität jetzt für Unternehmen zu einem der wichtigsten Aspekte wird, um sich auf dem globalen Markt erfolgreich durchzusetzen.

Welche Trends sehen Sie derzeit in der Kategorie „Haushalt und Küche"?
Haushalts- und Küchenprodukte sind eng mit der regionalen Kultur und Lebensweise verbunden. Um in den globalen Markt vordringen zu können, müssen Designer über ein grundlegendes Verständnis der Kulturen und Lebensstile auf den Zielmärkten verfügen, um die wirklichen Bedürfnisse der lokalen Verbraucher zu erfüllen. Im Westen ist ein Geschirrspüler zum Beispiel ein ganz normales Küchengerät, im Osten aber, vor allem in China, ist er nicht von Nutzen, da dort aus Schüsseln anstatt aus Tellern gegessen wird und Küchensterilisatoren viel weiter verbreitet sind als Spülmaschinen.

"Design helps people to be happier in three realms – social, cultural, and economic – while simultaneously contributing to the design industry and market development in the respective environments, contexts or regions."

„Design hilft den Menschen, in drei Bereichen glücklicher zu werden – dem sozialen, kulturellen und ökonomischen –, während es zugleich seinen Beitrag zur Designindustrie und Marktentwicklung in dem jeweiligen Umfeld, Kontext oder der Region leistet."

Prof. Carlos Hinrichsen

Professor Carlos Hinrichsen, born in 1957, graduated as an industrial designer in Chile in 1982 and went on to earn a Master's degree in engineering in Japan in 1991. He has since been heading research projects focused on innovation in design education, the implementation of new technologies, and the development and realisation of design concepts in close cooperation with the domestic manufacturing sector. In 1992, Hinrichsen assumed the position of director of the School of Design, Instituto Profesional DuocUC, at the Pontificia Universidad Católica de Chile. He has been a design process consultant for over two decades, focusing on product and strategic design. He is currently the design director for the Latin American Region of Design Innovation, a European design company with clients and prospects all over the world. Since 2002, Carlos Hinrichsen has been an honorary member of the Chilean Association of Design Firms (QVID). 2007–2009 he was president of the Icsid and has since served as senator within the organisation. Moreover, 2008–2009 he was lead chair of the International Design Alliance (IDA).

Professor Carlos Hinrichsen, geboren 1957, schloss 1982 sein Studium als Industriedesigner in Chile ab und erwarb 1991 zusätzlich ein Ingenieursdiplom in Japan. Seitdem leitet er Forschungsprojekte zu Innovationen in der Designausbildung, zum Einsatz neuer Technologien sowie zur Entwicklung und Umsetzung von Designkonzepten, die dabei mit der heimischen Fertigungsbranche kooperieren. 1992 übernahm Hinrichsen die Leitung der Designschule „Instituto Profesional DuocUC" der Pontificia Universidad Católica de Chile, und seit über 20 Jahren ist er als Berater im Bereich Design Process mit den Schwerpunkten Produkt- und Strategisches Design tätig. Gegenwärtig ist er zudem Design Director für die Region Lateinamerika bei Design Innovation, einem europäischen Designunternehmen mit Kunden und Interessenten aus aller Welt. Seit 2002 ist Carlos Hinrichsen Ehrenmitglied der chilenischen Vereinigung der Designfirmen (QVID). 2007–2009 war er Präsident des Icsid, dessen Senator er seither ist, und 2008–2009 Vorsitzender der International Design Alliance (IDA).

This year Professor Carlos Hinrichsen once again evaluated submissions in the categories "Life science and medicine" and "Bathrooms, spa and air-conditioning". From his perspective, "red dot is a great display of good design and leading-edge technologies applied to a wide range of solutions." Concerning the quality of design in the global market, he sees design quality, beyond the specific product or service, as a key process that he perceives "as tightly associated with itineraries between innovation and tradition, which enable the generation of proposals with high levels of differentiation and performance."

What, in your opinion, is the significance of design quality in the industries judged by you?
For me it has been a great opportunity because we have seen how products offer realistic, lively images of the desires and dreams of the users, as well as those of the designers and producers. In both product categories, design quality plays a key role in turning technological innovations into business success. Apparent is a wide variety of fields of use where product quality and performance, from a consumer standpoint, have also been improved.

Do you see a clear development in design emerging this year, for example with regards to the choice of materials and manufacturing techniques, or maybe even surprising innovations?
From the perspective of new ways of integrating innovation into products or services, I have noticed how companies are using design as a vehicle for innovation. That is, they are using design to appropriately augment innovations – both those coming from the R&D sphere and innovations associated with social and market changes – with the objective of successfully responding to people's new needs and requirements. In this regard, design can be seen as a vehicle for innovation in times of crisis.

Professor Carlos Hinrichsen begutachtete in diesem Jahr erneut die Einreichungen in den Kategorien „Life Science und Medizin" sowie „Bad, Wellness und Klimatechnik". Aus seiner Perspektive ist „der red dot eine vortreffliche Zurschaustellung guten Designs sowie der für ein breites Spektrum an Lösungen angewandten Spitzentechnologien." Was die Designqualität im globalen Markt angeht, versteht er Designqualität jenseits spezifischer Produkte oder Leistungen als einen Kernprozess, „den ich in enger Verzahnung mit den Abwägungen zwischen Innovation und Tradition verstehe und der die Generierung ausgeprägter Differenzierungs- und Leistungsangebote ermöglicht."

Wie würden Sie den Stellenwert von Designqualität in den von Ihnen beurteilten Branchen einschätzen?
Für mich war das eine großartige Möglichkeit zu sehen, wie Produkte die Wünsche und Träume der Benutzer ebenso wie die der Designer und Hersteller realistisch und lebendig darstellen. In beiden Produktkategorien spielt Designqualität bei der Umwandlung technologischer Innovationen in Geschäftserfolge eine Schlüsselrolle. Es lassen sich vielfältige Anwendungsfelder erkennen, in denen vom Standpunkt des Verbrauchers aus Produktqualität und Leistung ebenfalls verbessert wurden.

Sehen Sie in diesem Jahr eine sich klar abzeichnende Designentwicklung, beispielsweise im Hinblick auf Materialwahl und Herstellungstechniken, oder womöglich gar überraschende Innovationen?
Im Hinblick auf neue Ansätze, wie Innovation in Produkten oder Leistungen integriert wird, ist mir aufgefallen, wie Firmen Design als Medium für Innovation einsetzen. Das heißt, sie benutzen Design, um sowohl die Innovationen aus dem F&E-Bereich als auch soziale und marktbedingte Veränderungen entsprechend umzusetzen und so mit Erfolg auf die neuen Anforderungen und Bedürfnisse der Menschen zu antworten. So gesehen, kann Design als Medium für Innovation in Zeiten der Krise verstanden werden.

"Design is ... solving problems."   „Design bedeutet, Probleme zu lösen."

Dr. Thomas Lockwood

Dr. Thomas Lockwood holds a BA in visual design and marketing from Eastern Michigan University, United States, and an MBA and a PhD in design management from the Harrow Business School, University of Westminster, London. After his studies, Lockwood ran his own product and communication design firm for ten years, followed by another ten years of directing the global brand and design strategies for the companies Sun Microsystems and StorageTek. Today, Lockwood is president and board member of the Design Management Institute (DMI) in Boston, Massachusetts, and a designated expert in the areas of design management, methodology, strategy and leadership. His experience includes the development of design strategies for Fortune 500 companies as well as the design of the competition uniforms worn by the U.S. ski team at the Olympic Games. He has also taught as a visiting professor at the Pratt Institute in New York City.

Dr. Thomas Lockwood studierte Visuelle Gestaltung und Marketing an der Eastern Michigan University, USA, mit Abschluss B. A. und legte einen MBA sowie eine Promotion in Designmanagement an der Harrow Business School der University of Westminster in London ab. Anschließend führte er zehn Jahre lang ein Büro für Produkt- und Kommunikationsdesign und leitete weitere zehn Jahre die globale Marken- und Designstrategie der Unternehmen Sun Microsystems und StorageTek. Heute ist Lockwood Geschäftsführer und Vorstandsmitglied des Design Management Institute (DMI) in Boston, Massachusetts, sowie ein ausgewiesener Experte in den Bereichen Design Management, Designmethodik, Designstrategie und Design Leadership. Er entwickelte Designstrategien u. a. für „Fortune 500"-Organisationen und gestaltete die Wettkampfuniformen für das US-Skiteam bei den Olympischen Spielen. Darüber hinaus lehrt er als Gastprofessor am Pratt Institute in New York City.

Dr. Thomas Lockwood, who has been part of the jury board several times already, this year was jointly responsible for the adjudication in the categories "Gardens" and "Sport, games and leisure". He was particularly fascinated by the fact that, when compared to the product submissions in previous years, most of this year's judged products showed a clear step-up in terms of their design development and manufacturing techniques.
When asked about current trends in the category "Gardens", however, the acknowledged industry expert was more critical, and revealed: "The trends in the 'Gardens' category were more status quo, with only a few entries really demonstrating new innovation or exceptional quality."

What is, in your opinion, the significance of design quality in the industries judged by you?
Design quality is very significant in that design is a source of competitive differentiation. It is clear that the quality of product design is getting better and better in the major countries in the world, so competition by design will become more intense.

How important is design quality in the global market?
Design quality is extremely important in global competition. In fact, companies that do not have good design will not survive the future. Good design is becoming a baseline requirement of good business.

What current trends do you see in the category "Sport, games and leisure"?
The trends in the "Sport, games and leisure" category is better quality of design – greater simplicity, more refinements, simply more thoughtful design.

Dr. Thomas Lockwood, der dem Jurygremium bereits mehrfach angehörte, war in diesem Jahr für die Beurteilung der Bereiche „Garten" und „Freizeit, Sport und Spiel" mitverantwortlich. Im Vergleich zu den Einsendungen der vergangenen Jahre begeisterte ihn dabei besonders, dass die meisten der jurierten Produkte hinsichtlich der Entwicklung des Designs sowie der Herstellungstechnik eine deutliche Steigerung erkennen ließen. Zu den aktuellen Trends in der Kategorie „Garten" befragt, war der anerkannte Branchenexperte aber kritischer und verriet: „Die Trends in der ‚Garten'-Kategorie waren eher Status quo, und nur ein paar wenige Einreichungen bewiesen wirklich neue Innovationen oder eine außerordentliche Qualität."

Wie würden Sie den Stellenwert von Designqualität in den von Ihnen beurteilten Branchen einschätzen?
Designqualität hat einen hohen Stellenwert, denn Design stellt den Grundstein für die Differenzierung im Wettbewerb dar. Es ist klar, dass die Qualität der Produktgestaltungen in den einflussreicheren Ländern der Welt immer besser und der designorientierte Wettbewerb dadurch heftiger wird.

Wie wichtig ist Design im globalen Markt?
Im globalen Wettbewerb ist Designqualität außerordentlich wichtig. Tatsächlich werden Unternehmen, die kein gutes Design haben, die Zukunft nicht überleben. Gutes Design wird zur absoluten Grundvoraussetzung für den Geschäftserfolg.

Welche aktuellen Trends sehen Sie in der Kategorie „Freizeit, Sport und Spiel"?
Die Trends in der Kategorie „Freizeit, Sport und Spiel" sind eine bessere Gestaltungsqualität – höhere Einfachheit, optimierte Ausarbeitung, schlicht mehr durchdachtes Design.

"The red dot design award is the world standard today."

„Der red dot design award ist heute weltweit die Benchmark."

Wolfgang K. Meyer-Hayoz

Wolfgang K. Meyer-Hayoz, born in 1947, studied mechanical engineering, visual communication and industrial design and graduated from the Staatliche Akademie der Bildenden Künste in Stuttgart. The professors Klaus Lehmann, Kurt Weidemann and Max Bense had formative influence on the design philosophy he has today. In 1985, he founded the Meyer-Hayoz Design Engineering Group with offices in Switzerland (Winterthur) and Germany (Konstanz). The company offers consultancy services for business start-ups, small- and medium-sized enterprises, as well as world market leaders in design strategy, industrial design, user interface design, temporary architecture, and communication design and has received numerous awards. Meyer-Hayoz was president of the Swiss Design Association (SDA), from 1987 to 1993, and is among others a member of the Association of German Industrial Designers (VDID) and the Schweizerische Management Gesellschaft (SMG). Aside from his work as a designer and consultant, Wolfgang K. Meyer-Hayoz is also a guest lecturer at the University of St. Gallen and serves as a juror on international design panels.

Wolfgang K. Meyer-Hayoz, geboren 1947, absolvierte Studien in den Fachbereichen Maschinenbau, Visuelle Kommunikation sowie Industrial Design mit Abschluss an der Staatlichen Akademie der Bildenden Künste in Stuttgart. Prägend für seine heutige Gestaltungsphilosophie waren die Professoren Klaus Lehmann, Kurt Weidemann und Max Bense. 1985 gründete er die Meyer-Hayoz Design Engineering Group mit Büros in Winterthur, Schweiz, und Konstanz, Deutschland. Das Unternehmen berät Start-ups, kleine und mittelständische Unternehmen sowie Weltmarktführer in Design Strategy, Industrial Design, User Interface Design, Temporary Architecture und Communication Design und wurde bereits vielfach international ausgezeichnet. Von 1987 bis 1993 war Meyer-Hayoz Präsident des Schweizerischen Verbandes Industrial Designers (SDA); er ist u. a. Mitglied im Verband Deutscher Industrie Designer (VDID) und der Schweizerischen Management Gesellschaft (SMG). Neben seiner Tätigkeit als Designer und Consultant ist Wolfgang K. Meyer-Hayoz u. a. Gastdozent an der Universität St. Gallen sowie Juror internationaler Designgremien.

Wolfgang K. Meyer-Hayoz, a jury member for the "Bathrooms, spa and air-conditioning" and "Life science and medicine" categories, expects two different market strategies to prevail on the global scene: "On the one hand, low-cost products with a marginal, unique take on design and, on the other hand, intelligent, high-quality products with an authenticity that allows for strong corporate branding. For European companies, the latter strategy is the only road to success."

What, in your opinion, is the significance of design quality in the industries judged by you?
Our populations are aging. They want to live healthier and stay in shape, and at the same time they have a certain "longing for paradise" and a desire for authenticity meaning, and sustainability. This is in keeping with the new architectural trends featuring light-flooded and minimally furnished rooms. The products from these sectors reflect these preferences, resulting in the high priority given to adequate design quality.

What current trends do you see in the "Life science and medicine" sector?
This sector also shows a strong interest in health and fitness at old age, a predilection for natural materials, and the increasing demand of people to be given more information on the medical treatments and procedures they are offered. At the same time, cost pressure in medical product development is increasing rapidly, including enormous demands with regard to patient security, which often leads to a transfer of functions to software applications in an effort to minimise human error. We also see a strong trend toward the "aestheticisation" of medical devices.

Für die Zukunft macht Wolfgang K. Meyer-Hayoz, der die Einreichungen in den Bereichen „Bad, Wellness und Klimatechnik" sowie „Life Science und Medizin" jurierte, zwei unterschiedliche Marktstrategien aus, die sich global durchsetzen werden: „Ausgeprägte Low-Cost-Produkte mit einem marginalen, eigenen Anspruch an Gestaltung sowie qualitativ hochwertige und intelligente Premiumprodukte mit einer prägnanten, originären Gestaltsprache als Basis einer starken Unternehmensmarke. Für europäische Unternehmen", so der profilierte Designstratege, „kann mehrheitlich nur der zweite Weg zum Erfolg führen."

Wie würden Sie den Stellenwert von Designqualität in den von Ihnen beurteilten Branchen einschätzen?
Die Menschen werden immer älter. Sie wollen gesünder leben und sich fit halten und haben gleichzeitig eine gewisse „Sehnsucht nach dem Paradies" sowie den Wunsch nach Natürlichkeit, Sinnhaftigkeit und Nachhaltigkeit. Diese Trends finden auch in der neuen Architektursprache mit Räumen, die lichtdurchflutet und reduziert möbliert sind, ihren Ausdruck. Dementsprechend unterliegen die Produkte aus diesem Bereich den gleichen Anforderungen, und hieraus resultiert ein hoher Stellenwert für die adäquate Designqualität.

Welche aktuellen Trends sehen Sie im Bereich „Life Science und Medizin"?
Auch hier steht das Interesse an Gesundheit und Fitness im Alter, an natürlichen Materialien, die man sich im Umfeld wünscht, und an dem Anspruch, erklärt zu bekommen, was bei medizinischen Behandlungen mit einem passiert, im Vordergrund. Wir sehen aber auch den stark zunehmenden Kostendruck bei der Entwicklung von Medizinprodukten, einen enormen Anspruch bezüglich der Patientensicherheit von Geräten und daher auch oftmals ein Verlagern von Entscheidungen in den Softwarebereich, um menschliche Interpretationsfehler möglichst zu reduzieren. Ebenfalls zu beachten ist ein starker Trend zur Ästhetisierung medizinischer Geräte.

"Design is ... changing the existing physical and digital surroundings to allow people to live with a sense of well-being, comfort, independence, dignity and aesthetics."

„Design verändert die reale physische und digitale Umgebung und erlaubt so den Menschen, mit einem Sinn für Gesundheit, Komfort, Unabhängigkeit, Würde und Ästhetik zu leben."

Prof. Ron Nabarro

Professor Ron Nabarro, born in the Netherlands and active as a designer since 1970, is professor for Industrial Design at the Technion-Israel Institute of Technology. Between 1998 and 2001 he headed the School of Design and Art at the Holon Academic Institute of Technology and was executive board member of the International Council of Societies of Industrial Design (Icsid), for which he since then acts as a regional advisor. Nabarro focuses in particular on topics in the fields of age-friendly design, design management and design theories. He founded companies such as Innovation Design Ltd. (1973) und Design4all (2001) and is co-founder as well as co-director of Senior-Touch Ltd. (2003) und Scentcom Ltd. His works have received numerous awards, among them in 2009 the World Technology Network Award for Design, New York, and he is also active as a lecturer, author and manager of congresses and workshops, as well as a member of international design juries.

Professor Ron Nabarro, geboren in den Niederlanden und seit 1970 als Designer tätig, ist Professor für Industriedesign am Technion-Israel Institute of Technology. Zwischen 1998 und 2001 bekleidete er den Vorsitz der School of Design and Art am Holon Academic Institute of Technology und war Vorstandsmitglied des International Council of Societies of Industrial Design (Icsid), für den er seitdem als Regionalberater tätig ist. Nabarro befasst sich insbesondere mit den Bereichen Altersfreundliches Design, Designmanagement und Designtheorie. Er gründete Unternehmen wie Innovation Design Ltd. (1973) und Design4all (2001) und ist Mitbegründer sowie Co-Direktor von Senior-Touch Ltd. (2003) und Scentcom Ltd. Seine Arbeiten wurden mit zahlreichen Auszeichnungen prämiiert, u. a. 2009 mit dem World Technology Network Award für Design, New York; zudem ist er als Redner, Autor und Leiter von Kongressen oder Workshops sowie als Mitglied internationaler Designjurys tätig.

Professor Ron Nabarro adjudicated the entries in the categories "Bathrooms, spa and air-conditioning" as well as "Life science and medicine" and – towards the end of what he called a "highly professional, exacting, and highly meticulous design award competition" – made the observation that "today's global market is unforgiving towards companies who fail to achieve design quality. Design quality is the main part of the product that the user can understand and appreciate."

What is, in your opinion, the significance of design quality in the industries judged by you?
In the fields of "Life science and medicine" as well as "Bathrooms, spa and air-conditioning" design quality has not only to do with look and feel but with issues like safety, ease of operation, ergonomics, and user-interface solutions – especially for old age. Design quality is not complete without dealing with these issues.

What current trends do you see in the field of "Life science and medicine"?
The most interesting trend that is becoming more and more obvious in the field of "Life science and medicine" is that designers and producers are neglecting the traditional serious, scientific, severe look and are instead attempting to design less threatening and more user-friendly and colourful products.

What trends do you see in the category "Bathrooms, spa and air-conditioning"?
An ongoing trend that views bathroom and spa environments as spaces for living and leisure – as part of quality of life and maintenance of physical and mental well-being – is very much present in the designers' work in this field.

Do you see a clear development in design emerging this year?
Designers have always been early adopters of technologies and materials; it is only obvious and natural to see the employment of these materials and technologies in the new products that appear on the market.

Professor Ron Nabarro beurteilte die Einreichungen in den Kategorien „Bad, Wellness und Klimatechnik" sowie „Life Science und Medizin" und machte am Ende dieses „sehr professionellen, sorgfältigen und überaus genauen Designwettbewerbs" die Feststellung: „Der globale Markt von heute ist gnadenlos gegenüber Firmen, die keine Designqualität hervorbringen. Designqualität macht den Hauptanteil dessen aus, was der Nutzer an einem Produkt verstehen und goutieren kann."

Wie würden Sie den Stellenwert von Designqualität in den von Ihnen beurteilten Branchen einschätzen?
In den Bereichen „Life Science und Medizin" sowie „Bad, Wellness und Klimatechnik" hat Designqualität nicht nur mit Aussehen und Anmut zu tun, sondern mit Themen wie Sicherheit, Nutzerfreundlichkeit, Ergonomie und Bedienoberflächen mit Lösungen, die insbesondere dem hohen Alter gerecht werden. Designqualität bleibt bei Missachtung dieser Themen unvollständig.

Welche Trends sehen Sie derzeit im Bereich „Life Science und Medizin"?
Der interessanteste, immer offensichtlicher werdende Trend im Bereich „Life Science und Medizin" besteht darin, dass die Designer und Produzenten die traditionelle, seriöse, wissenschaftliche, strenge Anmut vernachlässigen und versuchen, weniger bedrohliche, bedienfreundlichere und farbenfrohere Produkte zu schaffen.

Welche Trends sehen Sie in der Kategorie „Bad, Wellness und Klimatechnik"?
Der anhaltende Trend, die Bad- und Wellnessbereiche als Lebens- und Entspannungsräume und so als Teil der Lebensqualität und des Erhalts der körperlichen und geistigen Gesundheit zu betrachten, ist in den Designerarbeiten dieses Bereichs sehr präsent.

Sehen Sie eine sich in diesem Jahr klar abzeichnende Entwicklung im Design?
Designer waren schon immer unter den Ersten, die sich der Technologien und Materialien angenommen haben; die Verwendung dieser Materialien und Technologien in neuen auf dem Markt erscheinenden Produkten zu beobachten, ist selbstverständlich und naheliegend.

"Design is ... for everyone."

„Design ist ... für jedermann.“

Lyndon Neri

Lyndon Neri received a Master's degree in architecture from Harvard University and a Bachelor's degree in architecture from the University of California, Berkeley. He began his career for more than ten years as director of projects in Asia for Michael Graves & Associates in Princeton as well as working for various architectural firms in New York City. Thereafter he founded his own firm, Neri&Hu Design and Research Office (NHDRO), based in Shanghai, together with his partner Rossana Hu. Aside from his practical work as an architect, Neri has been actively involved in teaching and research, among others as an author and also as a visiting critic at Princeton University, the Harvard Graduate School of Design, and Syracuse University. He is also the founder of Design Republic, a business concept for retail stores based in Shanghai offering unique product collections from the world's best design talents. Together with his partner, Lyndon Neri also launched the product line "neri&hu", which has earned many international awards.

Lyndon Neri erhielt einen Master of Architecture von der Harvard University und einen Bachelor of Architecture von der University of California, Berkeley. Bevor er zusammen mit seiner Partnerin Rossana Hu sein eigenes Büro NHDRO (Neri&Hu Design and Research Office) mit Sitz in Shanghai eröffnete, war er mehr als zehn Jahre als Projektleiter in Asien für Michael Graves & Associates in Princeton tätig und arbeitete für verschiedene Architekturbüros in New York City. Neben seiner praktischen Tätigkeit engagiert sich Neri in der Forschung und Lehre, u. a. als Autor sowie Gastkritiker an der Princeton University, Harvard Graduate School of Design und Syracuse University. Er ist einer der Begründer der „Design Republic", eines Geschäftskonzepts für den Einzelhandel in Shanghai, das besondere Produktkollektionen internationaler Designtalente anbietet. Zusammen mit seiner Partnerin entwickelte Lyndon Neri zudem die Produktreihe „neri&hu", die bereits mehrfach international ausgezeichnet wurde.

Lyndon Neri took part this year for the first time in the product evaluation process for the international award, supporting the red dot jury board in the category "Tableware". A versatile designer himself, he considers the red dot design award a very important platform for a society which, in his opinion, currently shows a lack of awareness of good design. His professional motto thus postulates the creation of products that are suitable for everyone.

What, in your opinion, is the significance of design quality in the industry judged by you?
In general the quality was quite good, and there were a few breakthroughs.

How important is design quality in the global market?
Design quality is extremely important. Good design quality in the everyday, the mundane, and the ordinary is imperative.

What current trends do you see in the category "Tableware"?
The companies are focusing on branding.

Do you see a clear development in design emerging this year, for example with regards to choice of materials and manufacturing techniques, or maybe even surprising innovations?
The few breakthroughs deal with new typologies, which are very exciting.

Lyndon Neri nahm erstmals an der Jurierung des internationalen Wettbewerbs teil und gehörte dem Gremium des Bereichs „Tableware" an. Den red dot design award erachtet der vielseitig tätige Gestalter als eine sehr wichtige Plattform für eine Gesellschaft, der es seiner Meinung nach an einem Bewusstsein für gutes Design mangelt. Seine professionelle Maxime lautet daher, Produkte zu entwerfen, die sich für jedermann eignen.

Wie würden Sie den Stellenwert von Designqualität in der von Ihnen beurteilten Branche einschätzen?
Im Allgemeinen war die Qualität ziemlich gut, und es gab auch ein paar Höhepunkte.

Wie wichtig ist Designqualität auf dem globalen Markt?
Designqualität ist außerordentlich wichtig. Gute Designqualität im Alltag, im Profanen und Gewöhnlichen ist eine zwingende Notwendigkeit.

Welche Trends sehen Sie derzeit in der Kategorie „Tableware"?
Die Unternehmen setzen den Schwerpunkt auf Markenbildung.

Sehen Sie eine sich in diesem Jahr klar abzeichnende Entwicklung im Design, beispielsweise bezüglich Materialwahl und Herstellungstechnik, oder womöglich gar überraschende Innovationen?
Die wenigen Höhepunkte drehen sich um neue Typologien, die sehr spannend sind.

"We designers have the task of creating responsible systems and products. I hope companies make use of these possibilities sooner than later in all the manufacturing sectors on our tiny planet."

„Wir Designer haben die Aufgabe, verantwortungsvolle Systeme und Produkte zu kreieren. Ich hoffe, dass sich Unternehmen aller Herstellungsbranchen auf unserem kleinen Planeten diese Möglichkeiten eher früher denn später zunutze machen."

Satyendra Pakhalé

Satyendra Pakhalé, born in 1967 in India, studied industrial design in Mumbai and advanced product design at the Art Center College of Design in La Tour-de-Peilz, Switzerland. He then worked as a senior product designer at Philips in Eindhoven, Netherlands, creating products in the areas of digital communication and transportation. In 1998 he founded his own design studio in Amsterdam and has since been working for clients such as Alessi, Bosa, Cappellini, Hästens, Magis, Moroso, Material ConneXion, and Tubes. He carved a unique position in the international design arena, resulting in a sensorial design language, which transcends conventional borders. The Design Academy Eindhoven invited him to develop and head the artistic direction of their master's programme in Humanitarian Design and Sustainable Living. Pakhalé's work is represented by Designer's Gallery Gabrielle Ammann, Cologne, and is held in several public collections, including the Stedelijk Museum, Amsterdam, and the Centre Pompidou, Paris.

Satyendra Pakhalé, 1967 in Indien geboren, studierte Industriedesign in Mumbai sowie Advanced Product Design am Art Center College of Design in La Tour-de-Peilz, Schweiz. Anschließend arbeitete er als Senior Product Designer bei Philips in Eindhoven, Holland, und entwarf Produkte in den Bereichen Digitale Kommunikation und Transportmittel. 1998 gründete er sein eigenes Studio in Amsterdam und arbeitet seither für Kunden wie Alessi, Bosa, Cappellini, Hästens, Magis, Moroso, Material ConneXion und Tubes. Mit einer die Sinne berührenden Gestaltungssprache, die herkömmliche Grenzen überschreitet, hat er sich in der internationalen Designszene eine einzigartige Position erarbeitet. Die Designakademie Eindhoven lud ihn ein, das „Master's Programme in Humanitarian Design and Sustainable Living" als Leiter zu entwickeln und die Art Direction zu übernehmen. Pakhalés Werke werden in der Designer's Gallery Gabrielle Ammann in Köln ausgestellt und befinden sich zudem in zahlreichen öffentlichen Sammlungen, z. B. im Stedelijk Museum in Amsterdam und im Centre Pompidou in Paris.

Satyendra Pakhalé, who complemented the expert jury in the category "Households and kitchens", explains in the interview with red dot that developing and designing products today naturally requires much more than merely satisfying the requirements of pure utility. "To have new, unique sensorial-symbolic qualities is essential in industrial design today," the versatile designer emphasises, adding that "the significant qualities that I like to see come from companies which have a culture of their own and create value in the true sense. We were glad to see that some companies have cultivated this sensibility in a relatively short amount of time."

How important is design quality in the global market?
Having a "design culture" inbuilt within manufacturing and distribution is of utmost importance today. We've seen some great examples; however, by and large, design is still not fully integrated into industrial culture. We hardly ever see designers responsible for top management tasks in multinational companies. It is rare to see design thinking applied in order to cultivate internal company culture and therefore shape every aspect of a manufacturing company. In today's context, sustainability and ecology-related matters are huge untapped design opportunities.

What current trends do you see in the category "Households and kitchens"?
There is more and more awareness of well-being these days, which is a great thing. The smart integration of new technologies and not-so-new technologies for effective use of space and energy, and also for maintaining a high level of hygiene, is core to household and kitchen products. This was evident in several products and entries that we judged in this category.

Satyendra Pakhalé, der die Expertenjury in dem Bereich „Haushalt und Küche" ergänzte, hebt im Interview mit red dot hervor, dass es bei der Gestaltung und Entwicklung von Produkten heute selbstredend um weit mehr als um die reine Zweckerfüllung gehen müsse. „Neue, einzigartige sinnlich-symbolische Qualitäten zu haben, ist für das Industriedesign von heute wesentlich", betont der vielseitige Designer. „Unternehmen, die eine eigene Kultur verfolgen und im wahrsten Sinne Wert schaffen, kreieren die bedeutende Qualität, die ich sehen möchte. Wir waren froh zu sehen, dass einige Firmen diese Sensibilität in relativ kurzer Zeit kultiviert haben."

Wie wichtig ist Designqualität im globalen Markt?
Eine in Herstellung und Vertrieb tief eingebundene Designkultur ist heute von allergrößter Bedeutung. Wir haben ein paar großartige Beispiele gesehen; im Großen und Ganzen aber ist Design immer noch nicht vollkommen in die Kultur der Branchen integriert. Fast nie trifft man Gestalter auf der Verantwortungsebene des Top-Managements multinationaler Unternehmen. Und selten findet man ein Designdenken, das an der Kultivierung einer internen Unternehmenskultur ansetzt und derart jeden Aspekt eines Herstellungsunternehmens prägt. Im heutigen Kontext stellen Nachhaltigkeit und ökologiebezogene Themen eine weitgehend unausgeschöpfte Chance im Design dar.

Welche aktuellen Trends sehen Sie in der Kategorie „Haushalt und Küche"?
Es gibt heutzutage ein immer breiteres Bewusstsein für das Wohlbefinden, was großartig ist. Die intelligente Integration neuer und nicht so neuer Technologien für die effektive Nutzung von Raum, Energie sowie dazu, einen hohen Grad an Hygiene zu halten, bildet den Kern der Haushalts- und Küchenprodukte. Das war bei mehreren von uns beurteilten Produkten und Einreichungen offenkundig.

 "Design is ... my way of life." 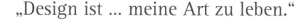 „Design ist ... meine Art zu leben."

Jorge Pensi

Jorge Pensi, born in Buenos Aires, studied architecture in his hometown. In 1975 he left Argentina and founded, together with designers Alberto Liévore, Norberto Chaves and Oriol Pibernat, the Group Berenguer in Barcelona. In 1984 he opened his own design studio, specialising in furniture and lamp design, among others for Amat, B.Lux, Cassina, Poggenpohl, Kusch+Co., and Thonet. Over the course of his long career, Jorge Pensi has received many international awards, and some of his early designs, such as the Toledo aluminium chair from 1986 and the Regina lamp from 1987, have become true icons of contemporary Spanish design. In the familial atmosphere of his studio he works on graphic design and other projects in cooperation with Diego Slemenson, Constanze Schutz, Roman Proubasta, Toni Casares and his wife Carmen Casares. Jorge Pensi places great value on close collaboration and friendly relations with his clients, whom he believes to be the key to success.

Jorge Pensi, geboren in Buenos Aires, studierte Architektur in seiner Heimatstadt. 1975 verließ er Argentinien und gründete 1977 zusammen mit Alberto Liévore, Norberto Chaves und Oriol Pibernat die „Group Berenguer" in Barcelona. 1984 eröffnete er sein eigenes Designstudio und spezialisierte sich auf die Gestaltung von Möbeln und Leuchten, u. a. für Amat, B.Lux, Cassina, Poggenpohl, Kusch+Co. und Thonet. Im Laufe seiner Karriere wurde Jorge Pensi vielfach ausgezeichnet, und einige seiner frühen Entwürfe wie der Aluminiumstuhl „Toledo" von 1986 und die Lampe „Regina" von 1987 gelten als Ikonen zeitgenössischen spanischen Designs. In der familiären Atmosphäre seines Studios arbeiten Diego Slemenson, Constanze Schutz, Roman Proubasta, Toni Casares und dessen Frau Carmen Casares, teils auch an Grafikdesign-Projekten. Jorge Pensi legt großen Wert auf eine enge Zusammenarbeit und einen freundschaftlichen Kontakt zu seinen Kunden, welche seiner Meinung nach der Schlüssel zum Erfolg sind.

Jorge Pensi joined the international board of jurors for the first time this year. The renowned designer, who has garnered international acclaim – above all for his elegant and carefully crafted furniture made from cast aluminium – evaluated the submitted product entries in the categories "Architecture and interior design" and "Offices". In an interview with red dot, he emphatically underscores how important it is for companies to demand the highest standards of design and manufacture.

What, in your opinion, is the significance of design quality in the industries judged by you?
Companies are investing a great amount of energy in improving the quality of design and manufacture, year after year.

How important is design quality in the global market?
It is absolutely important if you don't want to be a loser.

What current trends do you see in the realm of "Architecture and interior design"?
Attention is being paid to small details, noble materials, clean spaces, and a design that aspires to be timeless.

What trends do you see in the category "Offices"?
In this category I have seen good examples of a mixture of poetry and realism, ecological materials, and a focus on ergonomics and comfort.

Jorge Pensi war zum ersten Mal Mitglied des internationalen Jurygremiums. Der renommierte Designer, der vor allem mit seinen eleganten, sorgfältig gearbeiteten Möbeln aus Gussaluminium internationale Aufmerksamkeit erhielt, bewertete die eingereichten Arbeiten in den Kategorien „Architektur und Interior Design" sowie „Büro". Im Interview mit red dot betont er insbesondere die Bedeutung, die ein hoher Anspruch an die Gestaltung sowie die Ausführung hat.

Wie würden Sie den Stellenwert von Designqualität in den von Ihnen beurteilten Branchen einschätzen?
Firmen investieren viel Energie, um die Design- und Herstellungsqualität zu verbessern – von Jahr zu Jahr.

Wie wichtig ist Designqualität im globalen Markt?
Sie ist absolut wichtig, wenn man kein Verlierer sein will.

Welche aktuellen Trends sehen Sie im Bereich „Architektur und Interior Design"?
Große Aufmerksamkeit für kleine Details, edle Materialien, aufgeräumte Räume und ein gestalterisches Verlangen nach Zeitlosigkeit.

Welche Trends sehen Sie in der Kategorie „Büro"?
In dieser Kategorie sind mir gute Beispiele in einer Mischung aus Poesie und Realismus, ökologische Materialien und Sorgfalt in Ergonomie und Komfort begegnet.

"In the global market, design quality is the most important tool for market differentiation."

„Auf dem globalen Markt ist Designqualität das wichtigste Tool zur Differenzierung."

Robert Stadler

Robert Stadler, born in Vienna in 1966, studied design at the Istituto Europeo di Design in Milan and at the Ecole Nationale Supérieure de Création Industrielle in Paris. In 1992 he co-founded the RADI DESIGNERS group and has been working independently since 2000. Aside from his studio work, Stadler is a visiting professor at numerous universities and academies at home and abroad, among them the Escola Superior de Desenho Industrial, Rio de Janeiro, TU Delft, and the University of Fine Arts (HFBK) Hamburg. Robert Stadler is active in very diverse fields, questioning with his works the status of an object as either artwork or product and exploring the fine line between value and worthlessness, elegance and vulgarity, or the serious and the absurd. His work is held in numerous collections, including the Fondation Cartier and the FRAC Nord – Pas de Calais. He works for clients such as the Académie des César, the Costes Group, Dior, Ricard, and Take 5 Editions.

Robert Stadler, 1966 in Wien geboren, studierte Design am Istituto Europeo di Design in Mailand und danach an der Ecole Nationale Supériore de Création Industrielle in Paris. 1992 war er Mitbegründer der Gruppe RADI DESIGNERS und arbeitet seit 2000 eigenständig. Neben seiner praktischen Arbeit lehrt Stadler als Gastprofessor an zahlreichen Hochschulen im In- und Ausland, z. B. an der Escola Superior de Desenho Industrial, Rio de Janeiro, der TU Delft und der Hochschule für bildende Künste Hamburg. Robert Stadler ist in unterschiedlichsten Bereichen tätig; er stellt mit seinen Werken den Status des Objekts als Kunstwerk oder Produkt infrage und lotet die Grenze zwischen Wert und Wertlosigkeit, Eleganz und Vulgarität, Ernst und Absurdität aus. Seine Arbeiten sind in zahlreichen Sammlungen vertreten, etwa der Fondation Cartier und des FRAC Nord – Pas de Calais. Zu seinen Kunden zählen u. a. die Académie des César, die Costes-Gruppe, Dior, Ricard und Take 5 Editions.

As a first-time jury member of the red dot design award, Robert Stadler participated in the "Living rooms and bedrooms" and "Lighting and lamps" categories. He observed significant differences in the level of design quality in these sectors, with submissions ranging "from the best to the worst". In response to the question about current trends in the "Living rooms and bedrooms" sector, he stated seeing no clearly pronounced direction. Rather, companies seem to be playing it safe and resorting to classic and conservative solutions. Nevertheless, in the "Lighting and lamps" category, the recognised designer – who in his own work explores the limit between design and art as well as new forms of social interaction – did notice a trend towards immateriality, brought to the fore through the prominent use of LEDs.

Robert Stadler nahm zum ersten Mal an der Jurierung des red dot design award teil und unterstützte das Expertengremium in den Kategorien „Wohnen und Schlafen" sowie „Licht und Leuchten". Den Stellenwert der Designqualität schätzt er in diesen Branchen als sehr unterschiedlich ein, so habe es Einreichungen auf Niveaus „from the best to the worst" gegeben. Auf die Frage nach aktuellen Trends im Bereich „Wohnen und Schlafen" kristallisiert sich für ihn keine sich klar differenzierende Richtung heraus. Die Unternehmen gingen hier auf Nummer sicher und setzten auf eine klassisch-konservative Linie. In der Kategorie „Licht und Leuchten" dagegen macht der anerkannte Designer, der sich mit seinen Arbeiten an der Grenze zwischen Design und Kunst bewegt und neue Formen für die soziale Interaktion entwirft, einen Trend zur Immaterialität aus, der aufgrund der LEDs verstärkt zum Vorschein komme.

"The red dot design award is ultimate success achieved by design."

„Der red dot design award steht für durch Design errungenen ultimativen Erfolg."

Prof. Danny Venlet

Professor Danny Venlet, born in Australia in 1958, graduated with honours in architecture, interior design and art in Brussels in 1983. Thereafter, he gained professional experience at, among others, Peter Sands, Inarc design, and Rice and Daubney Architects. Following his cooperation with Neil Burley (1988) and Marc Newson (1988 to 1990), in which he started to attract international attention with interior projects such as the Burdekin Hotel in Sydney, Venlet eventually opened his own studio, Venlet Interior Architecture, in 1991. His interior projects are characterised by a contemporary international style and range from private houses, bars, exhibitions and restaurants, all the way to showrooms and offices of large companies such as Timberland and Mini. Danny Venlet has taught at several schools and universities in Belgium and Australia, and is currently a professor at the Royal College of the Arts in Ghent as well as at the private College of Advertising and Design in Brussels.

Professor Danny Venlet, 1958 in Australien geboren, schloss sein Studium der Architektur, Innenarchitektur und Kunst in Brüssel 1983 mit Auszeichnung ab und sammelte anschließend berufliche Erfahrungen u. a. bei Peter Sands, Inarc design, und Rice and Daubney Architects. Nach seiner Zusammenarbeit mit Neil Burley (1988) und Marc Newson (1988 bis 1990), in der er mit Innenraumprojekten z. B. für das Burdekin Hotel in Sidney international auf sich aufmerksam machte, eröffnete Venlet 1991 sein eigenes Studio Venlet Interior Architecture. Seine Einrichtungsprojekte reichen von Privathäusern, Bars, Ausstellungen und Restaurants bis zu Showrooms und Büros für große Unternehmen wie Timberland oder Mini und zeichnen sich durch einen zeitgemäßen internationalen Stil aus. Danny Venlet lehrte an verschiedenen Hochschulen in Belgien und Australien und ist heute Professor am Royal College of the Arts in Gent sowie an dem privaten College of Advertising and Design in Brüssel.

Danny Venlet defines design as "a tool for success". The architect and designer, who is a long-time member of the red dot jury, this year judged the product entries in the category "Tableware".

In the industry that you judged, what, in your opinion, is the significance of design quality?
Ergonomics, quality, the use of materials, innovation in the handling... Design makes the difference between a good product and an ordinary one.

What current trends do you see in the category "Tableware"?
I have seen little in the way of new trends, but we awarded some objects that were, in my eyes, catalysts that could start a new trend.

Do you see a clear development in design emerging this year, for example with regards to choice of materials and manufacturing techniques, or possibly regarding surprising innovations?
There were some really well-designed products, but this year we missed that one object that placed itself above the others.

Danny Venlet definiert Design als „ein Instrument für den Erfolg". Der Architekt und Designer, der die red dot-Jury bereits seit vielen Jahren unterstützt, beurteilte diesmal die Einreichungen in der Kategorie „Tableware".

Wie würden Sie den Stellenwert von Designqualität in der von Ihnen beurteilten Branche einschätzen?
Ergonomie, Qualität, Materialeinsatz, Innovation in der Handhabung ... Im Design besteht der Unterschied zwischen einem guten Produkt und einem nur gewöhnlichen.

Welche Trends sehen Sie derzeit in der Kategorie „Tableware"?
Im Sinne neuer Trends habe ich nur wenig gesehen, aber wir haben einige Produkte prämiiert, die in meinen Augen neue Trends auslösen könnten.

Sehen Sie eine sich in diesem Jahr klar abzeichnende Entwicklung im Design, zum Beispiel in Hinsicht auf Materialwahl oder Herstellungstechniken, oder womöglich gar überraschende Innovationen?
Da waren ein paar wirklich gut gestaltete Produkte dabei, doch in diesem Jahr haben wir dieses eine Objekt vermisst, das über allen anderen steht.

red dot award: product design
Design for a modern and comfortable lifestyle at home
Design für ein stilvolles und behagliches Leben zu Hause

All products presented in this book were distinguished in the "red dot award: product design" and address a discerning clientele. The created settings convey new visions of comfort and style. The seven chapters of "living" are grouped according to the type of product, featuring the latest and best design from the competition categories "Living rooms and bedrooms", "Households and kitchens", "Tableware", as well as "Lighting and lamps". The mature products are fine-tuned to a well-honed lifestyle and offer state-of-the-art technologies for energy efficiency, intelligent home systems, and atmospheric lighting. The chapter "Gardens" shows how gardens are increasingly viewed as an integral part of the ambiance and features products that allow to easily move lounges or candlelight dinners outside. The chapter also presents tools that make gardening easier and more fun. Readers who wish to redesign their bathrooms and get their home up to par with the latest technology can consult the "Bathrooms, spa and air-conditioning" chapter, which features many interesting innovations and bathroom furnishings for tomorrow's wellness oases. On the whole, this book provides the reader with a quick overview of all "living" categories of the "red dot award: product design", allows to discover design, cultivate one's own style, and even plan the furnishings of an entire home. The innovations and inspirations from the chapter "Architecture and interior design" will also guide readers in that regard. We invite readers to leaf through this book, obtain information, and get inspired by the large format photographs. The products are listed together with the corresponding company name and website, allowing readers to research any item that strikes their interest. Volume "living" addresses people who love exclusivity and comfort and for whom design is not just decoration but a way of life. In short, readers are bound to become captivated by the truly fascinating field of design.

Sie erschaffen Szenarien eines behaglichen und stilvollen Lebens, wie es sie noch niemals zuvor gab: Die Produkte in diesem Buch wurden allesamt im red dot award: product design ausgezeichnet und sie richten sich mit ihrem Design an anspruchsvolle Zielgruppen. In den sieben Kapiteln von „living" findet der Leser, sinnvoll nach Produkten geordnet, das neueste und beste Design aus den Wettbewerbskategorien „Wohnen und Schlafen", „Haushalt und Küche", „Tableware" sowie „Licht und Leuchten". Es sind sehr ausgereifte Produkte für einen hoch entwickelten Lebensstil in Verbindung mit zeitgemäßen Technologien für modernes Energiesparen, das Intelligent Home oder ein stimmungsvolles Beleuchten des Raumes. Dass auch der Garten mehr und mehr zum Teil des Ambientes zählt, zeigt im Anschluss das Kapitel „Garten" – die Lounge oder das Candle-Light-Dinner können mit diesen Produkten mühelos nach draußen verlagert werden. Passend dazu gibt es in diesem Kapitel auch Geräte, mit denen die Gartenarbeit überaus stilvoll und ohne großen Kraftaufwand vonstattengeht. Wer sich in seinem Zuhause technisch auf den neuesten Stand bringen oder gerade sein Bad neu gestalten will, der findet im Kapitel „Bad, Wellness und Klimatechnik" viele interessante Neuerungen und perfekt abgestimmte Badmöbel für die Wellness-Oasen der Zukunft. Rasch erhält der Leser so einen Überblick über alle Kategorien des red dot award: product design im Bereich „living" und wird feststellen, dass sich dieses Buch wunderbar dazu eignet, Design zu entdecken, den eigenen Stil zu pflegen oder sogar einen ganzen Hausstand zu planen. Hierzu ergänzen sich gut die Innovationen und Anregungen aus dem Kapitel „Architektur und Interior Design". Der Leser kann in diesem Buch blättern, sich eingehend informieren und von den großformatigen Bildern inspirieren lassen. Bei Interesse findet er zum Produkt schnell das passende Unternehmen und dessen Homepage. Er wird erfahren, dass Design eine überaus spannende Sache ist – die Produkte des Bandes „living" sprechen die Menschen an, die das Besondere und Komfortable lieben und für die Design nicht nur ein schmückendes Beiwerk, sondern auch eine Lebenseinstellung ist.

The competition
What designers and companies worldwide see in red dot

Throughout the world, there are designers who design good products and companies who have recognised how important design is for their success. For innovative products that have not been on the market for more than two years, the red dot design award is an attractive platform: It serves not only as a qualification and as orientation, but allows to communicate the product's quality by means of the "red dot" label, in turn contributing to an appreciation of quality by the public. The red dot design award is divided into three sections that are adjudicated independently from each other: "red dot award: product design", "red dot award: communication design", and "red dot award: design concept", the latter of which has been conducted yearly since 2005 in Singapore.

The red dot design award has been issued for more than 50 years on an international level. Just in the year of 2009, the contest listed in its three disciplines over 12,000 registrations from more than 60 nations and its "red dot" label has become one of the most coveted quality symbols worldwide for excellent design. Given that it is among the largest and most challenging design competitions, a participation in the red dot design award also represents the unique occasion to find out how well one's products fare in comparison to those of international competitors. Those who have won an award count among the best of the world and can communicate their success by means of the red dot – an internationally recognised seal of quality for design – thereby distinguishing themselves from their competitors.

The competition categories
Design in all its facets and possibilities

Products from nearly any field can be submitted to one of the 17 different categories of the "red dot award: product design". Each of these categories has its own selected expert jury that evaluates the respective products. Generally, products are submitted in their final form, i.e., not as drafts.

Der Wettbewerb
Warum Designer und Unternehmen ihn weltweit für sich nutzen

Auf der ganzen Welt gibt es Designer, die gute Produkte gestalten, und Unternehmen, die erkannt haben, wie wichtig Design für ihren Erfolg ist. Für innovative Produkte, die nicht länger als zwei Jahre auf dem Markt sind, ist der red dot design award eine attraktive Plattform: Er dient nicht nur der Qualifikation und Orientierung, sondern er macht die Qualität mithilfe des red dot kommunizierbar und rückt sie damit in den Fokus des öffentlichen Interesses. Der red dot design award unterteilt sich in drei Bereiche, die unabhängig voneinander ausgeschrieben und juriert werden: red dot award: product design, red dot award: communication design und red dot award: design concept, der seit 2005 jährlich in Singapur durchgeführt wird.

Der red dot design award blickt auf eine über 50-jährige Geschichte zurück und er agiert auf internationaler Ebene. Allein im Jahr 2009 erhielt der Wettbewerb in seinen drei Disziplinen mehr als 12.000 Anmeldungen aus über 60 Nationen, und seine Auszeichnung, der „red dot", hat sich international als eines der begehrtesten Qualitätssiegel für gutes Design etabliert. Da er zu den größten und härtesten Designwettbewerben weltweit zählt, bietet sich den Teilnehmern im red dot design award damit die einmalige Chance herauszufinden, wie gut sich ihre neuesten Produkte im internationalen Vergleich behaupten können. Wer hier gewonnen hat, zählt zu den Besten der Welt und er kann seinen Erfolg mithilfe des red dot, dem weltweit anerkannten Qualitätssiegel für Design, wirkungsvoll kommunizieren und sich von seinen Wettbewerbern absetzen.

Die Kategorien des Wettbewerbs
Design in all seinen Facetten und Möglichkeiten

In den unterschiedlichen Kategorien des red dot award: product design können innovative Produkte aus nahezu allen Bereichen eingereicht werden, in der Regel als Original. Da die Produkte überaus vielfältig sind, bietet der Wettbewerb siebzehn unterschiedliche Kategorien an. In jeder dieser Einzelkategorien werden die jeweiligen Produkte gesondert und von einer ausgewählten Fachjury bewertet.

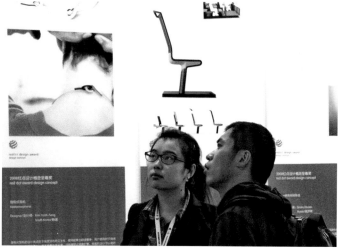

red dot on tour in Beijing

red dot on tour in Peking

The jury of the competition
Why their expertise is so important

Every product is different – in regard to its innovative content as well as its design quality. The products in the competition are based on very diverse design concepts. These implement new technologies and find new ways of interpreting the familiar. Also, their spectacular innovations often consist of only a single yet very decisive detail. In order to ensure due consideration to this complexity, the international jury of the red dot design award is composed of high-ranking members whose expertises match the respective categories. The jury is composed of eminent design leaders from around the world, who, as an international team, exclude national, cultural, or social partialities. Among these leaders are prominent figures from the design scene as well as representatives from international institutions from design and culture. Of import is, in particular, the strict rules concerning the autonomy and impartiality of every juror – who must decide on a completely independent basis. For that reason, only international experts who have not submitted products themselves are appointed to the jury. Moreover, the jury changes its composition regularly. The organisers of the red dot design award monitor the international design scene throughout the year in order to recruit new jurors and to thereby give the competition new impulses.

The accolades of the red dot design award
Evaluations that do justice to each product

Design is a process and a product is always the expression of many decisions and paths. Until it finally reaches its form, it usually passes through many stages during which it undergoes modifications. Seeking to fairly judge design quality in light of this background, the red dot design award encompasses three types of product awards: "honourable mention" distinguishes products that stand out for particularly successful detail solutions; "red dot" distinguishes products that stand out for their high design quality; and "red dot: best of the best" is issued to the best products of a category and is therewith the highest distinction a product can achieve in the red dot design award.

Die Jury des Wettbewerbs
Weshalb ihr fachliches Können so wichtig ist

Jedes Produkt ist anders – in seinem innovativen Gehalt und in seiner Designqualität. Die Produkte im Wettbewerb basieren auf den unterschiedlichsten Designkonzepten, sie fokussieren neue Technologien, interpretieren Bekanntes völlig neu und oft verbirgt sich eine spektakuläre Innovation in nur einem einzigen, aber entscheidenden Detail. Um dies in all seiner Vielschichtigkeit bewerten zu können, ist die internationale Jury des red dot design award sehr hochrangig besetzt und fachlich genau auf die zu bewertende Kategorie abgestimmt. Die Jury des red dot design award besteht aus international renommierten Designkoryphäen aus vielen Ländern und Erdteilen, damit national geprägte kulturelle und gesellschaftliche Aspekte keinen zu hohen Stellenwert einnehmen können: Persönlichkeiten der Designszene, aber auch Vertreter internationaler Institutionen aus dem Bereich Design und Kultur. Wichtig sind vor allem die strengen Maximen der Unabhängigkeit und Souveränität eines jeden Jurors – er soll schließlich völlig ungebunden entscheiden. Daher können auch nur internationale Experten in die Jury berufen werden, die keine eigenen Produkte eingereicht haben. Die Jury wechselt zudem regelmäßig ihre Zusammensetzung. Über das Jahr hinweg beobachten die Organisatoren des red dot design award die internationale Designszene, um die Jury durch neue Juroren zu ergänzen und dem Wettbewerb auf diese Weise neue Impulse zu geben.

Die Auszeichnungen im red dot design award
Bewertungen, die jedem Produkt gerecht werden

Design ist ein Prozess und ein Produkt ist stets der Ausdruck vieler Entscheidungen und Wege. Bis es schließlich zu seiner endgültigen Form gelangt, durchläuft es viele Stadien und wird möglicherweise immer wieder überarbeitet. Um der Designqualität eines Produktes auch vor diesem Hintergrund gerecht zu werden, gibt der red dot design award der Jury drei verschiedene Möglichkeiten der Bewertung eines Produktes vor: Mit einer „honourable mention" werden Produkte gewürdigt, die sich durch besonders gelungene Detaillösungen von der Masse abheben. Mit dem „red dot" werden diejenigen Produkte ausgezeichnet, die sich durch ihre hohe Designqualität von vergleichbaren Produkten unterscheiden. Der „red dot: best of the best" wird an die besten Produkte einer Kategorie vergeben und ist somit die höchste Auszeichnung, die ein Produkt im red dot design award überhaupt erhalten kann.

red dot award: communication design

How can it be quickly and clearly communicated that the new Citroën C5 model comes with cornering lights as a standard feature? The answer to this question was rewarded with a "red dot: best of the best" in the "red dot award: communication design 2009". This competition searches for first-class communication design achievements and awards them with a prize, because even the best product never stands alone. It is often part of a product line, needs to reflect elements of the corporate design and convey the company image. In short: the object has to communicate a message and at the same time becomes the object of communication. Packaging, brochures, manuals, advertising campaigns, websites, promotional items, and presentations in shops and at trade fairs, all this accompanies the product into and eventually in the market. Here design also plays a key role – when it comes to differentiate oneself from others, set accents, and attract attention.

This year, a special accolade for clients will be awarded for the first time: from this year on the title "red dot: client of the year" will honour a particularly courageous and decisive client who places the trust in designers and agencies that they need in order to realise new, creative approaches.

Wie lässt sich schnell und plakativ kommunizieren, dass Citroën jetzt ein Abbiegelicht im neuen C5-Modell serienmäßig anbietet? Die Antwort auf diese Fragestellung wurde beim red dot award: communication design 2009 mit einem „red dot: best of the best" belohnt. Dieser Wettbewerb sucht nach gestalterisch-kommunikativen Glanzleistungen und zeichnet sie aus. Denn auch das beste Produkt steht nie für sich allein. Es ist in vielen Fällen Teil einer Produktlinie, muss Elemente des Corporate Designs widerspiegeln und das Firmenimage transportieren. Kurz: Der Gegenstand muss kommunizieren und wird zugleich Gegenstand der Kommunikation. Verpackung, Broschüren, Gebrauchsanleitungen, Werbekampagnen, Internetpräsenz, Promotion-Artikel, die Präsentation in Shops und auf Messen, all das begleitet das Produkt in den und schließlich im Markt. Auch hierbei spielt gutes Design eine Schlüsselrolle, wenn es darauf ankommt, sich von anderen zu unterscheiden, Akzente zu setzen und die Aufmerksamkeit auf sich zu ziehen.

In diesem Jahr ist erstmals auch eine Sonderauszeichnung für Auftraggeber zu vergeben: Als „red dot: client of the year" wird künftig ein besonders mutiger und entscheidungsfreudiger Auftraggeber gewürdigt, der Designern und Agenturen das Vertrauen entgegenbringt, das sie brauchen, um kreative, neue Ansätze auch in die Tat umsetzen zu können.

The award-winning poster "Cornering Lights" was designed by Euro RSCG Düsseldorf for Citroën. It is among the 0.9 per cent of all entries that were awarded a "red dot: best of the best".

Das prämiierte Poster „Abbiegelicht" gestaltete Euro RSCG Düsseldorf für Citroën. Es gehört zu den 0,9 Prozent aller Einreichungen, die eine Auszeichnung mit dem red dot: best of the best bekamen.

Designers and companies entered more than 6,000 works to the comparison of achievements last year. BurdaYukom Publishing from Munich managed to impress the jurors with the 2008 online annual report for AUDI.

Mit mehr als 6.000 Arbeiten stellten sich Designer und Unternehmen im vergangenen Jahr dem Leistungsvergleich. Mit dem Online-Geschäftsbericht 2008 für AUDI konnte BurdaYukom Publishing aus München die Juroren überzeugen.

On the night of the awards presentation the spotlight is on the winners of the "red dot: best of the best" and "red dot: grand prix", such as the agency ART+COM, which received a "red dot: grand prix" for their kinetic sculpture for the BMW Museum.

Im Rampenlicht stehen am Abend der Preisverleihung die Gewinner des red dot: best of the best und des red dot: grand prix, wie die Agentur ART+COM, die einen red dot: grand prix für ihre Kinetische Skulptur für das BMW Museum verliehen bekam.

Also, every year an agency is awarded the special award "red dot: agency of the year" for continuously outstanding design achievements. Last year's winner was the agency KMS TEAM from Munich. Furthermore, in 2010 for the first time a company or institution will be awarded the title "red dot: client of the year".

Außerdem wird jedes Jahr eine Agentur für ihre kontinuierlich herausragenden Designleistungen mit der Sonderauszeichnung „red dot: agency of the year" geehrt, im letzten Jahr die Agentur KMS TEAM aus München. 2010 wird zudem erstmals ein Unternehmen oder eine Institution mit dem Titel „red dot: client of the year" ausgezeichnet werden.

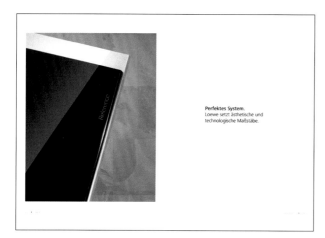

Last year, 527 works received an award, among them the Loewe 2008 annual report ("Das Wesentliche." – English: "The essential.") by Kuhn, Kammann & Kuhn AG, Cologne...

527 Arbeiten wurden im vergangenen Jahr ausgezeichnet, darunter auch der Loewe-Geschäftsbericht 2008 („Das Wesentliche.") von Kuhn, Kammann & Kuhn AG, Köln ...

... and this advertising campaign by J. Walter Thompson GmbH, Düsseldorf, for Nokia Navigation.

... oder diese Anzeigenkampagne der J. Walter Thompson GmbH, Düsseldorf, für Nokia Navigation.

At the awards presentation, every year approximately 900 creative professionals and representatives of the media, business and politics meet in the red dot design museum in Essen, Germany to honour the best in communication design.

Zur Preisverleihung treffen sich jedes Jahr rund 900 Kreative und Vertreter aus Medien, Wirtschaft und Politik im red dot design museum in Essen, um die Besten des Kommunikationsdesigns zu ehren.

The international yearbook communication design is an internationally established reference work of communication design. It presents the best design achievements from around the world on approximately 800 pages.

Das international yearbook communication design gilt als internationales Standardwerk für Kommunikationsdesign. Auf rund 800 Seiten werden die besten Gestaltungsleistungen aus aller Welt gezeigt.

The red dot design museum presents all award-winning works in the four-week winners' exhibition "Design on stage – winners red dot award: communication design". In a second special exhibition the current "red dot: agency of the year" presents itself with a cross section of sophisticated design achievements.

Das red dot design museum zeigt alle ausgezeichneten Arbeiten in der vierwöchigen Winners' exhibition „Design on stage – winners red dot award: communication design". In einer zweiten Sonderausstellung präsentiert sich die aktuelle red dot: agency of the year mit einem Querschnitt anspruchsvollster Designleistungen.

red dot on tour: A large crowd gathered for the opening of the exhibition "Quality has a form. red dot presents: Excellent communication design in Basel". Some 500 guests attended the vernissage in the exhibition area of the Basel School of Design on 12 April 2010 to inspect the award-winning works.

red dot on tour: Großer Andrang bei der Eröffnung der Ausstellung „Qualität hat eine Form. red dot präsentiert: Ausgezeichnetes Kommunikationsdesign in Basel". Rund 500 Gäste kamen zur Vernissage am 12. April 2010 in die Ausstellungsräume der Schule für Gestaltung, um sich die prämiierten Arbeiten anzuschauen.

red dot award: design concept

While in the "red dot award: product design" and the "red dot award: communication design" concrete products and works are awarded with a prize, designers and companies competing in the "red dot award: design concept" have the chance to prove their whole creative potential: with prestige and image enhancing projects such as concept cars or future scenarios as well as concepts for new products or entire environments, they can demonstrate their innovative strength. Winning an award in this competition shows that one is actively engaged, researches, experiments, and has visionary ideas – that one is someone to count on also in future.

However, concrete product ideas, prototypes and hand-sized models can also be presented to the jury in the "red dot award: design concept". The evaluation by the design experts can already anticipate the product's chance of being successful in the market some time in the future. All award-winning concepts and prototypes will be presented to the general public at the red dot design museum in the heart of the booming city state of Singapore for the duration of one year.

Während beim red dot award: product design und beim red dot award: communication design ganz konkrete Produkte und Arbeiten prämiiert werden, haben Designer und Unternehmen beim red dot award: design concept die Chance, ihr ganzes kreatives Potenzial unter Beweis zu stellen: Mit Prestige- und Imageprojekten wie Concept Cars oder Zukunftsszenarien können sie hier ihre Innovationskraft ebenso zeigen wie mit Konzepten für neue Produkte oder ganze Lebenswelten. Eine Auszeichnung in diesem Wettbewerb zeigt, dass man sich engagiert, forscht, experimentiert und Visionen hat – dass auch in Zukunft mit einem zu rechnen ist.

Doch auch ganz konkrete Produktideen, Prototypen und Handmodelle können beim red dot award: design concept der Jury vorgelegt werden. Das Urteil der Designexperten kann die Chance des Produkts, irgendwann auf dem Markt zu bestehen, schon antizipieren. Alle ausgezeichneten Konzepte und Prototypen werden ein Jahr lang im Herzen des boomenden Stadtstaates Singapur im dortigen red dot design museum der breiten Öffentlichkeit präsentiert.

Since the "red dot award: design concept" was launched in 2005, every year more designers, companies and institutions have submitted visionary concepts and prototypes to prove their innovative power and creativity.

Seit der red dot award: design concept 2005 ins Leben gerufen wurde, reichen jedes Jahr mehr Designer, Unternehmen und Institutionen visionäre Konzepte und Prototypen ein, um ihre Innovationskraft und Kreativität unter Beweis zu stellen.

Philips Design already impressed the jury with its "Skin" research project in 2007.

Bereits 2007 konnte auch Philips Design mit dem Forschungsprojekt „Skin" die Jury überzeugen.

The awards presentation in Singapore is the festive highlight of the "red dot award: design concept". In the impressive setting of the red dot design museum in Singapore, the city's creative scene celebrates the best with a spectacular event in the presence of more than 400 international guests from the international design industry.

Die Preisverleihung in Singapur ist der feierliche Höhepunkt des red dot award: design concept. In der eindrucksvollen Kulisse des red dot design museum in Singapur feiert Singapurs Kreativszene die Gewinner im Beisein von über 400 internationalen Gästen aus der Designbranche mit einer spektakulären Inszenierung.

Last year, the "red dot: luminary", which is worth US$ 5,000 and awarded to the best work of the entire competition, went to the SIRIUS Breast Cancer Scanner, which was developed by Design Exchange for Resource Medical.

Den mit 5.000 US-Dollar dotierten red dot: luminary gewann als beste Arbeit des gesamten Wettbewerbs im vergangenen Jahr der SIRIUS Breast Cancer Scanner, den Design Exchange für Resource Medical konzipierte.

Among the award-winners were concepts such as "Fresh Hands" by Samsung C&T...

Unter den Gewinnern beispielsweise Samsung C&T für das Konzept „Fresh Hands" ...

... and "Smart Pillow" by Trigem Computer.

... und Trigem Computer mit dem Konzept „Smart Pillow".

The Berlin-based designer Arman Emami has had great success with his design concept "USB Clip": In 2009 he won a "red dot: best of the best" in the "red dot award: design concept". Now he has once again impressed a jury of international experts: in the "red dot award: product design 2010" he also received a "red dot: best of the best", for outstanding design quality (see Vol. 2, doing, page 84/85).

Eine großartige Erfolgsgeschichte schrieb der Berliner Designer Arman Emami mit seinem Designkonzept „USB Clip": 2009 gewann er im red dot award: design concept einen red dot: best of the best. Jetzt überzeugte er erneut eine internationale Expertenjury: Auch im red dot award: product design 2010 erhielt er den red dot: best of the best (vgl. Vol. 2, doing, S. 84/85).

Many of the award-winning design concepts show interesting paths into the future and allow new perspectives. Particularly the re-interpretations of well-known problems and the creativity involved time and again fascinate the jury: the "Pininfarina Sintesi" concept car by the Italian design studio Pininfarina already received an award in 2008.

Viele der ausgezeichneten Designkonzepte zeigen interessante Wege in die Zukunft auf und lassen neue Sichtweisen zu. Insbesondere die Re-Interpretation bekannter Probleme und die damit verbundene Kreativität zieht die Jury immer wieder in ihren Bann: Bereits 2008 wurde das Concept Car „Pininfarina Sintesi" des italienischen Designstudios Pininfarina ausgezeichnet.

The red dot design museum in Singapore is the venue where the "red dot award: design concept", the awards presentation and the special exhibition take place. It is housed in the former red dot traffic, an impressive colonial style building painted in bright red, which ranks as the creative centre of Singapore today. The red dot design museum in Singapore offers the winners of the "red dot award: product design" the unique opportunity to present their award-winning products to the Asian public at the Asian hub, in the heart of the booming city state of Singapore.

Schauplatz des red dot award: design concept, der Preisverleihung und der Ausstellung ist das red dot design museum in Singapur, untergebracht im ehemaligen red dot traffic, einem eindrucksvollen Gebäude im Kolonialstil, das heute – leuchtend rot gestrichen – als kreatives Zentrum Singapurs gilt. Für die Gewinner des red dot award: product design bietet das red dot design museum in Singapur die einzigartige Möglichkeit, ihre ausgezeichneten Produkte auf der Drehscheibe Asiens, im Herzen des boomenden Stadtstaates Singapur der asiatischen Öffentlichkeit zu präsentieren.

Into the small hours the guests celebrate the winners and take advantage of the opportunity to exchange thoughts and ideas with design experts from all around the world, get inspired, and make new contacts over cocktails such as the red dot Bombay Sapphire, the official drink of the awards presentation.

Bis tief in die Nacht feiern die Gäste die Gewinner und nutzen die Gelegenheit, sich bei Cocktails wie dem red dot Bombay Sapphire, dem offiziellen Drink der Preisverleihung, mit Designexperten aus aller Welt auszutauschen, sich inspirieren zu lassen und neue Kontakte zu knüpfen.

The special exhibition, which presents all the award-winning products of the competition year, provides deep insights into the products and the world of tomorrow.

Tiefe Ein- und Ausblicke in die Produkt- und Lebenswelt von morgen gewährt die Sonderausstellung, in der alle ausgezeichneten Arbeiten eines Wettbewerbsjahres präsentiert werden.

Somfy GmbH
Felix-Wankel-Str. 50
D-72108 Rottenburg am Neckar
Page/Seite 423

Guangzhou Songdream Furniture Co., Ltd.
No. 85 Hantang Middle Street, RenheTown,
Baiyun District
Guangzhou 510470
China
Page/Seite 106

Sonlux GmbH
Licht- und Elektroinstallation GmbH & Co. KG
Frankenhäuser Str. 66
D-99706 Sondershausen
Page/Seite 30–31

South Asia International (HK) Ltd.
Unit 1101-1105, 11/F, Peninsula Square
18 Sung On Street, Hunghom, Kowloon
Hong Kong
Page/Seite 152, 160

Speck Pumpen Verkaufsgesellschaft GmbH
Hauptstr. 1-3
D-91233 Neunkirchen am Sand
Page/Seite 258

Spectral Lichttechnik GmbH
Bötzinger Str. 31
D-79111 Freiburg
Page/Seite 307

The Spiritree Forest Company
#996 Calle San Roberto
PR-00926 San Juan
Page/Seite 338

Vanguardia Europea
Stanza
Rubén Dario 560
MEX-44670 Guadalajara
Page/Seite 275

Stephalux Furniture
Jl. Raya Cibarusah km. 09
Cikarang Selatan
RI-Bekasi 17550
Page/Seite 83

Stern GmbH & Co. KG
Garten- und Freizeitmöbel
Maybachstr. 13
D-71563 Affalterbach
Page/Seite 348

Stuben–Hocker
Ralf Hennig
Am Strauchhof 4
D-50321 Brühl
Page/Seite 104

SunSquare
Hochäckerstr. 4-8
A-3430 Tulln
Page/Seite 415

Swissdent Cosmetics AG
Theaterstr. 18
CH-8001 Zürich
Page/Seite 252

T

Taiwan Order Furniture Corp.
3F, N. 84, Sec. 1, Wenhua 1st Rd. Linkou Shiang
Taipei 333
Taiwan
Page/Seite 93

Takata Lemnos Inc.
511 Hayakawa
J-Takaoka City, Toyama Prefecture 933-0957
Page/Seite 218

Take2 Designagentur GmbH & Co. KG
Goethestr. 38-40
D-83024 Rosenheim
Page/Seite 213

Tal
Joos De Ter Beerstlaan 33
B-8740 Pittem
Page/Seite 315

TECE GmbH
Hollefeldstr. 57
D-48282 Emsdetten
Page/Seite 262

Techmar B.V.
Elektrostraat 2e
NL-7483 PG Haaksbergen
Page/Seite 336

Tefal
Groupe SEB
Z.I. des Granges
F-74570 Rumilly
Page/Seite 227

Teka Küchentechnik GmbH
Sechsheldener Str. 122
D-35708 Haiger
Page/Seite 146

Telekom Deutschland GmbH
Landgrabenweg 151
D-53227 Bonn
Page/Seite 406

Tendo Co., Ltd.
1-3-10 Midarekawa Tendo
J-Yamagata 994-8601
Page/Seite 22–23

Terramanus Landschaftsarchitektur
Rheinallee 72
D-53173 Bonn-Bad Godesberg
Page/Seite 332

Tescoma s.r.o.
U Tescomy 241
CZ-76001 Zlin
Page/Seite 220

ToddlerCompany
Hellerupvej 3a
DK-2900 Hellerup
Page/Seite 214

Tong Yang Magic Co., Ltd.
Tyli Bldg., 10F #185-10, Euljiro-2(i), Jung-gu
ROK-Seoul 100-845
Page/Seite 163

Tormax
Landert Motoren AG
Unterweg 14
CH-8180 Bülach
Page/Seite 357

Toshiba Home Appliances Corporation
2-15, Sotokanda 2-Chome, Chiyoda-Ku
J-Tokyo 101-0065
Page/Seite 169–170

Toto Ltd.
Design Center
2-24-2, Sakurashinmachi, Setagaya-Ku
J-Tokyo 154-8540
Page/Seite 232

Transtek Electronics Co., Ltd.
Jin an Road, Minzhong
Zhongshan 528441
China
Page/Seite 154, 194

Trend Factory GmbH
Kraftwerk, Neckartal
D-78628 Rottweil
Page/Seite 398

TRILUX GmbH & Co. KG
Heidestr. 4
D-59759 Arnsberg
Page/Seite 308

Trimo, d.d.
Engineering of pre-fabricated buildings
Prijateljeva cesta 12
SLO-8210 Trebnje
Page/Seite 380

Tschannen Metallbautechnik AG
Gerberstr. 31
CH-3072 Ostermundigen
Page/Seite 408

Tunto Design
Tekijänkatu 8
FIN-04440 Järvenpää
Page/Seite 305

Tylö
Svarvaregatan 6
S-30250 Halmstad
Page/Seite 254

U

Unilux
12 avenue du Garigliano
F-91600 Savigny-sur-Orge
Page/Seite 302

V

V&B Fliesen GmbH
Rotensteiner Weg
D-66663 Merzig
Page/Seite 382

Vaillant GmbH
Berghauser Str. 40
D-42859 Remscheid
Page/Seite 260–261

Velux A/S
Aadalsvej 99
DK-2970 Hoersholm
Page/Seite 32–33

Vendinova
Statenlaan 25
NL-5223 LA Den Bosch
Page/Seite 193

Versor d.o.o.
Svetozarevska ulica 6
SLO-2000 Maribor
Page/Seite 424

Vestel White Goods
Organize Sanayi Bölgesi
TR-45030 Manisa
Page/Seite 144–145

Viessmann Werke Allendorf GmbH
Viessmannstr. 1
D-35108 Allendorf/Eder
Page/Seite 259

Viking GmbH
Hans Peter Stihl Str. 5
A-6336 Langkampfen/Kufstein
Page/Seite 344

Villeroy & Boch AG
Postfach 1120
D-66688 Mettlach
Page/Seite 233

VitrA Tiles
Ataturk Cad. Sifa Mah. Tuzla
TR-34941 Istanbul
Page/Seite 383

voestalpine AG
voestalpine Str. 1
A-4020 Linz
Page/Seite 394

Vorwerk Elektrowerke GmbH & Co. KG
Blombacher Bach 3
D-42270 Wuppertal
Page/Seite 167

V.R. Union Co., Ltd.
137/16 Moo 9, Phetkrasem 91, Suanluang,
Kratumban
T-Samutsakorn 74110
Page/Seite 275

W

W I L Langenberg GmbH
Corneliusweg 1-2
D-42499 Hückeswagen
Page/Seite 346

Herbert Waldmann GmbH & Co. KG
Peter-Henlein-Str. 5
D-78056 Villingen-Schwenningen
Page/Seite 302

Wästberg
Box 22212
S-25024 Helsingborg
Page/Seite 303

Weishäupl Möbelwerkstätten GmbH
Neumühlweg 9
D-83071 Stephanskirchen
Page/Seite 335

Robert Welch Designs Ltd.
Lower High Street
GB-Chipping Campden GL55 6DY
Page/Seite 215

Studio William Welch Ltd.
Unit C1, The Bridge Business Centre
Timothy's Bridge Road
GB-Stratford-upon-Avon CV37 9HW
Page/Seite 215

Wever & Ducré
Beversesteenweg 565
B-8800 Roeselare
Page/Seite 317

Whirlpool Corporation
Global Consumer Design Studios
Localita' Cassinetta, Biandronno
I-21024 Varese
Page/Seite 186

Whitespa
635 Sa-Ri, Seotan-Myeon
ROK-Pyeongtaek City, Gyunggi-do 451-852
Page/Seite 232

WIK Elektrogeräte
Schacht Neu-Cöln 12
D-45355 Essen
Page/Seite 192

Wilo SE
Nortkirchenstr. 100
D-44263 Dortmund
Page/Seite 428

WK Wohnen GmbH & Co. Möbel Marketing KG
Im Gefierth 9a
D-63303 Dreieich
Page/Seite 108

Wodtke GmbH
Rittweg 55-57
D-72070 Tübingen
Page/Seite 111

Norbert Woll GmbH
Heinrich-Barth-Str. 7-11
D-66115 Saarbrücken
Page/Seite 211

WOOREE Lighting
636-3 Sunggok-dong, Danwon-gu
ROK-Ansan 425-833
Page/Seite 318

Woven Image Ltd.
Page/Seite 383

Y

Yamagiwa Corporation
1-5-10 Soto-Kanda
J-Tokyo 101-0021
Page/Seite 304

Yantouch
5F, No. 5, Li-Hsin Road III, Hsinchu Science Park
Hsin-Chu 30078
Taiwan
Page/Seite 315

Z

Zehnder Group Vaux Andigny S.A.S.
5 rue des Parachutistes de la France Libre
F-2110 Vaux-Andigny
Page/Seite 246

Zumtobel Lighting GmbH
Schweizer Str. 30
A-6851 Dornbirn
Page/Seite 313

Zweibrüder Optoelectronics GmbH
Kronenstr. 5-7
D-42699 Solingen
Page/Seite 320–321

Imprint | Impressum

Editor | Herausgeber:
Peter Zec

Project management | Projektleitung:
Sabine Wöll

Project assistance | Projektassistenz:
Sabine Meier
Dijana Milentijević
Sarah Hockertz
Björn Schamberger
Weijing Le
Jan Derksen
Philipp Grewer

Editorial work | Redaktion:
Bettina Derksen, Simmern, Germany
Kirsten Müller, Essen, Germany

Text | Text:
Bettina Derksen, Simmern, Germany
Kirsten Müller, Essen, Germany
Ann Christin Artel, Essen, Germany
Burkhard Jacob (red dot: design team of
the year & Interview)
Sandra Kesseboom (Interviews designer
portraits I Interviews Designerporträts)
Bettina Laustroer, Rosenheim, Germany
Justine Otto (Trend spots | Trendberichte)
Astrid Ruta (red dot award: communication
design & red dot award: design concept)
Martina Stein, Otterberg, Germany

Proofreading | Lektorat:
Klaus Dimmler, Essen, Germany
Mareike Ahlborn, Essen, Germany
Dawn Michelle d'Atri, Kirchhundem,
Germany
Annette Gillich-Beltz, Essen, Germany
Karin Kirch, Essen, Germany
Schmidt & Knyhala GbR,
Castrop-Rauxel, Germany

Translations | Übersetzung:
Russell Cennydd, Cologne, Germany
Stanislaw Eberlein, Tokyo, Japan
Cathleen Poehler, Montreal, Canada
Jan Stachel-Williamson,
Christchurch, New Zealand
Bruce Stout, Grafenau, Germany
Andreas Zantop, Berlin, Germany
Christiane Zschunke, Frankfurt/Main,
Germany

Layout and cover artwork |
Gestaltung und Titelillustration:
oktober Kommunikationsdesign GmbH,
Bochum, Germany

Photographs | Fotos:
In-company photos | Werksfotos der Firmen
Enrico Basili for Dogma
(Portrait | Porträt Juror Massimo Iosa Ghini)
Robert Fischer
(Portrait | Porträt Designer Stefan Diez)
Katrien Franken
Tracy Kraft, Maui, Hawaii
Magnus Länje
(Portrait | Porträt Juror Robin Edman)
Jeroen Musch
Elisabeth Toll
(Portrait | Porträt Juror Robert Stadler)
Stian L. Solum
Judith Schulz
(Portrait | Porträt Designer Julien Fillion)
Thomas Wagner
(Portrait | Porträt Juror Jorge Pensi)
Andrew Zuckerman

Jury photographs | Jurorenfotos:
Georg Valerius, Cologne, Germany

Production, lithography and printing |
Produktion, Lithografie und Druck:
tarcom GmbH, Gelsenkirchen, Germany

Printing | Druck:
Himmer AG, Augsburg

Publisher + Worldwide distribution |
Verlag + Vertrieb weltweit:
red dot edition
Gelsenkirchener Str. 181, 45309 Essen
Germany
Phone +49 201 81 41-822
Fax +49 201 81 41-810
E-mail info@red-dot.de
www.red-dot.de

red dot design yearbook 2010/2011
Vol. 1, living, 978-3-89939-115-2
Vol. 2, doing, 978-3-89939-116-9
Set Vol. 1 & Vol. 2 (living & doing):
978-3-89939-114-5

©2010 red dot GmbH & Co. KG

red dot design yearbook 2010/2011
Vol. 1, living, 978-3-89939-115-2

Cover photos | Titelfotos:

Sudster™ Kitchen Cleaning Tools /
Küchen-Reinigungstools
Chef'n Corp, Seattle, USA
In-house design / Werksdesign:
Chef'n In-house Design Team
(Adam Jossem, Jonah Griffith, Matt Krus,
Dave Hull, David Holcomb)

Young w094
Desk Light / Schreibtischleuchte
Wästberg, Helsingborg, Sweden / Schweden
Design: Michael Young Ltd. (Michael Young),
Hong Kong / Hongkong

Extreme
Chair / Stuhl
Gaber S.r.l., Caselle d'Altivole (Treviso),
Italy / Italien
Design: Stefano Sandonà Design
(Stefano Sandonà), Selvazzano Dentro
(Padova), Italy / Italien

I-Zecure
Holding Bar / Haltegriff
Bathroom Design Co., Ltd., Bangkok, Thailand
In-house design / Werksdesign

Infinity
Desk Light / Schreibtischleuchte
Unilux, Savigny-sur-Orge, France / Frankreich
Design: 360 Design Industriel Design Global
(Patrick Jouffret), Toulon, France / Frankreich